(continued on back endsheet)

Publications of the
MINNESOTA HISTORICAL SOCIETY

STEPHEN H. LONG by Charles Willson Peale. Long sat for this portrait at Philadelphia in 1819. Courtesy Independence Hall Collection, Philadelphia.

THE NORTHERN EXPEDITIONS OF STEPHEN H. LONG

The Journals of 1817 and 1823 and Related Documents

Edited by Lucile M. Kane,
June D. Holmquist, and Carolyn Gilman

MINNESOTA HISTORICAL SOCIETY PRESS • 1978

Library of Congress Cataloging in Publication Data:
Long, Stephen Harriman, 1784–1864.
The northern expeditions of Stephen H. Long.

Includes index.
1. Mississippi River—Description and travel.
2. Northwest, Old—Description and travel.
3. Minnesota—Description and travel—To 1858.
4. Great Lakes—Description and travel. 5. Long, Stephen Harriman, 1784–1864. 6. Explorers—United States—Biography. I. Kane, Lucile M. II. Holmquist, June Drenning. III. Gilman, Carolyn, 1954–
IV. Title.
F597.L83 1978 917.7'04'2 78-5166

INTERNATIONAL STANDARD BOOK NUMBER: 0-87351-129-8

MANUFACTURED IN THE UNITED STATES OF AMERICA

FOR PUT-PUT HOLMQUIST

who always knew
what direction we were going

Preface

STEPHEN H. LONG, who was always impatient of any delay that impeded his travels, would not have approved of the length of time it has taken his editors to complete this book. But then Long knew where he was and what he was doing there, something it has taken us twelve years to figure out.

In fact, this book on Long's northern expeditions has been contemplated for so many years that some fellow members of the Minnesota Historical Society's staff point out that the idea is older than they are. The notion of publishing an annotated edition of Long's journals of 1817 and 1823 was first suggested in the 1940s by Dr. Grace Lee Nute, former curator of manuscripts at the society, who expressed surprise that so basic a document in western exploration as Long's 1823 journal had never been published. About the same time, the late Bertha L. Heilbron, then editor of *Minnesota History*, became interested in James E. Colhoun's 1823 journal and asked Lucile Kane to edit it for publication.

Little substantial work was done, however, until 1966, when Kane inveigled June Holmquist into joining her on the project. Frequently during the next decade, the editors announced, usually softly to one another, that they were almost finished, only to have yet another year pass while they attempted to find answers to further research questions. In 1976 fresh help arrived in the person of Carolyn Gilman, who took both Long and the other editors in hand and made a major contribution to the completion of the project by checking sources, reducing overlong footnotes, and researching the science of the period as well as the literary references in the Colhoun journal. In the latter task, Gilman received valuable aid from editorial assistant Mary Cannon, who valiantly broke the trail.

In many respects our journey with Long and Colhoun has been a pleasant one. Nevertheless, since at least one of the editors was not blessed with a keen sense of direction and a love of old maps, retracing his steps geographically consumed considerable time. One or the other of the editors has traveled over most of the area Long described, albeit in autos, canoes, and planes rather than in Dearborn wagons, six-oared skiffs, or on horseback. Only a few stretches of the most remote lakes Long traversed were not visited in person. Especially memorable were two glorious autumn trips. One took us to Long's home town of Hopkinton, New Hampshire, where a handsome house which once belonged to him still stands and the local historical society preserves a small model of his design for a truss bridge. The other followed the route of the National Road through the mountains of northern Maryland, where it is still possible to trace at least five earlier roads, including portions of the one Long followed in 1823. Less productive was a trip down the Mississippi River to view some of the geographic features described by the explorer, only to find them obscured by rain, fog, and steamy car windows.

The greatest pleasure has been in associations with the many, many people throughout the nation who have stopped in their work to answer our seemingly endless questions, welcomed us to their reading rooms, and responded generously by mail to requests for information. Our largest debt is to Oliver W. Holmes and the incomparable Sara D. Jackson. After the National Historical Publications Commission, of which Mr. Holmes was director, generously endorsed this project, both Mr. Holmes and Mrs. Jackson provided major assistance, patiently searching out obscure documents, securing photocopies, and extending warm words of encouragement—tasks Mrs. Jackson continued to perform up to the eve of publication.

Others to whom we owe very special thanks are our associates on the Minnesota Historical Society's staff, who not only put up with our never-ending Long project all these years but have also cheered us on and lent many a helping hand. We also wish to thank former colleagues Michael Brook and Janet White Cotter for research in Great Britain and Illinois; Raymond S. Baby of the Ohio Historical Society, Ellen Lee Barker of the Maryland Historical Society, and Herman Chilson of Webster, South Dakota, for sharing their detailed knowledge of their respective areas; Raymond J. De Mallie for his help with Long's often puzzling Dakota orthography; Caroline Dunn and Frances B. Macdonald of the Indiana Historical Library and the Indiana State Library, who remembered our problem even while on a picnic; M. Elizabeth Arthur and K. C. A. Dawson of Lakehead University in Ontario, Herman Friis of the National Archives of the United States, and Mildred Goosman of the Joslyn Art Museum for their fruitful suggestions; Josephine L. Harper of the State Historical Society of Wisconsin for repeated timely help; William E. Lass of Mankato State University, Philip P. Mason of Wayne State University, and Blake McKelvey of the Rochester, New York, city historian's office, who generously shared their specialized knowledge with us; Edwin McDill, who kindly allowed us to consult an unpublished portion of the Colhoun journal in his possession; Nancy C. Prewitt of the Western Historical Manuscripts Collection in the University of Missouri Library and Frances H. Stadler of the Missouri Historial Society, who must be rejoicing to be rid of us; Lester Smith, who smoothed our path through Buffalo, New York; Vaughn E. Whisker for help with Pennsylvania mountain geography; and Theresa G. Haynes, Jean Kirby, Jacqueline Cretzmeyer, Phyllis Sandstrom, and June Sonju for typing above and beyond the call of duty.

We are also grateful for the help we received from our supportive families: Donald C. Holmquist, to whom this book is dedicated, with unfailing good nature transported the editors to the sites of their choice, tolerated hours of discussion, and contributed his own knowledge of geography and science. He is indeed the "gentleman of the party." Ruth Coty Kane, descendant of voyageurs and fellow early-riser, whose greeting at daybreak on innumerable Saturday mornings was "I suppose you are off again to work on Stephen What's-his-name"; Leona Kane Eder, who cheerfully throughout a long scholarly career kept the home fires burning; and Sister Alora Kane for sharing home duties.

A grant from the Minnesota Historical Society's McKnight Foundation Research Fund was most helpful in the early research stages of the project. We are also appreciative of permission to publish two documents from the Thomas A. Smith Papers in the University of Missouri Library and a third in the Public Record Office, London. To the many other institutions and individuals who extended courtesies to us over the years, we say a sincere "thank you."

The journals here printed represent a literal transcription of the originals in the collections of the Minnesota Historical Society. Spelling and sentence structure were meticulously preserved, although paragraphs were created, and date entries and punctuation were regularized for greater clarity. The texts are complete with four exceptions: several groups of astronomical observations, lists of courses and distances, and miscellaneous accounting figures were omitted from Long's 1823 journal, and only a few of the day-to-day maps sketched by Long and Colhoun have been reproduced. Samples of all three groups of maps have been included, as have specific maps referred to in the journal texts. Complete copies of all three journals, including the omitted material, are available on microfilm from the Minnesota Historical Society.

The end sheet maps showing the routes of the 1817 and 1823 journeys reproduce the map prepared by Long for publication in the *Narrative of an Expedition to the Source of St. Peter's River*. The front end sheet reproduces the western half of the map, while the back end sheet shows the eastern portion. The two overlap for easy orientation. A broken line in brown ink has been added to indicate Long's 1817 route on the Mississippi River; this line, of course, did not appear on the map reproduced in the *Narrative*. The 1823 route, which was drawn in by Long, has been labeled by adding a date; it is shown by a solid line in brown ink.

The editors attempted to identify the people and places Long visited. Corrected personal names and current geographical names have been supplied in brackets where they first occur in the text. Unless corrections appear in brackets following mileages or other figures given by Long and Colhoun, the figures are approximately correct. The following abbreviations have been used throughout the footnotes:

AGO—Adjutant General's Office
GAO—General Accounting Office
MHC—Minnesota Historical Collections
MHS—Minnesota Historical Society
NARG—National Archives Record Group
OIA—Office of Indian Affairs
OCE—Office of the Chief of Engineers
WHC—Wisconsin Historical Collections
WHS—Wisconsin Historical Society

ST. PAUL, MINNESOTA

Lucile M. Kane
June D. Holmquist
Carolyn Gilman

Contents

ILLUSTRATIONS

Introduction

STEPHEN HARRIMAN LONG won his place in American history with a series of five exploring expeditions made from 1816 to 1823 as one of the initial group of United States topographical engineers who did so much to map the American West. Although he later made substantial contributions to river improvement, road surveys, railroad building, bridge design, and other fields, it was as an explorer probing the southwestern and midwestern reaches of the nation that he has been remembered. His travels covered an estimated 26,000 miles from the Atlantic Coast to the Rocky Mountains and from the headwaters of the Canadian River in New Mexico to Lake Winnipeg in Canada. As a leader of government-sponsored expeditions, Long was preceded in the West only by Meriwether Lewis, William Clark, and Zebulon M. Pike. He was unusual in his day not only for the extent of territory he traversed, but for the superior organization of his expeditions and the amount of information they gathered.[1]

This book deals with two of Long's trips—the only two for which his journals seem to have survived. The first, made in 1817, took him from Belle Fontaine, Missouri, up the Mississippi River to the Falls of St. Anthony in present-day Minneapolis, Minnesota, with a side trip up the Wisconsin River to what is now Portage, Wisconsin. The second, a more elaborate and longer expedition carried out under his direction in 1823, went westward from Philadelphia across the present states of Pennsylvania, Ohio, Indiana, Illinois, Wisconsin, and Minnesota, and returned eastward along the old fur trade canoe routes in the Canadian provinces of Manitoba and Ontario, through

[1] John Livingston, "Col. Stephen H. Long of the U.S. Army," in *Portraits of Eminent Americans Now Living; With Biographical and Historical Memoirs of Their Lives and Actions*, 4:477–489 (New York, London, and Paris, 1854). For an assessment of Long's contributions, see Roger L. Nichols, "Stephen Long and Scientific Exploration on the Plains," in *Nebraska History*, 52:51, 59–62 (Spring, 1971).

the Great Lakes and the newly opened portions of the Erie Canal in New York, and back to Philadelphia again.

Long was well prepared by heritage and education for his lengthy and notable career in the United States Corps of Topographical Engineers, a career which extended from 1816 to 1863, the year before he died. Born in 1784 at Hopkinton, New Hampshire, he was the son of Lucy Harriman and Moses Long, a cooper, farmer, and Revolutionary War soldier. Stephen was the second child and the eldest son among the 13 surviving children of Moses and Lucy, several of whom showed marked talents in scientific and scholarly fields. At Dartmouth College Stephen acquired the classical education then necessary for a career as a teacher. During his college career he was elected to Phi Beta Kappa and demonstrated a strong interest in music by joining the Handel Society.[2]

After his graduation from Dartmouth in 1809 at the age of 25, Long became the principal of an academy at Salisbury, New Hampshire, near his Hopkinton home. His stay at Salisbury was brief. Early in the winter of 1810–11 he accepted a position as principal of a public school in Germantown, Pennsylvania, a suburb of Philadelphia.[3]

Long seems to have been well fitted by temperament, if not by inclination, for the role of teacher. John Adams Dix, one of his students at Salisbury, described him as a firm teacher who was nevertheless "considerate and just, and I do not think there was a single pupil who did not love and respect him." This flattering view of Long's character was by no means universal. The fiery Giacomo C. Beltrami, who knew him in 1823 and disliked him, ridiculed his pompousness, and Christopher C. Baldwin, librarian of the Ameri-

[2] Richard G. Wood, *Stephen Harriman Long, 1784–1864: Army Engineer, Explorer, Inventor*, 22–34, 38, 262 (Glendale, Calif., 1966); Harvey Reid, *Biographical Sketch of Enoch Long, an Illinois Pioneer*, 32–41 (*Chicago Historical Society's Collection*, vol. 2—Chicago, 1884). Although the house Stephen Long was born in no longer stands, the handsome home he bought from his cousin Isaac in the 1830s survives in Hopkinton. A model of Long's truss bridge is preserved in the museum of the William H. Long Memorial Building there.

[3] Here and below, see Wood, *Long*, 34–36; J. C. Beltrami, *A Pilgrimage in Europe and America, Leading to the Discovery of the Sources of the Mississippi and Bloody River*, 2:321, 326 (London, 1828, and reprint ed., Chicago, 1962); American Antiquarian Society, *Diary of Christopher Columbus Baldwin*, 306 (Worcester, Mass., 1901); Reid, *Biographical Sketch of Enoch Long*, 33. The Peale painting is reproduced as the frontispiece, above; the later engraving is in Livingston, *Portraits of Eminent Americans*, 4:facing p. 477. The photograph opposite is from G. Frank Long, "A Revolutionary Soldier and Some of His Family," in *Journal of the Illinois State Historical Society*, 7:282 (October, 1914). On James, see below, p. 43.

A PHOTOGRAPH of Stephen H. Long probably taken in the early 1860s. Courtesy Illinois State Historical Library, Springfield.

can Antiquarian Society, who met him in 1834, commented that the explorer was a small man, "not remarkably imposing either in his looks or conversation." His face as delineated in Charles Willson Peale's painting of him in his thirties is lean, mild, and ascetic, while an engraving and the photograph above in later life have a strict and dour cast. He was nevertheless capable of warm and lasting friendships with John Harris, a gentleman farmer of Hopkinton, for example, and with the scientist Dr. Edwin James. He not only named a son for James, but entrusted his literary legacy to him.

Most of the surviving official letters from Long's pen are terse and peremptory, and the comments of his military colleagues generally cite his discretion, efficiency, diligence, and perseverance. These qualities pervade his official reports. Concisely written, logically organized, and displaying wide general knowledge, they are models of informative reporting. His personal journals, which were prepared as sources for official reports, reveal other qualities, notably an acute sense of military and personal propriety, a high moral tone, an inquisitive and disciplined mind, and a romantic concept of nature and aboriginal culture. His dogged cheerfulness at the physical discomforts of exploration is offset by an intolerance of any incompetence or irresponsibility that might jeopardize the fulfilling of his mission.

Long's reaction to Pennsylvania when he arrived there in 1810 was typical. Attracted to Philadelphia as a center of learning, he nevertheless condemned the inhabitants of other portions of the state as "brutishly ignorant, in everything but the art of amassing wealth." Showing his New England bias, he observed that "the Yankees know much better, how to appreciate real merits & talents, than their neighbors of the South." Despite these reservations about Pennsylvanians, he settled down in Philadelphia to the extent of joining the Harmonic Society and making a number of friends, among them the family of Martha Hodgkiss, his future wife.[4]

By 1812 Long was clearly discontented with his life as a school principal in Germantown. He confided to John Harris in Hopkinton that he was weighing an offer from a Philadelphia physician that would permit him to study the "profession of Physic." The offer attracted the restive schoolmaster, but he feared that his friends would consider him "fickle & unsteady" if he accepted a nonpaying apprenticeship while he still had debts. Somewhat embarrassed by these confidences, he showed a rare flash of humor at the conclusion of his letter to Harris: "I have nothing but Egotism, a squeamish dose, to offer you at this time—next time, if [I] can find nothing better, I will fill my letter with garden-seeds."[5]

While in Germantown, Long and an associate designed a hydrostatic engine for which they received a patent. This demonstration of "mechanical ingenuity" brought him to the attention of Brigadier General Joseph G. Swift, chief of engineers in the United States Army, who at first asked him to work as a civilian engineer on the defenses of New York harbor. Under Swift's patronage, Long's army career began propitiously when he was commissioned a second lieutenant in the Corps of Engineers in 1814. The following year he was appointed assistant professor of mathematics in the United States Military Academy at West Point.[6]

His stay at West Point was short but significant. At that time the school was one of very few in the country equipped to train scien-

[4] Wood, *Long*, 35–37, 72; Long to John Harris, June 10, September 28, 1811, in Harris Papers, Dartmouth College Archives, Hanover, N.H. The physician mentioned below who offered to instruct Long in medicine was William Dewees, the uncle of Martha Hodgkiss; see Wood, *Long*, 72n; C. C. Lord, *Life and Times in Hopkinton, N. H.*, 430 (Concord, N.H., 1890); Long to Harris, February 2, 1812, in Harris Papers, New Hampshire State Library, Concord.

[5] Long to Harris, February 2, 1812, in Harris Papers, New Hampshire State Library.

[6] A description and sketch of the engine are enclosed in Long to Harris, February 26, 1814, in Harris Papers, New Hampshire State Library. See also Wood, *Long*, 37.

tists for the young nation. Long's "liberal education" and his "general knowledge in the mathematical sciences & remarkable talent in mechanics," as Swift put it, made him one of a rare breed. Scarcely a year after his arrival at West Point he requested a commission as a topographical engineer. He was one of the first six officers assigned to this newly reorganized unit. He received his commission on April 29, 1816, with the rank of brevet major, and was dispatched to join Brigadier General Thomas A. Smith of the ninth military department, headquartered at Fort Belle Fontaine near St. Louis. Smith echoed Swift's enthusiasm for the major, declaring that his "character for science, industry, and perseverence is not surpassed by any topigraphisist in the American army."[7]

Long's assignment to the topographical engineers placed him in the pioneering era of a branch of government service that would play a crucial role in the exploration of the West. The unit was created during the War of 1812 to plot military positions and collect data in the field with the army; later its function was expanded to include western surveys. In 1818 it was made a bureau under the jurisdiction of the Corps of Engineers, and in 1838 it became a corps coequal with other divisions of the army. It was, in the words of historian William H. Goetzmann, "a central institution of Manifest Destiny," delineating boundaries, building roads, improving rivers and harbors, locating forts, and producing a remarkable body of maps, reports, and other data on the West. Staffed by men noted for their learning and ingenuity, the corps was a natural home for Stephen Long.[8]

When the newly commissioned officer reported to General Smith in St. Louis to begin his exploring career in 1816, the War Department was reassessing frontier defenses in the aftermath of the War of 1812. During that conflict, the Northwest had been a battleground of opposing forces contending for strategic positions. After the war, British influence in the area remained strong. Although Congress in 1816 excluded foreign traders from the country, British subjects found ways to circumvent the law. Moreover, they con-

[7] Wood, *Long*, 38; Henry P. Beers, "A History of the U.S. Topographical Engineers, 1813–1863," in *Military Engineer*, 34:287 (June, 1942); Smith to John C. Calhoun, February 14, 1818, Smith Papers, joint Western Historical Manuscripts Collection—State Historical Society Manuscripts, University of Missouri Library, Columbia. On Smith, see Howard L. Conard, ed., *Encyclopedia of the History of Missouri*, 6:8 (New York, Louisville, and St. Louis, 1901).

[8] Beers, in *Military Engineer*, 34:287, 288; William H. Goetzmann, *Army Exploration in the American West 1803–1863*, 4–13 (New Haven, 1959).

tinued to influence the Indians, many of whom had favored the British in battle as well as in trade. Observing efforts to lure Native Americans to trade northward across the border, a United States Indian agent reported that the British promised to "build a perpetual council fire so large that the blaze is to extend to the moon, that it may give light to all their children . . . that they may see to travel by night as well as by day."[9]

An elaborate rhetoric that flowed freely from British and American adversaries as well as competition for trade and intertribal conflicts contributed to the disquiet on the frontier. More important, however, was the movement of white men into what had been Indian country. In council with government agents, Native Americans might pledge to "wash the blood from the Land & Water & join hands with their great father the President," but as treaties extinguished their rights to tribal lands and white farmers settled on them, apprehension bred a bitterness that threatened open war. Resolved to remove the threat of Indian alliances with the British, strengthen the American fur trade, quell the intertribal wars, and open the way for white settlement, the United States government in 1815 made plans to erect a series of frontier fortifications. Long would help carry out those plans, examining the strategic importance and defensibility of existing posts, selecting sites for new forts, and building them.[10]

He would also contribute to another important government goal — securing information about the large western domain acquired in the Louisiana Purchase. Since 1804, when President Thomas Jefferson had dispatched Lewis and Clark across the continent to the Pacific, the government had shown a keen interest in learning about natural resources, geography, geology, natural history, and Native American peoples. A fine intellectual resource for digesting this broad spectrum of information existed in Philadelphia, "the scientific capital of the country." The community of scien-

[9] Henry P. Beers, *The Western Military Frontier 1815–1846*, 24, 35–37 (Philadelphia, 1935); Benjamin F. Stickney to Lewis Cass, October 6, 1815, U.S. Office of Indian Affairs (hereafter abbreviated OIA), Michigan Superintendency, Letters Received and Sent, Record Group 75, National Archives, Washington, D.C. Record groups in the National Archives are hereafter cited as NARG.

[10] Beers, *Western Military Frontier*, 27, 30–37, 50; William H. Puthuff to Cass, August 31, 1815, OIA, Michigan Superintendency, Letters Received and Sent, NARG 75; Francis P. Prucha, *Broadax and Bayonet: The Role of the United States Army in the Development of the Northwest 1815–1860*, 17–22 ([Madison, Wis.], 1953).

tists there, centering on the prestigious American Philosophical Society, strongly influenced the planning of western expeditions and provided the training for many of the scientists who accompanied them. Jefferson's instructions to Lewis and Clark, framed with the aid of the society, were the prototype of the instructions Long received for his various journeys, and the same society was responsible. At the request of Secretary of War John C. Calhoun, the organization advised Long on preparations for his first major scientific expedition in 1819. The major himself was closely associated with the society, submitting a paper on his explorations in 1817 and becoming a member in 1823.[11]

Long's first important exploration assignment after he joined General Smith in 1816 was a trip to Lake Peoria in Illinois to select the site for a new post to replace Fort Clark, a brief journey that was followed by visits to Chicago and Fort Wayne. During this "first scientifically recorded survey" of the Chicago region, Long mapped the Chicago Portage and gathered data for a recommendation that a canal be constructed between Lake Michigan and the waters of the Illinois River. His brief report on these journeys was typical of those he would write later. Explicit on the subject of fortifications and practical military data, it also included information on geography, topography, geology, and Indian tribes.[12]

By 1817 it was clear that the major had acquired a zest for exploration. In March he proposed to President James Monroe a plan to build a small steamboat and with it reconnoiter the main tributaries of the Mississippi, the Great Lakes, and the rivers flowing into

[11] For a review of the significance of the instructions given to Lewis and Clark and the army's role in exploration, see William H. Goetzmann, *Exploration and Empire: The Explorer and the Scientist in the Winning of the American West*, 4–7, 183, 303 (New York, 1966); and Prucha, *Broadax and Bayonet*, 189–195. See also John C. Calhoun to Robert Walsh, March 11, 1819; Walsh to Calhoun, March 30, 1819; Long, paper addressed "To the American Philosophical Society of Philadelphia," March 7, 1817—all in American Philosophical Society Library, Philadelphia; Wood, *Long*, 138.

[12] Wood, *Long*, 40–43; Wood, "Stephen H. Long's Plan for New Fort at Peoria," in *Journal of the Illinois State Historical Society*, 47:417–421 (Winter, 1954); Long to George Graham, March 4, 1817, Secretary of War, Letters Received, NARG 107. On the Chicago Portage exploration, see Robert Knight and Lucius H. Zeuch, *The Location of the Chicago Portage Route of the Seventeenth Century*, 103 (*Chicago Historical Society's Collection*, vol. 12—Chicago, 1928); *Letter From the Secretary of War, Transmitting Topographical Reports*, 7 (16 Congress, 1 session, *House Executive Documents*, no. 17—serials 31–32). The complete text of Long's 1816 report appeared in *National Register*, 3:193–198 (March 29, 1817). A canal similar to the one Long recommended was constructed in 1836–48.

them. General Swift would provide instruments, Long declared, and West Point cadets "well versed in the requisite branches of Education" could be employed to collect data.[13]

The eager explorer received an assignment in 1817, although his mission was more modest than the grand reconnaissance he had advocated to Monroe, and his conveyance was an old six-oared skiff rather than a steamboat. On May 31 he was ordered to chart the Mississippi River as far north as Prairie du Chien in present Wisconsin, follow the Wisconsin River as far east as the portage to the Fox River, describe the course of the Fox to Green Bay on the shores of Lake Michigan, and record information on the Indians and the country he traversed.[14]

Long departed from Belle Fontaine on June 1 in a six-oared skiff borrowed from William Clark of Lewis and Clark fame, who was then serving as Missouri Territory's governor and superintendent of Indian affairs. Pushing upstream against the Mississippi's current, he reached Prairie du Chien on June 23. Writing to Smith from there on the eve of his departure for the sortie up the Wisconsin River, he disclosed that his itinerary might differ from his original instructions. Reports about the disposition of the Indians on the Mississippi were not satisfactory, he remarked, "but I am in hopes they will be more flattering before my return, as I am very anxious to ascend to the Falls of St. Ant[h]ony." Perhaps to leave time for this northern excursion, he did not travel all the way to Green Bay, but turned back at the Fox-Wisconsin Portage. Upon his return to Prairie du Chien, he learned that the danger from hostile Indians was slight or nonexistent, and he decided to make the trip to the only major waterfall in the Mississippi, now the site of Minneapolis.[15]

The decision to extend the trip into what is now Minnesota gave Long an opportunity to examine two sites for military posts recom-

[13] Long to Monroe, March 15, 1817, Secretary of War, Letters Received, NARG 107.

[14] For Long's instructions, dated May 31, 1817, see Appendix 1, below. See also Wood, *Long*, 39, 46; Long to Smith, May (n.d.), 1817, in Appendix 1, below. Long was ordered to go to Prairie du Chien in 1816, but the plan was changed to permit him to design an arsenal at St. Louis. See William H. Crawford to Long, June 18, July 2, 1816, Secretary of War, Letters Sent Re Military Affairs, NARG 107.

[15] Wood, *Long*, 46; Long to Smith, June 24, 1817, May 12, 1818, in Appendix 1; see also pp. 49, 50, below.

mended by Lieutenant Zebulon Pike on his expedition of 1805–06. One of these was at the junction of the Mississippi and St. Croix rivers; another was at the junction of the Mississippi and Minnesota rivers. In 1806 the government had felt no urgency about building posts at either of these locations. After the War of 1812, however, the presence of Lord Selkirk's colony on the Red River of the North near present-day Winnipeg took on greater importance when coupled with other threats of British influence, and American military planners began to consider seriously the erection of northern forts.[16]

Leaving Prairie du Chien on July 9, Long reached the Falls of St. Anthony on July 16, spent one day reconnoitering the area, and then turned his skiff downriver toward Belle Fontaine, where he arrived on August 15. Although the voyage was swift, the New Englander executed thoroughly his responsibilities as a military engineer. He not only examined the sites Pike had recommended for new posts, he also inspected the fortifications at Forts Crawford (Prairie du Chien), Armstrong (Rock Island, Ill.), and Edwards (Warsaw, Ill.).[17]

His assignment to record information on the Indian tribes was also performed with diligence. Between Prairie du Chien and present-day La Crosse, Wisconsin, were villages of the Winnebago, some of whom had fought on the British side during the War of 1812 and who in the next decade would again turn on the Americans. North of the Winnebago were the villages of the Mdewakanton Dakota or Sioux, governed by hereditary leaders whose interests had often been wedded to the British cause. Long gave close attention to the Dakota, who had no resident Indian agent and were little known to white men other than fur traders and occasional travelers. In gathering information about the nation, he was assisted by his interpreter, the formidable Augustin Rocque, a longtime trader on the upper Mississippi bound to the great chief Wabasha by ties of blood. An additional informant was Wazecouta, or Shooter from the Pine Top, who accompanied Long to the falls, contributed legends, and gave the party an opportunity to know a Dakota in nonceremonial circumstances.[18]

[16] Beers, *Western Military Frontier*, 30–32, 39; William W. Folwell, *A History of Minnesota*, 1:90–94 (Reprint ed., St. Paul, 1956).

[17] See below, pp. 70–77, 110; Wood, *Long*, 47.

[18] On Rocque, Wazecouta, and the soldiers mentioned below, see Chapter 1, notes 1, 2, 22.

The instructions to make observations on the countryside must have presented difficult problems for a man of Long's precision. He had few instruments with which to record scientific data. Moreover, his soldier companions — six privates and a sergeant—were hardly the caliber of West Point cadets he had envisioned; in fact, three of them could not write their own names. Given these limitations, Long gathered a surprising amount of information, particularly on topography.

A month after Long returned from the upper Mississippi, General Smith ordered him to the Arkansas River, where he chose the site and prepared the plans for a post that was first named Belle Point and then Fort Smith. He was also instructed to collect the same kinds of information specified in the orders that had sent him to the upper Mississippi.[19]

Arriving back at Belle Fontaine in January, 1818, he wrote a report that included data gathered on both expeditions, as well as on his earlier travels and from other observers. Its scope was narrow, for the report was a response to written questions posed by Smith on the military situation in the West. It was submitted to Smith on May 12, 1818, but may not have reached Secretary of War Calhoun until late in the year. In the meantime, Calhoun instructed Major General Jacob J. Brown, commanding general of the army's northern division, to make arrangements for establishing a post at the mouth of the Minnesota River. When Calhoun communicated this intention to Congress on December 11, 1818, he submitted as supporting evidence another short report by Long, estimating "the line of our frontier . . . with the distance of some of the more remote posts from the seat of Government." Despite Long's later claims, his recommendation of the site at the mouth of the Minnesota may not have been the decisive factor in the establishment of what later became Fort Snelling, but his report probably confirmed Calhoun's inclination to the project.[20]

[19] Beers, *Western Military Frontier*, 58, 61; Smith to Long, September 15, 1817, U.S. General Accounting Office Records (hereafter abbreviated GAO), Second Auditor, Account No. 1433, NARG 217.

[20] Wood, *Long*, 53; Smith to Long, May 7, 1818, Smith Papers. Long's report, dated May 12, 1818, is printed in Appendix 1, below. It was apparently not available to Calhoun when he wrote Gen. Brown about the establishment of the post at the mouth of the Minnesota on October 17, 1818; in fact, Brown did not receive it from Calhoun until March 11, 1819. See Letter Book, pp. 123, 138, 141, Jacob Brown Papers, Library of Congress. For Calhoun's report to Congress, see *American State Papers: Military Affairs*, 1:779, 791 (Washington, D.C., 1832). For Long's claims, see p. 152, below.

Once he had disposed of these reports, Long found enough time between assignments to attend to some personal matters. He returned to Philadelphia, where on March 3, 1819, he married Martha Hodgkiss. They had five children between 1820 and 1832. Long seems to have been devoted to his family and diligent in promoting his children's interests. Although his peripatetic life made it impossible for him to be with his family for long periods of time, they accompanied him whenever the nature of his assignments made it possible to establish a home. One of his sons, Henry Clay Long, became a civil engineer; another, Richard Harlan, graduated from West Point to become an officer, and Lucy, his only daughter, was carefully educated.[21]

The modest assignments upon which Long had been engaged answered the needs of military planners but did not fulfill his ambition to lead a scientific expedition. He continued to urge that the topographical engineers be deployed to acquire knowledge useful "both in a military & civil point of view. Any influence you can exercise, with the President, for the accomplishment of such an object," he wrote General Swift, "would, I am confident, be of service to the Public, and at the same time lead to a very desirable issue as it respects myself."[22]

To abbreviate sharply a complex story—in 1818 Long was chosen to lead a scientific expedition westward to the Rocky Mountains. The journey, carried out in 1819–20 and usually referred to as the "Yellowstone Expedition," was the best-known and the most extensive of all his travels. Its modern repute rests in part on the fact that it was the first well-equipped scientific expedition to cover the expanse of land from the Missouri River to the sources of the South Platte, Arkansas, and Canadian rivers in present Colorado and New Mexico. The expedition is remembered, too, because Long endorsed Pike's earlier concept of the "Great American Desert."[23] Within the context of this volume, however, its importance lies in the pattern it provided for the 1823 journey.

[21] Wood, *Long*, 72; Reid, *Biographical Sketch of Enoch Long*, 33; W. T. Norton, "Mrs. Lucy Long Breckinridge," in *Journal of the Illinois State Historical Society*, 10:464 (October, 1917). Mrs. Long's maiden name is also variously spelled Hodkiss and Hotchkiss. See Long, in *Journal of the Illinois State Historical Society*, 7:283.

[22] Long to Swift, October 15, 1817, Office of the Chief of Engineers (hereafter abbreviated OCE), Miscellaneous Papers, Fortifications (Series A), NARG 77.

[23] Wood, *Long*, 59–119. For a discussion of the western desert concept, see Richard H. Dillon, "Stephen Long's Great American Desert," in American Philosophical Society, *Proceedings*, 111:93–108 (April, 1967); Appendix 1, notes 15, 26, below.

An influential part of the pattern was the nature of the instructions Secretary Calhoun issued to Long. Reminiscent of the broad mandate Jefferson had given Lewis and Clark, Calhoun advised Long to acquire "thorough and accurate knowledge" of the country he traversed. Furthermore, Calhoun sent a copy of the instructions to the American Philosophical Society, which responded by appointing an advisory committee to furnish guidance.[24]

Other elements important to the character of the 1823 trip were present. Long selected as members of the 1819–20 expedition men competent in several branches of knowledge—Thomas Say as zoologist; Edwin James as botanist, geologist, and surgeon; Titian Ramsay Peale as assistant naturalist; and Samuel Seymour as landscape painter—and he equipped them with scientific books and instruments. At the conclusion of the trip, James compiled a narrative from the party's notes. Published in 1823, the *Account* also included Seymour's sketches, astronomical and meteorological records, Indian vocabularies, Long's topographical report, and maps.[25]

Long had scarcely emerged from his labors on this book when Major General Alexander Macomb, chief of engineers, suggested another expedition. "From your knowledge & experience in the mode of exploring the Western regions," he wrote on March 8, 1823, "it has been proposed to order you on an expedition up the St. Peters [*Minnesota River*] this season." Conscious of the "arduous undertakings" in which Long had been engaged, Macomb gave him the option of refusing the assignment.[26]

Macomb's invitation must have come as no surprise to the major, for even before concluding the Yellowstone Expedition he had proposed a side trip into the Northwest to survey the Minnesota and St.

[24] A copy of the instructions, dated March 8, 1819, is in the American Philosophical Society Library. A separate military mission was assigned to Col. Henry Atkinson. On the expedition, see Cardinal Goodwin, "A Larger View of the Yellowstone Expedition, 1819–1820," in *Mississippi Valley Historical Review*, 4:306–310 (December, 1917); Wood, *Long*, 71.

[25] Wood, *Long*, 65–67, 94, 113–115; Edwin James, comp., *Account of an Expedition from Pittsburgh to the Rocky Mountains . . . Under the Command of Major Stephen H. Long* (Philadelphia, 1823).

[26] Macomb to Long, March 8, 1823, in Appendix 2, below. On Macomb's lifelong career in the army, see Francis B. Heitman, *Historical Register and Dictionary of the United States Army, From Its Organization, September 29, 1789, to March 2, 1903*, 1:680 (Washington, D.C., 1903); "Alexander Macomb," in *The National Portrait Gallery of Distinguished Americans*, 4:n.p. (Philadelphia, 1852).

Croix rivers and the Great Lakes. Another scheme, which he advanced on February 1, 1823, envisioned an astronomical survey of the nation to determine correct latitudes and longitudes, a survey which would ultimately result in "one entire and accurately digested Map of the U[nited] States." Among the critical points for examination, the ambitious engineer included the Canadian boundary line.[27]

Long's response to Macomb was both equivocal and enthusiastic. He hesitated to accept the appointment, he wrote on March 11, not because of his recent labors, but because he was thinking of renewing an application he had once made to the state of Virginia for the position of civil engineer. On the other hand, his inclination to accept Macomb's invitation was clear, for he included in his letter recommendations on personnel, route, instruments, objectives, and publication of a book at the conclusion of the expedition. A few days later he requested permission to prepare for the journey. "In case the charge of the Expedition should devolve upon some other officer," he wrote on March 19, "he might avail himself of the preparations already made." Long did not receive the Virginia appointment, and he moved swiftly to make arrangements for his second major scientific expedition and his second trip into the northern reaches of the nation.[28]

Macomb's proposal reflected the keen interest in the Northwest manifested by the government after Long's 1817 trip. The line of military occupation had moved up the Mississippi River to its junction with the Minnesota when Camp Coldwater was established there in 1819. In 1820 the camp had been supplanted by Fort St. Anthony, later renamed Fort Snelling. Then the nation's northwesternmost outpost, it stood on the eminence overlooking the two rivers—the magnificent site Long had recommended in 1817. The fort also overlooked the beginnings of a new fur trading center that would be called Mendota and an Indian agency established in 1819 for the Dakota and Ojibway or Chippewa nations. To the northeast at Sault Ste. Marie, Michigan, was another new post, Fort Brady, built in 1822, and an agency for the Ojibway.[29]

[27] Long to Calhoun, January 3, 1820, and to Christopher Vandeventer, February 1, 1823, printed in W. Edwin Hemphill, ed., *The Papers of John C. Calhoun*, 4:546, 7:452–455 (Columbia, S.C., 1969, 1973).

[28] Long to Macomb, March 11, March 19, April 15, 1823, and Macomb to Long, March 17, 1823, all printed below, Appendix 2. See also Wood, *Long*, 115.

[29] Folwell, *History of Minnesota*, 1:112n, 137–141; Beers, *Western Military Frontier*, 46.

Knowledge of the northern country Long was to examine had expanded dramatically in the six years that had elapsed between his two trips. Of the several expeditions to explore parts of the area, the most elaborate was one conducted in 1820 by Lewis Cass, governor of Michigan Territory. During the planning stages of Cass's expedition, Secretary Calhoun briefly considered ordering Long to accompany it on his way back from Washington, D.C., to Council Bluffs on the Missouri, where he had left his own 1820 expedition to wait out the winter while he traveled quickly back east. This plan was soon abandoned and Cass was instead accompanied by Captain David B. Douglass, professor of natural philosophy at West Point, Henry R. Schoolcraft, geologist and later a well-known observer of Indian culture, and others of Cass's own choosing. The party traveled westward from Detroit to the Mississippi by way of Lake Superior's south shore and the St. Louis River, down the Mississippi to the Wisconsin, and eastward by way of the Wisconsin and Fox rivers to Lake Michigan.[30]

In 1820, soon after returning from his tour, Cass informed Calhoun that Douglass was preparing an extensive report and map covering a broad area including the Great Lakes and the Mississippi as far south as Rock Island. To provide Douglass with additional information, Cass suggested that exploring parties be sent out from various frontier posts. Among the expeditions he proposed was one that would depart from Fort St. Anthony, travel up the Minnesota and then down the Red River of the North to the Canadian border.[31]

Although the 1823 expedition was not a direct implementation of the Cass proposal and differed from the one Long himself had suggested in 1820, it was part of the general American quest for information about the area. For this quest, Long prepared with characteristic thoroughness. In the weeks between receiving Macomb's invitation on March 8 and his departure from Philadelphia on April 30, he concerned himself with defining the route, articulating objectives, accumulating instruments, supplies, and equipment, estimating expenses, and engaging personnel.[32]

[30] Mentor L. Williams, ed., Schoolcraft, *Narrative Journal of Travels Through the Northwestern Regions of the United States*, 10–17, 306 (East Lansing, Mich., 1953); Wood, *Long*, 89.

[31] Cass to Calhoun, September 27, 1820, OIA, Michigan Superintendency, Letters Sent, NARG 75, printed in Williams, ed., Schoolcraft, *Narrative Journal*, 321–323. Cass suggested the command of the Red River expedition be given to Lt. Andrew Talcott, whom Long later requested as assistant for his 1823 expedition.

[32] Wood, *Long*, 121–124.

Long defined the route and the objectives of the expedition in letters to Macomb written on March 11 and April 15, and these suggestions were included almost word for word in the orders issued by Calhoun on April 25. The party, Calhoun directed, was to cross the country from Philadelphia via Wheeling (then in Virginia), Fort Wayne, and Chicago to the Mississippi at Fort Armstrong or at Dubuque's lead mines, then travel up the Mississippi to Fort St. Anthony, up the Minnesota to its source, down the Red to the 49th parallel, and homeward by way of the Great Lakes.[33]

As the expedition proceeded, Long made changes in the route. He opted for a short cut overland from Chicago to Prairie du Chien, passing north of Fort Armstrong and missing the lead mines; instead of following the Minnesota to its source, he abandoned it near present St. Peter, Minnesota, and moved overland to the sources of the Red; and instead of halting his northward journey at the 49th parallel, he followed the Red to Fort Douglas in Canada, a possibility entertained during the planning of the trip but not included in the orders. These changes were made in the interest of speed, and it was well that Long hurried his march. As it was, the party barely escaped from the northern lakes before the winter freeze-up.[34]

The stated objectives of the expedition were purely scientific—to investigate the character and customs of the Indians, describe many aspects of the country, and determine the latitude and longitude of important points. In his enthusiasm for the mission, Long on April 28 added another objective to the list: "I hope the names of our friends in the Administration will remain as long as the 'perpetual hills' and never be forgotten till 'the rivers shall cease to flow.' Should I find any rivers, mountains, cataracts, caverns or fountains worthy to bear their names, I shall cheerfuly [*sic*] assume the functions of the priest, so far as to christen them."[35]

Calhoun's orders did not mention the 49th parallel, which had been stipulated in a treaty of 1818 as the boundary dividing the United States from the British possessions to the north, but it is apparent that the first official location and marking of the line was an unspoken objective of Long's expedition. Americans had

[33] Long to Macomb, March 11, April 15, 1823; these and Calhoun's orders are printed below, Appendix 2.

[34] Long announced the route changes to Macomb in letters dated June 10, July 15, and August 8, 1823, printed below, Appendix 2. See also Calhoun to John Q. Adams, April 28, 1823, OCE, Miscellaneous Letters Sent, NARG 77.

[35] For details, see Calhoun to Long, April 25, 1823, and Long to Macomb, April 28, 1823, in Appendix 2, below.

gradually become aware that a good portion of Lord Selkirk's grant, as well as the British trading post at Pembina (now in North Dakota), were south of the border. The diplomacy involved in approaching or entering Canada was considered in the party's preparations. Long was eager to have a "letter of credence and pass-port," and Calhoun asked John Quincy Adams, secretary of state, to obtain one from Stratford Canning, British minister in Washington. Canning obliged with a generous letter, which Long received en route and which doubtless gained him the trust of many Canadian traders who gave assistance to the party; but the minister also took the precaution of reporting his action to George Canning, his cousin and Britain's foreign minister.[36]

While stressing the scientific nature of the expedition, Stratford Canning expressed concern about its possible hidden objectives. The minister knew that part of the Selkirk Colony was located below the 49th parallel, and he believed that a visit to the settlement "may form one of the express objects of Major Long's Instructions." Canning further reported that he had informed Lord Dalhousie, governor-in-chief of Canada, of the expedition and had submitted "to His Lordship's judgment how far it may be worth while to give directions for observing it's movements, and Endeavouring to ascertain more particularly the extent of its views."[37]

British representatives did watch the expedition carefully as it moved east from the Red River settlements toward the British posts on the border lakes. For example, in response to a request of May 28 from Canada's military secretary, the commander at Drummond Island in Lake Huron near Sault Ste. Marie promised that while treating Long's party with "the utmost degree of civility," he would do everything in his power to determine "the object they may have in exploring the Red River, and the adjacent settlements." After the expedition visited the Hudson's Bay Company post on Rainy River, Dr. John McLoughlin, the chief factor there, wrote Simon Fraser on September 14, 1823, that "it is said they came to ascertain the 49 Parallel of north Latitude" and "to acquire a Knowledge of the country . . . so as to be ready in case of war." George Simpson, governor of Rupert's Land, was also on the alert. Commenting on

[36] John E. Parsons, *West on the 49th Parallel Red River to the Rockies, 1872–1876*, 5 (New York, 1963); Long to Macomb, April 24, 1823, in Appendix 2, below; Calhoun to Adams, April 28, 1823, OCE, Miscellaneous Letters Sent, NARG 77. See also Canning to "Any Officer of His Majesty," May 1, 1823; Stratford Canning to George Canning, May 5, 1823—both printed below, Appendix 2.

[37] Canning to Canning, May 5, 1823, in Appendix 2, below.

Long's movement toward the British possessions, the Hudson's Bay Company official professed ignorance of the major's objectives, "unless it be to take formal possession of what they may consider their Territory in that quarter, probably with the view of establishing a Military Post so as to watch our motions."[38]

Long did indeed enter the Red River settlements north of the border, talk with the colony's turbulent population, and lay down the location of the 49th parallel, finding that all but one house in the town of Pembina lay south of the border. He nearly confirmed British suspicions when he had a member of his party draw up a petition to the United States Congress on behalf of the inhabitants of Pembina, requesting that their property rights be assured and that "such privileges as are enjoyed by the Citizens of the United States" be extended to them. Although the people of Pembina "stood so much in awe of the agents of the Hudson's Bay Company, that signatures were slowly & doubtingly put to it," 36 names were collected out of some 300 inhabitants before the petition was forwarded to Congress. The officials of the Hudson's Bay Company, who were under the impression that the petition was for an American military or trading post at Pembina, were irate, and the Catholic bishop of the Red River country had to deny vigorously that he had conspired to produce the document. Despite British concern, nothing came of the petition; it was tabled by the House Judiciary Committee on December 23, 1823.[39]

Although the specific objectives of the expedition were clouded by uncertainty about conditions on the northern border, there was clarity in Long's preparations for equipping the party. A pair of bayonet pistols, one percussion pistol, a "small gun," a rifle, and a

[38] John Gaff to Henry C. Darling, July 10, 1823, in *Michigan Pioneer and Historical Collections*, 23:524 (Lansing, 1895); Burt B. Baker, *The McLoughlin Empire and its Rulers*, 175 (Glendale, Calif., 1959); Simpson to Andrew Colvile, September 8, 1823 (25:228), Selkirk Papers, Public Archives of Canada, Ottawa. The Minnesota Historical Society (hereafter abbreviated MHS) has a microfilm copy of the latter collection.

[39] See p. 183, below. George Simpson disagreed with Long concerning how much of Pembina was south of the border; see Simpson to Colvile, May 31, 1824 (26:106), Selkirk Papers. The petition, dated August 8, 1823, is in Records of the House of Representatives, NARG 233. Also of interest are comments in James E. Colhoun, Journal, 26, in the possession of Edwin B. McDill, Abbeville, S.Car.; Grace Lee Nute, ed., *Documents Relating to Northwest Missions 1815–1827*, 416, 431 (St. Paul, 1942); 18 Congress, 1 session, *Journal of the House of Representatives*, 75, 86 (serial 92). Beltrami made fun of the petition, saying that no one would sign it, and George Simpson thought Long could get only 12 signatures. Beltrami, *Pilgrimage*, 2:356; Simpson to Colvile, May 31, 1824 (26:106), Selkirk Papers.

"double" gun, as well as priming wires and brushes, priming caps, flints, balls, and powder were purchased to arm the men. These did not constitute the total weaponry, for Long stated that all the "gentlemen of the party" were also armed with rifles or double-barreled guns and some of them with pistols.[40]

Except for the stretch along the Mississippi from Fort Crawford north to Fort St. Anthony, where some members of the expedition were transported in a mackinaw boat, and between Fort St. Anthony and Traverse des Sioux on the Minnesota River, where some traveled by canoe, horses furnished the party's means of transportation until its members reached the Red River Colony. On the journey across so large an expanse of country, the horses fared far worse than the men. When Long left Philadelphia, he may not have foreseen that he would become a horse trader, replacing worn-out mounts and buying and selling them as the numbers of his party expanded and contracted. In any event, his preparations in Philadelphia were minimal, for he purchased only three horses, with saddles, bridles, and other accouterments, and acquired two Dearborn wagons for the early part of the journey.[41]

Although Long's only recorded purchase of food supplies in Philadelphia was six pounds of portable soup (an early forerunner of bouillon), he recognized that providing sustenance for the party would be a problem. It proved to be a far greater one than he anticipated. His projected budget, submitted to Macomb on April 15, included only minimal subsistence expenses. He requested and was granted authority to secure supplies from military posts en route—a precaution that saved the party on more than one occasion. Even before the expedition reached Fort St. Anthony, Long was purchasing foodstuffs. After leaving that frontier fort—the westernmost on his route—his purchases from fur trading posts became heavy. Once across the Canadian border he often had to rely upon his personal credit to obtain food from Hudson's Bay Company posts.[42]

[40] Individual vouchers as well as a consolidated "Abstract of Expenditures," dated November 1, 1823, exist for the Long expedition in GAO, Third Auditor, Account No. 2303, NARG 217; see Vouchers No. 6, 7, 9, in the "Abstract," printed in Appendix 2, below; see also p. 156, below. Long also kept extensive and rather unorganized accounts at the end of his journals which were consolidated in the "Abstract" and hence have not been printed here. The Long journals have been microfilmed in their entirety and are available from the MHS.

[41] Vouchers No. 5, 12, 15, in "Abstract," Appendix 2, below; see also Chapter 3, note 10.

[42] Voucher No. 14, in "Abstract"; Long to Macomb, April 15, 1823; and Calhoun to Long April 25, 1823—all in Appendix 2, below. See also p. 248, below.

The miscalculation of needed food supplies was primarily due to the party's inability to live off the land to the extent Long had anticipated. In Philadelphia he supplied the expedition with fishing equipment and butcher knives in addition to the guns noted above, but because of the scarcity of game and the speed of travel, these tools were seldom used. At the beginning of the trip, while the men were crossing settled regions of Pennsylvania, Maryland, and Ohio, they bought meals at inns and taverns. After leaving Fort Wayne and civilization, the fare included bread, biscuits, pork, bacon, maize, coffee, and tea, with occasional variants such as ducks, turtle eggs, and at least one badger. The addition of a military escort at Fort Crawford precipitated the first serious concern about food supplies, and the group often traveled on short rations after that. Buffalo meat—fresh, jerked, and pounded into pemmican—was the staple food on the journey over the plains, varied by whatever sugar, salt, wheat, corn, potatoes, and salt pork could be procured from traders. Other meals consisted of dried moose meat, squirrel, and even elk's udder, most of them simply roasted on a stick over the fire. Indian hosts contributed more exotic dishes, such as swan, dog, and *tipsinna* or prairie turnips. The gentlemen and officers fared somewhat better than the soldiers and *engagés*, having a private store which probably included brandy and whisky as well as tea and sugar. However, when a severe food shortage occurred along Lake Superior, the gentlemen shared with their fellows a "nauseating" soup made from tripe-de-roche.[43]

The scientific objectives of the expedition were not neglected in Long's purchases of equipment. But due to "exaggerated reports of the difficulties in the country through which we were to pass" and other unspecified "accidental circumstances," the astronomical and surveying instruments formed a sad contrast to the lavish equipment Long had set out with in 1819. This was unfortunate, for the members of the party were totally dependent upon sextant, compass, and watch to determine their geographic position. The most common method of finding latitude in Long's time was based upon measuring with a sextant the angle of elevation of some celestial body above the horizon. The sextant, improved in accuracy from the simpler quadrants and octants of the 18th century, nevertheless utilized the same basic principles. Sightings were taken upon two

[43] Voucher No. 59, in "Abstract," Appendix 2; William H. Keating, *Narrative of an Expedition to the Source of St. Peter's River . . . under the Command of Stephen H. Long*, 1:189, 212, 292, 336, 337, 371, 432, 435, 2:10, 20, 95, 116, 187, 188 (Philadelphia, 1824); pp. 128, 154, below.

objects (usually the horizon and sun, moon, or star) by means of a telescope and movable mirror, the angle being read off from the angle of these two parts to one another. If the true horizon was obscured by trees or hills, the observer used an artificial horizon, a perfectly level mirror formed by a pool of specially distilled mercury sheltered from the wind with a glass plate. The observer could sight his sextant at the reflection of the star in the mercury instead of at the horizon, thus measuring exactly twice the star's true altitude from the horizon.[44]

Long's equipment included at least two sextants, one of them a pocket or "snuff-box" sextant bought for $20 in Philadelphia and one described as "a brass sextant, of five inches radius" made by William Cary, a prominent London instrument maker. The artificial horizon of mercury was carried in a boxwood case. The difficulties under which readings were taken and the smallness of the sextants accounted for the relative inexactness of some resulting measurements. It is a credit to the skill of Long and his astronomer James E. Colhoun that the most crucial measurement—that of the 49th parallel at Pembina— was so nearly correct. Despite cloudy weather and troubles with their instruments, they placed the border only 250 yards south of the correct line, a result that could hardly have been improved upon except by sheer accident, given the instruments available. Twenty-six years later, when Major Samuel Woods visited Pembina, he wrote that Long was reputed to have voiced suspicions that the post he placed to mark the 49th parallel was "some two or three hundred yards within our territory." If this was true, Long's and Colhoun's precision and sense of accuracy in using their small instruments is all the more remarkable.[45]

[44] Keating, *Narrative*, 2:402; Vouchers No. 85 and 86, March 15, 1819, Abstract 1, in Account No. 1020/1823, and Voucher No. 3, March 22, 1819, in Account No. 7261/1819, all in GAO, Third Auditor, NARG 217.

For a description of instruments and methods of the 1820s here and below, see Robert Gibson, *The Theory and Practice of Surveying; Containing All the Instructions Requisite for the Skilful Practice of This Art*, 337–348 (New York, 1821).

[45] Long to Macomb, March 11, 1823; Voucher No. 10, in "Abstract"—both in Appendix 2; Keating, *Narrative*, 2:401, 409. Lengthy lists of astronomical observations in Long's and Colhoun's journals have been omitted from the present edition; several mentions of the instruments are in the omitted material and can be found on pp. 70, 81, 106 of the manuscript versions of Long's journal in the Division of Archives and Manuscripts, MHS. On Cary, see Maurice Daumas, *Scientific Instruments of the Seventeenth and Eighteenth Centuries*, 245 (New York and Washington, 1972). Information on the location of the 49th parallel is from an interview of the editors, September 28, 1977, with William E. Lass, who has done extensive research on this subject for a forthcoming book; Maj. Samuel Woods to Gen. R[oger] Jones,

JAMES E. COLHOUN as a young man. Undated portrait by an unknown artist. Courtesy South Caroliniana Library, University of South Carolina, Columbia.

In the 1820s longitude presented more problems than latitude. Determining it required finding the exact difference in time between the place of observation and a fixed reference point (Long, like other British and American observers, used Greenwich), and clocks were at best unreliable. The most expensive single piece of equipment Long purchased for the expedition was a patent lever watch, made by Robert Roskell of Liverpool, which was in constant need of resetting and checking. Theoretically, the first reliable chronometers, developed about 1760, had made it possible for a

November 10, 1849, in 31 Congress, 1 session, *House Executive Documents*, no. 51, p. 19 (serial 577).

traveler to carry a watch set to Greenwich time and find the longitude by noting Greenwich time at local noon. Practically, however, it was necessary to check the watch by observing distinct astronomical occurrences which had been predicted for Greenwich. It was then possible to compare the local time of the occurrences with tables of Greenwich times published in the *Nautical Almanac*, an invaluable reference book that Long acquired before leaving Philadelphia. The predicted occurrences could include eclipses of Jupiter's moons, occultations of stars behind the moon, transits of planets across the sun, or simply the passage of stars across the meridian. The majority of observations taken during Long's journey were of lunar distances, a method whereby the moon's movement among the stars formed an astronomical clock whose running was measured by noting the angular distances between the moon and certain prominent stars.[46]

Another frequent observation was the measurement of amplitudes, or the angular distance of the sun along the horizon from true east at rising, or from true west at setting, a measurement helpful in finding the magnetic variation of the compass. To take this reading it was necessary to have an instrument which measured horizontal angles; the Long party seems to have made do with a surveyor's compass. This was simply a large magnetic compass divided into four quarters, each marked from 0 to 90 degrees, and having two projecting arms for sighting along a north-south line. Though it was "small and not nicely graduated," it seems to have served to triangulate the width of the Falls of St. Anthony as well as for amplitude readings and measuring the direction of travel. It needed frequent adjustment; since magnetic north does not coincide with true north, the party constantly had to check and correct the compass readings for magnetic variation.[47]

Other equipment on the journey included a protractor used in conjunction with the compass to draw sketch maps, a pocket compass, two lenses probably used as burning glasses, and a measuring tape. For recording observations and collecting specimens, there were blank notebooks, lead pencils, and tin boxes. Two thermometers served for meteorological data. Conspicuously miss-

[46] Vouchers No. 10, 11, in "Abstract," Appendix 2, below. On Roskell and the development of watches for finding longitudes, see G. H. Baillie, C. Clutton, and C. A. Ilbert, *Britten's Old Clocks and Watches and Their Makers*, 176–180, 186–202, 464 (7th ed., New York, 1959).

[47] Gibson, *Surveying*, 352; Keating, *Narrative*, 1:298; Long, manuscript journal, p. 100.

ing were the barometers, chronometers, circumferentors, and theodolites with which Long had been supplied in 1819.[48]

Engaging men to fill the key positions in the expedition was one of the most critical planning tasks Long faced. Interpreters, guides, a military escort, and boatmen he would engage in the West as they were needed, but the necessity for recruiting the persons whom he called "the gentlemen of the party" was immediate. Among his first suggestions were two men experienced in exploration—Captain Matthew J. Magee, to command the military escort, and Lieutenant Andrew Talcott, to serve as Long's assistant. The major's other suggestions included three seasoned men who had accompanied him in 1820: Dr. Edwin James, to serve as botanist, geologist, and physician; Thomas Say, naturalist and antiquary; and Samuel Seymour, landscape artist.[49]

Not all of these men joined the party. Magee's name disappeared from the correspondence early in the planning, and Long did not select a commander of the military escort until he picked up his first detachment of troops at Fort Crawford. There the position was assumed by Lieutenant Martin Scott, legendary on the frontier for his deadly aim and hunting prowess.[50]

Talcott was not present when the expedition left Philadelphia on April 30. Long left instructions for him to join the party at Wheeling. In the meantime, General Macomb had given Talcott another assignment, but not until April 30 did he write to inform Long about the change in plan. The major, who thus expected to meet Talcott in Wheeling, was disappointed not to find him there. The situation was clarified when the party reached Columbus, Ohio, where James Edward Colhoun was waiting. He gave Long the general's letter of

[48] Vouchers No. 2, 8, 10, 13, in "Abstract," Appendix 2, below. In Long to Macomb, March 11, 1823, in Appendix 2, below, Long indicated that barometers were too delicate to transport, and that he wished instead to determine atmospheric weight by measuring the boiling point of water.

[49] Long to Macomb, March 11, April 15, 1823, in Appendix 2, below; Valentine M. Porter, ed., "Journal of Stephen Watts Kearny," in *Missouri Historical Collections*, 3:15n (St. Louis, 1908).

[50] Long to Macomb, April 15, July 9, 1823, in Appendix 2, below. Scott, who joined the army as a second lieutenant in 1814 and was killed during the Mexican War, was a member of Company G, Fifth Infantry, at Fort Crawford when he joined Long. His exploits are recounted in J. F[letcher] Williams, "Memoir of Capt. Martin Scott," in *Minnesota Historical Collections*, 3:180–187 (1880); this series is hereafter abbreviated *MHC*. For his service record, see Heitman, *Historical Register*, 1:869; U.S. Adjutant General's Office (hereafter abbreviated AGO), Inspection Returns, Fifth Infantry, Company G, Fort Crawford, February, 1823, October, 1824, NARG 94.

April 30 and another communication announcing that Colhoun had been chosen as a substitute for Talcott.[51]

Perhaps the greatest disappointment Long experienced was in missing connections with Dr. James. While the major was making his final preparations in Philadelphia, James was en route from Albany, New York, to Belle Fontaine, Missouri. Fearing that James might be unable to join the expedition, Long asked William H. Keating to go along as mineralogist and geologist. Keating agreed to serve without pay should James be intercepted. Long continued to write the doctor letters en route, addressing one to Belle Fontaine fixing Fort Crawford or Fort St. Anthony as a rendezvous point. When James reached Missouri, Long's orders had not arrived there, and to his chagrin, he missed the trip. Keating, the substitute, not only ably performed scientific duties intended for James, but later compiled the narrative describing the expedition, as James had done for the southwestern journey.[52]

No untoward events forestalled Thomas Say and Samuel Seymour from making the journey, and when Colhoun joined the group in Columbus, the scientific complement was complete. The "gentlemen of the party" were talented, well educated, and energetic. And Talcott's replacement was extremely well connected. James Edward Colhoun (1796–1889) was the son of John Ewing Colhoun—a South Carolina planter, lawyer, United States senator, and a cousin of John Caldwell Calhoun, secretary of war. Soon after John Ewing's death in 1802, John Caldwell began taking a keen interest in the family. He counseled the widow, Floride, on the education of her sons and in 1811 he married her only daughter. Doubly related as second cousin and brother-in-law, he developed a close friendship with James Edward.[53]

It was through Secretary Calhoun that James, then 27 years old and a navy midshipman, was selected to join the Long expedition.

[51] Long to Macomb, April 28, May 12, May 23, 1823, and Macomb to Long, April 30, May 3, 1823, all in Appendix 2, below.

[52] Long to Macomb, April 28, May 1, May 12, 1823, in Appendix 2, below; Richard G. Wood, "Dr. Edwin James, A Disappointed Explorer," in *Minnesota History*, 34:285 (Autumn, 1955).

[53] Francis de Sales Dundas, *The Calhoun Settlement District of Abbeville, South Carolina*, 11–17 (Staunton, Va., [1950]); J. Franklin Jameson, ed., *Correspondence of John C. Calhoun*, 83, 99, 105, 130, 132, 196, 205 (American Historical Association, *Annual Report for the Year 1899*, vol. 2—Washington, D.C., 1900); Charles M. Wiltse, *John C. Calhoun, Nullifier, 1829–1839*, 161–163, 311 (Indianapolis and New York, 1949). See also p. 271, below. Wiltse, *John C. Calhoun, Nationalist, 1782–1828*, 407 (Indianapolis and New York, 1944) explains the variant spellings of the family name.

WILLIAM H. KEATING, an undated portrait by Hugh Bridport. Courtesy Franklin Institute, Philadelphia.

THOMAS SAY by Charles Willson Peale. The portrait was painted in Philadelphia in 1819. Courtesy Philadelphia Academy of Natural Sciences.

According to his later recollections, while they were breakfasting together, Secretary Calhoun, "as if thinking aloud, said: 'I'm sorry I can't spare Lt. Talcott.' 'For what?' I asked. 'Major Long ought to have an assistant engineer to aid him in exploring St. Peter's river.' 'Can I take the place?' 'Yes, if you wish.' The second night I was off in the stage to intercept Major Long and his party at Columbus, O." Colhoun arrived in Columbus bearing a brief note from Macomb announcing that the midshipman had volunteered his services and had been selected to take Talcott's place. If the casual exchange annoyed the meticulous major, he rose above it to express gratification "at the attainment of so valuable an acquisition to our part[y] as that afforded by the substitution of Mr. Calhoun [*sic*]."[54]

Secretary Calhoun's sponsorship of his kinsman, with whom he corresponded during the course of the expedition, probably eased his acceptance by Long and the other gentlemen. The young man, however, had qualities over and above his distinguished sponsorship that would recommend him to the party. Blue-eyed, of medium stature, and erect in bearing, he was kindly, affable, and though shy, a fine conversationalist. Moreover, he was widely traveled, for his tours of naval duty had carried him to South America and China. He was also well read, a background that enabled him to make a substantial contribution to the party's published *Narrative*. His scientific qualifications for his assignments as astronomer and assistant topographer were probably not outstanding. Although he produced the astronomical data that appeared in the *Narrative*, he made few maps and drew upon others for the inaccurate table of distances prepared for the book. After the expedition he returned to the navy until 1833, when he retired to begin a long career as a planter in Abbeville County, South Carolina.[55]

There was no doubt about the scientific qualifications of Thomas Say (1787–1834), one of the veterans of Long's 1819–20 journey who was selected to serve as antiquary, zoologist, botanist, and one of the literary journalists on the 1823 expedition. Son of Benjamin Say,

[54] Quoted in Dundas, *Calhoun Settlement*, 25. Colhoun was the recipient of numerous furloughs during his naval career. The one covering his service with Long is dated April 23, 1823, and is for eight months. It is in U.S. Office of Naval Records and Library, Naval Records Collections, Appointments, Orders, and Resignations, 13:79, NARG 45. See also Macomb to Long, May 3, 1823, and Long to Macomb, May 23, 1823, both in Appendix 2, below.

[55] Jameson, ed., *Correspondence of John C. Calhoun*, 211–213; Dundas, *Calhoun Settlement*, 13; Wiltse, *Calhoun, Nationalist*, 231; Colhoun to Keating, September 19, 1824, South Caroliniana Library, University of South Carolina, Columbia.

a physician and apothecary, Thomas was well established in the Philadelphia scientific community. He had begun studies in natural history after a brief formal education and practice as an apothecary, and in 1812 he became one of the founders of the Philadelphia Academy of Natural Sciences. His career between that date and 1823 included service as the academy's secretary, curator of the American Philosophical Society, and professor of natural history at the University of Pennsylvania. To collect and study fauna, he had made wide-ranging field trips, the most extensive of which was as a member of Long's earlier Yellowstone Expedition.[56]

The publications of this gentle and modest man extended Say's reputation as a natural scientist far beyond the intellectual circles of Philadelphia. By 1823 he had written on entomology and conchology, and he had laid down lines for major works that would be completed later. His contributions to the *Account* of Long's 1819–20 expedition, published in 1823, were substantial and were fully acknowledged in the book. His contributions to the *Narrative* of the 1823 expedition further enhanced his reputation. Through these and later works, he became known as the father of American conchology, American zoology, American entomology, and descriptive entomology.

Say's scientific dedication, combined with an amiable and conciliatory nature, made him a valuable member of the 1823 group. Even the mercurial Giacomo Beltrami, who had few compliments for the expedition members as he traveled with them from Fort St. Anthony to the Selkirk Colony, praised Say as a scientist and as a man "distinguished at once by modesty and merit."[57]

The sources relating to the expedition do not reveal any other reactions to this tall, spare, dark-complexioned scientist, who spoke with a lisp and went about his duties wearing a white beaver hat. But he must have been a man to remember. At one point on the journey he was so absorbed in collecting insects that an antelope came near him without his being aware of the delicate creature. On another occasion, while intently examining a dead rattlesnake's head, he punctured his thumb and was poisoned. He undoubtedly administered his own antidote, for in the absence of a physician he used his experience as an apothecary to treat anyone who needed

[56] For this and the paragraph below, see Harry B. Weiss and Grace M. Ziegler, *Thomas Say: Early American Naturalist*, 18, 24, 31–41, 54, 61, 79, 88, 93, 157, 190–201 (Springfield, Ill., and Baltimore, Md., 1931).

[57] Weiss and Ziegler, *Thomas Say*, 158; Beltrami, *Pilgrimage*, 2:370.

medicines. While he attended to medical duties that would have fallen to James, he also tried to carry out the doctor's assignment as botanist. Although Say collected plants, Keating commented, he did so "with that diffidence with which a man will attend to a task with which he does not profess to be conversant."[58]

Say's distinction as a scientist was matched by that of William H. Keating (1799–1840), the youngest member of the expedition and a man who also belonged to the same Philadelphia intellectual group that nourished the remarkable naturalist. The son of Baron John and Eulalia Deschapelles Keating, he was born in Wilmington, Delaware, and grew up in Philadelphia. In addition to receiving bachelor's and master's degrees from the University of Pennsylvania, he studied chemistry, mineralogy, mining engineering, and geology in France, Switzerland, Savoy, Germany, Holland, Scotland, and England. His *Considerations upon the Art of Mining . . . and the Advantages Which Would Result from an Introduction of This Art into the United States*, published in 1821, was said to be the first scientific work on this subject by an American.[59]

Keating's identification with Philadelphia's intellectual community was evidenced by his appointment in 1822 at the age of 23 as professor of mineralogy and chemistry at the University of Pennsylvania and by his association with the city's learned organizations. The Philadelphia Academy of Natural Sciences published his articles as early as 1821. In 1822 he became a member of the American Philosophical Society, and two years later he was one of the founders of the Franklin Institute, where he taught chemistry and issued a text on that subject in 1824. In that notable year of his young life, he also compiled the book describing Long's 1823 expedition, an assignment that made his name known far beyond scientific circles and probably overshadowed his later accomplishments in science, law, and politics.

Long selected Keating to accompany the expedition during the last days of his preparations for departure. The orders Secretary Calhoun issued on April 25 include no mention of the young man. Three days later Long informed Calhoun that he had offered Keat-

[58] Weiss and Ziegler, *Thomas Say*, 158; U.S. Department of the Interior, "Thomas Say, the 'Father of American Descriptive Entomology,'" 11, mimeographed memorandum for the press, September 24, 1938, copy in MHS library; Keating, *Narrative*, 1:12n, 180, 268, 270, 2:63, 118.

[59] For this and the paragraph below, see Wyndham D. Miles, "A Versatile Explorer: A Sketch of William H. Keating," in *Minnesota History*, 36:297, 298 (December, 1959); *Dictionary of American Biography*, 10:276 (New York, 1933).

ing the position of mineralogist and geologist, to which he added the assignment of literary journalist when it seemed probable that James would not be able to join the party. Although the major wrote that Keating "stands deservedly high as a Geologist" and expressed confidence in him, his letter was focused on the absent doctor rather than on the talented substitute. Keating recorded his enthusiasm for the appointment when he notified the trustees of the University of Pennsylvania on April 29 of his imminent departure for the West. "It has appeared to me," he wrote, "that the acceptance of this offer was by no means incompatible with the duties of the chair which you have been pleased to confide to my care, and that on the contrary you would approve of my lending my assistance to an undertaking which it is hoped will prove very serviceable to science, at the same time that I was making myself better acquainted with the resources and productions of our country."[60]

Still another Philadelphian was among the "gentlemen of the party." Like Say, Samuel Seymour, artist and engraver, was a veteran of Long's 1819–20 expedition. Unlike Say, very little is known of his life before and after his service with Long, and his artistic works are widely scattered. He may have been a native of England. His earliest known works in America are engravings dating from 1797. His friendship with William Russell Birch and his son Thomas Birch, two English artists living in Philadelphia, supplied him with employment, especially from 1798 to 1800 when the Birches were publishing a collection of Philadelphia views for which Seymour did some engraving. Rambles up the Schuylkill Valley with artists John Wesley Jarvis, Thomas Birch, and later Thomas Sully gave Seymour opportunities to sketch and paint Pennsylvania scenery. After 1800 Seymour executed many engravings published in Philadelphia, often from paintings by Birch. A major project from 1810 to 1812 was engraving illustrations for the Philadelphia edition of John Pinkerton's *General Collection of the Best and Most Interesting Voyages and Travels, In All Parts of the World*. In 1811 and again in 1814 he exhibited several paintings at the Pennsylvania Academy of the Fine Arts. The Philadelphia city directories began to list Seymour's name in 1808, although he must have been living in or near the city before then; by 1819 he was residing with Joseph H. Seymour, an engraver from Worcester, Massachusetts, who had

[60] Long to Macomb, April 28, 1823, in Appendix 2, below; Keating to the trustees of the University of Pennsylvania, April 29, 1823, in University of Pennsylvania Archives, Philadelphia.

been in Philadelphia since 1803. This joint residency continued until about 1822. In 1823 Joseph died while Samuel was traveling through Illinois with Long's expedition. After 1823 Samuel seems to have abandoned Philadelphia as a permanent residence, possibly moving to New York. He may have lived into the 1830s, for art historian William Dunlap referred to him in the present tense in 1834.[61]

As late in his planning as April 15, Long was not certain that Seymour would accompany the expedition as landscape painter, for he listed as an alternate the name of "Reader"—possibly Alexander Rider, another Philadelphia artist. Calhoun's orders of April 25, which throughout reflected Long's wishes, also listed "Reader" as an alternate. By April 28, however, Long reported that Seymour was ready to leave with the party. The reasons for the major's ambivalence concerning Seymour were not stated. The artist might have been difficult to reach or engaged in other work. Another factor might have been Long's experience with him while the *Account* of the 1819–20 expedition was in preparation. "I cannot get him to complete the Drawings for our Book," Long wrote in exasperation to the chief of the Topographical Bureau on June 29, 1822. "A strange infatuation seems to have seized him — and I know not when to expect his recovery." Seymour seems to have been reasonably active during the 1823 expedition, for there are frequent references to his sketches in Long's journal and in Keating's *Narrative*. In addition to these duties, he was in charge of recording temperatures at various times each day.[62]

[61] William Dunlap, *History of the Rise and Progress of the Arts of Design in the United States*, 2:259, 447 (New York, 1834); David M. Stauffer, *American Engravers Upon Copper and Steel*, 1:xiv, 244, 2:475–478 (New York, 1907); Martin P. Snyder, "William Birch: His Philadelphia Views," in *Pennsylvania Magazine of History and Biography*, 73:275, 280 (July, 1949); Anna W. Rutledge, comp. and ed., *Cumulative Record of Exhibition Catalogues: The Pennsylvania Academy of the Fine Arts, 1807–1870, The Society of Artists, 1800–1814, The Artists' Fund Society, 1835–1845*, 200 (American Philosophical Society, *Memoirs*, vol. 38—Philadelphia, 1955); *Philadelphia Directory*, 1803, 1808, 1819–21, 1824; George C. Groce and David H. Wallace, *The New-York Historical Society's Dictionary of Artists in America 1564–1860*, 570 (New Haven and London, 1957); Death Register, Archives of the City and County of Philadelphia, in City of Philadelphia, Department of Records; Robert Taft, *Artists and Illustrators of the Old West 1850–1900*, 379 (New York and London, 1953). For reviews of Seymour's career, see John F. McDermott, "Samuel Seymour: Pioneer Artist of the Plains and the Rockies," in Smithsonian Institution, *Annual Report*, 1950, pp. 497–509 (Washington, D.C., 1951); John C. Ewers, *Artists of the Old West*, 26–36 (New York, 1965).

[62] Long to Macomb, April 15, 28, 1823, and Calhoun to Long, April 25, 1823, all in Appendix 2, below. The quotation is in McDermott, in Smithsonian Institution,

The expedition gathered other members in its long trek of about 4,500 miles in six months. Andrew Allison, a black man, joined the party as a servant at St. Clairsville, Ohio, and troop detachments were added first at Fort Crawford and then at Fort St. Anthony. Among the guides and interpreters during various parts of the journey were noted frontiersmen—Joseph St. Peter Le Sellier, Augustin Rocque, Joseph Renville, and Charles Gasparde Brousse. At Fort St. Anthony they were joined by Giacomo Costantino Beltrami, traveler and litterateur from Bergamo, Italy, in self-imposed exile from his native country, whose impetuous disposition caused friction with Long until the Italian's furious departure from the party at Pembina. William Joseph Snelling, who was to earn a reputation as a writer, also traveled with the expedition from Fort St. Anthony to the Red River, the portion of the journey on which the party reached its maximum number of 32 men.[63]

Although the men who accompanied Long had heavy responsibilities and novel sights to stimulate their curiosity, boredom and a sense of isolation occasionally overcame them. For example, Keating wrote that the capture of two young wolves on the prairies in western Minnesota "created such a sensation in the party, as will not be readily conceived by those, who have not experienced how eagerly man seizes the first opportunity of being relieved from his own thoughts, when he has been left to the uninterrupted exercise of them for a certain length of time."[64]

For the most part, the trip was not marked by unusual events, even when passing through a region inhabited by Dakota tribes of uncertain disposition. In one instance an encounter with a mischievous band created uneasiness, an incident that probably inspired the exaggerated accounts that reached St. Louis of an attack on the expedition.[65] Although the usually spartan character of Long's journal and Keating's general objectivity in the *Narrative* precluded personal observations, the gentlemen seem to have treated one another with great civility. Furthermore, party mem-

Annual Report, 1950, p. 503. On Rider, see Rutledge, comp. and ed., *Cumulative Record of Exhibition Catalogues*, 183. On Seymour's temperature records, see p. 315, below.

[63] Keating, *Narrative*, 2:205; pp. 119, 135, 145, 155, below; Augusto P. Miceli, *The Man With the Red Umbrella: Giacomo Costantino Beltrami in America*, 71–81 (Baton Rouge, La., 1974).

[64] Keating, *Narrative*, 1:358.

[65] Maj. Gen. E. P. Gaines to John C. Calhoun, October 18, 1823, and Long to Macomb, August 8, 1823, both printed in Appendix 2, below.

bers had rewarding experiences with the many people they met on their travels: native leaders Wabasha, Red Wing, Waneta, and Metea, traders John McLoughlin and Donald McKenzie, and frontier notables James Riley and Lewis Cass. Even the delicate situation in the Selkirk Colony was handled with discretion, and in Detroit, where Governor Cass was their host, no questions about Douglass' master plan for collecting scientific data seemed to disturb the serenity of the reception.

On the journey, as well as in his preparations, Long was keenly aware of the fiscal duties that he must discharge when the expedition returned to Philadelphia. On April 15, he sent Macomb a detailed cost estimate amounting to $2,000, and Macomb promptly honored his initial draft for $1,000. By the time the party reached Fort Wayne, the major realized that expenses would exceed his estimates, and he asked Macomb to send an additional $500 to Detroit. When he reached Buffalo, New York, on the return trip, his message to Macomb was still more woeful—the expenses, he reported, would far outrun his estimates. And indeed they did. The abstract of expenditures he submitted on November 1 amounted to $4,370.04. Part of the gap between the estimate and the final account was due to the substitution of Keating and Colhoun for James and Talcott, for the latter were in the government's employ and would not have received additional salaries. Other elements Long mentioned were the high cost of "horse-keeping" and the amount of food he was forced to purchase because the military posts along the way could not provide enough to compensate for the scarcity of game. Macomb quibbled about some of the expenses, but the expedition costing less than $1.00 a mile would seem to have been a bargain for the United States government.[66]

Upon his return, Long took up the work of producing a book describing the journey—a project he had had in mind since the inception of the expedition. "Thinking it probable that some account of our researches, in a popular form, will be required," he wrote to Macomb on October 31, 1823, "I have already made some arrangements with a view to that object, but can do nothing decisive, till

[66] Long to Macomb, April 15, May 29, October 18, November 20, 1823; Macomb to Long, April 30, October 31, 1823; "Abstract"—all printed in Appendix 2, below. Some of the accounts were not finally settled until early in 1824. See GAO, Third Auditor, Accounts No. 3106, 3593, Long, NARG 217.

authorized by the Department." Macomb authorized the book, which was to be completed in nine months.[67]

The major then set about producing the volume that was to become a classic in the literature of western exploration—*Narrative of an Expedition to the Source of St. Peter's River, Lake Winnepeek, Lake of the Woods &c. &c.* He purchased writing and drawing paper, quills, ink, pencils, and wood to heat the rented office through the winter's work. The office undoubtedly had other accouterments, for Macomb suggested that the furnishings used while the *Account* of the 1819–20 expedition had been written would "answer your purpose." The major engaged Keating and Say to work on the narrative at a per diem rate and agreed to pay Seymour $3.50 for each drawing completed.[68]

Once again Long had difficulty getting Seymour to complete his work. Although the artist delivered 11 drawings in time for publication, 22 additional illustrations intended for the book were not finished until April, 1825. Their late delivery presented Long with a problem in arranging Seymour's reimbursement. "The drawings are very well executed, and make very handsome pictures," Long wrote to Macomb. "Their cost will be $77. . . . I will endeavour to retain them, subject to your instructions, but consider myself under no obligations to Mr. S. There is little doubt however, that the drawings will command the price above mentioned." Whether Macomb authorized the purchase of any of these Seymour pictures is unknown. The 22 paintings which Long listed were dispersed and may be lost; some may yet exist in private collections, but only a few have been surely identified at present.[69]

[67] Long to Macomb, October 31, 1823, in Appendix 2, below; Long to Macomb, November 6, 1823, OCE, Letters Received, and Macomb to Long, November 10, 1823, OCE, Letters to Officers of Engineers, both in NARG 77.

[68] "Abstract of Expenditures," December 23, 1824, with supporting Vouchers No. 1–7, GAO, Third Auditor, Account No. 3593, Long, NARG 217; Macomb to Long, November 10, 1823, OCE, Letters to Officers of Engineers, NARG 77; Long to Macomb, April 23, 1825, in Appendix 2, below. The total expenditure Long charged to the government for the book was $548.62.

[69] For the quotation, see Long to Macomb, April 23, 1825, in Appendix 2, below. McDermott discussed the works of art produced as a result of the 1823 expedition in Smithsonian Institution, *Annual Report*, 1950, pp. 503–508. The largest group of known Seymour watercolors belongs to the Beinecke Library of Yale University, but none of these is from the 1823 expedition. They were reproduced in the Imprint Society's edition of James, *Account* (Barre, Mass., 1972). Some 1823 paintings in other hands include the watercolor "Indian Encampment on Big Stone Lake," which has been published in *Kennedy Quarterly*, 12:173 (June, 1973) and in *Antiques*,

Long chose for himself the same role he had played in the *Account* of the 1819–20 expedition—map construction, preparation of a topographical report, and supervision of the project. His supervisory responsibilities were specified in a contract with the printers, H. C. Carey and I. Lea, the Philadelphia printing house that had also issued the *Account*. He seems to have worked in Philadelphia on the *Narrative* rather steadily from November, 1823, to May, 1824, when an impatient Macomb assigned him to investigate navigation on the Ohio River. In November, 1824, to Macomb's chagrin, he was back in Philadelphia working on the book that would be issued in late December. At times during the printing he was absent from the city, and some errors in the published volume are attributed to his absence.[70]

Chosen as compiler was Keating, who in amalgamating the journals and notes written by expedition members into a coherent narrative followed the earlier pattern established by James in the *Account*. Keating acknowledged the contributions other party members made to the book. In addition to the fields of their assigned responsibilities, he noted the debt to Colhoun for references to older writers, to Say for data on the Indians to supplement his own, and to Long for historical and descriptive material. He also credited contributions by members of the American Philosophical Society and the Academy of Natural Sciences. Among others acknowledged were Lewis D. von Schweinitz, who described the plants collected by Say, and Joseph Lovell, surgeon general of the United States Army, whose table on climate was used in preference to the data Seymour collected.[71]

An examination of the text of the *Narrative* makes it obvious that Keating drew substantially from the Colhoun and Long journals. Given the amount of interweaving he accomplished and in the absence of the original materials he and Say wrote, no definitive textual analysis can be made. However, his debt to Long seems to be

72:454 (November, 1957); and "View of Major Long's Party Crossing the Lower Falls on Winnepeek River, August 20, 1823," in the Sarah Ann Mordecai Collection of the American Jewish Historical Society, Waltham, Mass. Two untitled oil paintings of Seymour's which could possibly be from the 1823 expedition are in the possession of John C. Lord of Buffalo, N.Y.

[70] Long to Macomb, May 18, 1824, OCE, Letters Received; Macomb to Long, May 14, November 4, 1824, OCE, Letters to Officers of Engineers; Long to Macomb, February 1, March 1, December 1, 1824, OCE, Monthly Personal Reports of Officers, Long—all in NARG 77; Keating, *Narrative*, 1: errata page, viii. The contract has not been located.

[71] Keating, *Narrative*, 1: vii–xii.

particularly heavy. Extensive passages were taken verbatim from the 1823 journal, and many excerpts from the major's 1817 journal appear as well.

News of the return of Long's party was not without bitterness to the explorers who had accompanied Lewis Cass's 1820 expedition. Henry Schoolcraft expressed consternation at learning of Long's journey, which destroyed his own "cherished hope . . . of leading an expedition to the North." Schoolcraft had in fact been encouraged to expect the command of an expedition up the Minnesota River as late as April 29, 1823. Even keener was the indignation of David Douglass, who was still struggling to publish a map and journal of the Cass expedition. Upon learning of Long's intention to prepare a separate report, Douglass wrote Secretary Calhoun that "Until very lately indeed I had not entertained the smallest doubt that the party of Majr. Long was organized in pursuance of the plan recommended by Gov. Cass and myself; and for the purpose of collecting additional information in aid of the work upon which I have been for some time engaged." The publication, which, he stated, was "in a very good state of forwardness," had been purposely delayed to incorporate Long's information. Referring to his previous correspondence with Calhoun, Douglass said that he had been given full encouragement to believe Long's information would be given to him. He feared "a collission [with Long] which I am sure would be equally unpleasant to us both." Between Keating's *Narrative* and Schoolcraft's *Narrative Journal* of the Cass expedition, so much information was eventually published that Douglass' book was rendered unnecessary. Although Long referred to the volume Douglass was preparing in his description of the Mississippi River published in the *Narrative*, the book never appeared.[72]

Overt conflict came not with Douglass, but with Beltrami. He, too, wrote a book, which was published in French in New Orleans in 1824 and included harsh comments about Long. The major, answering in kind, added to the *Narrative* a footnote signed with his initials in which he criticized Beltrami's work for its "fictions and misrepresentations." When Beltrami spotted the note, he was incensed. Although he must have known that Long had written it, he

[72] Schoolcraft, *Personal Memoirs of a Residence of Thirty Years with the Indian Tribes on the American Frontiers*, 168, 175, 177 (Philadelphia, 1851); Douglass to Calhoun, November 3, 1823, OCE, Letters Referred, NARG 77; Keating, *Narrative*, 2:218. The conflict between Schoolcraft and Douglass over the same projected work is discussed in Sydney W. Jackman and John F. Freeman, eds., *American Voyageur: The Journal of David Bates Douglass*, xix–xxi (Marquette, Mich., 1969).

addressed a letter to Keating and the publishers asking who might give him an explanation for the "insolent" comment. Stephen H. Long, replied the addressees. The Italian then challenged Long, demanding satisfaction for this and other insults. So far as is known Long did not reply, but the offensive footnote was modified in later editions of the *Narrative*. Beltrami, however, did not let the matter rest. Blaming an imagined conspiracy on Long's part for a delay in the distribution of his book and for a derogatory review in the *National Gazette*, a Philadelphia magazine, the Italian continued to attack the major in letters to newspapers, in a pamphlet published in 1825, and in the expanded English version of his book issued in 1828.[73]

Beltrami's comments notwithstanding, the skillfully executed *Narrative* became a popular book. A London edition which adhered faithfully to the Philadelphia one was published by G. B. Whittaker in 1825, and another edition entitled *Travels in the Interior of North America* was issued by the same London publisher in 1828. Meanwhile, a German edition had appeared, considerably condensed into one slim volume, all charts, plates, and appendixes having been eliminated and the text reduced to a day-by-day description of the journey. The most recent edition to date is a photographic reprint of the first London edition published in Minneapolis in 1959.[74]

The reviews which appeared soon after publication of the *Narrative* both in America and England were mixed. The *North American Review*, a Boston magazine, praised it, saying that "Mr Keating has accomplished his task, as historiographer to the expedition, with much good judgment," although Jared Sparks, in the unsigned review, took exception to certain passages as "abounding in occasional superfluous epithets." The London *Monthly Review* declared that, with some exceptions, the book was "replete with valuable and interesting information," while the *Western Monthly Review*, published in Cincinnati, objected to the "foppery of display of barbarous and ear-splitting terms, in their disquisitions of natural history and

[73] Miceli, *Man With the Red Umbrella*, 122–129; Beltrami, *Pilgrimage*, 2:303, 315, 324, 483, 506; Beltrami to Keating and Carey and Lea, July 15, 1825, and to Long, July 19, 1825, in Biblioteca Civica di Bergamo, Italy, copy in Beltrami Papers, MHS.

[74] The 1825 London edition contained the following variations from the Philadelphia one: the errata were corrected; the footnote by Say appearing on p. xi of the Philadelphia edition was placed on a page by itself following the preface; six plates were eliminated, the rest were re-engraved, and some were hand-colored; the meteorological charts were printed on fold-out sheets; paging was altered. The German edition was *Forschungsreise in dem nordlichen Theile der Vereinigten Staaten von Nordamerica, im Jahre 1823* (Jena, 1826).

geology."[75] The reviewers' evaluations of the scientific contributions of the expedition in the areas of geology, natural history, geography, and ethnology were similarly varied. With modern hindsight it is possible to form a more balanced judgment of the expedition's achievements in these areas. The intellectual obstacles Long faced are nowhere more obvious than in his contemporaries' opinions of his accomplishments.

Geology was a topic of heated discussion in the mid-1820s, for the infant science was fast emerging as the study which would make the first scientific break with biblical interpretations of the world's history. The reactions of reviewers to Keating's conservative approach to the subject were predictably diverse. The *North American Review* was complimentary, saying that "The geological observations made by the expedition are mostly new, and very interesting." The more liberal *Monthly Review*, on the other hand, said the geological section was "the least satisfactory of any, as it adds little to the scanty information we before possessed. The gentleman who undertook this department appears much better qualified to examine mineral specimens in a cabinet, than to explore the geological character of an extensive region." The *Western Monthly Review* avoided specifics, remarking only that "A pedantic geologist must be the most tedious of all pedants."[76]

The truth lies somewhere between the extremes. To judge the expedition's contribution to geology, it is necessary to consider how little was known about the rocks of the inner American continent. Stratigraphy was in its infancy, and the day of systematic, government-sponsored geologic surveys was still in the future. Keating was the first professional geologist to explore the Minnesota and Red rivers, and his investigations earned praise for the Long expedition among later geologists, one of whom called it "the first attempt to apply the accurate methods of modern science to the exploration of any portion of Minnesota." But Keating was hampered in his interpretation of what he saw by the ponderous, outdated terminology of Abraham Gottlob Werner, the 18th-century

[75] *North American Review*, 21:189 (July, 1825); On Sparks, editor of the magazine, see Miles, in *Minnesota History*, 36:296n. See also *Monthly Review*, 108:125 (October, 1825); *Western Monthly Review*, 1:49 (May, 1827). Later and more unfavorable comments on the book appeared in *North American Review*, 22:61 (January, 1826), 27:95–98 (July, 1828); the first may have been written by Lewis Cass and the second by Henry Schoolcraft.

[76] *North American Review*, 21:183; *Monthly Review*, 108:123; *Western Monthly Review*, 1:49.

theorist whose work was still a standard geologic text in America in 1823, despite the fact that James Hutton's contrary theories of volcanism and erosion had been available since 1795 and William Smith's revolutionary delineation of English geologic strata had been published in 1815.[77]

The Wernerian system with which Long and Keating were burdened assumed that all rocks were formed out of the sediments of a primeval sea that at one time covered the globe. Rocks were divided into several classes: the oldest were the primitive, characterized by hard, unstratified rocks without fossils (such as granite, basalt, and schist); the youngest were the secondary, which were formed from the hardening of deposited sediments (sandstone, limestone, chalk, and coal); the transitional were a midpoint between these two (such as some schists, slate, and gypsum). Other categories were alluvial and volcanic, supposedly formed by the erosion or melting of the other three. These oversimplified Wernerian classes were a trial to the firsthand investigator, since they forced him to construct a complicated system of "intrusions" and "superimpositions" to explain the presence of young igneous rocks found above older sedimentary ones; nor did they account for the fact that geologic strata were not continuous throughout the globe. The latter difficulty led Keating to search exhaustively for parallels between American minerals and those of Germany and England, a somewhat futile exercise for which he was praised in the *North American Review*.

Keating was handicapped not only by the prevailing geologic theories of his day but also by the lack of satisfactory theories to account for what he saw. The expedition passed through a terrain shaped largely by glaciers. Keating observed the driftless area of southern Wisconsin and southeastern Minnesota, the moraines of the Minnesota Valley, the flatness of the former Glacial Lake Agassiz area of the Red River Valley, and the scoured Canadian Shield southeast of Lake Winnipeg. But he did not understand what he saw, for Louis Agassiz had not yet propounded his revolutionary

[77] A good summary of the *Narrative's* geologic contributions can be found in N[ewton] H. Winchell and Warren Upham, *The Geology of Minnesota*, 1:33–44 (*Geological and Natural History Survey of Minnesota*—Minneapolis, 1884). For this and the paragraph below, see also William E. Lass, "Introduction to the Reprint Edition," in George W. Featherstonhaugh, *A Canoe Voyage up the Minnay Sotor*, 1:xxx–xxxii (Reprint ed., St. Paul, 1970); Carroll L. and Mildred A. Fenton, *Giants of Geology*, 43–46, 56, 80 (New York, 1952); George P. Merrill, *The First One Hundred Years of American Geology*, 2–4 (New Haven, 1924); Keating, *Narrative*, 1:195–199; *North American Review*, 21:183. For examples of Long's reliance on Werner's theories, see pp. 66, 80, 115, 232, 254, below.

glacial theories. In the 1820s most travelers resorted to the ideas of Count Constantin F. Volney and Samuel L. Mitchill, who both proposed that the entire Mississippi watershed had once been a vast lake held in by a chain of mountain dams. At one point these natural dikes were supposed to have given way, causing a cataclysmic flood which deposited the remains of former islands and dikes in moraines over the land. This theory probably prompted Long to refer to the Coteau des Prairies, the height of land separating the Missouri and Mississippi watersheds in South Dakota and Minnesota, as a "grand dike." It was almost certainly in his mind when he observed evidence of ancient high water levels on the Mississippi in 1817. Long's contemporaries Henry Schoolcraft and John J. Bigsby proposed similar theories to explain ancient high water levels in the Great Lakes. Schoolcraft's 1825 argument that the Mississippi's level had once been 130 feet higher bears a definite resemblance to Long's observations on the area eight years earlier.[78]

Despite its lack of glacial theory and its steadfastly Wernerian terminology, the *Narrative* did contribute to the mineralogical map of North America. It astutely noted the precise limits of the driftless area of southern Wisconsin and Minnesota; it mentioned the limestone and sandstone formations on the lower Minnesota River; it was the first to locate accurately the Coteau des Prairies, though no detailed investigation of this important formation was attempted; it described accurately the extent of the glacial drift in the Minnesota Valley, though it did not account for this phenomenon; it gave a detailed mineralogical description of rocks found in parts of Illinois, Wisconsin, Minnesota, and Ontario. The book remained a standard geological report on the region until David Dale Owen surveyed Wisconsin, Iowa, and Minnesota in the 1850s. In 1884 it was still considered "a good preliminary account" of the geology of the area.[79]

The natural history section of the *Narrative* was a disappointment. The London reviewer complained that "the North American naturalists seem too well disposed to follow the example of cabinet-philosophers in Europe" by naming new species after little observation, noting that "no addition is made to our knowledge of the

[78] Merrill, *American Geology*, 28, 50–52, 68, 92; Fenton and Fenton, *Giants of Geology*, 124, 126, 132; Keating, *Narrative*, 2:224; Schoolcraft, *Travels in the Central Portions of the Mississippi Valley*, 216–219 (New York, 1825); p. 80, below.

[79] Lawrence Martin, "A Pennsylvanian's Discovery of the Driftless Area," in Geographical Society of Philadelphia, *Bulletin*, 21:140–147 (October, 1923); Miles, in *Minnesota History*, 36:296; Winchell and Upham, *Geology of Minnesota*, 1:34.

mammalia class." The latter objection was true; although Say's entomological survey was quite thorough, a scrutiny of the book reveals only 11 species of mammals recorded during the entire journey. The list of 53 birds included the first scientific record on the ornithology of the Minnesota area and mentioned several now-rare species breeding along the route of the journey. That the botanical section was inadequate was due to the lack of a trained botanist on the expedition. Say's collection of plants was first given to the widely traveled pioneer botanist Thomas Nuttall to evaluate for publication, but he had completed the classification of only five specimens when he was called away to England, and the work was completed by Lewis D. von Schweinitz. The loss of several boxes of specimens en route made the collection Schweinitz had to work with very small; he identified only 130 species, 11 of which he diffidently proposed as new. But the incompleteness of the specimens and the lack of information concerning where they were gathered combined to make the identifications uncertain; thus no significant discoveries were forthcoming. As early as 1879 botanists pronounced the 1823 expedition "unimportant as to botany."[80]

The geographic contributions of the expedition were more easily recognized. The *North American Review* claimed in 1825 that "Three fifths of our wide possessions are to this day a complete *terra incognita*, of which we know little more than we do of the geographical and political features of Monomotapa." The state of affairs was not as drastic as the magazine claimed in relation to the country Long visited in 1823; good maps were available from such American cartographers as John Melish, Henry S. Tanner, and the publishers Carey and Lea of Philadelphia. Maps of the Mississippi basin had been greatly improved after the Lewis and Clark and the 1819–20 Long expeditions had explored the western waterways. Nevertheless, Long wrote frankly in February, 1823, that "So defective is our Geography in the essentials of *Latitude* and *Longitude*, that I have little hesitation in asserting, that . . . these elements have not been determined with any considerable precision at more than eight or ten points." Although Long never was assigned to conduct the nationwide survey he proposed to correct this situation, his maps contributed substantially to the known geography of the nation he

[80] *Monthly Review*, 108:124, 125; Herbert Krause, "Ornithology of the Major Long Expedition, 1823," and "Mammals of the Major Long Expedition, 1823," in *Minnesota Naturalist*, September, 1956, pp. 39–42, Spring, 1957, pp. 1–4; Keating, *Narrative*, 2:379; Susan D. McKelvey, *Botanical Exploration of the Trans-Mississippi West 1790–1850*, 279 (Jamaica Plain, Mass., 1955).

served. Henry Tanner praised his work for its accuracy on the upper Mississippi, and John J. Bigsby called it "the best accessible map of the vicinity of the Lake Superior."[81]

Long mentions only three published sources he used in drawing up the map which appeared with the *Narrative* of the 1823 expedition: Zebulon Pike's map of the upper Mississippi, Joseph Bouchette's "Map of Upper and Lower Canada, Compiled from the Latest Surveys, and Adjusted from the Most Recent Astronomical Observations," and Henry Tanner's maps of New York, Pennsylvania, Ohio, Indiana, and Illinois. For the northern parts of the route Long may also have consulted the British map of Aaron Arrowsmith, which incorporated information gathered in the surveys of David Thompson and Peter Fidler. He probably also had access to Lewis and Clark's map of the West.[82]

These were all accurate maps for their day, and Long found little need to depart drastically from them or from his own earlier map drawn from the 1819–20 expedition notes. His principal contributions were in correcting the course of the Minnesota River, which had been shown flowing vaguely northwest as far as the sources of

[81] *North American Review*, 21:178. Melish's main work was "Map of the United States with the Contiguous British and Spanish Possessions," published in Philadelphia in 1816 and reprinted at least 22 times before 1823; Tanner's was "Map of North America, Constructed According to the Latest Information" (Philadelphia, 1822). Carey and Lea, the publishers of James's *Account* and Keating's *Narrative*, brought out *A Complete Historical, Chronological, and Geographical American Atlas* in 1822, including a "Geographical, Statistical, and Historical Map of Arkansas Territory" drawn by Long. On all of these see Carl I. Wheat, *Mapping the Transmississippi West 1540–1861*, 2:62, 81, 82, 218, 225 (San Francisco, 1958). For the quotations from Long, see Long to Christopher Vandeventer, February 1, 1823, in Hemphill, ed., *Calhoun Papers*, 7:452. For the contemporary assessments of Long's work, see Tanner, *New American Atlas Containing Maps of the Several States of the North American Union*, 7 (Philadelphia, 1825); Bigsby, *The Shoe and Canoe or Pictures of Travel in the Canadas*, 2:185 (London, 1850). See also Herman R. Friis, "Stephen H. Long's Unpublished Manuscript Map of the United States Compiled in 1820–1822(?)," in *California Geographer*, 8:82–86 (1967).

[82] Keating, *Narrative*, 2:251. On Bouchette's maps and Long's manuscripts, see Tanner, *New American Atlas*, 5, 17; most of the Tanner maps Long mentioned were revised and reprinted in this atlas. The approximate route of the 1823 expedition through Indiana, Illinois, and Wisconsin is shown as a road on Tanner's maps of those states. On Arrowsmith, see John Warkentin and Richard I. Ruggles, eds., *Manitoba Historical Atlas: A Selection of Facsimile Maps, Plans, and Sketches from 1612 to 1969*, 132, 137–140 (Winnipeg, 1970). For Long's mentions of Arrowsmith, see pp. 186, 194, below. Some good examples of the cartographic confusion over the Red and Minnesota rivers mentioned below are reproduced in Wheat, *Mapping the Transmississippi West*, 2:facing pp. 2 and 3. Nicollet's comments appear in *Report Intended to Illustrate a Map of the Hydrographical Basin of the Upper Mississippi River*, 107 (26 Congress, 2 session, *Senate Documents*, no. 237—serial 380).

the Mississippi, and in laying down the north-south orientation of the Red River, which had been confused with the Red Lake River and shown flowing east-west. He also located Devils Lake in the correct latitude, clearly marked the Coteau des Prairies, pinpointed the subtle divide at Lake Traverse, and clarified the orientation of the Canadian border waterways. The information gathered on more southerly areas also proved useful. Long's manuscript maps were at one point loaned to Henry Tanner, who was preparing his *New American Atlas* for publication in 1825; Tanner incorporated the major's information in a map of Illinois and Missouri which appeared in that volume. As it was at last published, Long's map for the *Narrative* contained refinements and details correct enough to win praise from later master map maker Joseph N. Nicollet, who attributed to Long the "first rectifications" of the course of the Minnesota River. The map appears on the end sheets of this book.

From the enthusiasm with which the *Narrative*'s reviewers received the book's information on Indian tribes of the West, it might have been supposed that the expedition's reputation was secure in the area of ethnology. The *Monthly Review* declared that the *Narrative* "contains, we think, the best and most authentic information respecting them [*the Indians*] which we have any where read," and the *North American Review* spoke warmly of the party's "praiseworthy diligence . . . rewarded by a large amount of valuable acquisitions." But even here a sour note was struck by a later reviewer (possibly Lewis Cass) who criticized the book's "numerous errors of fact and opinion" and pleaded, "Surely the intelligent gentlemen, who composed that expedition, will not demand from the readers of its history, their implicit belief in accounts thus collected and reported." Cass, if he was the critic, may have had reasons of his own for wishing to detract from Long's accomplishments, and the judgments of later historians have not sustained him. The expedition faced many difficulties in gathering information; its members did not have time for more than a cursory observation of any tribe's customs, and they lacked knowledge of any Indian languages. Under such circumstances, the information they gathered was bound to be superficial. But they had the good fortune to acquire excellent interpreters and informants—notably Joseph Renville, who knew the Dakota well—which partially compensated for other drawbacks. The uses ethnologists and historians have made of the *Narrative* over the years attest to the quality of its contributions. One historian concluded that "The accounts of the Potawatomi,

Sioux, and Chippewa Indians [in the *Narrative*] . . . are among the best sources of our knowledge of these nations."[83]

Though the published volume unquestionably had weaknesses, it furnished the only detailed information on Long's 1817 and 1823 expeditions available for many years. The work became a standard source on the Midwest of the 1820s, quoted profusely by authors of other travel accounts, historians, and scientific writers. Perhaps the best summary of the book and the expedition which produced it is that of historian William W. Folwell, who wrote: "If this expedition did not make large additions to existing knowledge, those it did make were reliable."[84]

With the publication of the *Narrative* in December, 1824—the month of Long's fortieth birthday—his career as an explorer came to an abrupt end. Ahead lay almost 40 years of more prosaic work for the Corps of Topographical Engineers, assignments that included river improvements, road, canal, and harbor surveys, and the construction of steamboats and marine hospitals. In 1827 he assisted in the first survey for the Baltimore and Ohio Railroad. He remained on this assignment for nearly three years, making good use of the opportunity to put into practice his theories on engineering; out of this experience came his patents on bridge design and his manuals on bridge construction and railroad surveying.[85]

Although he was an engineer of rare attainments, Long's advancement in the corps was slow. He was breveted lieutenant colonel in 1827, but he was not promoted to colonel until 1861. In the same year he was appointed bureau chief, a position he held until March, 1863, when the Corps of Topographical Engineers was again disestablished. A few months later he retired, returning to Alton, Illinois, where he had once made his headquarters and where several members of his family and his friend Edwin James had preceded him. He died there in 1864 at the age of 79.[86]

The major's interest in what he termed "the cause of Science" did not end when he turned to more prosaic work. For example, in 1832 he wrote to the Navy Department requesting that its officers in Florida co-operate with John J. Audubon, who was collecting

[83] *Monthly Review*, 108:123; *North American Review*, 21:186, 22:62; Folwell, *History of Minnesota*, 1:107.

[84] Folwell, *History of Minnesota*, 1:109.

[85] Wood, *Long*, 144–153, 156–160; Long's publications are listed on p. 279.

[86] Wood, *Long*, 147, 248, 254, 261–263.

specimens to illustrate his forthcoming publication. Audubon, Long astutely predicted, was an "enterprising and accomplished naturalist, who I think bids fair to rival his predecessors in this Department of natural history, and to become one of the most shining ornaments of this, his native country."[87]

Long's concern with publications about his explorations also continued throughout his career, and, characteristically, he entrusted the undertaking to another person. In 1855 he proposed to Edwin James the compilation of a three-volume work on his expeditions, supplemented by accounts of other travelers and entitled "Mississippiana." The "Bill of Fare," he wrote James, was submitted "for your consideration in catering an entertainment for the Public . . . seasoned in all respects according to your own taste & skill in cookery."[88]

When in 1860 Edward D. Neill, secretary of the Minnesota Historical Society, inquired about the journal kept on the 1817 expedition, Long's reply made no mention of "Mississippiana." "The notes & sketches taken by me, on this and many other tours of Exploration," he stated, "have all been committed to the keeping of Dr. Edwin James . . . with the understanding that he should be at liberty to make such use of them, as he might deem proper, more especially in the preparation of matter for publication in the Journal of the Historical Society of Chicago."[89]

Intent on publication of the 1817 journal, Neill then wrote to James, who responded by sending the portion of it describing Long's journey from Prairie du Chien to the Falls of St. Anthony and the return trip to Belle Fontaine. He did not send the first half of the two-part journal, because he assumed the Minnesota society would have no interest in it. Although he granted permission to publish the portion sent, he requested that it be returned to him for transmittal "in due time" to the Chicago Historical Society.[90] The Minnesota Historical Society in 1860 published the journal in its *Collections* under the title "Voyage in a Six-Oared Skiff to the Falls of Saint Anthony in 1817 by Major Stephen H. Long, Topographical Engineer United States Army."

[87] Long to Levi Woodbury, January 2, 1832, Office of Naval Records and Library, Naval Records Collections, Miscellaneous Letters, NARG 45.

[88] Long to James, February 28, 1855, Archibald Church Library, Northwestern University, Chicago. Accompanying the letter are a title page and an outline of the proposed book.

[89] Long to Neill, July 12, 1860, in Correspondence Files, MHS Archives. Neill's July 6 letter to Long has not been located.

[90] James to Neill, August 4, 22, 1860, Correspondence Files, MHS Archives.

Long was enthusiastic about the publication, complimenting Neill on the "manner & dress in which it has been put forth." He then commended to the society for publication his "notes" on the 1823 expedition, which were in James's possession, for he felt they were "quite as interesting as these already published." Neill asked James for the "notes," and on February 10, 1861, James forwarded three small leatherbound volumes containing Long's journal of the expedition. Seemingly forgetful of his previous plans for Long's papers, James commented that he hoped "you may find the volumes worthy of preservation in the Archives of your Society."[91]

After this episode, the society's records are silent upon the subject of the journals until 1866 when Henry C. Long, the major's son—then a civil engineer associated with Major General Gouverneur K. Warren in his survey of the upper Mississippi--asked for a copy of "Voyage in a Six-Oared Skiff" and inquired about the location of his father's papers. He expressed particular interest in the 1817 journal, for he felt it would be a valuable aid in noting changes that had taken place in the Mississippi Valley over a 50-year period. The society leaped to the conclusion that Long wanted to take possession of his father's manuscript and hurriedly offered to trace for him the maps not included in the publication. Long, surprised at the apprehension his request had created, assured the society that he had no intention of asking for the manuscript.[92]

Four volumes of Long's journals—one volume for the 1817 trip and three for the 1823 expedition — were thus preserved in the Minnesota collections. The fate of the first volume of the 1817 journal and the bulk of Long's papers remains a mystery. The Chicago Historical Society has no record of acquiring them, but the destruction of its building during the 1871 fire leaves room for doubt. It is certain that some of them passed to the family of Edwin James after his death in 1861, for his grandnephew had manuscripts of both Dr. James and Long as late as 1931. Other papers, E. C. James stated in 1931, were destroyed when his grandfather's home burned "more than thirty years ago." E. C. James died in the 1960s, and his widow, questioned by the editors in 1968, had no information about the material. When the Alton Board of Education, to which the E. C. James house was bequeathed, examined boxes

[91] Long to Neill, November 14, 1860; James to Neill, December 31, 1860, February 10, 1861—all in Correspondence Files, MHS Archives.

[92] Henry C. Long to Neill, November 20, 1866, January 31, 1867; and to J. F. Williams, February 27, 1867; Neill to the society, February 5, 1867; unsigned memorandum, n.d., 1867—all in Correspondence Files, MHS Archives.

stored in the attic, no papers were found. After more than a hundred years of migration, the trail of the papers is cold. However, elusive manuscripts have a way of turning up after persistent hunters have given up the chase, and the missing portion of the 1817 journal and Long's notes on other explorations may someday be located.[93]

The portion of James Edward Colhoun's journal covering July 1–29, 1823, published in this volume also has an intriguing history. It was acquired at an unknown date by James Durkin from a Mr. McDill of Abbeville, South Carolina, who may have gotten it along with the home of Armistead Burt, whose wife was John C. Calhoun's niece. Durkin gave the journal to his sister, Margaret Galligan of Lanesboro, Minnesota. The Minnesota Historical Society learned about the volume in 1918 and asked that it be donated or permission be given for photocopying.[94]

The society did not copy the journal until 1938. Dr. Mary D. Galligan, daughter of Margaret, gave the original manuscript to the St. Paul Seminary in 1966 and in 1970 the society purchased it from the seminary. A later section of Colhoun's journal, covering the weeks from July 30 to August 21, 1823, is in the possession of Edwin B. McDill, who intends to publish it and who kindly allowed the editors to examine it. When this portion appears, the presently known journals of Stephen Harriman Long's northern expeditions will at long last be available to illuminate a period in the region's history for which few other accounts of comparable substance exist.[95]

[93] Nine volumes of Long's papers dating from 1843 to 1862 were given to the Missouri Historical Society at St. Louis in 1958 by Ashley Breckinridge Taylor, a descendant of Long's daughter Lucy. Dorthea Barnes, Taylor's daughter, in 1968 gave to the Joslyn Art Museum, Omaha, a number of books from Long's library. See also E. C. James to Irving S. Cutter, April 3, 6, 1931; Cutter to James, April 4, 1931—all in Archibald Church Library, Northwestern University; Macy Pruitt, Alton, Ill., Board of Education, to the editors, May 19, 1971.

[94] Durkin to "Sister Madge," undated; MHS "Field Agent" to Mrs. John Galligan, October 22, 1918—both in Acquisition Files, Division of Archives and Manuscripts, MHS; Edwin B. McDill to MHS, January 24, 1965, in the possession of the editors; Wiltse, *Calhoun, Nullifier*, 312.

[95] Accessions Records, Division of Archives and Manuscripts, MHS; p. 271, below. Edwin B. McDill generously made available to the editors a copy of the second portion of Colhoun's journal for use in annotation only. Mr. McDill also has Colhoun volumes for 1825–26 and 1829–30. The other portions of the 1823 journal, which must have been in several volumes, have not been located.

THE JOURNAL
OF
STEPHEN H. LONG
1817

Wednesday July 9.

Learning that there was little or no danger to be apprehended from the Indians living on the Mississippi above Prairie Du Chien, I concluded to ascend for the purpose of reconnoitring still farther up the river. — Layed in provisions for sixteen days, and set sail at half past 8 this morning with a favourable wind. — — I took an additional soldier on board at the Fort, so that my crew now consisted of seven men. — My former Interpreter not being acquainted with the language of the Indians living on this part of the river, I had occasion to dismiss him and employ another. — The name of my present interpreter, is Roch or Roque, whose father was a Frenchman, & mother a squaw of the Sioux nation. — But as he was not acquainted with the English language, nor I with the French, sufficiently to converse with him, — I stood in need of some person to interpret his conversation in english. — A Gentleman by the name of Hempsted, a resident of Prairie du Chien, having some desire to ascend the Mississippi, had the politeness to volunteer his services as french Interpreter, and ascend the river in company with me. — The whole number on board of my boat was now, ten persons. — Mr Hempsted was a native of New London Connecticut, but has resided in this part of the country about 8 years. —

There sailed also in company with us, two young gentlemen from New York — by the name of King & Gun who are grandsons of Capt. J. Carver, the celebrated traveller. — They had taken a bark canoe at Green Bay, and were on their way to the northward, on a visit to the Sauteurs, for the purpose of establishing their claim to a tract of land granted by those indians, to their grandfather. — — They had waited at Prairie du Chien, during my trip up the Ouisconsin, in order to ascend the Mississippi with me. — On board their boat were three men beside themselves; — so that our whole party consisted of fifteen persons. — — — — Passed Yellow River on our left, about 2 miles from the Fort. It is navigable for Perogues, in time of high water, about 50 miles from its mouth. About 1 mile farther up is a Creek of considerable size coming in on the same side, called the Painted Rock. — One and a half miles higher is a small prairie on the east side, at the upper end of the Prairie du Chien, called the Prairie Des Sioux, at which the Sioux Indians are in the habit of stopping to dress & paint themselves, when they

THE OPENING PAGE of Stephen H. Long's journal for July 9, 1817, in the collections of the Minnesota Historical Society. The journal pages measure 8 by 12 1/2 inches in size.

1. Up the Mississippi in a Six-Oared Skiff

JULY 9 THROUGH 17, 1817

WEDNESDAY, JULY 9, 1817. Learning that there was little or no danger to be apprehended from the Indians living on the Mississippi above Prairie Du Chien, I concluded to ascend for the purpose of reconnoitring further up the river. Layed in provisions for sixteen days, and set sail at half past 8 this morning with a favourable wind.

I took an additional soldier on board at the Fort [*Crawford*], so that my Crew now consisted of seven men.[1] My former Interpreter [*Joseph Goe*] not being acquainted with the language of the [Dakota] Indians living on this part of the river, I had occasion to dismiss him and employ an other. The name of my present interpreter is [Augustin] Rock or Ro[c]que, whose father was a Frenchman & mother a squaw of the Sioux nation.[2] But as he was not acquainted with the

[1] On Fort Crawford, established at Prairie du Chien in 1816, see pp. 88–90, below. The fort site has been preserved.

The extra man was John Rollins of Capt. Edmund Shipp's company, Fort Crawford. Five of the six soldiers Long brought with him from Benjamin Birdsall's company at Belle Fontaine were Andrew and Samuel Love, Samuel and Thomas Porter, and Zachariah Stevens or Stephens. The sixth may have been Corp. Charles Sheffield, although his name does not appear in Long's accounts; see pp. 77, 96, below. The latter is listed as a private in his enlistment record. On all of these men, see AGO, Registers of Enlistments, 1815–28, 14:214, 15:170, 19:261, 275, 20:209, 22:52, 23:225, NARG 94. See also Vouchers C, F-J, in Appendix 1, below.

[2] Goe had served as Long's interpreter and guide since the party left Belle Fontaine. A Joseph Goe, Gaud, or Gow was a resident and landowner at Portage des Sioux, Mo.; see land title of John King under Joseph Gow, May 11, 1825, and Theodore Hunt, "Testimony Relating to Town & Village Lots," 1:84, 185, 234, copies in Theodore Hunt Papers, Missouri Historical Society, St. Louis. Goe (Gaud) was also listed in Oscar W. Collet, "Index to St. Charles Marriage Registers, 1792–1863," unpublished manuscript in Missouri Historical Society. Rocque or Roc, who replaced him, was the mixed-blood son of Joseph Roc or La Rocque, a trader and interpreter whose surname is spelled several ways. Augustin had a very limited English vocabu-

English language, nor I with the French sufficiently to converse with him, I stood in need of some person to interpret his conversation in english. A gentleman by the name of [Stephen] Hempste[a]d, [Jr.,] a resident of Prairie du Chien, having some desire to ascend the Mississippi, had the politeness to volunteer his services as french Interpreter and ascend the river in company with me. The whole number on board of my boat was now ten person. Mr. Hempsted was a native of New London, Connecticut, but has resided in this part of the country about 8 years.[3]

There sailed also in company with us two young gentlemen from New York by the name of [Jonathan P.] King & [Moses or Henry] Gun[n], who are grandsons of Capt. J[onathan] Carver, the celebrated traveller. They had taken a bark canoe at Green Bay and were on their way to the northward on a visit to the Sauteurs [*Ojibway*], for the purpose of establishing their claim to a tract of land granted by those indians to their grandfather. They had waited at Prairie du Chien during my trip up the Ouisconsin [*Wisconsin R.*] in order to ascend the Mississippi with me. On board their boat were three men beside themselves, so that our whole party consisted of fifteen persons.[4]

Passed Yellow River on our left [*west*] about 2 miles from the Fort. It

lary. See p. 145 and Vouchers A, D, in Appendix 1, below; H[enry] H. Sibley, "Reminiscences of the Early Days of Minnesota," in *MHC*, 3:249; "The Mackinac Register," in *Wisconsin Historical Collections*, 19:92 (1910); this series is hereafter abbreviated *WHC*.

[3] Hempstead, a merchant and contractor, moved from Connecticut to Missouri in 1808. By 1816 he was carrying on a contracting business at Prairie du Chien, where he also represented the fur trading interests of Manuel Lisa. See Mrs. Dana O. Jensen, ed., "I at Home by Stephen S. Hempstead, Sr.," in Missouri Historical Society, *Bulletin*, 13:32n, 311 (October, 1956, April, 1957); Florence Gratiot Bale to Peter L. Scanlan, September 19, 1927, Peter L. Scanlan Papers, State Historical Society of Wisconsin (hereafter abbreviated WHS), Madison.

[4] Carver, a captain during the French and Indian War, allegedly secured a land grant located in present-day Minnesota and Wisconsin from the Dakota, not the Ojibway, in a deed dated May 1, 1767. On this and later efforts to have the grant confirmed, see John Parker, ed., *The Journals of Jonathan Carver and Related Documents, 1766–1770*, 47–51 (St. Paul, 1976).

Carver's grandsons were Jonathan Parsons King, the son of Mary Carver and Simeon King, and either Moses Gunn, Jr., or Henry Gunn, sons of Olive Carver and Moses Gunn. The three men who accompanied King and Gunn have not been identified. See J. P. King to Mary L. Johnson, April 9, 1835, May 23, 1836; King to Emma Lincoln, July 29, 1857; Abbie Laura Pangborn to Emma Lincoln, May 1, 1860; and Bertha Clark, "The Johnson Line,"—all in Erma Johnson Kyle scrapbook, in the possession of Mrs. Claude C. Kyle, St. Paul, microfilm copy in MHS. See also *Vital Records of Montague, Massachusetts, to the End of the Year 1849*, 17, 24, 25, 63, 137 (Salem, Mass., 1934); Chapter 2, note 23, below.

is navigable for perogues in time of high water about 50 miles from its mouth. About 1 [*4 1/2*] mile farther up is a Creek of considerable size coming in on the same side called the Painted Rock [*Paint Creek*]. One and a half miles higher is a small prairie on the east side at the upper end of the Prairie du Chien called the Prairie Des Sioux, at which the Sioux Indians are in the habit of stopping to dress & paint themselves when they are on their way to visit the Garrison below.[5]

Passed a prominent part of the Bluffs on our left called Cape Puant. The circumstance from which it derived its name was as follows. The Sioux & Puants [*Winnebago*] were about to commence hostilities against each other, and a large party of the latter set out on an expedition to invade the territory of the Sioux and attack them by surprise. But the Sioux, gaining intelligence of their design, assembled a superior force & laid in ambush waiting for the Puants to land on this side. Immediately after their landing the Sioux rushed down from the Bluffs, attacked the Puants in a small recess between two promontories, drove them into the river, & massacred the whole party.[6]

Just above this is Garlic Cape, remarkable from the singularity of its appearance. In shape it resembles a cone cut by a perpendicular plane passing thro' its apex & base. Its height is about 450 feet. A little East of its base is a fine spring.

The valley of the river in this part is almost entirely occupied by the river, whi[ch] spreads in some places to the width of three or four miles, giving place to numerous islands, some of which are very large. The bluffs are generally between 4 & 5 hundred feet high, cut with numerous ravines, & exhibiting other signs of being the commencement of a very hilly & broken inland country.[7]

[5] On this area see Chapter 2, note 7, and p. 146, below.

[6] The massacre of the Winnebago by the Dakota at this location has not been verified in a contemporary source, although it is repeated in T. E. Courtenay, *A Guide to Pomerade's Original Panorama of the Mississippi River*, 38 (New York, 1849). The location may have been confused with a tradition concerning a Winnebago massacre by the Illinois Indians at Red Banks on Green Bay, Lake Michigan. Red Banks was also known as Le Cap des Puants. See Augustin Grignon, "Seventy-two Years' Recollections of Wisconsin," in *WHC*, 3:204 (1857); Publius V. Lawson, "The Winnebago Tribe," in *Wisconsin Archeologist*, 6:90, 92 (July, 1907).

Cape Puant and Garlic Cape, mentioned below, are in Allamakee County, Ia. Garlic Cape was also known as Cap à l'Ail and is now called Mount Capoli.

[7] The heights of the various bluffs in this region are summarized in Lawrence Martin, *The Physical Geography of Wisconsin*, 145, 169 (Madison and Milwaukee, 1965). Long is essentially correct.

The wind failed us about eleven A.M. and we had occasion to row the rest of the day. Encamped on the head of an island about sun set. Distance 28 1/2 miles.

THURSDAY, JULY 10, 1817. Our companions in the Birch canoe [*King and Gunn*] encamped on the same Island but about 4 miles below us. The weather calm this morning. Got under way at sunrise and came six miles before breakfast during which we caught 5 Catfish & 1 Drum.[8] A favourable wind then rising, we set sail.

Passed a small recess on our right formerly occupied by a party of Winnebagos as a village.[9] It now contained but two small wigwams, having been deserted by its former occupants in consequence of a disastre that befell one of their party. In time of the late war [of 1812], Gov. [William] Clark of St. Louis ascended the Mississippi for the purpose of establishing a Military post at Prairie du Chien.[10] On his arrival at that place, he found there eight indians who were inhabitants of this village and made prisoners of them, as they had taken part with our enemies. They were confined in the house now occupied by Mr. Hempstead and a guard set to keep them secure. Apprehending that they should be treated with severity, they were meditating a plan whereby to effect their escape, when one of the number hit upon an expedient which they afterwards adopted. His plan was for one of the party to break thro' a window & seize the centinel, when there should happen to be but one on post, & hold him fast till the rest should make their escape. But aware that the one who should execute this part of the plot must expose himself to almost certain death, he offered to sacrafise himself for the safety of the others; and an opportunity presenting he leaped thro' the window, seized the centinel whose attempts to stab him with his bayonet he effectually frustrated, and held him fast till the rest had got out of danger. He then released the centinel and attempted to make his escape, but was immediately fired upon by the centinel, &

[8] On the catfish of the upper Mississippi and the drum, or freshwater sheepshead, see Samuel Eddy and James C. Underhill, *Northern Fishes With Special Reference to the Upper Mississippi Valley*, 297–311, 332–334 (Revised ed., Minneapolis, 1974).

[9] The Winnebago village of Chief Winneshiek was later located in this vicinity on the east side of the river near De Soto, Wis. See "Major William Williams' Journal of a Trip to Iowa in 1849," in *Annals of Iowa*, 3rd series 12:259, 268 (April, 1920); Union Publishing Company, *History of Vernon County, Wisconsin*, 726 (Springfield, Ill., 1884).

[10] An expedition led by Clark occupied Prairie du Chien and built Fort Shelby there in 1814. It was captured by the British and renamed Fort McKay. See p. 90, below; Bruce E. Mahan, *Old Fort Crawford and the Frontier*, 52–57 (Iowa City, Ia., 1926).

received a wound in the knee of which he died a short time after, altho' it did not prevent him from effecting his escape at the time.[11]

Passed Little Ioway [*Upper Iowa*] River coming in from the west. There is a small village of Foxes about three miles up this River, consisting of 5 or 6 wigwams. The river is navigable in time of high water about 50 miles and at all times a little above the Indian village. Its current is generally rapid but not precipitate.[12]

Passed several Sioux Lodges or wigwams on our left, at which there was a small war party of 10 or 12 Indians. As soon as they saw our flag, they hoisted American colours, and we returned the compliment by discharging a Blunderbuss, upon which they fired two guns ahead of us. Finding we were not disposed to call on them (for we had a very fine wind), six of the young warriors, very fine looking fellows, took a canoe and waited on us. We slackened sail to enable them to overtake us. When they came up, their chief warrior gave me his hand & a few common place remarks passed between us.[13] I gave him some tobacco & a pint of whiskey, & they left us apparently very well satisfied. Passed Raccoon [*Coon*] Creek, an inconsiderable stream coming in from the East ward.

Since we left Prairie du Chien have not been able at any place to see both sides of the river at the same time, owing to the numerous Islands which the river imbosoms. The Bluffs generally make their appearance immediately upon the shore of the river on both sides. They are intersected by numerous ravines, which divides them into knobs & peeks towering 4 or 5 hundred feet above the level of the river. The rocky stratifications are almost exclusively sand stone of a

[11] For two conflicting contemporary reports on this Winnebago incident (neither of which agrees with Long's account), see [Thomas Forsyth] to Ninian Edwards, July 31, 1814, Forsyth Papers, 4:12, in Lyman C. Draper Manuscripts, WHS; Douglas Brymner, "Capture of Fort M'Kay, Prairie du Chien, in 1814," in *WHC*, 11:262 (1888).

[12] At various times the Fox and the closely related Sauk had villages on the Upper Iowa River, which marked the northernmost point on the Mississippi they claimed as their range. See W. E. Alexander, *History of Winneshiek and Allamakee Counties Iowa*, 19 (Sioux City, Ia., 1882); Emma H. Blair, ed., *The Indian Tribes of the Upper Mississippi Valley and Region of the Great Lakes*, 2:147 (Cleveland, 1912).

[13] Benjamin O'Fallon, an Indian agent who also visited the area in 1817, placed the Mdewakanton Dakota band led by Wabasha on the Upper Iowa River, where for many years they had a village in present-day Winneshiek County, Ia. Although the chief warrior cannot be certainly identified, he may have been White Dog, mentioned by O'Fallon as the "second chief," or a leading warrior named the Grand Partisan. See Benjamin O'Fallon to William Clark, May 10, 1817, May 20, 1818, in Clarence E. Carter, ed., *The Territorial Papers of the United States (Missouri)*, 15:263, 407, 411 (Washington, D.C., 1951); Newton H. Winchell, *The Aborigines of Minnesota*, 541, 544 (St. Paul, 1911). See also pp. 57, 146, below.

yellowish appearance, inclining to be soft & spongy rather than brittle & crumbling. Numerous bluffs of a semiconical form resembling Cape Garlic before described, only in many instances are much larger, are arranged along the sides of the river. Their faces are perpendicular cliffs of the above mentioned sand-stone.[14]

Passed the mouth of Root river on our left. It is navigable in high water about 40 or 45 miles and in low about 20. There are no Indians living upon it at present, but hunting parties frequently encamp in the neighbourhood of it.

The wind very favourable most of the day. Encamped on the west side of the river a little above the Root river at a late hour. Distance 50 miles.

FRIDAY, JULY 11, 1817. In the latter part of the night a violent storm from the north east, accompanyed with very heavy thunder, commenced & continued till morning. Got under way at sun rise, the weather calm & cloudy. Passed Prairie de la Cross on our right [*east*], upon which we observed a small enclosure which was the burying place of the son of an Indian chief. Upon his grave a pole was erected to which an American Flag was attached. The Flag was almost worn out, having been suspended for a considerable time.[15]

At the upper part of the Prairie was a small encampment of Winnibagos—the most civil of any of that nation I have met with. They gave us a large number of turtles eggs, of which they had collected nearly half a bushel, and in return I gave them some tobacco. This party belongs to a small band of Winnebagos living about 6 miles up the Prairie de la Cross Cr. [*La Crosse R.*], which comes in from the NE at the head of the Prairie. The band consists of 40 or 50 men besides women & children. These indians were peaceable during the late war & have always manifested a friendly disposition towards the Americans.[16]

[14] The St. Peter sandstone formation alternates with the Galena or Trenton limestone strata along the Mississippi from Minnesota to Illinois. See Winchell and Upham, *Geology of Minnesota*, 1:218.

[15] The grave may have been that of a member of the Decorah or Dekaury family once marked on Front Street in present-day La Crosse, Wis. See Charles L. Emerson, *Wisconsin Scenic and Historic Trails*, 70 (Madison, 1933). On the Winnebago custom of flying flags over the graves of distinguished members of the tribe, see, for example, "Williams' Journal," in *Annals of Iowa*, 3rd series 12:259.

[16] This was the village of One-Eyed Decorah or Dekaury, member of a notable Winnebago family. Long was mistaken about the band's friendly disposition. The chief participated in engagements against the United States during the War of 1812, and two additional rifle companies had been ordered to Fort Crawford in April, 1817, because of Indian hostility in the area. See Lawson, in *Wisconsin Archeologist*, 6:141;

Collected several specimens of curious, tho' not very interesting, minerals, amongst which were iron ore, red sand stone, some parts of which were of a vermillion hue, and sandstone of a yellowish cast containing abundance of extremely small shells and other organic remains.

Met three canoes of Sioux Indians. Passed the Black River on our right coming in from the NNE. It is navigable for perogues somewhat more than 100 [*40*] miles, where the navigation is obstructed by rapids. On this river is an abundance of pine timber of an excellent quality. Much of the pine timber used at St. Louis is cut here. This river has three mouths by which it discharges itself into the Mississippi, the lowermost of which is most passable and communicates with the Mississippi 12 or 14 miles below the junction of the valleys of the two rivers.[17]

The Bluffs along the river to day were unusually interesting. They were of an exceedingly wild & romantic character, being divided into numerous detached fragments, some of them of mountainous size, while others in slender conical peeks seemed to tower aloft till their elevation rendered them invisible. Here might the poet or bard indulge his fancy in the wildest extravagance, while the philosopher would find a rich repast in examining the numerous phenomena here presented to his view & in tracing the wonderful operations of nature that have taken place since the first formation of the world.

A little above the mouth of Black River both shores of the Mississippi may be seen at the same time, which is the only instance of the kind we have met with on our way from Prairie du Chien to this place. One mile further ahead the bluffs on both sides approach within 800 yards of each other, and the river in consequence is

David McBride, "The Capture of Black Hawk," in *WHC*, 5:297n (1868); Carter, ed., *Territorial Papers of the United States (Illinois)*, 27:495, 498 (Washington, D.C., 1950).

[17] Several rapids and waterfalls (notably at Black River Falls, Wis.) impeded navigation on the Black River. The river's three mouths are clearly shown on Joseph N. Nicollet, "Map of the Hydrographical Basin of the Upper Mississippi River" (1843). The channel and water level of the Mississippi here have since been altered by the construction of Lock and Dam No. 7.

No corroboration has been found for Long's statement regarding the use in St. Louis of pine timber cut on Black River, although the *Missouri Gazette & Public Advertiser* (see, for example, September 25, 1818) frequently mentioned white pine arriving in St. Louis from eastern points. A sawmill was built on the Black River in 1819; see A[bner] D. Polleys, *Stories of Pioneer Days in the Black River Valley*, 52 (Black River Falls, Wis., 1948); William F. Raney, "Pine Lumbering in Wisconsin," in *Wisconsin Magazine of History*, 19:76 (September, 1935).

narrower here than at any other place this side of Prairie du Chien. Notwithstanding this contraction of its channel, the river here imbosoms an island [*Minnesota I.?*] of considerable size. The wind hard ahead most of the day. Encamped about sunset on a small island [*Island 78?*]. Distance 26 1/2 miles.[18]

SATURDAY, JULY 12, 1817. Within a few yards of the island where we encamped is another considerable smaller, which for the sake of brevity I called the Bluff Island as its former name [*Trempealeau*] is very long & difficult to pronounce. It has been accounted a great curiosity by travellers. It is remarkable for being the third island of the Mississippi from the Gulf of Mexico to this place that has a rocky foundation similar to that of the neighbouring bluffs and nearly the same altitude. [Zebulon M.] Pike in his account of it states the height of it to be about 200 feet. We layed by this morning for the purpose of ascertaining its altitude, which we found, by a trigonometrical calculation which my instruments would not enable me to make with much accuracy, to be a little more than 500 feet. It is a very handsome, conical hill but not sufficiently large to deserve the appellation of Mountain, altho' it is called by the name of the Montaigne qui trompé de l'eau, or the mountain that is soaked in the water.[19]

When we stopped for break fast, Mr. Hempstead & myself ascended a high peek to take a view of the country. It is known by the name of the Kettle hill, having obtained this appellation from the circumstance of its having numerous piles of stone on its top, most of them fragments of the rocky stratifications which constitute the principal part of the hill, but some of them small piles made by the Indians.[20] These at a distance have some similitude of kettles arranged along up on the ridge & sides of the hill. From this or almost

[18] Long may here refer to the area near Perrot State Park, Wis., above Lock and Dam No. 6, which has changed the river level and its islands.

[19] Trempealeau Mountain, a well-known landmark in Perrot State Park, is at the upstream end of a line of hills known as Trempealeau Bluffs, which are actually detached portions of the river bluffs. The altitude of the mountain above the flood plain is almost 400 feet, while Trempealeau Bluffs are approximately 550 feet at the highest point. See "Additions and Corrections," in *WHC*, 10:506 (1888); Martin, *Physical Geography of Wisconsin*, 149–151. Trempealeau is not now an island. Pike's remarks are in Elliott Coues, ed., *The Expeditions of Zebulon Montgomery Pike*, 1:52, 307 (Reprint ed., Minneapolis, 1965). For Long's return visit to this spot, see p. 81, below; Keating, *Narrative*, 1:271.

[20] Kettle Bluff, the ridge projecting into the center of the present town of Homer, Minn., was known by that name as late as 1913. See Franklyn Curtiss-Wedge, ed., *The History of Winona County Minnesota*, 1:544 (Chicago, 1913).

any other eminence in its neighbourhood, the beauty & grandeur of the prospect would baffle the skill of the most ingenious pencil to depict & that of the most accomplished pen to describe. Hills marshaled into a variety of agreeable shapes, some of them towering in lofty Peeks, while others present brod summits embelished with contours & slopes in the most pleasing manner. Champaigns & waving vallies, Forests, lawns & Parks alternating with each other, the humble Mississippi meandering far below and occasionally losing itself in numberless islands, give variety & beauty to the picture, while ragged cliffs and stupendous precipices here & there present themselves as if to add boldness & majesty to the scene.

In the midst of this beautiful scenery is situated a village of the Sioux Indians on an extensive lawn called the Aux Aisle Prairie at which we lay by for a short time. On our arrival the Indians hoisted two American Flags, and we returned the compliment by discharging our Blunderbus & pistols. They then fired several guns ahead of us by way of a salute, after which we landed & were received with much friendship. The name of their chief is Wauppaushaw [*Wabasha*], or the Leaf, commonly called by a name of the same import in French La Fieulle [*Feuille*], or la Fye, as it is pronounced in english. He is considered one of the most honest & honourable of any of the Indians and endeavours to inculcate into the minds of his people the sentiments & principles adopted by himself. He was not at home at the time I called & I had no opportunity of seeing him.[21]

The Indians, as I suppose, with the expectation that I had something to communicate to them, assembled at the place where I landed & seated themselves upon the grass. I inquired if their chief was at home & was answered in the negative. I then told them I should be very glad to see him, but as he was absent I would call on him again in a few days when I should return. I further told them that our father, the new president [*James Monroe*], wished to obtain some more information relative to his red children, and that I was on a tour to acquire any intelligence he might stand in need of. With this they appeared well satisfied, & permitted Mr. Hempstead

[21] Wabasha, Wapasha, Red Leaf, or La Feuille was the second of four Mdewakanton leaders to bear that name and was considered the principal chief of the Dakota. Although this village at present Winona, Minn., was established sometime after the one on the Upper Iowa, it became the favorite residence of Wabasha's band. On the village and on Wabasha, see Winchell, *Aborigines*, 540–544, 546, 549; Frederick W. Hodge, *Handbook of American Indians*, 2:911 (Bureau of American Ethnology, *Bulletins*, no. 30—Washington, D.C., 1910); Lawrence Taliaferro Journal, undated entries (7:17, 31), Taliaferro Papers, MHS. See also pp. 80, 147, below.

& myself to go thro' their village. While I was in the wigwam, one of the subordinate chiefs whose name was Waz-ze-coo-ta, or Shooter from the pine tree, volunteered to accompany me up the river. I accepted of his services, and he was ready to attend me on the tour in a very short time.[22]

When we hove in sight, the Indians were engaged in a ceremony called the *bear-dance*, A ceremony which they are in the habit of performing when any young man is desirous of bringing himself into particular notice and is considered a kind of initiation into the state of manhood. I went on to the ground where they had their performances, which were ended sooner than usual on account of our arrival. There was a kind of flag made of Fawn skin dressed with the hair on, suspend[ed] on a pole. Upon the flesh side of it were drawn certain rude figures indicative of the dream which it is necessary the young man should have dreamed before he can be considered a proper candidate for this kind of initiation. With this a Pipe was suspended by way of sacrafice. Two arrows were stuck up at the foot of the pole and fragments of painted feathers &c. were strewed about the ground near to it. These pertained to the religious rites attending the ceremony, which consist in bewailing & self mortification that the good spirit may be induced to pity them & succour their undertaking.[23]

At the distance of two or three hundred yards from the flag is an excavation which they call the bears' hole, prepared for the occasion. It is about 2 feet deep and has two ditches about 1 foot deep leading across it at right angles. The young hero of the farce places himself in this hole to be hunted by the rest of the young men, all of whom on this occasion are dressed in their best attire and painted in their neatest style. The hunters approach the hole in the direction of one of the ditches and discharge their guns, which were previously loaded for the purpose with blank cartridges, at the one who acts the part of the bear; whereupon he leaps from his den, having a hoop in

[22] Wazecouta, or Shooter from the Pine Top, whose name is rendered in various ways, was probably a resident of the village of Red Wing rather than Wabasha. In some disrepute among whites, he was called by Taliaferro "a noted old rascal." Taliaferro Journal, May 4, 1829 (8:254), Taliaferro Papers; "Prairie du Chien in 1827: Letters of Joseph M. Street to Gov. Ninian Edwards, of Illinois," in *WHC*, 11:360. See also pp. 149, 273, below.

[23] Long's description of the bear dance here and below was published in Keating, *Narrative*, 1:273–275. Apparently his informant was Wazecouta. See also Samuel W. Pond, "The Dakotas or Sioux in Minnesota As They Were in 1834," in *MHC*, 12:419 (1908).

each hand & a wooden lance, the hoops serving as fore feet to aid him in characterizing his part and his lance to defend him from his assailants.

Thus accoutred he dances round the plane, exhibiting various feats of activity while the other Indians pursue him & endeavour to trap him as he attempts to return to his den, to effect which he is privileged to use any violence he pleases with impunity against his assailants, even to taking the life of any of them. This part of the ceremony is performed three times, that the bear may escape from his den and return to it again thro' three of the avenues communicating with it. On being hunted from the fourth or last avenue, the bear must make his escape thro' all his pursuers if possible & flee to the woods, where he is to remain thro' the day. This however is seldom or never accomplished, as all the young men exert themselves to the utmost in order to trap him. When caught, he must retire to a lodge erected for his reception in the field, where he is to be secluded from all society thro' the day, except one of his particular friends whom he is allow[ed] to take with him as an attendant. Here he smookes and performs various other rites which superstition has lead the Indians to believe are sacred. After this ceremony is ended, the young indian is considered quallified to act any part as an efficient member of their community.

The Indian who has had the good fortune to catch the bear and overcome him when endeavouring to make his escape to the woods is considered a candidate for preferment, and is on the first suitable occasion appointed a leader of a small war party, in order that he may further have an opportunity to test his prowess & perform some essential service in behalf of his nation. It is accordingly expected that he will kill some of their enemies & return with their scalps.

I regretted very much that I had missed the opportunity of witnessing this ceremony, which is never performed except when prompted by the particular dreams of one or other of the young men who never is complimented twice in the same manner on account of his dreams.

Passed several places where the prospect was very agreeable. The winds strong ahead all day. Encamped on a sand bar. Distance 21 miles.

SUNDAY, JULY 13, 1817. Caught several fish last night. The atmosphere loaded with vapour this morning—the mercury at 51°. Started at sunrise but had to lay by on account of the fog. A favourable breeze sprung up from the SE about 8 & we hoisted sail. Saw a numerous flock of pelicans. They flew up from a sand bar a little before us & continued sailing about us for some time, which is usual with them, till they arose to a very great height, when they disappeared. Passed Embarrass [*Zumbro*] River on our left coming in from the west. Just above its confluence with the Mississippi it unites its waters with Clear water Creek [*Whitewater R.*]. The former is navigable in high water 30 or 40 miles, the latter about 15 miles. The Indians frequently hunt in the neighbourhood of these rivers, but have no permanent establishment upon them.[24]

A little above this, our Indian companion informed us that he was fired upon seven times by a party of Chipeways [*Ojibway*] but rec[e]ived no injury. He was alone & unarmed at the time, but the Chipiways fled immediately after fireing upon him. Passed the Cabin also where my interpreter [*Rocque*] spent the last winter in trading with the Indians—at present unoccupied.[25]

Met the nephew of La Fieulle & another Indian who were on a hunting expedition. My interpreter inform'd the nephew, who is to succeed his uncle in the office of Chief, that a party of the Sioux Indians of his village had followed us to beg whiskey after we had given them all we thought it prudent to part with. He appeared much offended that they should have done so & eagerly enquired if his uncle was not at home to restrain them. We gave them some tobacco & whiskey & left them.[26]

Were much amused by the singing of our Chief [*Wazecouta*], who felt a disposition to be merry after taking whisky. He appears to be a man of veracity, firmness & bravery. He occasionally stands up in the boat & harangues with a loud voice, proclaiming who he is, where he is going, & the company he is with. Passed the river au Beuf [*Buffalo R.*] coming in from the North. It is of moderate size

[24] On the intricacies of the Zumbro River delta, much altered by man since Long wrote, see Franklyn Curtiss-Wedge, *History of Wabasha County Minnesota*, 133 (Winona, 1920); Coues, ed., *Pike*, 1:56–58n. See also Chapter 3, note 68, below. American white pelicans were abundant in the Mississippi Valley as far north as Canada; see Thomas S. Roberts, *The Birds of Minnesota*, 1:162–165 (Minneapolis, 1932).

[25] For many years Augustin Rocque had a trading post—one of several he and his family operated—near present Wabasha, Minn. Long's statement places him firmly in this location in 1816–17; see also Taliaferro Journal, October 23, 1838 (15:114), Taliaferro Papers; Winchell, *Aborigines*, 526.

[26] The usual version of relationships in the Wabasha dynasty is that Wabasha III (died 1876) was the son, not the nephew, of Wabasha II. See Hodge, *Handbook*, 2:911.

and is navigable in high water about 30 miles. Buffaloes are found on this river, which gives occasion to its name; the Indians hunt them here in all seasons; they are not however very numerous.

Opposite to the mouth of this river on the west side of the Mississippi is a large [*Wabasha*] prairie, situated between the Bluffs & the river, being about 2 miles in width. On a part of it is a scattering growth of timber. Should there be occasion to send troops into this quarter, they might be posted to advantage at this place, as the position would be secure and at the same time afford a tolerable command of the river. The elevation of the Prairie above the river is about 25 [*30*] feet. Upon the upper end of the Prairie is the Grand encampment, or place of general resort for the Indian traders during the winter for the purpose of traficing with the Indians.[27]

Arrived at the foot of Lake Pepin about dark.[28] The wind favourable but very gentle thro' the day. Distance 35 miles.

MONDAY, JULY 14, 1817. The wind blew violently from the SE thro' the night, but as it was too dark to take our courses, we could not avail oursilves of the advantage it otherwise would have been to us. Set sail at an early hour, but the wind soon shifted into the NW & was so strong ahead that we could make very little progress either by rowing or cordelling. Were in consequence delayed about 1 1/2 hours, during which Mr. H. & myself ascended the Bluff in order to enjoy a prospect of the neighbouring country. The place where we were was at the lower extremity of Lake Pepin. From the height we had a view, not only of the Lake and the majestic bluffs that bound it, but also of the surrounding country to a considerable extent. The contrast between this and the view we had two days before is very striking. The Bluffs are more regular and more uniform in their height. The back country is rolling rather than hilly and has comparatively but little timber upon it, particularly on the west of the river. The vally between the bluffs, which was before thronged with Islands, sandbars, pools & marshes, is here occupied by a beautiful expanse of water with nothing to obstruct the view upon its surface but the shores of the lake.

At the lower end of Lake Pippin, which has its general course

[27] On Grand Encampment or Teepeeota Point in present Wabasha, see G. Hubert Smith, "Carver's Old Fortifications," in *Minnesota History*, 16:158 (June, 1935); Porter, ed., in *Missouri Historical Collections*, 3:113; Coues, ed., *Pike*, 1:59n.

[28] Lake Pepin, a lake within the Mississippi River noted for its beauty and treacherous winds, reaches its widest point near Lake City, Minn. See also p. 80, below.

about ESE, is Chippeway [*Chippewa*] river coming in from the North [*northeast*]. It is about 500 yds. wide at its mouth and is navigable for perogues about 50 miles at all times and in high water much further. From its appearance, however, I should judge that its navigation must be much obstructed by sand bars.

After breakfast we passed up the lake about 2 miles & stopped [on] the east shore for the purpose of ascertaining the width of the lake & the height of the bluffs where the high lands commence. We found the lake a few yards short of 2 miles wide & the elevation of the hills 475 feet above the surface of the lake. About mid way of the lake passed the Lover's Leap, a prominent part of the bluffs with a perpendicular precipice of about 150 feet & an abrupt descent of nearly 300 feet from its base to the waters edge. At this place an unfortunate squaw [*Winona*] met with an untimely fate as the consequence of her parents obstinacy and persecution. The circumstances that led to this result were related by our Indian chief & were the following.[29]

Since his remembrance, a large party of the Sioux Indians of Le Fieulle's band were going on a visit from the river St. Peters' [*Minnesota R.*] to Prairie du Chien. When they arrived at the hill now called the Lover's Leap, they stopped to gather Blue Clay, which is found near the foot of the hill, for the purpose of painting themselves. Of this party was the young squaw [*Winona*] who is the subject of the story. She had for a long time received the addresses of a young hunter, who had formed an unconquerable attachment to her and for whom she entertained the strongest affection. Her parents & brothers were strenuous opposed to her choice, and warmly seconded the solicitations of a young warrior who was very much beloved by the nation for his bravery & other good qualities. To obviate her objections to the warrior as being destitute of the means of clothing and feeding her, in consequence of the life he must lead in order to perform the duties of his profession, her brothers were at the expense of procuring every thing that was necessary to the care & comfort of a family and presented them to the young warrior. This they did on the day of their arrival at the fatal spot with the hope that their sister would readily be prevailed upon to marry the young man when all her objections to him were thus obviated.

She still persisted, however, in the determination never to marry

[29] Long's version of the suicide of Winona at present-day Maiden Rock, Wis., was the most elaborate recorded up to 1817. It is repeated in Keating, *Narrative*, 1:280–285. See G. Hubert Smith, "The Winona Legend," in *Minnesota History*, 13:367–376 (December, 1932).

any but the object of her sincere affection, the young hunter; while her parents & brothers, finding they could not accomplish their purpose by gentle means, began to treat her with severity. They insisted on her complyance with their wishes, still summoning the arguments of filial duty & affection in aid of their cause. She replied—"She did not love the soldier & would live single forever rather than marry him. You call me daughter & sister as if this should induce me to marry the man of your choice and not of my own. You say you love me—yet you have driven the only man that can make me happy far from me. He loved me but you would not let us be happy together. He has therefore left me—he has left his parents and all his friends and gone to bewail in the woods. He cannot partake of the pleasures of this party. He can do nothing but mourn. You are not satisfied with all this. You have not made me miserable enough. You would now compel me to marry a man I do not love. Since this is your purpose, let it be so. You will soon have no daughter or sister to torment or beguile with your false professions of love."

The same day was fixed upon as the day of her marriage with the warrior, and the Indians were busily occupied in gathering clay & painting themselves, preparatory for the nuptial ceremony. She in the mean time walked aside from the rest of the party, ascended to the top of the hill, & called aloud to her parents and brothers, up braiding them for their unkind treatment. "You first refused to let me marry agreeably to my own choice. You then endeavoured by artifice to unite me to a man I cannot love, and now you will force me to marry him whether I will or not. You thought to allure[?] & make me wretched, but you shall be disappointed." Her parents aware of her design ran to the foot of the hill and entreated her to desist with all the tenderness & concern that parental fondness could suggest, rending their hair & bewailing in the bitterest manner, while her brothers attempted to gain the summit before she should execute her fatal purpose. But all in vain. She was determined & resolute. She commenced singing her death song and immediately threw herself head long down the precipice, preferring certain & instantaneous death to a lingering state of unhappy wedlock.

Passed a large encampment of Sioux Indians 2 miles further up the lake at which we left our Chief. As we hove in sight they hoisted the American Flags, which we saluted with a discharge of our blunderbuss. Our salute was returned by the discharge of several guns fired ahead of us. When we landed, a crowd of Indians came about us & were anxious that we should stop a while with them. But the wind being strong and favourable, we concluded it best to make as little delay as possible. We accordingly gave them some tobacco & proceeded on.[30]

Lake Pepin is about 21 miles long and of variable widths from 1 1/2 to three miles. Thro' the greater part of its length it occupies the whole width of the valley situated between the river bluffs. There are however two prairies of considerable size within the valley that appear possesed of an excellent soil and are advantageously situated in regard to their elevation above the water. There are a few unimportant Creeks emptying into the lake. About four [*five*] miles above the lake is a river coming in from the west called Cannon rivir. Its navigation &c. is similar to that of Root river before mentioned. It has a small band of Sioux Indians residing near its head.[31] Passed an Island a little above where two french traders were killed by an Indian a few years since.[32] Encamped on a sand bar at sunset. Wind favourable a part of the day. Distance 35 1/2 miles.

TUESDAY, JULY 15, 1817. Soon after we encamped last evening we received a visit from four Indians, two men & two boys, which gave me more satisfaction than any visit I had received from the Indians. They appeared very good humour[ed] & friendly. They asked for nothing. I gave them some Tobacco & whiskey for which they repeatedly thanked me. Gratitude is the noblest return that can be made for a kindness.

Set sail a half an hour before sunrise with a favourable wind. Break fasted a little below a place called the Crevasse, which is merely a fissure between two large rocks affording a passage to a small stream of water. Ascended the bluff which is here no more than about 175 feet high, which is the common level of the country

[30] Wazecouta left the party at Point au Sable or Sand Point, the site of present-day Frontenac, Minn. Although Red Wing the Younger was encamped there in 1817 (see below, p. 81), no evidence has been found that a permanent Dakota village was located on this site. See also p. 149, below.

[31] The roving Wahpekute Dakota lived on the headwaters of the Cannon River (see p. 278, below) as well as on the Blue Earth and Des Moines rivers. See Keating, *Narrative*, 1:386; Hodge, *Handbook*, 2:890; Lawrence Taliaferro, Sioux Census, September 1, 1834, OIA, St. Peter's Agency, Letters Received, NARG 75.

[32] It is possible that Long here refers to the murder of two French-Canadian traders named Landry and Décoteaux near the mouth of the St. Croix River in 1805. For a summary of this incident, see Edmund C. and Martha C. Bray, *Joseph N. Nicollet on the Plains and Prairies: The Expeditions of 1838–39*, 44n (St. Paul, 1976).

in this vicinity. Upon the slope of the bluffs observed a variety of pebbles & stones amongst which were the Agate of various hues, C[h]alcedony, Flint, Serpentine, Ruby Rock Chrystal [*rose quartz?*] &c. Pike in his journal describes the Mississippi for a considerable distance below the River St. Croix as of a reddish appearance in shoal water, but black as ink in deep. The reddish appearance is occasioned by the sand at the bottom which is of that complexion, the dark is no more than what is common to deep water that is moderately limpid. Met eight canoes of Indians headed by a leader whose name was the Elk's head. They were merely on a hunting expedition. I gave the Chief some tobacco.[33]

Passed the Saint Croix River on our right. Its mouth is about 100 yards wide, but immediately above it expands into a lake [*Lake St. Croix*] from 3/4 to 2 miles wide and about 30 [*24*] miles long. Throughout its whole extent it is deep and navigable for crafts of very considerable burden. Its general course from its head to its confluence with the Mississippi is about SE. About 20 [*26*] miles above the lake in the river St. Croix are rapids [*St. Croix Falls*] by which the navigation of the river is entirely obstructed. Above the rapids the river is navigable for a considerable distance in a direction towards Lake Superiour [*Superior*]. The water communication between Lake Superiour & the Mississippi is obstructed by a portage of moderate extent only, and is the channel of considerable intercourse between the British Traders & the Indians.[34]

The Indians have no permanent villages either on the Lake or river St. Croix. They resort here annually, however, in large hunting parties for wild game of almost all kinds, which is found in great abundance. Gen. Pike on his expedition negotiated with the Indians for a tract of land comprehending the confluence of the St. Croix & Mississippi and obtained a grant of 9 miles square.[35]

[33] Coues, ed., *Pike*, 1:77. No reference to an Indian named Elk's Head has been located.

[34] British and American traders reached Lake Superior from the St. Croix via a portage to Wisconsin's Brule River. Two long portages occurred in Minnesota on the Lake Superior-Mississippi River route: the Grand Portage of the St. Louis River, which was seven miles long, and the Savanna Portage, which was six miles long. All three portages are marked and preserved. June D. Holmquist and Jean A. Brookins, *Minnesota's Major Historic Sites: A Guide*, 158–163 (2nd ed., St. Paul, 1972). On the mouth of the St. Croix, see also p. 78, below.

[35] The Dakota ceded a tract of land at the junction of the St. Croix and the Mississippi, as well as one at the junction of the Minnesota with the Mississippi, in a treaty signed with Pike on September 23, 1805. See *American State Papers: Indian Affairs*, 1:754 (Washington, D.C., 1832). The narrowest part of the Mississippi, mentioned below, was near present Hastings, Minn.

About 4 miles above the mouth of the St. Croix, as it is said, is the narrowest part of the Mississippi below the Falls of St. Ant[h]ony. At this place we crossed the river from a dead start with 16 strokes of our oars. The river is here probably between 100 & 120 yds. wide—but as we had a favourable wind up the river we did not stop to measure it.

Upon the supposition that the country on ascending the Mississippi would loose its alluvial & secondary character after passing the Des Moin[es] Rapids and exhibit nothing but traits of primitive formations not only in its precipices but even upon its surface, I had expected to find on this part of the river not merely bluffs & knobs 5 or 6 hundred feet high but also mountains of vast height & magnitude. On the contrary, I now discover that we have long since passed the highest lands of the Mississippi and that we are now moving thro' a rolling Prairie country, where the eye is greeted with the view of extensive undulating planes instead of being astonished by the wild gigantic scenery of a world of mountains.[36]

The hig[h]lands on this part of the river are elevated from one to two hundred feet above the water level. The bluffs are more regular both in their height & direction than they are below Lake Pepin, and the valley of the river more uniform in its width. The Stratifications of the bluffs are almost entirely sand stone containing clay & lime in greater or less proportions. The pebbles are a mixture of Primitive & secondary stones of various kinds. Blue clay or chalk is frequently to be found.

Passed the Detour de Pin, or Pine turn [*Pine Bend*] of the Mississippi, which is the most westwardly bend of the river between St. Louis & the Falls of St. Antony. The distance from this bend across to the river St. Peters is about 9 miles, whereas it requires two days to go by water to the same place on the St. Peters'.

The Mississippi above the St. Croix emphatically deserves the name it has acquired, which originally implies Clear River.[37] The water is entirely colourless & free from every thing that would render it impure either to the sight or taste. It has a greenish appearance occasioned by reflections from the bottom, but when taken into a vessel is perfectly clear.

[36] The Des Moines Rapids were near present Keokuk, Ia. Long's use of the terms "primitive" and "secondary" indicates his awareness of the theories of Abraham Gottlob Werner.

[37] Long is in error regarding the name of the Mississippi, an Algonquian Indian word meaning "Great River" not "Clear River." See Warren Upham, *Minnesota Geographic Names: Their Origin and Historic Significance*, 4–6 (Reprint ed., St. Paul, 1969).

The wind was favourable thro' most of the day, but the river in this part is very crooked so that we could not sail with so much expedition as otherwise we might have done. Encamped at sun set on the east side of the river upon a handsome prairie. Distance 41 miles.

WEDNESDAY, JULY 16, 1817. Set sail at half past 4 this morning with a favourable breeze. Passed an Indian burying ground on our left, the first that I have seen surrounded with a fence. In the centre a pole is erected, at the foot of which religious rites are performed at the burial of an Indian by the particular friends & relatives of the dec[e]ased. Upon the pole a Flag is suspended when any person of extraordinary merit, or one who is very much beloved, is buried. In the enclosure were two scaffolds erected also about 6 feet high & six feet square. Upon one of them were two coffins containing dead bodies.[38]

Passed a Sioux village on our right containing 14 Cabins. The name of the Chief is the Petit Corbeau or Little Raven [*Little Crow*]. The Indians were all absent on a hunting party up the River St. Croix, which is but a little distance across the Country from the village. Of this we were very glad, as this band are said to be the most notorious beggars of all the Sioux on the Mississippi. One of their Cabins is furnished with loop holes and is situated so near the water that the opposite side of the river is within musket shot range from the building. By this means the Petit Corbeau is enabled to exercise a command over the passage of the river, and has in some instances compelled traders to land with their goods and induced them, probably thro' fear of offending him, to bestow presents to a considerable amount before he would suffer them to pass. The cabins are a kind of stockade buildings and of a better appearance than any Indian dwellings I have before met with.

Two miles above the village on the same side of the river is Carvers Cave, at which we stopped to breakfast. However interest-

[38] Many later travelers also mention a Dakota cemetery on the west bank near Kaposia, the village described in the paragraph below.

The village of Petit Corbeau or Little Crow, who was chief of the Kaposia band of Mdewakanton Dakota, was moved from the east bank, where Pike and Long found it, some time before 1834. Little Crow, like Wabasha, was a member of a dynasty of leaders bearing the same name. He was succeeded by his son upon his death in the winter of 1833–34. Donald Jackson, ed., *The Journals of Zebulon Montgomery Pike*, 1:201 (Norman, Okla., 1966); Taliaferro, Sioux Census, September 1, 1834, OIA, St. Peter's Agency, Letters Received, NARG 75; Willoughby M. Babcock, "Sioux Villages in Minnesota Prior to 1837," in *Minnesota Archaeologist*, 11:137 (October, 1945). See also p. 305, below.

ing it may have been, it does not possess that character in a very high degree at present. We descended it with lighted candles to its lower extremity. The entrance is very low & about 8 feet broad, so that a man in order to enter it must be completely prostrate. The angle of descent within the cave is about 25°. The flooring is an inclined plane of quick sand formed of the rock in which the cavern is formed. The distance from its entrance to its inner extremity is 24 paces, and the width in the broadest part about 9, & its greatest height about 7 feet. In shape it resembles a Bakers oven. The cavern was once probably much more extensive. My interpreter [*Rocque*] informed me that since his remembrance the entrance was not less than 10 feet high, & its length far greater than at present. The rock in which it is formed is a very white Sandstone so fryable that the fragments of it will almost crumble to sand when taken into the hand. A few yards below the mouth of the cavern is a very copious spring of fine water issuing from the bottom of the cliff.[39]

Five [*three*] miles above this is the Fountain Cave, on the same side of the river, formed in the same kind of sand stone but of a more pure & finer quality. It is far more curious & interesting than the former. The entrance of the Cave is a large windinding [*winding*] hall, about 150 feet in length 15 feet in width & from 8 to 16 in height, finely arched over head & walled on both sides by cliffs of sandstone nearly perpendicular. Next succeeds a narrow passage & difficult of entrance which opens into a most beautiful circular room, finely arched above and about 50 feet in diameter. The cavern then continues a meandering course, expanding occasionally into small rooms of a circular form.

We penetrated about 150 yards till our candles began to fail us, when we returned. To beautify and embellish the scene a fine chrystal stream [*Fountain Creek*] flows thro' the Cavern & cheers the lonesome dark retreat with its enlivening murmurs. The temperature of the water in the cave was 46° and that of the air 60°. Entering this cold retreat from an atmosphere of 89°, I thought it not prudent to remain in it long enough to take its several dimensions & mean-

[39] There is an extensive literature on Carver's Cave, where Jonathan Carver met with the Dakota in 1767, and Fountain Cave, discovered in 1811 and described in the following paragraph and p. 76, below. Several descriptive accounts containing mileages between the two caves which differ from Long's are analyzed in Coues, ed., *Pike*, 1:199–201n. The sites are marked within present-day St. Paul. See Sue E. Holbert and June D. Holmquist, *A History Tour of 50 Twin City Landmarks*, 5, 16 (St. Paul, 1966). Long's 1823 expedition also visited Fountain Cave, according to Keating, *Narrative*, 1:290, but the visit is not mentioned in the manuscript journals.

der its courses, particularly as we had to wade in water to our knees in many places in order to penetrate as far as we went. The fountain supplies an abundance of water as fine as I ever drank.

This Cavern, as I was informed by my Interpreter, has been discovered but a few years. That the Indians formerly living in its neighbourhood knew nothing of it till within six years past. That it is not the same as that described by Carver is evident not only from this circumstance, but also from the circumstance that instead of a stagnant pool and only one accessible room of a very different form, this cavern has a brook running thro' it and at least 4 rooms in succession one after the other. Carver's Cave is fast filling up with sand so that no water is now to be found in it, whereas this from the very nature of the place must be enlarging, as the fountain will carry along with its impact all the sand that falls into it from the roofs & sides of the Cavern.

A little above stopped to take a meridian altitude of the sun's lower limb, which we found to be 66° 42′.

Five miles above the River St. Peters comes in from the SW. We arrived at the mouth of this river at two P.M. & layed by to dine. The St. Peters is about 200 yards wide at its mouth & is navigable for Mackinaw Boats between 2 & 3 hundred miles in all stages of the water and in high water much farther.[40] For about 40 miles it has still & deep water; farther up there are occasional rapids by which there are portages of moderate extent.

There are three considerable Indian villages up this river, the first of which is about 9 miles above its mouth. They are all different bands of the Sioux nation.[41]

The country at the junction of the rivers I shall have occasion to describe on my return.[42]

The rapids below the Falls of St. Antony commence about 2 miles above the confluence of the Mississippi & St. Peter's and are so strong that we could hardly ascend them by rowing, poling, & sailing with a strong wind all at the same time. About 4 miles up the rapids we could make no head way by all these means, and were obliged to substitute the cordel in place of the poles & oars.[43]

[40] The total length of the Minnesota River from its mouth to Big Stone Lake is only 329 miles. See Chapter 8, note 2, below.

[41] On the villages, see p. 157, below.

[42] See p. 78, below.

[43] The rapids were created by the recession of the Falls of St. Anthony from the vicinity of Fort Snelling to the point approximately eight miles upriver, where Long found them. Although estimates of mileages differed with the type of craft making the

Arrived at the Falls of St. Anthony at a quarter past seven. Winds favourable a part of the day. Encamped on the east shore just below the Cataract. Distance 27 1/2 miles.

THURSDAY, JULY 17, 1817. The Place where we encamped last night needed no embellishments to render it romantic in the highest degree. The banks on both sides of the river are about 100 [50] feet high, decorated with Trees and shrubbery of various kinds. The Post Oak, Hiccory, Walnut, Lynden, Sugar tree, White Birch & the American Box, also various evergreens, such as the Pine, Cedar, Juniper &c. added their embellishments to the scene. Amongst the shrubbery were the Prickly ash, Plumb & cherry tree, the goosberry, the Black & red raspberry, the Choak berry, Grape vine &c. There were also various kinds of herbage & Flowers, among which were the wild parsley, rue, spikinard &c., Red & white roses, Morning Glory, and various other handsome flowers. A few yards below us was a beautiful cascade of fine spring water, poring down from a projecting precipice about 100 feet high, on our left was the Mississippi hurrying thro its channel with great velosity, and about 3/4 mile above us in plain view was the majestic cataract of the Falls of St. Anthony. The murmuring of the Cascade, the roaring of the river, and the thunder of the cataract, all contributed to render the scene the most interesting & magnificent of any I ever before witnessed.[44]

The perpendicular fall of the water at the cataract, as stated by Pike in his Journal, is 16 1/2 feet, which I found to be true by actual admeasurement. To this height however 4 or 5 feet may be added for the rapid descent which immediately succeeds the perpendicular fall within a few yards below. Immediately at the Cataract the river is divided into two parts by an Island [*Hennepin*], which extends considerably above & below the Cataract & is about 500 yards long. The channel on the right side of the Island is about three times

trip and with varying river depths, Long's assessment here and on p. 71, below, is essentially correct. See Frank Leverett, *Quaternary Geology of Minnesota and Parts of Adjacent States*, 145 (U.S. Department of the Interior, *Geological Survey Professional Paper*, no. 161—Washington, D.C., 1932).

[44] The descriptive literature on the Falls of St. Anthony is extensive. See Lucile M. Kane, *The Waterfall That Built a City: The Falls of St. Anthony in Minneapolis*, 1–9 (St. Paul, 1966). See also below, Chapter 4, note 3, and pp. 283–285. The spring has not been specifically identified. Pike commented that between the mouth of the Minnesota and the falls the "shores have many large and beautiful springs issuing forth, which form small cascades as they tumble over the cliffs into the Mississippi." Coues, ed., *Pike*, 1:311.

the width of that on the left. The quantity of water passing thro' them is not however in the same proportion, as about one third part of the whole passes thro' the left channel. In the broadest channel just below the Cataract is a small island [*Cataract*] also about 50 yards in length & 30 in breadth. Both of these Islands contain the same kind of rocky formations as the banks of the river & are nearly as high. Besides these, there are immediately at the foot of the cataract two islands [*Spirit and Upton*] of very inconsiderable size situated in the right channel also.[45]

The rapids commence several hundred yards above the Cataract & continue about 8 miles below. The fall of the water, beginning at the head of the rapids and extending 260 rods down the river to where the portage road commences below the Cataract, is accor[ding] to Pike 58 feet. If this estimate be correct, the whole fall from the head to the foot of the rapids is not probably les[s] much less than 100 feet. But as I had no instrument sufficiently accurate to level, where the view must necessarily be pretty extensive, I took no pains to ascertain the extent of the fall. The mode I adopted to ascertain the height of the Cataract was to suspend a line & plumbet from the table rock on the south side of the river, which at the time had very little water passing over it, as the river was unusually low.

The rocky formations at this place were arranged in the following order from the surface downward: A coarse kind of limestone in thin strata containing considerable silex. A kind of soft fryable stone of a greenish colour & slaty fracture probably containing lime, alumen & silex. A very beautiful stratification of shell lime stone in thin plates extremely regular in its formation and containing a vast number of shells all apparently of the same kind. This formation constitutes the table rock of the Cataract. The next in order is a white or yellowish sandstone so easily crumbled that it deserves the name of a sand-bank rather than that of a rock. It is of various depths from 10 to 50 or 75 feet and is of the same character with that found at the caves before described. The next in order is a soft fryable sand stone of a greenish colour similar to that resting upon the shell lime stone. These stratifications occupied the whole space from low water mark

[45] On Pike's measurements here and below and the portage road, see Coues, ed., *Pike*, 1:244, 311. Long's observations were made looking downriver. His "right" thus refers to the west side of the falls. Although his measurements differ from those of later engineers, his observations on the conformations are correct. Because of the construction of dams and navigation locks, the only remaining islands at the falls are Hennepin and Nicollet. The latter is located upriver above Hennepin.

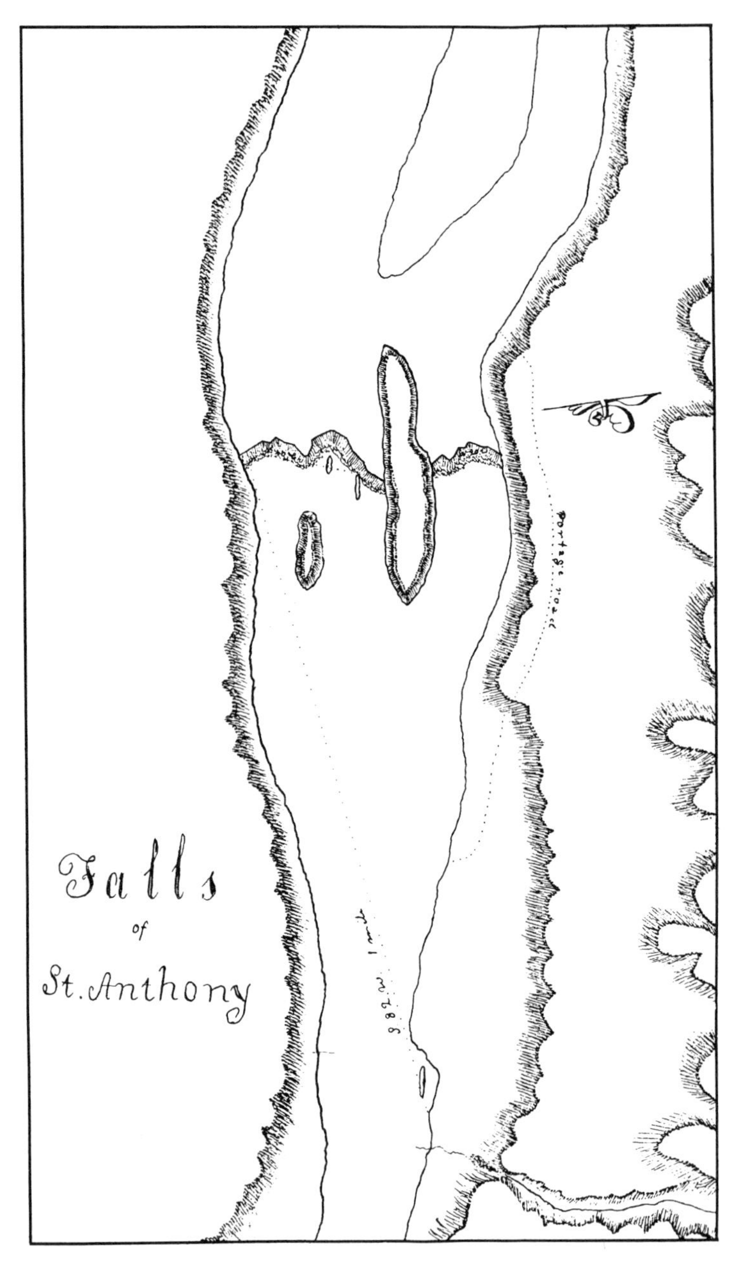

LONG'S SKETCH MAP of the Falls of St. Anthony (now within Minneapolis) in his 1817 journal.

nearly to the top of the Bluffs. On the east, or rather north side of the river at the Falls, are high grounds at the distance of half a mile from the river considerably more elevated than the Bluffs & of a hilly aspect.[46]

This remarkable part of the Mississippi is not without a tale to hallow the scenery & add some weight to the interest it is naturally calculated to excite. Our Indian Companion, the Shooter from the Pine Tree, related a story while he was with us, the catastrophe of which his mother witnessed with her own eyes.[47]

A young Indian of the Sioux nation had espoused a wife with whom he had lived happily for a few years, enjoying every comfort of which a savage life is susceptible. To crown the felicity of the happy couple, they had been blessed with two lovely children on whom they doated with the utmost affection. During this time the young man by dint of activity & perseverance signalized himself in an eminent degree as a hunter, having met with unrivalled success in the chase. This circumstance contributed to raise him high in the estimation of his fellow savages and draw a crowd of admirers about him, which operated as a spur to his ambition.

At length some of his newly acquired friends, desirous of forming a connexion that must operate greatly to their advantage, suggested the propriety of him taking another wife, as it would be impossible for one woman to manage his household affairs & wait upon all the guests his rising importance would call to visit him. That his consequence to the nation was every where known & acknowledged and that in all probability he would soon be called upon to preside as their Chief. His vanity was fired at the thought; he yielded an easy compliance with their solicitations and accepted a wife they had already selected for him.

After his second marriage it became an object with him to take his new wife home & reconcile his first wife to the match, which he was desirous of accomplishing in the most delicate manner that circumstances would admit. For this purpose he returned to his first wife, who was yet ignorant of what had taken place, and by dissimulation atempted to beguile her into an approbation of the step measure he

[46] Except for the lowest "fryable sandstone," Long's delineation of the strata is basically correct. See Winchell and Upham, *Geology of Minnesota*, 1:31n; Frederick W. Sardeson, "Beginning and Recession of Saint Anthony's Falls," in Geological Society of America, *Bulletins*, 19:33 (March, 1908).

[47] This is the legend of Dark Day, or Ampato Sapa, which Long seems to have been the first to record. There are many versions of the tale, most of them similar to that given here. See Kane, *Waterfall*, 2.

had taken. "You know," said he, "that I can love no one so much as I love you. Yet I see that our connexion subjects you to hardships and fatigue too great for you to endure. This grieves me much, but I know of only one remeday by which you can be relieved, and which with your concurrence shall be adopted. My friends from all parts of the nation come to visit me, and my house is constantly thronged by those who come to pay their respects, while you alone are under the necessity of labouring hard in order to cook their food and wait upon them. They are daily becoming more numerous & your duties, instead of growing lighter, are becoming more arduous every day. You must be sensible that I am rising high in the esteem of the nation, & I have sufficient grounds to expect that I shall ere long be their cheif. These considerations have induced me to take another wife, but my affection for you has so far prevailed over my inclination in this respect as to lead me to solicit your approbation before I adopt the measure.The wife I take shall be subject to your control in every respect and will always be second to you in my affections."

She listened to his narration with the utmost anxiety & concern & endeavoured to reclaim him from his purpose, refuting all the reasons & pretences [in] his duplicity he had urged in favour of it by unanswerable arguments, the suggestions of unaffected love & conjugal affection.

He left her however to meditate upon the subject, in hopes that she would at length give over her objections and consent to his wishes. She in the mean time redoubled her industry and treated him invariably with more marked tenderness than she had done before, resolved to try every means in her power to dissuade him from the execution of his purpose. She still however found him bent upon it. She plead all the endearments of their former life, the regard he had for the happiness of herself and offsprings of their mutual love to prevail on him to relinquish the idea of taking another wife. She warned him of the fatal consequences that would result to their family upon his taking such a step. Till at length he was induced to communicate the secret of his marriage. He then told her that a complyance on her part would be absolutely necessary. That if she could not rec[ei]ve his new wife as a friend & companion, she must admit her as a necessary incumbrance, at all events they must live together.

She was determined however not to remain the passive dupe of his hypocricy. She took her two children, left his house, & went to reside with her Parents. Soon after her return to her father's family, she joined them and others of her friends in an expedition up the Mississippi to spend the winter in hunting. In the spring as they were returning laden with peltries, she & her children occupied a canoe by themselves. On arriving near the Falls of St. Anthony, she lingered by the way till the rest had all landed a little above [the] shoot. She then painted herself & children, paddled her canoe immediately in to the suck of the rapids, & commenced singing her death song, in which she recounted the happy scenes she had passed thro' when she enjoyed the undivided affection of her husband and the wretchedness in which she was involved by his inconstancy.

Her friends, alarmed at her situation, ran to the shore and begged her to paddle out of the current, while her parents in the agonies of despair, wrending their clothes & tearing out their hair, besought her to come to their arms. But all to no purpose; her wretchedness was complete & must terminate only with her existence. She continued her course till she was born head long down the roaring cataract and instantly dashed to pieces on the rocks below. No traces either of herself & children or the boat were ever found afterwards. Her brothers, to be avenged of the untimely fate of their sister, embraced the first opportunity and killed her husband whom they considered the cause of her death, a custom sanctioned by the usage of the Indians from tim[e] immemorial.

After having viewed the falls upon this side of the river, we attempted to cross the rapids in our boat, but the water was so low & the current so rapid that we were compelled to return again to the same side, which we accomplish at the risk of having the boat recked upon a large rock which we were but just able to shun. Made a second attempt a little further down, in which we succeeded.

Having taken a view of the Cataract on both sides, we commenced descending the river at a quarter past 10 A.M. in hopes that we should arrive at the mouth of the St. Peters in time to take an observation for the Latitude of that place. But finding we were likely to be pressed for time, we stopped 1 1/2 miles above, where we found the altitude of the Suns' lower limb when on the Meridian to be 66°.

After arriving at the St. Peters, we lay by 2 or 3 hours in order to examine the country in that neighbourhood. At the mouth of this River is an Island [*Pike*] of considerable extent, separated from the main by a Slough of the Mississippi into which the St. Peter's discharges itself. Boats in ascending the former, particularly in low water, usually pass thro' this slough, as it affords a greater depth than the channel upon the other side of the island. Immediately above the mouth of the St. Peter's is a tract of flat Prairie extending far up this river & about 350 yards along the Slough above mentioned. This tract is subject to inundation in time of high water, which is also the case with the flat lands generally situated on both of these rivers. Next above this tract is a high point of land [*Pilot Knob*], elevated about 120 [250] feet above the water and fronting immediately on the Mississippi but separated from the St. Peters by the tract above described. The point is formed by the bluffs of the two rivers intercepting each other.

Passing up the river on the brow of the Mississippi Bluff, the ground risis gradually for the distance of about 600 yards, where an extensive broad valley of moderate depth commences. But on the St. Peters the bluff retains nearly the same altitude, being intersected occasionally by ravines of moderate depth. A military work of considerable magnitude might be constructed on the point and might be rendered sufficiently secure by occupying the commanding height in the rear in a suitable manner, as the latter would control not only the point, but all the neighbouring height to the full extent of a 12 pr.'s range. The work on the point would be necessary to controul the navigation of the two rivers. But without the commanding work in the rear would be liable to be greatly annoyed from a height situated directly opposite on the other side of the Mississippi, which is here no more than about 250 yds. wide. This latter height however would not be eligible for a permanent post on account of the numerous ridges & ravines situated immediately in its rear.[48]

Reembarked and descended to the Fountain Cave, where we landed again & went into the cave for the purpose of taking some [of] its dimensions. Owing to the different state of the atmosphere, we could not penetrate so far by about 50 yards as we did yesterday, before our candles went out. We measured the distance as far as we went on this occasion, which we found to be 150 yds. We embarked the third time, laid in a supply of wood for the night, kindled a fire in our cabouse, & concluded to float during the night.

We regretted exceedingly that we could not spend more time in the enjoyment of the scenes we had been witnesing to day, but were

[48] The site Long recommended here was later chosen as the location of Fort St. Anthony, better known as Fort Snelling. See pp. 282, 342, below.

induced to forego the pleasure from the circumstance that our provisions were nearly exhausted from a want of care in the distribution of them, that we had no whiskey remaining on the same account, which may be considered a necessary of life to those employed in the navigation of the Mississippi in hot weather.

These concerns I had entrusted to my Corporal [*Charles Sheffield*], as it was impossible for me to manage them & perform my other duties at the same time. But as he was appointed to officiate in that capacity at the commencement of the voyage, without ever having had the requisite experience before, he did not know how to distribute with proper economy, altho he was extremely anxious to do so.

2. *Down the Mississippi to Belle Fontaine*

JULY 18 THROUGH AUGUST 15, 1817

FRIDAY, JULY 18, 1817. Floated all night with no other inconvenience but occasionally running upon Sand Bars. Landed at the river St. Croix for the purpose of examining the ground situated below the mouth of that river. At this place [*Prescott, Wis.*] is a position well calculated for the command of both rivers, with the exception that there is an Island [*Prescott I.*] of the Mississippi several miles long situated opposite to the confluence of the two. On the west side of the Mississippi is a very small [*Vermillion*] Slough that separates the Island from the main land. This Slough is navigable in high water, but its navigation may be effectually obstructed by constructing a Chevaux di [*de*] frise & sinking them in the channel. With this exception, a military post might be established here to considerable advantage, & would be sufficiently secure by occupying a commanding ground situated in rear of the site proposed with an enclosed work constructed on the principle of the Martello Tower.[1]

About 20 miles below the St. Croix met the grandsons of Carver, before spoken of. We parted with them the second day after leaving Prairie du Chien and saw nothing more of them till this day. We stopped a few minutes with them and gave them some instructions to enable them to find the caves.

We lay by a while at a Sioux Village 4 1/2 miles above Lake Pepin in order to catch some fish, as we had nothing left of our Provisions but flour. Our whiskey also was all expended, & we had two hundred miles farther to go before we could obtain a fresh supply. Caught three very fine cat fish & killed a few [*passenger?*] pigeons.

[1] In his report of May 12, 1818 (see Appendix 1, below), Long did not recommend a post here on the land cession secured by Pike.

The village was kept in very nice order, exhibiting more signs of a well regulated police than any one I have met with on the voyage, with the exception of the Little Raven's before mentioned. The name of the chief of this village is Red Wing the elder. He and all his band were on a hunting tour at the time we were there.[2]

During our delay at this place, Mr. H[empstead] & myself ascended a hill about 1/2 mile far[ther] down the river called the [Mount La] Grange, or barn, of which it has some faint resemblance. Its length is 3/4 mile & its height about 400 [*345*] feet. Its acclivity on the river side is precipitous, that on the opposit very abrupt. It is completely insulated from the other hilands in the neighbourhood, which is also the case with many others within a moderate distance tho' not in quite so remarkable a manner; for this is not only surrounded by valleys, but is also nearly insulated by water, an arm or bay [*Colvill Bay*] of the river entering at the lower end of the hill & extending within 3 or 4 hundred yards of the river above.[3]

Immediately upon the highest part of the Grange is one of the numerous artificial mounds that are to be met with in almost every part of this western world. Its elevation above its base, however, is only about 5 feet; I have observed that the mounds on the Mississippi above the Illinois, tho' probably more numerous, are of a much smaller size generally than those below, having been erected perhaps by a different nation of aborigines.

From the summit of the Grange, the view of the surrounding scenery is surpassed perhaps by very few, if any, of a similar character that the Country and probably the world can afford. The sublime & beautiful are here blended in most enchanting manner, while the prospect has very little to terrify or shock the imagination.

To aid in forming an idea approximating in some degree to the reality of the scene, we may suppose that the country at the head of Lake Pepin, situated between the main bluffs of the grand Missis-

[2] The village was located at present-day Red Wing, Minn. This notable chief, who died in 1829, was also called Tatankamani, Walking Buffalo, and Aile Rouge; he was one of a succession of at least four tribal leaders (including Shakea, mentioned on p. 274, below) known as Red Wing. His band of Mdewakanton Dakota was closely associated with that of Wabasha. See Taliaferro Journal, March 19, 1829 (8:235), Taliaferro Papers; Hodge, *Handbook*, 1:678 (Washington, D.C., 1907), 2:365. See also below, pp. 149, 150.

[3] Mount La Grange, or Barn Bluff, is within the present city of Red Wing. It still constitutes a point not entirely surrounded by water. Keating, *Narrative*, 1:286, used much the same language in describing it. On the mounds mentioned below, see Winchell, *Aborigines*, 154, 164, 169.

sippi Valley, has once been inundated to the height of 250 feet above the present water level. That at this time the Lake embosomed numerous small Islands of a circular, oblong, & serpentine form. That from the main land also promontories and peninsulas projected into the lake on all sides, forming numerous Capes, Bays and Inlets. That the country bordering upon the lake was an extensive plane in many places variegated with gentle hills & dales of the same general level with the Islands & Promontories. We may then suppose that by some tremendous convulsion that must have shaken the earth to its centre this vast body of water has been drained off to its present humble level, & left the bed of the lake free of water & furnished with a rich & fertile alluvion well adapted to vegetation of all kinds. That afterwards the valleys & knobs assumed a verdant dress and those places which were once the haunts of the finney tribes now became the resorts of the feathered—and we shall have a faint idea of the outlines of the scene. But to be impressed with the sublimity & delighted with the bea[u]ty of the picture, a view of the original is indispensable.[4]

A favourable breeze springing up about dark we concluded to set sail as it was only 4 1/2 miles to the Lake, and after our arrival there we should sail without obstructions either of trees or Sand bars.

Saturday, July 19, 1817. We had got into the broadest part of the Lake about midnight, when the wind began to blow stronger, and there were at the same time strong indications of an approaching storm; we shifted our course and made for the shore as fast as possible, which we fortunately reached before the storm became violent. The night was so dark that we could find no harbour in which to secure our boat. We were engaged about one hour in towing her along the beach in hopes of finding one, but the violence of the storm increased and the boat began to fill with water, so that we were forced to take out all our baggage with the least possible delay, all of which we had the good luck to save with out its having received much injury. We then made fast the boat and left her to fill, as it was out of our power to prevent her filling while the surf ran so high & strong. We succeeded in pitching our tent after much trouble, & got our baggage deposited within it. Our next object was to kindle a fire, but on inquiry found that our apparatus for that

[4] Long, writing before Louis Agassiz had formulated his glacial theory, could not have known of the Glacial River Warren which at one time inundated the Mississippi Valley. This passage probably reflects the theories of Constantin F. Volney and Samuel Mitchill.

purpose was completely drenched in water. I then tore a piece of the lining from my coat sleaf, being the only place where I could find it dry, & kindled a fire with some dry rotten wood the men chanced to find in the dark.

The day dawned soon after & we began to make preparations for starting again, tho' the storm continued with some abatement. We found that the most important parts of our baggage had received but little injury & that our boat was not damaged. We embarked again at half past six, rowed out in to the lake till we could clear a point laying a little to the le[e]ward of us, hoisted sail, & ran with great speed. The surf ran so high & strong that we were in danger of filling several times, as the waves broke over the sides of our little bark.

Called at the Indian Village situated upon Sandy [*Sand*] Point, the same that we left our chief [*Wazecouta*] at on our outward Voyage. He had promised to return with us, but during our absence had been prevailed upon to join the Indians of the Village on a hunting expedition up the Chippeway River in which they were then about to embark. The name of the chief of this village was Red-Wing, the younger, son of Red wing spoken of yesterday. We delayed here but a very few minutes. Sailed thro' the lake with a strong wind. At evening the weather became calm, & we concluded to float thro' the night. Layed by a short time about sunset to collect wood & kindle a fire in our Caboose—during which caught three cat fish.[5]

SUNDAY, JULY 20, 1817. Met with no inconvenience in floating, except running foul of sand bars occasionally from which we easily extricated ourselves.

Passed Le Fieulle's or The Leaf's [*Wabasha's*] Village at which there were no Indians to be seen, all of them having recently gone on a hunting Campaign. Stopped at the Sand bar, where we took observations to ascertain the height of the Bluff [*Trempealeau*] Island on our passage up. Here we found our axe which we lost on that occasion. Landed again on Bluff Island for the purpose of ascending to the top of the hill, which I did in company with Mr. H. Here we had a view of the Indian Village on Aux-Aisle Prairie, as also of the beautiful scenery mentioned in my journal of Saturday, 12 inst. Here we discovered that what before appeared to be the main river

[5] Red Wing the Younger was probably Wacouta, son or stepson of the Red Wing whom Long mentioned above. Wacouta was elected chief of the band on May 18, 1829, soon after the elder Red Wing's death. See Taliaferro Journal, April 15 (8:247), May 18 (9:5), 1829, Taliaferro Papers.

bluffs on the left [*east*] just below the Island were a broken range [*Chicken Breast Bluffs*] of high bluff lands towering into precipices & peeks, completely insulated from the main Bluffs by a broad flat Prairie. This, ranged in connexion with the Island, may be considered a great curiosity, when we reflect that their sides have once been buffetted by the billows of a Lake at least 200 feet above the present water level.

A little below we saw three Indians on shore engaged in killing a rattle snake. They called to us and said that one of them had been bit on his leg by the snake, upon which we waited for them to come to us. Immediately after the wound was inflicted they had cut out a piece of the flesh containing the wounded part and applied bandages to the leg above. I proposed salt & water as a wash for the wound, but they objected, being prejudiced against admitting water to a wound in any case. I had no sweet oil or any thing else that I thought serviceable, & could do nothing more but advise them to return as soon as possible to their encampment.

Lay'd by a while to ascend another hill said to be the highest on the Mississippi. It is of a semi conical form as it presents itself to the view from the river, but after ascending it appears to be a ridge, the highest part of which projects towards the rivir forming a high prominent Peek cleft perpendicularly from its summit about 200 or 250 feet. From this point it declines gradually till it looses itself in the bases of other hills farther from the river. The view from its summit direct to the river is rendered exceedingly terrific by one of the most frightful precipices I ever beheld. Even the largest trees below appear like stinted shrubbery, and the river seems to be almost inaccessible from its vast depression. I took observations for estimating the height of the hill, agreeably to which its elevation above the water is 1000 feet, but I am inclined to think some mistake was committed either in the measurement of the base line or in reading the angles from my sextant, as by the estimate the hill is much higher than I should judge it to be from its appearance.[6]

From this hill we also had a view of Bluff Island & its neighbour-

[6] This area is lined with hills along both the Minnesota and Wisconsin sides of the river. Long may have been referring to Gwinn's Bluff some three miles north of Dakota in Winona County, Minn. Reputedly the highest on the river, it is 1,176 feet above sea level. Long carried no barometer and his measurement was indeed too high. The bluffs in this region vary from 500 to 600 feet above the river level. See Winchell and Upham, *Geology of Minnesota*, 1:243. The geological evolution of the river channel near Trempealeau, discussed below, is explained in Martin, *Physical Geography of Wisconsin*, 148–151.

ing heights on the left shore, as well as the main bluffs of the river as far as the eye could reach. The beauty, grandeur & magnificence of the scene completely baffles description. The most curious & wonderful part of the scenery was the passage of the river between the main bluffs on the right & the insulated range before mentioned on the left of the river. Here the river, not contented as in other places to meander thro' a valley several miles in width, seems to have left its original channel, preferring to cut a passage just wide enough for its accommodation thro' a cape or promontory 6 or 8 hundred feet high, rather than embellish an extensive & beautiful lawn with its peaceful waters. This phenomenon can be accounted for on no other principle than the existence of a Lake that once occupied the valley of the Mississippi, filling it to the height of many hundred feet above the present water level. This vast body of water may have given occasion to billows, which wore upon the Sand stone formations of the lake shores and in process of time formed inlets, bays, peninsulas & islands, so that when the water was drained off to its present level the hig[h] lands & valleys retained these singular conformations as testimonials of the great changes they had experienced.

On the top of the hill we collected many interesting specimens of minerals, such as chrystals of Iron ore, siliceous chrystalizations beautifuly tinged with iron, some of them purple, others red[d]ish, yellow, white &c., Crusts of sand stone strongly cemented with Iron & thick set with polished chrystals of quarts, &c. &c.

This Hill would seem to be entitled to the appellation of mountain were it not that the neighbourin[g] heights & the high lands generally in this part of the river have very nearly the same altitude.

MONDAY, JULY 21, 1817. Floated last night also, but made very little progress on account of head winds. While we stopped to breakfast caught several fish which, since we have no meat, are become essential to a healthy subsistence, particularly as my men have hard duty to perform.

Met 12 Canoes of Fox Indians on a hunting tour from the Upper Ioway River. There were three very aged squaws with them, one of whom was entirely blind. She was busily engaged in twisting strips of bark for the purpose of making rush mats. This labour, notwithstanding her blindness & great age, she performed with much expedition.

Passed The Painted rock on the right of the river 9 miles above Prairie Du Chien. It has obtained this name from its having numerous hyeroglyphics upon it painted by the Indians. These figures are painted on a cliff nearly perpendicular at the height of about 25 feet from its base. When ever the Indians pass this cliff, they are in the habit of performing certain ceremonie, which their superstition leads them to believe are efficacious in rendering any enterprise in which they may be engaged successful.[7]

Arrived at Prairie Du Chien a little after 9 o'clock in the evening, having accomplished the trip from this to the Falls of St. Anthony & back again in 13 Days, being three days sooner than I had expected to return at the time of my departure from this place.

TUESDAY, JULY 22, 1817. Found my friends at this place all very well, except Captain [William Le] Dufphey who had been bitten by a Rattle snake on the day of my departure.[8] He received the wound in the instep, where the tooth of the snake penetrated to the bone. He applied a bandage upon his leg in the first instance, & resorted to medical aid as soon as it was practicable. When he was bitten, he was in the woods 4 miles from home, consequently the poison must have had a considerable time to diffuse itself before he could apply a remedy. His foot and leg swelled very much & became black, but the remedies applied proved efficacious, & he is now past danger & is so far recovered that he is able to walk about with ease.

WEDNESDAY, JULY 23, 1817. Dr. Pearson [*William H. Pierson*], Lt. [William] Armstrong & myself took horses & rode about the neighbourhood this morning, for the purpose of discovering a position better calculated for a military post than the present site of Fort Crawford.[9] We went down the Prairie to the Ouisconsin, then fol-

[7] The Painted Rock near the mouth of Paint Creek 1/2 mile north of present Waukon Junction, Ia., was an Indian landmark described as "a great cliff overlooking the Mississippi . . . formerly bearing paintings supposed to represent the water spirit." Mentioned by many early travelers, it was a gathering place of Dakota tribes going to Prairie du Chien. See Works Projects Administration, *Iowa: A Guide to the Hawkeye State*, 433 (New York, 1938); Charles Reuben Keyes, "Ancient Sites," in *Palimpsest*, 8:211 (June, 1927); Beltrami, *Pilgrimage*, 2:175; Lawrence Taliaferro, "Auto-Biography," in *MHC*, 6:206 (1894). The prairie opposite contained an ancient habitation site excavated in 1925–26. See David Baerreis, "The Bookshelf," in *Wisconsin Archeologist*, new series 44:186–189, 191 (September, 1963). Both sites have been destroyed; see Marshall McKusick, *Men of Ancient Iowa As Revealed by Archeological Discoveries*, 53 (Ames, Ia., 1964). See also p. 146, below.

[8] On Dufphey, who commanded Fort Crawford from August, 1816, to April, 1817, see Heitman, *Historical Register*, 1:386; Peter L. Scanlan, *Prairie du Chien: French, British, American*, 124 (Menasha, Wis., 1937).

[9] On Armstrong and Pierson, who was surgeon's mate in the Rifle Regiment in 1817, see Heitman, *Historical Register*, 1:170, 792; "Report of Surgeons and Mates of

lowed the course of that river about three miles above the commencement of the high lands, but could discover no position that was not objectionable in very many respects. The Prairie itself is separated from the Ouisconsin by a broad marshy tract of land annually subject to inundation, which is the case also with some parts of the Prairie. The high lands are intersected by numerous ravines and exhibit a constant succession of hills, ridges, and valleys of various depths. They are inaccessible from the river at many points and overlook it at none, the view as well as the command of the river being effectually obstructed by the numerous islands which it embosoms.

Altho' there was no opportunity to accomplish the object of our reconnoitre, still however we had occasion to be high[l]y gratified with a survey of curiosities that have baffled the ingenuity & penetration of the wisest to account for them. The curiosities alluded to are the remains of ancient works constructed probably for military purposes, which we found more numerous & of greater extent upon the high lands just above the mouth of the Ouisconsin than any of which a description has been made public that have yet been discovered in the Western Country. They consist of ridges or parapets of earth and mounds variously disposed so as to conform to the nature of the ground they are intended to fortify, the surface of which is variegated with numerous ridges, hills, valleys & ravines. The works of course have no regular form. The parapets are generally about three and a half feet high with no appearance of a ditch upon either side, and are intercepted at short intervals by a gateway, or sally ports, most of which are flanked by parapets or mounds. The parapets are mostly situated upon ridges; some few, however, are disposed after the manner of Traverses, being carried across the interiours of the works in various directions. The mounds are from 4 to 6 feet in height, at present of a circular form tho' square probably when first constructed. They are arranged in a straight direction, are about 20 feet asunder, and form continuations of the fortified lines having the same direction as the Parapets. Wherever there is an angle in the principal lines, a mound of the largest size is erected; the parapets also are generally terminated by

the Army," March 31, 1819, in Secretary of War, Letters Received, Unregistered Series, NARG 107; [Stella M. Drumm, ed.], "Letters of William Carr Lane, 1819–1831," in *Glimpses of the Past*, 7:63 (July–September, 1940); excerpt from a manuscript by Samuel Williams, "Memoir of Eliza Armstrong Williams," in William Armstrong Papers, WHS.

mounds of this description at the extremities of lines, as also at the Gate ways. In many places the lines are composed of Parapets & mounds in conjunction, the mounds being arranged along the Parapet at their usual distance from each other, and operating as flank defences to the lines. These works exhibit abundant evidence of having been erected at the expense of a vast deal of labour. Works of a similar Character are to be found scattered thro' this part of the country in various directions. At what period they were constructed, and by what race of people, must in all probability forever remain a desideratum.[10]

THURSDAY, JULY 24, 1817. Capt. Dufphey, Lt. Armstrong, Mr. Hempstead, & myself took an excursion into the neighbouring high lands to day in order to ascertain in some measure of what character they are, and to visit some of the remains of ancient fortification. We rode across the country about 20 [*15*] miles to Kickapoo Creek [*Kickapoo R.*], & returned again in a course different from that in which we travelled out.

The country is divided into numerous hills, or rather ridges of various shapes & dimensions but generally of an equal altitude, by valleys & ravines, some of which have fine streams of spring water running thro' them. The hills are generally elevated from 3 to 4 or 5 hundred feet above the valleys, handsomely rounded upon their tops, but abrupt & precipitous on their sides and almost inaccessible except thro' the numerous ravines by which they are cut. The vallies are many of them broad and appear well adapted to tillage & pasture. The highlands also appear well calculated for the raising of grain. The country is generally Prairie land, but the hills & valleys are in some places covered with a scattering growth of fine timber consisting of White, Red, & Post Oak, Hiccory, White Walnut, Sugr. Tree, Maple, White & blue ash, American Box &c.

The antiquities were of a similar character with those described yesterday. Of these we saw numerous examples upon the hills and

[10] Although Long said nothing about crossing the river, the extensive formations described here resemble those now preserved in the spectacular highlands of Wyalusing State Park at the junction of the Wisconsin and Mississippi rivers in present Wisconsin. Described as a "procession of mounds," they were first surveyed in 1873–74 by Moses Strong of the Wisconsin Geological Survey. His report, "Observations on the Pre-historic Mounds of Grant County, Wisconsin," is in Smithsonian Institution, *Annual Report*, 1876, pp. 428–431 (Washington, D.C., 1877). For a more recent description, see E. G. Bruder, "Archeological Remains in Wyalusing State Park," in *Wisconsin Archeologist*, new series 32:97–107 (December, 1951). It is also possible that these formations are among those covered by notes 11 and 18, below.

ridges as also a few in the valleys. These on the ridges had the appearance of being designed to resist an attack on both sides, being for the most part a single parapet of considerable extent, crossed at rig[h]t angles by traverses at the distance of 20 or 30 yds. from each other and having no ditch upon either side. These in the valleys appeared to have been constructed to command the passage of the particular valley in which they were situated. Some appeared as if they had been intended to defend against the attack of Cavalry, as they were constructed across the heads of ravines thro' which horses must pass in order to get upon the top of the hills. We saw no works that exhibited signs of having been complete enclosures, but the whole were in detached parts, consisting of Parapets, Traverses, & mounds forming lines & flanks.[11]

We had designed also to visit a natural curiosity upon [the] banks of the same Creek [*Kickapoo R.*], but were not able to find it. Agreeably to the representations of several Indians whom I consulted on the occasion, it is a gigantic figure of stone resembling the human shape. It stands erect in a niche or recess formed in a precipice, the brow of which projects forward so as to over hang the figure. There are prominent parts of the precipice also upon either side of the figure resembling the jambs of a fire place. The Indians pay religious homage to this figure, sacrifising Tobacco & other things they deem valuable at the feet of it.[12]

The history they give of it is that a long time since a very bloody battle was fought at Prairie Du Chien in which vast numbers were slain and the Inhabitants of the Prairie vanquished. That a very good woman after having received several wounds made her escape from the carnage and fled to the neighbouring hills, where she was like to famish for want of provisions. That the good spirit pitying her condition converted her in to this monument of veneration and for a long time killed every indian that dared approach in sight of it. But at length being tired of this havoc, he stayed his hand, and now suffers them to approach & worship it with impunity.

[11] The north bank of the Wisconsin River from its mouth to the Kickapoo River in Crawford County, Wis., was rich in aboriginal remains. The precise group referred to by Long has not been pinpointed. For a listing, see Charles E. Brown, "A Record of Wisconsin Antiquities," in *Wisconsin Archeologist*, 5:301–306 (April–October, 1906). See also Keating, *Narrative*, 1:239–242; p. 93, below.

[12] The driftless area of southwestern Wisconsin abounds in oddly shaped natural formations of weathered sandstone or limestone. The story recounted by Long below sounds remarkably like one mentioned by Jonathan Carver. See Parker, ed., *Carver Journals*, 87.

FRIDAY, JULY 25, 1817. Spent the day in measuring & planning Fort Crawford & its buildings. The Work is a square of 340 feet upon each side and is constructed entirely of wood, as are all its buildings, except the Magazine which is of stone. It will accommodate five companies of soldiers. The enclosure is formed principally by the quarters & other buildings of the Garrison, so that the amount of all the pallisade work does not exceed 350 feet in extent. The faces of the work are flanked by two Block Houses, one of which is situated in the SE and the other in the NW Corner of the Fort, being alternate or opposite angles.

The Block Houses are two stories high with Cupolas, or turrets, upon their tops. The first stories are calculated as flank defences to the Garrison, the second afford an obliq[u]e flank defenc[e], and at the same time guard the approach to the angles in which the Block-houses are situated, being placed diagonally upon the first. The turrets are fortified with oak plank upon their sides and furnished with loop holes for muskets or wall Pieces.

The Quarters, Store Houses &c. are ranged along the sides of the Garrison, their rear walls constituting the faces of the work, which are furnished with loop holes at the distance of 6 feet from each other. The buildings are constructed with shed roofs, sloping inwards, so that their outward walls are raised 20 feet from the ground, thus presenting an insurmountable barrier to an assailing enemy. The buildings are all rough shingled except the Block Houses, which are covered with smooth shingles.

The rooms are generally about 19 feet square, most of them floored with oak plank, and all that were designed for quarters furnished with a door & window each in front. The magazine is 24 by 12 feet in the clear, the walls 4 feet thick, and the arch above supported by a strong flooring of timber. It has at present no other covering but the arch; preparations are making, however, to erect a roof over it & cover it with shingles.

The works are, fore the most part, constructed of square timber, and the crevices in the walls of the buildings plaistered with lime mortar in such a manner as renders them comfortable habitations, excepting that the roofs are not well calculated to shed rain. The troops however are at present busily occupied in dressing shingles, cutting timber &c. in order to repair the defective parts of the works & make additions where they are found necessary. Piazzas are to be built in front of all the quarters, floors to be laid, ceilings &c. to be made, all of which are necessary to cleanliness & a well regulated police within the Garrison.

The building of these works was commenced on the 3rd of July 1816 by the troops stationed here under the command of Col. [William S.] Hamilton, previous to which no timber had been cut or stones quarried for the purpose. These articles were to be procured at the distance of from 2 to 5 miles from the site of the Garrison and transported to it in boats. The country where they were to be procured was so broken & hilly that teams could not be employed even to convey them to the boats, but all must be done by manual labour. With all these disadvantages & hardships and still more with a corrupt & sickly atmosphere have the soldiery at this place had to contend, in order to construct works of sufficient magnitude & strength to guard this part of our frontier. A considerable part of the work was done in the winter season, when at the same time, they were compelled to get their fuel at the distance of 2 or 3 miles from the Garrison and in many instances to draw it home by hand. Yet no extra compensation either in pay or clothing has been allowed them in a single instance, altho' the whole of this labour was unquestionably extra duty.[13]

In regard to the eligibility of the site up on which Fort Crawford is erected, very little can be said in favour but much against it. Its relation to other parts of the country would seem to give it a high claim to consideration as a military Post, as also its central situation with respect to our Indian neighbours. But the disadvantages, under which works of moderate expense particularly must lay in this neighbourhood, are too numerous to admit a doubt of the impropriety of placing confidence in works of a similar character with those now constructed while in a state of war.

The first objection that presents itself is that the situation from the nature of the place must be unhealthy. It is almost surrounded with stagnant waters at a short distance from the Fort. The country about

[13] On Hamilton, see Heitman, *Historical Register*, 1:494; Scanlan, *Prairie du Chien*, 123, 124. Although the usual extra compensation for such service was 15 cents a day and a ration of spirits, the troops received only an extra ration of whisky. See Adjutant and Inspector General's Office, *Articles of War, Military Laws, and Rules and Regulations for the Army of the United States*, 85 (Washington, D.C., 1817); Alice E. Smith, *The History of Wisconsin From Exploration to Statehood*, 97 (Madison, 1973); Maj. Willoughby Morgan Orders, August 2, 1816, AGO, Letters Received, NARG 94; William H. Crawford to Maj. Gen. Jacob Brown, June 13, 1816, Letter Book, p. 24, Brown Papers. The troops assigned to build Fort Crawford arrived on June 20, 1816. See Scanlan, *Prairie du Chien*, 123.

it abounds in marshes & low lands annually subject to be over flowed, and the part of the river lying immediately in front of the place is very little better than a stagnant pool, as its current is hardly perceptible in low water.

In a military point of view the objections to the present site, as also to any other that might be fixed upon in the neighbourhood, are various and cannot easily be obviated. No complete command of the river can be had here on account of the islands which it embosoms. Directly opposite to the Fort, and at the distance of 650 yards from it, is an island [*unnamed*] 2 1/2 miles in length & 700 yards in breadth separated from the east shore by a channel 500 yards & from the west by a channel 250 yds. wide. Both above & below this are numerous others effectually obstructing the command of the river from any single point. At the distance of about 600 yards from the Fort to the South & east of it is a circular valley thro which troops might be conducted, completely under cover & secure from the guns of the fort. At the entrance of this valley the enemy's troops landed in time of the late war [of 1812], and under cover of a small mound a little in advance of it, commenced can[n]onading the old Garrison (which occupied the highest part of the site of the present Fort) with a three pounder, and soon compelled them to surrender.[14]

Immediately in rear of the place are the main river bluffs at the distance of about 1 1/2 miles from the Fort. These are heights elevated 420 feet above the site of the Garrison & overlook the whole of The Prairie Du Chien. The site has been repeatedly subject to inundation, which is always to be apprehended when excessive floods prevail in the river. Indeed, the Military features of the place generally are so faint & obscure that they would hardly be perceptible, except by occupying several of the neighbouring heights with castles & Towers in order to protect an extensive Work erected in the Prairie below.

SATURDAY, JULY 26, 1817. Prairie Du Chien is a handsome tract of low land situated on the east side of the Mississippi immediately above its confluence with the Ouisconsin. It is bounded on the east by the river bluffs, which streach them silves along upon that side in

[14] The fort was located on what is now Prairie Street, a part of Prairie du Chien separated from the rest of the town by Marais de St. Friol. Long repeated his criticisms and recommended that the post be abandoned in his 1818 report. See Appendix 1, below. The "old garrison" was Fort Shelby, captured by the British in 1814. See Mahan, *Old Fort Crawford*, 53–57.

nearly a straight direction and are occasionally intersected by ravines & valleys, which afford easy communications with the hilly country situated back of the bluffs. The Prairie is about 10 [*8*] miles in length & from 1 to 2 1/2 [miles] in breadth. In some parts it is han[d]somoly variegated with swells & valleys that are secure from the inundations of the river, but in others flat marshy lands, sloughs, and pools of water present them silves, which, altho' they add some embellishments to the scenery, serve to render the place unhealthy. Many parts of the Prairie, which are sufficiently dry for cultivation in the summer season, are subject to be overflowed whenever floods prevail in the river. The southerly part of the Prairie is separated, both from the Mississippi & the Ouisconsin, by a large tract of marshy woodland, extending along the shores of both rivers and from 1/2 to 1 1/2 miles in breadth. This tract in many places is cut by sloughs of moderate depth communicating with the main channels of the two rivers. The view of both rivers from the Prairie is generally obstructed by the trees & shrubbery growing upon the marshy lands, as also by the numerous islands which both rivers embosom, so that neither of them can be seen except in a very few instances.

The Bluffs on the west side of the Mississippi present them selves in gigantic forms immediately along the margin of the river, and extend up the river many miles till they appear to be intercepted by those on the East. South of the Ouisconsin, the Bluffs of the two rivers intercept each other & form a stupendous promontory [*Signal Point*], between which and Pikes hill on the west opens a broad vista thro' which the two rivers flow after having mingled their waters.[15]

The village of Prairie Du Chien, according to Pike, was first settled by the French in 1783. A man by the name of [Basil] Giard, who died suddenly during my voyage up the Ouisconsin, is said to have been the first settler. He was of French & Indian extraction. Pike mentions two others, Mr. [Pierre Pelletier, *dit*] Antaya & [Julien] Dubuque, who established themselves here at the same time with Giard. The ground occupied by these settlers was at a little distance below the present villag[e].[16]

[15] "Pike's hill," now known as Pike's Peak, is preserved in Pike's Peak State Park, Ia. The "stupendous promontory" of Signal Point on Sentinel Ridge opposite is preserved in Wyalusing State Park, Wis.

[16] Pike was mistaken in listing Dubuque among the three Prairie du Chien pioneers; it was Augustin Angé who settled there with Giard and Pelletier in 1781, rather than 1783. All three were traders who married Indian women. They were not, however, the first white occupants of the site. At the time of Long's visit Prairie du

Exclusive of stores, work shops & stables, the village at present contains only sixteen dwelling houses occupied by families. These are situated on a street parallel with the river & about one half mile in length. In rear of the village at the distance of 3/4 mile are four others. Two & a half miles above are five, and at the upper end of the prairie 5 miles from the village are four dwelling houses. Besides these there are several houses situated upon different parts of the Prairie, in all not exceeding 7 or 8, so that the whole number of family dwellings now occupied does not exceed 38. The building[s] are generally of logs, plaistered with mud or clay, some of them comfortable habitations, but none of them exhibit any display of elegance or taste. The Inhabitants are principally of French & Indian extraction. There are very few of them that have not savage blood in their veins. If we compare the village & its inhabitants in their present state with what they were when Pike visited this part of the country, we shall find that instead of improving they have been degenerating. Their improvement has been checked by a divertion of the Indian[s] into other channels, and their degeneracy accellerated, not only by a consequent impoverishment of the Inhabitants, but in addition to natural decay [by] their inconquerable slothfulness & want of enterprise.

About one mile back of the village is The Grand Farm, which is an extensive enclosure cultivated by the inhabitants in common. It is about 6 miles in length & from 1/4 to 1/2 mile in width, surrounded by a fence on one side & the river bluffs on the other, and thus secured from the depredations of the cattle and horses that run at large upon The Prairie. Upon this farm, corn, wheat, Potatoes, &c. are cultivated to considerable advantage, and with proper care no doubt large crops of these articles, together with fruits of various kinds, might be raised. The[y] never have yet taken pains to seed the ground with any kind of grain except the summer wheat, which is never so productive as the fall or winter wheat. Wry, Barley, oats, &c. would undoubtedly succeed well upon the farm.[17]

Chien was still a major fur trade center largely dominated by traders sympathetic to the British. Here and below, see Coues, ed., *Pike*, 1:303; Louise P. Kellogg, *The British Régime in Wisconsin and the Northwest*, 171 (Madison, 1935); Peter L. and Marian Scanlan, "Basil Giard and His Land Claim in Iowa," in *Iowa Journal of History and Politics*, 30:219–223 (April, 1932); "Prairie du Chien, in 1811," in *WHC*, 11:249n; Scanlan, *Prairie du Chien*, 166, 180; Mahan, *Old Fort Crawford*, 187–191.

[17] Long is referring to a complex of about 40 farms enclosed as a common field. According to James H. Lockwood, the farmers lived in the village rather than on the land. The term "Grand Farm" was also applied to a 640-acre tract owned by James Aird and sold by his estate to Alexis Bailly in 1827. The Canadian practice of farming

The soil of the Prairie is generally a silicious loam, containing more or less black mould, and is of various depths from 1 to 3 feet. Below this is a bed of sand and small pebbles extending probably to a considerable depth & alternating with veins of clay and marl.

There are numerous antiquities discoverable upon various parts of the Prairie, consisting of Parapets, Mounds, and Cemetaries, relative to which the Indians have no traditions & the oldest of them can give no account. They only suppose that the country was once inhabited by a race of white people like the present americans, who have been completely exterminated by their forefathers. This supposition is grounded upon the circumstance of their having discovered human bones in the earth buried much deeper than the Indians are in the habit of burying their dead, & never accompanyed by any implements of any kind, which the Indians have always been accustomed to bury with the body of their proprietor. Tomahawks of brass [*copper*?] and other implements different from any the present indians make use of have also been f[o]und under the surface of the ground.[18]

They consider also the ancient Fortifications another pro[o]f of the correctness of this opinion, as none of the Indians are in the habit of constructing works of a similar character & indeed are unacquainted with the utility of them.

Mr. [Michael] Brisbois, who has been for a long time a resident of Prairie du Chien, informed me that he saw the Skeletons of eight persons, that were found in digging a cellar near his house, laying side by side.[19] They were of gigantic size, measuring about eight feet from head to foot. He remarked that he took a leg bone of one of them and placed it by the side of his own leg in order to compare the length of the two. The bone of the skelleton extended six inches

in strips back from a river was transplanted to French settlements in the Mississippi Valley. See Louise P. Kellogg, *The French Régime in Wisconsin and the Northwest*, 389 (Madison, 1925); James H. Lockwood, "Early Times and Events in Wisconsin," in *WHC*, 2:120 (1856); Deed of Ezekiel Lockwood to Alexis Bailly, September 20, 1827, in Alexis Bailly Papers, MHS.

[18] The antiquities at Prairie du Chien were more completely described by Increase A. Lapham, *The Antiquities of Wisconsin*, 66–68 (*Smithsonian Contributions to Knowledge*, vol. 7—Washington, D.C., 1855); Alfred Brunson, "Ancient Mounds or Tumuli in Crawford County," in *WHC*, 3:181–183; and Peter L. Scanlan, "Map of 1821 Borough of Prairie du Chien," in Scanlan Papers. See also Keating, *Narrative*, 1:239.

[19] Michael or Michel Brisbois was a fur trader who settled at Prairie du Chien in 1781. His house there is preserved. WHS, *Dictionary of Wisconsin Biography*, 49 (Madison, 1960).

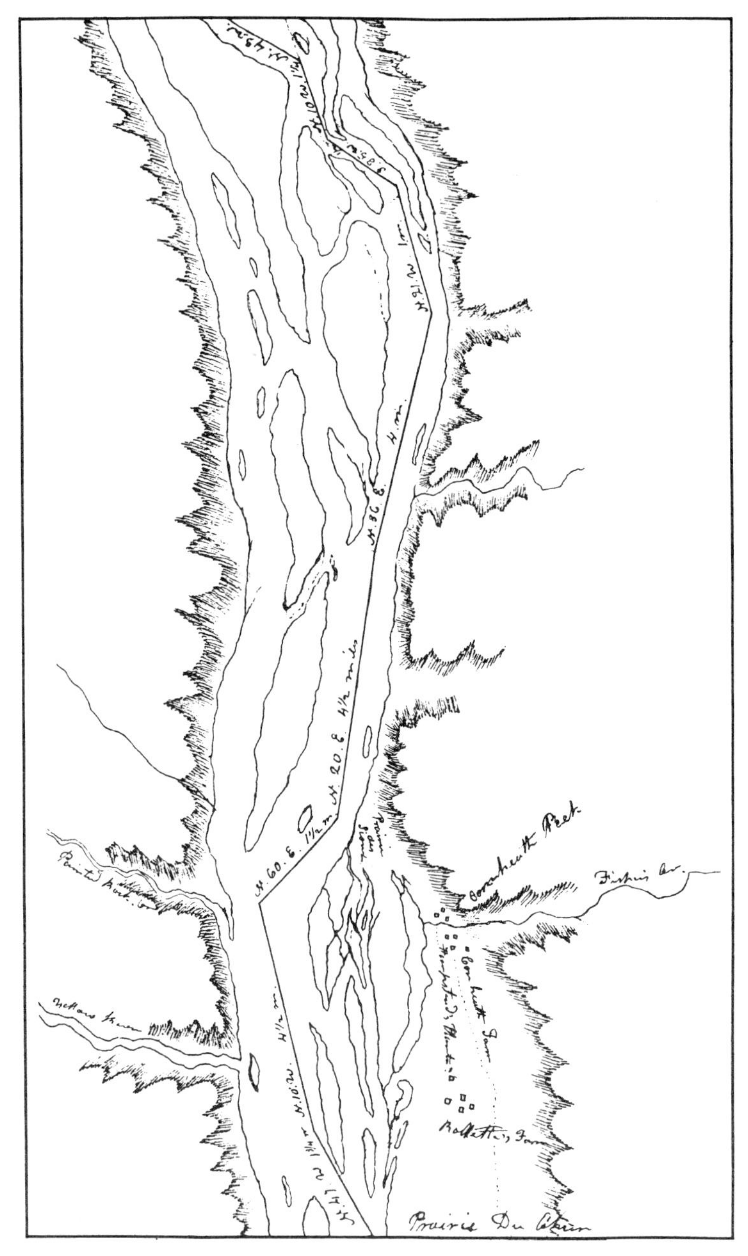

LONG'S SKETCH MAP of Prairie du Chien, Wisconsin, and the Mississippi River in his 1817 journal.

above his knee. None of these bones could be preserved, as they crumbled to dust soon after they were exposed to the atmosphere.

The mounds probably were intend[ed] both as Fortifications & cemetaries, as most of them (perhaps all) contain human bones, and at the same time appear to serve as flank defences to fortified lines. Whether the bones they contain are of the same character with those described by Mr. Brisbois I have not been able to ascertain.

The Prairie Du Chien or Prairie of the Dog derives its name from a family of Indians formerly known by the name of the Dog Indians headed by a chief called the Dog. This Family or band has become extinct. The Indians have some tradition concerning them. They say that a large party of Indians came down the Ouisconsin from Green Bay [*of Lake Michigan*]. That they attacked the family of the Dogs, and massacred almost the whole of them, and returned again to Green Bay. That a few of the Dogs, who had succeeded in making their escape to the woods, returned after their enemies had evacuated the Prairie & reestablished them selves in their former place of residence, and that these were the Indians inhabiting the Prairie at the time it was first settled by the french.[20]

The Inhabitants of Prairie Du Chien have lately caused two small schools to be opened, in one of which the English language is taught & in the other the French. This augers well of the future respectability of the place, if at the same time they would barter their slothful habits for those of industry.[21]

SUNDAY, JULY 27, 1817. Having accomplished my business at the Prairie, I took leave of my friends, the officers of the Garrison, to whom I feel greatly indebted for the politeness and attention they have shown me, & particularly to the Commanding Officer Capt. Dufphey. The Suttler [*Alexander McNair*] also Capt. Owins [*Wilfred Owens*] evinced his friendship for me & the cause in which I was engaged by cheerfully supplying me with funds, without which I could not have prosecuted my voyage with expedition or comfort. We reembarked at 10 o'clock A.M. to descend the Missis-

[20] Prairie du Chien may have been named for the Dog band of the Fox, a chief of that name, or both. Although the origins of Indian settlement there are obscure, a Fox village was recorded as early as 1732. The massacre tradition recounted here is probably related to an attack on the Fox by the French and their Indian allies in the 1730s. See Parker, ed., *Carver Journals*, 88, 186; Kellogg, *French Régime*, 329.

[21] The English school was taught by Sgt. Samuel Reeseden, who also operated a post school. Charles Giasson taught the French school. See Samuel Peters Diary, September 6, 10, 1817, William H. Bell Papers, WHS; W. C. Whitford, "Early History of Education in Wisconsin," in *WHC*, 5:330, 332.

sippi. My Crew now consisted of only five men, the same I took with me from Belle fontaine with the exception of Sheffield.[22]

Last evening Mr. Gun & King arrived at the Prairie from the Falls of St. Anthony. Whether they accomplished the object of their trip, viz. to establish their claim to the tract of country ceeded by the Indians to their Grand father, Carver, I had no time to enquire, but presume there is no ground for supposing they did, as they before told me they could find but one Indian who had any knowledge of the transactions or was in the least disposed to recognize the Grant. That they do not consider the cession obligatory upon them is very evident from their having ceeded to the United States, thro' the negociations [of] Pike, two parcils of the same tract specified in the Grant in favour of Carver.[23]

Just before night we met the contractor Mr. [Hugh] Glen[n] on his way to Prairie Du Chien with provisions for the supply of the Garrison at that place. He left St. Louis on the 8th June, 7 days after I commenced my voyage, and has been almost constantly engaged in ascending the river ever since. When he left St. Louis, his boat was very heavily laden, having provisions on board for the supply of Forts Edwards, Armstrong and Crawford for 9 months. He found both [Rock and Des Moines] rapids very difficult to pass & has been frequently delayed by Sand-bars. We spent some time with him, & I supped on board his boat.[24]

[22] Sutler McNair later became governor of Missouri. Owens, a Kentuckian, was one of his clerks. See Thomas A. Smith to Talbot Chambers, Letter Book, March 26, 1818, Smith Papers; Nancy C. Prewitt, University of Missouri Library, to the editors, July 2, 1973; John G. Gregory, ed., *Southwestern Wisconsin: A History of Old Crawford County*, 1:171 (Chicago, 1932).

[23] King and Gunn were unsuccessful in their mission. They left the alleged treaty with trader Joseph Renville with a request that he pursue the matter with the Dakota. On this incident, see Dr. Samuel Peters' remarks concerning the report of the Committee on Private Land Claims made to the House of Representatives on January 28, 1825, in Bell Papers. See also Milo M. Quaife, "Jonathan Carver and the Carver Grant," in *Mississippi Valley Historical Review*, 7:3–25 (June, 1920).

[24] On Glenn, a Cincinnati merchant who was awarded the contract to supply the posts in January, 1817, and his later associations with Long, see Harry R. Stevens, "Hugh Glenn," in LeRoy R. Hafen, ed., *The Mountain Men and the Fur Trade of the Far West*, 2:161–174 (Glendale, Calif., 1965).

The Rock and Des Moines rapids were the most serious obstacles to navigation on the Mississippi River below the Falls of St. Anthony. They are now the sites of Lock and Dam No. 15 at Rock Island and No. 19 at Keokuk. Descriptions of them appear in reports by Robert E. Lee in 1837 and by Long and Gouverneur K. Warren in 1853, in 25 Congress, 2 session, *Senate Executive Documents*, no. 139, and 33 Congress, 1 session, *House Executive Documents*, no. 104 (serials 316, 725). See also pp. 98, 104, 105, below.

MONDAY, JULY 28, 1817. We floated last night till a strong head wind induced us to lay by. Had a shower of rain accompanyed by heavy thunder about 2 A.M. Passed several canoes of Sack [*Sauk*] Indians. The country on this part of the Mississippi, which apeard beautiful in a very high degree when we ascended the river, seems to have lost half of its charms since we have visited the more noble scenery above.

Had strong head-winds most of the day, so that our progress was very slow. Passed Dubuques mines in the morning and arrived opposite the mouth of the River La Fievre [*Galena R.*] at evening, where we lay by to fish a little while & afterwards commenced floating.[25]

TUESDAY, JULY 29, 1817. At 10 o'clock last night there came on a violent thunder Storm so that we were obliged to put into shore. It continued with short intervals of abatement thro' most of the night. The lightning appeared almost one continued blaze, & the thunder seemed to shake the earth to its centre, while the rain pored down in torrents. Our boat was in danger of filling from the vast quantity of rain that fell, so that we had frequent occasions to bale in order to prevent her sinking.

Started early this morning with a gentle breeze in our favour, which soon failed us & was succeeded by a calm. The scenery we have passed to day, altho' in many respects it is far less interesting than many views farther up the river, yet has numberless beauties that give pleasure to the eye of the beholder, amongst which precipices of red sand stone fronting the river are some of the most striking. They give to the Bluffs a blushing appearance which affords a very pl[e]asing contrast when viewed in connexion with the verdant attire in which they are clad.[26]

Passed opin Prairie a little before night, where we had another view of the beautiful scenery of this part of the river. But the idea that this beautiful tract has for ages unfolded its charms with none to

[25] The main lead mines of Julien Dubuque, who secured a permit from the Sauk and Fox to operate them in 1788, were located near present-day Dubuque, Ia. Subsidiary mines existed along the Galena and Apple rivers in Wisconsin and Illinois. See Reuben G. Thwaites, "Notes on Early Lead Mining in the Fever (or Galena) River Region," in *WHC*, 13:279, 280, 282 (1895); p. 141, below.

[26] Long was in the vicinity of Mississippi Palisades State Park north of Savanna, Ill. The precipices he saw were dolomite—brown, yellowish brown, and pinkish brown—which appears red when wet. The "opin prairie" below probably refers to the lowlands located on both sides of the Mississippi above the mouth of the Wapsipinicon River.

admire but unfeeling savages, instead of having delighted thousands that were capable of enjoying them, casts a gloom upon the scenery, which added to the solemn stillness that every where prevails in these solitary regions robs the mind of half its pleasure.

WEDNESDAY, JULY 30, 1817. The night was very fine & we floated about 15 miles. This morning we passed Mer a Dogé [*Marais d'Ogée*] Prairie, before spoken of. Should there ever be occasion to station troops above the head of La Roche [*Rock*] rapids—the first eligible position may be found on this prairie, as there are many positions where a complete command of the river may be had, and troops stationed upon them would not be exposed to the sudden annoyance of an enemy, as there would be no difiles thro' which he w[ou]ld approach with out being discovered. Descended the La Roche Rapids without much difficulty, altho' the water was very low & we had no one on board who was acquainted with the course of the channel. Arrived at Fort Armstrong at about 12 o'clock.[27]

THURSDAY, JULY 31, 1817. Spent the day in recoinnoitring the country about the Fort. Took observations for the Latitude of Fort Armstrong, which I found to be 41° 32′ 33″ [*41° 31′*] N.

FRIDAY, AUGUST 1, 1817. Having made the necessary surveys, I spent the day in plotting them & making a plan of the country adjacent to the site of Fort Armstrong. The Island on which the Fort is situated is called Rock Island from the circumstance of its being founded upon a rocky basis. It is situated immediately at the foot of La roche Rapids, is about 3 miles in length, and of various breadths, not exceeding 1 mile in the broadest part. At the lower extremity is the site of the Fort over looking a large sheet of water in to which the Mississippi spreads immediately below, also extensive tracts of flat Prairie situated on either side of the river within its valley.

[27] "Mer a Dogé" is undoubtedly Marais d'Ogée near Albany, Ill. See J. P. Colton to A. J. Hill, July 12, 1869, in Archaeological Records, MHS, and map in [Samuel A. Mitchell], *Illinois in 1837: A Sketch Descriptive of the . . . Country* (Philadelphia, 1837). For variations in the spelling of the name, see Coues, ed., *Pike*, 1:26n. The phrase "before spoken of" perhaps refers to Long's upriver trip in the missing first half of this journal.

Fort Armstrong was constructed in 1816 and garrisoned until 1836. For its history and a schematic drawing made in 1819 and corresponding closely to Long's description on pp. 100–102, below, see *A Short History of the Island of Rock Island 1816–1966*, 2–5 (*Rock Island Arsenal Pamphlets*, no. 870–1—Rock Island, Ill., 1967); "Extract from the Report of Major M. Marston, September 10, 1819," in OCE, Fortifications Map File, NARG 77. Long's plan of the fort has not been located. The island is now the site of the Rock Island Arsenal, a national cemetery, a museum, a reconstructed blockhouse, and other points of interest.

The valley is here about two miles wide & is boundered on both sides by bluffs of gentle acclivity, cut in many places by ravines of moderate depth. The elevation of the country back of the bluffs or hills is generally about 100 feet above the water level, that of the Prairies within the valley 8 or 10, and that of the site of the Fort, which is nearly at an intermediate distance between the bluffs, is 32 feet. The general course of the river past the Island is WSW. The width of the north channel is 640 yards, that of the South 275, and the width of the whole river immediately below the island is about 1400 yards, which is the average width for about one mile below. Four miles below the Island Rock River comes in from the NE. Upon the point of land situated between this river & the Mississippi above their confluence is an extensive level prairie with a few scattering trees; this also is in full view from the Fort. To the South of the lower end of Rock Island is another small [*Wilson's*] island annually subject to inundation, tho' sufficiently elevated to admit of cultivation in the summer season. It is separated from Rock island by a very narrow slough. It is 97 yards wide at its lower end and tapers off to a point about 800 yards farther up.

Immediately opposite to the Fort on the south side of the River is a village of Fox Indians containing about 30 cabins with two fires each. The number of souls at this village is probably about 500. On Rock River two miles above its mouth and three across the point from Fort Armstrong is a Sack village, consisting of about 100 Cabins of 2, 3, and in some instances 4 fires each. It is by far the largest Indian village situated in the neighbourhood of the Mississippi between St. Louis & the Falls of St. Anthony. The whole number of Indians at this village amounts probably to between 2 & 3 thousand. They can furnish 8 or 9 hundred warriors, all of them armed with Rifles or fusees. The Indians of these two villages cultivate vast fields of corn, which are situated partly in the low ground & extend up the slopes of the bluffs. They have at present several hundred acres at present under improvement in this way.[28]

[28] These Sauk and Fox villages were the principal towns of the two closely allied tribes. Thomas Forsyth, who visited Fort Armstrong in 1817, estimated that the Fox town consisted of about 20 lodges and 200 warriors, while the Sauk village (Black Hawk's town) had 100 lodges and 1,000 men. See "Letter-Book of Thomas Forsyth—1814–1818," in *WHC*, 11:348; Sara J. Tucker and Wayne C. Temple, *Indian Villages of the Illinois Country: Historic Tribes*, 93, 103, 111–113 (Illinois State Museum, *Scientific Papers*, vol. 2, pt. 2—Springfield, Ill., 1958). For the locations of the villages, see John H. Hauberg, "Black Hawk's Mississippi From Rock River to Bad Axe," in *Journal of the Illinois State Historical Society*, 22:98 (April, 1929).

The soil of this part of the country is generally of an excellent quality well adapted to the cultivation of Corn, Grain, Pulse, Potatoes, Flax, mellons &c. The natural growth consists principally of Oak, Black Walnut, Cherry, & Hiccory, affording excellent timber for building & other purposes. Rock Island itself furnishes an abundance of these articles, being altogether wood land except the lower end of it which was cleared for the accommodation of the Fort. The Prairies yield an abundance of fine grass, and the country generally is well adapted for grazing. The country back of the river bluffs is rolling and in some parts hilly, but is every where accessible by gentle ascents & declivities. The surface of Rock Island is undulating, inclining to hilly in the upper parts.

The Site of Fort Armstrong in a military point of view is elligible in many respects, and at the same time has fewer objections than any other position that can be found on the Mississippi from St. Louis to the River St. Peter's. Its advantages are a healthful situation, an effectual command of the river and of the neighbouring Prairies to the full extent of cannon shot range, security from the attack of an enemy armed with any thing less than heavy artillery. Timber and lime stone of a good quality & in great abundance, rich grounds for gardens situated immediately above the Garrison, a copious spring of fine water issuing from the cliffs a few rods above the site, &c. Its disadvantages are a commanding rise elevated 15 feet above the site at the distance of 200 yards in an Easterly direction, which if occupied by a suitable work would be an important advantage, as it would give to the place a more extensive command; rising ground to the NE at the distance of half a mile. The river blluffs NNW 1300 and those to the south 1650 yards from the site, the want of a convenient harbour for boats in low water. These disadvantages compared with those of every other position I have seen upon the river below the St. Peter's are of little weight in point of objection. The advantages in point of locality are the facilities of communication either by land or water between this and other important parts of the country, which will be mentioned in their proper place, as also its central position in relation to the Indians.

SATURDAY, AUGUST 2, 1817. Took the dimensions of the Fort & its buildings, & made a plan of them. The Fort is situated immediately upon the lower extremity of Rock Island, at which place the shores are perpendicular cliffs of limestone 30 feet high. In some instances the cliffs project over their base and even some parts of the Fort over hang the water.

The Fort has two entire faces only, the other two sides being sufficiently fortified against an assault by the cliffs before mentioned. The east face commences immediately upon the top of the cliff, where there is a Block House (No. 1) 2 stories high & 21 feet square. The front upon this side is 277 feet including a Block House (No. 2) at the NE corner of the Fort 26 feet square. The North face forms a right angle with the east & extends from Block House No. 2 to the North Channel of the River, where it is terminated by Block-House No. 3 of the same dimensions as No. 1., presenting a front on this side of 288 feet. Both faces are flanked by Block House No. 2, the other Block Houses being placed in such a manner as to form a part of the Front of the two faces.

The Block Houses are all two stories high, their second stories being placed diagonally upon the first. No. 2 has also a basement story which is used as a store house. The faces are made up principally by the rear walls of the Barracks and store houses. They are about 20 feet high and furnished with two rows of loop holes for muskets. The spaces between the buildings are fortified by walls of stone about 8 feet high supporting a breast work of timber 5 feet high.

The buildings ranged along the Faces contain 7 rooms 20 feet square upon each side; 8 of which are occupied as soldiers quarters, 3 as hospital, 2 as store houses, & 1 as Guard House. On the South and west sides detached from other parts of the works are situated 2 other buildings [*one word illegible*], 64 feet long & 16 wide, containing four rooms each, designed for officers quarters. In the SW corner is a 2 story building with low wings designed as quarters for the comdg. Officer and Offices for the use of the Garrison. The body of the building is furnished with Piazzas on both sides, & the whole combines a degree of taste & elegance worthy of imitation at all other military posts in this part of the country.

The works are constructed principally of square timber, the lower part of the block houses including lower embrasures is of stone. The Magazine also is of stone, 7 by 10 feet in the clear, its walls 4 feet in thickness. Besides these there are a few other buildings outside of the Garrison, viz. a smith's shop, suttler's & contractor's stores, a stable &c.

The plan of defence is at present incomplite, there being three points where an enemy might approach the garrison completely under cover from the works. The first is at the lower point of the Island directly under the brow of the cliffs, which streach along that extremity in nearly a straight direction 150 yards from the Fort eastwardly. The second is the rise beforementioned East ward of the Fort, beyond which there is a gentle declivity to the waters' edge thro' an expanding valley. The third is a kind of bay situated just above a prominent part of the Island upon the North side by which the fire from the Fort in to the bay would be obstructed. In this Bay also is situated the spring before described so that a command of this place is the more desirable on that account.

To remedy the first defect, a water battery may be constructed immediately at the point of the island, which will give a far more complete command of the river below than the present works designed for that purpose, and at the same time, its east face would completely flank the cliffs in that direction. To obviate the second & third defects, the Block Houses No. 1 & No. 3 might be removed & erected, one on the commanding rise to the East & the other on the eminence to the North of the Garrison. These Block Houses in their present situation have no command that they would not have after being removed to the places proposed, and where the[y] now stand a breast work would be a far better substitute. No. 3 particularly is badly situated. It projects considerably over the water & is partly supported by woodden props, so that should the river continue to undermine the bank, there would be great danger of its being precipitated into the water.

Having completed my plans, we reembarked at 3 P.M. to descend the river. Passed Rock River 4 miles below the Fort. This river in high water is navigable about 300 miles to what are called the Four Lakes, but in its present stage, which is the usual height at this season of the year, it is with great difficulty that a canoe can ascend it even three or four miles.[29] There are numerous Rapids which make their appearance in various parts of the river when the water is low, but at other times there are none perceptible thro' out the above mentioned distance.

The Indians residing upon this river, beside the Sack Village before mentioned, are principally Winnebagos with some few of the Ioways & Fols Avoins [*Menominee*], most of whom have their residence in the neighbourhood of the Four Lakes. Between the Head waters of the Rock River & those of Lake Michigan is a portage of

[29] Long probably confused the mileage between the mouth of the Rock and Four Lakes (Madison, Wis.) with that between the mouth and the river's source in Fond du Lac County, Wis. The former is about 281 and the latter is 304. See Reuben G. Thwaites, *Historic Waterways*, 26 (Chicago, 1888); Royal B. Way, ed., *The Rock River Valley: Its History, Traditions, Legends and Charms*, 1:8 (Chicago, 1926).

moderate extent thro' which some trade is carried on with the Indians.[30]

At evening when we had got 20 miles from the Fort I discovered that I had left my Sextant, which made it necessary for us to encamp for the night in order to send a man back for it in the morning, as it would be impossible for me to take observations for the latitude without it.

SUNDAY, AUGUST 3, 1817. Dispatched a man for the Sextant early this morning with orders to return to Fort Edwards either in the contractors boat which is daily expected down, or in the Express boat which must come in a few days to Fort Edwards. Started a little after sun rise. The Wind strong ahead all day. Encamped on the East side at the Red banks, the wind being too strong to admit of floating.[31]

MONDAY, AUGUST 4, 1817. Started at an early hour. Went on shore in the after noon to visit the ruins of Fort Madison. There was nothing remaining but old chimneys left standing and a covert way leading from the main garrison to an elevated ground in the rear upon which there was some kind of an out work. The covert way was fortified with pallisads only. There were a number of Fruit trees also standing upon the ground formerly occupied as a garden, amongst which were the Peach, the Nectarine & the apple tree.[32]

[30] The presence of the Winnebago, Iowa, and Menominee on the Rock River, with a Winnebago concentration in the Four Lakes region of Madison, Wis., and on nearby Lake Koshkonong, has been well established. For a review of village sites and migrations, see N. W. Jipson, "Winnebago Villages and Chieftains of the Lower Rock River Region," in *Wisconsin Archeologist*, new series 2: 125–139 (July, 1923); William Harvey Miner, ed., *The Iowa*, 36 (Cedar Rapids, Ia., 1911). The portage between the headwaters of the Rock and Lake Michigan via the Fox River and Green Bay was in Fond du Lac County, Wis., near the lower end of Lake Winnebago. On the importance of the portage, which connected the Great Lakes and Mississippi River waterways, see James M. Phalen, *Sinnissippi: A Valley Under a Spell*, 10 (Washington, D.C., 1942).

[31] For Long's description of Fort Edwards downriver in present-day Warsaw, Ill., see p. 105, below. For the derivation of the names Red and Yellow Banks near present-day Oquawka, Ill., see a report by Thomas Forsyth enclosed in his letter to James Barbour, June 15, 1826, OIA, Letters Received, NARG 75. See also Coues, ed., *Pike*, 1: 19n.

[32] Fort Madison, located at present-day Fort Madison, Ia., was called Fort Bellevue during the first few months after its establishment in 1808. The "covert" or covered way connected one of three blockhouses situated on level ground near the river with a fourth on a ridge about 250 feet from the main stockade. On September 3, 1813, the garrison, under heavy Indian siege, evacuated and burned the post. The charred chimneys that remained were long a landmark to travelers. A monument now marks the approximate site of the fort. See Donald Jackson, "Old Fort

Descended the Rapids De Moin a little before sun set, but as none of us was acquainited with the channel and the water very low, we ran foul of rocks a number of times, which occasioned a leak in our boat so that we had to keep one man constantly bailing to prevent her filling with water. Arrived at Fort Edwards about dark, the men very much fatigued with rowing & getting the boat across the rapids.

TUESDAY, AUGUST 5, 1817. Gave the men an opportunity to rest themselves while I took an excursion on foot about the place.

WEDNESDAY, AUGUST 6, 1817. Concluded to ascend the Rapids again and take a short Tour into the country above. In this excursion I was joined by Dr. [William Carr] Lane & Capt. Colhoun [Joseph Calhoun, Jr.].[33] Having a fair wind, we set sail about 11 A.M. but after passing half way up the Rapids, the wind failed us and we had recourse to rowing. Ascended with[in] 4 miles of the head of the Rapids & encamped for the night.

THURSDAY, AUGUST 7, 1817. Started early & arrived at the head of the Rapids at Ewing's Plantation (formerly known by the name of the U. States Agricultural Establishment) at half past 8 oclock.[34] Here we breakfasted, and as the wind was strong ahead concluded to leave the boat & travel on foot farther up. The two gentlemen before mentioned, myself & two soldiers made up the party. We

Madison—1808–1813," in *Palimpsest*, 39:11–15, 19, 33–35, 37, 40, 61, and inside back cover (January, 1958); Jacob Van der Zee, "Old Fort Madison," in *Iowa and War*, January, 1918, p. 38.

[33] Dr. Lane arrived to serve as surgeon at Fort Edwards in July, 1817. He had served at both Forts Crawford and Armstrong during the year. See Lane to Joseph Lovell, June 14, 1818, in AGO, Medical Records, Personal Papers of Medical Officers, Lane, NARG 94. Calhoun, a distant cousin of James E. Colhoun, whose 1823 journal is printed in Chapters 7 and 8, below, was listed as commanding at Fort Edwards in Monthly Returns, April, 1817, and as "permitted to visit Nashville" or "on furlough" in the October–December, 1817, returns; see AGO, Returns of Military Organizations, 1800–1916, Rifle Regiment, 1817, NARG 94. See also Long to Smith, June 24, 1817, in Appendix 1, below; possibly the tour above the rapids was connected with the mineral speculation mentioned there. Both Lane and Calhoun resigned from the army in 1818. Lane moved to St. Louis, where he practiced medicine and was elected the first mayor in 1823. See [Drumm, ed.], in *Glimpses of the Past*, 7:47–53; Heitman, *Historical Register*, 1:274, 614; William Hyde and Howard L. Conard, eds., *Encyclopedia of the History of St. Louis*, 3:1227 (New York, 1899); A. S. Salley, *The Calhoun Family of South Carolina*, 13 (n.p., [1906?]).

[34] William Ewing of Pennsylvania, agricultural agent to the Sauk and Fox in 1805–07, established the "plantation" on the site of present-day Nauvoo, Ill. See Donald Jackson, "William Ewing, Agricultural Agent to the Indians," in *Agricultural History*, April, 1957, pp. 4–7.

accoutred ourselves with Rifles, ammunition & two day's supply of provisions, having a pack horse which was sent up for the purpose to convey our baggage. We pursued the course of the River on the east side about 20 miles to a prairie a little above Fort Madison. We then turned to the right and travelled due east about 6 miles, where we encamped for the night near a small [*Camp?*] Creek running north. Near the place of our encampment observed a tree marked by the surveyors as follows, R7N, T7W, S[ec.] 9, being the corner bound of one of the Towns recently surveyed in this part of the Country.[35] The country in a direction due east from the River in this place is considerably broken, being intersected by numerous water courses & ravines. But the season being unusually dry, few of them contained any water at the time we were there.

FRIDAY, AUGUST 8, 1817. Started about sunrise & travelled about SW and came upon an extensive prairie about 2 miles from the place of our encampment. We had not proceeded far when we struck upon an Indian trail leading nearly in the direction we contemplated to take, viz. WSW. We accordingly pursued it 15 miles and arrived at our boat about 12 o'clock. The whole of this distance lay thro' an extensive prairie, cutting off but a very small fraction of it. This vast tract of level country occupies most of the space included between the Mississippi & Illinois, commencing at Rock River on the Former & Fox River on the latter, and extending downward nearly to the junction of the two.

After dining we commenced descending the river again. Passed the Rapids with less difficulty than before. Killed a Pelican. Stopped a while at the Foot of the Rapids to examine the Stratifications, which we found of a similar character with those generally along the Mississippi. While we were engaged in this examination, one of the men found a hive of bees which they soon took and found in it about 2 gallons of honey. Arrived at the Garrison about 5 P.M.

SATURDAY, AUGUST 9, 1817. Spent the day in sketching the Country about Fort Edwards, the Garrison &c. Fort Edwards is situated on the East side of the Mississippi 3 miles below the foot of De Moyen Rapids. The Mississippi at this place is about 1400 yards wide; the main channel is on the west side; the passage on the east, particularly in low water, is obstructed by sand bars. Directly opposite to the Fort are two Islands, dividing the De Moyen [*Des Moines*

[35] Long was near Dallas City, Hancock County, Ill. On the Illinois surveys, see Solon J. Buck, *Illinois in 1818*, 45–47 (Springfield, Ill., 1917).

R.] which comes in on the west at this place into three mouths; about 1 mile above the Fort on the same side of the [Mississippi] river is an Island [*Nassau I.*] of considerable extent. The Bluffs at this place approach immediately to the water's edge on the East, but on the west are separated from the river by an extensive tract of bottom land covered with a fine growth of Cotton wood, Sycamore, and Black Walnut. The site of the Fort is elevated 100 feet above low water mark. Its distance horizontally from the river is about 60 yards. At the distance of half a mile from the Fort in a SW direction is the Site of Cantonment Davis, which has been abandoned since the erection of Fort Edwards. The country situated between the two sites is cut by deep ravines, which have meandering courses and approach in some places within musket shot range from both sites.[36]

To the NE of Fort Edwards is a commanding height at the distance of 600 yards, separated from the site of the Fort by a broad ravine and elevated 50 feet above it, or 150 feet above the river. The Country adjacent to the Fort to the East & NE is considerably broken & abounds in ravines. South eastwardly of the Fort the country has nearly the same level as the site on which it is built. The ground generally in this neighbourhood is covered with a scattering growth of Hiccory, Oak & Walnut; the Hill to the NE however is covered with deep woods.

In regard to the military character of the place, many objections present them selves. 1st. No effectual command of either river can be had, not only on account of the great width of the Mississippi, but also a Slough leading to the west of the rive[r] from which it is separated by an Island about one mile wide and communicating with the Mississippi at the distance of one mile below & 1 1/2 miles above the site of the Garrison. Thro' this Slough the De Moyen discharges its waters, and Boats may pass with facility in time of high water. 2nd. The ravines before mentioned would facilitate the approach of an

[36] Fort Edwards succeeded Fort Johnson, which was built and evacuated in 1814, and Cantonment Davis (or Davies), established in 1815 and abandoned when the new post was constructed. Built in 1816–17 near the site of the earlier posts, Fort Edwards was garrisoned intermittently until 1824. A 50-foot granite monument now marks the site. See William L. Talbot, *Fort Edwards, Military Post and Fur Trade Center*, 6–11, 14–18, 24 (Carthage, Ill., 1968). Long's sketch, referred to above, has not been located. The two islands he saw may have been created by channel changes or may have been those later known as Big Muddy and Little Muddy. See U.S. Army Corps of Engineers, *Navigation Charts Middle and Upper Mississippi River*, no. 24 (St. Louis, 1946); Robert E. Clevenstine, Corps of Engineers, Rock Island District, and Doris A. Foley, Keokuk Public Library, to the editors, December 18, 1972, February 16, 1973.

enemy to within musket shot range of the Garrison completely under cover from its fire. 3rd. The commanding heig[h]t to the NE would render the position untenable, tho' ever so strongly fortified, provided an enemy should occupy it with ordnance of moderate caliber. 4th. From the situation of the place no important end can be answered by keeping up a Garrison at it, except perhaps in time of actual war fare with the Indians. The only object that presents itself in this point of view is its proximity to the rapids above & the protection that might be afforded by the Garrison to supplies, stores &c., in their passage up the Rapids. But in this respect no advantage would be derived from a Garrison at this place more than at any other upon the river, provided transports of every kind are conveyed up & down the river in their proper season, viz. from the 1st of April to the middle of June when there is always a sufficient depth of water to pass the rapids with a current but little more accellerated than is to be met with in other parts of the river.

The distance from this place to Fort Clark on the Illinois is about 75 [*100*] miles across a level tract of Prairie Country; and about 120 [*170*] to Fort Osage on the Missouri across a level country principally Prairie. In the neighbourhood of rivers & Creeks in this direction the country is some what broken.[37]

Fort Edwards is a pallisade work constructed entirely of square timber. It is intended to contain two block houses situated in alternate angles of the Fort, a magazine of stone, Barracks for the accommodation of one company of soldiers, Officers Quarter's, hospital, store rooms &c. — all to be constructed in a simple but neat style, but on a scale too contracted for comfortable accommodations. The works are in such a state of forwardwardness [*forwardness*] that they will probably be nearly completed this season. The Magazine is still to be built as are also the Officer's Quarters, Hospital &c. They have been wholely executed by the soldiery stationed there since June, 1816.

SUNDAY, AUGUST 10, 1817. Had to finish my plans of Fort Edwards & the adjacent country and make preparations for resuming

[37] Long had visited Fort Clark, built in 1813 at the site of present-day Peoria, Ill., during his 1816 expedition. See Wood, in *Journal of the Illinois State Historical Society*, 47: 417–421. Fort Osage, near present-day Sibley in Jackson County, Mo., was built in 1808 and occupied intermittently by troops until 1819. It has been partially restored. See Kate L. Gregg, "The History of Fort Osage," in *Missouri Historical Review*, 34: 439, 444, 456, 478 (July, 1940); James Anderson, "Fort Osage: An Incident of Territorial Missouri," in Missouri Historical Society, *Bulletin*, 4: 175 (April, 1948).

my voyage. I yesterday took an observation for the Latitude of the place and found the meridian altitude of the Sun's Lower limb to be 65° 12′ 46″.

MONDAY, AUGUST 11, 1817. Started at half past 6 A.M. in company with Dr. Lane to ascend the River De Moyen a few miles. We entered at its lowermost mouth, passed the middle which at this time had no water passing thro' it, and ascended about 2 miles to the uppermost, thro' which is the principal discharge of the De Moin in low water. We ascended the River about 3 miles higher, where the channel was completely obstructed by sand bars, affording not even a sufficiency of water for the navigation of the smallest canoes. The water in the river, how ever, was at this time unusually low. Nevertheless, there is seldom a sufficiency of water at this season of the year to admit boats to ascend very far. In the spring of the year deep floods usually prevail in the river, which render it navigable for Mackinaw boats 160 or 200 miles.

The river is about 120 yards wide near its confluence with the Mississippi. Its upper mouth affords a considerable depth of water in all stages, but the channel is narrow & crooked and almost blocked up in many places by drift wood, snags & sawyers. The passage by the lower mouths is much bro[a]der but obstructed in many places by sand-bars that are impassable in low water. The principal part of the Ioway Indians reside up this river at the distance of about 120 mil[e]s from its mouth.[38]

Observed many fragments of coal apparently of a good quality scattered upon the sand bars in this river.

Returned about 12, dined, and took my leave of Dr. Lane and Capt. Ramsay [*Thomas Ramsey*], commanding officer of the garrison.[39] To Dr. L. in particular I feel much indebted for his politeness & attention. Capt. Colhoun was about to take his departure on a visit to his friends, & I invited him to take a passage to Belle Fontaine in my boat, with which he complyed. We started at two P.M.—the wind ahead. Met several canoes of Indians.

[38] Although there is conflicting evidence concerning the location of the Iowa village, Long's comment on its distance from the mouth of the Des Moines agrees with that made by Thomas Forsyth. This would put it near what is now Oskaloosa, Ia. See Forsyth to John C. Calhoun, September 26, 1821, OIA, Letters Received, NARG 75. For speculations on other locations, see Mildred Mott, "The Relation of Historic Indian Tribes to Archaeological Manifestations in Iowa," in *Iowa Journal of History and Politics*, 36:252–257 (July, 1938).

[39] Ramsey was the officer in charge of building Fort Edwards; he died in 1818 of a wound suffered in a duel. See Heitman, *Historical Register*, 1:814; *Missouri Gazette & Illinois Advertiser*, August 7, 1818.

TUESDAY, AUGUST 12, 1817. Floated till one at night, when we were compelled to lay by on account of an unfavourable wind accompanied with rain. Started again at Sun rise. A favourable wind sprang up at 1 P.M. and we were able to sail the rest of the day.

WEDNESDAY, AUGUST 13, 1817. Floated all night, and arrived at Burris Tavern early in the morning. Were able to sail most of the day moderately. Arrived a[t] Little Cape Gris [*Little Cap au Gris*] about dark and encamped.[40]

THURSDAY, AUGUST 14, 1817. Capt. Colhoun, my self & one of the men took an excursion across the country this morning & went in sight of the shores of the Illinois. Independant of the Bluffs, there is a ridge of land elevated about 18 feet above the water level extending from the Mississippi to the Illinois. The distances between the two rivers along this ridge is about 4 1/2 miles. The Bluffs of the two rivers meet each other at the distance of about 1 mile in rear of the ridge, being a succession of Knoles forming an extensive curve between the two rivers. The soil is of a good quality, inclining to sandy in some places. Growth principally Oak, Hiccory, Black & White Walnut, Sycamore, Cotton wood, Pirsimmon, Pawpaw. Upon the [*Calhoun*] point below the ridge is a large prairie extending to the Illinois. There are five settlements at this place, including two immediately upon the Mississippi at Little Cape Gris. Started at half past 8. Weather rainy. Called at Portage De[s] Sioux, [Mo.]. Arrived at the Mouth of the Missouri about 6 P.M., and ascended it 1/2 mile, where we encamped for the night.[41]

[40] No information on Burris Tavern has been found. Little Cap au Gris, located about 12 miles below Cap au Gris, in Calhoun County, Ill., was at or near the town later known as Deer Plain. See Porter, ed., in *Missouri Historical Collections*, 3: 130; J. M. Peck, *A Gazetteer of Illinois*, 172 (Philadelphia, 1837).

[41] The five settlements Long referred to may have been any of the following, which existed on Calhoun Point between the Illinois and the Mississippi at various times before 1823: Bountyville, Hamburg, Colesgrove (Gilead), Monroe (Mepper?), and Little Cap au Gris (later Milan or Deer Plain Ferry). See Lewis C. Beck, *A Gazetteer of the States of Illinois and Missouri*, 93, 101, 117, 140 (Albany, N.Y., 1823); George W. Carpenter, *History of Calhoun County*, 11, 12 (Jerseyville, Ill., 1934); *History of Pike County Illinois*, 197 (Chicago, 1880). Long himself was interested in a speculation for a new town at the mouth of the Illinois. See Long to Smith, September 19, 1817, June 20, 1818, Smith Papers; and to Swift, October 15, 1817, OCE, Miscellaneous Papers, Fortifications (Series A), NARG 77.

Portage des Sioux, an early French settlement in St. Charles County, Mo., was a favorite crossing place of the Indians between the Mississippi and the Missouri rivers. The town, established about 1799, was described in 1825 as "a straggling French village of perhaps forty buildings" by Schoolcraft, *Travels in the Central Portions of the Mississippi Valley*, 298. See also *History of St. Charles, Montgomery, and Warren Counties, Missouri*, 261–263 (St. Louis, 1885).

FRIDAY, AUGUST 15, 1817. Arrived at Belle Fontaine [Mo.] at 9 in the morning, all in good health. Three of my men had experienced a short illness of one day each, having been attacked with the Fever and ague. But by a seasonable application of remedies neither of them had a return of the chill. The mode of treatment I adopted towards them was to administer a cathartic of Calomel & Jallap soon after the Shake or Chill wor off, and the next day sometime before the return of the fever was expected requir the Patient to take freely of wine & Bark, which invariably had the desired effect.

The time occupied in the voyage was 76 days.

Lat. in the Mississippi 1 1/2 miles above the mouth of the St. Peters 45° 7′ 8″ [*44° 54′ 25″*]

Lat. at Prairie du Chien 43° 7′—by a Lunar observation 43° 6′ 14″ [*43° 3′ 30″*]

Fort Armstrong, Rock Island 41° 27′ 29″ [*41° 31′*]

At Fort Edwards, De Moyen [R.] 40° 22′ 19 [*40° 21′ 30″*]

At the Wisconsan Portage 44° — [*43° 32′ 15″*]

THE JOURNAL
OF
STEPHEN H. LONG
1823

Topographical Journal

Wednesday Apr. 30. 1823.

An Expedition having
been authorised by the War
Department, for exploring
a portion of the U. S Terri
tory situated westwardly
and Northwestwardly of
Lake Superior, and Maj.
S. H. Long of the Top'l. Engrs
having been duly appointed
to the command of it, the
gentlemen selected as ~~coad~~
coadjutors in the enter
-prise, assembled this morn
ing at 10 o'clock, and
immediately took their
departure from Philadel-
phia. — The party now
consisted of Maj. L. as comdg
officer of the Expedition
Professor T. Say, as Zoologi

THE OPENING PAGE (actual size) of the first volume of Long's journal for April 30, 1823, in the collections of the Minnesota Historical Society.

3. Overland from Philadelphia to the Mississippi River

APRIL 30 THROUGH JULY 2, 1823

WEDNESDAY, APRIL 30, 1823. An Expedition having been authorized by the War Department for exploring a portion of the U.S. Territory situated westwardly and Northwestwardly of Lake Superior, and Maj. S. H. Long of the Topl. Engrs. having been duly appointed to the command of it, the gentlemen selected as coadjutors in the enterprise assembled this morning at 10 oclock and immediately took their departure from Philadelphia. The party now consisted of Maj. L. as comdg. officer of the Expedition, Professor T[homas] Say as Zoologi[s]t and Antiquary, Professor [William H.] Keating, Geologist & Mineralogist (these gentlemen being also appointed as literary Journalists to the Expedition), & Mr. Samuel Seymour, Landskip Painter and designer. Lt. Andrew Talcott of the Corps of Engineers had been appointed by the Chief Engineer to accompany the Expedition in the capacity of Assistant Topographer & Astronomer, also as second in command with the view of conducting detachments or of taking charge of the Expedition in case of the sickness or other misfortunes of the Comdg. officer. This gentleman, however, not having arrived at Philadelphia in season to join the party before mentioned, was directed by orders from the Comdg. officer left at the Post Office to repair to Wheeling [*now in West Va.*] or Columbus [Ohio] and there join the party. We travelled to Downingstown [*Downingtown, Pa.*], where we arrived at an early hour and put up for the night. Dist. 30 m.[1]

[1] On the members of the expedition and the substitution of Colhoun for Talcott, see pp. 23–30, above. From Philadelphia to Lancaster, Pa., Long followed the nation's first turnpike, completed in 1794. See Joseph A. Durrenberger, *Turnpikes: A Study of the Toll Road Movement in the Middle Atlantic States and Maryland*, 51–58 (Valdosta, Ga., 1931).

THURSDAY, MAY 1, 1823. Started at 7 A.M. and arrived at Lancaster [Pa.] at 1/4 past 5 P.M. Distance 32 miles.

FRIDAY, MAY 2, 1823. Started at 1/2 past 5, having procured some few articles necessary for our journey. Break fasted at Columbia, dined at Little York, and put up for the night at King's, a very indifferent tavern [*in Abbottstown, Pa.*] tho the best on the road for a considerable distance. Distance 33 miles.[2]

SATURDAY, MAY 3, 1823. Started at half past 5. Breakfasted at Oxford, dined at Gettysburg, and put up for the night at Millerstown [*now Fairfield, Pa.*]. From Philadelphia to Gettysburg we travelled the Turnpike road, which was for the most part exceedingly rough, especially from Little York to Gettysburg. At the place last mentioned we left the turnpike with the view of crossing to the Cumberland road, the route in this direction to Wheeling having never been examined for the purpose of scientific description.[3]

In the vicinity of Millerstown is a copper-mine situated in the immediate neighbourhood of the South Mountain, which is a continuation of the Blue Ridge. Mr. Keating collected some information relative to the localities of this mineral together with some account of the rocks &c. in the neighbourhood.

Millerstown is situated eastwardly of the Blue Ridge at the distance of about 2 miles from its base. It contains about 30 houses partly of brick. Distance 26 miles.

[2] Long's route ran along present U.S. 30 to Gettysburg and along Pa. 116 to Fairfield. It may be traced most clearly on D. Small and W. Wagner, "Map of York & Adams Counties, 1821," in the collections of the Pennsylvania Historical and Museum Commission, Harrisburg. The MHS has a photocopy. See also Carey and Lea, *American Atlas*, map 18. King's Tavern at Abbottstown was operated by Michael King as early as 1799; see *History of Cumberland and Adams Counties, Pennsylvania*, part 3:217 (Chicago, 1886). For Keating's comments on the road, see *Narrative*, 1:24–28.

[3] According to S. K. Stevens, Pennsylvania Historical Commission, to the editors, March 3, 1969, "Long could not have left the Philadelphia-Lancaster Turnpike at Gettysburg because it did not extend that far." He was apparently following another highway "which was usually known as the Old Pennsylvania Road."

The first portion of the Cumberland or National Road (now U.S. 40) was authorized by Congress in 1806 and completed in 1818. Long followed its route from Hagerstown, Md., to Zanesville, Ohio, touched it again at Columbus, Ohio, and then diverged from it completely. On the road and the towns along it, see Philip D. Jordan, *The National Road*, 74, 89 (Indianapolis and New York, 1949); [William N. Blane], *An Excursion through the United States and Canada During the Years 1822–23*, 82–92 (London, 1824); [John Melish], *The Traveller's Manual*, facing p. 111 (New York, 1831). For the copper mines and Jacks Mountain, mentioned below, see Small and Wagner, "Map of York & Adams Counties"; Keating, *Narrative*, 1:15.

SUNDAY, MAY 4, 1823. Millerstown or Fairfield is situated in a kind of Cove or semi basin formed at the base of the South Mountain or Blue Ridge by two projecting spurs, on[e] of which on the SE is called Jacks Mountain. The circumjacent country, occupying the cove as above, is remarkable for containing a limestone conglomerate similar to that found near the Potomac in Maryland and employed in the construction of the Capital at Washington.

Started at 6. Struck the Turnpike road leading from Baltimore [Md.] to McConnels T. [*McConnellsburg*] Pa. at the base of the Blue Ridge, and on this road crossed the mountain, on the top of which we breakfasted. Arrived at Hagerstown, Md., at 4 P.M. and put up for the rest of the day. Dist. 25 m.[4]

MONDAY, MAY 5, 1823. The road from Gettysburg to Hagerstown was very bad—with the exception of about 7 miles, including the passage of the Blue Ridge, which as before remarked is turnpike. It however leads thro' a country highly interesting to the Mineralogist & Geologist, which in a great measure compensates for the difficulty of travelling it. The Blue Ridge exhibits numerous indications of copper, and ore of this mettal contains from 15 to 30 per cent of copper has been found. The mountain abounds in rocks apparently of a primitive type, while the vallies on the route exhibit extensive ranges of stratified lime stone, inclined in an angle of 25 to 80 degre[es] and running in a direction nearly parallel to that of the mountain. The soil of the vallies is generally good, as also on most of the hills. The growth of the former consists of oak, hiccory, ash, maple, and of the former [*latter*] white pine and chesnut in addition to those just ennumerated.

Started a little before six, break fasted at the Clear spring, crossed the North mountain, passed thro' Hancock [Md.], crossed the Sideling hill, near the top of which is a most extensive and romantic view of the country situated E & SE of our road—and put up for the night at Norris Tavern at the foot of the hill.[5]

The valleys generally present blue limestone in strata highly in-

[4] On this turnpike, known as the Bank Road, and Long's route of May 5–8 below, see Edward C. Papenfuse *et al.*, *Maryland: A New Guide to the Old Line State*, 49–60 (Baltimore and London, 1976); Ellen Lee Barker, Maryland Historical Society, to the editors, March 13, 1969. It seems probable that Long crossed the Monterey Summit of the Blue Ridge on a route now approximated by Pa. 16.

[5] On the use of the geological term "primitive," see p. 38, above. On the tavern kept by Thomas Norris, see Thomas B. Searight, *The Old Pike: A History of the National Road*, 201 (Uniontown, Pa., 1894). The stone bridge mentioned below is still in existence seven miles west of Hagerstown, Md.

clined, the hills clay slate dipping to the NW—and the mountains sandstone, having an inclination similar to that of the rock last mentioned. In the immediate vally of the Potomac (along which our way lead for a considerable distance) Cleyy slate appeared to be the prevailing formation.

The Cumberland Road or Turnpike, which we entered at Hagerstown and on which we travelled thro' the day, is very good, greatly surpassing the Pittsburg[h] both in the style of its execution and in the comfort and ease with which it may be travelled. It crosses the Conegocheague river [*Conococheague Creek*] on a very fine stone bridge, constructed with seven arches of blue lime stone, which is said to have cost $9000. Distance 36 miles.

TUESDAY, MAY 6, 1823. The weather last night exceedingly cold for the season. A heavy frost observable this morning and ice on the stagnant pools of water.

Started at half past 5. Crossed Town hill and Green ridge before breakfast. Breakfasted at Pratt's. Crossed Polish Mountain and afterwards Martins Mt.—the latter of which differs materially from the others in its geological character. The valley between these two mountains contains limestone in abundance of a very dark complexion, nearly black. As we ascended Martins mt., we observed the same kind of stone but gradually assuming a lighter complexion. Descending upon the west side, the lime stone continued to present itself, intermixed with sandstone, till we had passed about two thirds down the mountain, where slate clay became the prevailing formation. Arrived at Cumberland [Md.] at 4 P.M. where we put up for the night. Dist. 30 miles.[6]

WEDNESDAY, MAY 7, 1823. In the neighbourhood of Cumberland coal of an excellent quality is found in abundance. It burns with a brisk & lively flame and occasions but little smoke and no smell of sulphur.

Started at half past 7. The weather being rainy we took break fast previously. Crossed Wills Creek over which is a chain bridge of remarkably slender construction tho' strong enough to admit the passage of the heaviest loaded waggons.

[6] Town, Green, and Polish mountains are now in Green Ridge State Forest, Md. Martin Hill is on the border between Rainsburg, Pa., and Cumberland, Md. On Pratt's tavern, located in what is now Pratt Hollow, Md., see Searight, *Old Pike*, 202. The structure stood on property at the east foot of Polish Mountain owned in 1968 by Howard Robinette.

Crossed Wills', Dan's, Savage & Alleghany [*Allegheny*] mountains, Red Ridge, meadow mountain, Shade hill, and Negro mountain and put up for the night at Stod[d]ards on the top of Keisers [*Keyser's*] Ridge. No part of the road travelled today can be considered as level for a distance of half a mile in a place. The road very rough as well as hilly. Dist. 29 miles.[7]

THURSDAY, MAY 8, 1823. Started at 1/4 past 5. Breakfasted at Smithfield [*now Somerfield, Pa.*] situated on the Yohogany [*Youghiogheny*] river, over which the road passes on a well constructed stone bridge of three arches. Crossed a broad mountain [*Laurel Hill*] the name of which we could not learn—also Laurel [*Chestnut*] Ridge, the last of the Alleghany Range in this direction. In the valley between these two ridges and at the distance of about 400 yards from the road is the site of Fort Necessity, memorable on account of its construction by Gen. [George] Washington in his first campaign [*1754*] against the Indians in this part of the country. It is situated in a low bottom on the margin of a small creek [*Great Meadow Run*], is of a triangular form, and covers an area of about 200 square yards. The only traces of it now distinguishable are low parapets rising from one to two feet above the natural surface, with a small trench inside of the parapets. It is about 10 miles east of Union Town [Pa]. About 1 1/2 miles from this place is the spot where the body of Gen. [Edward] Brad[d]ock was buried, immediately in the road bearing his name.[8]

Arrived at Union Town a little past 4 and put up for the night. Dist. 32.

[7] A detailed description of the early Cumberland coal fields may be found in J. Thomas Scharf, *History of Western Maryland*, 2:1312–1318 (Philadelphia, 1882). See also Keating, *Narrative*, 1:20. According to a marker near the site in 1968, the chain bridge was replaced by a stone one in 1834. For the mountains mentioned here, see Archer B. Hulbert, *The Old National Road: A Chapter of American Expansion*, facing pp. 22, 36 (Columbus, Ohio, 1901). On the tavern kept by James Stoddard, see Searight, *Old Pike*, 211.

[8] The site of the Youghiogheny bridge, built in 1818, is marked in the present Somerfield, Pa., Recreation Area. See also Works Projects Administration, *Pennsylvania: A Guide to the Keystone State*, 593 (New York, 1940). On Fort Necessity National Battlefield and Braddock's grave, also in Pennsylvania, see Robert Bruce, *The National Road*, 60–62 (New York and Washington, D.C., 1916); Robert G. Ferris, ed., *Explorers and Settlers: Historic Places Commemorating the Early Exploration and Settlement of the United States*, 163 (National Park Service, *National Survey of Historic Sites and Buildings*, vol. 5—Washington, D.C., 1968). The sites are marked and the fort has been reconstructed. See also Keating, *Narrative*, 1:28–30.

FRIDAY, MAY 9, 1823. Started at 1/4 before six, breakfasted at Brownsville on the Monongahela river, crossed the river by ferriage. Mr. Seymour took a sketch of the Town, river, &c. from a commanding view on the west side of the river. The Country very hilly, tho' not mountainous. Passed thro' several small villages, the most considerable of which on the west of the Monongahela were Bellsville [*Beallsville*] & Hillsborough [*now Scenery Hill*]. Arrived at Washington [Pa.] at 1/2 past six after a fatiguing day's journey. Distance 36 m.[9]

SATURDAY, MAY 10, 1823. Started at 1/2 past 5, breakfasted at Claysville [Pa.] & arrived at Wheeling at 1/2 past 4 P.M. Distance 32 miles.

Having occasion to make new arrangements for the farther prosecution of our journey, we resolved to remain at Wheeling a few days for that purpose. From inquiry relative to the condition of the roads thro' the State of Ohio, we were convinced that it was not advisable to pursue our journey farther in Dearborns, and accordingly measures were taken to exchange one of them for horses. In the trafic for horses, two horses and a dearborn belonging to Maj. L. were exchanged for 4 horses that were thought suitable for the journey before us. Our outfit now consisted of 5 horses and one dearborn waggon, the equipments necessary for the former having been procured & brought with us from Philadelphia.

We had anticipated the pleasure of finding Dr. [Edwin] James at this place but were disappointed in this respect. The Dr., who was to have been of our party, having taken his departure from Albany [N.Y.] on his journey to Belle Fontaine [Mo.] by order of the Medical Department, where he no doubt expected to join us. But our route leading us in a different direction, we are likely to fore go the advantages of his cooperation.[10]

WEDNESDAY, MAY 14, 1823. Having completed our arrangements at Wheeling, we resumed our journey again this morning at 8 o clock. Our cavalcade no[w] contained five horses and one dearborn waggon, so that in addition to a horse for each individual of the

[9] On the Monongahela ferry site, see Bruce, *National Road*, 70, 71. Seymour's sketch is not among the completed paintings listed in Long to Macomb, April 23, 1825, in Appendix 2, below. It has not been found. All the towns in this paragraph are in Pennsylvania.

[10] Dearborns were light wagons or carriages. See Nick Eggenhofer, *Wagons, Mules and Men*, 130 (New York, 1961). The horse trade was not an even one; see Voucher No. 16, in "Abstract," Appendix 2, below. On James, see p. 24, above.

party, we had one extra, which we intended for the use of a servant as soon as we should be able to find one. We crossed the Ohio riv. in ferry boats, one of which plying between Wheeling and the iland directly opposite to the town and bearing its name, is propelled by two horses labouring upon a horizontal wheel and is of a remarkably cheap and convenient construction. From the island to the north side of the river we crossed in a common scow. On entering the state of Ohio, we found the roads in a condition exceedingly bad and discouraging, owing in a great measure to the excessive rains that had recently fallen. That leading from the Ohio up Indian Wheeling creek to the point where we reached the high lands was so muddy and rough that it was with extreme difficulty that a single horse could draw the dearborn without a load. We dined at St. Clairsville [Ohio], where we procured a black man as a servant, whose name is Andrew [Allison]. Arrived at Morristown about 6 P.M. where we put up for the night. Distance 21 miles.[11]

THURSDAY, MAY 15, 1823. Started at 1/4 past 5. Found the road exceedingly bad in many places, so that it proved extremely difficult for the horse to draw our waggon thro' the mud without a load. Break fasted at Fair View, where we got some shoes set upon two of our horses. Travelled to [Old] Washington or Beamastown [*Beymerstown*], where we arrived a little after 4 P.M.—and having met with a slight accident to the dearborn and our horses being fatigued, we lay by to make repairs &c. Dist. 25 miles.

FRIDAY, MAY 16, 1823. Started at 5—it commenced raining soon after, and at half past 8 a violent rain commenced which continued at intervals till eleven. During this time we were delayed at Cambridge, where we breakfasted. The travelling rendered much more difficult by the recent fall of rain, which rendered the surface of the ground exceedingly slippery. Arrived at [John S.] Dugan's, half way from Cambridge to Zanesville, where another shower fell, & our

[11] On the ferry and Long's route through Wheeling, see Bruce, *National Road*, 82; Gibson L. Cranmer, *History of Wheeling City*, 144, 172, 175 (Chicago, 1902). For Indian Wheeling Creek on the west bank of the Ohio, see Samuel Cumings, *The Western Pilot*, facing p. 8 (Cincinnati, 1825). Keating, *Narrative*, 1:139, identified the black servant as Andrew Allison.

Long's route through Ohio may be traced in Tanner, *New American Atlas*, map 11. From Wheeling to Zanesville, the party followed in part Ohio's first road, the famous Zane's Trace marked out by Ebenezer Zane and authorized by Congress in 1796. See Hulbert, *Old National Road*, 48. For a contemporary account of this portion of the route, see Karl Bernhard, *Travels through North America, During the Years 1825 and 1826*, 2:153–157 (Philadelphia, 1828).

horses being somewhat fatigued, we put up for the night at 4 P.M. Dist. 22 m.[12]

SATURDAY, MAY 17, 1823. On harnising our horses, we discovered that one of them (the dear-born horse) was very lame, owing no doubt to a strain he received in his left hind leg in passing some difficult part of the road yesterday. He was nevertheless able to travel slowly, and we started a little before 5 o clock and proceeded to Zanesville, where we succeeded in exchanging our waggon for another horse, paying $35 into the bargain. Having now to arrange our baggage for transportation on horseback, we spent the day at Zanesville for that purpose. Distance 13 miles.[13]

SUNDAY, MAY 18, 1823. Having completed our arrangements at Zanesville yesterday, we resumed our journey this morning at 1/4 past 4 o-clock, all on horseback. Breakfasted at Irville, where we observed several Indian mounds—two of which had been opened and were found to contain human bones. In one of them was found a plate of copper about 5 inches broad & 6 or 7 long, as we were informed by our landlord.[14]

Our way led us up the vally of Licking Creek, which abounds in fine tracts of land well adapted to cultivation. The growth of the Lowlands consists of Sugar tree, maple, ash, Elm, oak &c. and the under growth of hazle, spice wood, &c. indicative of a good soil. On the road to Newark [Ohio] and a few miles short of that place we witnessed the effects of the gale so generally prevalent on Easter Sunday of this year. An entire orchard of apple trees were prostrated by it, a house unroofed, a barn blown down, together with the various other indications of a powerful tornado. It was remarkable that the wind here blew from the SW, whereas at Philadelphia it

[12] Dugan kept a tavern known as the Sign of the Green Tree, which opened in 1817. See Hulbert, *Old National Road*, 108; J. F. Everhart, *History of Muskingum County, Ohio*, 93, 94 (Columbus, Ohio, 1882).

[13] See Voucher No. 19, in "Abstract," Appendix 2, below. At Zanesville, Long left what later became the National Road to follow the older route through Newark to Columbus, now approximated by Ohio 146 and 16. For Keating's comments on Zanesville, see *Narrative*, 1:38–44.

[14] A mound at Irville, which later disappeared, is described in Everhart, *History of Muskingum County*, 401; four mounds nearby are mapped by William C. Mills, *Archeological Atlas of Ohio*, plate 60 (Columbus, Ohio, 1914). In a letter to the editors on March 5, 1969, Raymond S. Baby, Ohio Historical Society, reported that two mounds had been surveyed in the vicinity in 1946—one south of Irville on the Potwin-Jenkins farm and one northwest of the town on the Van Voorhis property. Keating, *Narrative*, 1:49, mentioned the expedition's unsuccessful attempt to visit the well-known earthworks now preserved near Newark, Ohio.

had an opposite direction. Arrived at Newark at 4 P.M. Dist. 25 miles.[15]

MONDAY, MAY 19, 1823. At Newark we met with the celebrated Capt. [John C.] Symmes with whom we had much conversation upon the subject of his singular theory of the earth. His theory, in addition to other absurdities, suppose[s] a magnetic equator forming with the true equator angles of 12 deggrees, and that the *verge* terminating the polar openings is formed on section parallel to his magnetic equator. On the road from Newark to Columbus are no hills of much size to be met with—the country is generally flat and swampy, or what is commonly termed the Beech-wood-land. Arrived at Columbus at 6 P.M. Dist. 33 m.[16]

TUESDAY, MAY 20, 1823. The following observations [*of equal altitudes of the sun*] were made at Comlumbus for the purpose of determining the Lat. & Longitude. . . . [*Observations omitted.*]

At Columbus I obtained from a Mr. Jos. Ridgway the following items of intelligence concerning surveys recently made by Judge [James] Geddes, Engr. of the N. York [*Erie*] Canal, for ascertaining the practicability of constructing Canals connecting the waters of Lake Erie with those of the Ohio, on five different routes, viz.

1st By way of the Miami [*and Maumee*] and Oglaze [*Auglaize*] rivers.

Summit above Lake Erie	399 ft.
Above the mouth of Mill Cr. just be low Cincinnati	550 ["]
2nd Between Scioto and Sandusky rivers.	
Summit above the Lake	354 ft.
above the mouth of Scioto R.	455 "
3rd Between Muskingum [R.] and Black R. of Lake Erie	
Summit above the Lake	337 ft.
above mouth of Muskingum R.	361 "

[15] While it seems commonplace today, Long's comment on the wind direction of the Easter storm shows him to have been a keen observer. See also Keating, *Narrative*, 1:49. Storms received little scientific attention in the United States until the 1830s, and James P. Espy's influential book, *The Philosophy of Storms*, was not published until 1841. For a summary of the development of thought on weather phenomena, see David M. Ludlum, *Early American Tornadoes 1586–1870*, 158–194 (Boston, 1970).

[16] Symmes, formerly of the U.S. Army, announced a theory in 1818 that the earth was hollow, open at the poles, and habitable within. See John A. Vinton, *The Symmes Memorial*, 95–98 (Boston, 1873); John W. Peck, "Symmes' Theory," in *Ohio Archaeological and Historical Publications*, 18:29–42 (Columbus, Ohio, 1909).

4th Between Cuyahoga [R.] of Lake Erie and the Tuscarawa[s branch] of the Muskingum.

Summit above Lake Erie	404 ft.
above mouth of Muskingum	428 ["]

5th Between Grand river of Lake Erie and the Mahoning of Big-Beaver.

Summit above Lake Erie	342 ft.
above Mouth of Big-Beaver	214 [*224 ft.*]

Surveys made by and under the direction of Judge Geddes.[17]

A violent hail storm and gust took place this after noon which did considerable injury to the houses in different parts of the town. Three of the chimneys of the State house had their tops blown down. We were prevented by cloudy weather from completing our observation for Lat. & Longitude.

At Columbus we found Mr. James Calhoun [*Colhoun*] waiting our arrival. He had been substituted in the place of Lt. Talcott, agreeably to instructions of the Chief Engineer, & had arrived more than a week before us with the view of joining the Expedition at this place. We were not a little gratified at this acquisition to our party. Remained at Columbus thro' the day for the purpose of making some new arrangements proper for the continuance of our journey, as also for Astrono. Observations.

WEDNESDAY, MAY 21, 1823. Our party now consisted of six persons, including the black boy [*Allison*] I had employed as waiter for the party, and seven horses all in good condition.

Started a little after sun-rise and travelled to Mechanicsburg. Roads exceedingly muddy. Country very flat. Soil generally a black loam, such as is common to Beach wood land of this part of the country. The flat lands are said to be healthy, while the ridges,

[17] There were two Joseph Ridgways in Columbus in 1823. It seems probable that Long was referring to Joseph, Jr. (1800–50), an engineer who later worked on Ohio canals, rather than his uncle Joseph, Sr. (1783–1861), who operated an iron foundry. See *Biographical Directory of the American Congress 1774–1961*, 1520 (85 Congress, 2 session, *House Documents*, no. 442—serial 12108); *Biographical Encyclopaedia of Ohio of the Nineteenth Century*, 373 (Cincinnati and Philadelphia, 1876).

Geddes, an Onondaga County, N.Y., judge and one of the principal engineers of the Erie Canal, was engaged by the state of Ohio in 1822 to make surveys. See Joshua V. H. Clark, *Onondaga; or Reminiscences of Earlier and Later Times*, 2:45–49 (Syracuse, N.Y., 1849); Chapter 6, note 42, below. The data Long presented on the routes were probably drawn in part from Geddes, *Canal Report*, a 14-page pamphlet published in Columbus in 1823. For the last figure Long originally wrote 324, then crossed it out. On the measurements, see also Keating, *Narrative*, 1:69–75. On Colhoun, below, see p. 24, above.

which are elevated but a little above the flat lands, are found generally unhealthy, fevers and Augues prevailing. The black soil is said to be equally as good for wheat as that of a lighter complexion but not so good for Ind. Corn. Distance 32 miles.[18]

THURSDAY, MAY 22, 1823. Started at 1/2 past 5. Break-fasted at Urbana. The country since leaving Columbus and even Zanesville generally flat. Large tracts often present them selves with scarcely an undulation to variegate their surface. The soil of such tracts is usually very thin and of a black colour, and is under laid by a stratum of sand, gravel, and pebbles. The growth of the country is principally beach, which prevails especially on the flat lands. Also of Oak, Ash, Elm, hiccory, sugar tree, wild cherry, Walnut (black), and occasionally Sycamore and Cottonwood, together with Poplar and Aspen. Best crops of Indn. corn amount to about 50 bushels p[e]r acre. Of wheat to about 30. Roads very muddy most of the distance travelled to day. Put up for the night at a private house where we met with very indifferent accommodation. Distance 32 miles.

FRIDAY, MAY 23, 1823. Started at 5 o clock, travelled to Pequa [*Piqua, Ohio*], where we spent the day for the purpose of examining the Antiquities found here, writing letters, and making additional preparations for our journey. Dist. 6 miles.[19]

SATURDAY, MAY 24, 1823. During our deleay at Piqua we visited not only the antiquities on the Town site but several in the neighborhood but on the opposite side of the [Miami] river, of which the gentle men of the party too[k] particular note, after having surviyed and assertained their dimentions.

Started at half past 5, and were accompanied about 3 miles by Maj. [William] Oliver, agent of the Land office at Pequa, and with him examined the ruins of an antient work situated at that dis-

[18] Long's exact route from Mechanicsburg to the Ohio-Indiana border is not entirely clear; the first part is perhaps shown in Henry Howe, *Historical Collections of Ohio*, facing p. 592 (Cincinnati, 1848); the route from Fort St. Mary's north may be that shown in Tanner, *New American Atlas*, map 11. The private house mentioned below has not been identified.

[19] On the five groups of antiquities near Piqua, described here and below, see Keating, *Narrative*, 1:55–67; E. G. Squier and E. H. Davis, *Ancient Monuments of the Mississippi Valley*, 23, 88 (*Smithsonian Contributions to Knowledge*, vol. 1—Washington, D.C., 1848). Keating believed erroneously that the works were "as yet undescribed"; see Daniel Drake, *Natural and Statistical View, or Picture of Cincinnati and the Miami Country*, 209 (Cincinnati, 1815).

tance from Town. It consisted of a wall of rolled stones, taken probably from the bed of the river which was distant about 700 yards, and exhibited an enclosure of an oval form, having its longest diameter about 500 and its shortest about 300 yards. The wall appeared to have been intercepted by numerous gate ways, and the work also presented several traces of mounds of the same kind of stones distributed in some parts of its interior. Its site elevated about 30 feet above the river *bottom* and may be considered as commanding. Our entertainment was of the worst order, but the charge higher than we have usual paid on other similar occasions. The roads better than we have found them of late, tho very muddy in places. Arrived at Fort St. Marys at 5 P.M. and put up for the night. Distance 32 miles.[20]

SUNDAY, MAY 25, 1823. Started at 5. The first 12 miles of our road was exceedingly bad. We were compelled to be satisf[ie]d with walking our horses, and that very moderately thro' the whole of that distance. The country swampy and flat.

At the end of this distance we met the celebrated Capt. [James] Riley, whose travels in Africa have given him considerable distinction. We had but a moments conversation with him, as we had about 6 miles farther to travel before breakfast. Travelled 18 miles and breakfasted at Shanesville [*now Rockford, Ohio*] on the St. Mary's [River], where we arrived at 12 o'clock. At Shanesville we crossed the St. Mary's by swimming our horses and transporting our baggage in a canoe. Travelled 14 miles after breakfast over roads exceedingly muddy and difficult at [*and*] put up for the night at half past 6 P.M. Dist. 32.[21]

[20] Oliver, who served with Ohio troops during the War of 1812, was appointed receiver for the Piqua land office in 1823. His surety bond, dated April 7, 1823, is in Records of the Bureau of Accounts, NARG 39. See also B[ert] J. Griswold, *The Pictorial History of Fort Wayne Indiana*, 1:206 (Chicago, 1917).

For contemporary descriptions of Fort St. Mary's, built in 1794 within present St. Mary's, Ohio, see Keating, *Narrative*, 1:75; Thomas S. Teas, "Journal of a tour to Fort Wayne and the adjacent country, in the year 1821," in Harlow Lindley, ed., *Indiana as Seen by Early Travelers*, 252 (*Indiana Historical Collections*, vol. 1—Indianapolis, 1916).

[21] The meeting took place at Willshire, Ohio, a settlement James Riley laid out in 1822 and named for William Willshire, an Englishman who rescued him from captivity with the Moors. Riley's adventures are told in his book, *An Authentic Narrative of the Loss of the American Brig Commerce, Wrecked on the Western Coast of Africa* (Hartford, Conn., 1817). See also Riley, "Founding of Willshire," in *Northwest Ohio Quarterly*, 16:41–44 (January, 1944). The party probably ate at Anthony Shane's tavern in the Ohio town named for him. See Teas, in Lindley, ed., *Indiana as Seen by Early Travelers*, 252, 254.

MONDAY, MAY 26, 1823. Learning that we should meet with no house on the road on this side of Fort Wayne [Ind.], we thot best to take an early breakfast, which we obtained at sunrise, and resumed our journey at a little past 5. The country generally flat, much of it inundated at this time in consequence of the wetness of the season. Our road of course remarkably bad. Travelled to Fort Wayne, where we arrived at half past 2 P.M. Dist. 25 miles.[22]

TUESDAY, MAY 27, 1823. At Fort Wayne we met with a kind reception from Gen. [John] Tipton, Indn. agt., Mr. Kercheville [*Benjamin B. Kercheval*], assistant Agent, and particularly Capt. [James] Hackley, formerly of the army.[23] Having additional arrangements to make in order to prosecute our journey in the wilderness, we purposed to delay some time for this and other purposes.

The following observations were made with the view of ascertaining the Lat. &c. . . . [*Observations omitted.*] We in vain sought opportuni[ty] to complete our observations, the weather continuing cloudy during our delay at Ft. Wayne.

THURSDAY, MAY 29, 1823. Having completed our arrangements for entering the wilderness and laid in provisions for eight days, we took our departure at half past nine this morning. Crossed the St. Marys by swimming our horses and transporting our baggage in a canoe. We had now two pack-horses loaded with provisions and camp-equipage; we had also detained one of the expresses [*Pvt. Jesse L. Bemis*] sent from Chicago to Ft. Wayne, one day, in order to avail ourselves of his services as guide to the former place. Thus

[22] By the time of Long's visit, a small settlement had grown up at Fort Wayne, a military post in present Indiana established in 1794 and evacuated by the army in 1819. An Indian agency was located there until 1828. See Bert J. Griswold, *Fort Wayne, Gateway of the West 1802–1813*, 1–4, 20 (*Indiana Historical Collections*, vol. 15—Indianapolis, 1927). Long had visited Fort Wayne in 1817; for his description of it, see the enclosure dated March 4, 1817, in Long to Monroe, March 15, 1817, Secretary of War, Letters Received, NARG 107. See also Wood, *Long*, 41.

[23] Tipton, a major general in the Indiana militia, was Indian agent at Fort Wayne from 1823 to 1828. Kercheval, a former American Fur Company trader, served as subagent beginning in 1821. Hackley became a trader after his resignation from the army in 1818; he committed suicide in 1826. Keating, *Narrative*, 1:88, acknowledged the party's debt to Kercheval for information about the Indians, and Long's purchase of supplies from Hackley is entered as Voucher No. 25 in "Abstract," Appendix 2, below. On these men, see Glen A. Blackburn, comp., and Nellie A. Robertson and Dorothy Riker, eds., *The John Tipton Papers*, 1:xvi, 298n, 314n (*Indiana Historical Collections*, vol. 24—Indianapolis, 1942).

our party consisted of seven persons and was supplied with eight horses.[24]

Crossed Eel river of the Wabash, which we were able to ford with some difficulty. The travelling muddy. Country for the most part flat, sometimes rolling. Crossed Blue Creek and encamped on its banks. Dist. 20 m.

During our stay at Ft. Wayne I accepted the polite invitation of Cap. Hackley and lodged at his house. Mrs. [Rebecca] H. is the daughter of Capt. [William] Wells formerly of this place, who fell a victim to savag[e] fury at the bloody massacre of Chicago. Her mother was a squaw of the Miami nation of the family of Little Turtle, one of the most celebrated chiefs of his age.[25]

Mrs. H., altho' completely an American lady in her deportment, dress and education, still retains a strong regard for the Indians of this part of the country and especially for those of the Miami nation. She has made herself acquainted with many peculiarities of their character. As I was too much occupied in completing my arrangements for the further prosecution of our journey to converse with her much in relation to the Indians, I can only record the following particulars. They believe in the existance of a good Spirit who is the source of all good, and in that of an evil spirit who is the cause of all evil. The former is to be worshipped, while the latter is to be propitiated that he may cease to inflict evils. They believe in the existence of the soul after death, but have no idea of Heaven or hell

[24] Bemis, the expressman, accompanied the party as far as Fort Crawford, Wis. See pp. 133, 136, below; AGO, Fort Dearborn Post Returns, August, 1820, and Registers of Enlistments, 1815–21, 27:181, both in NARG 94; Keating, *Narrative*, 1:139, 245.

At Fort Wayne the expedition left the settled region and plunged into the wilderness, following a route through Indiana roughly approximating present U.S. 33. Because the party was unable to ford the Elkhart River, its route was some 16 miles longer than the usual "trace" between Forts Wayne and Dearborn (at Chicago), according to Keating, *Narrative*, 1:161. The trace was not an established road, and its route shifted with the seasons and the water levels. Over it a military express carried mail monthly or fortnightly between the two forts. See Milo M. Quaife, *Chicago and the Old Northwest 1673–1835*, 267 (Chicago, 1913); Henry H. Hurlbut, *Chicago Antiquities*, 527–529 (Chicago, 1881); Logan Esarey, *A History of Indiana*, 1:355 (Indianapolis, 1915); [William] Johnston, "A Trip from Fort Wayne to Fort Dearborn in 1809," in *Indiana Magazine of History*, 36:45–51 (March, 1940).

[25] Rebecca Wells married James Hackley in 1817. Her father, William Wells, was captured by the Indians as a boy, adopted by the celebrated Miami chief Little Turtle, and killed in 1812 while assisting in the evacuation of the Fort Dearborn garrison (see note 44, below). Little Turtle has been cited for his courage, intelligence, and leadership qualities by many writers. See Keating, *Narrative*, 1:85–87; Griswold, *Fort Wayne, Gateway*, 30–34, 55, 56, 310n; Works Projects Administration, *Indiana: A Guide to the Hoosier State*, 196, 306 (New York, 1947).

any farther than that good men are to be placed in a better country and the bad in a worse country than that they now dwell in, their pursuits after death being supposed similar to those of the present life. They are exetremely superstitious, believing that the souls of departed friends cannot rest unless they are furnished with food to subsist on during their passage to the other world, & have the custom of placing food at the grave of a deceased person.

In their treatment of diseases, the indians appear to have very little skill; in some few instances, however, they are more successful than the whites. In cases of fever, bloodletting is sometimes resorted to, as also swetting. The former is performed by means of flints, while the latter is effected by a variety of means, some of the most remarkable of which are the following—stones are heated and a small pile of them collected and the patient made to stand over them enclosed in a blanket. Water is sometimes thrown upon them to produce steam which increases the effect. The patient is sometimes buried in a heap of fresh boiled corn, where he lays till he experiences relief. This is considered one of their most effectual remedies.[26]

FRIDAY, MAY 30, 1823. Started at 6 A.M. and travelled 18 miles before dinner. Proceeded 12 miles farther and reached the Elk heart [*Elkhart*] river, which we found so swollen that it was impracticable for us to cross it; we accordingly encamped for the night on the bank of the river, without being able to find pasture for our horses except what a bottom, densely timbered, would afford. Dist. 30 miles.

SATURDAY, MAY 31, 1823. Finding it almost impracticable either to ford or raft the river on account of its depth and rapidity, we resolved to pass down on the South of it thro the bottoms, which were densely wooded and destitute of roads. Having been delayed till near eight o'clock in consequence of our black man [*Allison*] having lost himself while searching for the horses, we took our departure.

Our progress slow and obstructed by thickets, swamps, and creeks. Crossed a creek of considerable size, which we found too deep for fording. We were so fortunate as to find a tree fallen across the river which served as a bridge to cross our baggage upon, while

[26] For information collected by expedition members from Mrs. Hackley and other informants on the Miami and Potawatomi, see Keating, *Narrative*, 1:91–138.

our horses got over by swimming. Encamped at 1/2 past 6 in a dense wood, where we found but little feed for our horses. Distance 20 miles.[27]

SUNDAY, JUNE 1, 1823. We were exceedingly annoyed by musquetoes at our encampment of last night. Our horses also suffered much by them and more for want of pasture, for we were situated in a thick forest with swamps in almost every direction.

Our fare since leaving Fort Wayne consists of Pork, ham, biscuit, Coffee, tea and sugar, and at mealtimes we are seated upon the ground using tins instead of cups and saucers, while our fingers serve as substitutes for plates. Our cooking utensils consist of a Tin kettle, Coffeepot, 1/2 doz. of Tin-cups, together with knives, consisting of knife, fork & spoon such as are made for the use of hunters.

Started at 1/2 past 6. Travelled thro' thickets that were difficult to penetrate, over swamps in which our horses were repeatedly in danger of miring, our course leading us thro a dense forest thro' which there were no traces to be seen but those of its bestial tenants. Travelled 10 miles and dined, having reached the banks of the Elk-heart in pursuit of which we had been struggling thro' the wood ever since we crossed the stream mentioned yesterday. Proceeded down the river 3 miles and had the good fortune to strike the trace leading to Chicago at the lowermost fording place of the Elk heart, which was still too high by several feet to admit of fording. Travelled ten miles farther on our road and lay by on the bank of Devil river. Distance 23 miles.[28]

MONDAY, JUNE 2, 1823. As usual we found the musquetoes exceedingly numerous and troublesome. Started at 6 o'clock, passed several small creeks, and the remains of several indian and one

[27] It seems probable that the stream referred to was Solomon Creek in Nobles County, Ind., a few miles west of present Benton. Long's route here is so uncertain, however, that the stream may be the larger Turkey Creek near present Waterford. See Keating, *Narrative*, 1:143.

[28] Fords existed at the present towns of Benton and Goshen. See H. S. K. Bartholomew, *Stories and Sketches of Elkhart County*, 2, 8 (Nappanee, Ind., 1936); Anthony Deahl, ed., *A Twentieth Century History and Biographical Record of Elkhart County*, 15, 33 (Chicago and New York, 1905). No present Devil River has been located. Although it is known that this was an early name for Baugo Creek west of Elkhart, it seems unlikely that the expedition had traveled so far at this point. Perhaps Long is here referring to Yellow Creek west of present Goshen. On the route here and below, see Keating, *Narrative*, 1:147. For the comments of missionary Isaac McCoy, who traveled this route a month earlier than Long, see his *History of Baptist Indian Missions*, 186–189 (Washington, D.C., and New York, 1840).

French village. The former are known by the names of the Strawberry & Rum's villages, and the latter by that of the St. Joseph's. Passed a trading establishment belonging to a Frenchman whose name is Rous[s]eau. He and another frenchman, probably his partner, had squaws for wives. At this place we obtained some milk, which proved a very savory biverage.[29]

Passed [Joseph] Bertrand's, a French trader who resides on the north of the St. Joseph's [River].[30]

Having a desire to visit the [Carey Mission] school & missionary establishment under the care of the Rev. Mr. [Isaac] McCoy, we proceeded down the [St. Joseph] river by a circuitous route of 6 miles and arrived at the place of our intended visit. Here we were gratified with meeting with an institution embracing every preliminary appropriate in an establishment for reclaiming and civilizing the savages. Seven months only have elapsed since the site occupied by the establishment was clad in a forest.[31]

Mr. McCoy, the principal, was unfortunately absent on a visit to [*the Ottawa Indians at*] Grand river of Lake Michigan at the time of our visit, but the result of his labours, zeal and industry spoke loudly in his praise. A large and comfortable dwelling house, a schoolhouse, a Black smith's shop, and other out houses, a large garden,

[29] Rum's village (Potawatomi) was located on the south edge of South Bend, Ind., in what is now Rum Village Park; Caroline Dunn, Indiana Historical Society, to the editors, April 30, 1968. Strawberry's village and St. Joseph have not been specifically located. The latter is not the noted St. Joseph established as a mission in the late 17th century near Niles, Mich.

The traders were the brothers Dominique and Charles Rousseau, whose alternate surname was Paget. Trading for Joseph Bailly and others, they moved their post many times. McCoy, *History of Baptist Indian Missions*, 182, placed it 15 miles from his mission in 1823. See also Benjamin B. Kercheval to McCoy, January 14, 1823, in Isaac McCoy Papers, Kansas State Historical Society, Topeka; L. W. Royse, *A Standard History of Kosciusko County, Indiana*, 1:85 (Chicago and New York, 1919); Account Books, 1802–21, *passim*, Joseph Bailly Papers, Indiana State Library, Indianapolis.

[30] Bertrand, who was associated with the American Fur Company in the 1820s, had a post at what is now Bertrand, Mich., in 1823. Many letters in the American Fur Company Mackinac Letter Book, 1820–25, in Stuart House, Mackinac Island, Mich., express his varying relationships with the firm. See also Augustin C. Rand, S.J., St. Louis, to the editors, June 7, 1971; "Mackinac Register," in *WHC*, 19:83; Otho Winger, *The Potawatomi Indians*, 115–119 (Elgin, Ill., 1939).

[31] From 1822 to 1830 McCoy operated the Carey Mission within present Niles, Mich. See *Guide to the Microfilm Edition of the Isaac McCoy Papers*, 3–5 (Topeka, Kan., 1967); George A. Schultz, *An Indian Canaan: Isaac McCoy and the Vision of an Indian State*, 59–94 (Norman, Okla., 1972); *Michigan State Atlas*, 18 (Rockford, Ill., 1966). Seymour completed a painting of the mission which has not been located; see p. 392, below.

pasture ground, enclosed with a good fence, together with a large field of plowed ground planted with corn, &c. &c.—are among the fruits of his industry and perseverance. But a still stronger proof of his worth was exhibited in the improvement of his Indian pupils. He has now under his charge no less than about 40 pupils, about half of them the children of indian parents and the other half of mixed blood, Indian & French. Of this number 14 are girls, who are taught reading, writing, arithmetic, plain & ornamental needle work, or [k]nitting, & spinning, together with the various business of the kitchen. The residu are boys who are taught in the same branches of education, and during their leisure from study and the requisite amusements are gradually initiated into the art of agriculture. Particular attention is paid to their morals & deportment, and the pupils appear uniformly to conduct themselves with as much decorum and propriety as are usually to be met with in schools of white children of the same age. They appear to be of all ages from 6 or 7 to about 17. Their course of instruction is altogether in the English language, & many of them appear to make very rapid proficiency.[32]

Mrs. [Christiana P.] McCoy is a lady of about 35 years of age, and appears admirably fitted to matronize an establishment of this kind. Her disposition is remarkably mild, her deportment winning, and her attention the most sedulous. She seems to entertain a mothers affection for them all, while they appear to treat her invariably with the respect and love of children. There are two young men [*Thomas C. Wright and Johnston Lykins*] who officiate as subordinate teachers, as also a young lady [*Angeline Wright*], who instructs the girls needle-work &c.[33]

The school is made up of children from the Potawotomies, Miamis, and Otaways [*Ottawa*]. The number is expected to be enlarged as soon as more buildings can be erected for their accommo-

[32] McCoy was visiting the proposed site of the Thomas Mission to the Ottawa Indians, which operated from 1826 to 1836 near Grand Rapids, Mich. See Schultz, *Indian Canaan*, 65; *The Missionary Jubilee: An Account of the Fiftieth Anniversary of the American Baptist Missionary Union*, 467 (Revised ed., New York, 1871). A month after Long's visit, McCoy reported 47 students enrolled at Carey and described the mission's objectives and facilities much as Long did. See McCoy to Lewis Cass, July 1, 1823, McCoy Papers.

[33] Mrs. McCoy also taught, directed the girls' activities, and managed the domestic affairs of the mission. The McCoys were married in 1803. See Schultz, *Indian Canaan*, 8; Emory J. Lyons, *Isaac McCoy: His Plan of and Work for Indian Colonization*, 11, 18 (Fort Hays Kansas State College, *Studies*, no. 9—Topeka, Kan., 1945); Financial Statement, September 9, 1823, and McCoy to Cass, July 1, 1823, McCoy Papers; Nyle Miller, Kansas State Historical Society, to the editors, May 18, 1971.

dation. Timber is already prepared for the construction of as many more as are now built. While every effort is made by those immediately connected with the establishment to advance its interests and utility.

Among the difficulties they have had to encounter, one of the most formidable was that of procuring the requisite supply of provisions, which they have hitherto been under the necessity of transporting by land over bad roads from Kentucky and Ohio. So precarious was this dependence that, sometimes owing to the impracticability of transportation and at others to the losses of provisions accidentally incurred on their passage, they have occasionally been reduced to the last extremities.

In order to guard against future embarrassments of this kind, arrangements are making to procure ample supplies from agriculture at the establishment itself. A field of about 50 acres is to be planted with corn and potatoes. A large stock of cattle is provided for, and 100 sheep are now at the disposal of the institution. The wool of these is to be spun and woven by the girls and is supposed sufficient to clothe the children of the establishment.

For the support of this establishment, government has appropriated $1,000 p[e]r annum to be expended in support of a teacher & black smith. Additional support to a very considerable amount is afforded by the Baptist Missionary and other charitable institutions and casual donations.

It is denominated the Carey Mission station and is exclusively under the management of the Baptist Missionary Society of Washington City. A similar establishment, under the auspices of the same society, is contemplated at the Forks of Grand river of Lake Michigan. Distance 25 miles.[34]

TUESDAY, JUNE 3, 1823. It is contemplated to adopt the Lancast[e]rian mode of education at this establishment as soon as they can render their organization more complete. This mode has been practised by Mr. McCoy at Fort Wayne (where he first commenced

[34] A treaty signed in 1821 authorized the annual payment of $1,000 and a land tract for a mission to the Potawatomi and $1,500 and a land tract for an Ottawa mission on the Grand River. See Charles J. Kappler, ed., *Indian Affairs: Laws and Treaties*, 2:200 (Washington, D.C., 1904); McCoy, *History of Baptist Indian Missions*, 113–115, 145–151. According to the Baptist Mission Board, Minutes, January 18, 1822, McCoy was authorized to draw $3,000 annually, minus contributions received from other sources. A copy of the minutes as well as other items attesting to McCoy's efforts to secure contributions of money, clothing, food, livestock, and tools are in McCoy Papers. On the mission's name, see Schultz, *Indian Canaan*, 64.

the duties of his mission) with much success, and was found peculiarly well adapted to the dispositions and capacities of Indian youths.[35]

At this place we got the shoes of some of our horses refitted by the assistance of the smith of the institution.

The site of the institution had been formerly occupied by a populous village of the Potawotomies, no traces of which now remain except the corn-hills upon the ground then under cultivation.[36] These appearances are both numerous & extensive, covering not less than 1,000 acres of ground now clad in a deep growth of timber and furze. Arrow-points, knives &c. are found distributed over the whole in considerable plenty. According to the statements of the Indians, the village after having dwindled for many years must have been finally abandonned between 50 and 100 years since. Aged squaws recalling to mind the scenes of their youth which they enjoy[ed] here, speak of them with tears and sighs. They point out the particular spots on which the cabins of their parents and kinsmen stood, and recount the scenes of their younger days till utterance is suppress[ed] by the most heart-rending sobs.

We took our leave of this interesting establishment at half past 7 A.M., leaving the good people to whom its management was entrusted with harts as heavy at the separation as they were glad at our arrival. Secluded from civilized society, they are exceedingly happy to receive visits from those with whom they are able to associate and converse.

On our route we entered what is called the 14 mile prairie at the distance of about 9 miles from McCoys and lay by for dinner at the site formerly occupied by the village of the Grand Coit (or Quoit).[37]

[35] The Lancasterian system, developed in England by Joseph Lancaster, used student monitors and emphasized reading, writing, and arithmetic. It was recommended by the federal government for Indian education. McCoy established the Fort Wayne school in 1820, after operating another near Terre Haute, Ind., for a brief period. See John C. Calhoun to William Staughton, American Baptist Board, September 3, 1819, and Circular Letter, August 29, 1821, in Secretary of War, Letters Sent Relating to Indian Affairs, vol. D:318–320, vol. E:151, NARG 75; Paul Monroe, *Founding of the American Public School System*, 363–372 (New York, 1940); Franklin G. Adams, "Rev. Isaac M'Coy," in Kansas State Historical Society, *Transactions*, 2:271 (Topeka, 1881).

[36] The former presence of a Potawatomi village is supported by McCoy, *History of Baptist Indian Missions*, 244; McCoy to Cass, August 22, 1822, July 1, 1823, McCoy Papers.

[37] The 14-mile prairie, usually called Portage Prairie, lies between Buchanan, Mich., and the Kankakee River, Ind. See Albert F. Butler, "Rediscovering Michigan's Prairies," in *Michigan History*, 31:277, 278, 33:120–124 (September, 1947,

Across this prairie is a low marshy tract connecting the St. Joseph's river with the source of the Kankakee. In time of excessive freshets boats have been known to pass and repass between these rivers.[38]

While we were at dinner, the express for Chicago, whom I had directed to wait at Fort Wayne till the next mail should arrive, overtook us, bringing three letters from Mrs. L. and one from Dr. James. By the last we were informed that Dr. J. had arrived at Wheeling two days after our departure from that place, and learning that we had proceeded on our journey, continued his route to Bell[e] Fontaine. Thus we are deprived of all expectation of his being able to join us. The express [*Bemis*] was accompanied by two men, one of whom [*David McKee?*] was on horseback. Thus reenforced we proceeded 15 miles farther & encamped. Dist. 30 m.[39]

WEDNESDAY, JUNE 4, 1823. Started at 1/4 past 5 and travelled 11 miles to Lake Michigan. In this distance we had to cross the rivier de Chemin, or Trail R., twice, which we found no difficulty in fording. The bottoms of this creek are extensive and swampy. Passed two mirey places, in one of which, while attempting to lead my horse thro', I fell into a deep mud-hole and was in danger of being over-

June, 1949). The Indian village may be the one which was a prominent landmark in German Township, St. Joseph County, Ind. See George A. Baker, *The St. Joseph-Kankakee Portage*, 14 (Northern Indiana Historical Society, *Publications*, no. 1—South Bend, Ind., 1899). In the 18th century a Grand Coit (whose name variations include Couette, Quoete, and Quet) was a chief of the Piankashaw, a tribe that at one time lived in the area of the St. Joseph and Wabash rivers. See *American State Papers: Indian Affairs*, 1:338; H. W. Beckwith, ed., "Letters from Canadian Archives," in Illinois State Historical Library, *Collections*, 1:396 (Springfield, 1903); Hodge, *Handbook*, 2:240.

[38] The St. Joseph-Kankakee Portage was known and used by white men from the days of French exploration. On its location, see Baker, *St. Joseph-Kankakee Portage*, 10–21, [49]; Tanner, *New American Atlas*, map 11. Lt. James S. Swearingen, who passed that way in 1803, remarked that "In the spring there is no portage, the two waters connect." See his journal in Quaife, *Chicago and the Old Northwest*, 375.

[39] The second man may have been McKee, who was on his way from Cincinnati to Chicago, where he was to join the Indian agency as a blacksmith. See John Wentworth, *Early Chicago*, 22, and "Obituary: David McKee," 155, in *Fergus' Historical Series*, nos. 7, 14 (Chicago, 1876, 1881).

From Bertrand, Long's party apparently followed the usual express route between Fort Dearborn and Detroit. Originally known as the Great Sauk Trail connecting the Mississippi River and the Detroit area, the route was later adopted for a stage road. It ran on a diagonal southwest from Bertrand to present La Porte, Ind., then northwest to Michigan City, Ind. (present U.S. 35), and along the beaches of Lake Michigan to Chicago. The literature on the trail is extensive. See Milo M. Quaife, *Chicago's Highways Old and New*, 38–41 (Chicago, 1923); Works Projects Administration, *Calumet Region Historical Guide*, 71–73 ([Gary, Ind.], 1939). The route can be traced in Tanner, *New American Atlas*, map 11.

run by my horse. Fortunately, no other damage was sustained than that of getting myself covered with mud from head to foot and having my gun immersed in the same element. In the other, one of our horses sunk in the mir[e] and we were compelled to help him out. Struck the Lake immediately at the mouth of Trail Creek.[40]

After striking the Lake, we travelled along its beach about 21 miles and encamped at the mouth of the Grand Calamick [*Calumet*] river, which enters at the southerly extremity of the Lake. Immediately back of the beach are huge sand hills, formed no doubt by sand drifted by the wind from the Lake shore. These are sometimes naked but more generally covered by a scrubby growth of white pine & furze. In rear of the hills spreads a level country supporting a scattering growth of white pine, oak, Beach, Hop-hornbeam, &c. Dist. 32 m.[41]

THURSDAY, JUNE 5, 1823. Last evening (June 4) Mr. Calhoun and myself attempted observations for Lat., but found it very difficult to ascertain the altitudes of the stars [*Arcturus and the last star in the tail of Ursa Majoris*] on account [of] a mist that hung over the Lake and some clouds that streached along the distant horizon. The observations were as follows. . . . [*Observations omitted.*]

Started a little before 5 and travelled 16 miles to the mouth of New River, where we lay by to rest and let our horses graze.[42] In this distance the horse, which we brot. with us from Philadelphia and which had been for some time disordered with the distemper,

[40] Keating, *Narrative*, 1:157, wrote that the party followed the Trail Creek Valley in northwestern La Porte County, Ind., to Lake Michigan. The mouth of Trail Creek is within present Michigan City, Ind. On the stream's name, see Jacob P. Dunn, *True Indian Stories with Glossary of Indiana Indian Names*, 308 (Indianapolis, 1909). On the beach trails of this area, see Armanis F. Knotts, "Indian Trails, Towns and Mounds In Lake County," in John O. Bowers, Arthur G. Taylor, and Sam B. Woods, eds., *History of Lake County*, 90–95 (Lake County Historical Association, *Publications*, vol. 10—Gary, Ind., 1929); Powell A. Moore, *The Calumet Region: Indiana's Last Frontier*, 53–58 (*Indiana Historical Collections*, vol. 39—[Indianapolis], 1959).

[41] The Calumet region has been greatly altered by industrial development, and the river's course was reversed at least as early as 1845. The mouth of the Grand Calumet has receded to a lagoon in what is now Marquette Park, Gary, Ind. On the evolution of the name of Calumet River, map sources, and the dune area, see Virgil J. Vogel, *Indian Place Names in Illinois*, 17 (Illinois State Historical Society, *Pamphlet Series*, no. 4—[Springfield], 1963); Moore, *Calumet Region*, 1–3, 9–14, 16–21; Works Projects Administration, *Calumet Region Guide*, 8–10, 69–71, 129–135, 186, 248.

[42] Keating, *Narrative*, 1:159, recorded that the party, seeking shelter from a strong wind, left the beach and went inland to the prairie. The mileages and Long's map place New River near the Indiana-Illinois border at the southeast edge of present-day Chicago, suggesting that the stream may have been a new outlet of Wolf Lake.

failed and was no longer able to keep up with the party without either load or rider. It was accordingly thought best to leave him at the mouth of New River. Bearing of the mouth of Trail river from that of New River, as found by observation, S 85° E.

Proceeded 3 miles farther and crossed the Little Calamick [*Calumet*] (or Conomeconse) r. on the mouth of which the boundary line between the States of Indiana & Illinois strikes the Lake. This river not being fordable, we crossed our baggage in a canoe and caused our horses to swim.[43]

Passed thro' the field of action where the Massacre of Chicago took place. Arrived at Fort Dearborn, Chicago, at half past 3 P.M. at which place additional arrangements were to be made for the prosecution of our journey. Dist. 32 m.[44]

FRIDAY, JUNE 6, 1823. Last evening at half past 11 o'clock (May [*June*] 5) observed Doub. Mer. Alt. of Arcturus was 43° 15′ Index Error −4′. Observation probably a little too late.

Observations (at Chicago) for ascertaining Error of Watch. . . . [*Observations for June 5 and 7, 1823, omitted.*]

MONDAY, JUNE 9, 1823. Cloudy and unfit for Observations. . . . [*Observations for June 10, 1823, omitted.*]

WEDNESDAY, JUNE 11, 1823. Having procured four horses as substitutes for the same number, which had been over-done on our Journey, hired a Frenchman by the name of [Joseph St. Peter] Le Sellier to accompany us to Prairie du Chien [Wis.] in the capacity of guide and interpreter, we took leave of our friends at Chicago at 9 A.M. For an account of our enquiries and the intelligence obtained at Chicago, also of a trip to the River de Pleins [*Des Plaines*] (Maple R.), See notes of Mrs. Say, Keating, and Calhoun. Our number now consisted of eight persons supplied with nine horses. One private

[43] The nature and course of the Little Calumet River have been altered by man. What used to be its mouth became an outlet from Lake Michigan near Calumet Harbor in South Chicago, about a mile northwest of the Indiana-Illinois boundary. See Moore, *Calumet Region*, 10, 13.

[44] The massacre took place on August 15, 1812, when soldiers and civilians evacuating Fort Dearborn were attacked by the Potawatomi who were escorting them. See H. A. Musham, "Where Did the Battle of Chicago Take Place?" in *Journal of the Illinois State Historical Society*, 36:21 (March, 1943). On Fort Dearborn, established in 1803, burned by the Indians in the 1812 battle, and rebuilt in 1816, see Francis P. Prucha, *A Guide to the Military Posts of the United States 1789–1895*, 71 (Madison, Wis., 1964).

from the troops at Chicago had been added to our party—his name Bemus [*Bemis*].[45]

Travelled 10 miles (Course S 80° W, 9 m.) to the river des Plein, which we forded with some difficulty, the water taking our horses nearly to their backs. Immediately after crossing the river a shower commenced and we encamped for dinner. Two indians with two lads, the sons of one of them, visited us from their village situated a short distance above us on the river. They were Potawatomies.[46]

Travelled 7 miles farther (N 80° W, 6 m.) and encamped on the river du Page, which enters the Illinois about 1/2 mile below [*above*] the mouth of the Des Pleins.[47] On overhalling our baggage, we found some of it wet, but no serious injury was done, tho' we were apprehensive of it. Distance 17 miles.

THURSDAY, JUNE 12, 1823. The flat tract of country in which

[45] On Le Sellier, a fur trader who lived at various posts on the Rock River, see Voucher No. 26, in "Abstract," Appendix 2, below; William D. Barge, *Early Lee County*, 1–10 (Chicago, 1918); Frank E. Stevens, "Pierre La Sallier: Lee County's First White Settler," in *Journal of the Illinois State Historical Society*, 30:345–352 (October, 1937).

The trip to the Des Plaines was made on June 7. For this and the notes on Chicago, see Keating, *Narrative*, 1:162–171. Say's notes were incorporated by Keating on p. 169. In addition to Bemis, the other seven persons in the party were: Long, Keating, Say, Seymour, Colhoun, Le Sellier, and Allison. The Des Plaines was so named by the French from the maples on its banks, according to Vogel, *Indian Place Names*, 29; Henry Gannett, *The Origin of Certain Place Names in the United States*, 93 (United States Geological Survey, *Bulletins*, no. 197—Washington, D.C., 1902).

[46] In recording the expedition's courses and distances, Long often abbreviated or omitted the word "miles." These are more clearly recorded on the numerous sketch maps in his manuscript journal which have been omitted here.

Tucker and Temple, *Indian Villages of the Illinois Country*, 146, theorized that the Des Plaines crossing was made at the Riverside ford. An Indian village near there is shown on a map of "Indian Trails and Villages of Chicago," compiled by Albert F. Scharf ([Chicago], 1900) and reproduced in Quaife, *Chicago's Highways*, facing p. 237. Keating, *Narrative*, 1:173, indicated that the party crossed the Des Plaines about four miles above the Chicago portage road; if Keating's mileage is correct, the party may have been north of Riverside, perhaps following the Lake Street Trail (Ill. 64) due west through what is now Chicago to St. Charles. See Dena E. Shapiro, "Indian Tribes and Trails of the Chicago Region," 52–55, 91, master's thesis, University of Chicago, 1929. On Long's 1816 explorations of the Des Plaines, see p. 7, above.

[47] Assuming progression in the northwesterly direction shown on his maps, Long could have crossed Salt Creek and missed the Du Page, traveling just north of its headwaters more or less along the route of present U.S. 20 to Elgin. Since his mileage figures from Chicago to the Fox River are approximately correct, he may have confused Salt Creek and the Du Page. Long also seems confused in his remark about the Du Page's mouth; both Tanner, *New American Atlas*, map 16, and Long's map in Keating, *Narrative*, vol. 1, show the Du Page flowing into the Des Plaines River a few miles above the latter's mouth, as it does today.

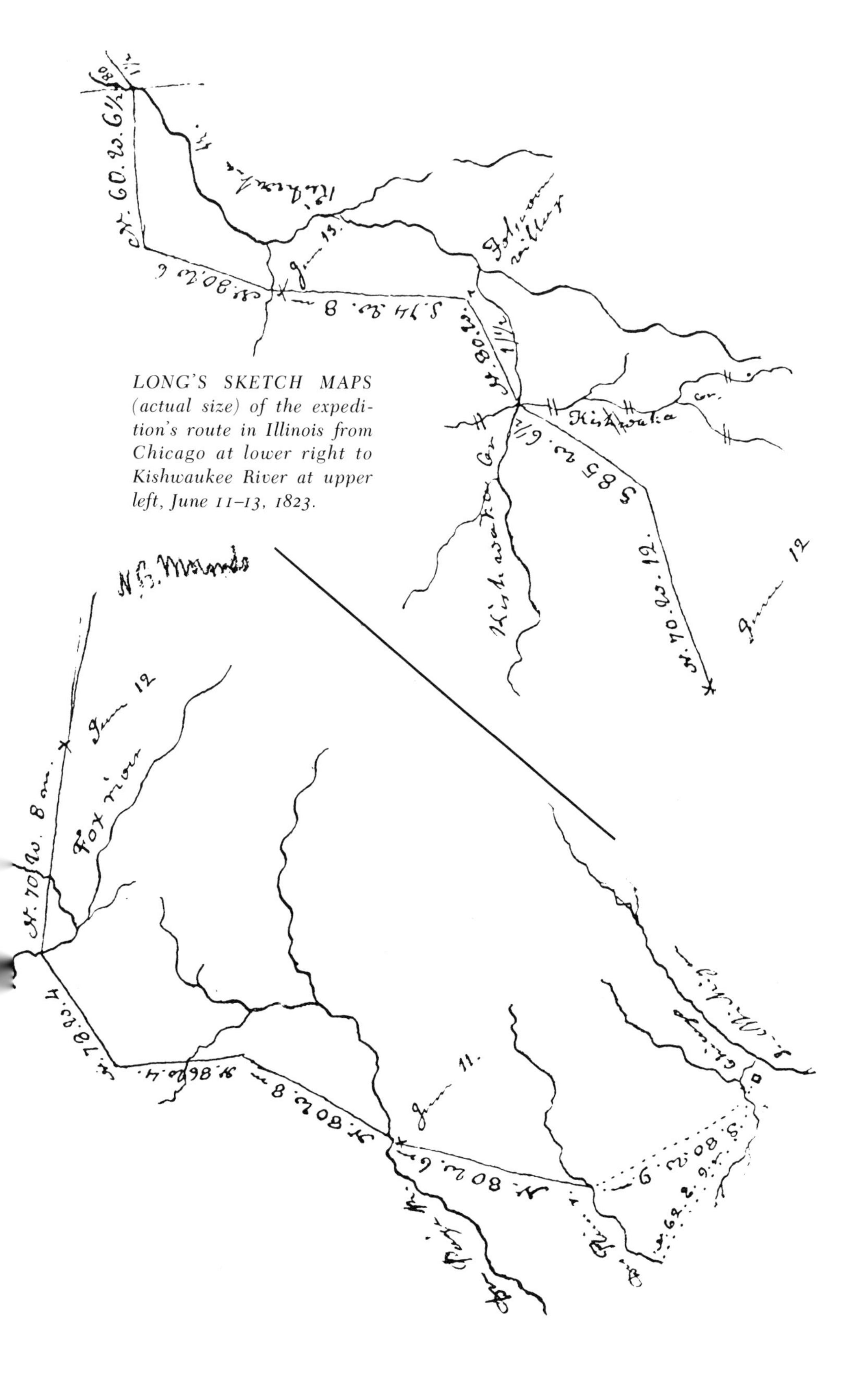

LONG'S SKETCH MAPS (actual size) of the expedition's route in Illinois from Chicago at lower right to Kishwaukee River at upper left, June 11–13, 1823.

Chicago (Pole Cat) is situated extends with scarcily an undulation to the River Des Pleins or Maple river, a distance of 9 miles.[48] The country passed since leaving that river is very similar but possesses a surface somewhat undulating. With the exception of narrow skirts of timber on the margins of water-courses, no woodlands appear. This region appears too flat and moist to be well adapted to cultivation, but the soil is unquestionably rich.

Last evening Mr. Say and Mr. Calhoun were both troubled with headache, also Andrew, the black boy, but all are better this morning.

Started at half past 5. Crossed the du Page near our camp, travelled N 80° W, 8 miles and N 86° W, 4 miles, by our route 13m., and lay by for dinner at half past 9—a shower impending. Crossed Fox river 5 miles from the last encampment. It is about 120 yards wide, shoal and easily fordable. On the west side of the river are situated several works of antiquity, consisting of mounds of a small size 20 to 30 feet in length, about 10 broad and from 3 to 5 high. They are situated upon a rising ground about 250 yards from the river. We counted no less than twenty six of them, evidently the work of an[cien]t[s].[49]

Encamped at half past 4 in order to dry our baggage, which had got considerably [wet in] a shower that happened this after noon. Courses P.M. N 78° W, 4 [miles], N 70° W, 8 miles. Distance by our route to-day 26 m.

FRIDAY, JUNE 13, 1823. Started a little after 5. Country swampy for 12 miles, afterwards more elevated. Not more than 1/16 woodland. Cours[es] N 70° W, 12 [miles] and S 85° W, 6 1/2 m., by our route 20 m. Encamped for dinner on Kish-wah-ka [*Kishwaukee*] Cr. tributary to Rock-river. Its course northward.

After dinner travelled 1 1/2 m. and came to a village of Mennomonie [*Menominee*] Indians consisting of 4 or 5 bark lodges and situated on the south bank of the Creek just mentioned. Here we delayed half an hour, gave some Tobacco & powder to the[m], and received in return some sugar (Maple) of which we stood in some need, our supply of that article being small. Travelled till 1/2 past 3

[48] The meaning and spelling of "Chicago" have been debated at length. Skunk or polecat, garlic, wild onion, or skunk weed are among the usual explanations. For a summary of the problem, see Vogel, *Indian Place Names*, 23–25; "Origin of the Names of Stations on the line of the Illinois-Central Railroad Company," in William K. Ackerman, *Early Illinois Railroads*, 109–115 (*Fergus' Historical Series*, no. 23—Chicago, 1884).

[49] Keating, *Narrative*, 1:174, 176, offered slightly different figures on the width of the Fox River and the number of mounds.

P.M. and encamped for the night. Courses P.M. N 80° W, 1 1/2 [miles], and S 74° W, 8 m. By our route to day 32 miles.[50]

SATURDAY, JUNE 14, 1823. Having experienced a slight attack of fever yesterday, I took a cathartic at the time of our encamping which proved efficatious in restoring my health. Started at 5 A.M. Travelled N 80° W, 6 miles & N 60° W, 6 1/2 miles, where we arrived at a small Ind. Village on the north bank of Kishwaka riv. which we crossed again at the village.[51]

The village consists of 7 Lodges—is called Kishwaka vil. and is inhabited by Potawatomies and others. We here made arrangement with the Indians to aid us in crossing Rock-river, & a boy was according dispached to a village situated some distance above the Ford in quest of a canoe. On our arrival at the river, which is at the distance of 1 1/2 miles from the Kishwaka village, the boy arrived with a small canoe in which we crossed our baggage and the party and encamped on the north side for dinner. Rock river is called in the indian Language, Sini-ce-pe, which is of the same import as its name in english.[52] It is about 1 hundred yards wide and at this time too deep for horses to ford, but in a moderate stage of water may be forded without difficulty. Course from the village to the river, N 80° W, 1 1/2 m.

Having crossed the river, we travelled N 78° W, 7 miles, and having an extensive Prairie before us about 15 miles over, we encamped early near wood & water. Distance travelled 23 miles. . . . [*Observations of the sun and moon omitted.*] The foregoing observations were taken at the place of our evening encampment.

SUNDAY, JUNE 15, 1823. Started a little before 5, travelled N 87° W, 9 [miles] & N 83° W, 9 miles thro Prairie. No Wood land on our route.

[50] Keating, *Narrative*, 1:178, identified this Menominee village as "Wakesa" and the chief as "Kakakesha" (Crow). Although the discrepancies in mileages given by Keating and Long make correlation hazardous, the village may be the "Wahkesah" shown in Tanner, *New American Atlas*, map 16, located on the Sycamore, an alternate name for the Kishwaukee River. Long's probable route across Illinois is also shown on this map. See Vogel, *Indian Place Names*, 54.

[51] Kishwaukee village was probably located southeast of present Rockford, Ill., near the ford of the Rock River just above the mouth of the Kishwaukee River. Keating, *Narrative*, 1:180, 181; Way, ed., *Rock River Valley*, 1:118; Jipson, in *Wisconsin Archeologist*, new series 2:134.

[52] Long is correct, although the more usual spelling is "Sinissippi" or "Sinnissippi." See Charles A. Church, ed., *History of Winnebago County*, 628 (Newton Bateman and Paul Selby, eds., *Historical Encyclopedia of Illinois*, vol. 2—Chicago, 1916); Vogel, *Indian Place Names*, 138.

Land roolling and possessed of a good soil. Lime-stone occasionally appears *in place*. Encamped for dinner on a handsome Creek called Little Peck-ta-no [*Pecatonica*], or Lit[tle] Muddy River. It enters the Peck-ta-no a short distance from where we crossed it. The latter is one of the most considerable tributaries of Rock-river, and receives a considerable stream from the north 6 miles above its mouth called Sugar river.[53]

Our way lead us within the view of the valley of the Peck-ca-no [*Pecatonica R.*], which appeared to possess a good soil and in places was well-wooded. It may be remarked that the name given by the Indians to this river is of the same import with that given to the Missouri—and in the Sauke [*Sauk*] Langu[a]ge is the same name.

At our mid-day encampment I was attacked again with a fever, which raged so violently that we were under the necessity of remaining encamped for three hours. During this time our guide [*Le Sellier*] proceeded forward two miles to an indian-village situate on the river Peck-ca-no for the purpose of hiring and [*an*] additional guide. We were visited by several Indians at our camp, and on arriving at their village I asked for some Lye Homony which I saw cooking, having had no appetite for my dinner. We engaged the brother of the Chief of the village [*Wanebea*] as our guide and proceeded 4 miles farther and encamped on the Peck-ca-no for the night, where we were again visited by the Indians, whom on this occasion we found unwellcome guests. They had no provisions at home and out of our scanty supply We could ill afford to part with any. Encamped at 3 o'clock. Course P.M. N 83° W, 6 miles. Distance by our route 25 miles.[54]

MONDAY, JUNE 16, 1823. Started before 5. Courses N 76° W, 7 m., N 58° W, 5 1/2, and N 60° W, 7 m. We have no longer a trace to

[53] Various spellings and explanations of "Pecatonica" are recorded, including "muddy"—the meaning of "Missouri" to which Long refers below. See Church, ed., *History of Winnebago County*, 628; Vogel, *Indian Place Names*, 107; Keating, *Narrative*, 1:187.

[54] Keating, *Narrative*, 1:188, 190, stated that the Sauk chief of the village was "Wabetejec" or White Cedar and that the guide's name was "Wanebea," "Wennebea," or Spinning Top. A sketch of the latter appears in Keating, *Narrative*, plate 3. Long's mileage, however, puts him near present-day Freeport, Ill., where the usual village described is that of the Winnebago chief Winneshiek, whose name is not usually translated as "white cedar." See Edward L. Burchard, "Early Trails and Tides of Travel in the Lead Mine and Blackhawk Country," in *Journal of the Illinois State Historical Society*, 17:579, 582 (January, 1925); Jipson, in *Wisconsin Archeologist*, new series 2:132; Tanner, *New American Atlas*, map 16.

pursue, but follow our Indian guide who appears to have a good knowledge of the country. Our way leads thro' prairies skirted in the distant horizon with wood lands. The surface becomes more undulating or rolling as we proceed northward.

Encamped for dinner at the head of a small creek tributary, as we suppose, to the Mississippi.

Afternoon we travelled N 38° W, 4 m. and N 55° W, 3 1/2 miles and encamped on a small creek called Wa-Was-Se-mo Cr., or Ceepo, after the name of an Indian Chief formerly resident on the Creek. Wawassemo in the Sauke Lang. implies Lightning, which was the Chief's name. Our journey to day lay thro' a single prairie in which we approached no wood land execep[t] a small point at the place of our mid-day encampment. Our way lay along the dividing grounds between the Mississippi & Rock River. The stream on which we encamped at evening is tributary to the Peck-ta-no. Distance by the rte. 30 m.[55]

TUESDAY, JUNE 17, 1823. Started before 5. Course N 55° W, 16 1/2 miles—by the route 19. Country more undulating. Passed the source of the Fever [*Galena*] River on our left. At no great distance from the Mississippi Lead mines have been found on this river. They are included in the region denominated Dubuque's Lead Mine. At the distance of about a mile on this side of our camp of last night had a distant view of the Smoky Mountain [*Blue Mounds, Wis.*], which bore N 12° E about 30 miles dist. Twelve miles from the same camp saw Dubuque's hill, bearing S 45° W, Dist. about 20 miles. The Land Mark by which we have travelled to-day is two hills [*Belmont and Platte mounds*] of considerable elevation standing insulated in the Prairie to which the Indians give the name of Enne-shot-te-no, or the two hills. They are situated at the distance of 1 1/4 miles assunder, bearing from each other E & W. One of our horses failed to-day thro' fatigue of the journey, and it was with much difficulty that we were able to urge her on the way without a load. Courses P.M. N 55° W, 3 miles to the two hills, No. 40° W, 5

[55] The expedition was at this time passing through present Lafayette County, Wis., and the creek in question may be Ames Brook near Darlington or Wolf Creek at Gratiot. Although there was a Piankashaw chief named Lightning, a Winnebago named Coming Lightning, and a Potawatomi called Gibos or Gebo, no village bearing the names recorded by Long has been found. On the chiefs, see Kappler, ed., *Indian Affairs*, 2:73; Jipson, in *Wisconsin Archeologist*, new series 2:128; Maj. John Whistler to Lewis Cass, April 22, 1815, OIA, Michigan Superintendency, Letters Received and Sent, 1:54, NARG 75.

1/2, and N 60° W, 1 1/2 miles to a small Cr. on which we encamped for the night at 5 P.M. Distance by our route 29 miles.[56]

WEDNESDAY, JUNE 18, 1823. The country traversed for a few days past is of a very rolling aspect. Wood lands seldom appear, and never in greater proportion to the Prairies than as 1 to 40 or 50. Whenever they present them selves their growth consists principally of scrubby oaks and poplar. The soil in many places appears of a pretty good quality. Lime stone of a pretty good quality prevails, streams of pure water are frequent tho' not copious, and in all probability at some future period not far distant, this region will be populated by an agricultural people who will enjoy plenty as the reward of their industry. That part of the country thro' which we have passed since the 13th inst. exhibits sym[p]toms of its relationship to the lead mine region of the Mississippi. The stones are of a similar character and a similar conformation of surface generally prevails.

Started a little before 5. As we approach the Wisconsan [River], the country becomes more hilly and in some places broken. Precipices of Lime and Sand stone occasionally present themselves along the creeks. Pines appear upon some of the hills. Crossed a small creek called She-quak—or Pine Creek. Courses N 75° W, 2 [miles], W 1 1/2, N 75° W, 7 1/2 and N 80° W, 2. Encamped for dinner on a small branch of She-quak cr.[57]

After dinner our courses were as follow[s]: 80° W, 6 [miles], S 75° W, 5 1/2, N 40° W, 1 mile. We encamped on a small Cr. at an early hour, 1/2 past 4, on account of a storm approaching. The country we have travelled this afternoon is beautifully variegated with hills & valleys and checkered with lawns and woodlands. The soil is of an indifferent quality. Lime & sand stone frequently occur in horizontal strata. The growth of the wood lands is principally scrubby oak and poplar with som[e] maple, Elm and hiccory. Dist. 27 mil[e]s.

[56] Belmont and Platte mounds are near present Leslie in Lafayette County, Wis. See also Keating, *Narrative*, 1:193, 202, 212.

[57] Long's published map in Keating, *Narrative*, shows Shequak or Pine Creek as tributary to the Mississippi; it was probably the present Platte or Little Platte River. On the name, see Herbert W. Kuhm, "Indian Place-Names in Wisconsin," in *Wisconsin Archeologist*, new series 33:15, 113 (March, June, 1952). Keating, *Narrative*, 1:212, remarked that the creek below on which the party camped for the night was tributary to the Wisconsin River; it may have been Fennimore Fork of Blue River in Grant County, Wis.

THURSDAY, JUNE 19, 1823. The storm of last evening terminated in wind with out rain. The musquetoes were extremely troublesome as usual. Our horses this morning had strayed a considerable distance from our Camp. Started a little before 5. Courses N 80° W, 2 1/2 [miles]—N 35° W, 1 m. and N 60° W, 2 1/2, where we struck the Wisconsan, and down the river S 40° W, 1 1/2 to a place where we concluded to cross the river. On arriving at this point, we dispatched an express [*Bemis*] across the river on a small raft constructed for his use to the Comdg. Officer of Fort Crawford with a note requesting him to send us a boat and men to aid us in crossing the river.[58]

The Wisconsan, like the Ohio, appears to approach the Mississippi thro' a hilly country, the surface being cut by numerous ravines. Crossd a small Creek tributary to the Wisconsan—called the Eske-po-ka-po-wuck or Blue [*Big Green R.*] Creek. The hills rise to the height of 150 to 200 feet. The country appears possessed of an indifferent soil. Numerous small creeks make their appearance. Lime stone in horizontal strata, surmounted by a fine grained sand-stone in horizontal strata, frequently presents itself along the declivites of the hills. Distance A.M. 9 miles.

Our Interpreter Le-Selier was Interpreter at Waynes treaty.[59]

Our Indian guide [*Wanebea*] proved well acquainted with the country and was able to conduct us by a very direct and practicable route with out regarding the trace usually pursued on this part of our journey. But it was manifest that he was guided by noted landmarks at considerable distances from each other, rather than by any extraordinary sagacity as is usually attributed to the Indians. For in cloudy weather he frequently varied his course when out of sight of his Land-mark, but immediately rectified his mistake on seeing it.

He was affable and communicative without being loquacious. The following is a brief summary of the intelligence he gave us.

A good Indian will provide well for his family — he will be hospi-

[58] Long's text here and below indicates that the party struck the south bank of the Wisconsin River above the mouth of Big Green (not the Blue) River. From this point to Prairie du Chien his maps show only 11 1/2 miles; Keating, *Narrative*, 1:212, 213, gives this distance as 15 miles. The present Blue River is over 30 miles from Prairie du Chien and cannot be Long's "Blue Creek." For Long's route, see John Farmer, "Map of the Territories of Michigan and Ouisconsin" (Detroit, 1830); Scanlan, "Map of 1821 Borough of Prairie du Chien," in Scanlan Papers.

[59] "Wayne's Treaty" probably refers to the Treaty of Greenville, made on August 3, 1795, by Anthony Wayne. Le Sellier's name is not among the interpreters; see Kappler, ed., *Indian Affairs*, 2:45.

table and kind to strangers. He will treat the young men of his nation with kindness and hospitality. He will seldom be intoxicated. He will be kind, obliging and good humoured to his wives and children. He will provide amply for all their wants. He will never be guilty of fornication before marriage, nor adultery afterwards. He will never yield his wives or daughters to the embrace of other men. He will never be guilty of sodomy, buggery, incest, murder, or theft. While the bad man is characterized by qualities directly opposite.

The good woman must be chaste and virtuous—true to her husband and careful and diligent in family concerns. She will love & cherish her children and respect and obey her husband. She will never submit to the embrace of a man before marriage and only to that of her husband afterwards.

The duties of the man consist in hunting, tending their horses, making canoes, bows, arrows, and occupations which require strength, such as the hewing of timber, constructing of wigwams &c. &c.—while those of the women enbrace all kinds of domestic drudgery, dressing and cooking of meat, cultivation of corn, dressing of skins, collecting fuel, &c. in some of which the men occasionally participate, not from a sense of duty but from a disposition to oblige.

At 6 P.M. [Willoughby] Morgan and Lt. [Martin] Scott with two boats well manned arrived for the purpose of aiding us in crossing the river.[60] After partaking of a bottle of wine which the Col. brought with him for our refreshment, we embarked our baggage on board of one of the boats and employed the other in swimming our horses across the river. It was sunset when we were ready to resume our march to Prairie du Chien. Col. M. & Lt. S. accompanied us mounted on two of our horses, and we arrived at Fort Crawford at half past 10 P.M. Course S 78 W, Dist. 10 miles, whole distance travelled to day 19 miles.

WEDNESDAY, JUNE 25, 1823. We were delayed at Prairie du Chein till this morning. During our delay the several gentlemen of the party were employ[ed] in their appropriate pursuits. A variety of astronomical observations were taken by Mr. Calhoun for determining the Lat. Lon. & Mag[netic] Var[iation], a record of which is here subjoined viz. . . . [*Observations omitted.*]

[60] Morgan commanded Fort Crawford intermittently from 1816 until 1832; Heitman, *Historical Register*, 1:726; Mahan, *Old Fort Crawford*, 72. On Scott, see Introduction, note 50.

At the requisition of Maj. L. a detachment, consisting of one non commissioned officer and nine privates under the command of Lt. Scott, was detailed to accompany the Expedition.[61] Two horses were furnished in place of two others that we had bro't with us from Wheeling, these having been rendered unfit for immediate service by the fatigue of our late journey. A Mackinaw boat was also furnished for the transportation of our baggage and several of our party up the [Mississippi] river.

Having made additional arrangements for the journey before us, we took our leave of the Fort this morning at half past nine, crossing our horses and baggage in a large flat or scow, while the gentlemen of the Expedition embarked on board of the Mackinaw boat. We all ascended the Mississippi about 3 miles to the mouth of Yellow river, up which we had to ascend 1 1/2 miles in order to find a landing for our horses. Here the party separated into two detachments, one consisting of Maj. L., Mr. Calhoun, two soldiers [*George Bunker and John Wade*], one Sioux indian [*Tommo or Tamaha*] employed as a guide, and our black-boy [*Allison*], supplied with eight horse, to cross the country to the mouth of the St. Peters—the other consisting of Mrs. Say, Keating and Seymour, accompanied by Mr. [Augustin] Ro[c]que, a metif [*métis*] of French & Sioux origin as interpreter of the Sioux Language, together with Lt. Scott and his men to ascend the Mississippi to the same place. Our separation took place at 1/4 before 12 at noon, and both partyes proceeded on their journey.[62] Courses A.M. N 28° W, 3 [miles], N 50° W, 5 1/2, and

[61] AGO, Fort Crawford Post Returns, June, 1823, NARG 94, show one corporal and six privates from Company G, and one musician (the interpreter John Wade) and three privates from Company K on command with Long. The names of the men from Company G were Corp. Joshua Sanders, Pvts. Loamiah Butterfield, Solomon Balsom, Samuel Ripley, James Wilcox, George Bunker, and George Shields. The names of the privates from Company K have not been found. See AGO, Inspection Returns, Fifth Infantry, Companies G and K, Fort Crawford, June, 1823, NARG 94. Bemis left the party at Prairie du Chien.

[62] For an account of the water party's trip and on Bunker and Wade, see Keating, *Narrative*, 1:246, 250, 264–294, 397. For Colhoun's journal, see Chapters 7 and 8, below. George Bunker, an 18-year-old private who had enlisted at Prairie du Chien only two months before Long arrived, and John Wade, a 16-year-old musician, are listed in AGO, Inspection Returns, Fifth Infantry, Company G, Fort Crawford, October, 1824; and AGO, Registers of Enlistments, 1815–28, 35:59, 36:17—both in NARG 94. Tommo, characterized in Keating, *Narrative*, 1:246, 263, and p. 280, below, may have been Tamaha, a Mdewakanton. See Lafayette H. Bunnell, *Winona (We-No-Nah) and Its Environs on the Mississippi in Ancient and Modern Days*, 143, 148 (Winona, 1897); Hodge, *Handbook*, 2:680. On Rocque, who accompanied Long in 1817, see Chapter 1, note 2, above; Voucher No. 27, in "Abstract," Appendix 2, below; Keating, *Narrative*, 1:245. Long had visited this area in 1817; see Chapter 1.

we stopped to dine on the Painted Rock Cr. [*Paint Creek, Ia.*], which we found so miry as to be fordable with difficulty. After dinner we proceeded N 35° W, 10 miles and encamped a little after sun-set.

The country very rolling and elevated, the soil apparently between 2nd & 3rd rates. Much woodland appears at some distance both on our right and left, growth rather stinted in some places—consists of Hiccory, Hackberry, Ash, Post & white oak, white walnut, Sugar tree, Maple &c. Distance by our route 20 m.

THURSDAY, JUNE 26, 1823. On searching for our horses this morning we ascertained that they had gone back on the trace, and we were compelled to pursue them at least eight miles before we overtook them. This delayed us till 9 o'clock, when we resumed our march. The country is so much variegated with abrupt hills and deep vallies that we find it impracticable to maintain a direct course.

In our progress we are continually winding our way thro some deep ravine or along the declivity of a towering eminence. The scenery is often picturesque in a very high degree. Hills rising to the height of 5 or 6 hundred feet, and occasionally presenting precipices of stupendous hieght—knobs of various elevation with summits beautifully rounded and clad in a rich coat of verdure—conical peaks rising like a pyramid from the vally and vieing in altitude with the hig[h]est hills, and the valleys of water-courses sunk far below the general surface covered with a rich carpet of grass and flowers, and exhibiting their crystal streams meandering in graceful folds conspire to give both beauty and majesty to the landscape.

Crossed the Upper Ioway [*Iowa*] riv. about 4 miles above its mouth at a small village of Sioux (Dacota) Indians. It is about 25 yds. wide and is easily fordable at the present time. Encamped a little before sunset at a copious spring of excellent water. Dist. 23 miles.[63]

FRIDAY, JUNE 27, 1823. A violent thunder shower commenced early this morning and continued until near 7 o'clock. We were in consequence delayed until 8 o clo[c]k, when we resumed our march. Near our encampment were two very copious springs of fine water, their streams uniting formed a creek of considerable magnitude tributary to Upper Ioway riv.

Travelled over elevated prairies presenting numerous knobs

[63] On the Dakota village, see p. 53, above. The spring-fed stream, below, may have been either French Creek or Clear Creek in Allamakee County, Ia. The expedition was nearing the present Iowa-Minnesota border.

completely insulated and exhibiting perpendicular precipices of horizontal Sand stone. At 1 P.M. were overtaken by a shower and encamped for dinner. After dinner we had to wind our way thro' woody vallies, crossing creeks at short intervals, some of which were of a respectable size, particularly one which we suppose to be the same as that called Rood [*Root*] river. Encamped a little after sun set. Dist. 31 miles.

SATURDAY, JUNE 28, 1823. Our Indian guide [*Tommo*] last evening killed 3 ducks which afforded us a very agreeable repast for breakfast this morning. Started about 5 and crossed the Hokah or Root riv. about 1/2 a mile from our camp.[64]

Our way lay thro' vallies for the distance of 10 miles, after which we ascended the high lands. The soil of the vallies is light and loamy, that of the high lands somewhat similar tho' not so rich. The growth of the former consists of Oak, sugar tree, hiccory, black-walnut, ash, elm, hop-hornbeam, Linden, &c. together with an undergrowth of grape-vine, pea-vine, prickly ash, Snakeroot, &c. and that of the latter of scrubby oak, aspen, and some pine. Our pack horse in crossing a muddy creek got mired, and we were detained a considerable time in extricating him—not being able to find water we continued our morning ride till near two P.M.

Resumed our march again after a short delay and travelled down a beautiful valley bounded on both sides by high bluffs and precipices. It terminated in the broad valley of the Mississippi, where we ent[e]red on an extensive plain limited by that majestic river on one hand and by stupendous bluffs, on the other. In front appeared Wabasha's village, towards which we were directing our course. On arriving at the village, the enchantment of the scene vanished. We were assailed by a host of yelping dogs that were attended by their masters and a throng of children, which occasioned so great an annoyance that we were glad to take our leave with as little delay as possible. We visited the chief, Wabasha, (the leaf) but for want of a suitable interpreter could hold but very little conversation with him.[65]

We tryed to procure a small supply of corn and meat, but none was to be had. After delaying half an hour we proceeded up the

[64] *Hokah* is the Dakota word for root, according to Upham, *Minnesota Geographic Names*, 12. On the crossing, see Keating, *Narrative*, 1:247.

[65] The "beautiful valley" may have been Gilmore Valley in Winona County, Minn. On the Dakota chief, Wabasha, see Chapter 1, note 21, above; Keating, *Narrative*, 1:249, 272, 385.

Mississippi about 2 miles and encamped on its margin. Distance 32 miles.

SUNDAY, JUNE 29, 1823. Started at 1/4 past 5. Our way lay along the river bottom and at the base of the bluffs. There being no trace that we are able to pursue and our route a rugged one, we are compelled to be content with a slow progress.

Near our encampment of last evening there were several antique mounds of artificial structure arranged in nearly a right line along the margin of the river. The[y] are of inconsiderable hieght but cover a large surface.[66]

A short distance from our camp we crossed a creek of considerable size called in the Sioux Language E-aw-ne-me-ne-maw Cr. or Rolling stone [*Rollingstone*] cr. While we lay encamped for dinner, our boat hove in sight but at too great a distance for us to wait for her arrival. Continued along the river valley, occasionally ascending the bluffs a little in order to find a passage. The travelling very difficult and fatiguing to ourselves & horses. Crossed a creek of considerable size called Me-ne-skah, or white water [*Whitewater R.*], also several others of inconsiderable magnitude.

A little before night we passed thro a beautiful prairie elevated about 75 feet above the bottom lands and presenting a surface almost a dead level. It is about 3 miles long and from 1/2 to 3/4 mile wide. A portion of it, about 3/4 mile long and 1/4 broad, is peculiar for evenness of surface and its being entirely destitute of Bushes and weeds. In this beautiful spot are located numerous indian mounds of high antiquity. This probably is the place alluded to by [Jonathan] Carver as being situated a few miles below Lake Pepin. Encamped at sun-set. Mr. C. took observations for Latitude. Distance 33 miles.[67]

MONDAY, JUNE 30, 1823. Last evening Mr. C. took an altitude of Arctures and of the moon this morning, for the purpose of ascertaining the Lat. Started at half past 5. Crossed a considerable creek called Waz-zee-o-zhu creek [*Zumbro R.*]. It unites with the Me-

[66] Several groups of mounds between Winona and Minnesota City are described in Winchell, *Aborigines*, 87. On Rollingstone Creek and the Whitewater River in the paragraph below, see Upham, *Minnesota Geographic Names*, 583, 584.

[67] Carver, who visited the area in 1766, described an elaborate series of mounds and earthworks he believed to be aboriginal fortifications in his *Travels through the Interior Parts of North America*, 56 (Reprint ed., Minneapolis, 1956). For a review of the nature and location of the supposed works, including Long's contribution to the controversy, see Smith, in *Minnesota History*, 16: 152–165.

nes-kah near the Mississippi and forms what has generally been called by the French hunters Embarrass [*Zumbro*] river. On this river we observed a numerous and crowded assemblage of antient tumuli. They were situated on a plain elevated at least 75 feet above the river valley. On an area of a few acres we discovered near a hundred of these structures. They were mostly of an oblong form, raised to the height of 3 to 6 feet, disposed in general without order, but in a few instances arranged in right lines, and in one instance in two parallel rows not more than ten feet asunder.[68]

On arriving in view of Lake Pepin, we halted to take lunar distances which were as follows. . . . [*Observations omitted.*]

Delayed a short time for dinner and resumed our march with the view of reaching the village of Elle-rouge [*Red Wing*] before night. Our way lead us considerably south of the lake (Pepin) along a tract of valley country separated from the lake by a considerable body of insulated high lands, which bound the upper part of the Lake on the South. Reached the village a little before night and encamped a few yards above it. Were visited by the chief and many of the Indians in the evening and amongst these was Wazze-coota, or the shooter from the pine top, who accompanied me in 1817 from Wabasha's village upward to point du Sable [*Sand Point*] of Lake Pepin. Distance 31 mile.[69]

TUESDAY, JULY 1, 1823. Having taken a supply of provisions sufficient only for 6 days, in which time we expected to arrive at Fort St. Anthony, and finding that supply now nearly exhausted while a journey of 3 days was still before us, we were induced to wait the arrival of our boat in order to replenish our stores.

In the morning we were visited again by Wazze coota, the Red-Wing, and several other Indians to whom the object of our journey and the route we purpose to take were explained very much to their satisfaction. On showing them my map of the country, they appeared much struck at the practicability of constructing one in the manner

[68] *Wazi Oju*, meaning "pines planted," was the Dakota name for the present Zumbro River. The French name *Embarrass* is said to have referred to a natural raft of driftwood which obstructed the river's mouth. Upham, *Minnesota Geographic Names*, 210. Long's Meneskah Creek or Whitewater River does not unite with the Zumbro now, but may have done so in his day; see Nicollet, "Hydrographical Basin." Several groups of aboriginal burial mounds in Wabasha County resemble Long's description; see Winchell, *Aborigines*, 136–139.

[69] On Red Wing and Wazecouta, see Chapter 1, notes 22, 30, Chapter 2, note 2, and p. 273, below. Keating, *Narrative*, 1:251, 261, 286, noted that Wazecouta "scarcely recollected" accompanying Long in 1817.

that was done. The[y] accounted it mysterious in a high degree that intelligence could be collected and retained so as to construct a map of so large an extent of country and embracing so many rivers, Lakes and other geographical features. Th[ey] expressed much surprise at witnessing the operations of the Magnetic needle and particularly at the weight and fluidity of mercury, especially when we showed them that iron would float upon it as buoyant as cork on water. To all these things, which appeared mysterious in their conception, they attached the epithet of Manitou, intimating that it was the work of the Great Spirit.

Agreeably to our wishes, the boat arrived about 10 o'clock, after which the party repaired to the Chiefs' lodge, where with considerable formality a conversation took place between us and the elder & younger Red Wing, chiefs of the village, in the presence of their principal men who were assembled on the occasion.[70] The objects of our Expedition were explained to them, friendship mutually declared, the views and wishes of our government in relation to the Indians briefly explained, and on their part professions of attachment and respect for the americans, &c.

The ceremony was prefaced by smoking of which we all partook, after which Maj. L. commenced the conversation by stating as above, and was replied to first by the Elder Red Wing and afterwards his son. The pipe of Peace was then lighted and passed round by an indian deputed for that purpose, who held the pipe in his hand and presented the stem to each individual present and after wards presented the handle of it to Maj. L. as a token of respect to the party. We then took our leave, shaking each of the indians by the hand. In the course of the conversation, we were reminded that a little whiskey would be acceptable, but it was stated in reply that we carried none of that article with us except for the use of the sick, that it never ought to be used but as a medicine, and was never intended to by [*be*] drunk like water, and that we should on no occasion give it to the Indians. This of course put a stop to their importunities.

We then returned to our camp, partook of a dinner, obtained a scanty supply of provision from the boat (of which their stock was

[70] On the Red Wing dynasty, see Chapter 2, note 2; Keating, *Narrative*, 1:251. On the peace-pipe ceremony below, see George A. West, *Tobacco, Pipes and Smoking Customs of the American Indians*, 231–270 (Milwaukee Public Museum, *Bulletins*, vol. 17—Milwaukee, 1934); pp. 274, 280, below.

very limited), again took our leave of our companions on board, and resumed our march at 2 P.M.

Crossed a small creek, also another of considerable magnitude called Ea-mo-sin-da-tu or Big stone Cr. [*Cannon R.*]. We left the valley of the Mississippi for the purpose of prosecuting our journey on the high lands. Crossed several small plains on which are to be seen antient tumuli more numerous than I ever before witnessed. Travelled till near 6 P.M. and encamped. Dist. 14 m.[71]

WEDNESDAY, JULY 2, 1823. Started at 20 minutes before 5. A thunder storm soon commenced and continued till 9 A.M. Travelled over a rooling country, sandy in many places and destitute of a timber growth excep[t] such as was of a dwarfish character. The country less elevated than we have usually found it this side of Prairie du Chien. Crossed a considerable Creek called by the Sioux name ochth-pi-ta, or rapid water creek [*Vermillion* R.].[72] Encamped for dinner near a small pond surrounded by a quag mire so soft that our horses could not approach it. Distance by our route before dinner 21 miles. Travelled 7 miles after dinner and arrived at Fort St. Anthony at 1/2 past 3 P.M. Dist. 28 m.

[71] On the Cannon River's name, see p. 278, below. Winchell, *Aborigines*, 150, identified a group of 173 mounds along the Cannon in T113N, R15W, Sec. 29, 30, as those referred to by Long.

[72] On p. 281, below, Colhoun rendered the Vermillion's name "Hethpoita" and also translated it as rapid current. According to Raymond J. De Mallie, Indiana University, to the editors, June 1, 1977, it is impossible to identify the Dakota word these renderings derived from. The Dakota for "rapid water creek" would contain *kadusya*, swiftly flowing, and *watpa*, stream. For a discussion of later names for the Vermillion, see Upham, *Minnesota Geographic Names*, 169.

4. Exploring the Minnesota and Red Rivers

JULY 3 THROUGH AUGUST 15, 1823

JULY 3–8, 1823. In the summer of 1816 [*1817*] I ascended the Mississippi by order of Gen. T. A. Smith, then commandant of the 9th Mily. Department, for the purpose of examining the Mily. features of the country along the river and other Topographical purposes, and was required to report thereon after my return. In conformity to his instruction, I reported in favour of occupying the site on which Ft. St. Anthony stands with a military work large enough to accommodate 5 companies of soldiers. My report on this and other subjects was submitted to the Hon. Secy. of War, Mr. [John C.] Calhoun, in the summer of 1818, who immediately took measures for the establishment of a post at this place.[1]

Lt. Col. [Henry] Le[a]venworth with a detachment of 7 companies of the 5th Regt. Infantry was ordered to repair to the mouth of the St. Peters [*Minnesota R.*] in the spring of 1819 and to commence the erection of Works. He arrived at the place of his destination on the 25th [*24th*] August of the same year and erected huts for the winter-canton-ment of his troops on the S side of the St. Peter's, immediately at its junction with the Mississippi. In june following he was induced to remove from this cantonment in consequence of sickness which prevailed among his troops, which he supposed was occasioned by the lowness of the situation (the site occupied being a part of the river bottom, low and marshy and subject occasionally to inundation) and to badness of the water used for culinary purposes. He accordingly selected another position as a temporary residence for his command about 1 1/2 miles above the first on the right [*west*]

[1] Long here referred to his report of May 12, 1818, in Appendix 1, below. On his role in the founding of Fort St. Anthony, see p. 10, above.

bank of the Mississippi at a copio[u]s spring called Cold Water. This site was also in a bottom subject to occasional inundation.[2]

Soon after the erection of the huts &c. at this place, Col. Josiah Snelling [*in August, 1820*] succeeded to the command of the 5th Regt. and immediately took measures for the construction of a permanent Work. He selected for the site of the garrison the very spot I had previously pointed out. Timber of a good quality was procured. Stones remarkably well adapted to the construction of buildings quarried at the very spot where the buildings were to be constructed, and the work commenced on a scale of suitable extent and respectable character. In the fall of 1821 the Barracks and other buildings were ready for the occupancy of the troops, who then composed 5 [7] companies of 51 men each. Col. S. has been continued in command ever since, and by his attention & perseverance has brought the works to a state of forwardness highly reputable to his command. For a further description of this place, See Messrs. Say & Keating's notes.[3]

During our delay at this place the gentlemen of the party were busily engaged in their appropriate pursuits. Astronomical observations for Lat. & Londe. were taken. The falls of St. Anthony and the Little [*Minnehaha*] falls visited, the country around the Fort examined and described, several interesting Landskips sketched, and much valuable intelligence concerning the indians obtained.

Mr. Calhoun and myself were kindly entertained at the table of Col. Snelling, and Messrs. Say, Keating & Seymore at that of Lt. Nathan Clark, whose hospitality and kindness were bestowed in the most cordial and friendly manner.

[2] For copies of Leavenworth's 1819 orders and on his troops, see Henry R. Schoolcraft, *Summary Narrative of an Exploratory Expedition to the Sources of the Mississippi River*, 35 (Philadelphia, 1855); AGO, Regimental Returns, Fifth Infantry, August, 1819, NARG 94. The winter location, known as Cantonment New Hope, was within present Mendota. Leavenworth stated that the move to Camp Coldwater was made in the spring of 1820. Leavenworth to Gen. T. S. Jesup, June 18, 1823, Quartermaster General's Office, Consolidated Correspondence, Fort Snelling, NARG 92; Folwell, *History of Minnesota*, 1:137.

[3] On Snelling, see Heitman, *Historical Register*, 1:906; Charlotte O. Van Cleve, "A Reminiscence of Ft. Snelling," in *MHC*, 3:77n; AGO, Regimental Returns, Fifth Infantry, August, 1820, NARG 94. AGO, Inspection Returns, Fifth Infantry, Fort St. Anthony, October, 1821, NARG 94, list seven companies with a total complement of 318 men present. The fort, which was later renamed for Snelling, has been restored. Minnehaha Falls, mentioned below, is a well-known landmark within present Minneapolis. On that and the Falls of St. Anthony, see Holmquist and Brookins, *Minnesota's Major Historic Sites*, 33–40; pp. 70–75, above. See also Keating, *Narrative*, 1:294–311; pp. 283–285, below. Seymour completed a painting of the Falls of St. Anthony which has not been located; see p. 392, below.

The party that ascended by water from Prairie du Chien arrived late on the evening of the 2nd Inst., and Lt. Scott with the boats crew and boat was ordered back to Ft. Crawford on the 4th for the purpose of bringing back with him a detachment of 20 men to supply the place of those that were to be added to our party. He was directed to return as soon as possible, that he might overtak[e] us on our march and join our party.[4]

No time has been lost in preparing and expediting the means of our departure.

WEDNESDAY, JULY 9, 1823. At Ft. St. Anthony we were furnished with a guard of 22 men, including one Sergeant and two corporals, who were placed under the immediate command of Lt. [St. Clair] Denny, detailed for the service of the Expedition till relieved by Lt. Scott and allowed to accompany us farther in case he should wish to perform the tour.[5]

We were here also supplied with 12 additional horses, 8 pack-saddles, 4 draggoon Saddles, and other equipments for our horses. The provisions laid in at this post for the exigencies of the journey were as follows, viz. 480 lb. of hard biscuit, 350 lb. Pork, 70 lb. Ham, 100 lb. Sugar, 15 lb. Coffee, 6 lb. Tea, and a few other articles. Beside Lt. Denny, Mr. [William] J. Snelling, son of Col. S., volunteered to accompany us to Red river. Having spent considerable time up the St. Peter's in the capacity of Indian trader, he had acquired a pretty good knowledge of the Sioux Language, as also of the manners & customs of the indians. Mr. [Giacomo C.] Beltrami, and [*an*] Italian gentleman of the order of Noblem., also joined our party as an amateur traveller. He had ascended to Ft. St. Anthony in the Steam boat Virgin[ia] (which had made two trips to this post laden with public stores early in the season and is the first that has ever ascended the river above the Demoyen [*Des Moines*] rapids) and learning that our expedition was on the march, waited 3 weeks for our arrival with the view of accompanying us.[6]

[4] On Clark, above, see Van Cleve, in *MHC*, 3:77n. Long found it necessary to exchange the military escort secured at Fort Crawford because of its poor performance during the trip from Prairie du Chien. Only Pvt. Bunker from Fort Crawford remained with the expedition. See Keating, *Narrative*, 1:264, 267, 311; p. 286, below.

[5] On Denny, see Heitman, *Historical Register*, 1:367; Charlotte O. Van Cleve, *Three Score Years and Ten*, 26 (Minneapolis, 1888). Scott caught up with the expedition on July 27, 1823; see p. 174, below. Denny remained with the party until it reached Mackinac. See p. 373, below.

[6] William Snelling is best known for his writings, particularly *Tales of the Northwest* (Boston, 1830). For his career, see John T. Flanagan, "Introduction: William

Mr. Reynville [*Joseph Renville*], a distinguished interpreter of the Sioux language, was employed to accompany us to the Red river, and a young Metiff [*métis*] named Louis Demarest [*Desmarais?*] was engaged for the route to Mackinaw. They are both Metiffs of French fathers and Indian mothers.[7]

The following list will show the names of the persons composing the Expedition, and the capacities in which they serve.

Maj. S. H. Long, comdg. officer Expedi.
Prof. T. Say, Zoologist } Lity. Journalis.
" W. H. Keating, Geologist }
Mr. J. E. Calhoun A. A., Topr. & Astronom.
Mr. S. Seymour, Ld. Skp. Painter & Designer
Lt. St. C. Denny A. A., Topr. and Comdg. guard
Mr. [William] Jos[ep]h Snelling, volunteer guid[e] &c.
Mr. G. Beltrami, Amateur traveller.
Mr. Jos. Reynville [*Renville*], guide & Sioux interprer.
Mr. Louis Demarest [*Desmarais?*], Chipy. Interprete.

Sergeant	Geo. Day	5th Infany., Reg.	Co. E
Corporl.	J. W. [*West H.*?] Anderson	Do.	Co. A
Corpl.	Geo. Moore	Do.	Co. H
Privt.	Thos. Lyons	Do.	Co. A
"	Saml. Swazey	"	" "
"	Hugh Frazier	"	" "
"	Rich. S. Johnson	"	" "
"	H[oward] Newman	"	Co. C
"	T[homas] Taggart	"	" "
"	J[ohn] Irvin 2nd	"	" "

Joseph Snelling," in Snelling, *Tales*, vii–xxv (Reprint ed., Minneapolis, 1971). On his trade with the Indians, see note 18, below.

Beltrami, who was not a nobleman but had held several official posts in Italy, arrived at Fort St. Anthony on May 10, 1823, aboard the "Virginia." Lawrence Taliaferro, Indian agent at the fort, who was also aboard the steamboat, gave Beltrami a horse and provisions for his journey with Long's party. See p. 31, above; William J. Petersen, "The 'Virginia,' the 'Clermont' of the Upper Mississippi," in *Minnesota History*, 9:347–362 (December, 1928); Taliaferro, in *MHC*, 6:240–242.

[7] Renville spent most of his life trading with the Dakota. When Long met him in 1823 he was a member of the Columbia Fur Company with headquarters at Lake Traverse. See Gertrude W. Ackermann, "Joseph Renville of Lac Qui Parle," in *Minnesota History*, 12:231–246 (September, 1931).

Demarest is called "Pellais" by both Colhoun, p. 285, below, and Keating, *Narrative*, 1:315. His name does not appear in the accounts Long submitted to the War Department, and he seems to have left the party at Pembina. He may have been the fur trader Louis Desmarais (with variant spellings) who is mentioned frequently in the Taliaferro Papers for the 1820s and 1830s. See, for example, Taliaferro Journal, February 2, 1836 (14:13), Taliaferro Papers.

"	Jac[o]b Slaughter	"	Co. E
"	J[ohn] McPhail	"	" "
"	J[ohn] O'Neal	"	" "
"	N[athaniel] Brown	"	" "
"	J[ohn] Russick	"	Co. H
"	J[ame]s Gardner	"	" "
"	L[inus] Scott	"	" "
Privt.	M[athew] Cunningham	5th R[eg]t.	Co. I
"	J[ame]s Dougherty	"	" "
"	J[ame]s Fletcher	"	" "
"	Peter Wicoff	"	" "
"	Geo. Bunker	"	Co. G[8]

The gentlemen of the party were armed partly with Rifles and partly with double barrelled guns. Many of them were furnished with pistols and the apparatus proper to be carried with their arms. Four of the men were armed with rifles and their accompanying accoutrements, and the residue with Muskets, bayonets & Cartridge-boxes. Our travelling apparatus embraced also five tent flies as substitutes for tents, together with the usual allowance of Camp equippage and several articles of extra furniture, such as tin kettles, 1 copper kettle, two small brass kettles, &c. for the use of the gentlemen of the party.

Thus furnished & equipped we took our leave of our friends at Ft. St. Anthony and commenced our journey up the St. Peter's at half past 5 P.M.

Maj. L. took charge of a party to ascend by water, consisting of Mr. Keating, Mr. Seymour, Mr. De Reynville, one corporal, and 12 privates, while the residue proceeded with the horses by land. It was our purpose to meet occasionally on the river, and the circumstance that the Land party must avail themselves of our aid in crossing the river rendered this measure necessary.[9]

The party by water were embarked in a skiff and 4 canoes and had charge of most of the provisions, baggage &c. The other party

[8] The names of the soldiers are given in AGO, Inspection Returns and Muster Rolls for the appropriate companies, Fifth Infantry, Fort St. Anthony, August, 1823, NARG 94. Corp. J. W. Anderson is not listed; perhaps Long meant Corp. West H. Anderson of Company B. If by "A.A." Long meant to indicate that Colhoun and Denny were professional American army men, the designation is confusing, for Colhoun was a navy midshipman. See Introduction, note 54. Also present in the party was Andrew Allison, the black servant. See p. 192, below.

[9] For an account of the land party, composed of Colhoun, Say, Denny, Desmarais or Pellais, and nine soldiers, see pp. 285–288, below.

took a few days allowance of provisions only that they might proceed with as little fatigue to the horses as practicable.

On our way up the river we met Mr. [Lawrence] Taliafer[r]o returning. He had been up about 6 miles to the 2nd Sioux village, and learning that the Indians at the mouth of Terre blue (Blue Earth) river were absent on a hunting expedition, gave over his purpose of ascending higher. Passed two Sioux villages, one 3 and the other six miles above the mouth of the St. Peter's. Encamped at an Indian lodge, where we found protection from the annoyance of the musquitoes. Distance 6 1/2 miles.[10]

THURSDAY, JULY 10, 1823. Started early, passed another Sioux village on the north side of the river called the Old village. Breakfasted at the ruins of a recent trading establishment. Travelled about 24 [*12*] miles and arrived at the village of the Six, situated on the north side. It was now vacated, its inhabitants having recently gone on a hunting expedition.[11]

Having met with our companions about 2 miles below this village and given them instructions to proceed to the village where [we] would aid them in crossing the river, we waited for their arrival a long time when three of the river party went in search of them. But returning without having seen them, we concluded they had proceeded onward, and accordingly resumed our voyag[e] at half past 5 P.M.

[10] Taliaferro served as Indian agent at Fort Snelling from 1820 to 1839; he had set out to hold a council with the Sisseton in Long's presence. See Helen M. White, *Guide to a Microfilm Edition of The Lawrence Taliaferro Papers*, 5–11 (St. Paul, 1966). Keating, *Narrative*, 1:328. While there are many discrepancies in the distances and locations of the Minnesota River Dakota villages, the three-mile one on the left bank in present Bloomington, Hennepin County, may have been that of the White Bustard mentioned in Thomas Forsyth, "Fort Snelling: Col. Leavenworth's Expedition to Establish It, In 1819," in *MHC*, 3:156, or some less permanent village. See also Coues, ed., *Pike*, 1:89n. The six-mile village on the right bank in Dakota County was that of Black Dog or Wamendetanka. On this and the Blue Earth band of Sisseton, see Keating, *Narrative*, 1:326, 342, 345, 380, 385; Bray and Bray, eds., *Nicollet on the Plains*, 43, 255, 256; Taliaferro, Sioux Census, September 1, 1834, September 30, 1836, OIA, St. Peter's Agency, Letters Received, NARG 75.

[11] The Old Village, usually known as that of Chiefs Penichon (with variant spellings) and later Good Road, was near the mouth of Nine Mile Creek in present Hennepin County. The trading establishment has not been identified. The largest village on the Minnesota River, headed by Chief Shakopee or Six, a well-known Mdewakanton leader, was for some years located on the left bank, as Long indicated. It is so shown on Taliaferro's map in James B. Rhoads, "The Fort Snelling Area in 1835: A Contemporary Map," in *Minnesota History*, 32:26 (March, 1956). Later it was moved to the right bank in present-day Shakopee. See Babcock, in *Minnesota Archaeologist*, 11:130; Bray and Bray, eds., *Nicollet on the Plains*, 43, 45, 255, 256; Beltrami, *Pilgrimage*, 2:306; Keating, *Narrative*, 1:328, 329, 385.

During this delay, we had an opportunity of visiting the Indn. corn fields, which were extensive, as also several scaffolds erected for the use of the dead. We observed a recent grave at which a crucifix had been erected, also a dog suspended in one of the corn fields with his head decorated with feathers and horse hair dyed red, probably offered in sacrifice for the security of their fields & h[o]uses during the absence of the Indians.

The village consisted of 14 large wigwams constructed of bark and poles, each large enough to accommodate from 30 to 50 inhabitants living in the manner of savages.

On the south side of the river opposite to the village is one wigwam and a corn-field besides several enclosures of small pickets intended probably as cemetaries. On the same side of the river are situated numerous antient tumuli, some of them of pretty large size. They occupy a large extent of the prairie on which they are situated. In one part of the prairie they formed a line of about 1/2 mile in a direction parallel to the river from which it was distant about 300 yards. Thro'out this distance they were arranged at intervals of from 12 to 15 yards asunder, and when viewed at one end of the line appeared to form a ridge or parapet. Encamped a few miles above the village at sunset. Dist. 32 miles.[12]

FRIDAY, JULY 11, 1823. Started at dawn of day. Proceeded about 6 miles and discovered our Land-companions encamped and waiting our arrival. They informed us that their reason for not coming to the village where we expected them was that they found themselves separated from it by a swamp which they deemed impassable. We aided them in crossing the river, which delayed us a little more than 2 hours.

Passed a shoal [*Carver Bar*] in the river extending across it with scarcely a sufficient depth of water to admit our boats.

Passed the Little [*Carver*] rapids, which are said to be 60 [*35.8*] miles from the mouth of the river. They are formed by two rock bars of sand stone extending across the river and occasioning an aggregate fall of about 7 feet. The channels across them were narrow &

[12] Seymour completed a painting of a scaffold burial as well as a drawing; see pp. 308, 392, below. Several groups of mounds in the Shakopee area are described in Winchell, *Aborigines*, 189–191. See also Theodore H. Lewis to Alfred J. Hill, October 12, 1882, in Archaeological Records, Division of Archives and Manuscripts, MHS.

the current rapid, but we were able to pass them with our baggage on board.[13]

Having crossed the rapids, we dined and resumed our march. Arrived at a small Sioux village about 5 miles above the rapids at 3 P.M.[14] The indians were all absent on a hunting expedition, and we could only gratify our curiosity by visiting their Wigwams, burying places &c. We observed two scaffolds on which as many dead bodies had been deposited. On one of them, erect[ed] about 12 feet high & situated on a rising ground, was a rude coffin covered with calico and containing a corpse. Immediately under the scaffold, a post was set about 6 ft. high on which were inscribed several rude figures of Indians by the friends of the deceased, purporting to be victims or prisoners taken in battle who had preceded him on their march to the other world, and who were thus offered as guides or companions of the deceased to conduct him on his way. On the other, the friends of the deceased had evinced their grief by wrenching locks of hair from their heads and offering it at the scaffold in token of their friendship. At both scaffolds were burying grounds in which the remains are depositd when the coffin shall have decayed, as is customary among the Sioux.

At this place we had also mad[e] arrangements to meet our Land companions and expected to find them waiting for us on our arrival.

SATURDAY, JULY 12, 1823. Started at break of day and proceeded 11 miles before break fast. Soon afterwards met Mr. Farribo [*Faribault*] of St. Anthony descending from an indian village above with a large canoe manned by two french men. Finding our skiff in a leaky condition and in other respects illy suited to the navigation of the river, we effected an exchange for his canoe, giving him instructions to Col. Snelling with a request that the Col. would satisfy him for the canoe. We found this vessel a very useful as well as convenient addition to our little fleet, which now consisted of 5 canoes. Entered a considerable forest [*Big Woods*] called by the French Bois Franc from the circumstance of its containing timber trees of a

[13] The Upper and Lower Little Rapids, now known as Carver Rapids, are between Scott and Carver counties, T115N, R23W, Sec. 31. A total fall of 7.28 feet was recorded by G. K. Warren, *Minnesota River*, 25 (43 Congress, 2 session, *House Executive Documents*, no. 76—serial 1645). See also p. 288, below.

[14] This was the Sand Creek village, but at this date it seems to have been located several miles above the mouth of Sand Creek near present Jordan. See below, p. 288; Beltrami, *Pilgrimage*, 2:207; Bray and Bray, eds. *Nicollet on the Plains*, 46; Featherstonhaugh, *Canoe Voyage*, 1:291; Keating, *Narrative*, 1:332, 385.

few varieties only. Elm and Oak are the prevailing trees in addition to which there are occasionally cotton wood and white maple. Encamped a little before sunset, distance 35 miles.[15]

SUNDAY, JULY 13, 1823. Started at the break of day and proceeded about 3 miles to an Indn. village recently established where we expected to find our Land-companions waiting for us, but were again disappointed in this respect. Left the village and proceeded 4 miles above it around a bend of the river, across the gorge of which the distance was little more than 1 mile. Here we purposed to wait the arrival of the party, after having breakfasted.[16]

The St. Peters (a name supposd to have been corrupted for Sans Pierre, which had formerly been given by the French to this river from the circumstance that no stones are found in it for a considerable distance from its mout[h]) is a very serpentine river, of a sluggish current, and varying in width from 30 to 70 yards. The first forty miles from its mouth the river is deep and navigable for battaues, at the end of which enters a small stream from the north, supposed to be Carvers river, at the mouth of which is a shoal extending across the river.[17]

Having waited some time and the party not appearing, we resumed our voyage again, and after ascending several miles higher we lay by for dinner at a place near which we discovered the trace of our Land companions, and soon afterwards their encampment a few

[15] Both Jean Baptiste Faribault and his son Alexander, fur traders, resided in 1823 at Mendota rather than at the Falls of St. Anthony or the fort, as Long indicates. See Folwell, *History of Minnesota*, 1:438; Warren Upham and Rose B. Dunlap, comps., *Minnesota Biographies 1655–1912*, 216 (*MHC*, vol. 14—1912).

The *Bois Francs*, or Big Woods, a distinctive area of deciduous hardwoods, has been described by many travelers. See p. 289, below; Winchell and Upham, *Geology of Minnesota*, 1:72, 636, 2:115–117 (St. Paul, 1888); Carl O. Rosendahl, *Trees and Shrubs of the Upper Midwest*, 10 (Minneapolis, 1955); Bray and Bray, eds., *Nicollet on the Plains*, 48.

[16] This may be the village of Red Eagle or Quilliou (with variant spellings), located about 20 miles above Sand Creek on the east bank of the Minnesota opposite present Henderson. See p. 289, below; Bray and Bray, eds., *Nicollet on the Plains*, 47; Featherstonhaugh, *Canoe Voyage*, 1:295; Michael J. Smith, "Historic Sites in the Minnesota River Valley," 15, in Division of Archives and Manuscripts, MHS. Keating, *Narrative*, 1:334, indicated that members of the Sand Creek village had recently moved there. Beltrami and Taliaferro also associated Red Eagle with the Sand Creek band; see Beltrami, *Pilgrimage*, 2:207, 309; Taliaferro Journal, August 19, 1827, February 8, 1828 (8:57, 161), Taliaferro Papers.

[17] For a thorough discussion of the naming of the St. Peter's, now the Minnesota River, see Upham, *Minnesota Geographic Names*, 2–4. Carver, *Travels*, 74, gave his own name to an unidentified stream 40 miles from the Minnesota's mouth. Today's Carver Creek joins the Minnesota at the village of Carver, Carver County.

miles above us. After dinner we proceeded on and overtook them at about 4 P.M. Having supplied them with a little more provision, we again embarked and had proceeded but a short distance when a canoe containing the principal part of our ammunition and all of our Indian tobacco unfortunately overset. The tobacco was all lost and the powder so much injured that we could save no more than one half of it. To add to our misfortunes, a violent thunder-storm soon came on, the rain pouring in torrents, & continued at short intervals thro' the night. This did further damage to our ammunition and injured our bread so much that we apprehend the loss of a considerable part of it.

These accidents added to the other delays prevented our proceeding as far as we might other wise have done with care. Distance 23 1/2 mile[s].

MONDAY, JULY 14, 1823. On examining our baggage this morning we found much of it wet and our provisions, especially the biscuit, much injoured, tho' less than we had anticipated. The boats had been bailed several times during the night and the baggage sheltered under bearskins and other coverings as well as our circumstances would permit. But so violent was the storm that no pains or care we could bestow were sufficient to protect either our persons or baggage from its ravages.

Started at a little past 5 o'clock and proceeded to the trading house formerly occupied by Mr. Snelling, one of our party. Arrived at this place at 9 A.M. and commenced overhawling our baggage. Our land companions soon came up with us, crossed the river by our aid and proceeded a short distance up the river, where they waited our arrival. In the mean time, haveing dryed our baggage, breakfasted &c., we proceeded up the river and arrived at their encampment at half past two P.M.[18]

The part of the river where we now were [camped] has been called the Crescent, from a remarkable bend in its course. Here it was determined to make a new disposition of the party & proceed by land. Out of the men constituting our guard, 22 in number, 13 were selected as the more active and efficient, and the residue, 9, sent back to Ft. St. Anthony with two canoes that had been borrowed,

[18] It seems probable that Snelling's trading house was at or near Traverse des Sioux. In 1822 he was trading for the Columbia Fur Company, which did business at the Traverse. See "A list of Licenses Granted at the Indian Agency at St. Peters Upper Mississippi in the year 1822," in Taliaferro Papers.

one from Mr. [Duncan] Campbell & the other from Mr. Farribo, both of St. Anthony. Distance 16 1/2 miles.[19]

TUESDAY, JULY 15, 1823. Having arranged our baggage in such a manner as that we could pack the whole upon horses, including all our provisions &c., All personal baggage belonging to the gentlemen of the party was to be on their respective horses. Our three remaining canoes (3) were drawn up into the bushes on a bottom to remain till some of the party should return & take them down. Letters were written to the War-Dept. and to our friends. And we were ready to resume our march at half past 10 A.M. Courses N 75° W, 1.25 [miles], S 75° W, 9 and S 30° W, 3 miles. Country prairies surrounded by woo[d]lands. Surface undulating. Small Lakes & swamps abound. Crossed two of the latter in which our horses were in danger of being mired. Mr. Calhoun took observations for Longitude near our evening encampment. Encampe[d] near a small lake called Swan Lake, or rather belonging to a group called Swan Lakes. Dist. 14 1/4 m.

WEDNESDAY, JULY 16, 1823. Started at half past 6, having been delayed till this time in consequence of making some new arrangement of our baggage.

In the course of yesterday we passed the entrance of Blue Earth river at a very considerable distance on our left. This river is the first stream of any considerable magnitude tributary to the St. Peters. It enters on the south side and has its sources in the Coteau de[s] Prairie[s]. At no great distance from its mouth is found a sort of Blue Clay used by the Indians in painting themselves; hence the river derives its name.[20]

[19] The Crescent, an early name applied to a bend of the Minnesota in Nicollet and Le Sueur counties, came to be better known as Traverse des Sioux. See Upham, *Minnesota Geographic Names*, 373. On the consolidation of the two groups, see Keating, *Narrative*, 1:337; p. 291, below. Campbell is recorded in "A list of Licenses . . . 1822," Taliaferro Papers. He was trading on the Minnesota River, not at St. Anthony, in the 1820s. See Thomas Forsyth to William Clark, October 3, 1819, Forsyth Papers, Missouri Historical Society, copy in MHS; Taliaferro Journal, February 11, 1826 (7:69), Taliaferro Papers.

[20] For Long's letter to the War Department from Traverse des Sioux, mentioned above, see Appendix 2, below. Keating, *Narrative*, 1:341, indicated that the party did not see the mouth of the Blue Earth River because they passed north of it. On its name, see Upham, *Minnesota Geographic Names*, 57. Its sources are in Kossuth and Winnebago counties, Ia.

Long was among the first to apply the name Coteau des Prairies (highland of the prairies) to the extensive elevated plateau that is a prominent feature of southwestern Minnesota and northeastern South Dakota. It is more fully described below, pp. 168,

Encamped for dinner immediately on the bank of the St. Peters, which we forded at our camp without difficulty. A small stream from the west called by the French rivier aux Liard, or Cotton Wood river, entering just above the same place. This stream has been wrongly called the White wood [*basswood*], the cotton wood having been mistaken for that tree.[21]

Proceeded along the valley of the river on the SW Side. Its valley spreads in some places to the width of 1 1/2 miles and is bounded by bluffs like those of most of our western rivers. The bluffs rise to the height of about 50 feet. They are abrupt in places where the bed of the river ap[p]roaches near them but els[e]where of gentle acclivity. Primitive rocks in rolled masses abound, also pebbles of various formations. Encamped at half past 5, having travelled most of the day in rainy weather. Dist. 20 1/2 miles.

THURSDAY, JULY 17, 1823. At our encampment of last evening we were exceedingly annoyed by musketoes. Our horses appeared to suffer exceedingly by them, and were hovering round our camp in order to protect themselves from the attacks of these blood-thirsty insects in the smoke of our fires.

Resumed our march at half past 5 A.M. The country less marshy than below, tho' swamps frequently occur. Wood-lands occupy a smaller proportion of the country than on the lower part of the river. Travelled 16 miles before dinner.

In the afternoon our progress was slow owing to hindrances occasioned by the breaking of pack-saddles &c.—travelled only 5 1/2 miles after dinner and encamped a little before sunset at a place where we were excessivly annoyed by musquitoes. Dist. 21 1/2 m.

FRIDAY, JULY 18, 1823. Altho' the air was somewhat chilly last night, still it was not sufficiently cool to prevent the musquitoes from preying upon us thro' the night, and the[y] proved exceedingly troublesome. Started at 5 and pursued our way westward along the river, whose valley was constantly in view. Crossed a considerable stream called in the Sioux Languag Chon-sa-a-pi, or Red-tree river,

170, 306, and was most thoroughly explored and described by Nicollet, *Report*, 9. See also P. K. Sims and G. B. Morey, eds., *Geology of Minnesota: A Centennial Volume*, 573 (St. Paul, 1972).

[21] On the name of the Cottonwood, see p. 292, below; Upham, *Minnesota Geographic Names*, 149, 453. The bluffs mentioned below usually attain a higher elevation than Long implies, but the first terrace bordering the river rises only 30 to 50 feet as he reports. See Warren, *Minnesota River*, 46.

from the circumstance that a tree on its banks had been painted red by the Indians. It has hence been denominated in english the Red Wood river. It has its source in the Coteau de Prairie and enters the St. Peters by computation 120 leagues from the mouth of that river and 5 leagues below Pattersons Rapids, which are situated about 3 miles from our noon-day encampment.[22]

As we advance on our journey Swamps & ponds of water become less frequent, the surface less flat, and wood-lands less abundant. Granitic rocks, in rolled masses of all sizes from enormous to minute, are in many places strewed in profusion over the surface. This afternoon it appeared manifest in several places that the granite showed itself in place along the valley of the river, rising to an elevation of about 35 feet above the water, while the height of the bluffs was about 50 feet. The Surface of the country generally exhibits undoubted evidence of secondary formations, if we except the Granitic elevations just alluded to.

Our courses A.M. were N 75° W, 11 [miles], N 70° W, 1.5, and P.M. the same as the last of A.M. viz. N 70° W, 6 [miles], N 60° W, 3 and West 1.5. Encamped at 6 immediately on the bank of the St. Peters. Dist. 24 mile[s].

SATURDAY, JULY 19, 1823. Our usual companions the musquetoes were by no means remiss in their attentions thro the night. Started at half past 5, proceeded some distance along the river valley in which numerous granitic eminences presented them selves. Ascended the bluffs, which were steep, and entered upon the vast prairie on which we travelled yesterday. Scarcely a skirt of woodland intercepted the view except the narrow groves that fringed the margin of the water courses. Travelled West 1.75

[22] On the name of the Redwood River, which rises in Lyon County, Minn., and enters the Minnesota 186.8 miles above its mouth at present Redwood Falls, see p. 293, below; Upham, *Minnesota Geographic Names*, 448. The Long party did not see Patterson's Rapids, which are about 14 miles above the mouth of the Redwood in T114N, R37W, Sec. 24, Renville County. They are shown on many maps, including Nicollet, "Hydrographical Basin," and Greg Breining and Linda Watson, *A Gathering of Waters: A Guide to Minnesota's Rivers*, 55 (St. Paul, 1977). On the measurement of leagues, see p. 181, below.

John Walker's system of indicating the pronunciation of vowels by numerals, described in his book entitled *A Critical Pronouncing Dictionary, and Expositor of the English Language*, 29–42, 88 (5th ed., London, 1810), was used by all the expedition members because Long wished their vocabularies to be consistent with the ones printed in James, *Account*. The marks correspond to the following sounds: f$\overset{1}{\text{a}}$te, f$\overset{2}{\text{a}}$r, f$\overset{3}{\text{a}}$ll, f$\overset{4}{\text{a}}$t; m$\overset{1}{\text{e}}$, m$\overset{2}{\text{e}}$t; p$\overset{1}{\text{i}}$ne, p$\overset{2}{\text{i}}$n; n$\overset{1}{\text{o}}$, m$\overset{2}{\text{o}}$ve, n$\overset{3}{\text{o}}$r, n$\overset{4}{\text{o}}$t; t$\overset{1}{\text{u}}$be, t$\overset{2}{\text{u}}$b, b$\overset{3}{\text{u}}$ll; $\overset{32}{\text{o}}$il, p$\overset{33}{\text{o}}$und. See Keating, *Narrative*, 2:449, 450.

LONG'S SKETCH map of the Grand Portage at Granite Falls in the Minnesota River passed by the expedition on July 19, 1823.

[miles], N 83° W, 3.25, N 55° W, .75, and N 63° W, 1.5 miles, and encamped on the upper side of the Yellow Medicine river near its mouth for dinner. It is called in the Sioux Language Pa-zhe-o-ta-Ze-Ze Wa-te-pa, and with the other S Westarly tributaries of the St. Peters has its source in the Coteau de prairie.[23]

Resumed our march at 12 o'clock and travelled N 85° W, 4 [miles], N 60° W, 2.75, N 20° W, 1.25, N 48° W, 5, and encamped on the bank of the river. In the course of the afternoon passed a

[23] On the Yellow Medicine River, see Upham, *Minnesota Geographic Names*, 593.

rapid of the river called the Grand Portage on account of the necessity of transporting the loads of canoes &c. around it. Its length is about 1 mile. At the same place (5 miles below our encampment) granitic ridges appear in the valley of the river, having a direction nearly east & west.[24]

At evening two Indians of the Gens du Lac, who belonged to a small encampment just below us on the opposite side of the river, came to see us and offered us some Jerked Buffaloe meat, which proved very acceptable. Distance 23 miles.

SUNDAY, JULY 20, 1823. Soon after we encamped last evening the indians arrived in a canoe, bringing their lodges and a small supply of Jerked buffaloe meat. They pitched their lodges near our camp and cooked their buffaloe meat, intending to give us a feast of that kind of food. We partook of it, and altho' we had just supped, we ate with considerable appetite. Took our leave of them at a little past 5 A.M. and travelled N 65° W, 1.25 [miles], N 75° W, 6.25, N 55° W, 2, N 25° W, 1.25, N 52° W, 2.5, N 70° W, 1.5, and N 50° W, 2.25.

A ride of about 8 hours brought us to the Lower end of Lac qui parle, where we encamped for the rest of the day at 1 P.M. In this distance we crossed two inconsiderable Creeks, the larger of which enters the St. Peters about 1 mile below the lake just mentioned and is called Cha-pa or beaver creek [*Lac qui Parle R.*]. The Sioux have another name for this stream which implies the river that ends the river, indicating that the St. Peters takes that name from the confluence of this creek.[25]

About 6 miles above our camp of last night enters a considerable stream from the north called by the French, the Chippeway [*Chip-*

[24] The Minnesota River Grand Portage, bypassing Granite Falls and a succession of rapids, was located in the present city of Granite Falls in Yellow Medicine County. See Featherstonhaugh, *Canoe Voyage*, 1:333; Arthur P. Rose, *An Illustrated History of Yellow Medicine County Minnesota*, 162 (Marshall, 1914); Winchell and Upham, *Geology of Minnesota*, 2:211–213; p. 294, below.

Long probably used the term *Gens du Lac*, below, as an equivalent to Mdewakanton, in contradistinction to *Gens du Large*, a second major division of the Dakota that included the Sisseton, Wahpekute, Wahpeton, Yankton, Yanktonai, and Teton. The encampment referred to was evidently not a permanent one. See Keating, *Narrative*, 1:380; Bray and Bray, eds., *Nicollet on the Plains*, 257, 258; Hodge, *Handbook*, 1:490; p. 294, below.

[25] The Lac qui Parle River's name was rendered *Entapa*, *Intapa*, or *Cha Intpah* by other travelers, meaning "river at the head" rather than Beaver Creek. See p. 295, below; Keating, *Narrative*, 1:357; Warren, *Minnesota River*, 68; Upham, *Minnesota Geographic Names*, 292.

pewa] river, and by the Indians Mi-a-wa-kong or Medicine bark river. It is said to have a common origin with one of the branches of Red [*Otter Tail*] river, which is also the case with another tributary of the St. Peters [*Pomme de Terre R.*] entering on the same side of this river.

Our sunday encampment is on an eminence near the foot of the [*Lac qui Parle*] Lake commanding an extensive prospect adorned with this beautiful sheet of water. Distance 20 miles.[26]

The country as we advance becomes more elevated, but as yet no hills of magnitude except the bluffs of rivers and creeks make their appearance. These have generally an alt[i]tude of about 100 feet, sometimes higher, and are the boundaries of extensive planes destitute of timber and gently undulating. No woodlands appear except narrow skirts situated along the margin of water-courses.

MONDAY, JULY 21, 1823. Started at 1/4 past 5 and pursued our course along the South side of Lac-qui-parle at some distance from its shore. Courses N 75° W, 2 [miles], N 60° W, 3.75, which brought us opposite the upper end of the Lak[e]. Then N 70° W, 2, N 60° W, 5.5, N 80° W, 5, & N 58° W, 2.25. The country remarkably level and free from undulations. A creek here and there occurs fringed with bushes, and copses of woodland occasionally present themselves along the vally of the river, which has been gradually diminishing in size till it now hardly merits the name of creek. At our noon-day encampment, which was immediately on the bank of the river, the bed of the stream was overgrown with wild rice and nothing of a river more than a mere stagnant pool of water was presented.

While encamped an Indian of the Sioux with his squaw & a young daughter came to our camp. They were on an expedition down the river to ascertain the prospect of the wild rice harvest in the ensuing August. They informed us that the prospect was very flattering. Resumed our march and travelled West 2.75 [miles], N 60° W, 1.5 and S 73° W, 5.25. Our way lay along the valley of the river, which was clad in a thin growth of grass, presents an even surface with few or no swamps, and is bounded by hills of gentle acclivity and moderate height. The latter are elevated about 40 feet above the valley.

[26] On the name of the Chippewa River, above, which enters the Minnesota about 12 miles below Lac qui Parle, see Upham, *Minnesota Geographic Names*, 102. Keating, *Narrative*, 1:357, rendered the meaning as "river of the spirit banks." This entry marks the end of Long's first manuscript notebook.

Besides large fixed bodies of primitive rock, rolled fragments of the same rocks are strewed in profusion over the surface. Encamped at 20′ before 6 near the mouth of a considerable creek heading in the Coteau de Prairie and called by the Sioux Tsha-wa-kon, or Spirit Mountain creek [*Yellow Bank R.*] from a hill or eminence in its vicinity called by the same name. Distance 25 1/2 miles.[27]

TUESDAY, JULY 22, 1823. A very copious rain fell in the night from which we were protected by our fly tents, except that the water upon the ground made its way in brooks across our camp and some of us got wet. Started at 6 A.M. Crossed the creek on which we were encamped, and 5 1/2 miles farther on another of about the same size called E-zoo-za-zoo or Sand-stone creek [*Whetstone R.*], entering the St. Peters about three miles below Big Stone Lake. On our arrival at this Lake, we were met by a large party of Indians, some on foot and some mounted. The[y] received us in a very friendly manner, and the Chief [*Nunpakea?*] invited us to his Lodge, which with 29 others stood on the margin of the Lak[e], where we partook of a feast, very much to our gratification. The first course consisted of Pemikin, or buffaloe meat dried and pounded, the second of Pom[m]e Blanche [*prairie turnip*] pounded and prepared after the manner of hominy, and a third for which we could not wait was to consist of boiled buffalo, dog, and Pemikin. The objects of our journey were explained to the Indians and appeared to give them satisfaction.[28]

Our way hence led us along the bluffs of Big-stone Lak[e] which occasionally presented itself as we ascended the swells of the Prairie. But by far the grandest object in view was the Coteau de

[27] On wild rice and the Dakota use of it, see Albert E. Jenks, "The Wild Rice Gatherers of the Upper Lakes," in Bureau of American Ethnology, *Nineteenth Annual Report*, 2:1021–1037, 1043–1047, 1056–1074 (Washington, D.C., 1900). The Yellow Bank River is shown on Nicollet, "Hydrographical Basin," flowing from "He Wakan or Spirits Hill." C. E. Davis translated the name of the river as "mound of the Great Spirit." See Chief of Engineers, *Report*, 446 (44 Congress, 1 session, *House Executive Documents*, no. 1, part 2—serial 1675). See also Upham, *Minnesota Geographic Names*, 291; Lewis to Hill, September 20, 1887, Archaeological Records, MHS; p. 296, below.

[28] Long, on his manuscript map 19, and Keating, *Narrative*, 1:368, identified these Indians as Wahpeton. On p. 386 Keating named Nunpakea as the chief of the Wahpeton, but did not specify Big Stone Lake as his residence. See also pp. 297, 312, below. On pemmican and prairie turnip or *tipsinna* (*psoralea esculenta*), see "Pemmican and How to Make It," in *The Beaver*, Summer, 1964, pp. 53–55; Melvin R. Gilmore, "Uses of Plants by the Indians of the Missouri River Region," in Bureau of American Ethnology, *Thirty-Third Annual Report*, 92 (Washington, D.C., 1919). Seymour completed a painting of Big Stone Lake; see Introduction, note 69.

Prairie, of which we first got a sight at the lower end of the Lake. It is an extensive range of high land, rising about 1000 feet above the common level of the country and presenting towards the NW a regular slope of gentle acclivity in some places but some what abrupt in others. At the top of the Coteau a rolling prairie country commences, more undulatory than that over which we travel. This Coteau is succeeded by another [*Coteau du Missouri*] of similar character at the distance of one day's travel from the first. Between them passes the river Jacque or James, which has a course parallel to that of the Missouri. The second has a similar appearance to that of the second [*first*].[29]

Having promised our host, the chief, some tobacco if he would send for it at the trading hous[e] of Mr. Moore [*Hazen Mooers*] 9 miles above, we took our leave and proceeded up the Lake to that establishment, where we arrived at half past 4 P.M. and met with a very kind reception from Mr. M.[30] A small encampment of indians consisting of three or four Lodges was situated near the trading house, whose chief Ta-tanka-wick-ash-ta, or the Buffalo-man, invited us to a feast and gave us a most friendly reception. Our repast consisted of a profusion of buffaloe meat, well selected, and Pemikin of an excellent quality of which we partook freely. After the feast he made a short speech, highly appropriate & pertinent. (See copy of the Speech in Mr. Keatings notes.) Some tobacco & powder were promised him and we took our leave.[31]

Courses to-day N 75° W, 5.5 [miles], N 50° W, 4.25, N 45° W, 3.75, & N 80° W, 8 miles. Distance 22 miles.

WEDNESDAY, JULY 23, 1823. Having procured from Mr. Moore 100 lb. of flour and two bushels of Indian corn & transmitted it by water to the head of the Lake, and having on the evening of our arri[val] at Moore's dispatched an Indian as an express to Lake Traverse for the purpose of delaying 6 carts which we learnt were

[29] The Coteau du Missouri is situated between the James and Missouri rivers in North and South Dakota. Both coteaux are clearly shown on Nicollet, "Hydrographical Basin."

[30] Mooers, a veteran fur trader, was at this time employed by the American Fur Company. His post on Big Stone Lake is shown on Long's and Colhoun's manuscript maps near present Hartford Beach in T122N, R48W, Secs. 3–4, Roberts County, S. Dak. See also Upham and Dunlap, *Minnesota Biographies*, 519; Smith, "Historic Sites," 46.

[31] Keating described the meeting with Wahpeton Chief Buffalo Man, whose name he rendered "Tatanka Wechacheta," and gave the text of his speech; see *Narrative*, 1:371–375. See also p. 298, below.

about to proceed thence to Pembina without loads, we resume[d] our march at 7 o'clock and proceeded along the Lake to its western extremity, from which, varying our course to the northward, we reached Lake Travers[e] at half past 3 P.M. On arriving at the Trading establishment of the Columbia Fur Company situated on the eastern shore of this Lake, we were greeted by a discharge of musketry from their fort and from an encampment of Indians near it. The fort is a square stockade of small size containing huts sufficient to accommodate thos[e] necessary to carry on the affairs of the establishment.[32]

Soon after our arrival we were invited to a bountiful feast prepared for the entert[a]inment of our party by Wan-no-taw [*Waneta or Wahanantan*]—the Charger, who is a respectable chief of the Sioux nation.[33] The repast of which we all partook, soldiers as well as gentlemen, consisted of 2 or 3 dogs in a high state of obesity, select parts of jerked buffaloe meat, and Pome Blanche, some of it boiled after the manner of potatoes and some of it pounded and cooked after the manner of hominy in the fat of Buffaloe.

The reception we met with both from the gentlemen of the establishment and the Indians was highly gratifying. Distance 24 miles.

The Coteau de Prairie, of which mention has already been made, is a very remarkable feature in the Topography as well as geology of the country. It has an elevation to all appearance of nearly or about 1000 feet—Begins to assume its peculiar character at about Lat. 45° N and extends in a curved line bounding its easterly slope in a direction about NNW to the Assiniboin[e] river in Lat. about 49° N. The concavity embraced by the line appears to conform in some degree to the curvature of the St. Peter's river, whose SW tributaries for the most part have their sources in the Coteau.

It was intended that Mr. Keating should visit this remarkable eminence, but learning that its summit was at the distance of 36 miles and that the slope leading to it presented no rocky pricipices or

[32] The Columbia Fur Company post is located on Long's manuscript map 20. The firm's official name was Tilton and Company. Organized in 1821 by Joseph Renville, William Laidlaw, Daniel Lamont, and Kenneth McKenzie, it was purchased by the American Fur Company in 1827. See Alan R. Woolworth and W. Raymond Wood, "Excavations at Kipp's Post," in *North Dakota History*, 29:239 (July, 1962); Alvin C. Gluek, *Minnesota and the Manifest Destiny of the Canadian Northwest: A Study in Canadian-American Relations*, 33–37 (Toronto, 1965); p. 307, below.

[33] Waneta, a well-known Yanktonai chief, was more fully described in Keating, *Narrative*, 1:429–431, 436; Bray and Bray, eds., *Nicollet on the Plains*, 106; p. 309, below.

rocks in *situ*, also our delay at this place being necessarily too limited to allow sufficient time for the examinations, the enterprise was given up.

THURSDAY, JULY 24, 1823. It commenced raining this morning and we were unable to make any astronomical observations. In the after noon the weather became fair, and a series was commenced.

Learnt that a band of more than 100 Lodges of the Indians denominated the Gens des Perches were engaged in hunting buffaloe near the route before us. At evening Wan-ni-taw, the chief to whose hospitality we were yesterday indebted for a feast, came to see us in his proper costume (for a description of it, see notes of the gentlemen of the party). Mr. Seymour sketched his figure &c.[34]

Soon afterwards a small band of the Indians, by special request, came to entertain us with a dance. A speciman of their music is exhibited on a preceding page [*below*].[35] The day spent in preparation for our journey.

FOUR BARS of Indian music inserted by Long in the 1823 journal. Keating identified them as accompaniment for the dog dance of the Dakota Indians.

FRIDAY, JULY 25, 1823. Spent the day in making arrangements to prosecute our journey. Three of our horses that were too lame to

[34] The *Gens des Perches* were a division of the Yanktonai. See Bray and Bray, eds., *Nicollet on the Plains*, 107, 258. On Waneta's costume and portrait, see Keating, *Narrative*, 1:frontispiece, 432; pp. 172, 311, below.

[35] On the dance and the music, reproduced in a different key with some changes and entitled "Dog Dance of the Sioux," see Keating, *Narrative*, 1:437–439, plate 5; p. 310, below.

WANETA AND HIS SON, a drawing by Samuel Seymour engraved by J. Hill for publication in the Narrative *of the 1823 expedition published in 1824.*

travel were exchanged for 2 of indifferent character. One that had been rendered unfit for service by an accident that happened to him on the day of our departure from Ft. St. Anthony was given over to the Interpreter as past recovery.

Three carts were engaged for the service of the Expedition that were about to return to Pembina, also two others partially freighted with our baggage. Horses exchanged &c. in a manner to accommodate the party. Provisions purchased &c.

SATURDAY, JULY 26, 1823. Our arrangements having been completed, and our outfit now embracing 28 horses including several that were hired, 5 carts with three drivers (two of them being supplied by our own men), one guide and one interpreter [*Joseph Jeffryes*], 360 pounds of dry buffaloe meat, 106 pound of Pemakin, a large canister of fat (of buffaloe) together with 100 lb. of flower & 2 bushels of Indn. corn, which we added to our supplies at Moore's trading house, now augmented our baggage very considerably. Three of the carts being chartered exclusively for our use, they were loaded with our baggage to the weight of about 400 lb. each. We obtained of the Columbia Fur company provisions & other necessaries to the amount of more than $230.[36]

On taking our departure from the establishment this morning, which was at 8 o'clock, we ascended the bluff, and from its summit returned a salute in answer to that given on our arrival.

Procceede[d] along the east side of the lake norwardy, crossed a considerable creek called Hare creek [*Mustinka R.*], on which we stopped to dine.[37] Soon after dinner we came in sight of buffaloes, and two of them were pursued on hors[e]back and killed by some of the gentlemen of the party.

Arrived at an indian encampment where we were invited to partake of a part of a swan which was ready cooked. While enjoying this repast, one of the carters attached to our party went off about 500 yards and killed a third buffaloe.

[36] Six carts rather than five were engaged for the journey to Pembina, and Antoine Le Gros was the driver hired. The provisions purchased from the Columbia Fur Company totaled $234.75, including the rental of a horse and the services of a guide. See Vouchers No. 28, 35, in "Abstract," Appendix 2, below; Voucher No. 35, in GAO, Third Auditor, Account No. 2303, NARG 217. Jeffryes, the guide and interpreter, was a Scottish fur trade veteran employed by the Columbia Fur Company as a clerk. See Keating, *Narrative*, 2:6; pp. 307, 312, below; Taliaferro Journal, October, 1827, (8:143), Taliaferro Papers; Grace Lee Nute, "Hudson's Bay Company Posts in the Minnesota Country," in *Minnesota History*, 22:283 (September, 1941).

[37] The names "Mustinka" and "Lievre" (given to this river by Colhoun, p. 312, below) both translate as hare or rabbit; Upham, *Minnesota Geographic Names*, 554.

The exercises of the chase were like to prove fatal to one of the objects of our expedition. Mr. Calhoun, our Astronomer and one of the pursuers, lost from under him the saddle bags containing all our astronomical instruments. After much delay and trouble in searching for them, we were so fortunate as to find them. Encamped at an early hour on an arm of the Lak[e] called buffaloe Lake [*Lake Traverse*]. Distance 18 1/2 mile[s].[38]

SUNDAY, JULY 27, 1823. Started at 5 o'clock and proceeded about 6 miles when we were overtaken by Lt. Scott accompanied by Mr. [William] Laidlaw of the Columbia Fur co. Mr. S., having returned from Prairie du Chien, obtained from the comdg. Officer of Ft. St. Anthony 2 men, one guide, and two horses and started on the 14th with the view of overtaking the Expedition. But one of his horses failing on the first day, he was under the necessity of returning again to the garrison and seeking another mode of conveyance. He again resumed his journey on the 16th in a canoe and ascended the river about 110 miles, where he obtained an Indian guide and his horse to aid him on his way. The horse served for the transportation of a small quantity of baggage, while Mr. S., with two attendants and his Indn. guide, proceeded on foot. The Indian having accompanied him a considerable distance was under the necessity of returning to his family, but had the generosity to leave his horse in the service of Mr. S., who pursued us with all practicable speed.[39]

On arriving at the lower extremity of Big-stone Lake, he left his attendants with a party of Swiss on their way from Pembina down the St. Peters with whom the men were to return. Mr. S. proceeded with haste to Moore's Trading House, where he obtained an Indian guide and reached the Establishment of the Columbia Fur company at a late hour of the night succeeding the day of our departure. As soon as the moon arose Mr. Laidlaw, having offered to conduct him on our route, they sat out together and came up with us, as before stated.

[38] On this incident, see p. 313, below. The marshy area north of the Mustinka River, which Long called Buffaloe Lake, is now considered a part of Lake Traverse.

[39] Laidlaw, a Scot who emigrated in 1816 to Lord Selkirk's Red River Colony where he managed an experimental farm, left the settlement in 1822 to begin a long career in the fur trade. See Ray H. Mattison, "William Laidlaw," in Hafen, ed., *Mountain Men*, 3: 167–172 (Glendale, Calif., 1966); Robert Laidlaw to Andrew Colvile, April 29, 1818 (14: 302), and George Simpson to Colvile, May 20, 1822 (24: 98–100), Selkirk Papers. The Swiss referred to below and p. 312 were probably among the disappointed settlers who left the colony and made their way to the United States between 1821 and 1827, often traveling via the route Long mentioned. See Gluek, *Minnesota and Manifest Destiny*, 13, 28.

Soon after this occurrence we arrived at the encampment of Wanitaw, the Indn. Chief who feasted us at Lake Travers, and partook of a collation of fresh buffaloe meat at his Lodge. He was engaged with a few indians of his nation in hunting buffaloe, which were exceedingly numerous in this part of the country. At the suggestion of one of the party, he offered to give us a specimen of his skill in hunting on horse-back with a bow and arrow, and was accompanied by some of the party who were much pleased with his adroitness.[40]

Passed a Water course now destitute of water called the [Bois de] Sioux river, which is the out let of Lake Travers and tributary to Red River. Encamped at half past one at a place called the Bois des Sioux, whi[c]h is the first woodland we have seen to-day and is situated on the [Bois de] Sioux river.[41]

It being stormy in the afternoon, we remained encamped. Distance 21 miles.

MONDAY, JULY 28, 1823. Started at half past 6 A.M. and proceeded down the [Bois de] Sioux river to Red river, which we crossed about 5 miles below its confluence with the former. On crossing the river an accident happened which required considerable time to repair. The cart loaded with our dry meat overturned as it was descending to the water thro' the carelessness and obstinacy of its driver, and the contents of the cart precipitated into the water. We accordingly halted on the east shore of the river to dry the meat.[42]

Red river has its source in a Lake about 5 miles wide and 24 long called Otter-tail Lake, which is situated in a N easterly direction from the Trading establishment at Lake Travers at the distance of about 150 miles. Near the source of this river are high lands, visible at our noon day encampment, denominated the Leaf mountains.

[40] Beltrami claimed credit for suggesting that Waneta "give us the sight of a buffalo hunt with bows and arrows," implying that only he and Renville participated while the rest of the party moved on. See *Pilgrimage*, 2:330–332; p. 316, below.

[41] The term "Bois des Sioux" as used in this sentence referred to "insulated patches of wood" or "isles of woods" on the prairie. See Keating, *Narrative*, 2:12; Bray and Bray, eds., *Nicollet on the Plains*, 56.

[42] The present Bois de Sioux and Otter Tail rivers join at Breckenridge, Minn., to form the Red River of the North. Long's party had crossed the Bois de Sioux and encamped on the west side. Here they crossed back to the east side of the Red River a few miles north of the site of Breckenridge. As Long explained in the following paragraph, the Otter Tail River below Otter Tail Lake was then considered to be the Red River, a usage that persisted into the 20th century. The total length of the Otter Tail is about 150 miles; it extends farther north than Otter Tail Lake in Otter Tail County, Minn., which is some 60 miles from Lake Traverse as the crow flies. On this and the Leaf Mountains, see Upham, *Minnesota Geographic Names*, 390, 396, 404;

After drying our meat, which we were able to do pretty effectually, we resumed our march and travelled downward on the east side of the river. Innumerable buffaloes thronged the prairie and a large herd of elk, consisting probably of more than 100, presented themselves and were pursued by three gentlemen of the party, who killed one of them. This success however was likely to bring upon us serious evil. For while three of the party, including our guide & interpreter [*Jeffryes*], were employed in this enterprise, the main party encountered a group of about 35 indians of the band called the Gens de la feuille, notorious for their rudeness and barbarity, whose deportment towards us was by no means destitute of these attributes.[43]

They attempted to stop us on our march and demand presents, insisted upon our encamping at a place they would choose, but to no purpose but that of making us more determined in the course proper for us to take. We encamped about 5 miles above them thinking our horses, baggage &c. would be more secure from their depredations. We were very apprehensive that our companions who had engaged in the chase would be illy treated by them, but fortunately they arrived safely at camp at a late hour in the evening. Encamped at sunset. Dist. 22 1/2 miles.

TUESDAY, JULY 29, 1823. Apprehending no friendly disposition of the indians towards us from the reception they gave us as well as from their known character, we took every precaution in our power to protect our horses and baggage from depredation. The former were pinioned with long lines, or hobbled, and then arranged in such a manner as to answer the purpose of a bre[a]st work. A guard consisting of all our military strength, viz. 13 soldiers of the army was posted, forming two reliefs of six men each under a sergeant. Most of the gentlemen of the party kept watch, and so much caution was observed by all that a lurking enemy could have found no encouragement to annoy us. Still feeling that our position was inse-

Keating, *Narrative*, 2:13, 14; Winchell and Upham, *Geology of Minnesota*, 2:511, 534, 546–549; Thomas F. Waters, *The Streams and Rivers of Minnesota*, 109, 113 (Minneapolis, 1977).

[43] Keating, *Narrative*, 2:16, stated that the *Gens des Feuilles* ("people of the leaves") were Wahpekute ("shooters in the leaves"), while Beltrami, *Pilgrimage*, 2:337, claimed the band was "the very same who had feasted us at the lake of the Big Rock," or Wahpeton ("dwellers among leaves"). To further complicate matters, the Assiniboin also had a band of this name. See Hodge, *Handbook*, 1:626, 2:890, 891; "Abstract of presents delivered by John F. A. Sanford," December 31, 1834, William Clark Papers, State Historical Society of Kansas; p. 320, below.

cure and that some difficulty might accrue for the want of an interpreter well skilled in the Sioux Language,[44] and still more from the want of presents to satisfy their exorbitant demands, it was deemed most prudent to avail ourselves of the light of the moon, which arose about 10 P.M., and resume our journey by night. We accordingly started at midnight with as little bustle as possible, and indeed were so silent about it that one of the indians who slept in camp with us was not awakened till we were about departing.

Travelled 12 miles over an unvaried plain and encamped at sunrise for breakfast on the bank of the river. Proceeded 8 miles farther and dined Just below the entrance of the Fol[le avoine] or Wild rice river, which rises near the Coteau de Prairie at the distance of about 40 miles NW of Lake Traverse.[45] Encamped a little before sun-set on the bank of the river. Dist. 33.

WEDNESDAY, JULY 30, 1823. Were particular also last night in taking the same precautions to guard against spoliations by the Indians that we did the night before. No accident of the kind happened. Started this morning a little before 3 o'clock. Travelled 8 miles and arrived at a small river called Buffaloe [*Buffalo*] river empt[y]ing into Red river a little below the mouth of the Shienne [*Sheyenne*], which enters from the SW. In crossing the former a few miles from its mouth, we found some difficulty, owing to the muddiness of its bottom. It rises near a large tract of wood land called by the French, grand-bois, in a chain of small Lakes. Its course is about NW and its length about 80 miles. The Shienne is a river of clear water and considerable size, being at least equally as large as the Red river above their junction. The locality of its source is not known. Its general course is about NE.[46]

Proceeded on after breakfast, travelling a little west of north. Killed a buffaloe — arrived at a considerable river called Wild-rice

[44] Renville left the party on July 27, and on July 28 Jeffryes was absent with Colhoun and Beltrami on a hunting trip. See Keating, *Narrative*, 2:13; Beltrami, *Pilgrimage*, 2:335; p. 320, below.

[45] The present Wild Rice River enters the Red River from the west some seven miles south of Fargo, N. Dak. Its source in Sargent County, N. Dak., is approximately 40 miles from Lake Traverse. Long's manuscript map 23 and Keating, *Narrative*, 2:37, 39, referred to this stream as the "Pse"; the latter stated that the party's information regarding the west shore was obtained from Jeffryes. The expedition was still traveling on the east side of the Red River.

[46] The Buffalo River enters the Red from the east near today's Georgetown, Minn., and rises about 88 miles farther east in Tamarac Lake in the woodlands of present Becker County, Minn. The Sheyenne enters the Red River from the west near present Fargo, N. Dak. It rises in Sheyenne Lake in Sheridan County, N. Dak.

river and crossed it about 9 miles from its mouth. It has its rise in a Lake about eighteen miles in diameter, and from the abundance of wild rice growing in it, is denominated Wild rice [*Upper Rice*] Lake. The supply of this article of food yielded by the lake is said to be inexhaustible. At the outlet of the lake was formerly a trading establishment belonging to the N[orth] W[est] Comy. under the superintendance of Mr. [Alexander] Kennedy. Two other similar establishments were situated on different parts of the river. The length of the river is about 120 [*160*] miles, and its general course parallel to that of the Buffaloe river.[47]

A violent thunder storm commenced immediately after we had crossed the river and we were constrained to remain at our camp thro' the rest of the day. Dist. 22 miles.

THURSDAY, JULY 31, 1823. The morning being foggy we could not start so early as we intended. Resumed our march before 5, and not finding water travelled 15 miles before breakfast. At the end of this distance we found a stagnant pool in a watercourse called Plum Creek [*Marsh R.*], which at present has no running water. Killed an Elk.

Note. [Wild] Rice river, the same on which encamped last night, is said to be the boundary between the Sioux & Chippeway's, or rather that the Chippeways claim the country northwardly of this river while the Chippeways [*Dakota*] are desirous of extending their claims to the Grand Fork farther north, corresponding to their claim on the West of Red river, which is limited by the Turtle river entering near the confluence of the Grand Fork & Red river.[48]

Passed the Sandhill Creek and encamped on its bank. This water course is similar in all respects to Plum Creek. Distance 27 miles.

FRIDAY, AUGUST 1, 1823. Resumed our journey at the dawn of day this morning. Observations for Longitude were taken last night and repeated this morning some distance from Camp. After a tedi-

[47] Upper Rice Lake in T145N, R36, 37W, Clearwater County, Minn., now has a diameter of less than five miles. It is known that Kennedy was employed by the North West Company, but no positive evidence has been found placing him at the posts Long mentioned. Research Report, Hudson's Bay Company to the editors, May 6, 1971.

[48] The Red River Valley portion of the Ojibway-Dakota boundary line was later formalized in article five of the 1825 treaty with these tribes. It was then described as running down the Buffalo River to the Red, then up the Red to the mouth of Goose River near present Caledonia, N. Dak., or slightly farther south than Long described. The Turtle River enters the Red in what is now Walsh County, N. Dak., some 25 miles north of Grand Forks. See Kappler, ed., *Indian Affairs*, 2:252.

ous and winding course, occasioned by a mistake of our guide, we arrived at the most considerable tributary of Red river called the Grand or Red Fork [*Red Lake R.*]. The circumstance of its originating in Red Lake probably occasions the name of Red river, which has been given to the whole stream along the vally of which we direct our course. The red fork at this place is equally as large as Red river at any of the places where we have thus far had an opportunity of seeing it. This river, as before mentioned, rises in Red Lake.

Red Lake is about 50 [*40*] miles long and 20 [*25*] broad, and of an irregular shape resembling a demi-lune, its back to the SW.

The American Fur or S[outh] W[est] company have a trading establishment on the lake. The general cours[e] of the Red Fork from this lake is about NW. It receives several small tributaries, the most considerable of which is Clear [*Clearwater*] river entering about 30 [*76.8*] miles from its mouth on the SW side, and Thief river, from the north, 90 [*58*] miles from the Lak[e]. It is navigable for batteaus in a high stage of water, and for canoes in all stages, with some obstructions by shoals & rapids.[49]

Timber growth of the Red river country. Several varieties of the oak, Elm (white and some red), Linden, Ash (gray), Red Maple, Cotton-wood (Liard), Aspen, Hackberry, Iron-wood, Hop-hornbeam, white & red pine on the heads of the most considerable streams, Fir, Sugar tree & birch on Red Lake, Willow, Wild cherry, Plum, crab-apple, Hazle, barbary [*cranberry?*], Cedar (Red & white) near the sources of the rivers, grape vine, gooseberry, Currant, wild hop, raspb[e]rry, Briars.

The woodlands of this country are mere fringes along the water-courses except near the sources of some of the tributaries, particularly those from the SE where tracts of woo[d]lands are numerous. This region is remarkably flat and equally as remarkable for its want [of] creeks, brooks, springs, and even ravines. There is nothing to variegate the land-scape except the serpentine beds of the rivers, adorned with a skirt of timber growth of moderate size.

Crossed the Red Fork by fording. Our carts passed with their

[49] Keating, *Narrative*, 2:38, remarked that the information on Red Lake was obtained from Jeffryes. The size given suggests the combined Upper and Lower Red Lakes in Beltrami and Clearwater counties, Minn. The American Fur Company was trading there by 1816. The trade may have been carried on initially in the name of the South West Company, a firm organized in 1811 and dissolved in 1817. See David Lavender, *The Fist in the Wilderness*, 148–150, 253 (New York, 1964); John P. Pritchett, "Some Red River Fur-Trade Activities," in *Minnesota History Bulletin*, 5:408 (May, 1924).

loads secure from getting wet. Width of river about 60 yards. Travelled down the Fork 7 miles and encamped. Dist. 27 miles.

SATURDAY, AUGUST 2, 1823. Started this morning at break of day as usual. Travelled a circuitous route to avoid swamps, and dined at one of the numerous stagnant pools which present themselves along this part of the river. Encamped on the bank of Red river, a little above the mouth of Turtle river which enters from the SW. It is formed by the junction of two forks about 40 miles from its entrance into Red river. It is about as large as the Wild Rice or Menomena, mentioned in the journal of the 30th ult. Game of all sorts has become again very scarse. Occasionally we see an Elk at a distance, which affords but a poor prospect of getting supplies of fresh meat. Encamped at 5 P.M. Distance 23 miles.

SUNDAY, AUGUST 3, 1823. Started at Sun-rise. Pursued our a way along a blind road made by the people of Pembina on their hunting excursions.[50]

Crossed a small stream called Marsh or Swamp Cr. [*Snake R.*] from the abundance of swampy land on its banks. Passed in the course of the day the entrances of two considerable streams entering from the SW. The first is called Big Salt Cr. [*Forest R.*] & rises in a Lake of considerable size called Big Salt [*Ardoch?*] Lake which is about 1 1/2 miles in circumference. The second is Park River, which is supplied by numerous small tributaries, the most considerable of which are Little Salt, Cart, Sand Bar and the Peak Creeks. Little Salt Creek [*Park R.*] rises in a small lake whose water is employed by the french in making Salt. The country traversed to-day is some-what marshy and covered in many places with willow bushes. Timber growth as usual along the water courses. Encamped at 5. Dist. 23 miles.[51]

MONDAY, AUGUST 4, 1823. At our encampment of last night was a spring slightly impregnated with Sulphur. The discharge of water is very inconsiderable. Started as soon as day light appeared. The country still flat and uninteresting and apparently more sunken than

[50] Hundreds of people were involved in the highly organized excursions of the Red River buffalo hunters. See p. 182, below; Alexander Ross, *The Red River Settlement*, 242–274 (London, 1856).

[51] The Forest River flows through Lake Ardoch, the largest of four salt lakes in Walsh County, N. Dak., but its headwaters are farther to the west. Except for Cart River, the other tributaries listed by Long are now named as branches of the Park River. The small lake employed by the French in making salt may have been present Salt Lake or North Salt Lake in Martin Township, Walsh County.

before. Saline appearances are frequent, and no doubt salt water might be found by boreing to a moderate depth. No rocks, stones or pebbles appear upon the surface. No trees are to be seen except those that fringe the water-courses. No hills and vallies variegate the land-scape. Scarse do we pass a single ravine in the course of a days travelling. Arriv[e]d at a small water course called Bois pierce Cr. [*Tamarac R.?*] in which we found a stagnant pool of water, from which we supplied both ourselves and our horses with that necessary article, and here we breakfasted, having travelled 11 miles. At 12 an observation was taken for Latitud[e], which gave for our noon day encampment, 48° 39′ 55″ [*about 48° 45′*]. After noon we crossed two considerable creeks called the Two-rivers, which unite their waters about 10 miles above their junction with Red riv. Near the former point [*the confluence*] is a salt spring, from which considerable salt is manufactured. Having crossed these streams, we encamped near the last at 6 o'clock. Distance 23 miles.[52]

TUESDAY, AUGUST 5, 1823. Started at break of day and travelled a distance, as estimated by the French, of three Leagues, but according to our estimate 15 miles, where we arrived at Pembina at 9 A.M. We have remarked that the estimates of distances made by the Canadians of this part of the country differs materially from those of the French on the Mississippi & Missouri. In the former case a league extends thro' the distance of about 3 1/2 or 4 miles, while in the latter its average length by the customary rate of reckoning distances is about 2 1/3 miles. On our arrival we crossed the [Red] river at a ferry and were very kindly received and hospitably entertained by Mr. Nowlan [*Augustin Nolin*], one of the most respectable inhabitants of the place. Distance 15 miles.[53]

[52] Keating, *Narrative*, 2:36, 39, reported that the Long party did not actually see any salt springs. They were, however, numerous in the region. See Chapter 8, note 30, below; Winchell and Upham, *Geology of Minnesota*, 4:128–130 (St. Paul, 1899); Elliott Coues, ed., *New Light on the Early History of the Greater Northwest*, 1:62, 85 (Reprint ed., Minneapolis, 1965). The lack of stones and the extremely flat topography of the region were, of course, caused by Glacial Lake Agassiz.

[53] As Long indicated, the exact distance covered by a league was not standardized. In English-speaking countries it is now usually taken to be three miles. John F. McDermott, *A Glossary of Mississippi Valley French 1673–1850*, 93 (St. Louis, 1941), defined a French league as 2.4229 English miles, while fur traders variously reported it as both two miles and three miles. See Don W. Thomson, *Men and Meridians: The History of Surveying and Mapping in Canada*, 1:207 (Ottawa, 1966).

The ferry was a barge owned by Nolin; see p. 184, below; Keating, *Narrative*, 2:41. Of the several Nolins living there, Augustin, a fur trader residing at Pembina, is known to have met and talked with Long. See Augustin Nolin to Andrew Colvile, August 1, 1824 (26:187–189), Selkirk Papers. Seymour completed a portrait of Nolin which has not been located; see p. 392, below.

WEDNESDAY, AUGUST 6, 1823. Pembina (An-na-pem-me-nan in Chippeway) a name given to a certain berry resembling the barberry, contains about 60 log houses, including a Catholic church of logs about 70 by 40 feet and house for the residence of a clergyman. The settlement of the place was commenced about 9 years ago under the auspices of Lord Selkirk. For further account of the history &c. of this place, see notes of Messrs. Say, Keating, Calhoun &c.[54]

At the time of our arrival the inhabitants were mostly absent on a hunting expedition, an occupation which employs a large portion of their time. The few that remained at home appeared well pleased with our visit and the object of it. At evening we again accepted of the polite invitation of Mr. Nolan and supped at his house.

THURSDAY, AUGUST 7, 1823. A little before noon the inhabitants of the village (here denominated freemen in contradistinction to Engagees, or such as are in the employ of the British N. W. Co.) arrived laden with an abundance of provisions (dried Buffaloe meat, grease &c.) sufficient not only for the exigencies of this place but for those of Fort Douglass, the inhabitants of both being in pressing want of provisions.[55]

Their train embraced no less than 115 carts heavily loaded with meat and more than 200 horses. It comprised 80 men beside boys, women and children, about 300 persons in all. On arriving at our Camp they signifyed their pleasure at our visit by a discharge of

[54] "Pembina" is usually thought to refer to *viburnum opulus* Linnaeus, the high-bush cranberry common in the region. See Upham, *Minnesota Geographic Names*, 276. Settlers began arriving at Pembina in 1812. The mission, called St. Francis Xavier, was established in 1818 and discontinued shortly before Long's arrival. See John P. Pritchett, *The Red River Valley 1811–1849: A Regional Study*, 83 (New Haven, Toronto, and London, 1942); Nute, ed., *Documents Relating to Northwest Missions*, xv, xvii, 189, 410. Colhoun's comments on Pembina are in his Journal, 14–42, in the possession of Edwin B. McDill. See also Keating, *Narrative*, 2:41–53.

[55] On the term "freemen" see Marcel Giraud, *Le Métis Canadien: Son rôle dans l'histoire des provinces de l'Ouest*, 364–371 (Paris, 1945). The North West Company no longer existed in 1823, having merged with the Hudson's Bay Company two years earlier. See E. E. Rich, *The History of the Hudson's Bay Company, 1670–1870*, 2:397 (London, 1959). Fort Douglas, headquarters of the governor of Assiniboia and the Selkirk Colony, was built in 1815 a mile below the confluence or "forks" of the Red and Assiniboine rivers in present-day Winnipeg. Badly deteriorated by 1824, it was rebuilt at the forks beside Fort Garry. It was virtually destroyed in the flood in 1826. William Douglas, "New Light on the Old Forts of Winnipeg," in Historical and Scientific Society of Manitoba, *Papers*, 3rd series, no. 11, pp. 54–61, 86 (1956). On the boundary and the petition mentioned below, see pp. 15–17, 20, above.

Musketry, those on horseback (about 50) forming and advancing in line.

Our main object at this place being to de[te]rmine some point in the 49th deg. of N Latitude, no opportunity was suffered to pass by Mr. Calhoun without embracing it for Astronl. Observations. The result of his observations gave for the Latitude of our Camp, to which in honour of the President of the U.S. we gave the name of Camp Monroe, 48° 59′ 57″. Our Flag Staff, which was erected in front of the Camp, prove[d] to be located but a few feet south of the line, or the 49th deg. of N Lat.

This Parallel crosses the river at a point below all the settlements of Pembina except a single house standing near the left bank of the river. The Inhabitants appeared highly gratified to ascertain that they were included within the U.S. Territory, and steps were immediately taken to make a representation to Congress in a respectful petition of their condition, views & wishes.

FRIDAY, AUGUST 8, 1823. Having made the necessary observations for determining the Lat. tho' not favoured by clear weather, a post was erected on the bank of the river at the point determined upon as the 49th deg. of N Lat., and upon the north side of the post, G.B. was inscribed and on the south side U.S. Our men were then paraded, the Flag hoisted, and a national salute fired under the following declaration viz. "By authority of the President of the U. States, and in presence of these witnesses I declare the country situat[e]d on Red river above this point to be comprehended within the territory of the U. States.["]

By our observations the Flag staff of Camp Monroe proved to be only 207 1/2 feet S 44° W from the post of demarkation.

Inasmuch as a different mode of conveyance was now to be resorted to, a variety of new arrangements were to be made, such as the transfer of our horses, saddles, &c. for provisions, and the services of boatmen, the employing of a suitable guide, and bows-men & steers-men for canoes, the outfit of a portion of our party and horses to return to Fort St. Anthony, the procuring of groceries and merchandise for distribution amongst the indians on the route before us &c. &c. &c.

Of the character of the inhabitants of Pembina, very little can be said by way of encomium, on the contr[ar]y, if we admit them to a rank in any degree elevated above that of the milder savage tribes, they will have very little occasion to complain of the grade allowed them. To this general opinion there are many happy exceptions, however, particularly in relation to those of Canadian or foreign extraction, but these exceptions do not apply to all the individuals of those descriptions. By far the greater proportion of the inhabitants are of mixed blood, the descendents of Canadians and Indians, or Foreigners, viz. Swis[s], Scotch, Italians &c., and Indians.

In their manners they exhibit few traits indicative of a higher refinement than their savage neighbours. The songs or rather chantings of the half breeds (here denominated Bois Broule) is very similar to those of the former. Their style of living is very similar, except that their habitations are more comfortable & more skillfully constructed. In dress they approximate some what nearer to the American, altho' they retain many of the tawdry trappings common to the Indians. Some few of the more respectable of this community have very descent habitations, keep cows, and cultivate small plantations. Indeed there is scarsely an individual who does not grow more or less of wheat, Indn. Corn, Potatoes, Barley, Oats, Beans, Peas, Turnips, Pumpkins, Carrots, onions, cabbage, tobacco, mellons &c. Tobacco is said to succeed well.[56]

SATURDAY, AUGUST 9, 1823. Mr. Beltrami, our Italain companion, having taken offence at the party generally and being highly provoked at my objecting to his turning an indian out of our Lodge, left the party in a very hasty and angry manner.

Having made such a disposition of the party as circumstances required, it was thought best that Maj. L. should proceed by land to Fort Douglass, and make such arrangements at that place as might be requisite to the prosecution of our journey, by the time the party who were to descend the river in canoes should arrive at that place. He accordingly started, attended by one man [*Bunker*] of the party and two Canadians employed as boatmen for the voyage from Ft. Douglass. The residue of the party were to proceed the next morning in company with Mr. Nowlan's barge, which was not yet ready to sail. (Mr. Snelling and three of the men, viz. McPhail, Irvin, and Newman, also Mr. Jeffrys, our guide from Lake Travers, having

[56] In defining the origins of the *métis* or *bois brûlé* Long may have used the term "Canadian" in the sense of French Canadian, the predominant element in the mixed-blood population of Red River. Scottish-Indian alliances were also common, but no references to *métis* of Italian descent have been found. The presence of a substantial admixture of Swiss is also doubtful. On this and the culture and farming of the *métis*, see Giraud, *Le Métis Canadien*, 291, 348, 614–618, 637–640, 651, 671, 724, 761.

proceeded as far as was contemplated when they joined the Expedition, were to return hence with 4 horses and two mules on the morning of to morrow.)

Travelled down on the west side of the [Red] river. Weather cloudy & sometimes rainy. Crossed two small streams, the first called Marsh [*Rivière aux Marais*] and the last Scotchman's Cr. [*Plum R.*]. Encamped on the bank of the river near the mouth of the latter. Distance 22 miles.[57]

SUNDAY, AUGUST 10, 1823. The weather stormy thro' the nigh[t]—remarkably cool this morning, the wind blowing strong from the NW. Started at 8. Passed a small creek [*Rivière Sale*], whose water is pretty strongly impregnated with salt and is occasionally employed in the manufacture of that article. Country somewhat more undulating than we found it above Pembina—soil apparently good. Wood lang [*land*] observable only in skirts along the principal water courses. Rolled stones occasionally appear on the surface.

Travelled 14 1/2 miles after dinner, crossed the river and encamped, or rather put up, at the cabin of a mr. [Magnus] Spence at 6 P.M. Distance 27 miles.[58]

MONDAY, AUGUST 11, 1823. Mr. Spence, our land lord, was a native of the Orkney's of Scotch extraction. Had resided in this country about 38 years, 30 of which he spent in the service of the Hudson Bay co. on the river Sas-katch-aw-in [*Saskatchewan*], where he was married to a woman of the Kre [*Cree*] or Kenisteno nation. He has several children who converse in the Eng. Lang. with ease. We were here informed that the Mud-river (Maria's R.) [*Piegan*] Indians were the most numerous of any nation in that quarter. They are said to amount to 6000 strong, exclusive of old men women & children, and reside on Muddy [*Marias*] Riv. The Fols or Wild-rice [*Fall*] Indians reside on Red Dear [*Deer*] riv., a branch of the former, and amount to about 200 men. The Cold

[57] On the subsequent frictions between Long and Beltrami, see p. 35, above. Bunker was named as Long's companion in Colhoun, Journal, 25, in the possession of Edwin B. McDill. The two Canadians have not been identified. The water party's trip was described in Keating, *Narrative*, 2:61–64. The streams mentioned enter the Red near Letellier and St. Jean Baptiste, Man., respectively.

[58] On the salt spring near present St. Norbert, Man., see Keating, *Narrative*, 2:63. Long's landlord was probably Magnus Spence, Sr., an employee of the Hudson's Bay Company from 1783 to 1821, according to Research Report, Hudson's Bay Company to the editors, May 6, 1971.

Indns. reside in the same neighbourhood and are of the same race. The Black Feet also reside on Red Dear R. and number about 400 men. The Blood Indns. live on the same riv. and number about 200 men. The Sussee [*Sarsi*] Indns. are a band distinct from those above mentioned and reside on Red Dear Lake. They number about 150 men.[59]

Red Dr. Riv. heads in the Rocky Mountains, runs an easterly course, and enters the Saskatchawin about 150 [*385*] miles from its mouth after receiving a large tributary called the South Branch. Red Dr. Lake is situated southerly of the [North] Saskatchawin about 2/3 pts. of the way from Lake Winnipeek [*Winnipeg*] to the Rocky Mts.[60]

[Aaron] Arrowsmith's map of this part of the country is said to be pretty correct. Started at 8 A.M. and arrived at the Farm belonging to the H. B. Co. at 10 1/2.[61] Here we allighted, obtained milk to drink, examined the improvements which are on an extensive & respectable scale tho' deficient in taste or eligance, and proceeded 3 miles farther, which brought us to the confluence of the Red and Ossinnaboin [*Assiniboine*] rivers at half past 12. Settlements are distributed in every direction along the last three miles of our morning's ride, at all of which Corn, wheat, barley, potatoes &c. in small patches are cultivated. The name given to the tract comprehending the settlements, which are scattered in every direction around the bifurcation of these rivers, is Ossinnaboia [*Assiniboia*]. Fort Douglass [*Garry*], or as it is commonly called, the [Hudson's Bay] Com-

[59] The Marias River is in northern Montana. Piegans, Bloods or Kainah, and Blackfeet were the three subtribes of the Blackfoot nation. The Cold were a band of the Blackfeet, and the Sarsi were closely allied. Long probably misunderstood his informant regarding the "Fols," which he translated as "wild rice" (*folle avoine*), the term for the Menominee. The tribe meant was probably the Fall or Atsina who lived on the Red Deer River. On these tribes and their ranges, which were more extensive than Long indicated, see Hodge, *Handbook*, 1:113, 359–362, 643, 2:246, 467, 570; Coues, ed., *New Light*, 2:524; Alice M. Johnson, ed., *Saskatchewan Journals and Correspondence*, 15n, 19n (London, 1967); Richard Glover, ed., *David Thompson's Narrative 1784–1812*, 239, 240, 252 (Toronto, 1962).

[60] The Red Deer River referred to here and above rises in what is now Banff National Park, Alba., and flows into the South Saskatchewan River near the present Alberta-Saskatchewan border. Red Deer Lake is approximately 60 miles southeast of present Edmonton, Alba. See James G. MacGregor, *Blankets and Beads: A History of the Saskatchewan River*, 17–19 (Edmonton, Alba., 1949).

[61] On Arrowsmith's maps, see p. 41, above. The farm, called Hayfield, was started for the Selkirk Colony and taken over by the company as the first of three experimental farms. It was located about four miles south of Fort Garry, and it is so shown on Long's manuscript map 28. See William Laidlaw to Selkirk, July 22, 1818 (15:303–306), Selkirk to Robert Laidlaw, April 21, 1819 (18:152), Simpson to Colvile, May 20, 1822 (24:93), all in Selkirk Papers; Rich, *Hudson's Bay Company*, 2:511–514.

pany's Fort, is located on the West side of Red river immediately below the debouchere of the Ossinniboin. Besides this there is another Fort on the same side of the river about 1 mile below also called Fort Douglas, or the Colony's Fort, which is mor[e] immediately under the jurisdiction of the representatives of the estate of the Earl of Selkirk. In the former [*Fort Garry*] is the residence of the Agent of the H. B. Compy. & in the latter [*Fort Douglas*] is that of the governour of the colony planted by Ld. Selkirk. On my arrival at the former I received a polite invitation from the Agent of the Company, Mr. McKenzy [*Donald McKenzie*], to take up my abode in his quarters which I thankfully accepted. Distance 12 miles.[62]

TUESDAY, AUGUST 12, 1823. Gov. [Andrew] Bulger, who has recently presided over the affairs of the Colony, was now absent, having embarked a few days since on his voyage to the entrance of Hudson's Bay whence he purposes to sail for England. He left a Mr. [William] Kemp[t] to officiate in the capacity of Actg. Gov. till the arrival of a successor, who is now on his way hither and shortly expected to arrive.[63]

I visited the Actg. Gov. [Kempt] at the colony's fort, where I met with a very kind reception and offers of any assistance in his power to render towards the further prosecution of our journey. The kind letter of Mr. [Stratford] Canning, the British Minister at Washington, proves of great consequence in the attainment of all necessary aids and attentions of the public officers at this place, altho' from their friendly disposition and deportment [and] even countenances support might be expected.[64]

Mr. McKenzie, the present Chief Factor for the H. H. B. Co. on

[62] On Fort Douglas, see note 55, above. The Hudson's Bay Company post at the forks within present-day Winnipeg was Fort Garry. At least three forts of that name existed between 1822 and 1835. See Leslie F. Hannon, *Forts of Canada: The Conflicts, Sieges and Battles that Forged a Great Nation*, 178–184 (n.p., 1969); Keating, *Narrative*, 2:64, 70, 76. McKenzie had served the North West and Pacific Fur companies before his appointment as a chief factor of the Hudson's Bay Company in 1821. He was in charge of the Red River district 1823–33 and served as governor of Assiniboia, 1825–33. See Cecil W. Mackenzie, *Donald Mackenzie "King of the Northwest,"* 141–148 (Los Angeles, 1937); E. E. Rich and R. Harvey Fleming, eds., *Colin Robertson's Correspondence Book, September 1817 to September 1822*, 233 (Toronto, 1939).

[63] Bulger became governor of the colony in 1822. He left Red River on August 6, 1823. Kempt, a Scotsman who went to the colony as a surveyor, was succeeded by Robert P. Pelly, who arrived on October 2, 1823. See William Kempt Journal, August 6, 1823 (25:267), Simpson to Colvile, November 1, 1823 (25:284), both in Selkirk Papers; Thomson, *Men and Meridians*, 1:200.

[64] For the Canning letter, see Appendix 2, below.

this station, is of the family of the celebrated Sir. Alexander McK. [*Mackenzie*], the distinguished traveller. Mr. McK. has spent 24 years in trafic with the Indians, making discoveries &c., during which time he has traversed the country in various directions from Montreal & Hudson's Bay to the Pacific Ocean. In the employ of Mr. [John J.] Astor of N. York and in company with Messrs. [Wilson P.] Hunt, [Ramsay] Crooks, Stewart [*Robert Stuart*], & [William W.] Mat[t]hews in the same employ, he visited the mouth of the Columbia river and traversed much of the country in that quarter. In the course of his rambles he ascended the Walla-mut [*Willamette*] (commonly but erroneously called the Multnoma) river about 600 [*300*] miles, accompanied with Mr. Mathews and a considerable party fitted out for the purpose by orders of Mr. Hunt, then superintendant of Astor's Trading establishment [*Astoria*] at the mouth of the Columbia. The account he gives of the country of the Wallamut is in a high degree interesting.[65]

The [Willamette] river is very crooked—its vally broad and exceedingly prolific. On both sides of the river, and within a mile or two of it, commences a country beautifully rolling, variegated with rounded knobs of moderate height and gentle acclivity, having their summits crowned with spreading oaks arranged in open order after the manner of an orchard of fruit trees. A rich carpet of luxuriant grass decorated with flowers of every hue covers the surface and gives the most beautiful finish to the land-scape.

Beavers and smaller vellifuous [*?*] animals abound on the water courses, while deer in the greatest plenty abound along the whole extent of the river.

WEDNESDAY, AUGUST 13, 1823. The party who were to descend [the Red R.] by water from Pembina were expected yesterday but did not arrive till after noon of this day. A cordial welcome awaited them. The Company's Flag was hoisted at the Fort, which had also been done on the arrival of the commandg. officer two days before.

Mr. McKenzy gave us some account of the Rocky mountain Sheep [*goat*], which inhabits that elevated region between the 48th

[65] Donald McKenzie, a cousin of explorer Sir Alexander Mackenzie, helped establish Astoria at the mouth of the Columbia River in 1811. McKenzie and Matthews made the trip in 1812 to the Willamette River, called the Multnomah by Lewis and Clark. See Mackenzie, *Donald Mackenzie*, 21; Lavender, *Fist in the Wilderness*, 130–134, 137, 156; Edgar I. Stewart, "Donald McKenzie," in Hafen, ed., *Mountain Men*, 5:227–231 (Glendale, Calif., 1968); Philip A. Rollins, ed., *The Discovery of the Oregon Trail: Robert Stuart's Narratives*, lvii, 31–33, 278–280 (New York and London, 1935). Long later met Robert Stuart; see p. 246, below.

and 60th deg. of N Latitude. They are found in abundance on the head waters of the north fork of Columbia river, where they constitute a principal item in the subsistence of the natives. They are found scattered in various directions thro out that portion of the country but are seldom seen at a distance from the mountains. They are generally about as large as the common sheep, have white fleeces, interspersed with long hare standing erect upon the surface of their bodies. Their horns and hoofs are black, while the other parts of the animal are uniformly white. The former are slightly curved and incline backward, scarcely protruding beyond the wool. Their flesh at best not very palatable & of a musky odour. Not difficult of access to the hunter.[66]

THURSDAY, AUGUST 14, 1823. At Ft. Douglass a Church has been constructed for publick worship by the Protestant Episcopalians, at the expense of the English bible society, at which however they now have no minister; also a school connected with it. A Catholic chapel [*St. Boniface Mission*] has also been built at the expense of the Earl of Selkirk's estate, over which a Bishop [*Joseph-Norbert Provencher*] presides with one assistant who officiates occasionally at Pembina and a third person who has the charge of a school. In addition to these institutions, a school has been established by the Catholics for the education of indian children, and is conducted on a similar plan and with similar success with that of McCoy's on the river St. Joseph's.[67]

[66] This rather confused description refers to the Rocky Mountain goat rather than the bighorn sheep. The latter is an elusive animal difficult to hunt, and its horns do not incline backward but project out at the sides. Both animals were observed by the Astorians, according to Gabriel Franchère, "Narrative of a Voyage to the Northwest Coast of America," in Reuben G. Thwaites, ed., *Early Western Travels*, 6:360 (Cleveland, 1904).

[67] John West, an Anglican, established a Protestant mission and school in 1820 supported by the Church Missionary Society rather than the British and Foreign Bible Society to which Long referred. West left the settlement in June, 1823. His Presbyterian successor, David T. Jones, arrived in October. Provencher, who was named titular bishop in 1820, established St. Boniface Mission at the forks in 1818. In 1823 his assistants were Father Thomas Destroismaisons and Jean Harper. A separate school for Indian children was not operating at this time, as Long stated. Although Selkirk was interested in the Lancasterian system of education (see Chapter 3, note 35), its use in the colony has not been verified. See John West, *The Substance of A Journal During a Residence at the Red River Colony . . . 1820–1823*, x–xii, 3, 18, 19, 62, 66, 143, 172 (Vancouver, B.C., 1967); Harry Shave, "Pioneer Protestant Ministers at Red River," and C. J. Jaenen, "Foundations of Dual Education at Red River 1811–34," in Historical and Scientific Society of Manitoba, *Papers (Transactions)*, 3rd series, no. 6, pp. 36, 39, 40, no. 21, p. 36 (1951, 1965); G[eorge] Dugas, *Monseigneur Provencher et les Missions de la Rivière-Rouge*, 20, 69, 76–79, 88, 97, 315 (Montreal, 1889). See also p. 192, below.

FRIDAY, AUGUST 15, 1823. Had an interview with a Chippeway chief called the Black man, from Red Lake. The views & objects of our Expedition were explained to him, and the purposes of the American Govt. in relation to the Indians. He appeared highly pleased with the interview.[68]

[68] On Black Man (Kayajieskebinoa), see Alexander Morris, *The Treaties of Canada with the Indians of Manitoba and the North-West Territories*, 298–300 (Toronto, 1880); Keating, *Narrative*, 2:75. A sketch of him by Seymour is in Keating, 1:plate 3.

5. *A Canoe Trip in British Territory*

August 16 through September 14, 1823

Saturday, August 16, 1823. No time had been lost in making preparations for our departure [from Fort Garry]. A guide [*Jean Baptiste Desmarais*] was employed for 800 livres (6 to the dollar), three bowsmen [*François Fournier, Antoine Le Frenière (Le Frenier), and Louis Morain*] at the rate of 400 livs. each, and three steersmen [*Peter George, Joachim Ranger, and Jean Baptiste Robillard*] at the same rate, also two [*three*] middlemen [*Moses Le Fevre, Baptiste La Fontaine, and Joseph Plante*] at $1 pr. day each. All engaged for the voyage to Ft. William. An interpreter [*Charles G. Brousse*] of the Chippeway language was also employed at a dollar pr. D. during his term of service. Three bark canoes about 28 feet in length, called North canoes, were procured for the transportation of our persons and baggage. The provisions laid in for the use of the party amounted to about 1000 lb. of Dry buffaloe meat most of which was pounded and packed in bags (called Pemakin)—also 4 bushels of wheat meal, buffaloe fat, vegetabl[e]s &c. &c.[1]

[1] Desmarais or Demarest, Robillard (also called Lambert), and La Fontaine (also Lafontaine or Fontaine) were North West Company employees; the latter two men lived at Red River. See A[drien] G. Morice, *Dictionnaire Historique des Canadiens Et des Métis français de L'Ouest*, 89, 261, 335 (2nd ed., Quebec, Montreal, and Winnipeg, 1912); Red River Census, 1838, p. 45, in Manitoba Provincial Library, Winnipeg, copy in MHS; *Report of the Proceedings Connected with the Disputes between the Earl of Selkirk and the North-West Company . . . 1818*, 183 (London, 1819); see also Vouchers No. 37–49 in "Abstract," Appendix 2, below, which have additional information on these and the other voyageurs, wages, and purchases at Red River.

Brousse, a resident of the Red River Colony and a former employee of the North West Company, settled near what is now Stillwater, Minn., in 1838. See Flavien Bonduel to Society for the Propagation of the Faith, November 15, 1847, in the Society's archives, Paris (a translation is in the MHS); [John Halkett], *Statement Respecting The Earl of Selkirk's Settlement Upon the Red River*, 99, xlvii (London,

SUNDAY, AUGUST 17, 1823. Our arrangements having been completed, we resumed our journey by water in 3 canoes at a little before 11 o'clock this morning. During our stay at Ft. Gerry [*Garry*] we received the kindest attentions from Mr. McKenzy [*Donald McKenzie*], who with the utmost hospitality entertained all the gentlemen of the party at his table. Nor would he suffer us to depart without bestowing upon us several important and highly useful articles of provisions and a number of very acceptable volumes from his library, for which we could make no return but by grateful acknowledgments. Our Party now consisted of Maj. L., Messrs. Say, Keating, Calhoun, Seymour, Scott & Denny, ten Canadian Boatmen, one interpreter [*Brousse*] of the Indn. Language, ten soldiers of the U.S. Army, and one black man [*Allison*], amounting in all to 29 persons.

The settlements continue on the [Red] River, extending downwards about 15 miles below the confluence of the Red & Ossinnaboin [*Assiniboine*] rivers. At this place is situated the Catholic chapel [*St. Boniface Mission*] on the right bank of the river. The Protestant Episcopal Church stands on the Left Bank about 4 miles below. Passed the Buffaloe factory on the Right, where we procured 4 yds. of cloth made of Buffaloe wool and 20 pr. Mocasins of the tanned hide of the same animal. Travelled till sunset and encamped on a small island. Dist. 34 miles.[2]

MONDAY, AUGUST 18, 1823. It is customary in voyaging with bark canoes to discharge their cargoes every night and draw the canoes on shore. This is done with much dispatch by the Canadians, and any leaks in the canoe easily stopped with gum or turpentine. Embarked at break of day and started immediately. Passed an encampment of Chippewas at the mouth of the river de Mort [*Netley Creek*], called in the Indn. Lang. Onepo or river of Death from the

1817); Robert Campbell, "Driving Sheep from Kentucky to the Hudson's Bay Country," in *Annals of Iowa*, 15:244 (April, 1926).

Since the usual crew of a North canoe consisted of a guide or bowman, a steersman, and six middlemen, some of the soldiers attached to Long's party also functioned as paddlers; see Keating, *Narrative*, 2:78. On the North canoe's size and crew, see Edwin T. Adney and Howard I. Chapelle, *The Bark Canoes and Skin Boats of North America*, 138–142, 145 (Smithsonian Institution, *Bulletin*, no. 230—Washington, D.C., 1964); Grace Lee Nute, *The Voyageur*, 24, 27 (Reprint ed., St. Paul, 1955); Keating, *Narrative*, 2:76–79. On Fort William, see note 52, below.

[2] The factory and a tannery were established by the Buffalo Wool Company, a subsidiary of the Hudson's Bay Company organized in 1820 and managed by John Pritchard. He did not make a success of the venture and it ceased operations in the mid-1820s. See Rich, *Hudson's Bay Company*, 2:427, 508.

circumstance that 2 or 3 hundred Lodges of Chippeways were massacred by a party of Sious on its banks many years since.[3]

In the diary of yesterday it should have been remarked that we passed what is called the [*St. Andrew's*] Rapids of Red river, which are about 9 miles long and at present afford but a moderate depth of water. Our canoes struck the bottom in several places, and one of them sustained some slight injury. Rocks make their appearance along this part of the river.[4]

Along the rapids, the banks of the river rise about 30 feet and exhibit numerous rolled stones together with stratifications of lime stone in a few places. Country generally wooded, much of it marshy. Swamps are numerous. Passed two encampments of Chippeways. They were engaged in fishing, an important means of subsistence not only with the Indians but with many of the whites of this country.

Entered Lake We-ne-peek [*Balsam Bay of Lake Winnipeg*] at half past ten A.M. This extensive sheet of water, as its name imports, is of a sallow-muddy appearance, its length is about 270 [*240*] miles, and its greatest breadth about 80 [*55*], & its least about 15 [*1*]. Its general direction is about NNW or SSE. Its Eastern coast presents high lands faced with occasional precipices, while the country on the west abounds in swamps & low-grounds, the coast being much indented.[5]

[3] Canoes were usually gummed with resin from several types of pine or black and white spruce; see Adney and Chapelle, *Bark Canoes*, 17. Long's explanation of the name Death River is the usual one found with varying details in early travel narratives. A later version stated that the deaths were caused by a smallpox epidemic. The location, a popular Indian encampment spot, was occupied in 1823 by an Ojibway band named Onepowesepewenenewak ("people of Death River"), also called the Nibowisibiwininiwak. See Coues, ed., *New Light*, 1:41; Geographic Board of Canada, *Place-Names of Manitoba*, 62 (Ottawa, 1933); Keating, *Narrative*, 2:82, 153; Hodge, *Handbook*, 2:69, 128.

[4] Many travelers mentioned the St. Andrew's (sometimes called Grand or Pelican) Rapids between Lower Fort Garry and present Winnipeg. They were eliminated by the construction of St. Andrew's dam in 1910. See Henry Y. Hind, *Narrative of the Canadian Red River Exploring Expedition of 1857*, 1:128–131, facing p. 172 (Reprint ed., New York, 1969); Malvina Bolus, Hudson's Bay Company, to the editors, June 4, 1971.

[5] The name of Lake Winnipeg, which is of Cree origin, is variously spelled and translated as "dirty water" or "muddy water." See Charles N. Bell, *Some Historical Names and Places of the Canadian North-West*, 3 (Manitoba Historical and Scientific Society, *Transactions*, 1st series, no. 17—Winnipeg, 1885); J. A. Rayburn, "Geographical Names of Amerindian Origin in Canada," in *Names*, 17:152 (June, 1969); Keating, *Narrative*, 2:81. None of the two specimens of convolvulus (bindweed) or the roses (below and p. 206) brought back by the expedition was a new species. A rose was named *Rosa Sayi* by Lewis D. von Schweinitz, but this classification did not persist. See Keating, *Narrative*, 2:384–388.

Our course in the Lake was first a little east of N about 16 miles, then due north by the compass [*blank in ms.*] miles. The eastern shore constantly in view, but no appearance of land to the west. Landed at a place called the Grand Marais (or Marsh) for dinner. The shore sandy & pebbly. A singular Cherry, also a new variety of convolvulus, and also of the rose, beside other curiosities, were found here. Passed near two points projecting into the lake, our course still north. Encamped on the bank a little before sun-set. Dist. 48 mil[e]s.

TUESDAY, AUGUST 19, 1823. Arrowsmiths Map of N. Americas is said to exhibit a pretty correct delineation of this part of the continent. He received his surveys and discriptions, however, from a Mr. [Peter] Fidler, late surveyor for the H. B. Co. now deceased. Mr. F. first came to this country in the capacity of servant to Mr. Turner [*Philip Turnor*] who had been appointed Surveyor for the Co.; Mr. Turner died soon after his arrival with out having accomplished any of the objects of his mission, and his books, instruments, &c. fell into the possession of Mr. F., who very laudably availed himself of this opportunity to become acquainted with the art of surveying, in which he afterwards succeeded very well and became the successor of Mr. Turner. In our observations & surveys we have generally found a coincidence with those of Mr. Fiddler, tho' on many occasions a discrepancy was manifest.[6]

Started 1/4 before 4 A.M. Pas[s]ed round a prominent point and entered a channel lying between the Point & Elk Island, which we left to the west. A sand bar here extends across the channel and is impassable for canoes in a very low stage of water. The place of passage across this is known by the name of the Indian Portage. Having crossed the portage, our course was changed to a due east direction [*in Traverse Bay*]. Breakfasted a little past the portage, and the wind being fair, our Boatmen soon prepared masts, yards, &c. and converted our Tent Flies into sails, and we were at once prepared to avail ourselves of the breeze. Elk Il. is about 4 miles

[6] Fidler began his studies in 1790 with Turnor, the Hudson's Bay Company's first surveyor who also trained David Thompson. Fidler was Turnor's assistant, not his servant, and he had his own instruments, chosen for him by Turnor. He was already an experienced surveyor by the time Turnor died in 1799 or 1800. See J[ames] G. MacGregor, *Peter Fidler: Canada's Forgotten Surveyor 1769–1822*, 6, 20, 21, 27, 41, 90, 255 (Toronto and Montreal, 1966); J. B. Tyrrell, ed., *Journals of Samuel Hearne and Philip Turnor*, 62, 92, 93 (Toronto, 1934). On Arrowsmith's use of Fidler's work, see Wheat, *Mapping the Transmississippi West*, 1:178–183 (San Francisco, 1957).

long & 3 broad. Eastwardly of it at the distance of about 10 miles is situated another called Pembina Island.[7]

This morning we past the most remote [northern] point of our Tour, the latitude of which is about [*blank in ms. —50° 44′*] deg. Hence our course was eastward, or S 70° E. Thus have we accomplished our outward journey without misfortune or even distressing accident worthy of particular notice in 112 days, having travelled in that time about 2100 miles. However gratifying the business of travelling in new regions, we were not a little rejoiced at the idea of turning our faces homeward, altho' a wilderness region of vast extent still separated us from our homes.

Passed up an arm [*Traverse Bay*] of the lake in a direction for the mouth of Wenepeek [*Winnipeg*] riv., where we arrived at 11 o'clock. The river here spreads to the width of a mile and is rather a bay. At the distance of 3 miles up the bay is situated one of the H. Bay trading establishments called Fort Alexander, which stands on the South [*southwest*] side of the river. Finding one of our canoes in bad condition and being able to procure bark and gum proper for repairing it, we concluded to remain here for the day to accomplish that object.[8]

Ft. Alexander was founded by the N. W. Co. about 25 years ago, and was intended as the principal Depot of the Co. and was indeed such till the coalition between the two companies took place, which was in the year 1820 [*1821*]. Since that period, York Factory, situated at the mouth of Nelson [*Hayes*] river of Hudson's Bay, has served as the principal Depot for the N. W. & H. B. Coms. consolidated.[9] The country back of this place, and generally around the southern extremity of Lake W., if we except several elevated promontories and some few tracts of high-land, is generally low & marshy. Dist. 26 miles.

[7] Keating, *Narrative*, 2:83, reported that the party floated over the bar at Indian Portage. Pembina Island is shown on Long's manuscript map 29.

[8] For a list of materials purchased for canoe repair, see Voucher No. 36, in "Abstract," Appendix 2, below. Fort Alexander, or Bas de la Rivière post, was first built in 1792 by the North West Company on the left bank of the Winnipeg River. See Ernest Voorhis, comp., *Historic Forts and Trading Posts of the French regime and of the English Fur Trading Companies*, 30, 38 (Ottawa, 1930); J. Bartleman, "H.B.C. Posts, Keewatin District," in *The Beaver*, September, 1927, p. 66.

[9] Grand Portage and later Fort William, rather than Fort Alexander, were usually considered the "principal" North West Company depots. York Factory on the north bank of the Hayes River near its outlet into Hudson Bay had a long history as a Hudson's Bay Company post from the 1680s to its closing in 1957. At least one frame structure from the 1830s still remains under the protection of Canada's National Historic Sites Service. See *The Beaver*, Winter, 1957, pp. 3–59.

WEDNESDAY, AUGUST 20, 1823. We were delayed at Ft. Alexander till 3 P.M. waiting for the repairs of the canoe, at which time we took our departure with a fair wind. To the kindness of Mr. [John] Bell, one of the Clerks of the H. B. Co. who at present is superintendant of this establishment, we feel much indebted for his hospitality.[10]

The bay on which Ft. Alexn. is situated is called Bas de La Rivier [*Rivière*], or entrance of the river, in contradistinction to the entrance of the lake mentioned yesterday. Its extent inland from the Lake is about 6 or 7 miles, where the River Wenepeek has its estuary. On entering this interesting stream we had first a rapid [*Manitou Rapids*] to contend against and soon after a considerable cataract [*Pine Falls*], around which we were compelled to transport our canoes & baggage by land, and the latter is hence called a Portage. Ascending higher, we encountered numerous rapids and had to tow our Canoes up some of th[e]m, carrying our baggage across the rocks that present themselves in such places. Our boatment [*boatmen*] perform their services on such occasions with remarkable dispatch. Our canoes and baggage were transported round the firs[t] portage [*Manitou Portage*] and we were all reembarked again in the space of about 15 minutes. Ascended to the Lower [*Silver*] falls which exhibit one of the most beautiful & majestic water falls that is to be met with in any country. Its roar is tremendous and a view of it awful in a high degree. Mr. Seymour took a sketch of this remarkable part of the river. Here are two portages within a very short distance of each other. Encamped at sunset at the head of the uppermost. Dist. 14 miles.[11]

[10] Bell, who was with the North West Company before the 1821 coalition, was appointed clerk at Fort Alexander in 1823. See E. E. Rich and R. Harvey Fleming, eds., *Minutes of Council Northern Department of Rupert Land, 1821–31*, 54, 427 (Toronto, 1940).

[11] On Seymour's sketch, see Introduction, note 69; Keating, *Narrative*, 2:92. Up the Winnipeg River (now much altered by power dams) and eastward to Lake Superior, the party followed fur trade routes described by many travelers. For a list of portages and for a comparison of features with the waterways today, see Hind, *Narrative*, 2:402; Eric W. Morse, *Fur Trade Canoe Routes of Canada/Then and Now*, 80–92 (Ottawa, 1968). The expedition's rate of canoe travel was slower than the average of 50 miles a day and considerably slower than that of Nicholas Garry's crack crew of voyageurs, who in 1821 covered in 13 days the route from Fort William to Lake Winnipeg which Long traversed in the opposite direction in 25. See Adney and Chapelle, *Bark Canoes*, 145; "Diary of Nicholas Garry," in Royal Society of Canada, *Proceedings and Transactions*, 2nd series, vol. 6, sec. 2, pp. 118–134 (Ottawa, Toronto, and London, 1900). For Keating's comments on the route, see *Narrative*, 2:86–142, 144–147.

THURSDAY, AUGUST 21, 1823. The Lower Falls of the Wenepeek, at the head of which we encamped, have probably an aggregate descent of at least 30 feet in the distance of about 500 yards. There are two principal cascades down which the torrent is precipitated in the wildest and most majestic manner — besides a continued rapid thro' the whole extent of the falls.

Started at break of day. Passed three other portages [*White Mud, Petit Roche, and Big Bonnet*] and encamped for breakfast at the head of the third. This last is one mile in length, passing along the north side of the river. The falls [*Great Falls and McArthur Falls*] we have passed this morning are all beautiful and majestic, but by no means equal in grandeur to the Lower Falls.

The river varies in width from 4 to 12 hundred yards, being contracted at the several rapids, and expanding into lakes in the intervening spaces. Islands of small size occasionally present themselves, but the character of the river is very little affected by them, except where they are connected with the rapids and based upon the rocks that give occasion to these interesting objects, in which cases they contribute greatly to the beauty of the scenery. Bear [*Maskwa*] riv. enters from the north.

Our Canoes having sustained some injury in the passage of the rapids and portages, we were induced to lay by awhile for repairs. Started again at 12 1/2 P.M. Passed another [*Cap du Bonnet*] portage, on the south of the largest Island we have yet met with in the river. At the distance of one mile farther passed another [*Bonnet*] portage with an island still larger, situated as before. Having passed this we entered Bonnet Lake [*Lac du Bonnet*], which has an arm extending about 3 miles in a direction N 65° E from the point of our entrance, and then receives a small river called Covert r. [*Pinawa Channel*] from its being sheltered by woodlands & cliffs. This stream is merely a channel making out from Wenepeek riv. and is passable for canoes in times of high water. It separates from the Wenepeek about 30 miles above its entrance into the Lake. Continued our course thro' the lake, and encamped a little before sunset about one mile below its upper extremity.

Bonnet Lake is about 15 [*20*] miles long and from 600 yards to 4 miles in width. In many places about mid-way of the Lake it is much contracted in width, and a strong current is manifest. Its shores are much indented, and it embosoms several small islands based upon rock. In passing the Lake an Indn. canoe came from the shore to meet, having the dried meat of the Mo[o]se on board, of whic[h] we purchased some. Dist. 27 miles.

Friday, August 22, 1823. Started at the usual time and passed out of the Lake 1 mile above our encampment. Shoals and rapids commence immediately above the lake, and the navigation is rendered difficult and even hazardous for canoes of frail construction like ours by reason of the rocks that abound in this part of the river. The extent of these rapids is 9 miles. At the head of them enters a small stream from the south called White [*Whitemouth*] river. Immediately above the mouth of this riv. is a considerable [*Seven Sisters*] fall and Portage. (N.B. In my acct. of courses & distanc[e]s, P. stands for portage, and r. for rapids where we had to use the towing line to ascend them). The portage here mentioned is one of seven that succeed each other at short intervals. All of these Portages occur in the distance of 4 miles following the meanders of the river, which here varies in width from 5 to 10 hundred yards. The [*Seven Sisters*] Falls at these places have an average descent of at least 15 feet.[12] We succeeded in towing our canoes up one of them but it is seldom passed in this manner. The average descent of the several portages we have passed before to-day may be estimated at the same rate, tho' their descent is by no means uniform.

Passed all these portages in the space of 2 3/4 hours and dined at the uppermost, where we had occasion to repair our Canoes by the application of pitch. Passed a remarkable portion of the river abounding in rapids & islands, two of which latter were of considerable magnitude. Our way lay thro' a very narrow channel to the north of them. (See sketch below). Ascended 7 1/2 miles from our dining place [*through Natalie, Sylvia, and Eleanor lakes*] and arrived at another portage [*between Margaret and Dorothy lakes*], where are situated a considerable Fall improperly called the Grand Rapids [*or Otter Falls*] of the Wenepeek. The Fall at this place is no more than 5 or 6 feet at the principal cascade. Ascended thro a small Lake, which we call Sturgeon Lake [*Dorothy and Nutimik lakes*], 2 miles long & 1 1/2 wide. Two Creeks enter this Lake, one from the SW[13] and the other [*unnamed*] from the NE. At the head of the Lakes [*between Nutimik and Numoa lakes*] is a Fall (Sturgeon Falls)

[12] See pp. 199, 226 for samples of Long's courses and distances. Others in this chapter were omitted. The total drop of Seven Sisters Falls is 48 feet.

[13] The stream to which Long referred is probably the Whiteshell River; it enters from the southeast, not the southwest. See also p. 203, below.

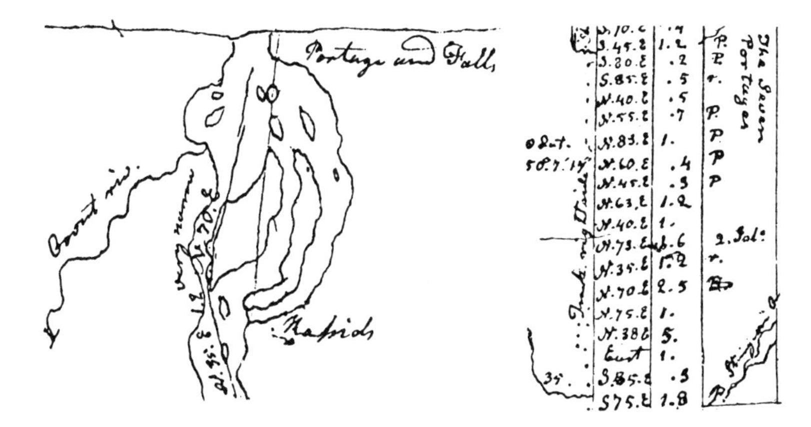

LONG'S SKETCH MAP of August 22, 1823 (left) and his record of courses and distances (right) for the portion of the Winnipeg River from Seven Sisters Falls through present Margaret and Dorothy lakes (actual size).

and a portage. Encamped at the Portage some time after sunset. Distance 30 1/2 miles.

SATURDAY, AUGUST 23, 1823. Started at sun-rise, having been delayed for some time in repairing our canoes. Passed several islands, some of which were of considerable size. The hills along the river become more elevated. Eight [*six*] miles above our Camp of last night, we came to a most romantic and beautiful Fall down which the whole river is precipitated with singular majesty. It is called Ah-wa-ka-ne or Slave Falls from the circumstance that an Indian prisoner, in attempting to make his escape from his pursuers, passed down the cataract in a canoe and was never heard of after wards.[14]

The river is here contracted to the width of about 80 yards, and falls about 20 [24] feet in the distance of less than 100 yards. The banks are here composed of granitic rocks and rise at least 35 feet above the water at the head of the falls. Mr. Seymour took a sketch of this beautiful scene, which we consider as second only to any thing of the kind we have hitherto met with on the journey, the Lower Falls having the precedancy. Past the Slave Falls is a portage of about 400 yards, at the upper end of which we stopped for break fast.

[14] Slave Falls is now the site of one of the many power dams on the Winnipeg River. On the name, see Bell, *Some Historical Names*, 2; Geographic Board of Canada, *Place-Names of Manitoba*, 82; Keating, *Narrative*, 2:98. Seymour's sketch mentioned below appeared in *Narrative*, 2:plate 9.

Another [*Petite Pointe du Bois*] Fall (15 ft.) and [*Rocher Brulé*] Portage (100 yards) occurred 2 1/2 miles above that just mentioned. One mile above these Falls is another singularly grand and beautiful, which by way of distinction we denominate the Upper Falls [*Pointe aux Chênes Falls and Pointe du Bois Falls*] of the Wenepeek. They are formed by two distinct chains or bars extending across the river, the lowermost [*Pointe aux Chênes Falls*] of which occasions a fall of at least 15 feet and the uppermost 10 feet within the distance of 200 yds. The lower chain is intercepted by two small islands between which are cataracts of peculiar beauty, the main channel passing eastwardly of both of them and foaming with terrific majesty. A sketch was taken by Mr. Seymour, but not in the most favourable position, no convenient landing being found elsewhere. We are of opinion that this place vies in beauty with the Lower Falls, if it does not exceed them.[15]

Having Passed these Falls by 2 Portages, we were delayed awhile to repitch our canoes which had again become leaky. Immediately above the Falls the river expands into a Lake of considerable extent. Islands are again numerous, and the scenery along the river picturesque and romantic.

The woodland growth on the lower part of the river consists principally of small aspens interspersed with white birch, with spruce, and Tamarac, none of which attain any considerable magnitude. The under-growth is exceedingly dense and consists of stinted oaks, choak-cherry, hazle, haw[thorn], Pembina shrub, service-berry, arrow-wood, wild plum, raspberry, briar bush, huckle-berry, Sumac, raspberry, wild rose, sand cherry (large & black) with a variety of other shrubbery. Country abounds in small Lakes and swamps. Hills are based on primitive rocks and rise only to a moderate height.

Ascended seven miles farther and passed another very beautiful fall called Jacks [*Jacob or Lamprey*] Falls. The bar or chain here forms a salient angle projecting downward, at the lower part of which is a small Island dividing the river into two channels. The descent of the falls is about 15 feet in the distance of 30 yards. It is surpassed in grandeur only by the Three falls before particularly noticed.

The hills along the river to day are evidently more numerous and

[15] Petite Pointe du Bois (or Eight Foot Falls) and Grande Pointe du Bois Falls in this stretch of the Winnipeg River have been altered by the Pointe du Bois Dam. For Seymour's sketch, see Keating, *Narrative*, 2: plate 10.

SLAVE FALLS in the Winnipeg River, a drawing by Samuel Seymour engraved by J. Hill for publication in the Narrative *of the 1823 expedition published in 1824.*

more elevated than we have before observed them to be. The white birch becomes more abundant. The [é]pinette [*black or white spruce*], a small species of pine whence the gum used in the construction of the bark canoe is usually extracted, has been seen interspersed here and there among the other growth, but now becomes considerably abundant. In size and appearance it resembles the spruce of dwarfish growth; its timber is used for small spars and Masts as also for laths used in lining the bark canoe. A small species of Pitch-pine called by the Canadians Cypress [*jack pine?*] begins to make its appearance. It is of a scrubby appearance and yields a gum or resin suitable for pitching canoes. Its bark is similar to that of the Pitch-Pine.

Since passing the last Falls, the river spreads to a great width [*Eaglenest Lake*], embosoming innumerable islands, most of them small and based upon rock. Encamped a little before sunset on an island. Distance 32 miles.

SUNDAY, AUGUST 24, 1823. In the course of the remarks upon the country made yesterday it should have been observed that the soil is very thin, and that the earthy covering of the rocks is total[l]y wanting in many places and scarsely hides them in others. The stinted growth of the woodlands and the dwarfish appearance of the vegetation generally is to be attributed to this cause.

Started early. Weather rainy. River still abounds in islands. Ascended about 14 miles and breakfasted at the Island Portage [*Portage de l'Isle*], so called from an island [*Boundary I.*] situated near the middle of the river at this place. Descent of the rapid about 7 feet. At the distance of 1 1/2 miles above this [*Boundary*] Fall[s], a bifurcation of the river occurs. A river equal in size to the Wenepeek above their junction, called the English river, enters from the NE. It resembles the Wenepeek also in character, abounding in small Lakes, Islands, Falls, rapids, and portages. It has its sources and interlocks with those of Albany river and is the principal channel of intercourse between Lake Wenepeek and Albany of Upper Canada.[16]

It should have been remarked before that the islands of the river are equally as elevated and broken as the hills of the circumjacent

[16] On the English River-Albany River route linking the Winnipeg River and James Bay, see Morse, *Fur Trade Canoe Routes*, 100. The sources of both rivers are in western Ontario; the English heads in Lac Seul, the Albany in nearby Lake St. Joseph. The north channel of the Winnipeg River described below has not been altered by the Whitedog Dam, which flooded the south channel.

country. Indeed the country may be considered as made up of islands, the water having receded from the valleys and left a dry, broken, and stirile region with earth upon the hills scarsely sufficient to cover the rocks, and valleys possessing a soil made up of the coarse and unproductive detritus of inorganic rocks. Passed the entrance of a smal[l] channel which is separated for a long distance from the main river. Such channels are frequent.

At the distance of 18 miles above the last Portage we had a [*La Cave*] rapid to pass by which our baggage was carried by land. Just above this is a [*Terre Blanche*] Portage of about 150 yards and a Fall of 10 feet. One mile still above is another carrying place [*Petit Rocher or Charette Décharge*], descent of water 4 feet. A few yards above this is also another [*Terre Jaune*] Portage of about 80 yards and a Fall of at least 25 feet. The [north] Channel along which we passed is but a small portion of the [Winnipeg] river, separated from the main channel by an island extending thro'out the distance included within the Portages and rapids. Passed another rapid [*Grand Décharge*], fall about 5 feet, and ascended the same channel to the head of the Island, which we found 5 1/2 miles long. The main channel no doubt affords much picturesque scenery, as a great body of water is discharged thro' it and the descent thro' it cannot be less than 50 or 60 feet, but we had not leisure to examine any part of it. Encamped 1/2 mile above the island a little before 6 o'clock. Distance by our route 38 miles.

MONDAY, AUGUST 25, 1823. Started at break of day and travelled 9 miles before breakfast. White pine begins to make its appearance along the river. Hills more elevated, Islands more numerous. Were it not for the current, which is every where apparent and in many places rapid, the greater part of the [Winnipeg] river might be called a Lake or series of lakes.

Twelve miles above our morning encampment is a remarkable streight called the Dalles, thro' which the water is hurried with great rapidity. The whole river is here contracted to the width of 40 yards and is bounded on both sides by perpindicular precipices of Granite for the distance of about 40 yards. The current is very rapid, but by the strong exertions of our watermen we succeeded in prising it with our paddl[e]s. Passed an out-let on our right [*Locke Bay?*] within a short distance of the Lake of the Woods which supplies Sturgeon [*Whiteshell*] river, before noticed [*p. 198, above*] as entering a lake of that name. Passed a Fall on our left which serves as the out let of

The Lake of the Woods and proceeded some distance beyond it in a small lake [*Darlington Bay*], from which we passed to the Lake of the Woods by a short portage known by the name of the Rat Portage. Its length is about 100 yards. Here we encamped at 4 1/2 P.M. Distance 31 miles.[17]

TUESDAY, AUGUST 26, 1823. The point at which we entered the [*Portage Bay of*] Lake of the Woods is situated near the N westerly part of the Lake within 9 or 10 miles of its northerly extreme. The commissioners appointed to perambulate the boundary line between the U.S. and the British Territory had arrived at this place within two weeks past in the performance of the duties assigned them and had returned again to Lake Superiour. We could discover no land-marks, however, that had been fixed by them. The Lake of the woods appears to be elevated about 12 or 15 feet above the Wenepeek river at the point where we left it.[18]

Soon after our arrival in the afternoon of yesterday a storm commenced and continued thro' a considerable part of the night, which prevented us from examining the place, visiting the Falls at the out let, and taking observations for Latitude and Longitude.

Started before 3 A.M. Passed eastwardly thro' a small arm [*Portage Bay*] of the Lake 1/4 mile, where we entered the lake itself. The numerous islands with which the Lake is thronged prevented our having an extensive view in any direction. Encamped for breakfast on an island, having travelled 16 miles. The island furnished a variety of small fruit, such as small red & black cherries, the former of which was similar in taste to the domestic one called the (Morella) and both quite free from astringency. A singular berry was also found upon the island growing upon a small shrub strongly resembling the hemlock. This fruit is of a bright red, about as large as a currant, sweetish to the taste, has a slimy pulp, and seeds about as large as those of common hemp. Currants (black), and goosberries,

[17] On the three outlets of Lake of the Woods and the location of Rat Portage in modern Keewatin, Ont., see International Joint Commission, *Final Report on the Lake of the Woods Reference*, 131, 214–216 (Washington, D.C., 1917); Morse, *Fur Trade Canoe Routes*, 87; Keating, *Narrative*, 2:106. The falls at the outlets mentioned here and below in present Keewatin and Kenora, Ont., are now used for hydroelectric power.

[18] The international boundary problem in the Lake of the Woods area dated back to the Treaty of Paris in 1783, and it was not fully resolved until the 20th century. For summaries of the problem and the commission travelers of 1823, see Robert McElroy and Thomas Riggs, eds., *The Unfortified Boundary: A Diary of . . . Joseph Delafield*, 63–123 (New York, 1943); Grace Lee Nute, *Rainy River Country*, 25–27 (St. Paul, 1950); Thomson, *Men and Meridians*, 1:260; Keating, *Narrative*, 2:106–108.

also huckle berries, together with the service berry, were also found here.[19]

A rocky formation of different characters from those we have usually met with occurred yesterday and becomes abundant, even the prevailing rock to-day. The rock alluded to is a Slate, in some instances Lamellar, but usually hard and in large blocks when disengaged from their native precipices. Masses of rolled stone are also numerous and seem to abound most on the south sides of the islands. The islands are uniformly based upon rocks, and like those of Wenepeek river, attain the same elevation as the hills of the circumjacent country. It is remarkable that neither on the margins of the Lake of the woods nor on those of Wenepeek river are bottom lands to be met with, nor even are sand-bars or beaches to be found connected either with the islands or shores.

Pitch pine and white pine gradually becomes more abundant. The timber-growth generally attains a larger size. A great variety of grasses, flowers and weeds has prevailed pretty generally along the rivers and Lakes. We have seen but very little Wild Rice till our arrival at the Lake of the Woods, but in the coves and recesses of the lake it is abundant. It is now in its mature state and the indians are engaged in gathering & preparing it for their winter sustenance.

At our Breakfast encampment observations were attempted for Latitude and Longitude, our delay at that place having been 3 1/2 hours; it is presumed, however, that they were incomplet[e] for want of observations to determine the rate of the time piece.

Proceeded 14 miles farther and arrived at the Portage du Lac [*du Bois or French Portage*], where we encamped again for dinner. Here it commenced raining again. This is a portage to save distance in passing round a [*Aulneau*] peninsula, the neck across which we passed is about 100 yards. It appears that the portage of the Lake is merely across an isthmus joining two peninsulas, which together constitute an island.[20]

The Lake of the Woods deserves a high rank on the scale of beauty when compared with other Lakes. Its scenery is wild and romantic in a high degree, its shores being faced with precipices and

[19] For Seymour's sketch of the breakfast encampment on what Keating called Cosse's Island, and for a description of the cherry mentioned here, see Keating, *Narrative*, 2:110, 387, plate 11. The cherry may be the Canada plum (*Prunus nigra*) and the berry may be the fruit of the American yew (*Taxus canadensis*).

[20] French Portage Narrows and a boat channel now follow this route across Aulneau Peninsula, and a dam has raised the water level, covering the portage. See Morse, *Fur Trade Canoe Routes*, 85.

capped with hills & knobs of variable heights clad with a dense foliage of shrubbery and evergreens. Its surface is beautifully studded with countless islands of various sizes and formes, disclosing between them the continued sheet of its wide-spreading waters, the extent of which enlarges upon the view as the traveller advances upon them till the main land is shut out from his view by the islands that multiply around him.

The rain continuing we were induced to remain encamped during the rest of the day. Distance 30 miles.

WEDNESDAY, AUGUST 27, 1823. The weather becoming fair and the wind favourable, we set sail at an early hour and pursued our voyage with considerable speed. As we approached the SE extremity of the Lake an arm [*Muskeg Bay*] of considerable extent extending in a southerly direction appeared on our right. The passage to the Fork of Red river (Ft. Douglass) leads thro' this arm, across a portage, down Red river before spoken of, and to the place above mentioned. The time required by a traveller on snoe-shoes to perform the journey from the Lake of the Woods to Fort Douglass by this route is 4 days travelling expeditiously.[21]

We daily witness occasions for regrets that we have not a botanist attached to our party. Mr. Say, who is in some measure competent to the collection of new plants, embraces every opportunity to furnish an herbarium with new specimens out of the abundance and variety that come under our observation. The islands on which we land occasionally afford a great variety of plants and shrubbery many of which are no doubt rare and valuable. Several were collected on that where we break fasted this morning. Among others a beautiful little shrub bearing a white berry, also a new variety of the convolvulus (white), and a rose bush apparently new were found here.

At noon we stopped at Red Rock island and took an alt. of the Sun for the Latitude.[22]

[21] It seems probable that Long here referred to an overland trail and water route long known to the Indians and fur traders; it ran from Muskeg Bay of Lake of the Woods, up the Warroad River with a portage to Hay Creek and the Roseau River, and then down the Roseau to the Red River. See Earl V. Chapin, "The Early History of the Roseau Valley," in *Minnesota History*, 24:319, 321 (December, 1943); Coues, ed., *New Light*, 1:70; Gordon C. Davidson, *The North West Company*, facing p. 144 (University of California, *Publications in History*, vol. 7—Berkeley, 1918).

[22] The rose was not a new type. Red Rock Island or Rocher Rouge was a usual stopping point for canoes. McElroy and Riggs, eds., Delafield, *Unfortified Boundary*, 427, 431, described it as a granite point of an island (probably Painted Rock) northeast of the traverse. Morse, *Fur Trade Canoe Routes*, 85, noted that the Grand Traverse, mentioned below, was normally made between Bigsby Island and the mouth of Rainy River. See also Keating, *Narrative*, 2:110–113.

Having passed numerous other islands, some of which were large, we entered a part of the Lake almost entirely destitute of them. Our course S 24° E, 7.5 [miles], led us thro what is called by the voyageurs the Grand Traverse. It is situated in the South part of the Lake. To the SW of it no islands or land appears, but an arm of the Lake about 14 miles in length and 4 or 5 in breadth extends in that direction beyond the reach of our vision. In the opposite direction its extent is very considerable. Having crossed the Traverse, which is passable only in still weather for bark canoes, we entered a channel separated from the main Lake by a chain of rocks imbedded in sand, and hence denominated the Isle du Sable [*Sable Islands*]. The channel runs parallel to the shore of the lake and is distant from it no more than 100 or 150 yards. In windy weather canoes are obliged to lay by and not cross the Traverse till they are favoured with a calm.

Encamped in the channel above mentioned a little before sun-set. Distance 47 1/2 miles.

THURSDAY, AUGUST 28, 1823. Wenepeek river and the Lake of the Woods may be regarded as worthy of a rank amongst the most singular and curious of Natures works in the formation of rivers and Lakes. It seems as if Nature here had established her re[a]lm so firm and unchangeable as to bid defiance to the power and art of man either to overthrow or mutilate it. The country, both main[land] & islands, is so cased and covered with rocks that no part of it appears susceptible of cultivation, while the water-courses are so bent with rapids & cataracts formed by the hardest and most unmanageable of rocks, that the human strength and art would seem a[l]together inadequate to any purpose of changing or controlling their direction or commanding their services.

Started at half past 4. Proceeded 5 1/2 miles and arrived at the entrance of Rainy river of which we commenced the ascent.[23] At the mouth of this river is an extensive marsh covered with a luxuriant growth of grass & weeds and intersected by numerous small runs, or creeks, of stagnant water. The Island of sand [*Sable Islands*], before mentioned as separating the channel thro' which we passed from the Lake, is about 7 miles long. This and other sandbars in the

[23] From this point eastward to Lac la Croix, the party traveled for the most part along the present boundary between Minnesota and Ontario. These waters were part of the "main line" of the fur trade. From Lac la Croix, two well-known canoe routes led eastward to Lake Superior: the so-called Kaministikwia River route, which Long followed to Fort William (now Thunder Bay, Ont.), and the Grand Portage route farther south along the boundary to Grand Portage, Minn. See Morse, *Fur Trade Canoe Routes*, 75–84.

neighbourhood of the mouth of Rainy-r. are all that we have seen in the Lake.

By an Observation at our Camp of last night, the Lat. was found to be 48° 54′ 10″ N. At our Breakfast encampment, 8 1/2 miles up the river, observations were also taken for Longe.

Since leaving the Lake of the Woods a manifest change in the aspect of the country has taken place. Rocks seldom make their appearance along the banks or channel of the river. The soil of the country is deeper & of a better quality, the hills are less numerous, and the surface less broken, while a more dense and larger growth of timber is uniformly prevalent thro' out the circumjacent country. Rainy river thus far bears equally as strong a contrast with the Wenepeek. It has generally a uniform width of 4 or 5 hundred yards, is destitute of islands, its current very moderate, and its shores exhibit very few rocky precipices. The prevailing growth is still aspin, tho' pine abounds at a little distance from the river. The white birch becomes more plentiful and attains a larger size.

Passed a considerable stream entering from the south called the river of the Rapids [*Rapid R.*] from a handsome Fall situated at its mouth. It heads in Lakes and swamps, having an extent of 70 or 80 miles.

The animals that abound on these waters, especially on the tributaries of the principal rivers, are the following viz. Beaver, otter, musk-rat, martin, fisher, loup-cervier [*Canada lynx*], carcajou [*wolverine*], the bear, moose. Carabou, porcupine, fox, squirrel, weazle &c. are also inhabitants of this region.

Ascended to the mouth of Pine [*Pinewood*] river, where we encamped a little before sun-set. This river enters from the NW and is about 30 yards wide at its mouth. Distance 38 miles.

FRIDAY, AUGUST 29, 1823. Started at an early hour. The wind being ahead, as was generally the case yesterday, our progress was slow. The current of the [Rainy] river continues moderate. Its width somewhat less, averaging about 250 or 300 yards. The country apparently becomes better as we advance. The white [*silver*] maple begins to make its appearance. The forest trees are larger. The pine more abundant.

The means of acquiring a knowledge of the country are very defective. Our engagees are illy calculated to give a satisfactory account of it, and it is difficult to draw from them what little information they are able to give.

The statement of one of our engagees, [La] Fontaine, who has traversed the country by land from the southern extremity of the Lake of the Woods to Pembina, represents it as possessing an aspect little varied or interesting. In the vicinity of the Lake the country is rocky, swamps and marshes next occur, extending about one day's march from the river, this part of the route impracticable for horses—farther on savannah, or prairies, abounding in marshy and low grounds, make their appearance. Copses of wood-land occasionally appear but their growth is small. No hills of any considerable magnitude are to be met with. The same man has also travelled by land from Rainy Lake to the Grand Portage [*of the St. Louis R.*] near Fond du Lac. The country on this route is very rugged, hills numerous, and in some instances very high. Very little timber to be found on them. Wood-lands present themselves in the low grounds and swamps but the growth is small. Swamps and marshs abound in the vallies.[24]

Passed several stakes probably set by the commissioners at the lower end of an island for ascertaining the width of the channels. Five miles above our morning camp we reached the [*Long Sault*] Rapids of Rainy river, which we ascended with some difficulty. They are about one [*one and one-half*] mile long — the current rapid and the Fall considerable [*about seven feet*]. The principal Fall is occasioned by a chain of rocks streaching across the river, past which we were compelled to debark and tow our canoes. Rocks — a hard slate — river some what reduced in width.

Mr. Robillard, another engagee, who has traversed the country of the Nippegon [*Nipigon*] river of Lake Superior, gives the following statement. This river is about [*half*] as long as Rainy riv. It has but 3 inconsiderable rapids and is navigable for north canoes thro' the year. It heads in Red [*Nipigon*] Lake situate[d] northwardly of its mouth. It traverses a hilly and rocky country, destitute of soil in

[24] La Fontaine's description of both regions was quite accurate. On the area from Lake of the Woods to Pembina, see S[imon] J. Dawson, *Report on the Exploration of the Country between Lake Superior and the Red River Settlement*, 14 (Toronto, 1859). On the Grand Portage of the St. Louis River, now within Jay Cooke State Park near Duluth, see Holmquist and Brookins, *Minnesota's Major Historic Sites*, 158–163. The St. Louis River route, connecting Lake Superior and Rainy Lake (via the Pike River, Lake Vermilion, Vermilion River, Crane Lake, Little Vermilion Narrows, and then west along the present border) figured in the boundary negotiations between England and the United States. See William E. Culkin, "Northern Minnesota Boundary Surveys in 1822 to 1826, Under the Treaty of Ghent," in *MHC*, 15:384–388 (1915). The route is shown on Nicollet, "Hydrographical Basin."

many places, but in some instances corn and potatoes are cultivated by the people of the Hudson-B. co., who have four trading establishments on its banks. Back from the river the country abounds in swamps and marshs, alternating with rugged hills of moderate height.[25]

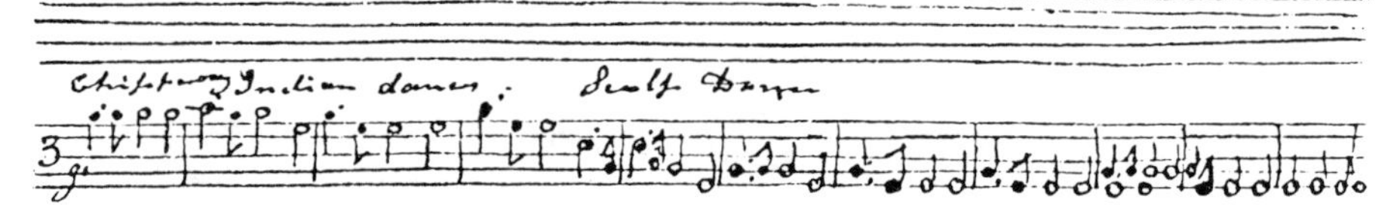

A BAR of Ojibway or Chippewa music to accompany a scalp dance inserted by Long in his journal at this point.

Several of our engagees, among whom is Demarest [*Desmarais*], our guide, have frequently travelled in the capacity of watermen westwardly and N westwardly to the Rocky Mountains. From them have we gleaned the following items of intelligence. A region of great extent, no doubt a continuation of the Great American desert, streaches alonong [*along*] the eastern side of the mountains, possessing a sandy surface and dest[it]ute of vegetation, except in the vallies of water-courses.[26]

It is represented as producing a growth of grass early in the season when the ground is filled with moisture, but it soon withers as summer advances and the prairies or plains are left destitute of verdure. The mountains there, as is the case in lower latitudes, rise abruptly out of the plains, attain a great elevation, and are covered with perpetual snow. Saskatchawin [*Saskatchewan*] river has a general width of about 800 yards. Its current is gentle, its water some-

[25] On Robillard, see note 1, above. His account of the Nipigon River was inaccurate. It heads in Lake Nipigon, Ont., and flows south into Nipigon Bay on Lake Superior's north shore. It is not open throughout the year, is only about half as long as the Rainy River (40 miles and 85 miles respectively), and contained at least six portages, two of which were over three miles long. Although little used by fur traders in later years, it was known to the French and re-explored by Edward Umfreville of the North West Company in 1784. See Umfreville's journal in R. Douglas, ed., *Nipigon to Winnipeg: A Canoe Voyage through Western Ontario*, 13–15 (Ottawa, 1929). On the fur posts, see E. E. Rich, *The Fur Trade and the Northwest to 1857*, 177 (Toronto, 1967).

[26] On the Great American Desert, see p. 11, above; Keating, *Narrative*, 2:242. The music was reproduced in a different key and entitled "Chippewa Scalp Dance," in Keating, *Narrative*, 1:plate 5.

what muddy, its shores destitute of rocks, and no rapids are to be met with below the Forks, a distance of ten days travel or about 200 [*340*] miles from its mouth. Rapids are to be met with in both branches of the river a short distance above their junction. The forks are narrow at their confluence but expand greatly on ascending them. The country wooded below this point but almost entirely destitute of a timber growth above.[27]

The Athabaska [*Athabasca*] is a very large river. From the description given it does not in aptly compare with the Missouri in extent, magnitude, and character of its waters. Its current is considerably rapid. No rocks appear in its bed for a long distance from its mouth. The country along its margins is clad in a dwarfish growth of Aspens, pines, birch, &c. Lake Athabaska [*Athabasca*] is situated 25 days journey above the estuary of the river. Several tributaries, some of which are very large, discharge themselves into the Lake & river. In ascending the river, the soil first met with is sandy, afterwards, as is stated, pitchy, probably charged with petrolium and thus of a black and unctuous character.[28]

A storm commenced soon after we encamped for dinner, and we lay by for the residue of the day. Distance 25 miles.

SATURDAY, AUGUST 30, 1823. It continued rainy thro' the night. Resumed our voyage this morning at 4. Ascended two miles and passed another [*Manitou*] rapid formed by a single chain of rocks extending across the river. We occasionally pass small islands, but they are not numerous in any part of the river. The maple becomes

[27] The Saskatchewan, Canada's fourth longest river, had been known to British fur traders since the mid-1700s. It heads in the Rocky Mountains and flows across prairies, some of them arid, in Alberta and Saskatchewan, emptying into Lake Winnipeg at Grand Rapids, Man. The junction or forks of the north and south branches occurs about 30 miles east of present Prince Albert, Sask., 340 miles from the outlet at Lake Winnipeg. Five sets of rapids, some now dammed, existed below the forks, including Grand Rapids at the outlet. See MacGregor, *Blankets and Beads*, 15–22; Bruce Peel, "First Steamboats on the Saskatchewan," in *The Beaver*, Autumn, 1964, pp. 16–21.

[28] Long was misinformed about the Athabasca River, which is 765 miles in length compared to 2,714 for the Missouri. Fur traders led by Peter Pond penetrated the Athabasca region of present Alberta at least as early as 1778, and the area became known to the literate world with the publication of Alexander Mackenzie, *Voyages from Montreal, on the River St. Laurence, through the Continent of North America* (London, 1801), describing his journeys of 1789 and 1793. See also Rich, *Fur Trade and the Northwest*, 172–185. The oil sand deposits of the Athabasca near Fort McMurray, Alba., were not developed until the mid-20th century, although they were known to the Geological Survey of Canada at least since 1897. Robert Kroetsch, *Alberta*, 200 (New York, 1968).

more plentiful along the river. The Elm & cotton wood sometimes occur.

Passed Black river, a small stream ent[e]ring from the SE. It rises in swamps and small lakes at no great distance from its mouth. About twenty five miles below Rainy Lake the [Rainy] river receives a large tributary called the Grand [*Big*] Fork, which yields a supply of water nearly equal to that received from the Lake. It rises in or near Lake Wenepeek? [*Lake Winnibigoshish*] of the Mississippi, between which is a direct water-communication for canoes without the interruption of a portage. Throughout the whole extent of the Fork, a distance of six days travel with light canoes, there are but two places of rapids, past one of which is a portage. This fork receives a tributary from the SW [*Moose Brook or Caldwell Creek*] which affords a communication with Red Lake. It enters three days journey from the mouth of the Grand Fork. The country is said to be destitute of high hills, abounds in marshes, is generally timbered, and possesses a pretty good soil. Rocks are not abundant. Boulders appear in the river.[29]

About 8 miles above the entrance of the Grand Fork is that of a considerable stream from the SW called the Little Fork, which has no great extent, nor is it a channel of communication between any important points. At the confluence of this and Rainy riv. is a settlement on the American side at which improvements have been made on a small scale.[30]

The aspect of the country appears to be materially changed for the better, compared to that we have passed since we entered the Lake Wenepeek. The surface is far less rocky and broken, no rocks appear in the river, except boulders occasionally along the shore and the rocks that present themselves at the rapids. The timber growth, besides being larger and more thrifty, presents a variety of trees not to be found below, such as the white oak, the ash, the hiccory, the

[29] The Big Fork River, which rises near Lake Winnibigoshish, Minn., provided a connecting route to both the Red River and the Mississippi watersheds. The river's course contains many sets of rapids and two waterfalls; see Waters, *Streams and Rivers of Minnesota*, 100. Keating, *Narrative*, 2:116, wrote that the information on it was obtained from Mr. (William?) Davenport of the American Fur Company's Rainy River post, which used the route in its trade. On the name variations of Lake Winnibigoshish, see Upham, *Minnesota Geographic Names*, 96–98.

[30] The Little Fork River, Minn., is about 150 miles long. The "settlement" was the farm of Vincent Roy, a former North West Company employee. See Nute, *Rainy River Country*, 30, 33.

water maple, the white walnut, the Linden &c. The beautiful shrub called the Larche [*white spruce*] is also found here; the black alder frequently occurs along the river.

The soil appears much deeper and more fertile. Indeed the change of aspect is no less striking than the transition from the rugged hills and craggy cliffs of a Primitive region to the gentle swells and undulating plains of a secondary. And in fact, we are disposed to think that we are actually making this transition.

Arrived about sun-set within 4 or 5 miles of Rainy Lake and encamp[e]d. Dist. 39 m.

SUNDAY, AUGUST 31, 1823. Started at our usual hour, travelled 5 miles, and arrived at the [*Koochiching*] Falls situated at the out-let of Rainy Lake at 5 1/2 o'clock A.M. Where we lay by to repair our canoes, procure a fresh supply of provisions &c.

At the Falls of Rainy river are situated two trading establishments, the one belonging to the Hudson Bay company situated on the British side, and the other belonging to the American Fur company on the American side of the river directly opposite.[31] Not finding such supplies as we stood in need of at the latter, we fix[ed] our encampment near the former, where we were very kindly received by Mr. [Simon] McGillivray, [Jr.], the superintendent.[32] Dist. 5 miles.

MONDAY, SEPTEMBER 1, 1823. Deeming it expedient to leave one of our canoes at this place, in consequence of the shattered condition to which our voyage added to former services had reduced her, and having occasion to make material repairs in the other two, we were necessarily delayed thro' this day to accomplish this purpose. The weather also, being continually cloudy and sometimes rainy since our arrival, retarded our work very considerably. All

[31] The Hudson's Bay Company Fort la Pluie to which Long referred was built in 1818 and named Fort Frances in 1830. The fort, located in present-day Fort Frances, Ont., has been reconstructed. The American Fur Company post was established in 1822 as part of that firm's campaign to keep the British traders north of the boundary. See Nute, in *Minnesota History*, 22:270–275; Morse, *Fur Trade Canoe Routes*, 84; McElroy and Riggs, eds., Delafield, *Unfortified Boundary*, 422, 432, 434; Ramsay Crooks to Robert Stuart, December 5, 1821, April 8, 1822, Mackinac Letter Book, 1820–25, Stuart House, Mackinac Island, Mich., copy in MHS.

[32] McGillivray became a chief trader of the Hudson's Bay Company in 1821 after earlier service with the North West Company. He was appointed to Rainy Lake in 1822. See E. E. Rich, ed., *Journal of Occurrences in the Athabasca Department by George Simpson, 1820 and 1821, and Report*, 451 (Toronto, 1938).

articles necessary for our subsistence on the voyage to Fort William were procured without much difficulty — such as Wild Rice, Indn. Corn, Wheat meal, potatoes &c. No meat of any description was to be had.

The [*Koochiching*] Falls of Rainy River, agreeably to a measurement made this morning, have a descent of 25 feet. A grist mill of rude construction has been erected on the margin of the river, or rather upon the rocks on the shore, at which wheat is ground for the use of the H. B. establishment at this place. Mr. Seymour has taken a sketch of this interesting fall and the neighbouring scenery.[33]

Wheat, potatoes, and some indian corn, together with other culinary vegetables, are cultivated to advantage for the use of the establishment. The wheat fields in particular are very fine, but the season for harvest is but now commencing.

TUESDAY, SEPTEMBER 2, 1823. At the H. Bay Co.'s Fort we met with an American by the name of [John] Tanner, who had remained here for some time disabled by a wound received from an indian, who fired upon him as he was making his retreat from the Indian country with his wife (a squaw) and two of his children (daughters, the one about 15 and the other about 12 years old). His history is a very eventful one, sketches of which have been circulated thro' the medium of the Newspapers of the U. States. He had been taken prisoner by the indians at the age of about nine years and had continued resident among them till within 2 or three years, measures having been taken by his friends and relations to reclaim him. He had resided among the savages for a period of about 30 years, had lost all knowledge of his native language, and in every respect but complexion had become completely a savage. Since the discovery of his family and the intercourse he has had with the Americans in connexion therewith, he has acquired a knowledge of the English Language sufficient to enable him to converse intelligibly. For a more particular account of this man, see the notes of Mr. Say.[34]

[33] For the expedition's purchases, see Voucher No. 36, in "Abstract," Appendix 2, below. Construction of the water-powered mill at Koochiching Falls (now dammed at the towns of Fort Frances, Ont., and International Falls, Minn.) was announced in John McLoughlin to Dougald Cameron, February 15, 1815 (28: 153), Selkirk Papers. Seymour's painting of the falls has not been located. See p. 392, below.

[34] The story of Tanner's kidnapping by the Indians from his Kentucky home in 1789 has been told many times, with varying details. See Edwin James, ed., *A Narrative of the Captivity and Adventures of John Tanner*, 266–279 (New York, 1830); P. G. Downes, "John Tanner Captive of the Wilderness," in *Naturalist*, Fall, 1958, pp. 30–32. Say's information was included in Keating, *Narrative*, 2: 117–128.

As Mr. Tanner was very desirous to prosecute his journey to Mackinaw [*Mackinac, Mich.*] and had no other means of accomplishing it, we managed to give him a place and passage on board of our canoes as soon as we should be able to take our departure.

The weather so cold and rainy that we could not complete our canoes. Sometime after dark Dr. McGlauplin [*John McLoughlin*] arrived from York Factory, having been sent to this post to take charge of it in behalf of the Company as Superintendent.[35]

The deportment of this gentleman at the short interview we had with him this evening was calculated to leave on our minds the most favourable impressions as to his humanity and hospitality. A circumstance had occurred which required the friendly intraposition of some person of influence connected with the Trading establishment, and the arrival of the Dr. at this juncture seemed to be ominous of good fortune to the parties concerned.

The two daughters of Tanner had obtained the consent of their father to go into the fort and take leave of a woman that had been particularly kind to them during the confinement and sickness of Mr. T. But as they did not return at the time appointed, the father became anxious and unhappy on account of their delay. He proceeded to the fort in company with our interpreter, Bruce [*Brousse*], to make inquiry concerning them, but was repulsed in a rude if not inhuman manner by some of the Engagees of the establishment. This being reported, Maj. L. & Mr. Say proceeded to the Fort for the purpose of inquiry, and were informed that the girls were not in the fort nor in any of the buildings appertaining to it, but had probably made their escape in a canoe down the river to join their mother who was now at the Lake of the Woods. No efforts however were volunteered towards discovering the route taken by the girls till the arrival of the Dr., when inquiry, tho' unsuccessful, was immediately made. The night being extremely dark, no search could be made till morning. This morning inquiry and search was commenced in order to ascertain what had become of them. A reward was offered to any indian who would discover and bring them back, and two, the only ones about the fort that could engage

[35] Dr. McLoughlin, a Canadian trained as a physician, was a former employee of the North West Company who was named a chief factor of the Hudson's Bay Company in 1821. He was appointed to Rainy Lake the following year. He commented favorably upon Long and his care of Tanner in his 1823–24 journal, vol. B105/a/9, in the Hudson's Bay Company Archives, Winnipeg. See also Kenneth L. Holmes, "John McLoughlin," in Hafen, ed., *Mountain Men*, 8:235–245 (Glendale, Calif., 1971); Grace Lee Nute, "Border Chieftain," in *The Beaver*, March, 1952, pp. 35–39.

in the search, immediately started in pursuit of them. After an unsuccessful search thro' the day, no intelligence could be had concerning the girls.

A new Alt. of the sun was observed to-day from which the Lat. of the Falls was found to be 48° 26′ 27″ [*48° 36′ 30″*]. The weather became fair a little before noon—the first fair weather for many days. The gentlemen of the party all engaged in their appropriate pursuits. Provisions were purchased at enormous prices, for example—£3 9s. Sterling per half bushel or bag of hulled corn!—and a few other articles in due proportion. The Dr. kindly presented us with two pounds of tea, as many potatoes as we choose to take, turnips &c.[36] Our canoes were now nearly completed, and we were again in readiness to embark to morrow.

WEDNESDAY, SEPTEMBER 3, 1823. Having completed our arrangements, we delayed our departure till 10 A.M. in the hope that some intelligence might be had relative to the two daug[h]ters of Tanner, but were altogether disappointed in this respect, notwithstanding the search that had been made for them. Tanner, however, with a heavy heart concluded to embark with us, believing it highly probable that the girls had gone in pursuit of their mother and that all further enquiry for them would prove ineffectual, especially in his present disabled condition. He accordingly prepared to accompany us to Mackinaw, where one of his wives (he had two, one of whom also, that at the Lake of the Woods, had a second husband) and several children now resided.

We took leave of our newly acquired friends of the H. B. Co. with demonstrations of kindness and good wishes on the one part and of thankfulness on the other. We had been entertained in the most hospitable manner at the table of the Superintendent, and on taking our leave from him were pressed to take on board vegetabl[e]s and other conveniences, some of which we accepted. Having ascended Rainy river 2 1/2 miles above the Falls, we encountered a rapid [*unnamed*] situated immediately at the out let of Rainy Lake.

Finding that the motion of the canoe affected his fractured arm and rendered travelling exceedingly painful to him, Mr. Tanner, tho' with reluctance, chose to aban[don] the purpose of returning with us and concluded to wait some future opportunity when his arm should be restored to soundness again. He accordingly landed at an encampment of a young Canadian in the employ of the H. B.

[36] See Voucher No. 36 in "Abstract," Appendix 2, below.

Co. with whom he could easily return to the Fort either by land or water. The fatigue of travelling had occasioned considerable inflammation in his wounded limb, accompanied with febrile symptoms.

The wind being fair, we set sail on entering the Lake and proceeded rapidly about 15 miles, when we were induced to lay by on account its blowing too hard.

Sailed again at 5 P.M. with a fair and strong wind and arrived at the commencement of the Grand Travers at a little after sun-set. Dist. 28 m.

THURSDAY, SEPTEMBER 4, 1823. Rainy Lake, like the Lake of the Woods, abounds in islands & is bounded by rocky shores. At its eastern extremity also is a very broad part of the lake destitute of islands and called the Grand Travers. The rocks of the islands and shores are slate in the western, and granite in the eastern part of the Lake. Reef of rocks often occur, sometimes rising above the surface of the water and in many places are sunk to a moderate depth below, rendering the navigation hazardous.

Started early, the morning very fine. Crossed the Grand Traverse, which has an extent of about 12 miles, and encamped for breakfast. The part of the Lake in which the Travers is situated is of a width from 1 to 3 miles. Proceeded about 3 miles farther and passed out of the Lake into a small stream called New Portage river [*Canadian Channel and Bear R.*] along which our way lay, which proved very crooked. Arrived at a portage 3 miles from the Lake and a second [*Bear Portage*] about 700 yards farther on. Small Lakes or pools and swamp abounding in wild rice are of frequent occurrence. Passed the second portage at a little before 11 o'clock and entered another small [*Namakan*] lake.[37]

After leaving the [*Rainy*] Lake, we observed a water fall [*Kettle Falls*] on our right, at which there is a Portage called the Kettle P. by which canoes usually pass up the river [*Kettle Channel*] in a low

[37] Seymour completed a painting, not located, of Rainy Lake; see p. 392, below. The traverse of the eastern part of Rainy Lake was usually made roughly along the line of the international boundary from the Brûlé Narrows area east to Oakpoint Island at the southeastern end of Rainy Lake. The New Portage route confusingly described here usually followed the Canadian Channel along Oakpoint Island, bypassed Kettle Falls through Hale Bay of Rainy Lake, and entered Namakan Lake via Bear Portage, then called Nouvelle, Neuf, or Nu Portage. The route was not "new" when Long passed that way; Alexander Mackenzie passed over it as early as 1789. See W. Kaye Lamb, ed., *The Journals and Letters of Sir Alexander Mackenzie*, 105 (Cambridge, England, 1970); Morse, *Fur Trade Canoe Routes*, 79, 84.

stage of water. But in high waters as at present the route we have taken is preferred as being much shorter. By the other route, which lies along the main river [*Kettle Channel and Squirrel Narrows*], there is but one Portage, but the great length of the way by that route to Lake Nam-máka-kon [*Namakan*], or Sturgeon Lake, which we entered at the second [*Bear*] portage before mentioned.

Having travelled 15 miles in this [*Namakan and Sand Point*] lake, we entered a narrow straight [*Little Vermilion Narrows*] about 1/4 mile long, which communicates with Vermillion Lake [*Little Vermilion*], thro' which our way lead us. Having passed this lake, which is only 3 1/2 miles long, we entered the river de la Croix [*Loon R.*]. This a small stream exceedingly crooked, its folds almost doubling upon one another. Its general courses only were attempted. Wild rice and Reed grass are abundant along its shores. Its valley, irregular, but of considerable width and bounded by rugged hills 60 to 100 feet high. Ascended to the first Portage, about 6 miles by the meanders of the river. Encamped at this place after sun set. Distance 40 miles.

FRIDAY, SEPTEMBER 5, 1823. Started a little after 4 A.M. Travelled 1/2 mile and passed another [*Loon Falls*] Portage, after which we entered a small [*Loon*] Lake & travelled in it 4 1/2 miles its whole length. At the end of it, passed another [*Beatty*] portage and entered Lac de la Croix [*Lac la Croix*], which has no immediate water communication with the small lake just mentioned.

The main water channel between Lac de la Croix and Sturgeon or Nam-ma-kon Lake before mentioned is situated to the north of our course and is called Nam-ma-kon [*Namakan*] river. This stream rises in Lac de la Croix about 11 miles from the [*Beatty*] Portage last mentioned and enters Na-ma-kon Lake a short distance above [*east of*] the second [*Bear*] portage mentioned yesterday morning, and is the principal channel thro which the waters of the neighbouring country descend to Rainy Lake. There are four portages on that route; the river is made up of a series of small lakes alternating with straights. At the distance of seven miles from the point where we entered the lake [*Lac la Croix*] is an island on which the Catholics, when accompanied by a priest from the time of the French being in possession of the country, have been accustomed to stop and say mass. Hence the name given to the Lake.[38]

[38] The Namakan River, as Long indicated, flows north and west from Lac la Croix to the eastern end of Namakan Lake. The number of portages on the route apparently

Passed an inlet on our right which is the entrance of a small stream communicating with Lake Superior by way of the Grand Portage.[39] The communication is made up of a succession of small lakes & streams. Two miles farther on we passed the out-let of Lake de la Croix, thro' which the Namakon or Sturgeon river receives its supply of water. This river is the principal channel for canoes between lake de la Croix & Sturgeon L. as before remarked.

Lake de la Croix is 20 [*30*] miles long and from 300 yards to 3 or 4 miles wide. Like the lakes of this country generally, it embosoms many rocky islands, and its shores are lined with rocks which in some instances rise into stupendous precipices.

At the head of the lake we entered a small stream called the Malign[e] or Wicked river, which we ascended 2 1/2 miles and arrived at its first [*Island*] portage, where we dined. At this place is a considerable Fall [*Twin Falls*] in the river to which we give the name of Tanner's Falls, it being near the spot where he was wounded by an indian. This deed was perpetrated about 40 days since and occasioned the wound with which the unfortunate Tanner, before mentioned, it still disabled.[40]

The channel we are now ascending is called the Malign river on account of the numerous rocks, rapids, and portages that impede its

varied from three to five depending upon the direction of travel and the water levels. See Hind, *Narrative*, 1:70–74, 2:401; Great Britain War Office, *Notes on the Routes from Lake Superior to the Red River, and on the Settlement Itself*, 9 (London, 1870).

No verification has been found for Long's explanation of the name of Lac la Croix. Lamb, ed., *Mackenzie*, 104n, remarked that it was probably named for "Sieur de la Croix, who accompanied Jacques de Noyon . . . in 1688 and was drowned in Lac la Croix"; Mackenzie and others said it was named "from its shape." The distances given would place the party near present Island 45.

[39] Long's inlet was probably a general reference to the southern arm of Lac la Croix, where the Grand Portage route left the lake via Bottle River and Crooked Lake and continued eastward along the international boundary to Grand Portage, the fur trade center now a national monument in Cook County, Minn. A vast literature exists on this route. See, for example, Grace Lee Nute, *The Voyageur's Highway: Minnesota's Border Lake Land* (St. Paul, 1945); Morse, *Fur Trade Canoe Routes*, 75–79; Holmquist and Brookins, *Minnesota's Major Historic Sites*, 152–156. On the route followed by Long, see Keating, *Narrative*, 2:130–150.

[40] Seymour completed a painting of this spot; it has not been located; see p. 392, below. Although Long's name for the falls did not persist, a widening in the Maligne River east of this point is now known as Tanner Lake. McElroy and Riggs, eds., Delafield, *Unfortified Boundary*, 437, called the Maligne River portages here and below Portage de l'Isle, McKay Portage, Little Island Discharge, Third Portage, and Grosse Roche Portage. For additional details on the Maligne route, see Keating, *Narrative*, 2:146; Grace Lee Nute, "Campfires Along The Dawson Road," in *Naturalist*, Winter, 1958, pp. 51–57; Great Britain War Office, *Notes on the Routes from Lake Superior to the Red River*, 8, 12, 28.

navigation. The length of the river is only about 13 miles in which distance there are no less than three portages, two carrying places, and numerous rapids, besides shoals infested with large rocks. We had the misfortune to run one of the canoes upon one of the rocks, which injured it, but not materially. Encamped at a late hour at the head of the upper most portage of Malign river. Distance 40 miles.

SATURDAY, SEPTEMBER 6, 1823. Started early, passed another portage at the distance of 1/2 mile from that where we encamped last night & entered Little Sturgeon [*now Sturgeon*] Lake.

About 3/4 of the way thro' the lake (Lit. Sturgeon) enters a small stream from the SE, which affords the principal communication with Lake Superior by way of the Grand Portage. On this route is situated a small lake called Saganaga, also several others of small size connected by straights & rapids. Saganaga L. is about half the size of Rainy Lake.[41]

Little Sturgeon Lake is 18 miles long and of various breadths, embosoms many islands, and in other respects resembles the lakes below. Having passed the Lake, we entered a narrow winding channel, quite small, called Hay Creek, which we ascended to a [*Deux Rivières*] portage about 1200 yards long, exceedingly hilly and rough. Bridges and causeways have been constructed along it to facilitate the passage but are now in bad condition for want of repairs. Proceeded 1 1/2 miles farther thro' a small lake called the Lake of the Dead [*Pine Portage Lake*] from the death of a voyageur occasioned by an accident in passing one of the portages, and arrived at another [*Pine*] Portage, where his remains were deposited. This portage is about 450 yards long. The channel of the river or creek up which we are travelling is remote from this portage, being at a distance on our right.[42]

[41] Long's reference to a canoe route from Sturgeon Lake to the Grand Portage is misleading; as he indicated, a small unnamed stream connects to the southeast with Russell Lake from which it is possible to reach Cache Bay of Saganaga Lake on the Grand Portage border route through a series of lakes including Kawnipi and Saganagons. The "principal communication" with the border route, however, was that via the south arm of Lac la Croix; see note 39, above. Saganaga (19,610 acres) is far less than half the size of Rainy Lake (220,800 acres); Minnesota Department of Conservation, Waters Section, *An Inventory of Minnesota Lakes*, 105, 368 (St. Paul, 1968).

[42] Delafield, who passed this way a month before Long, noted the recent grave of a Canadian at Pine Portage. See McElroy and Riggs, eds., Delafield, *Unfortified Boundary*, 438. Keating, *Narrative*, 2:132, identified the fish mentioned below as "Hyodon tergissus, Lesueur," which would be the Mooneye (*Hiodon tergisus*). The Goldeye, which Long mentioned below, is classified as *Hiodon alosoides* Rafinesque. Eddy and Underhill, *Northern Fishes*, 139, 140. Seymour completed a painting of Pickerel Lake which has not been located; see p. 392, below.

On leaving Dead Man's [*Pine*] Portage we entered a [*Pickerel*] lake, the name of which in the indian language implies Gold-eyed [*Mooneye?*] Fish, and to which we give the name of Hyodon Lake, which is of the same import. That description of fish is said to be very abundant in the lake. The lake has numerous islands, and its coast is deeply indented by bays and recesses. Its length is about 13 miles, and its breadth exceedingly variable. On leaving the lake, we entered a small stream, very crooked, called Deep [*French*] river, which we ascended about 2 1/2 miles and entered a small [*French*] lake 1 1/2 miles in diameter. Having crossed this, we encamped at a [*French*] Portage a little after sunset. Dist. 41 m.

SUNDAY, SEPTEMBER 7, 1823. Finding the portage impracticable for the transportation of our canoes, our voyageurs proceeded by water while the residue of the party remained behind and crossed the [*French*] portage by land. The length of this portage is 2 1/4 miles, the road rendered difficult to travel by reason of hills and swamps. Embarked a little after noon, the canoes having arrived after a circuitous route by way of a small channel uniting Fourch [*French*] Lake, at which we encamped last night, to Sandy Lake, which is a short distance above the portage. Passed thro' a suc[c]ession of small Lakes and winding channels and arrived at another portage, or carrying place, by which we were able to tow the canoes. At this place we entered a small Lake called Cannibal or Wan-de-go [*Windigoostigwan*] Lake from the circumstance that an Indian woman, compelled by hunger, participated in devouring the dead bodies of 24 persons who died of hunger at this place.[43] Our way to-day lay thro a series of small lakes connected by narrow-winding channels thro' which there was a considerable current. Cannibal Lake is the most considerable, and is about 7 miles long but of moderate width and does not embosom many islands. Crossed another [*Brûlé*] portage and encamped early to secure ourselves against an approaching storm. Dist. 20 miles.

MONDAY, SEPTEMBER 8, 1823. Started at 5 A.M. and travelled thro another small Lake called McKay's [*Baril*] L. before breakfast. Its length is 7 1/2 miles, breadth from 1/4 to 2 miles. Its islands numerous. At the upper end of it is a [*Baril*] portage about 300 yds. long. Having passed this portage, we entered an extensive sheet of water called The Thousand Lakes [*Lac des Mille Lacs*] on account of

[43] The name "Sandy Lake" does not appear on modern maps. Keating, *Narrative*, 2:132, reported the cannibalism incident more fully, saying that it occurred in 1811.

the numerous arms, bays, and inlets which it presents. Its islands are numerous, rendering the route thro' it exceedingly intricate. Its length is 25 miles by the route we travelled—its arms branched out in all directions and extended to a very considerable distance. Having traversed this Lake, which is the last [*next to last*] of the chain tributary to Lake Wenepeek on this route, we entered Savanna [*Savanne*] river, which takes its name from the character of the country thro which it flows, which is exceedingly swampy. Having ascended the river six miles, we encamped for the night on an elevated part of the swamp. Dist. 42 mil[e]s.

TUESDAY, SEPTEMBER 9, 1823. A Thunder-storm commenced early this morning and continued till 8 o'clock, when we resumed our voyage. Savanna river is a sluggish stream very menandering in its course, has a good depth of water, and is well suited to the navigation of canoes, except that the channel is much obstructed by fallen timber, which rendered our progress up it very slow. The country along its banks is one continued swamp, covered with a dense growth of spruce, larche, some pine, and furze.

Arrived at the Savanna [*Savanne*] Portage at 1 P.M., having ascended the river 18 miles above our camp of last night. The Portage is about 1 1/2 miles long and in its whole length traverses a swamp. The road is made of small timbers hewed on one side and supported at their ends by cross sills, and is thus rendered quite easy to travel with baggage.[44] A storm commenced at the time of our crossing the portage, and we were compelled to encamp in the swamp for the residue of the day. Dist. 18 miles.

WEDNESDAY, SEPTEMBER 10, 1823. Took leave of our dreary and wet encampment, at sun-rise the weather cloudy. Crossed a small lake called Savanna L. [*Lac du Milieu*] about 2 miles long and arrived at the Middle Portage [*Portage du Milieu*], which we crossed. Its length is 1/2 mile; the tract thro' which it past is swampy most of the way, and the road of a similar construction with that we crossed yesterday. A small lake called Muddy [*Height of Land*] L. intervenes between this and the Prairie Portage, only 1/4 of a mile across. Having crossed the lake, we stopped for breakfast at the commencement of the Prairie Portage. This Portage crosses the

[44] "Diary of Nicholas Garry," in Royal Society of Canada, *Proceedings and Transactions*, 2nd series, vol. 6, sec. 2, p. 121, stated that the Savanne Portage road was built by the North West Company. By 1830 it was in a "decayed state"; see Grace Lee Nute, ed., "Journey for Frances," in *The Beaver*, March, 1954, p. 16.

dividing ridge between the waters of Lake Wenepeek and Lake Superior. Its length is little more than 2 1/2 miles. The road good.

The highest ground between the waters as above is not more than 150 feet above the water level by the route of the Portage. The descent is rather towards Lake Superior, the water at the SW extremity of the portage being somewhat more elevated than at the NE extremity. Having passed this portage, we entered a small pool called Cold Water Lake, which is only 150 yds. long and 20 wide. It receives its water from a copious spring a few yards above it. The temperature of the water in the Lake is 42 deg. Faht. and of the Spring above, 40 deg. This, as before remarked, is the first water of Lake Superiour we have yet met with on the route.

The Custom of voyageurs, viz. that of a treat from strangers who never before crossed the dividing ridge between the waters of Hudsons Bay and those of the Gulph of St. Lawrence, was here complied with. Three pints of strong Brandy were issued to the party and drunk with eager appetites.

Crossed Cold W. Lake and arrived at another short portage at which we dined.

Commenced descending the [*Jourdain*] creek leading from the Lake and passed thro' a series of small ponds, and by a meandering route thro a distance of about 5 miles and entered Dog river, a considerable stream from the North. Dog river has a very serpentine course and but one considerable [*Barrier*] rapid in the distance travelled to day. Descended it about 15 miles and encamped on its bank about sunset. Distance 27 miles.[45]

THURSDAY, SEPTEMBER 11, 1823. The night cold for the season, a severe frost this morning. Started at 5 A.M. The river exceedingly crooked. Descended 25 miles and entered Dog Lake. The country on Dog river exhibits a better aspect than we have hitherto witnessed on the streams of this part of the country. Extensive tracts of bottom land occasionally present themselves, but are in general too low for cultivation. The hill[s] rise to the height of 100 to 150 feet, but are less rocky than those we have met with since leaving Lake Wenepeek. The growth is similar, but larger. Spruce abounds, also Red & White Epinette, and attain a respectable size. Passed the entrance of a considerable stream from the SW called Cypress

[45] On the portages and the spring mentioned above, see Morse, *Fur Trade Canoe Routes*, 79, 82; Keating, *Narrative*, 2:134, 136. For a fuller description of the height of land ceremonies, see Nute, *The Voyageur*, 67.

[*Fisher*] riv. Encamped for breakfast on the Lake shore, one mile from the entrance of Dog-river.

Dog Lake is 12 [*16*] miles long, from 1 to 4 or 5 broad, and has but few islands. Its coast is much indented. It receives the waters of several tributaries of respectable size, among which is one that is said to have its rise in the Thousand Lakes, before mentioned. This stream [*Shebandowan R.?*] has its course southwardly of the route we travelled—abounds in rapids and falls, and is very difficult to navigate. Another of the tributaries of Dog Lake is also said to rise near English river, before mentioned, with which it affords a water communication for Canoes. Dog Lake takes its name from the fancied resemblance of [a] Dog made near the Portage road leading from its southern extremity, which is called the Dog Portage from the same circumstance. The figure is no longer discoverable. It was constructed of earth after the manner of the figure of the same animal depicted on skins & by indians with coal or paint. It is said to have been made by a war party of Sioux who are accustomed to similar practices.[46]

Dog Portage is 1 3/4 miles long and many parts of the route are extremely rugged. The Dog riv. passes to the right of the portage and has a very great descent in the distance, probably not less than 50 feet, the whole descent being divided between four principal schutes or falls.[47] Having crossed the portage and been delayed for some time waiting for the baggage, the opportunity was improved for astronomical observations for Lat. & Lon.

Encamped at Devil Portage at Sunset. Distance 42 miles.

[46] It is unclear which rivers Long referred to as connecting Dog Lake, English River, and Lac des Mille Lacs, since a height of land separates these watersheds. No tributary of Dog Lake (other than Dog River) communicates directly with Lac des Mille Lacs. The sources of the Dog River are the nearest to the English River of any stream falling into Dog Lake. The Shebandowan River, a major stream south of Long's route to which he refers below, does not rise in Lac des Mille Lacs.

The effigy mound was located and investigated in 1962 by K. C. A. Dawson, who described it as "well preserved" and having "the generalized outline of a dog-like creature." For his report and discussion of its possible origins, see Dawson, "The Kaministikwia Intaglio Dog Effigy Mound," in *Ontario Archaeology Publication No. 9*, 25–34 (June, 1966). See also Keating, *Narrative*, 2:137. Seymour completed a painting, not located, of Dog Lake; see p. 392, below.

[47] The four falls, proceeding downriver to Little Dog Lake, are High Falls, Silver Falls, Dog Falls, and Silver Falls Dam. Two control dams have "virtually obliterated" these falls, according to K. C. A. Dawson to the editors, October 13, 1971. Seymour completed a painting, not located, of this area which may have depicted either Dog Portage or a spot mentioned four paragraphs below farther down the Kaministikwia; see p. 392, below.

FRIDAY, SEPTEMBER 12, 1823. Started before sun-rise. Passed three[?] considerable rapids, all of which we descended in our canoes without accident. The part of the river situated below Dog Lake is called by the Indians K$\overset{3}{a}$-m$\overset{3}{a}$-n$\overset{1}{a}$, te-k$\overset{1}{o}$-e-ah [*Kaministikwia*], which implies a river of many channels. The Ka-ma-na is made up of several tributaries, the principal of which is Dog riv. before mentioned. It appears to discharge about double the quantity of water afforded by the river just noticed.[48]

Resumed our voyage after breakfast, having encamped earlier than usual on account of a dense fog which prevented our navigating in safety this dangerous part of the river. Rapids are numerous & the channels thro' them intricate. Passed 3 considerable ones, having an aggregate fall of about 10 ft. And came to the mouth of a considerable stream [*Shebandowan R.*] heading in the Thousand [*Shebandowan*] Lakes, as was said of that beforementioned, but affording a more safe and less difficult navigation. It is called by the Indians Sha-boon-da-wan Ma-t$\overset{3}{a}$-way, or Long-lodge Fork. Passed several other rapids, the apparent descent of which are noticed in the Table of courses & distances. [*See page 226.*]

At the distance of about 14 miles below our breakfast camp, we passed three considerable portages of moderate length. The third is called the Island Portage, at which there is a very beautiful cascade and Fall of about 15 feet in the distance of 30 yards. Mr. Seymour took a sketch of this and the one next above it. The river is here divided into two unequal parts by an Island. The most considerable Schute is that noticed above. Two miles below this is another [*Ecarté*] Portage and fall, the latter having an aggregate descent of about 18 feet and the former a length of 1/2 mile. The road is exceedingly rugged, being thickly set with sharp stones, the cliffs and fragments of a hard slate which is more prevalent than any other rock in this part of the country.

At the portages on this side of the dividing ridge in particular, we frequently meet with rude crosses indicating the places where the

[48] Many possible meanings and spellings have been offered for the Kaministikwia. The Shebandowan River, mentioned below, which heads in the Shebandowan lakes, not Lac des Mille Lacs, is said to mean "long wigwam." See M. J. L. Black, "Place Names in the Vicinity of Fort William," in Thunder Bay Historical Society, *Sixteenth and Seventeenth Annual Reports*, 15, 19 ([Fort William, Ont., 1926?]); Geographic Board of Canada, *Eighteenth Report*, 141 (Ottawa, 1924). For a listing of the rapids mentioned here and below, see Great Britain War Office, *Notes on the Routes from Lake Superior to the Red River*, 7, 11, 14. Most of them have now been obliterated by hydroelectric development.

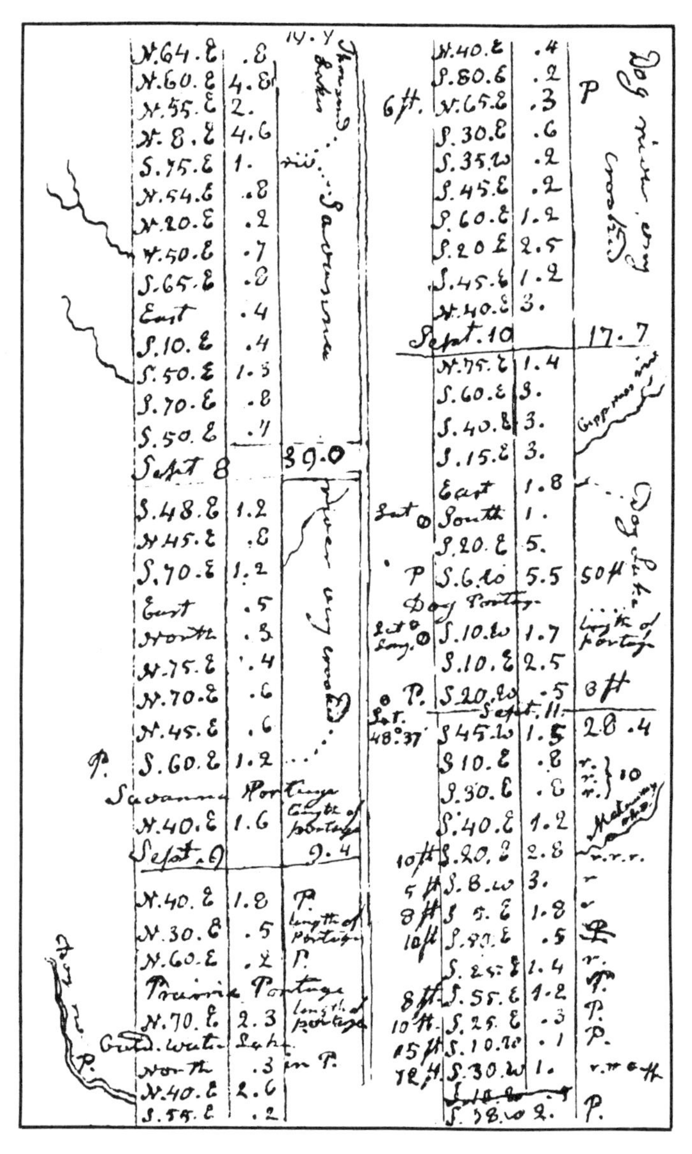

Course	Distance	Course	Distance
N.64.E	.8	N.40.E	.4
N.60.E	4.8	S.80.E	.2
N.55.E	2.	N.65.E	.3
N.8.E	4.6	S.30.E	.6
S.75.E	1.	S.35.W	.2
N.54.E	.8	S.45.E	.2
N.20.E	.2	S.60.E	1.2
N.50.E	.7	S.20.E	2.5
S.65.E	.8	S.45.E	1.2
East	.4	N.40.E	3.
S.10.E	.4	Sept. 10	17.7
S.50.E	1.3	N.75.E	1.4
S.70.E	.8	S.60.E	3.
S.50.E	.7	S.40.E	3.
Sept 8	39.0	S.15.E	3.
S.48.E	1.2	East	1.8
N.45.E	.8	South	1.
S.70.E	1.2	S.20.E	5.
East	.5	S.6.W	5.5
North	.3	Dog Portage	
N.75.E	.4	S.10.W	1.7
N.70.E	.6	S.10.E	2.5
N.45.E	.6	S.20.W	.5
S.60.E	1.2	Sept. 11	28.4
Savanna Portage		S.45.W	1.5
N.40.E	1.6	S.10.E	.8
Sept. 9	9.4	S.30.E	.8
N.40.E	1.8	S.40.E	1.2
N.30.E	.5	S.20.E	2.8
N.60.E	.2	S.8.W	3.
Prairie Portage		S 5.E	1.8
N.70.E	2.3	S.80.E	.5
Great water lake		S.25.E	1.4
North	.3	S.55.E	1.2
N.40.E	2.6	S.25.E	.3
S.55.E	.2	S.10.W	.1
		S.30.W	1.
		S.38.W	2.

A PAGE (actual size) of Long's courses and distances covering the expedition's route in Ontario from Lac des Mille Lacs on September 8, 1823, to Dog River on September 11, 1823.

remains of unfortunate voyageurs, who have fallen sacrifices to the hazardous and laborious duties they have to perform at such places, have been deposited. In transporting the baggage and especially the canoes across the portages, the labour is not only excessive but perilous in a high degree, and the sufferers who sustain irreparable injury are by no means few.

At the distance of 1/4 mile farther down the river is another Portage of 3/4 mile in length, which is the last on our route to Lake Superiour. It is called the Mountain Portage from its being situated in the vicinity of an elevated hill called Thunder mountain, which is of a hemispherical form and somewhat higher than any of the neighbouring hills.[49]

At this portage is a remarkable cataract [*Kakabeka Falls*] in the river which deserves a high rank among curiosities of this kind. The perpendicular pitch is 130 feet. Having visited this interesting fall, we regaled ourselves with Raspberries & huckleberries while dinner was in preparation for us. These circumstances, added to that of our having passed all the portages on the route, contributed to render the scene more gratifying than any other that has occurred.

The Indians give to this remarkable water fall the appellation of Ka-ka-be-ka, or the falls of the Cleft Rock, from the circumstance that the channel of the river for a considerable distance below passes thro a deep chasm worn in the slaty rock upon which the country is here based. The river is here bounded by perpendicular cliffs on both sides, rising to the height of more than 130 feet and exhibiting the most frightful precipices. The banks for a distance of 1/3 of a mile below are completely insurmountable, rising perpendicularly and in many places overhanging their base.[50]

Resumed our voyage a little before 5 P.M. and descended a continued rapid for a distance of 8 miles. In this distance passed a considerable stream entering from the west called White Fish [*Whitefish*] river. It rises in a lake of the same name and affords a water-communication connecting with the route of the

[49] The Mountain or Kaministikwia Portage has been marked in Kakabeka Falls Provincial Park near present-day Thunder Bay, Ont. Long's description is insufficient to positively identify the present-day hill which he calls Thunder Mountain. He referred below (p. 228) to a Thunder Mountain which is evidently Mount McKay, but he was apparently not speaking of the same hill here.

[50] For a fuller description of Kakabeka Falls, see Keating, *Narrative*, 2: 138–141, plate 12. Bell, *Some Historical Names*, 1, interpreted the name as "Cleft Rock," although more recent studies seem to favor "steep rock" or "high cliff falls." See Black, in Thunder Bay Historical Society, *Sixteenth and Seventeenth Annual Reports*, 15; Rayburn, in *Names*, 17: 151.

Grand Portage [*via Little Whitefish and Arrow rivers*]. Encamped at sunset at the lower-most rapid of the river, at which there is a carrying-place [*Décharges de Paresseux*]. Distance 35 miles.

SATURDAY, SEPTEMBER 13, 1823. The woodland growth of the country on the Kamana river is similar to that we have generally met with since leaving lake Wenepeek, but much larger. Spruce is the prevailing timber tree; Red or Pitch and White pine are plentiful in many places. The Fir is occasionally to be met with. Red and white Epinette [*spruce*], the latter of which is more generally called the Larche, are every where abundant. The maple sometimes occurs. A variety of the Poplar sometimes called the Balm of Gilead is scattered thro' the country and in many places attains a large size. The Pembina bush often presents itself loaded with its crimson fruit along the water-courses. The wild plum now begins to appear. The Huckle-berry & raspberry are common, also cherries of various kinds. Hazle begins to abound together with a great variety of other shrubbery constituting a dense undergrowth. We have also witnessed a great variety of grasses, among which the sweet scented grass (Antoxantum odoratum) frequently occurs.

The country below the Falls of Kakabeka assumes a more interesting character and improves rapidly as we descend the river. The timber growth becomes indicative of a good soil, and the luxuriant appearance of the grass, weeds, vines &c. strengthen the impression. Passed the ruins of an establishment formerly occupied by the Hudson B. Co. called Fort Muron [*Fort de Meuron*], situated on the left bank of the river. Several miles below passed along the base of a high, insulated hill called the Thunder Mountain [*Mount McKay*]. It appears to be a relict of the slaty formation which once covered this part of the country, and which from its more durable structure has survived the waste of the stratifications that once surrounded it. Its heigh[t] is not less than about 450 feet, probably having the same elevation as that of the Slate hills at the falls above mentioned.[51] At half past 10 A.M. we arrived at Fort William situated near the mouth of the river, where we were kindly received by Mr. [Roderick]

[51] The post at Point de Meuron was established by De Meuron soldiers during the conflict between the North West Company and the Red River Colony in 1816. It was maintained by the Hudson's Bay Company as late as 1818. See Rich and Fleming, eds., *Colin Robertson's Correspondence Book*, 54n, 230; Peter McKellar, "The Historic Land Marks in Thunder Bay," in Thunder Bay Historical Society, *Seventh Annual Report*, 10 ([Fort William, Ont., 1916?]). Mount McKay was called Thunder Mountain by the Indians of the area; see Black, in Thunder Bay Historical Society, *Sixteenth and Seventeenth Annual Reports*, 16.

McKenzie, superintendant of the establishment. Here we had not a little occasion to rejoice at the idea of having performed a long and hazardous voyage of near 700 miles without a serious misfortune or even accident. Distance 24 miles.[52]

SUNDAY, SEPTEMBER 14, 1823. Our Voyageurs & Interpreters, having been employed for the journey to this place only, were now to be paid and discharged with a canoe and provisions to enable them to return to Red river, where they embarked with us. Four of them however concluded to remain with us and serve as boatmen [*Le Fevre, Plante, La Fontaine, and Ranger*] till we should arrive at the Sault of St. Mary's [*Sault Ste. Marie*], two of them having a knowledge of the route engaged to serve as polots [*pilots*].[53]

Finding it expedient to change our mode of transportation in order to traverse the Lake [Superior] in greater safety, we substituted a Batteau or Mackinaw boat in place of our canoes. The Boat had been in the employ of the American Commission while engaged in the survey of the U.S. Boundary on this frontier, but being the only suitable craft that we could procure at the place, we ventured to take it in to our service. It needed repairs which were attended to without loss of time, while other arrangements were making to expedite our departure with the least possible delay.

[52] Fort William, within present Thunder Bay, Ont., was called Fort Kaministikwia when it was built between 1801 and 1804 to succeed Grand Portage as the North West Company's headquarters. It was renamed in 1807 for William McGillivray. Although it declined in importance after 1821, it remained in operation until 1878. It has been reconstructed upriver some distance from its original site. See W. Stewart Wallace, *The Pedlars from Quebec and Other Papers on the Nor' Westers*, 73–80 (Toronto, 1954). Its superintendent was veteran trader Roderick McKenzie; see W. Stewart Wallace, ed., *Documents Relating to the North West Company*, 479 (Toronto, 1934); p. 230, below. Keating, *Narrative*, 2:142, gave the total distance as 820 miles traversed in 27 days.

[53] The supplies Long purchased are listed in Voucher No. 45, in "Abstract," Appendix 2, below. Le Fevre and Plante were engaged as voyageurs, La Fontaine as pilot, and Ranger as guide. See Vouchers No. 46–49 in "Abstract." Keating, less restrained than Long, described the newly acquired boat, below, as "very old and crazy." See *Narrative*, 2:175. Long's entry for September 14 marks the end of the second manuscript volume.

6. *Through the Great Lakes and the Erie Canal*

SEPTEMBER 15 THROUGH OCTOBER 27, 1823

MONDAY, SEPTEMBER 15, 1823. Fort William is situated on the east side of Kamana Tekoea [*Kaministikwia*] river at the distance of nearly a mile above its entrance into Lake Superiour. The country around it to a considerable extent is level, rising gradually from the lake shore till it mingles with the highlands at the distance of 4 or 5 miles from the Lake. Fort William till within a few years was the principal Depot for the Indian Trade of the N. W. Co., and has been constructed on a scale corresponding to the former importance of the station. But since the consolidation of the N. W. & H. B. Companies and the establishment of Depots in other places, it has dwindled in importance and begins to wear the aspect of decline. The numerous buildings of the establishment are still however in a good state of repair, tho' they have in some measure lost the attentions formerly bestowed upon them. The buildings consist of a large dining hall, a council room, a large stone ware-house, fire-proof— several store houses, offices, quarters for superintendants & clerks, work shops, boat stores, &c. &c. The works are on a scale so extensive that about forty partners of the company, and as many clerks, with their families have been accommodated all at the same time with separate quarters or rooms.

During our stay at the Fort every desirable attention was paid us and every needful aid that we required, so far as was practicable, was cheerfully bestowed. The gentlemen of the party were all admitted as guests at the well furnished table of the Superintendant, whose hospitality towards us was manifested in various other ways.

Having settled with and discharged our voyageurs (four excepted) and made other arrangements necessary to the prosecution of our voyage, we embarked on board of our Batteau at a little past 1 P.M. The wind being favourable we were able to sail with considerable speed.

On leaving the river, we entered a broad and deep arm of the lake (Superior) called Kamana [*Thunder*] Bay, at the entrance of which are situated a cluster of islands called the Pie islands. They are all based upon rocks, and some of the[m] present circular hills from 100 to 150 feet high and flat on their summits from which circumstance they have derived their name. Having crossed the Bay, which is 15 miles wide, we passed a promontory called Thunder Point [*Thunder Cape*] remarkable for the stupendous precipices it exhibits on both sides. The hill is about 800 feet high. At ev'ning the wind subsided and the weather became calm. We lay by for supper a little after sunset, but having an open traverse of considerable extent across the entrance of another [*Black*] bay to pass, it was thought best to continue the voyage by moon-light, availing ourselves of the quiet state of the Lake in order to pass the Traverse in greater safety. We accordingly ran till 2 o'clock A.M. when we encamped on an [*Edward?*] island. Distance 37 miles.[1]

TUESDAY, SEPTEMBER 16, 1823. Having allowed some time for our men to refresh themselves with sleep, we breakfasted and got under weigh at 9 o'clock, the wind strong ahead. Passed two singular hills of a conical form situated near to each other and denominated the Mamelles [*Paps*]. Proceeded but 8 1/2 miles and lay by for dinner.

The Islands along the coast are numerous, but none of them of any considerable magnitude. Most of them are based upon rock, and some of them rise to the height of 4 or 500 feet above the Lake.

We have had Isle Royal[e] in view yesterday and to-day. It is the

[1] Keating, *Narrative*, 2:176, pointed out that only one of the islands in Thunder Bay was called Pie "from its form," as it is to this day. On the geology and the route along the north shore of Lake Superior, see Morse, *Fur Trade Canoe Routes*, 67–69; Keating, *Narrative*, 2:176–204. Keating's geological comments are similar to those of John J. Bigsby, whom the Long party met at Sault Ste. Marie on his tour of the lake; see *Narrative*, 2:107, 180, 251. When he wrote, Keating had not seen Bigsby's remarks, which were published as "Notes on the Geography and Geology of Lake Superior," in *Quarterly Journal of Science, Literature, and the Arts*, 18:1–34, 228–267 (October, 1824, January, 1825), and later revised for inclusion in *Shoe and Canoe*, 2:178–237. In his article (pp. 3, 5) Bigsby attributed various measurements to Long. The information Long obtained from Bigsby consisted of a list of 16 mileages and latitude and longitude readings at Rat Portage (Lake of the Woods) and at various points on Lakes Huron and Superior, which Long entered in the final pages of the third volume of his manuscript journal. These readings have not been printed here.

largest of the islands of Lake Superior, being about [*blank in ms.*] miles long and [*blank in ms.*] broad.[2] Its surface is some what broken, rising into elevated hills in some parts and presenting swells in others. We passed its eastern extremity to-day. Islands continually numerous. Occasional openings between them display extensive views of the Lake. These openings are called by the voyageurs Traverses, which are difficult and even dangerous to pass when the wind is strong and blows towards the Lake shore. We attempted to pass one this afternoon but were compelled to return again after having gone one third of the way across it. The wind continuing to increase, we encamped in a small harbour which we found near the shore at a little past 4 P.M. Distance 18 miles.

WEDNESDAY, SEPTEMBER 17, 1823. The storm continued thro' the night during which considerable rain fell. At the point where we encamped and generally along the lake-shore, the rocks are secondary trap containing numerous nodules of precious stones such as agate of various descriptions, carnelion, chalcedony, &c. &c. Numerous precipices of great height are presented along the shore of the lake, as also upon the islands. The rocks are what are sometimes denominated by Geologists Basaltiform, tho' they are not distinctly marked as of Basaltic formation.

The wind continued strong from the NW thro' the day, squalls towards evening. Encamped early, the men being fatigued with rowing and the Lake continuing boisterous. Dist. 23 1/2 miles.

THURSDAY, SEPTEMBER 18, 1823. Started early, the weather unsettled. Met two barges returning to Fort William. The[y] belonged to a British schooner ["*Recovery*"] employed by the British Govt. in making a survey of lake Superior under the command of Lt. [Henry W.] Bayfield. The schooner had sailed on monday last for Fort William. At 2 P.M. a favourable wind sprang up from the SW and we sailed with much speed till after dark, when we ran into a small harbour [*Bottle Cove*] well protected from the wind. Distance 50 1/2 miles.[3]

FRIDAY, SEPTEMBER 19, 1823. The wind continued to increase thro' the night, and this morning blew a gale. It rained considerably

[2] Isle Royale, Mich., now a national park, is 45 miles long and nine miles wide; its highest point has an elevation of 1,307 feet. See also Keating, *Narrative*, 2:239.

[3] Bayfield served as an admiralty surveyor on the Great Lakes from 1817 until

thro' the night and violently most of the forenoon. We conclude it to be the equinoct[i]al storm with which we are now visited and have no alternative but to wait its termination. Our encampment is by no means eligible for stormy weather. The ground is low and swampy, its surface covered with a dense and deep moss which retains much moisture, and the woods are not sufficiently dense to protect us from the wind. We however contrive to make ourselves tolerably comfortable by building large fires and sheltering ourselves under our tents and sail. The lake is put in great commotion by the storm, its billows lashing the shore with great violence.

SATURDAY, SEPTEMBER 20, 1823. The storm continued thro' the night with unabated violence. The ground this morning is covered with snow. There being a prospect of a change of weather, however, we held ourselves in readiness to start. The storm having abated and the wind blowing from the shore, we started at noon and proceeded slowly till one P.M. when we were able to hoist sail, the wind being more favourable. The weather continued squally thro' the day and the wind strong from NNW, rendering the lake very rough. Passed a trading establishment of the H. B. Co. situated on the lake shore near the entrance of a small [*Pic*] river. Finding a safe harbour, we encamped about sunset. Dist. 32 miles.[4]

SUNDAY, SEPTEMBER 21, 1823. As we were about to start this morning, one of our men, [Nathaniel] Brown, a private of the 5th Regt. co. E., was missing and not to be found. On examining our baggage, we discovered that a rifle, a coatee belonging to our black man [*Allison*], a ham of bacon, and some few articles beside were missing and had probably been taken by the deserter. Brown, it is said, has repeatedly been guilty of the same crime, but his motive in the present case must be entirely without an object. His time of service had nearly expired. Pay and emoluments to a considerable amount were now due him, and he was now travelling homeward. He had given no previous intimation to any one that such was his

1825. See Thomson, *Men and Meridians*, 1:186–191. On Bottle Cove, see Keating, *Narrative*, 2:182.

[4] The Pic post, located at the mouth of the Pic River near modern Marathon, Ont., was operated by the North West Company from the late 18th century until the consolidation with the Hudson's Bay Company in 1821. See Grace Lee Nute, "Peninsula, the Pic River Region, and Modern Marathon," in *Inland Seas*, 4:3–14 (Spring, 1948). Keating, *Narrative*, 2:183, 184, indicated the party did not stop at the post (which was closed), but camped a short distance beyond it.

intention, nor had he manifested any dissatisfaction at the service in which he was at present engaged.[5]

Started a little after sunrise, the weather squally. Proceeded but a few miles, when the wind being rather unfavourable and the lake very rough, we were induced to lay by till a change of weather should take place. For this purpose we encamped at the entrance of a small river behind some small islands that effectually protected us from the surf of the Lake.

The islands which have hitherto lined the coast are now very seldom to be met with. The coast continues to be rocky bound and exceedingly broken. No very high hills appear, but the country appears to be made up of hills of moderate elevation every where paved with rocks, which are often destitute of the least covering of earth. Few if any places of considerable magnitude are to be seen susceptible of cultivation. The growth is generally stinted and consists principally of cedar, spruce, white and yellow birch, balm of Giliad, or Liard, aspen, black alder, &c. &c.

The weather continued squally, considerable snow, sleet & rain fell in the former part of the day, but at 2 P.M. the wind shifted in to the NW, and for the first time for many days, we were again gratified with the prospect of good weather. To the harbour in which we sheltered ourselves from the storm, it being one of the safest and most secure of any we have met with on the lake, we give the name of Sunday harbour in honour of the day we spend in it.[6]

Resumed our voyage at 3 P.M. and ran till dark, and encamped at an indifferent harbour, where we could find no place to pitch our tents and had to sleep upon the rocks of the shore. Dist. 18 miles.

MONDAY, SEPTEMBER 22, 1823. Started early but our progress was slow, the wind being unfavourable. Lay by for break fast, after which we resumed our voyage again, but the wind being so strong ahead as to prevent in a great measure our progress and the lake so rough as to render our safety extremely uncertain, we were compelled to run into the first harbour for security, and were so fortu-

[5] Brown's period of service was to expire on November 10, 1823. On his many desertions see AGO, Inspection Returns, Fifth Infantry, Company E, Fort St. Anthony, October 31, 1821, June 30, August 31, December 31, 1822, April 30, December 31, 1823; and AGO, Muster Rolls, Fort St. Anthony, August 31, 1821—all in NARG 94.

[6] Several small unnamed streams fall into Lake Superior in the area southeast of Pic River, Ont. Sunday Harbor might have been today's Playter Harbor or the Sewell Point area, where there are a number of small islands. The harbor on September 22, below, was possibly today's Oiseau Bay.

nate as to find one that completely protected us from the storm. The wind cont[in]ued violent thro' the day and we were compelled to remain encamped. Dist. 8 miles.

TUESDAY, SEPTEMBER 23, 1823. The country along the Lake is one of the most dreary imaginable, considering its Latitude and the facilities with which it may be approached. Its surface is exceedingly rocky, broken, and unproductive even in the natural growth common to rugged regions. Its climate cold and inhospitable; Its means of subsistence so circumscribed that savages cannot fix their abode in it; Even the game common in other regions of the same Latitude seem to have deserted it for want of sustenance. Tho' fertile vallies may possibly be found in some parts of the country, yet they are so hemmed in by rocky hills and precipices that they never can subsist a dense population. Indeed to estimate its future population from present appearances, it would be an exag[g]erated allowance to admit a single inhabitant for every thousand acres of the country.

The wind continuing violent thro' the day, we were compelled to remain encamped. In the course of the last night, the storm increasing and the surf running high in our little harbour, we were under the necessity of raising the boat upon skids to protect her from the waves. Finding her still insecure this morning, we drew her on shore upon rude ways which we constructed for that purpose.

As we had not anticipated the delays we find ourselves compelled to make on the voyage, no provision had been made for our subsistence on such occasions, and as we begin to be apprehensive of a scarsity, we to-day gather moss from the rocks called *tripe de roche* by the french, of which we made a tolerable soup which we consider nutritive tho' not palatable. When boiled it forms a sort of mucilage similar to that of a solution of Gum Arabic.[7]

WEDNESDAY, SEPTEMBER 24, 1823. A change having taken place in the weather, we resumed our voyage at 10 A.M. and rowed diligently thro' the remainder of the day. Passed a beautiful cataract [*Cascade Falls*] on the lake shore occasioned by a small stream [*Cascade R.*], which was precipitated down a cliff of rocks with a fall of 30 or 40 ft. Of this Mr. Seymour took a sketch. A short distance in

[7] The region remains sparsely populated, as Long predicted, above. Tripe-de-roche (*Umbilicaria dillenii*), a common lichen, was often eaten and disliked by traders and explorers of the north. Keating, *Narrative*, 2:187, wrote that the party "made two meals upon the rock tripe, and . . . we have never tasted a more nauseating food." Three other wild plants were used by the expedition to make tea; see *Narrative*, 2:117.

advance of it is a remarkable promontory called the Otter's head, from a huge rock standing perpendicularly near its summit at least 30 feet high and having a fancied resembl[a]nce to that object. Encamped a little after sunset. Dist. 24 m.[8]

THURSDAY, SEPTEMBER 25, 1823. Started early. Our provisions being nearly exhausted, we were limited to very short allowance.

Passed a considerable island on our left about 15 miles from the Lake shore called Michipocotton [*Michipicoten*] Island, probably the same that is called on our Maps the Maurepas Island. Entered Michipicotton Bay and encamped near the mouth of a small stream called rivier La Chien [*University R.?*] at a place where we could find no eligible position for our tents. We however made shift to dispose oursilves upon the rocks and slept tolerably well till it was time to resume our voyage. Distance 32 miles.[9]

FRIDAY, SEPTEMBER 26, 1823. Started at half past two in the morning. Penetrated the Bay of Michipocotton to its eastern extremity and ascended the river of the same name 3/4 mile to an establishment of the Hudsons Bay company, with the view of obtaining a supply of provisions for the residue of our voyage thro' the Lake. To our great satisfaction we here found every thing we stood in want of, and a willingness on the part of the superintendent, Mr. [John] McIntosh the younger, to accommodate us. On our landing we were invited to his table to breakfast, and found it loaded with every thing calculated to tempt the appetite and gratify the palate. Among other articles of diet to which we had for a long time been strangers were the trout and white fish, the former of which in its delicacy of flavour and marrow-like consistency proved a luxury of the highest order.[10]

[8] Keating, *Narrative*, 2:188, also recorded that Seymour sketched this falls. The artist finished two views of Lake Superior which have not been found; see p. 392, below. The coast of Lake Superior "somewhat west" of Otter Head is depicted in *Narrative*, 2:plate 13.

[9] During the French regime Michipicoten Island bore the name of French statesman Jean Frédéric Maurepas, and various spellings of it appear on late 18th- and early 19th-century maps of Lake Superior. It is perpetuated in Point Maurepas on present Michipicoten Island. The use of "Maurepas" may indicate that Long did not have with him any of the Arrowsmith maps produced after 1802, for after that date the British cartographer usually mapped the island under its present name.

Keating, *Narrative*, 2:188, noted that the party passed between the shore and Michipicoten Island, coasting Michipicoten Bay. La Chien River is shown on Bigsby's map in *Shoe and Canoe* as Dog River, perhaps the present University River east of Point Isacor, Ont., or nearby Eagle River.

[10] For a time both the North West and Hudson's Bay companies had rival posts on opposite sides of the Michipicoten River, and the latter operated one on the east side

Beside the La Chienne and Michipocotton, the Bay of Michipocotton receives a considerable stream called the rivier de La Dorèe [*Doré*], or Hyodon river, on which there is a handsome cateract at a short distance from its mouth. The cataract is visible at a distance on the Bay, presenting itself as if interposed among the trees and verdant foliage with which the hill is covered. Numerous other streams of inferiour magnitude enter the bay, some of which are precipitated down rocky bluffs of stupendous stature—the streams disclosing themselves to the view in foaming sheets and rustling cascades.

The weather continued stormy thro' the day; some snow fell. The wind so strong up the bay and the Lake so rough that we were compelled to remain at Michipocotton during the day and were treated with the utmost attention and hospitality. We had an opportunity to regale ourselves on huckle-berries, which grow here in great abundance.

Mr. Robinson [*John Robertson?*], a clerk of the H. B. Co. who has ascended the Michipocotton to the dividing ridge between that and Moose river of Hudson's Bay, (which afford a water communication, by the help of short portages between this place and Moose Factory) gave us some account of the route and country in this direction. The former has no serious obstructions, and the voyage may be performed with loaded canoes in about 16 days, the distance being estimated at 160 leagues. The route abounds in lakes, some of which are of considerable magnitude.[11]

The country is hilly and broken, similar to that which presents itself on the north side of Lake Superior, to the distance of about 75

of the river off and on at least into the 1890s. The last of its buildings were dismantled in 1952. Agnes W. Turcott, *Land of the Big Goose: A History of Wawa and the Michipicoten Area from 1622 to 1960*, 18, 23–26, 28, 32–34, 47, 51, 61, 126 (Dryden, Ont., n.d.). For fuller descriptions of the post and its fishery in 1823, see Keating, *Narrative*, 2:191–194; Bigsby, *Shoe and Canoe*, 2:202–205. For the purchases, see Voucher No. 50 in "Abstract," Appendix 2, below.

John McIntosh, who served the Hudson's Bay Company from 1821 until his death in 1844, was the son of the superintendent, Donald. The latter was absent on a trip to Sault Ste. Marie at the time of Long's visit. See p. 242, below; Research Report, Hudson's Bay Company to the editors, May 6, 1971; Keating, *Narrative*, 2:191.

[11] Robertson was a clerk or interpreter in the Lake Superior district in 1822–24. Research Report, Hudson's Bay Company to the editors, May 6, 1971.

A fur trade route connected Lake Superior and James Bay via the Michipicoten, Missinaibi, and Moose rivers; see Turcott, *Land of the Big Goose*, 15, 17; Morse, *Fur Trade Canoe Routes*, 71. Moose Factory, a Hudson's Bay Company post on Factory Island in James Bay, was first occupied in 1672, captured and recaptured by the French and English, and rebuilt by the latter in 1730. See Eric Arthur, Howard Chapman, and Hart Massey, *Moose Factory 1673 to 1947*, 4–6 (Toronto, 1949).

miles up the Michipocotton, beyond which a rolling country of moderate extent presents itself and is succeeded by a region of level aspect, extending northwardly to the dividing ridge before mentioned. The subjoined sketch constructed from the intelligence given by this gentleman.

The storm continued violent thro' the day. Weather exceedingly squally at evening. Dist. 18 miles.

SATURDAY, SEPTEMBER 27, 1823. The weather still stormy, attended with occasi[o]nal squalls of snow, sleet & hail. Being anxious to return, we took our leave of the Michipicotton establishment at 7 A.M. But when we had proceeded 4 1/2 miles were compelled to put into a small harbour, the weather being too unfavourable for the voyage & the wind strong ahead. We were compelled to remain

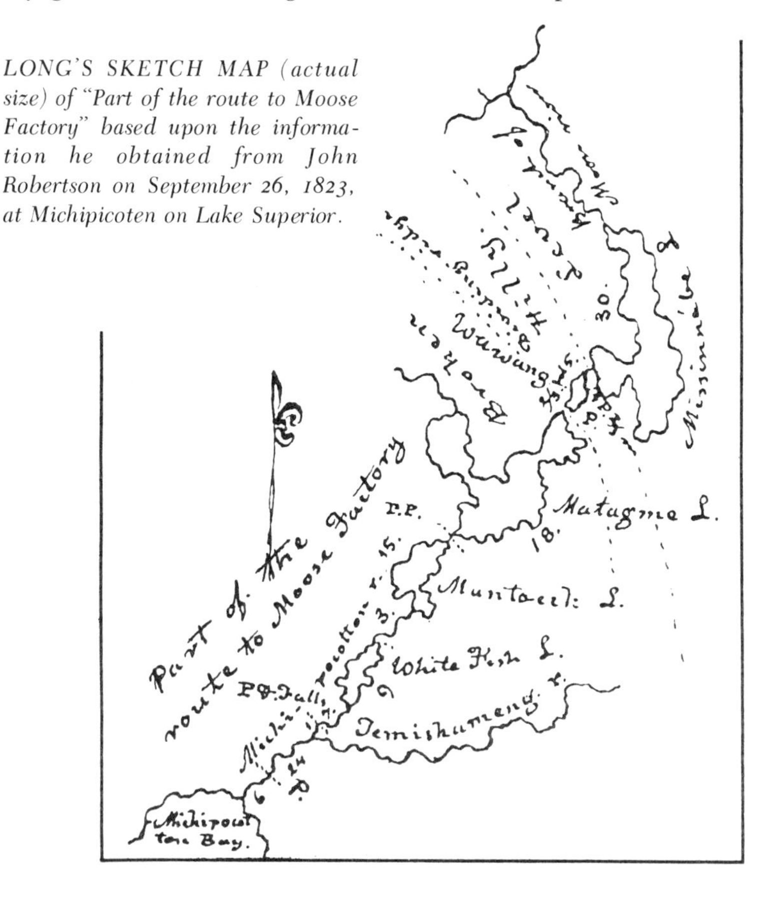

LONG'S SKETCH MAP (actual size) of "Part of the route to Moose Factory" based upon the information he obtained from John Robertson on September 26, 1823, at Michipicoten on Lake Superior.

encamped thro' [the] day, and the Lake became so rough that we were under the necessity of dragging our batteau out of the water. Dist. 4 1/2 miles.[12]

SUNDAY, SEPTEMBER 28, 1823. Considerable snow and sleet in the course of the night. This morning the weather and wind being favourable, we set sail at sunrise and ran with speed to the mouth of Michipocotton, or broad Bay. On this side of the bay at its junction with the lake is a remarkable promontory, together with several small islands studded with rocks of a gigantic stature, the whole denominated by the French [as] Point Gargantau [*Cape Gargantua*]. Here we lay by for breakfast at 10 oclock A.M., having sailed 22 miles. The wind still favourable, we prosecuted our voyage with speed. Passed a considerable island on our right, less elevated and rocky than we have usually seen them, denominated Fox [*Leach*] Isl.

Took a traverse across a broad bay 26 miles in length. On the easterly side of the bay are situated several small islands, low and level, called the Montreal Islands, at which are good fisheries, sandy beaches which are seldom to be met with on the Lake being here numerous and extensive. Encamped a little after sun-set at the end of the Traverse before mentioned. Distance 60 miles.

MONDAY, SEPTEMBER 29, 1823. The night cold and squally. Considerable snow fal[l], so that the surface of the ground appears white with it. Started at sunrise and travelled ten miles before breakfast. Ressumed our voyage again a little before 11 and entered an extensive traverse which we found to be 32 miles long.

In this distance we passed 2 small islands, called Maple islands, situated about 10 miles from the Lake shore.[13] From these we had a view of White-Fish Point on the opposite side of the lake near its eastern extremity. This point separates the Lake from an extensive [*Whitefish*] bay that passes directly round the SE part of the Lake. About 30 miles up [*north of*] the bay is the entrance of a respectable river called Montreal river, which has been considerably frequented by persons engaged in the Indn. Trade. Directly opposite the mouth

[12] The small harbor may have been in the Beauvier Point or Old Woman Bay areas southeast of Michipicoten.

[13] According to Bigsby, *Shoe and Canoe*, 2:189, Ile Parisienne was then called Maple Island, but the group referred to here was the lesser Maple Islands, probably including North and South Sandy as well as present Maple Island. Alexander Mackenzie referred to the existence of trading posts on the Montreal River route, mentioned below, "from the year 1782." See Lamb, ed., *Mackenzie*, 121.

of the bay just mentioned is another of smaller size [*Goulais or Batchawana bays*] on the north side of the lake. Encamped opposite the mouth of the former at a Point called Grand Cape [*Gros Cap*], having travelled till after dark in order to reach it. Dist. 43 miles.

TUESDAY, SEPTEMBER 30, 1823. Started at sun-rise after a comfortable night's repose, which we enjoyed upon the rocks secured from the inclemency of the weather by pitching our tent in the form of an indian lodge. Having run about 16 miles, we arrived at the Sault of St[e]. Marie at 10 o'clock A.M. Distance 16 miles.[14]

WEDNESDAY, OCTOBER 1, 1823. The Sau[l]t de St. Marie is a remarkable Fall situated immediately at the out-let of Lake Superiour [*St. Marys R.*] occasioned by a bed of secondary Sand stone in horizontal strata which here extends across the channel. The entire descent of the water, the whole of which is comprehended within a distance of 1/2 mile, is about 19 feet. The slope is very gradual, being formed after the manner of small steps by the breaking of the Lamina of the rock above mentioned.

A canal has recently been cut on the American side by the troops stationed at this place, for the purpose of supplying a saw-mill which is constructed at its lower extremity, and is intended for the passage of Canoes and Barges between the Lake and the [*St. Marys*] river below the Sault. The construction of the Canal, or rather race, has been attended with very little trouble or expense compared with the apparent magnitude of the undertaking. In no part of its route does the ground rise more than three feet above the level of the Lake. In the excavation the workmen had nothing of difficulty to encounter but cutting thro' the lamina of a fragile sand-stone, which required very little labour in breaking it up. The Saw-mill is a very good one and performs its labour with very great dispatch. In operation it performs 140 strokes per minute.[15]

At this place is an American Garrison containing five companies of the 2nd Rgt. of the U.S. Infantry at present under the command of Maj. [Enos] Cutler. The Fort constructed by them is a square

[14] Keating, *Narrative*, 2:201, noted that the Lake Superior crossing accomplished by the party in 15 days "was considered very short considering the season." It could be made by canoe in as little as four days, although seven or eight days was usual. See Turcott, *Land of the Big Goose*, 37. Seymour completed a painting of Sault Ste. Marie which has not been found; see p. 392, below.

[15] The canal was built in 1822–23, and the sawmill produced the lumber used to build Fort Brady, below. See Otto Fowle, *Sault Ste. Marie and Its Great Waterway*, 375 (New York and London, 1925).

stockade of about 460 feet on a side, containing comfortable quarters and other buildings sufficient for the accommodation of the troops intended for its support. The present works were intended merely for the temporary accommodation of the force and are not yet completed. The[y] are however constructed in a very neat and comfortable manner, considering the obstacles and disadvantages that must necessarily be encountered in a position so remote from a civilized population. They were commenced about a year since, the Troops having arrived at the place under the command of Col. [Hugh] Brady in the month of July 1822. The Post in its present form has received the name of Cantonment Brady in complement to the Comdg. officer of the 2nd Regt.[16]

Immediately above the cantonment is a vacant piece of ground [*Ashmun Hill*] a little more elevated than the circumjacent tract, reserved as the site of a permanent work should circumstances ever justify the construction of such a one. Next above this is a small village [*Sault Ste. Marie, Mich.*] commenced and increasing with the rise of the fancied importance of the place. It now contains many small houses, which appear comfortable tenements inhabited for the most part by loungers who appear to have no other objects in view, for the attainment of a livelihood, but illicit trafic with the soldiers of the garrison and speculations built upon the claims of former occupants of the present site of the public works. Below the Fort are also several houses in the possession of private individuals, at one of which Mr. [Henry R.] Schoolcraft, Indn. Agent for this place, has fixed his present residence.[17]

Directly opposite to the Cantonment on the British side is an establishment of the H. Bay Co. situated immediately at the foot of the Saute.[18]

[16] Cutler took command shortly before Long's arrival. Col. Brady and his men arrived at the Sault on July 6, 1822. They built Cantonment Brady, later called Fort Brady, on a site near the St. Marys River. In 1893 the post was moved from the original site to nearby Ashmun Hill, mentioned below by Long. See Heitman, *Historical Register*, 1:239, 349; John C. Calhoun to Henry R. Schoolcraft, September 19, 1823, Secretary of War, Letters Sent Relating to Indian Affairs, 1800–24, NARG 75; Joseph E. and Estelle L. Bayliss and Milo M. Quaife, *River of Destiny: The Saint Marys*, 77–80, 193 (Detroit, 1955); Prucha, *Guide to the Military Posts*, 61.

[17] Schoolcraft, who was appointed Ojibway agent at the Sault in 1822, found it difficult upon his arrival to find quarters for the agency. Before building a combined residence and agency in 1826–27, he occupied at least two different structures, described in his *Personal Memoirs*, 94, 109, 274. For a contemporary description of the village, see Williams, ed., Schoolcraft, *Narrative Journal*, 95.

[18] This post, built by the North West Company after an earlier one at the Sault was destroyed during the War of 1812, was used by the Hudson's Bay Company after the

About a mile below this is a considerable village [*Sault Ste. Marie, Ont.*] containing several houses of very decent appearance, among which is one conspicuous for its magnitude & elegance of structure. It belongs to a gentleman by the name of Hermitager [*Charles O. Ermatinger*], much respected in this neighbourhood.[19]

To-day we visited the H. B. Establishment for the purpose of making settlement for the supplies we obtained at Michipocotton. A gentle man by the name of [John] McBean presides at the establishment in the capacity of chief Factor, who gave us a very kind reception. Here we also met with Mr. Mackintosh [*Donald McIntosh*] of Michipocotton, who had left that place on his way hither eight days before us but did not arrive till three hours after we reached the Sault.[20]

THURSDAY, OCTOBER 2, 1823. Spent the day in settling with and discharging our voyageurs and making preparations for the further prosecution of our voyage. Spent part of the day with Mr. Schoolcraft, who politely furnished us with Topographical sketches of the Southern coast of Lake Superior and of the country situated between that lake and the Mississippi. He also gave us an opportunity of seeing his collection of minerals, shells, and Indian curiosities, which afforded us much gratification. His politeness manifested itself in a uniform readiness to afford us any intelligence in his power to give.

FRIDAY, OCTOBER 3, 1823. It is notorious that the soldiery of the U.S. Army especially in time of peace are addicted to intoxication.

consolidation in 1821. A list of the structures existing there in 1823 is in "Report of Buildings of Northwest Company at St. Mary's," in *Michigan Pioneer and Historical Collections*, 23: 436–438. See also Bayliss, Bayliss, and Quaife, *River of Destiny*, 82, 253.

[19] Ermatinger was a partner and agent of the North West Company before he became an independent trader. He began building his "Elegant Mansion" in 1814, and it remained unfinished in 1823. Located on Queen Street East, Sault Ste. Marie, Ont., the restored house is now a historic site open to the public. See Wallace, ed., *Documents Relating to the North West Company*, 438; Lavender, *Fist in the Wilderness*, 268; for a contemporary description of the house and the village, see G. P. de T. Glazebrook, ed., *The Hargrave Correspondence 1821–1843*, 5, 6 (Toronto, 1938).

[20] Both McBean and McIntosh were former North West Company men. After the coalition in 1821 McBean became a chief factor of the Hudson's Bay Company in charge of the Lake Huron district, while McIntosh was placed in charge of the Michipicoten district. The former spent the summer of 1823 at the Sault supervising the post there. See Wallace, ed., *Documents Relating to the North West Company*, 461, 472; Glazebrook, ed., *Hargrave Correspondence*, 8; Research Report, Hudson's Bay Company to the editors, May 6, 1971.

This deplorable circumstance grows out of the dissipation and corrupt principles contracted by those composing the army previously to enlistment. In a country like ours it can hardly be supposed that there can be any very strong inducement for young men of sober habits and upright characters to enter the service in time of peace, when they have nothing to expect but a very moderate compensation for services of the most arduous kind. It is obvious from a variety of considerations that none but the most profligate and abandoned of young men would enter the army in time of peace.

It proved perfectly in character with our guard that when we were ready to resume our voyage, they should be found so much overcome with liquor as to be illy fitted for the duties of boatmen. Nevertheless, as there was no prospect of their being in better trim than at present, we got ready to start soon after sunrise, and having taken leave of the gentlemen of the garrison for whose politeness we felt ourselves under many obligations, and proceeded on our voyage.

Our progress very slow till near 12 o'clock, when a favourable breez[e] sprang up and we were able to sail with speed. Passed a considerable [*Sugar*] island situated in an enlarged part of the river St. Marie [*St. Marys*] called Lake George. The main or Ship Channel [*Lake George*] passes on the East side of it, but is about 20 miles farther round than the Boat Channel [*Lake Nicolet*] by which we passed. The island is called Sugar I. from the Sugar Tree which abounds upon it, and is about 12 [*16*] miles long by four [*two to nine*] broad. St. Joseph's [*St. Joseph*] Island commences immediately below it and is of equal [*larger*] magnitude. On the west side of this is a considerable Lake called Mud [*Munuscong*] L. about 10 [*15*] miles long and 3 to 6 broad. Several small [*Lime*] islands are situated in the lower extremity of the Lake, which terminates at the South east end of St. Joseph's Island. On this part of the island are the ruins of several houses that were erected during the late war [of 1812] by the British soldiery. Two or three of the buildings only are now in a tolerable state of repair.[21]

Proceeded 4 miles below the Island and encamped opposite to

[21] The modern ship channel follows Long's route. His explanation of the name of Sugar Island is the usual one. A British post known as Fort St. Joseph was established on St. Joseph Island in 1796 and maintained until 1814, when it was burned by American troops. It was reoccupied by only a few soldiers who guarded the magazine until 1828. In 1977 it was being excavated by the Canadian government. On these points and the portion of the St. Marys River described here and below, see Bayliss, Bayliss, and Quaife, *River of Destiny*, 120–126, 153, 163.

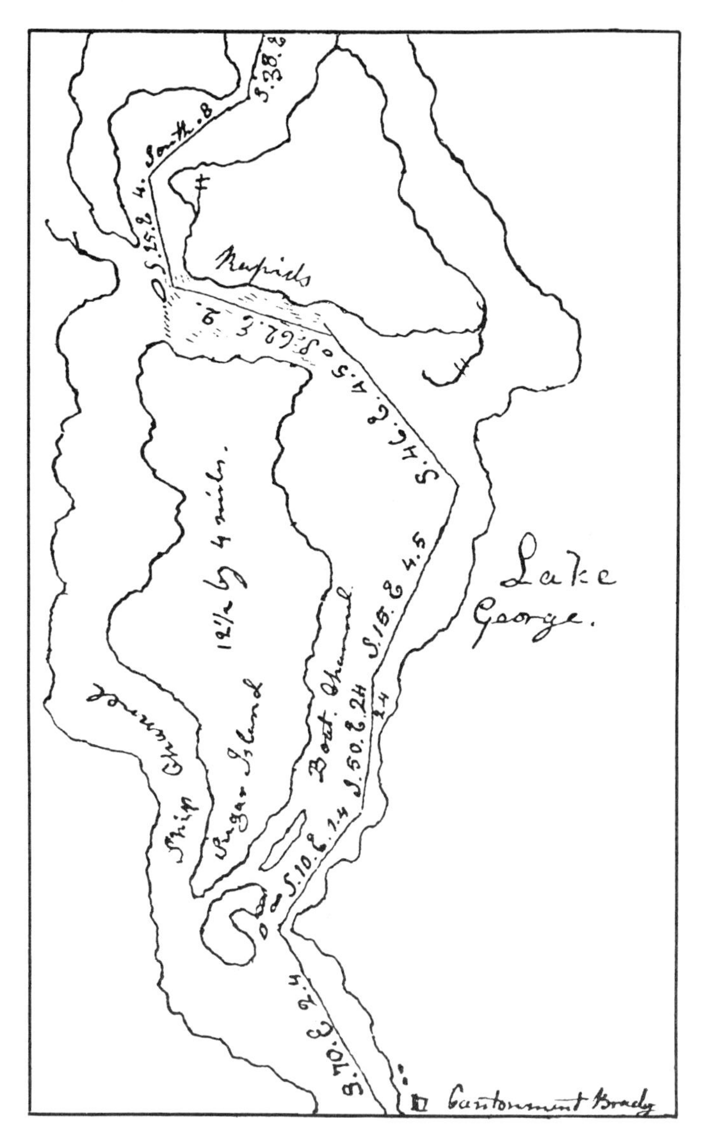

LONG'S SKETCH MAP *(actual size) of October 3, 1823, showing Lake George, Sugar Island, and the boat channels with Cantonment Brady (Sault Ste. Marie) at lower right.*

Drummond's Island on the American side at 1/2 past 6 o clock. Dist. 42 miles.

SATURDAY, OCTOBER 4, 1823. The Island of St. Joseph is about 24 [*20*] miles long and of variable width from 2 to 6 [*11*] miles. The main or Ship Channel passes on the west side of it; the [*St. Joseph*] channel on the other side being suitable for batteaus and other light craft. The lakes we passed yesterday are shoal, abounding in sand-bars covered with a moderate depth of water.

The country below the Sault of St. Marie, especially along the river, is for the most part low and swampy. High-lands occasionally present themselves but seldom approach the river or lakes. Large tracts of fresh meadow land are occasionally to be met with but are mostly over grown with willows and other bushes. At the distance of about 14 miles below the Sault is an extensive tract of this description from which the garrison at that place obtain their supplies of hay, of which they have made about 70 tons this season.

The growth of this part of the country consists principally of Spruce, Sugar-tree, maple, pine, white Birch, cedar &c.

Started early and passed into Lake Huron [*via Detour Passage*], leaving Drummond's Island on our left. We did not pass sufficiently near the island to observe the buildings and improvements made upon it.[22] A gentle head wind prevailed thro' the day, so that we were compelled to depend entirely upon our oars.

Passed numerous small [*Les Cheneaux*] islands on our right, none of which were of sufficient size to merit a name.[23] Arrived at Michilimakinak [*Mackinac, Mich.*] at about 9 o'clock in the evening after a fatiguing days voyage. Dist. 42 m.

SUNDAY, OCTOBER 5, 1823. Fort Mackinaw is at present commanded by Brevet Maj. [William] Whistler whose company is now the only force stationed here. Maj. W. has been resident here but a few weeks, having relieved Capt. [Benjamin K.] Pierce of the Artillery, late commandant of the Post. The gentlemen of the party were invited to accept of quarters and other accommodations at the mansion of the American Fur Company, where they were treated with

[22] The British built Fort Drummond on Drummond Island, then supposed to be outside the limits of American territory, in 1815. It replaced posts at St. Joseph Island and Mackinac. An establishment was maintained there until 1828, although a boundary survey completed earlier in the decade made it clear that the island was American territory. Bayliss, Bayliss, and Quaife, *River of Destiny*, 125, 129–139.

[23] On the later names of the approximately 50 Les Cheneaux Islands, see Frank R. Grover, *A Brief History of Les Cheneaux Islands*, 14, 103–110 (Evanston, Ill., 1911).

the utmost politeness & attention by Mr. [Robert] Stuart, the agent, and other officers of that institution.[24]

MONDAY, OCTOBER 6, 1823. Mackinaw, or Michilimakinak, is a name given to the Island on which a Fort and village, both of which bear the same name, are situated, and imports the Turtle, or Great Turtle, it having been given on account of the fancied resemblance of the island to that animal. The island is about 9 [*6*] miles in circumference, of an oval form, and is more elevated than any other point within the full extent of vision in every direction. The site of the Fort is about 150 feet above the level of the lake, which it overlooks for a great distance. A short distance northwardly of the Fort is a commanding eminence, occupying a small portion of the island and affording an extensive and grateful view of the straights and adjacent country. This eminence is elevated about 150 feet above the site of the Fort, or 300 above the water.[25]

It was formerly occupied by a military work constructed by the British, which has received the name of Fort Holmes in commemoration of the death of Maj. [Andrew H.] Holmes who fell in an attack made on the place by the Americans under the command of Col. [George] Croghan in Aug. 1814. While in the possession of the British, it was Called Fort George.

At the commencement of the late war, the american govt. kept a small force at this place, which was surprised by a more powerful one sent hither by the British for the purpose of reducing the place before the news of the declaration of war had reached it. They succeeded in their purpose, and for the sake of greater security built Fort George.[26]

[24] Fort Mackinac, occupied by American troops in 1796, captured by the British in 1812, and restored to the United States in 1815, was maintained intermittently until 1895. It has been restored and is open to the public. See Prucha, *Guide to the Military Posts*, 89; George S. May, *The Forts of Mackinac*, 3, 9–13 (Mackinac Island, Mich., 1962). On Pierce and Whistler, see Heitman, *Historical Register*, 1:791, 1026. Stuart, one of the Astorians mentioned on p. 188, above, managed the American Fur Company's business at Mackinac from 1819 until 1834. The "mansion" constructed after his arrival is now operated as a museum. See Lavender, *Fist in the Wilderness*, 134, 295, 417; David A. Armour, Mackinac Island State Park Commission, to the editors, October 16, December 14, 1970.

[25] For a discussion of the name and a review of its numerous spellings, see Walter Havighurst, *Three Flags at the Straits: The Forts of Mackinac*, x–xii (Englewood Cliffs, N.J., 1966).

[26] For a concise account of the capture of Fort Mackinac by the British and on Forts Holmes and George, see Reuben G. Thwaites, "The Story of Mackinac," in *WHC*, 14:12–14 (1898). Sugar Loaf and Arch Rock, mentioned below, are still points of interest on Mackinac Island. Seymour's views of Mackinac Island and Sugar Loaf have not been located; see p. 392, below.

The surface of the island is variegated with hills, precipices and valleys. There is a remarkable rock called the Sugar Loaf on the island, having an altitude of about 80 [75] feet and completely inaccessible at its summit. Also a singular rock [*Arch Rock*] disposed in such a manner as to form an arch of remarkable appearance. Mr. Seymour took sketches embracing these two subjects, as also an interesting view of the Village and Fort.

TUESDAY, OCTOBER 7, 1823. Finding no other means of prosecuting our voyage so agreeable to our wishes, we applied to Mr. [John W.] Mason, Acting Collector for the Port of Mackinaw, for a passage to Detroit on board of the Revenue Cutter A. J. Dallas, Capt. [Gilbert] Knapp, which was to sail in a few days for Erie as a wintering port. Mr. M. very kindly and frankly acceeded to the proposal and permitted the Cutter to sail whenever it should suit our convenience. Having taken our leave of Mr. Stuart, to whom we feel under many obligations for his polite and hospitable treatment as also of our other friends, we embarked and got under weigh at 2 h. 20′ P.M. The wind favouring, we continued the voyage thro' the night. At mid night we had made the Dist. 45 mile.[27]

WEDNESDAY, OCTOBER 8, 1823. In the morning early we had passed the Thunder Bay and five islands situated at its mouth cal[led] by the same name [*Thunder Bay, Sugar, Gull, Crooked, and Round*]. Passed the Entrance of Saganaw [*Saginaw*] Bay, which has a travers of more than 30 miles across its mouth. In passing this we found the Lake (Huron) very rough, the wind blowing heavily down the Bay. On this part of the voyage we were for a considerable distance out of sight of Land. The day stormy, but the wind would allow of keeping our course. At mid night our Distance was 112 miles.

THURSDAY, OCTOBER 9, 1823. It continued stormy thro' the

[27] Mason, acting or deputy collector of customs, was also postmaster and an employee of the American Fur Company. See "Collection of Manifests and Other Maritime Papers," 1821–23, in the Peter Barbeau Papers, Bayliss Library, Sault Ste. Marie, Mich., microfilm copy in MHS; Robert Stuart to Ramsay Crooks, October 26, 1823, Mackinac Letter Book; Dwight H. Kelton, *Annals of Fort Mackinac*, 123 (Detroit, 1884). Knapp, a captain in the U.S. Revenue Marine Service, was placed in command of the "A. J. Dallas" in 1819. For information on his colorful career in the service which later became the Coast Guard, see *Racine* [Wis.] *Daily Journal*, August 1, 1887; Records of the U.S. Coast Guard, Applications File and Service Record of Knapp, and Applications File of Daniel Dobbins, NARG 26. At Mackinac, Scott, Denny, and the ten remaining soldiers left the expedition to return to their posts on the Mississippi via Green Bay and the Fox-Wisconsin waterway. See Keating, *Narrative*, 2:204.

night. In the morning the wind became somewhat more favourable. Weather squally. At 3h. 15m. P.M. we arrived at the bottom or out let of the Lake [Huron], having sailed since mid-night 63 miles. Here commences St. Clair river, affording a navigable communi-[cation] with Lake St. Clair 45 miles below. At the head of St. Clair river on the American side is the site of Fort Gratiot, which appears secure and commanding. It is now occupied only by a missionary school at which are about 20 indian children. At midnight we had descended about 25 miles down the river, making in the last 24 hours the Distance of 93 miles.[28]

FRIDAY, OCTOBER 10, 1823. The river St. Clair meanders thro' a very beautiful country, apparently well adapted to cultivation. On its banks, especially on the American side, the settlements are pretty numerous and exhibit a flourishing aspect.

Passed into Lake St. Clair, a beautiful sheet of water, about 20 [*26*] miles long and 10 to 15 [*24*] broad. On its shores are numerous settlements in a flourishing condition and a few villages of respectable size. Seven miles below the Lake [*on the Detroit R.*] is the Town of Detroit, [Mich.] at which we arrived at 3 o'clock P.M. Dist. 50 miles.[29]

SATURDAY, OCTOBER 11, 1823. At Detroit we expected to receive letters from our friends and a fresh supply of funds from the War Department, but with respect to the latter were completely disappointed, none having been transmitted and no prospect of their arriving in season to answer our purpose. On our departure from Philadelphia no more than $500 were taken to meet the exigencies of the Expedition, which was thought a sum sufficient to defray our expenses till we had passed beyond the settlements. Thence to this place it was expected that game of one description or another sufficient for the subsistenc[e] of the party would be taken, but we were very much deceived in this calculation, the whole of

[28] An Indian school at former Fort Gratiot was maintained in 1821–23 by John S. Hudson and John Hart, Presbyterians acting for the Northern Missionary Society. The military post, built in 1814 and vacated in 1821, was reoccupied intermittently and finally abandoned in 1879. A marker at Stone and State streets in Port Huron, Mich., commemorated the site. See William L. Jenks, *St. Clair County Michigan: Its History and Its People*, 1:95–103, 271 (Chicago and New York, 1912); Lewis Cass to Hudson, August 30, 1822, OIA, Michigan Superintendency, Letters Sent, NARG 75; Gayle D. Harmer, St. Clair County Library, to the editors, June 9, 1972.

[29] The sailing course from northeast to southwest through Lake St. Clair was normally 18 miles in length. Many travelers commented on the contrast between the development on the Canadian and American shores. For a discussion of this and descriptive information on Lake St. Clair and the Detroit River, see Harlan Hatcher, *Lake Erie*, 341–355, 367–370 (Indianapolis and New York, 1945).

the game taken on the tour being no more than was necessary for our support for a single week. To make up for these miscalculations, recourse was had to the credit of the expedition, and by means of the polite credential furnished by Mr. Canning, the British minister, to the comdg. Officer, as also by the credit of the latter with some of his friends whom we chanced to meet with on the journey, all needfull supplies were obtained at his own individual responsibility. In order to cover the expenses of our journey from this place to Philadelphia, $500 had been called for in two different communications with an earnest solicitation to the War Department (thro' Gen. McComb [*Alexander Macomb*]), that this small sum might be transmitted in season for the use of the party on their arrival at Detroit. But being disappointed, as before remarked, we again had recourse to the private responsibility of Maj. L., who succeeded in raising a sum sufficient for our present purposes.

At Detroit we were politely received by Gov. [Lewis] Cass who today invited the gentlemen of the party to a dinner given by himself on their Account.[30]

SUNDAY, OCTOBER 12, 1823. We were invited to attend church by Governor Cass and accordingly accompanied him, not a little gratified that we again were within the land of religious instruction. The clergyman was a presbyterian and had for his subject the Decalogue on moral law, which he expounded in a very able tho' not elegant manner.

The religious societies of Detroit consist of Presbyterians, Catholics and Methodists, of which the two former have each a house of public worship. That of the Catholics was constructed at a very considerable expense, but the elegance of the building is by no means answerable to its cost. It is a very spacious building, has two steeples, two cupolas, and in the centre a dome. It is built principally of stone. The Presbyterian Church is of respectable size, and in its external has considerable claim to neatness if not elegance.[31]

[30] On Cass's career, see Frank B. Woodford, *Lewis Cass: The Last Jeffersonian* (New Brunswick, N.J., 1950).

[31] By 1823, $30,000 had been spent on the Catholic Church of St. Anne. The Protestant Church, a wooden structure, was used by the Episcopalians as well as the Presbyterians. Rev. Joshua Moore was the Presbyterian minister from 1822 to 1824. The Methodists laid the foundation for a church building in 1823 and it was virtually completed by the end of that year. *Detroit Gazette*, June 12, 1818, January 29, 1819, March 7, 1823, January 2, 1824; C. C. Trowbridge, "History of the Episcopal Church in Michigan," in *Michigan Pioneer and Historical Collections*, 3:214, 215 (Lansing, 1881); Fred Carlisle, comp., *Chronography of Notable Events in the History of the Northwest Territory and Wayne County*, 93 (Detroit, 1890).

MONDAY, OCTOBER 13, 1823. For an account & description of Detroit, also some sketch of its history, see notes of Messrs. Say and Keating.[32]

The country below the Sault of St. Marie assumes a very different aspect from that above. Its rocks are uniformly of a secondary character, its surface undulating, exhibiting hills of moderate height and gentle acclivity with occasional precipices, which is characteristic of a large proportion of Michigan Territory. The country is well timbered, its forests comprising an extensive variety of timber-trees and shrubbery. Among the former the sugar tree, maple, hiccory, oak, ash, beach, black-walnut &c. are plentiful, & among the latter are the Hazle, the arrow-wood, grape vine, wild hop, rasberry &c. &c.

The Lake shores present extensive sand beeches in many places, tho' the coast is more generally rocky bound and precipitous. The rivers St. Clair and Detroit are merely straights, the former communicating between Lakes Huron and St. Clair, and the latter between the Lake last mentioned and Lake Erie. They have a current of about 2 1/2 miles an hour, which moves with an accellerated velocity in one or two places in the river St. Clair called rapids.

Lake St. Clair is a beautiful sheet of water of moderate depth and consequently of difficult navigation in many parts of it, and is handsomely adorned with numerous flourishing settlements which have been recently formed on its margin. A number of wind-mills which have been erected at the lower end of the lake gave additional beauty and interest to the scene.

It is obvious to the travel[er] that the settlements on the American side are much more flourishing and numerous than on the Canada shore.

Detroit is situated about 4 miles below Lake St. Clair on the west, or rather SW, bank of the river bearing its name. It extends along the shore of the [Detroit] river about one mile, and occupies a portion of the beautiful plain commencing at the margin & reaching back from the river nearly a mile, where it is terminated by low woodlands. Indeed, the country along the banks both of St. Clair and Detroit rivers is of a similar character, presenting very many sites eligible for settlements, many of which are already occupied. A short distance below Detroit on the opposite side of the [Detroit]

[32] Keating's *Narrative* ends with the party's arrival at Sault Ste. Marie, devoting only a brief paragraph to the trip back to Philadelphia via New York. The notes here referred to have not been located.

river is the small village of Sandwich [*Windsor, Ont.*], which like most of the English settlements in this quarter exhibits no very thriving aspect.

TUESDAY, OCTOBER 14, 1823. During our stay at Detroit we were treated with much politeness, especially by His Excellency Gov. Cass, who kindly volunteered his carriage for the transportation of the gentlemen of the party to such places as they wished to visit, and with the utmost hospitality invited us to participate in the viands of his bountiful table.

Having waited for the Steam Boat ["*Superior*"] from Buffalo, which arrived early this morning, we embarked on board of her at 4 o'clock P.M. and proceeded on our voyage.[33] Passed Fort Malden situated on the Canada side of the [Detroit] river 18 miles below Detroit. At this place is a considerable village called Am[h]erst-burg [Ont.]. Entered Lake Erie a few miles below. Passed three Islands called the Three Sisters near [*north of*] which the naval battle took place in which the Gallant [Oliver H.] Perry gained his splendid victory. Arrived at Sandusky bay in the course of the night. Dist. 72 miles.[34]

WEDNESDAY, OCTOBER 15, 1823. The entrance into the bay being intricate, we lay by till day-light appeared in order to keep within the ship channel, which is very narrow and crooked. The Bay is very capacious, and affords a sufficient depth of water after having passed a bar streaching nearly across its mouth and obstructing the passage of vessels of any considerable draft.[35]

A few miles up the bay on the south side is the site of a village called Sandusky [Ohio], containing several houses and stores of decent appearance. The place is said to be sickly, which is particularly

[33] Long's departure from Detroit occasioned newspaper comment. The "Superior" was a new steamboat plying between Detroit and Buffalo, N.Y. The captain was Jedediah Rogers. See *Detroit Gazette*, October 3, 17, 1823.

[34] Fort Malden or Amherstburg, established by the British in 1796 after they abandoned their fortifications in Detroit in conformity with provisions in the treaty of 1794, was maintained as a military post until 1851. Remnants of the fort are preserved in Fort Malden National Historic Park in Amherstburg, Ont. See "Notes and Comments," in *Canadian Historical Review*, 29:124 (March, 1948). The naval battle of Lake Erie, fought against the British on September 10, 1813, was won by the American fleet under the command of Perry. A memorial stands at Put-in-Bay on South Bass Island. Middle, East, and West Sister islands off the Ohio and Ontario coast are still landmarks in Lake Erie. See Hatcher, *Lake Erie*, 80–90, 257, 258.

[35] Sandusky Bay is about 18 miles long and five miles wide. It is sheltered on the north by Marblehead Peninsula and on the southeast by Cedar Point Peninsula, which extends partly across the mouth of the bay as Long indicated.

the case at the present time. Three miles farther up the Bay on the same side is another small village called Venice, now nearly deserted on account of the insalubrity of its situation. The country on this part of the lake [Erie] is generally low and flat. Swamps abound, among which the dreary and inhospitable region called the Black Swamp, about 40 miles long and 25 broad, situated between the Sandusky and Maumee rivers. This tract is very flat, covered with a dense and heavy growth of timber impervious to the rays of the sun, and continually inundated with water in most places.[36]

Having exchanged a few passengers, we resumed our voyage, passed several small villages and numerous settlements on the lake shore and touched at Cleaveland [*Cleveland, Ohio*], where we landed a few passengers and took others on board. Cleaveland is situated at the mouth of Cuyahoga Cr. which affords a safe and commodious harbour for small craft. Its site is elevated, rising about 60 [75] feet above the level of the Lake. Here commences a region more elevated than we have heretofore met with on the lake, connected no doubt with the hilly country on the north of the Ohio river.

Passed the mouth of Grand river [*Fairport Harbor, Ohio*] at which we also touched for the purposes before mentioned. At mid night we had made our Distance 108 miles.

THURSDAY, OCTOBER 16, 1823. The settlements on the shore still to be seen scattered at short intervals. Passed the town of Erie [Pa.] about noon where we again exchanged passengers. This is a village of respectable appearance situated at the entrance of a large harbour formed by a singular point of land called Presque Isle. The entrance of the harbour is obstructed by a bar extending across it and preventing the passage of vessels drawing more than 5 or 6 feet of water. Measures however are about to be taken for the purpose of opening a navigable channel into the harbour.

The town is situated about mid-way of that part of the State of Pennsylvania which borders upon the Lake, is fast rising in importance, and bids fair to become one of the most considerable in this part of the country in a commercial point of view. Its site is elevated, and the adjacent country is moderately hilly, possessed of a prolific

[36] The Black Swamp, stretching some 100 miles along Lake Erie between the Maumee and Sandusky rivers, was a well-known feature of early Ohio and was considered unhealthful and malarial. Long's remarks were echoed by many travelers. For a fuller description of the area in 1823, see Alfred Brunson, *A Western Pioneer*, 1:276–278 (Cincinnati and New York, 1872).

soil and well timbered. At evening we had a strong wind to contend against, and the Lake became very rough. The pitching and tossing of the Steam Bo[a]t produced sea-sickness among a great number of the passengers. At midnight we had made the Distance of 104 miles.

FRIDAY, OCTOBER 17, 1823. At 7 o'clock this morning we arrived at Buffalo, [N.Y.] situated at the easterly extremity of Lake Erie, having travelled 46 miles. The town is in a very flourishing condition, tho' it may yet be considered as in its infancy, having had but a few year's growth. The Grand [*Erie*] Canal of N. York is to have its western termination at this place, which will no doubt contribute to raise it higher on the scale of importance than any other place on the Lake.[37]

Having breakfasted at Buffalo, we resumed our journey by travelling [north] in the mail stage and, having passed a small village called Black Rorck [*Black Rock, N.Y.*] (at which resides Gen. P[eter] B. Porter) and several other places memorable on account of the scenes that were acted in the course of the late war [of 1812] with Great Briton (Conjockaty Creek, Ft. Erie, Chippeway [*Chippawa*], &c.), we arrived at the Falls of Niagara, 22 miles down the river of the same name, where we purpose to delay a short time to gratify our curiosity with a view of the magnificent scenery of the place. Dist. 68 miles.[38]

[37] The Erie Canal was commonly called the Grand Canal as well as the Great Western Canal and the Big Ditch. Begun in 1817 and completed in 1825, it connected the waters of Lake Erie with those of the Hudson River and was 363 miles in length. When Long made his trip, the section between Brockport and Albany, N.Y., had been finished. Buffalo was selected as the canal's western terminus in 1823 after a spirited contest with neighboring Black Rock. See Ronald E. Shaw, *Erie Water West: A History of the Erie Canal 1792–1854*, 84–86, 101, facing p. 130, 157, 181, 237 (Lexington, Ky., 1966).

[38] Porter, who settled at Black Rock (now part of Buffalo) in 1810, was a militia general during the War of 1812, lawyer, congressman, secretary of war, international boundary commissioner, and businessman. See note 42, below; *Guide to the Microfilm Edition of the Peter B. Porter Papers in the Buffalo and Erie County Historical Society*, 1 (Buffalo, N.Y., 1968). During the War of 1812, several engagements occurred at the sites on the Niagara frontier Long mentioned. Scajaquada or Conjockety Creek (variously spelled) is within the present limits of Buffalo. Fort Erie, at the Lake Erie entrance of the Niagara River opposite Buffalo, was one of a succession of posts built in the vicinity from 1764 to 1814. It has been restored and a monument commemorating the siege of 1814 stands in Old Fort Erie Park, Ont. The most notable battle fought at Chippawa (now a suburb of Niagara Falls, Ont.) was on July 5, 1814. It is memorialized by a monument south of the village on the Niagara River Parkway. See Ronald L. Way, *Ontario's Niagara Parks: A History*, 222, 258–268, 319, 321 (Hamilton, Ont., 1946); Louis L. Babcock, *The War of 1812 on the Niagara Frontier*, 184–187 (Buffalo, N.Y., 1927).

SATURDAY, OCTOBER 18, 1823. The celebrated Cataract denominated the Falls of Niagara is formed by a pricipice of s[e]condary rocks streaching obliquely across the river, over which the whole body of water discharged by Lake Erie is precipitated in extensive and unbroken sheets. It is divided into two parts nearly equal in extent by the lower side of Goat Island, which occupies a space of about 300 yards of the middle portion of the precipice. That part of the cataract situated below the island is on the American side, and hence denominated the American Fall, while that above is called the British Fall, it being situated on the Canada side. The perpendicular pitch of the latter is less by 12 or 14 feet than that of the former, but the quantity of water passing over it is considerably greater. The perpendicular descent of the water in the American Fall is 172 feet and in the British 160. The precipice in its diagonal course across the river is about 1200 [*1,691*] yards long, running in a zigzag manner on the American side, and forming a curve or waving line resembling the letter S on the British side, and hence denominated the Horse-shoe.[39]

Goat island (to which the name of Iris has been attempted to be given in commemoration of the Rainbow with which the falls is ever embellished when the sun shines, but without success) is of an oval form, its diameters being 6 by 5 hundred yards, and has its longer diameter nearly at right angles with the general direction of the Falls. Between this island and the American shore are several small islands, the largest of which is about 75 yards long and 40 broad and is called Bath [*Green*] Island from a small building erected thereon for a bathing hous[e.][40]

[39] The top stratum of rock forming the precipice of the falls is Lockport limestone. A profile sketch showing this and other strata appears in *The Preservation of Niagara Falls: Final Report of the Special International Niagara Board*, 157 (Ottawa, 1930). Contrary to Long's statement, Goat Island divides the cataract into unequal parts. The Canadian or Horseshoe Falls are 2,300 feet wide and carry about 80 per cent of the water, while the American Falls are 1,100 feet wide. The perpendicular pitch of the cataract varies with the location. The Canadian Falls average 176 feet and the American 182 feet. However, many of these measurements may have changed due to recession and development of the falls since 1823. Maurice W. Barnes, Niagara State Park and Recreation Commission, to the editors, April 9, 1974. See also Peter A. Porter, *Official Guide: Niagara Falls—River—Frontier*, 188–191 (Buffalo, N.Y., 1901); Joseph W. Spencer, *The Falls of Niagara*, 2, 259 (Ottawa, 1907).

[40] Goat Island's average dimensions are 1,257 by 383 yards. Bath (now Green) Island measures 268 by 143 yards. See Barnes to the editors, April 9, 1974. On the baths, see Victor H. Paltsits, "Judge Augustus Porter, Pioneer of Niagara Falls," in *New York History*, 18:151 (April, 1937). A map showing Goat, Green, and other islands appears in Peter A. Porter, *Goat Island*, facing copyright page (n.p., 1900).

A bridge has been constructed leading from the American shore to Bath island 120 yds. long, and another from this island to Goat island 80 yards long. These structures are situated only about 350 yards above the Cataract and must have been built with im[m]inent hazard and danger to the workmen. The waters of the [Niagara] river over which they are built rushes like a torrent beneath them. The channels on both sides of Goat island abound in cascades succeeding each other at short intervals, making an aggregate descent of about 40 feet in a distance of 800 yards. The bridges were built by Judge [Augustus] Porter, who is at present their proprietor and owns also the islands with which they communicate. The surface of Lake Erie is elevated [about] 336 feet above that of Lake Ontario.[41]

Surveys embracing both the Hydrography & Topography of the interesting country between these two Lakes have been made by the Hon. Judge Porter, Judge [James] Geddes & others, but no opportunity presented of getting access to their documents.[42]

On the American side is situated a small village called Manchester [*Niagara Falls, N.Y.*] at which is a large and commodious mansion [*Eagle Tavern*] occupied as an inn, also the elegant mansion of Judge Porter, besides several mills, a store &c. On the Canada side directly opposite is the memorable tract [*of battlefields*] comprehending Bridgewater, Christlers Fields, Lundy's Lane &c. A superb mansion [*the Pavilion?*] three stories high overlooking the Falls has

[41] The bridges were first built in 1817 by Augustus Porter, Niagara County judge, who purchased the Goat Island group the year before. These bridges washed away and Porter replaced them in 1818 with another pair located farther downstream. These were the bridges Long saw. For varying descriptions of how they were built, see McElroy and Riggs, eds., Delafield, *Unfortified Boundary*, 222; Porter, *Official Guide*, 37–39. See also Charles M. Robinson, "The Life of Judge Augustus Porter A Pioneer in Western New York," in Buffalo Historical Society, *Publications*, 7:250, 259–261, 265 (Buffalo, N.Y., 1904). Long's figure for the descent of the river from the head of the rapids to the apex of the falls is approximately correct, although this distance varies with the irregular shape of the crestline and for other reasons. James Geddes (see note 42, below) estimated the level of Lake Erie above Lake Ontario at 334 feet; see *Laws of the State of New York, in Relation to the Erie and Champlain Canals*, 1:20 (Albany, N.Y., 1825). A more usual figure is 326 feet. See, for example, *The Preservation of Niagara Falls*, 10.

[42] It is not certain which of the Porter brothers Long had in mind. Judge Porter was a surveyor in western New York from 1789 to 1806. His brother, Gen. Peter B. Porter, participated as an American boundary commissioner in surveys of the Niagara River, which were concluded in 1822. See Robinson, in Buffalo Historical Society, *Publications*, 7:235–239, 243; McElroy and Riggs, eds., Delafield, *Unfortified Boundary*, 35–41, 58–61. Geddes surveyed the Niagara River in 1809. His report to the New York surveyor general appears in *Laws . . . in Relation to the Erie and Champlain Canals*, 1:18–24.

been here erected and appropriated to the accommodation of visitants to N[iagara] Fa[ll]s. Having examined this magnificent spectacle at a variety of interesting points on both sides of the river, and visited the memorable field of battle called Christler's fields or Lundy's Lane, we took our departure at 4 P.M. and travelled down the [Niagara] river to Lewiston, [N.Y.] situated at the termination of the high lands connected with the scenery of the Falls, and opposite to the town of Queenston, [Ont.] and the heights bearing that name. Dist. 7 miles.[43]

SUNDAY, OCTOBER 19, 1823. The heights of Queenston are elevated about 336 [*453 maximum*] feet above the level of Lake Ontario and are somewhat higher than the corresponding heights [*153 feet maximum*] on the American side.

Lewiston is 7 miles distant from the estuary of Niagara river at which Fort Niagara [N.Y.] is situated [*on Lake Ontario*]. It is a place of some importance, being situated at the head of ship navigation on that river. Here is a ferry across the river, which is the first commodious one below the Falls of Niagara and is much frequented by teams &c. The village or town contains about 100 houses including stores and work shops, many of them well built.[44]

Took our departure hence in the stage at 3 in the morning. Passed

[43] On the Eagle Tavern operated by Parkhurst Whitney, the various mills, the store owned by Samuel de Veaux, and the mansion built by Augustus Porter to replace an earlier structure destroyed during the War of 1812, see *History of Niagara County, N.Y.*, 300–304 (New York, 1878); Paltsits, in *New York History*, 18:142, 147, 149–151. There were two inns on the Canadian side, the Ontario and the Pavilion. Long probably meant the Pavilion operated by William Forsyth. See Ernest Green, "The Niagara Portage Road," in Ontario Historical Society, *Papers and Records*, 23: facing p. 260, 289 (Toronto, 1926).

Chrysler's or Crysler's Farm battlefield was not synonymous with Lundy's Lane. Crysler's Farm, where a battle took place on November 11, 1813, is on the St. Lawrence River, while Lundy's Lane, also known as the battle of Bridgewater, was fought on July 25, 1814. See Reginald Horsman, *The War of 1812*, 128–130, 178 (New York, 1969); Mabel V. Warner, "Memorials at Lundy's Lane," in Ontario Historical Society, *Papers and Records*, 51:43–47 (Toronto, 1959).

[44] Lewiston, head of navigation below Niagara Falls, was connected by a portage road with Schlosser, the point above the falls where navigation on the Niagara River continued to Lake Erie. The ferry, which plied between Lewiston and Queenston, was mentioned by other travelers. See Green, in Ontario Historical Society, *Papers and Records*, 23:260, 304; *History of Niagara County*, 249, 251.

Fort Niagara, at the mouth of the Niagara River at Lake Ontario, was built by the French in 1726, captured by the British in 1759, relinquished to the Americans in 1796, recaptured by the British in 1813, and again returned to the United States at the close of the War of 1812. The site, which includes several original buildings, is preserved. See S. Grove McClellan, "Old Fort Niagara," in *American Heritage*, Summer, 1953, pp. 32–38.

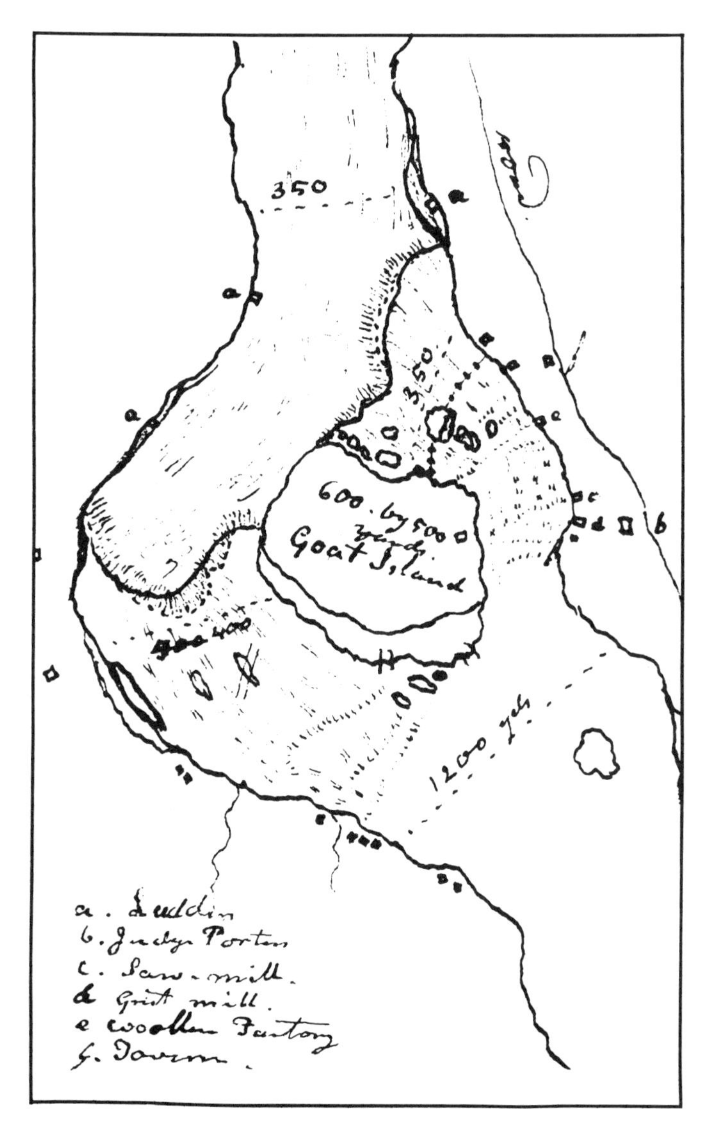

LONG'S SKETCH MAP of Niagara Falls and Goat Island, which he visited on October 18, 1823.

thro' a country remarkably well timbered, having occasional settlements scattered along the road. The timber growth consists principally of White, Red and black oak, Sugar-Tree, Maple, Walnut, Hiccory, Poplar (American), Beech, Ash &c. On the road are situated severall small villages of flourishing appearance, the most considerable of which is called Clarkson, [N.Y.] within a few miles of Genesee river.

The road we travelled is called the Ridge Road, from the circumstance of its passing along a remarkable ridge of land running parallel to the shore of Lake Ontario at the distance of about 6 1/2 miles from it. The summit of the ridge is elevated about 150 feet above L. Ontario, the ascent from the L. to the summit being gradual. South of the ridge is a valley about 3 miles in width, along the southern slope of which passes the route of the Grand [*Erie*] Canal of N. York in a direction generally parallel to the ridge and the Lake shore. Proceeding still farther Southward, the ground continues to rise gradually to the general elevation of the high lands, which may be regarded as a continuation of Queenston Heights and have nearly the same altitude. The Ridge commences 3 miles from Lewiston and extends to Oswego [N.Y.] a distance of 110 [*153*] miles [*east,*] interrupted only by watercourses, the most considerable of which is Genesee river. Thro'out its whole extent it maintains its parallel direction with the Lakeshore. Having travelled on the ridge nearly to Genessee river, we changed our course and proceeded upward [*south*] a few miles near the river valley and arrived at Rochester [N.Y.] at a quarter befor[e] 12 at night. Dist. 77 m.[45]

MONDAY, OCTOBER 20, 1823. Rochester is situated on the left bank of Genessee river about 6 miles above its mouth.[46] It contains about 200 houses, many of them large and handsomely built. It has been settled but a few years and owes its growth to the Grand Canal which passes thro' it. The country around it is said to be very productive, but it is presumed that its growth will be in some measure checked by the completion of this part of the canal, upon the con-

[45] Long described only a portion of the ridge, which was also discernible beyond Oswego. The section of the famed road that ran along the ridge from Lewiston to Rochester (now U.S. 104) is approximately 82 miles long. See Thomas F. Gordon, *Gazetteer of the State of New York*, book 1, p. 23 (New York, [1836]); Works Progress Administration, *Rochester and Monroe County*, 298, 302 (Rochester and New York, 1937).

[46] By 1823 the village limits of Rochester included areas on both sides of the river. See Blake McKelvey, *Rochester the Water-Power City 1812–1854*, 103 (Cambridge, Mass., 1945).

struction of which vast sums of money have been expended. The canal is here carried across the river by a stone Aqueduct, of which the annexed description published in the Rochester Telegraph of the 14th inst. [*October 14, 1823*] is given by Judge [David S.] Bates, the Engineer who superintended its construction.[47]

["]*The Aqueduct.* —Judge Bates, the Engineer who superintended the construction of this splendid work, has politely, at our request, furnished the following description:

["]This stupendous fabric, which forms a prominent link in the great chain of our inland communication, is built on one of the rifts which compose a part of the extensive falls of the Genesee river, about eighty rods south of its greatest fall. It is situated nearly in the centre of the village of Rochester, parallel to the great leading western road, and crosses the Genesee river about 80 yards south of it. The approach of the Erie Canal to the Genesee river, from the east, is for a considerable distance confined to a steep, bold bank; at the foot of which formerly run a raceway. This artificial water-course, on the immediate bank of the river, was compelled to give place to the Erie Canal, and has been placed outside of it, till at the instant of its crossing it is passed under it in an arch of twenty-six feet chord[.] The natural and artificial scenery, here presented, is grand and peculiarly interesting. The river, with its rapids, is surmounted by the race, above mentioned; which, in its turn, is surmounted by the Erie Canal, which is again overtopped by the table land in the vicinity, on the extreme edge of which is an important street of the village of East-Rochester. The Aqueduct, from the eastern extremity of its parapet walls to its western termination is 804 feet long, and is built on eleven arches, one above named of twenty-six feet chord, under which passes the water necessary for a number of important flouring mills, &c. nine of fifty feet chord, and one on the west side of the river of thirty feet chord, under which passes water for a number of flouring mills and other hydraulic establishments in West-Rochester. The structure is founded on solid rock, in which nitches were cut to found the piers, which are thirty-six feet long

[47] Bates was a division engineer on the Erie Canal at the time he directed construction of the aqueduct, which was completed in September, 1823, and replaced by a new structure in 1842. See *National Cyclopaedia of American Biography*, 18:171 (New York, 1922); Shaw, *Erie Water West*, 129; Noble E. Whitford, *History of the Canal System of the State of New York*, 1:112, 171 (*Supplement to the Annual Report of the State Engineer and Surveyor . . . 1905*—Albany, N.Y., 1906). A clipping from the *Rochester Telegraph* is pasted in Long's manuscript journal at this point. It is transcribed below.

and ten feet wide, including at each end a pedestal and dome, out of which rises a pilaster. The height of the piers is about four and an half feet; the rise of the arch eleven feet; its thickness at the foot three feet; at the apex, two and an half feet. The parapet walls or sides of the trunk, are five and an half feet high, including the coping, which is so constructed as to form a capital to the whole trunk. The whole of this immense building is of cut stone; many of them, particularly the piers, of very great size. These are trenailed to the rock by large iron bolts, and so cramped and cemented as nearly to form a mass which possesses the consistency and firmness of a single unbroken rock. The stones of which the walls are composed are red sand, intimately blended with a small proportion of iron. The pilasters and coping, of gray silecious lime stone. On the north wall, which is of sufficient thickness for the towing path, is an elegant iron railing; and at the west end the whole is terminated by a highway and towing-path bridge of the most solid and elegant workmanship.

["]The work was commenced by Mr. Alfred Hovey, the Contractor, on the 17th of July, 1822, and completed on the 11th of September, 1823.["][48]

The Falls of Genesse river are contiguous to the town [of Rochester] and add greatly to the interest a traveller would take in the place. They are divided into two cataracts at the distance of little more than a mile assunder. The uppermost is situated about 400 yards below the aqueduct and has a perpendicular pitch of 67 feet. The other cataract has a fall of between 40 & 50 feet, the sheet being broken and diverted from a perpendicular descent by reefs of rocks that occur between its summit and base. The river is navigable for steam boats 4 miles upward from its mouth or within two miles of the Town. Several mills and other machinery have been erected on the river at the upper cataract, which gives occasion to choise mill-sites in great numbers.[49]

It having been our intention to visit the Grand Canal, which

[48] The clipping ends here. The first work on the aqueduct was done by William Brittin in 1821. Hovey and two associates took over the contract in December, 1821. See New York State, *Journal of the Assembly*, 1824, p. 515 (Albany, N.Y., 1824); Richard N. Wright, Canal Society of New York State, to the editors, March 22, 1969.

[49] In 1823 there were four falls of the Genesee within the present limits of Rochester. Schooners, steamboats, and other craft plied the four miles of navigable water between Lake Ontario and the lower falls. For varying figures on the falls, the industries at the upper falls, and the navigation, see McKelvey, *Rochester the Water-Power City*, 13n, 59, 86–88; McKelvey to the editors, March 31, 1972.

deservedly ranks among the noblest works of our country, we embarked on board of one of the Packet-boats which ply daily upon the canal, and took our departure from Rochester at half past 8 o'clock this morning.

The Packet Boat in which we travel is 74 feet in length and 13 feet in width at the broadest part. Its bottom is flat, and terminated by curve lines which meet at the bow and stern, and is about 10 feet wide in the centre. The Cabin is about 50 feet long occupying the central portion of the boat, and is divided into two apartments, one of which is used as a mess room and the other being furnished with births as a sleeping apartment. About fifteen passengers can be accommodated on board of her, little or no freight being allowed. The Crew, besides the Boatswain who is styled Captain, consists of a steward, two boatmen, a cook and waiters. The boat is propelled or rather towed by three horses in single file driven by a boy who rides the hindmost, the towing line being about 30 yards long and attached to the side of the boat about 1/4 of its length from the bow. Thus equipped we move at the rate of 4 miles per hour, a greater speed being prohibited on account of the damage that the banks of the canal would sustain by the washing or surf occasioned by a more rapid movement.[50]

The Canal has been completed and rendered navigable from Brockport 20 [*15*] miles above [*west of*] Rochester to Albany, a distance of 287 miles. West ward of that place it is in an unfinished state, tho' much labour has been bestowed upon that portion of it. At a place called Lock Port, about 40 [*45*] miles beyond [*west of*] Brock-port, the Canal passes up the acclivity that divid[e]s the high lands before mentioned from the low country north of them. The passage is to be effected by several double Locks of 12 feet lift each, which circumstance gives name to the Town located at the place.[51]

The route of the Canal, necessarily conforming to the nature of the country and particularly to that of the watercours[e] whence it

[50] On the construction of packet boats, see Shaw, *Erie Water West*, 201–203. The law limiting packet boat speed to four miles an hour was enacted in 1822. Even so, "bank wash" was a continuing problem that necessitated extensive repairs, and the canal commissioners in 1825 complained of the damage caused by the packets and suggested raising tolls. See *Laws . . . in Relation to the Erie and Champlain Canals*, 2:94, 258, 315.

[51] Official figures on the length of the canal from Brockport to Albany were slightly less than, but close to, Long's. Five double locks were constructed at Lockport. Although the contracts were let in 1821, they were not completed until June 24, 1825. See *Laws . . . in Relation to the Erie and Champlain Canals*, 2:102, 108; Shaw, *Erie Water West*, 130–133.

derives its supply of water, leads thro the flattest and least interesting portions of the country, leaving the towns and villages that were formed previously to its location in the most eligible tracts remote from the canal. Numerous sites however have since been occupied along the canal, and many villages are now rapidly rising in situations where, but for the construction of this great work, no settlements would ever have been made within the present century. Among these are Pittsford, Perrington [*Perinton*], Palmyra, Newark, Lyons, Clyde, Montezuma, Jordan, Canton [*Memphis*], Geddesburg [*Geddes*], Syracuse, &c. &c. by far the greater part of which have been built since the location of the Canal.

Passed several swamps in which Cedar is the prevailing growth. American Poplar, Oak, Hiccory, Maple &c., are abundant on the high lands. At midnight we had travelled about the Distance of 60 miles.

TUESDAY, OCTOBER 21, 1823. At 4 this morning we passed the flourishing village of Montezuma, situated at the out let of Cayuga Lake. At midday arrived at Onondaga Lake, in the neighbourhood of which are the celebrated salt springs and works bearing that name. Here a branch canal has been constructed, leading from Cyracuse [*Syracuse*], a small village thro' which the Grand Canal passes, to the Lake, to facilitate the exportation of salt manufactured there, and also to constitute part of a water-communication between the Grand Canal and Lake Ontario, the difference of levels being here about 140 [*194*] feet, or the pound at Cyracuse haveing that elevation above Lake Ontario.[52]

The process of making salt by solar evaporation has been here attempted, but the experiment is not yet completed, and it is still to be ascertained if this mode has any advantage over that by boiling. The supply of salt water strongly impregnated is abundant and inexhaustable. It is not easty [*easy*] to form an estimate of the great benefit that will result to the State [of New York] from the manuf[act]ure of salt at this place.

Here we entered a summit level of the Canal which extends 69 miles without the intervention of a single lock. In this distance many

[52] By 1823 there was an extensive production of salt at the Onondaga springs, which had been administered by the state since 1797. The solar evaporation process mentioned below later became successful. See Clark, *Onondaga*, 2:11, 27, 32. A lateral canal was built between 1819 and 1823 from the Erie at Syracuse to Lake Onondaga. The extension to Lake Ontario, completed in 1828, was called the Oswego Canal. See Whitford, *History of the Canal System*, 1:446–452, 958, 987.

extensive tracts of swampy and flat country occur, but settlements and villages in their incipient state occasionally present themselves. This summit passes the dividing ridge between the waters of Lake Ontario & those of the Mohawk river. Distance before midnight 80 miles.[53]

WEDNESDAY, OCTOBER 22, 1823. At half past 7 o'clock this morning we arrived at Utica, 160 miles from Rochester. This is a flourishing town which has had a growth exceedingly rapid and bids fair to rise much higher on the scale of importance and respectability. The canal passes immediately thro' it, affording every facility for commercial pursuits, which, added to the circumstance of its being situated in the heart of a fertile country, cannot fail to enhance greatly the interest of the place. The Mohawk river here presents itself winding in graceful meanders thro' its beautiful and fertile valley, which last is every where environed by hills of gentle slope crowned with the mellow and sombre garb of autumn and che[e]red with fields and forests. The canal passes along the southerly slope of the Mohawk's valley, intersecting fertile fields and flourishing villages in its passage downward.

Altho' it may seem invidious, if not abusive, to pass any strictures upon the manner in which the Canal has been constructed, which is certainly a work that reflects the highest credit upon those who were concerned in its execution as well as on its projectors, yet we will venture to notice a few defects that will sooner or later prove serious impediments to the utility of the canal.[54]

There are not a sufficient number of Stop-Gates, particularly in the extensive pounds which occur in all parts of the route. In the event of a cravass formed in the bank, there will be no means of stopping the water till the whole shall have been drained off thro the breach, which will be enlarged more or less in proportion to the capacity of the pound or to the quantity of water to be discharged thro' it.

The Waste Weirs are not sufficiently numerous, thereby giving

[53] On the construction of the summit level of the canal and the dividing ridge near Rome, N.Y., see *Laws . . . in Relation to the Erie and Champlain Canals*, 1:367–375.

[54] Some of the defects Long noted below were remedied after the canal was completed, including the rebuilding of many bridges. For examples, see Whitford, *History of the Canal System*, 1:132; *Laws . . . in Relation to the Erie and Champlain Canals*, 2:250–253. Puddling was a process of working clay with water to make it more compact and impervious.

occasion for too great a rise of water in the canal and increasing the liability to the formation of breaches or crevasses. Moreover many of them are so constructed that they are themselves liable to be enlarged into breaches by the washing of the water.

The process of puddling seems not to have been adopted but in very few, if any, parts of the Canal with the exception perhaps of the Locks & Aqueducts, altho' there are obviously numerous places where this mode [of] securing the work against leakage and breaches ought certainly to have been practised. As an instance where the work ought to have been modified in this manner, we would mention a high embankment on the western section, where the canal is carried across a deep valley requiring an embankment of more than 70 feet high with nothing but sandy loam for its construction.

The numerous road and accommodation bridges on the Canal are for the most part careles[s]ly built, independantly of the rudeness of their structure. In many instances their piers, which are merely a wooden frame-work, have an embankment of earth serving as an abutment to support [them], which has already occasioned a slight inclination in some of them.

Altho' these and a few others that might be enumerated are obviously defects, yet they are not here recorded with the view of detracting from the merits of this great work, which in every point of view ought to be considered as highly reputable and ennobling to the genius of our country.

In the afternoon we passed the Little Falls of the Mohawk at which there is a handsome little village [*Little Falls, N.Y.*] which, contrasted with the wildness of the place, affords a most picturesqu[e] scenery. Here the [Mohawk] river passes thro a rugged valley bounded by abrupt hills and precipices that approach near to its bed. On its southerly bank the Canal winds along the base of an impending precipice, gradually descending by five successive locks of 8 or 10 feet fall each to the level of the plain below. This part of the canal is constructed by walling with stone from the margin of the river to the summit of the Canal, from 14 to 20 feet high. At this place is an Aqueduct handsomely built of stone, supported on three arches, serving as a feeder to conduct the water across the river from the old canal situated on the opposite side of the river and communicating with it at the head of the Falls. The passage on this part of the route must be considered amongst the most arduous and expensive of any of equal extent on any part of the line of the canal, that of the high lands and a part of the route from Schenectady to Albany perhaps being superiour in these respects.[55]

The utility of the Old Mohawk Canal has been almost entirely superseded by the Erie or Grand Canal and is entirely neglect[ed] and suffered to go to decay, with the exception of such portions of it as could be made subservient to the latter, as feeders &c. A short portion of it above the Little Falls now constitutes a part of its great rival, extending only about 400 or 500 yards. Distance travelled at midnight 75 m.

THURSDAY, OCTOBER 23, 1823. Travelled 25 miles and arrived at Schenectady at 8 o'clock, where we breakfasted. As our passage down the Mohawk has been mostly in the nigh[t], we have missed the opportunity of enjoying the beauty of the scenery on this part of our route, which is excelled by that of very few places in the country.

The Canal passes immediately thro the town of Schenectady, which stands on the bank of the Mohawk commanding an extensive and charming view of that river. This town was in a flourishing condition and had already attained a respectable size previously to the construction of the Canal, but its growth will no doubt be greatly accellerated that great work being now nearly completed.

Union College, which ranks high among the literary seminaries of our country, is situated on a beautiful plain just below the town, sufficiently elevated to overlook the town and afford an extensive prospect along the valley of the river, which is decorated with an unusual variety of artificial works to facilitate the pursuits both of agriculture and manufactures. This institution embraces two college edifices built of stone [*brick*], displaying much taste in their style of Architecture. They are four stories high and in other respects large and commodious. Having breakfasted, we resumed our voyage in the Packet Bt. for Albany at half past 9 A.M.[56]

[55] The 1,184-foot aqueduct was completed in 1822. The incorporation in 1820 of a portion of the old Mohawk Canal, mentioned here and below, into the new Erie Canal is explained in Nathan Miller, "Private Enterprise in Inland Navigation: The Mohawk Route Prior to the Erie Canal," in *New York History*, 31:398, 410 (October, 1950). On this section of the canal, see *Laws . . . in Relation to the Erie and Champlain Canals*, 2:110; Shaw, *Erie Water West*, 17, 134; Whitford, *History of the Canal System*, 1:955, 958.

[56] The buildings, begun in 1812, were designed by Joseph Jacques Ramée. They are still standing. See [Franklin B. Hough], *Historical Sketch of Union College*, 7, 13, 23 (Washington, D.C., 1876). On the wooden aqueduct and feeders at Alexander's Mills (now called Rexford), mentioned below, see *Laws . . . in Relation to the Erie and Champlain Canals*, 2:72–75; Shaw, *Erie Water West*, 135.

The Canal between Schenectady and Albany was opened for navigation on the 8th of the present month, not having been ready for that purpose till that time. It winds along the base of the high lands on the south side of the [Mohawk] river, as before remarked, occasionally approaching to the margin of the river, where it is supported by walled embankments on the river-side and bounded by abrupt precipices on the opposite side. At the distance of four miles below Schenectady [*at Rexford*] is a woodden Aqueduct, supported by sixteen stone Piers and two stone abutments, conveying the canal across the Mohawk at an elevation of 30 feet above the surface of the river. On the north side of the river are three Locks and a Feeder from the river furnished with a grand lock, all handsomely constructed of the lime-stone, which abounds in this part of the country and which is admirably adapted to the purposes of Masonry.

As an obvious and general defect in the construction of this part of the canal, we would notice the want of puddling. The sides and embankments are often composed of a sandy soil, intermingled with fragments of slate, which last in many instances seem to constitute the great body of the work. Such materials without the process of puddling, or some similar operation, can never be rendered impervious to water, and in relation to the canal, it is observable that a percolation is continually going on by which much of its water is wasted.

The process substituted instead of puddling, in many places where that mode was required, is to line the interiour slopes of the Canal with clay rammed at right angles with the slopes. By this mode it is manifest that the angles between the bottom and sides of the canal must be left insecure, inasmuch as the ramming would tend to loosen rather than consolidate the earth about those parts of the canal.

Twelve miles below the Aqueduct last mentioned is another [*at Fonda's Ferry*] by which the Canal is again conveyed across the river. It is of similar construction to the former, supported on 25 Piers beside the Abutments, and has an elevation of 25 feet above the river. Two [*four*] miles below this Aqueduct is the remarkable Falls of the Mohawk called the Cohoez [*Cohoes*], which we visited and of which Mr. Seymour took a sketch. The fall is occasioned by a precipice of slate rock extending across the river over which the whole body of the water is precipitated with singular majesty and beauty. The perpendicular pitch is said to be nearly 50 [*70*] feet. The scenery on both sides is romantic and bold, and its interest not a little enhanced by the passage of the canal, which is effected by deep excavations thro hills of solid rock and embankments across deep and rugged ravines.[57]

About 1 1/2 miles below the Cohoez the Mohawk enters the Hudson, into which it is precipitated over a dam that has been constructed across its mouth to subserve the purposes of the Champlain Canal, which unites with the Grand Canal about 1 1/4 miles below. From the pound in which the Aqueduct last mentioned is situated, the water is brought down to this point (the Junction) by means of eighteen Locks. The Champlain canal has one Lock between the Junction and the mouth of the river, which serves as a feeder to both canals below. Between Schenectady and Albany, which is a distance of 28 miles, there are no less than 28 [*29*] Locks and two Aqueducts across the Mohawk, besides numerous walled embankments and deep cuttings, all of which must have rendered this portion of the canal more difficult and expensive in the construction than any other of equal extent thro-out its whole extent.[58]

To the defects in the construction of the Canal already enumerated may be added a want of care and nicety in the mason-work of the Locks, some of which have jets of water pouring into them, very much to the annoyance of boats in their passage—as also a general roughness and want of permanency in the character of the banks.

The time requisite for the passage of a lock varies from 5 to 10 minutes, being considerably protracted in many of the locks by leakages in the upper gates and hatches.

Below the Junction [*near Waterford, N.Y.*] there are 4 locks, which bring us to the level of tide-water at Albany, the difference of level between these two points being about 42 feet. Arrived at Albany a little before eight in the evening. Distance 53 miles. Whole distance travelled on the Canal from Rochester to Albany is 274 miles.

[57] The aqueduct at Fonda's Ferry was near the present town of Halfmoon, N.Y. Seymour completed a painting of the Cohoes Falls at Cohoes, N.Y., which has not been found, see p. 392 below. The precipice of the falls is 70 feet with additional drops in the rapids above and below the cataract. See Whitford, *History of the Canal System*, 1:106; Nelson Greene, ed., *History of the Mohawk Valley*, 1:87 (Chicago, 1925).

[58] The Champlain Canal, connecting Lake Champlain and the Hudson River, was built by the state of New York between 1817 and 1823. Its terminus on Lake Champlain was near Whitehall, and its meeting point with the Erie near Waterford was called the Junction. The difficult portion of the Erie Canal between Schenectady and Albany opened on October 8, 1823. As Long predicted below, the embankments proved troublesome. See Whitford, *History of the Canal System*, 1:410–416, 979; *Laws . . . in Relation to the Erie and Champlain Canals*, 2:120, 172–174.

FRIDAY, OCTOBER 24, 1823. No Steam Boat running to N. York city, we spent the day in rambling about the town. Visited the Basin of Albany, an important appendage of the Canal, forming not only a commodious harbour for boats but a very convenient one for shipping. It is formed by an extensive pier or dock running along the river para[le]lled to its western shore at the distance of about 150 yds. from it. The Basin is separated from the Canal by a single Lock of 11 feet lift, which unfortunately gave way soon after it was filled, the foundation not being firmly laid.[59]

SATURDAY, OCTOBER 25, 1823. Embarked on board of the Steam Boat Richmond at 10 A.M. and continued our journey down the North [*Hudson*] river. The weather stormy, snowing rapidly. Arrived at N. York [City] at 4 in the morning. Dist. 160 [*145*] m.

SUNDAY, OCTOBER 26, 1823. Resumed our journey on board the Stm. Bt. Wm. Penn at 9 A.M. Took stage at [Perth] Amboy [N.J.] and arrived at Bordentown [N.J.] at 10 o'clock in the evening. Dist. 62 miles.

MONDAY, OCTOBER 27, 1823. In the remarks of yesterday it should have been observed that Messrs. Say, Calhoun and Seymour, wishing to remain a short time in N. York city, were left by Mr. Keating and myself at that place. Embarked on board the Stm. Boat Pennsylvania [on the Delaware R.] at 5 1/2 o'clock A.M. and arrived at Philadelphia a little before 10. Distance 30 miles.

[59] The difficulties of maintaining the lock connecting the canal and the basin are discussed in *Laws . . . in Relation to the Erie and Champlain Canals*, 2:256. An extensive bibliography on the Albany basin may be found in Whitford, *History of the Canal System*, 2:1260–1262.

THE JOURNAL OF JAMES E. COLHOUN 1823

July 1st 1823. We remained in our
camp, about 100 yards above Red-wing's
village, waiting for the arrival of
the boat to replenish our bread bag.
Early in the day, Wa[3]ze[2]ko[2]ta[4] (Shooter
from the pine-top,) a talkative old
Indian, came to visit us. Before proceeding further, I will remark, that
Father Hennepin tells us the chief of
the Issati or Nadouessies was named
Ouasicoudé, which he interprets Le
Pin Percé. Carver mentions, as one of
the bands of the Sioux of the Plains,
the Asrahcootans. And the Treaty
of St. Louis, made in 1816, recites as a
party to it "the Sioux who shoot
in the Pine Tops." Wazekota had only around his eyes smutted, the

THE OPENING PAGE (actual size) of James E. Colhoun's journal of July 1, 1823, in the collections of the Minnesota Historical Society.

7. Up the Minnesota River with Long

JULY 1 THROUGH 22, 1823

THE FOLLOWING JOURNAL *overlaps and supplements Long's account of the expedition's journey from July 1 to 29, 1823. Kept by Colhoun, the young second cousin and brother-in-law of Secretary of War John C. Calhoun who had joined the group on May 20, 1823, as a replacement for Lt. Andrew Talcott, it takes up the story while the party was encamped on the shores of picturesque Lake Pepin near modern Red Wing, Minnesota, and carries on up the Minnesota River Valley and into the watershed of the Red River. Colhoun's is the only other journal of the expedition known to have survived.*

Differing greatly in tone from Long's matter-of-fact prose, Colhoun's journal testifies to the young navy midshipman's erudition and reflects his travels, largely in South America and the Orient. It also bears witness to the greater leisure under which it was produced, for internal evidence indicates that it was written (or rewritten) by Colhoun in 1824, after the conclusion of the Long expedition but before the Narrative *was published. In his preface to the* Narrative, *Keating acknowledged his debt to Colhoun's "manuscripts," which, he said, "have been very valuable in furnishing the greater part of the references to older writers."* [1]

Colhoun's first entry is typical of the journal's tone and of its inclusion of voluminous excerpts from earlier authors. It is obvious that he had a wide reading knowledge, access to a substantial library, and some familiarity with at least four foreign languages—

[1] Keating, *Narrative*, 1: vii. On Colhoun, see pp. 24, 46, above. Information here and below was drawn from Dundas, *Calhoun Settlement*, 11–19; the 1877 letter appeared in Dundas, p. 25. The date at which the Colhoun journal was written can be deduced from Colhoun's reference to a letter of Epaphras Chapman published in the *Evangelical Magazine* "for January of this year" (1824). See Chapter 8, note 36, below.

French, Spanish, Latin, and Greek. In supplying citations to older writers, Colhoun indicated them by using Greek letters, an accomplishment not unusual in an educated person of that period. Many of the volumes he cited are now very rare and little known. In its literary allusions and in other respects, Colhoun's description of the journey provides an interesting contrast to the hurried, factual entries Long set down on the march.

His trip with Long was to be James Colhoun's only experience in exploring. The two men met at least once more in the years after the expedition. In a reminiscent letter written in 1877, Colhoun recounted how he tried to interest Long in the area near Pendleton, South Carolina, where his brother-in-law maintained a magnificent estate. On his way back to naval duty in 1825, Colhoun said that he "fell in" with Long and told him "That a canal communication with the West should be sought for" in the Pendleton area because "the character of the mountains changed from an unbroken range northward to isolated masses toward the South. . . . We arranged to make an early reconnaissance," wrote Colhoun, "for it so happened that his mind had been long occupied with the project of uniting the waters of the Mississippi with those of the Atlantic, somewhere through the Alleghanies [Alleghenies]. *But, as he wrote me, a certain influence with the government had procured his employment far away. I was promoted* [*in 1826*] *and went to sea." Nothing further apparently came of the idea.*

Colhoun served in the navy from 1816 until 1833 with frequent furloughs to permit him to travel abroad or to manage his landholdings near Abbeville and what is now Calhoun Falls, South Carolina. He married while in the navy, but his wife died while he was at sea soon after the birth of their first child. The child also died. Colhoun never remarried. He left active duty in 1829, resigned from the navy in 1833, and devoted the rest of his life to managing "Millwood," an extensive cotton and sugar cane plantation that stretched for seven miles along both sides of the Savannah River near the Georgia-South Carolina border. Apparently possessed of excellent health, he lived out his long life as a wealthy planter and country squire in South Carolina, where he died in 1889 at the age of ninety-three. After his death a sale of 11,664 acres of land was conducted in connection with his estate, and he willed his personal library to the town of Greenwood as the beginning of a public library.

TUESDAY, JULY 1, 1823. We remained in our camp about 100 yards above Red-Wing's village waiting for the arrival of the boat to replenish our bread bag.[2] Early in the day W$\overset{3}{a}$z$\overset{2}{e}$k$\overset{2}{o}$t$\overset{4}{a}$ (Shooter from the pine-top), a talkative old Indian, came to visit us. Before proceeding further I will remark that Father [Louis] Hennepin tells us the chief of the Issati or Nadouessies [*Dakota*] was named Ouasicoudé, which he interprets le Pin Percé. [Jonathan] Carver mentions as one of the bands of the Sioux of the Plains the Asrahcootans. And the Treaty of St. Louis made in 1816 recites as a party to it "the Siouxs who shoot in the Pine Tops."[3]

Wazekota had only around his eyes smutted; the other Indians in company had soot or charcoal more bountifully bestowed about their cheeks, and some had the face entirely smeared in mourning. Almost all the colors have been used for this purpose, but man kind are generally agreed to adopt black as the symbol of grief. The Assiniboins, however, rejoicing for victory blacken their faces & clothing, while in mourning they cover the hair & every part of the dress with white mud. [Jean Baptiste Léonard] Durand informs us that the Moorish women on the Senegal River blacken the face forty d[a]ys in joy for the birth of a son; for the birth of a daughter only one half the visage & for half that time. With the last there is some propriety; inhabiting a tropical region, the night is their season of gaiety, for performing the duties of hospitality, for travelling, for eating, & thus darkness, black, conveys to them the associations of society, of relief from heat &c.[4] I cannot account for the practice of the Assiniboins, unless the appearance of snow be to them the signal for suffering, or by supposing it depends upon some tradition.

But to return. I was gratified at witnessing again the ready apprehension of the Indians. They understood at once a map we

[2] It will be recalled that the 1823 expedition had divided into two sections at Fort Crawford to ascend the Mississippi by land and boat; the land party traveling up the west side of the river consisted of Long, Colhoun, Pvts. George Bunker and John Wade, the Dakota guide Tommo, and the servant Andrew Allison. Thus Colhoun's journal covers many of the same features of the route described by Long in 1817 and again in 1823. Full annotation for route features, expedition personnel, etc., appears on pp. 49–110, 144–151, above, and is not repeated here.

[3] On the numerical orthography system, see Chapter 4, note 22. The editions used by Colhoun were Hennepin, *Description de la Louisiane, Nouvellement Decouverte au Sud'Oüest de la Nouvelle France*, 260 (Paris, 1683); Carver, *Three Years Travels through the Interior Parts of North-America, for More Than Five Thousand Miles*, 40 (Philadelphia, 1789). On the Dakota treaty of June 1, 1816, see Kappler, ed., *Indian Affairs*, 2:128.

[4] Durand, *Voyage au Sénégal, Fait dans les Années 1785 et 1786*, 2:92 (Paris, 1807).

spread before them; they traced several rivers, told their names & pointed out portages. Wazekota laid his finger on the Falls of St. Anthony, which he called Hāhā-Wŏtēpȧ, but he often suspended his remarks to utter the monosyllable of Indian John in the Pioneers; that together with his oft repeated How d'ye do, Good bye, completed his whole stock of our language.[5]

The water party arrived in the course of the forenoon. We were invited soon after to the Chief's lodge, over which was hoisted the Flag of the United States. It was a large bark cabin like those we saw near Rock River. We were received in due ceremony. Shȯkeȧ [*Red Wing*], the chief, & his son Tȧtŭnkȧmēnė [*Red Wing, the younger*] were seated next to the entrance. They shook hands with each of us as we entered & ranged ourselves on the same frame they occupied. The frame opposite was appropriated to the warriors; no women were present. The Pipe of Peace was in the centre of the lodge, the bowl resting on the ground & the stem leaning against & sustained by a forked stick stuck down for the purpose. Red-Wing got up, shook each of us by the hand, took the Pipe & holding the bowl turned towards himself with the stem elevated, delivered a speech. Very often in the course of it the commencement of a sentence was in the concluding words of the one preceding. The warriors frequently signified their approbation of what he said by uttering ah hah in strong nasal & guttural tones, reminding me of the deep toned responses of the Baptists & Methodists. The Chief, as if in return for their applause, [in] concluding stated that many of those present had their faces blackened in sorrow for deceased relatives, & begged that some of his "Great Father's Milk" might be given them to gladden their hearts. Major Long, in replying to that part of his address, said that we were unprovided with any strong drink & that if we had rum, it would be an improper present.[6]

A young Indian lighted the Pipe, presented [it] first to the Major, then to each of us, to the warriors & chief, back to the Major again, supporting it all the time, & after each one had taken a whiff, he drew off the bowl, which was of a red [pipe]stone & gave the stem to the Major for the President. His duties ended with shaking the

[5] Indian John's monosyllable was "good." See James Fenimore Cooper, *The Pioneers, or the Sources of the Susquehanna; A Descriptive Tale*, 2:77 (New York, 1823). See also Keating, *Narrative*, 1:261. On Cooper's dependence on James, *Account*, as a basis for *The Prairie*, see Howard R. Lamar, "Introduction," in James, *Account*, xxx (1972).

[6] On the bark cabins at Rock River and the chiefs of the Red Wing dynasty, see Keating, *Narrative*, 1:179, 251.

hands of all present. Tatunkamane then stood up & spoke a short time with great vehemence & also shook hands all round. Both he & his father repeated a good deal. The speeches of neither were remarkable, nor were their gestures varied or significant. The council or interview concluded with the speech of Tatunkamane & we soon after departed; but first each of us shook hands with every individual in the lodge. Metea at Fort Wayne before delivering his speech walked round the room & shook each of us by the hand.[7]

Shaking hands is often mentioned both by Latin & Greek authors, proving that kind of salutation in their days to have been the common one, & in their poetry, at least, they give the practice to ancient times & to various nations. It is extremely difficult to say which of the many modes of salutation is the most natural, & if we find nations widely apart & speaking different languages agreeing in any of these modes, whether we consider them instinctive, founded on reason or artificial & arbitrary, it is a coincidence well calculated to arrest the attention. It would be remarkable should we find our expression of good will, derived from our British ancestors, originally used by the natives of this continent. With a view to ascertain the fact, I have examined many authorities, some of which are here subjoined.

Miantonimo [*Miantonomo*], after a conference with the Governor, gave him his hand for the absent magistrates.[α] He was a Narraganset chief. But this was subsequent to 1637. [John] Lawson informs us that shaking hands was a token of friendship among the Indians of Carolina.[β] And [Le Page] Du Pratz says the same, referring to the Natchez in particular & to the Indians on the Mississippi

[7] Metea, who furnished extensive data on Potawatomi history and customs, is described in Keating, *Narrative*, 1:88–91; Seymour's sketch of him appears as plate 3. For a biographical account, see Frederick W. Hodge and David I. Bushnell, eds., Thomas L. McKenney and James Hall, *The Indian Tribes of North America With Biographical Sketches and Anecdotes of the Principal Chiefs*, 2:205–212 (Edinburgh, 1934). Colhoun's dissertation, with notes, on shaking hands, below, was used by Keating in *Narrative*, 1:254–260.

[α] Hubbard's Narrative of Indian Wars, Brattleborough 1814.[α8]

[α8] Footnotes α through ψ were supplied by Colhoun. He referred here to William Hubbard, *A Narrative of the Indian Wars in New-England*, 54 (Brattleboro, Vt., 1814). On Miantonomo and his conferences with the governors of the Massachusetts Bay Colony, see Hodge, *Handbook*, 1:855.

[β] A New Voyage to Carolina by John Lawson Gent. London. 1709. p. 42.[β9]

[β9] John Lawson, *A New Voyage to Carolina; Containing the Exact Description and Natural History of That Country*, 42 (London, 1709), referred to the custom of scratching the shoulder in greeting, not shaking hands; Lawson did say on p. 201, however, that the Indians shook hands.

in general.[γ] These writers, however, visited America after there had been intercourse of many years between the Indians & Europeans, &, therefore, I do not consider their testimony as decisive against my opinion that the practice was acquired by the former from the Whites. I have nowhere seen it distinctly asserted that the Indians greeted in this manner among themselves.

While on this subject, I will enumerate a few of the methods by which the aborigines of North America welcomed a visiter. The salutation, about the mouth & west of the Mississippi,[δ] low down on the St. Lawrence,[ε] on some parts of our Atlantic coast,[ζ] among the Sioux[η] & in many of the intermediate spaces,[θ] was for the Indian to stroke with his hand his own breast, arms & legs & afterwards those of the stranger. The Clamcoets [*Karankawa*] near the Bay of St. Bernard [*Matagordo Bay, Tex.*] sometimes saluted one by blowing in his ear.[ι] The Cenis [*Caddo*], on their northern limit, had a different manner. Twelve old men with the right hand raised to the

[γ] Histoire de la Louisiane par Du Pratz, à Paris 1758. Tome 2. p. 237.[γ10]

[γ10] Le Page du Pratz, *Histoire de la Louisiane, Contenant la Découverte de ce vaste Pays*, 2:237 (Paris, 1758).

[δ] Naufragios de Alvar Nuñez Cabeza de Vaca, Cap. Journal Historique du Dernier Voyage de M. le Sale par Joutel à Paris 1713. p. 74. ou Histoire de la Nouvelle France par Charlevoix Paris 1744. Tome 3. p. 17.[δ11]

[δ11] The version of Cabeza de Vaca's book probably used by Colhoun was *Navfragios de Alvar Nuñez Cabeza de Vaca; y Relacion de la Jornada, que Hizo a la Florida con el Adelantado Panfilo de Narvaez*, 27 (Andris Gonzalez de Barcia Carballido y Zuñiga, *Historiadores Primitivos de las Indias Occidentales*, vol. 1—Madrid, 1749). This was a reprint of a volume first published under the title *La relacion que dio Aluar nuñez cabeça de Vaca de lo acaescido enlas Jndias enla armada donde yua por gouernador Pãphilo de narbaez* (Zamora, 1542) and reprinted with the author's *Comentarios* at Valladolid in 1555. See also Joutel, *Journal Historique du Dernier Voyage que feu M. de la Sale fit dans le Golfe de Mexique*, 74 (Paris, 1713); Pierre François Xavier de Charlevoix, *Histoire et Description Generale de la Nouvelle France*, 3:17 (Paris, 1744).

[ε] Histoire de la Nouvelle France, par Lescarbot à Paris 1618 p. 254 & p. 302.[ε12]

[ε12] Marc Lescarbot, *Histoire de la Novvelle-France*, 254, 302 (3rd ed., Paris, 1618).

[ζ] The "Voy. of Captains Amadas & Barlowe to part of the countrey now called Virginia" Hakluyt's Collection; London 1589. p. 729. The General History of Virginia by Capt. John Smith, London 1632. p. 3. Lescarbot ut supra p. 254.[ζ13]

[ζ13] "The first voyage made to the coastes of America, with two barkes, wherein were Captaines Master Philip Amadas, and Master Arthur Barlowe," in Richard Hakluyt, *The Principall Navigations, Voiages and Discoveries of the English nation*, 729 (London, 1589); John Smith, *The Generall Historie of Virginia, New-England, and the Summer Isles*, 3 (London, 1624); Lescarbot, *Histoire*, 254.

[η] Description de la Louisiane par Hennepin à Paris 1683. p. 270.

[θ] Alvar Nunez ut supra Cap.[θ14]

[θ14] Cabeza de Vaca, *Navfragios*, 30.

[ι] Joutel ut supra p. 84.

head ran up with loud cries & embraced the French.[κ] Embracing appears to have been the usage amongst some of the Esquimaux [*Eskimo*],[λ] in the island of Croatoan [*Croatan*] on the coast of North Carolina,[μ] & among the Shoshonees.[ν] Garcilaso de la Vega tells us that the chief Muscoço welcomed Juan Ortiz, who fled to him for protection, by embracing him & kissing his face.[ξ] He also mentioned prostration[ο] & kissing of hands,[π] but both were always to superiors & probably the last was in imitation of the Spaniards. At Hochelaga, [*an Iroquois village*] now Montreal, the French were welcomed by the women, who kissed their faces.[ρ]

[Henri] Joutel found Indians west of the Mississippi who had practice of washing the traveller's feet on his arrival.[σ] We are told also that at the Island of Roanoak, [N. Car.] Granganimeo's [*Granganameo's*] wife had the feet of her guests washed in warm water.[τ] Of

[κ] Idem. p. 220.[κ15]

[κ15] Joutel, *Journal Historique*, 214.

[λ] Davis' Second Voyage in 1586. Hakluyt's Collection ut supra p. 781.[λ16]

[λ16] "The second voyage attempted by Master John Davis with others, for the discouery of the Northwest passage, in Anno 1586," in Hakluyt, *Principall Navigations*, 781.

[μ] Hakluyt's Collection p. 767.[μ17]

[μ17] Thomas Harriot, "The fourth voyage made to Virginia, with three shippes, in the yeere, 1587," in Hakluyt, *Principall Navigations*, 767.

[ν] History of the Expedition under the command of Capts. Lewis & Clarke. Philadelphia 1814, vol. 1. p. 363.[ν18]

[ν18] Paul Allen, ed., *History of the Expedition Under the Command of Captains Lewis and Clark, to the Sources of the Missouri*, 1:363 (Philadelphia, 1814).

[ξ] La Florida del Inca. Madrid 1722. p. 28.[ξ19]

[ξ19] Garcilaso de la Vega, *La Florida del Inca*, 28 (Madrid, 1723).

[ο] Idem, Lib. 4. Cap. 5. Also mentioned in Narrative of de Soto's Invasion, written by a gentleman of Elvas, & translated by Hakluyt. London 1609 p. 96.[ο20]

[ο20] Vega, *La Florida del Inca*, 178; Richard Hakluyt, trans., *Virginia richly valued, By the description of the maine land of Florida, her next neighbour . . . Written by a Portugall gentleman of Eluas*, 96 (London, 1609). The latter book was republished in 1611 under the title, *The Discovery and Conquest of Terra Florida, by Don Ferdinando De Soto*.

[π] La Florida del Inca, p. 33. et alibi.

[ρ] Lescarbot ut supra p. 327.

[σ] Joutel ut supra p. 273. & in translation of Hennepin's Travels inserted in the Archaeologia Americana it is said "The young savages washed our feet & rubbed them over with the grease of deer, wild goats, & oil of bears."[σ21]

[σ21] Joutel, *Journal Historique*, 273, stated that the Indians washed their faces, not their feet. Louis Hennepin, "Discovery of the River Missisippi and the Adjacent Country," in *Archaeologia Americana*, 64 (American Antiquarian Society, *Transactions and Collections*, vol. 1—Worcester, Mass., 1820).

[τ] Hakluyt's Collection of Voyages, London. 1589. p. 731.[τ22]

[τ22] "The first voyage made to the coastes of America," in Hakluyt, *Principall Navigations*, 731. On Granganameo, a Secotan leader, see Hodge, *Handbook*, 1:503.

the Indians in the interior of N. Carolina, it is said that "They are free from all manner of Compliments, except Shaking of Hands, & Scratching on the Shoulder, which two are the greatest marks of Sincerity & Friendship, that can be shew'd one to another."[υ] Some of the Esquimaux have practice of pointing to the sun & then striking their breasts violently; when the action is imitated they approach with confidence.[φ] They also kiss the stranger's hand. Capt. [John] Ross met with one of their tribes whose mode of salutation was to pull the nose.[χ] Capt. [John] Smith & his companions, exploring the country about Chesapeake Bay, had the following curious reception, whether it was a salutation merely or a reverence I am unable to decide. "Landing at Kecoughtan, the Savages entertay[n]ed them with a doleful noyse, laying their faces to the ground, & scratching the Earth with their nayles."[ψ]

We of the land party left Red-Wing's Village at 2 P.M. & after riding one mile crossed a stream [*Hay Creek*] 6 yards wide. One mile beyond it we saw a great number of artificial mounds, none of them, however, larger than those we have seen for several days past. One mile & a quarter further crossed a brook [*Spring Creek*] 4 yards wide, where were again many tumuli. Thence one mile to another 5 yards wide, & half a mile beyond we forded $\overset{1}{\text{E}}\overset{2}{\text{a}}\text{m}\overset{1}{\text{o}}\text{z}\overset{2}{\text{i}}\text{nd}\overset{2}{\text{a}}\text{t}\overset{2}{\text{a}}$ or High Rock creek [*Cannon R.*], which is 18 yards wide & has a rapid current. Its name is derived from a white pyramidal rock of considerable height a few miles above where we crossed. We were anxious to pass by it, but the guide, from superstition or some other cause, was unwilling to conduct us that way; it would have added very little to our journey. It is said to be an object of veneration with the Indians.[26]

[υ] Lawson ut supra p. 201.

[φ] Hakluyt's Collection ut supra p. 778. Pinkerton's Voyages & Travels in America, Vol. 2, p. 187.[φ23]

[φ23] "The second voyage attempted by Master Iohn Dauis," in Hakluyt, *Principall Navigations*, 778; John Pinkerton, *A General Collection of the Best and Most Interesting Voyages and Travels in All Parts of the World*, 12:187 (London, 1812).

[χ] Ross' Voyage. London, 1819. p. 86.[χ24]

[χ24] John Ross. *A Voyage of Discovery*, 1:110 (2nd ed., London, 1819).

[ψ] Purchas his Pilgrimage. Lon. 1614 p. 768.[ψ25]

[ψ25] Samuel Purchas, *Pvrchas his Pilgrimage, or Relations of the World and the Religions Observed in All Ages and Places discouered*, 768 (2nd ed., London, 1614). Purchas was not quoting Smith in this passage, but a manuscript of "Master George Percie." Kecoughtan was a small village of Powhatan at the mouth of James River near present Hampton, Va., in 1607; see Hodge, *Handbook*, 1:670.

[26] Colhoun's "Eamozindata" comes from *inyan bosndata*, the Dakota name for Castle Rock; for a description of this formation, see Bray and Bray, eds., *Nicollet on the Plains*, 121; Winchell and Upham, *Geology of Minnesota*, 2:76–80.

Between the two last streams were several acres of well tended maize beginning to tassel. Like all the Indian crops we have seen, it was without any fencing & yet we observed no person watching it, nor was any habitation in sight. Here again the corn was planted in hills without regularity, but with people who are unacquainted with the plough & to whom land is not valuable, there is no adequate motive for a more orderly disposition.

4 or 5 miles from the village we ascended from the ravines running towards the [Mississippi] river to undulating prairie. Yesterday & today we found the soil of the prairie containing [a] considerable mixture of sand but still of good quality. From the lower extremity of Lake Pepin, the bluffs on this side have lost their abruptness & one half of their elevation; when I last saw the [Mississippi] river, those on the other side continued unaltered.

The numerous Tumuli we have seen during the last three days furnish unquestionable evidence that a very dense population once occupied the borders of Lake Pepin. To what travellers in the "way of all flesh" these vestiges belong may never be determined. The splendid antiquities of the East minister to the pride of man; they are glorious trophies of victory gained by human genius & power over time. History tells us the interesting circumstances connected with them; they in turn confirm her story. But here ferocious conquerors have torn her pages or they remain unfilled by a posterity forgetful it is a duty to cherish her, not only for instruction but that the benefactors of mankind may receive their fame. Here there is nothing to rescue *ab injuria oblivionis.* So rude & concise are the epitaphs, so faint & time-worn are the characters on these tombs, that we strain our eyes in vain; we can read no further, than *Hic jacet* x x x x x x.

The *qu[a]estio vexata* as to the probable authors of the ancient works to be seen in many parts of our country appears to me to have been improperly considered. The advocates of either side have not sufficiently studied the accounts left us by the early travellers & historians of this continent. Before I consulted these authorities, almost the only reading I possessed on the subject was in defence of the opinion of those who maintain that they were constructed by a people more refined than our Indians & totally differing from them. But contrary to my anticipation, a slight examination has convinced me that they were erected by the immediate ancestors of the Indians or by a similar race of men. I find enough in those writers pourtraying the primitive condition of the aborigines to justify expectation of works of at least equal magnitude & of as great ingenuity as is possessed by any of those remains that exist in our territory, nay, more, they describe distinctly works of the same character, & I doubt not it could be shewn that they actually speak of some of the very monuments about which there is so much controversy. Should I find leisure to pursue the inquiry I will give the result in an Appendix. Distance today 13 miles.[27]

WEDNESDAY, JULY 2, 1823. Though Tommo appears to be a listless fellow, he rides hard & we [are] constantly obliged to check him. I observe that he draws attention in the manner of the Portuguese by a kind of hissing. His hair is cut square at the forehead like most of the Indians we have seen; it is parted on the top of the head, & he has a plait behind each ear. He generally carries his light Makinaw gun thrust through the belt that confines his blanket to his waist. There never was a more incessant smoker. His tomahawk is his pipe. It is in the shape of a shingling hatchet: that part corresponding to the hammer is hollowed for the bowl & the handle is perforated to serve for the stem. I made the interpreter [*Augustin Rocque*] ask him what he conceived to be the advantages of the habit to which he was so much addicted. He answered that smoking is the Indian's resource in hunger; that while unassisted he could not unless with pain go without food for 24 hours, with the aid of his pipe he could easily fast two or three days.[28]

In the account of [Sir John] Hawkins' Voyage performed in 1564 even greater benefit is said to be derived from the practice. It is there stated that the Indians of Florida put a dried herb into an earthen cup at the end of a cane & burnt it; by sucking the smoke they were enabled to do without meat or *drink* for four or five days. This is one of the earliest accounts we have of tobacco smoking. The Indians may perhaps with impunity be inveterate in this habit, because they do not, as we, use the herb alone & in all its strength, but they render it mild by mixing with it various ingredients. I have

[27] Colhoun referred here to the now-discredited theory of the mound builders, a superior people different from the prehistoric forebears of the Indians. See Robert Silverberg, *Mound Builders of Ancient America: The Archaeology of a Myth* (Greenwich, Conn., 1968). Neither of the known volumes of Colhoun's journal contains the appendix he mentions. The three Latin phrases mean "from the injustice of oblivion," "Here lies . . ." and "frustrating investigation."

[28] Tommo was the party's Dakota guide. On the "Mackinaw gun," commonly called the "Northwest gun," see Charles E. Hanson, Jr., *The Northwest Gun*, 2 (Nebraska State Historical Society, *Publications in Anthropology*, no. 2—Lincoln, Neb., 1955). On tomahawk pipes, see West, *Tobacco, Pipes and Smoking*, 317–325.

never heard of an Indian who snuffed or chewed tobacco. I believe those modes of using it to have been invented by the Whites.[29]

Tommo's specific when unwell is to climb a tree, to cut the top so that it will bend & to let himself drop from it to the ground. He is a very good marksman & supplies us with wild [*passenger?*] pigeons. I observe that he uses an excellent kind of wadding, the scrapings of a cherry stick. He gave us [a] piece of the bulbous root of a plant he calls T$\overset{2}{e}$ps$\overset{2}{i}$n [*prairie turnip*], which grows here a foot high. Taking off a thick rind, it was in the shape of [a] hen's egg, but somewhat larger, & resembled in color & taste a half ripe chesnut.

13 miles crossed a rapid stream 6 yards wide called H$\overset{2}{e}$thp$\overset{3}{o}\overset{2}{i}t\overset{4}{a}$ [*Vermillion R.*]: first syllable sounded strongly guttural. The name, I believe, is expressive of its rapidity of current. 10 miles beyond it, we stopped to dine near a pond. Here we again saw granitic boulders, the first met with since leaving Rock R. Thence 7 miles to the mouth of St. Peter's [*Minnesota*] River, where it is about 90 yards wide. A boat took us across to Fort St. Anthony. Travelled today over sandy, undulating prairie. Rain in the afternoon. Distance 30 miles.[30]

The whole distance travelled from Prairie du Chien 211 miles in 8 days, giving a per diem average of 26 3/8 miles. The distance would have been shortened had we proceeded on the chord instead of the arc: we kept as near to the Mississippi as the nature of the country would permit. So far as we can learn, we are the only white men who have travelled on the right [*west*] bank of the river the whole way from Prairie du Chien to the mouth of St. Peters R. There seems to be deficiency of game in this region. From Chicago to this place, a distance of 440 miles, we have see[n] only a herd of Elk, two wolves, a deer & a badger. And not many birds.[31]

THURSDAY, JULY 3, 1823. Our boat got nearly up to the Fort last

[29] "The voyage made by the worshipful M. Iohn Haukins Esquire," in Hakluyt, *Principall Navigations*, 541. Colhoun was wrong in saying that snuffing and chewing tobacco were not practiced among the Indians. On these and other smoking customs and attitudes, see West, *Tobacco, Pipes and Smoking*, 48, 93–97, 99, 105.

[30] The reappearance of granitic boulders noted here was one of the observations of glacial drift contributing to the expedition's accurate pinpointing of the driftless region.

[31] An approximate measurement of the party's route on modern maps shows Colhoun's mileage to be almost exactly correct. Long underestimated the distance traveled as 408 miles from Chicago to Fort St. Anthony and 180 miles from Prairie du Chien. According to Keating, the party saw only a single coyote or prairie wolf (*Canis latrans* Say) in this part of the route. On the scarcity of game and for the observations of these animals, see Keating, *Narrative*, 1:193, 212, 232, 247, 292.

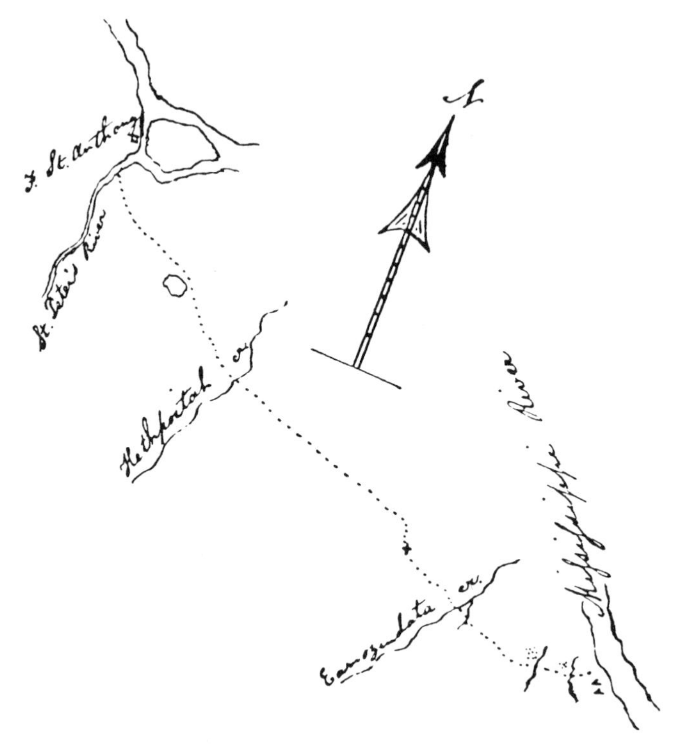

COLHOUN'S SKETCH MAP (actual size) of the land party's route from Red Wing's village on the Mississippi River overland to Fort St. Anthony at the mouth of the Minnesota River on July 1 and 2, 1823. The rivers crossed were the Cannon and the Vermillion.

night & our companions rejoined us this morning. Their passage up in not quite 8 days is considered an uncommonly quick one.[32]

The mouth of St. Peter's R. was first occupied by troops under the command of Col. [Henry] Leavenworth in August 1819. They were cantoned that year at the base of the Pilot-bluff [*Pilot Knob, Mendota*] on the south side of St. Peter's R. where they suffered much from sickness, especially from the scurvy. Fort St. Anthony, the permanent station, & now occupied though not completed, is a stone work on a bluff about 110 feet above the water of the Mississippi. It is placed immediately at the junction of that river with the St. Peter's & between them. The garrison consisting of about 200 men is under the command of Col. [Josiah] Snelling. The com-

[32] For an account of the water party's trip, see Keating, *Narrative*, 1:264–294.

mander calculates that in a year or two the troops will raise enough bread stuffs for their support. This is the remotest Northwestern military post. Its site perfectly healthy, the fertility of the surrounding country, the beauty of its prospect & its commanding & interesting location render this by far the most desirable as a residence of all the Outposts I have seen. This spot was visited for the first time by a Steam Boat [*the "Virginia"*] a few weeks since.[33]

We embraced an early opportunity to visit the Falls of St. Anthony, which by measurement are found to be 9 miles by water & little more than 7 miles by land distant from the mouth of the St. Peter's, notwithstanding Breckenridge [*Henry M. Brackenridge*] says the distance between them is 40 miles. Two miles & a half from the Fort, we turned a few steps from the road to view a beautiful cascade called Brown's [*Minnehaha*] Falls. A limpid stream about 15 feet wide leaps 44 feet from a jutting mass of limestone. This little water fall is regular in its features, simple, comparatively noiseless & easy of access, all [of] which may deter us from bestowing upon it the epithet romantic, yet of its kind I have seen none more pleasing. If I am not misinformed, the stream is the outlet of a Lake [*Minnetonka*] in a Northwestern direction, first known to the garrison about twelve months ago. That Lake is here thought to be equal in size to L. Champlain: I doubt the correctness of that opinion.[34]

After satisfying [our] curiosity, we proceeded to the Falls of the [Mississippi] river. With them, I confess, I was at first disappointed from the difficulty of embracing the whole at once. I thought the islands & the piles of rocks in front rather caused unpleasant obstruction of the view than lent savage grandeur to the scene. But

[33] On the elevation of Fort St. Anthony, see Josiah Snelling to Thomas S. Jesup, August 16, 1824, Office of the Quartermaster General, Consolidated Correspondence File, Fort Snelling, NARG 92, where it was said to be 110 feet above the low-water mark. Keating, *Narrative*, 1:294, placed it at 105 feet. AGO, Inspection Returns, Fifth Infantry, Fort St. Anthony, August, 1823, NARG 94, listed the total complement at the fort as 238 and the number of men present as 205.

On farming efforts at Fort Snelling, see Keating, *Narrative*, 1:295; John E. Wool to Col. G. Gibson, November 25, 1823, and Snelling to Jesup, August 16, 1824, March 1, 1826, Office of the Quartermaster General, Consolidated Correspondence File, Wool and Fort Snelling, NARG 92.

[34] Brackenridge, *Views of Louisiana; Together with a Journal of a Voyage up the Missouri River, in 1811*, 49 (Pittsburgh, 1814). On Minnehaha Falls and the creek's source in Lake Minnetonka, which according to legend was first visited in 1822 by Joseph R. Brown, a fifer at Fort Snelling, and William J. Snelling, see Alan H. Potter, "Minnesota's Most Famous Spot: Minnehaha Falls," in *Gopher Historian*, Spring, 1965, pp. 8–13; Edward D. Neill, *The History of Minnesota: From the Earliest French Explorations to the Present Time*, 331 (Minneapolis, 1882). Lake Minnetonka is less than one-tenth the size of Lake Champlain in New York.

they possess a peculiarity: the sheet of water, furnishing every variety of cataract in shape & shade, continues unrent, though alternately salient & retiring, sometimes for many feet. A wooded [*Hennepin*] island, projecting 100 yards beyond the Falls, divides them into two unequal parts. The eastern division, though least extended, has perhaps the greatest volume & fall of water.

I measured with a rough water level the height of the Falls near the western bank & found them to be a little short of 15 feet. Major Long some years ago [*in 1817*] with a line determined the height to be 16 feet, agreeing with the measurement made by [Zebulon M.] Pike. Father Hennepin, who discovered these Falls in 1680, stated them to be 50 or 60 feet high. Carver, the next writer who saw them, reduced the height to 30 feet. I am unable to account for the statement of Mr. [Henry R.] Schoolcraft in 1820 that the river has here a perpendicular pitch of 40 feet. Mr. Say & I by measurement made the width of the river just above the cataract on the West side of the Island 1009 feet & on the East side 473 feet. Including the island, therefore, the river at that place is about one third of a mile wide. This measurement, however, must be considered as only an approximation: the compass was small & not nicely graduated, & we were unable to measure the base line otherwise than by handing the tape from one to the other, holding it over the water.[35]

Half a mile below the river is compressed to 200 yards. We waded entirely across a few yards above the cataract. Although the water was nowhere deeper than to the middle of the thigh, yet was there some risque in the enterprise, for the slippery nature of the bottom made us perpetually liable to falling from which there could have been no recovery. It is here that the river overcomes the limestone stratum, which it continues to remove very rapidly. From the large fissures in the rock in the rapids above, the process is evidently by washing away the substratum of frail sandstone, which causes large projecting masses, deprived of support, to split off. The operation of the Falls of Niagara is doubtless similar but infinitely more tardy.

[35] On the Falls of St. Anthony, see above, pp. 70–75. The measurements mentioned are in Pike, *An Account of Expeditions to the Sources of the Mississippi*, part 1 appendix, 51 (Philadelphia, 1810); Carver, *Three Years Travels*, 35; Schoolcraft, *Narrative Journal of Travels . . . to the sources of the Mississippi River*, 289 (Albany, 1821). The figure given by Colhoun appeared in Hennepin, *Nouvelle Decouverte d'un tres grand Pays Situé dans l'Amerique*, 313 (Utrecht, 1697), a work Colhoun may have used but which he has not previously cited. Hennepin, *Description*, 200, gave a figure of 40 or 50 feet for the falls.

Winchell and Upham, *Geology of Minnesota*, 2:313, 335–340, reviewed the statements of these authors and commented on the erosion mentioned below. On the surveying equipment, see above, p. 19.

A very good saw-mill & a grist-mill have been erected by the garrison at the Falls. This must be from [its] appearance a country of water-fall & the Mills might have been placed nearer to the Fort, but I presume in the location regard was had chiefly to constancy of stream & to the facility of rafting timber, which is brought down the river from a considerable Distance. While at the Falls, an old Sergeant gave us for dinner a very fine black bass. That fish is taken here in great abundance, as also catfish, pike, pickerel &c. Antonio [de] Ulloa speaking in reference to the lower Mississippi says the coldness of the water is the cause of its having no more than two or three species of fish & that those are neither numerous or delicate. He would not have thought so had he visited the upper Mississippi. If in truth there are so few fish lower down, it is to be attributed to the muddiness of the water & in some degree perhaps to the limestone of the region. One of those causes banishes the brook trout from all the eastern tributaries of the Mississippi & from the western also except about their sources. The same may be the case with other species of fish. There are many beautiful lakes between the two rivers [*the Minnesota and Mississippi*]. Few places are superior to Fort St. Anthony in having in their neighborhood a greater variety & number of interesting natural objects inviting to little excursions over fine plains. During our stay at Fort St. Anthony, I made the following Observations. . . . [*Observations omitted.*][36]

WEDNESDAY, JULY 9, 1823. At 5 P.M. we took leave of our hospitable entertainers of the Fort & proceeding 4 miles in a Southwesterly direction encamped in the prairie. Our company has augmented to 33 [*32*] persons. Besides those composing the integral part of the expedition, we have Mr. [William] Joseph Snelling, the Colonel's son, who has before ascended the St. Peter's & having some knowledge of the Sioux or Dacota Language, has volunteered to accompany us; Mr. [Giacomo C.] Beltrami, an Italian gentleman, on his travels; Joseph Rainville [*Renville*], a half breed trader, our guide & Sioux interpreter; Louis Pellais [*Desmarais?*], another half breed & our interpreter for the Chipeways; & Lieut. St. Clair Denny, who commands the escort furnished us at Fort St. Anthony,

[36] The sawmill and grist mill were built at the falls between 1821 and 1823. The logs were driven down the Mississippi from the Rum River. See Kane, *Waterfall*, 9. On the brook trout, pike and pickerel, catfish, and bass, see Eddy and Underhill, *Northern Fishes*, 161–165, 198–208, 297–311, 340–350. For Ulloa's comment, see *Noticias Americanas: Entretenimientos Phisicos-Historicos, Sobre La América Meridional*, 173 (Madrid, 1772).

consisting of a Sergeant, two Corporals & nineteen Soldiers. Lieut. [Martin] Scott was ordered to return with all his men except George Bunker, who is of our party. That alteration was made because the men could not be conveniently spared from Fort Crawford; besides their terms of service had nearly expired.

Major Long & Mr. Keating with the water party ascend the St. Peter's with a small batteau & 4 canoes; Mr. Say, myself & another portion of our company follow the course of the river with 20 horses. Our expedition is fairly commenced, as [we] are about to enter the *terra incognita.*[37]

I remarked before that the St. Peter's is 90 yards broad at its mouth. It has there no perceptible current & it is deep. The Sioux call it W$\overset{3}{o}$t$\overset{2}{e}$p$\overset{4}{a}$ M$\overset{1}{e}$n$\overset{1}{e}$s$\overset{1}{o}$t$\overset{2}{e}$ or the River of Muddy Water. Carver is probably right in his conjecture that the [*Pike*] island at its mouth hid this river from the view of Father Hennepin. The earliest notice of it that I have met with is by Charlevoix, who states that [Pierre Charles] Le Sueur was sent by M. [Pierre le Moyne, sieur] d'Iberville to make an establishment in the Sioux country & to take possession of a copper mine he had there discovered (*que Le Sueur y avait découverte.*) He ascended the St. Peter's 40 leagues to la Riviere Verte [*Blue Earth R.*], which comes in on the left. Though only the last of September, the ice hindered him from ascending that river more than a league. He therefore built a fort & passed the winter at that spot. In April 1702 he went up la Riviere Verte to the mine, which was only three quarters of a league above his winter establishment. In twenty two days they got out more than 30,000 lbs. *de matiere* (ore) of which 4000 lbs. were selected & sent to France. The mine was at the foot of a mountain ten leagues long, that seemed to be composed of the same substance. After removing a black, burnt crust hard as a rock, the copper could be scraped with a knife. Several reasons, particularly the want of funds, hindered le Sueur from following up the entreprise.* Distance today 4 miles.[38]

THURSDAY, JULY 10, 1823. At daylight moderate rain; wind SW.

[37] For an account of the water party's journey, see above, pp. 156–161.

* Histoire de la Nouvelle France par Charlevoix. Tom. 4. p. 165 & 166. [*Colhoun's note.*]

[38] On the name of the St. Peter's, see Chapter 4, note 17. See also Carver, *Three Years Travels*, 33; Charlevoix, *Histoire*, 4:164–166. Keating, *Narrative*, 1:316–321, used Colhoun's information here and expanded upon it. Le Sueur was mistaken in thinking the blue-green clay of the Blue Earth River was copper; on Le Sueur, see Mildred Mott Wedel, "Le Sueur and the Dakota Sioux," in Elden Johnson, ed., *Aspects of Upper Great Lakes Anthropology: Papers in Honor of Lloyd A. Wilford*, 157–163 (St. Paul, 1974).

3 miles to a brook [*Nine Mile Creek?*] 3 yards wide. 4 miles further to another stream [*Purgatory Creek?*] of the same size. Soon after leaving it, saw a great number of Tumuli on a bluff rising from the river. The largest one, about 7 feet high & 20 feet diameter of base, bore from Six's [*Shakopee's*] village N 31° E. We stopped near it & sent to the village to inquire whether the Major had passed with the boats. Our messenger found it deserted, this being the season in which the Indians go to the plains in pursuit of the buffalo. Flourishing corn fields were around it. Before the messenger returned, the water party came in sight. They hailed us & endeavored to concert a rendezvous; it being deemed prudent that both parties should unite every evening if practicable.[39] The river at that point winds through the northern part of its fertile valley, which is there three miles wide & nearly destitute of trees.

At sunset we encamped in the Little Prairie [*Chaska*] on the bank of the river. In the forenoon we rode over prairie, rather broken: in the afternoon the travelling very bad, through ravines, thickets & on the edge of bluffs, frequently crossing small runs of water, with quick-sand beds & about them grew grape vines & willows. Mr. Say pointed out wild hops. Saw ripe raspberries but had no time to profit by the discovery. About our camp the growth is principally oak: willow thickets line the water's edge. Fair weather the greater part of the day. Distance 18 miles.[40]

FRIDAY, JULY 11, 1823. About sunrise the water party came up & put us across the river: the horses swam. We could have forded the river a little above Six's village. The river where we crossed is 70 yards wide. Its current, though accelerated by a Southwest wind, was by no means rapid. The color of the water is a sort of drab, the bottom muddy.

We proceeded on the right bank of the river on a course Southwesterly. While in the low grounds, we were often retarded by bogs. In one instance, we had to fill the bed of a stagnant brook 6 yards in width, & then crossed with great risk to the horses. On high grounds & the sides of bluffs we were opposed by a very dense growth of butternut, lyn [*linden or basswood*], maple, ash, grape vines &c. We were so badly guided by Pellais that I found it impossible to take the courses; he was often lost & had to retrace, besides the thickets confined my sight to a few yards. Could we have kept

[39] On the mounds in this area, see Winchell, *Aborigines*, 248–252.

[40] Chaska was known as Little Prairie into the 1840s; see J. Fletcher Williams, *A History of the City of Saint Paul, and of the County of Ramsey, Minnesota*, 115 (*MHC*, vol. 4—1876).

two or three miles out from the river, we would have had prairie to travel upon, but it is thought advisable to separate the two parties as little as possible. Saw limestone & sandstone in place, also granitic masses. Ripe strawberries.

In the afternoon crossed a [*Sand*] creek 7 yards wide. 3 miles beyond it we came to Weăkăotē, a settlement of two houses without inhabitants at present. It is la Batture aux Fievres of the traders.[41] The water party was there waiting for us & when we rode up, its members were looking at a scaffold on which a dead body was placed. In the morning we had witnessed another mode in which the Sioux treat the dead. The body was laid in a grave which was not filled in or covered with earth, but protected by small logs stuck in the ground & disposed like a roof, rising to the height of 4 or 5 feet. When we met, Mr. Beltrami & Rainville joined the land party: Pellais & I the water party. Went up the river 2 1/4 miles & encamped on the left [*north*] bank of the river, but on the right hand with respect to our course. Distance today 15 miles.[42]

SATURDAY, JULY 12, 1823. At 3:42 A.M. we embarked & continued up the river. Came to a rapid of a single pitch over a small ledge of sandstone; the canoes were able to paddle up it. Finding the boat not a good one, we exchanged it for a canoe with a Mr. Ferribaud [*Faribault*], a fur trader we met descending the river. In the course of the day passed 12 islands, the largest not exceeding 200 yards in length and 30 yards in width. They, as well as the margin of the river, thickly clothed with willows. We saw no habitations. Our view from the canoes obstructed by forests of cottonwood, elm, oak, &c., in the afternoon occasional prairie. The river banks varied from 5 to 16 feet in height; they are abrupt & disclose a pale, loose & deep soil. Average & almost constant width of the river, 60 yards. The current increased from one mile to one mile & a half per hour. Frequently large trees half exposed above the water. Sometimes there are freshe[t]s in this river that inundate its valley at least about the mouth. Now it is a shallow stream, & in the latter part of the summer at some of the places passed today, batteaux & even large canoes have to be lightened.

The deepness ascribed by Carver to this river must have been

[41] The name "Weakaote" comes from *Wiyaka otidan watpa*, the Dakota name for Sand Creek. *Batture aux Fièvres* was the French name for this stream, which was known as Fever River into the 1860s. See Bray and Bray, eds., *Nicollet on the Plains*, 46.

[42] Colhoun has now joined Long in the water party.

owing to the season of the year. "Carver's River" exists only in that traveller's narrative, unless indeed it be one of the few brooks crossed by the land party the second day, unusually swollen when Carver passed, which was in the latter part of November 1766. At 6:45 P.M. we stopped for the night in a prairie on the left bank of the river. A remarkable hill on the opposite side at least 150 feet high bore from camp East & distant half a mile. At 9:23 P.M. Mer[idian] Alt[itude] of Star η Ophiuchi was 59° 59′ 00″; hence Latitude 44° 33′ 59″, index error −4′. Distance 30 miles.[43]

SUNDAY, JULY 13, 1823. Began our voyage at 4 A.M. & directly after entered into an acceleration of current called Rapids of the Islands, so named from three islands at this place in immediate succession. 3 miles from camp brought us to two Indian lodges on right bank of the river, where we stopped to ask if the land party had passed. They were at the upper termination of the Bois Franc [*Big Woods*], a term, according to Pellais, that expresses a forest of some *one* kind of hard wood but here it is applied to a mixture of oak & elm. Thence 10 miles to the mouth of a shallow stream [*Rush R.?*] 6 yards wide entering on our right. Beyond it 7 miles to Prairie de pierre au Fleche [*Arrow Prairie*], where we found the land party. Stopped to speak to them. In the Prairie there was [a] block of granite of about 80 lbs. weight painted on the top with red & crowned with a grass fillet, within which were deposited several twists of tobacco, the myrrh & frankincense of the Indians: feathers were stuck arou[n]d the stone.[44]

Soon after we reembarked, the baggage canoe upset, by which accident we lost all the tobacco intended for presents to the Indians & ten pounds of our best powder. One mile above the Prairie we put ashore on account of threatening clouds. Average width of the

[43] On Carver, see Parker, ed., *Carver Journals*, 94; Chapter 4, note 17, above. The "remarkable hill" has not been identified, but the bluffs on the east side of the river reach altitudes of 280 feet above river level south of Blakeley in Scott County.

[44] Colhoun's "Rapids of the Islands" may have been Coon Rapids about four miles below Henderson, where C. E. Davis, an engineer who surveyed the Minnesota in 1868, found several substantial sand islands, one of them 10 feet high and wooded. See Warren, *Minnesota River*, 55. *Prairie la Flèche* (Arrow Prairie) was an area 30 miles in circumference north of and opposite Traverse des Sioux, between the present towns of Le Sueur and Ottawa; it was later known as Le Sueur Prairie; see Martin McLeod to "Mr. Editor," August, 1851, McLeod Papers, MHS; William G. Gresham, *History of Nicollet and LeSueur Counties Minnesota*, 1:363 (Indianapolis, 1916); Bray and Bray, eds., *Nicollet on the Plains*, 48n. Sacred stones were common among the Dakota. On beliefs and practices concerning them, see H. C. Hovey, "Eyay Shah: A Sacrificial Stone Near St. Paul," in *American Antiquarian and Oriental Journal*, 9:35 (January, 1887). See also p. 296, below.

river today, 80 yards, consequently it was more shoal, the sand spits more numerous & more extensive. Just before encamping last evening we observed the first collections of rolled fragments of granite, sandstone, &c. at the river margin; today those collections have been more numerous & the stones larger. The river banks same as yesterday. In some places the current was equal to two miles the hour. Twelve islands; the largest 300 yards long & 30 yards wide.

There cannot be a more crooked river or one more silent, scarcely even a bird to be seen. Two Swallow-tailed Hawks [*kites?*] soared over our heads.[45] A very heavy gust of thunder, vivid lightning & torrents of rain detained us for the night, where we stopped: I have rarely seen its equal between the tropics. The whole party, with a single exception, have the advantage of robust health to support them against inclemencies of the weather. One of the soldiers for three days passed has had a slight attack of fever & ague, which militates against the reported exemption of this river; however, it is no doubt true in general. 21 miles.

MONDAY, JULY 14, 1823. Left the shore at 5 A.M. 11 miles to the White Rock, a limestone bluff on the right bank of the river; on a sandy point opposite we saw an Indian family encamped.[46] They informed us that those of their nation living about the sources of the river were reduced almost to a state of starvation by the delayed visit of the Buffalo. 6 miles further to a vacant log-house on the left bank & formerly a trading establishment [*at or near Traverse des Sioux*]. We landed a little above & on the same side with it. The land party came to the bank opposite at the same time, forded the river & joined us. Nine islands today; not larger than those heretofore seen. The banks sometimes higher, sometimes lower than yesterday: current about the same. General width of the river, 70 yards.

We continued where we landed [the] greater part of the day, drying our biscuit, other provision & baggage much damaged by last night's rain. Making preparation also to send back some of our guard [and] to mount [a] greater part of the remainder, leaving the canoes. Though it is our wish to fullfil the intention of government to navigate the river as far as practicable, there is good reason for this alteration of plan. The loss of time a continuance on the river would

[45] Colhoun probably meant the now-vanished swallow-tailed kite; see W. J. Breckenridge, "A Century of Minnesota Wild Life," in *Minnesota History*, 30:230 (September, 1949).

[46] On White Rock Bluff at present Ottawa, see Winchell and Upham, *Geology of Minnesota*, 1:36, 637. Colhoun's mileage is exaggerated here.

occassion; the necessity for reducing our numbers that we may have enough provision when entering a scarce country towards the expiration of its comparatively plentiful season; the damage of three firearms rendering as many soldiers inefficient &c. We are permitted so to act by the improbability of meeting large bands of Indians at this season near the river.

In afternoon moved higher up the river about a mile & encamped in a prairie on the left bank of the river at a remarkable bend called the Crescent. Distance 18 miles. . . . [*Observations omitted.*][47]

TUESDAY, JULY 15, 1823. A corporal & eight men were sent away with orders to return to Fort St. Anthony, a subtraction that leaves with us one Sergeant, two Corporals & ten Privates, making in all a party of 24 persons. We still have 20 horses & mules. According to Major Long's estimate, it is about 130 [*85*] miles by water from the mouth of the river to the Crescent. We abandon the weary task of following the sinuosities of this devious river with the less regret because we already perceive its importance is much overrated, as is its magnitude exaggerated. Breckenridge in his views of Louisiana gives it a length of 1000 miles, others of 1200, but the traders, who always make large estimates, allow it no more than 600 miles.[48]

At 11 A.M. we left the river & proceeded on our journey over flat prairie, passing between several small lakes of the Swan groupe & crossing some fenny places with great difficulty. Our course carried us near to the frames of some Indian lodges; on a scaffold in the midst of them we observed a corpse wrapped up in skins & a blanket. On one of the posts supporting it were 15 horizontal black lines, which Rainville explained to denote the aggregate number of scalps taken by those who danced in honor of the deceased & presented to him by this formality. I rode before the party to the camping ground in a grove on the Southwest border of Great Swan Lake, & made the following Observations. . . . [*omitted*]. Distance travelled 14 miles.[49]

[47] The omitted astronomical observations were "made to determine the position of the Crescent" at present St. Peter.

[48] On the length of the Minnesota River, see Brackenridge, *Views of Louisiana*, 49; Chapter 8, note 2, below. It is possible that Colhoun arrived at the 1,200-mile figure by misreading a statement in Carver, *Three Years Travels*, 38, which indicated that the Minnesota and the Missouri entered the Mississippi 1,200 miles apart. No other source for 1,200 miles as the length of the Minnesota has been located.

[49] Great Swan Lake, now Swan Lake, Nicollet County, was the site of a major village of South or Lower Sisseton. See Taliaferro Journal, September 2, 1830 (9:108), Taliaferro Papers; Hodge, *Handbook*, 2:580; Bray and Bray, eds., *Nicollet on the Plains*, 49–52.

WEDNESDAY, JULY 16, 1823. Last night we heard the barking of the Prairie Wolf [*coyote*]. I strove in vain to measure the Altitudes of some stars; the mosquitoes overpowered me. We killed a species of garter snake, which makes only the third or fourth of all species seen in our whole route. Rainville says that Great Swan Lake is the limit of the rattle snake & that last year it was the limit also of the wanderings of the buffalo. He likewise informed me that the mouth of the Terre Bleue [*Blue Earth R.*] is 20 [*15*] miles Southeasterly from that Lake. It enters the St. Peter's at its extreme southing, where it makes the greatest bend. The Sioux call it Wotepah M$\overset{2}{\text{a}}$k$\overset{2}{\text{a}}$t$\overset{1}{\text{o}}\overset{1}{\text{o}}z\overset{2}{\text{e}}$ i.e. the River where blue earth is gathered. My informant denies that it is neutral ground. He called some small excavations I pointed out Forts. Five miles from the Lake saw two mounds that appeared to be artificial.[50]

All the forenoon we were in sight of the line of woods marking the course of the river and gradually approaching it; elsewhere prairie of good soil but inferior, Rainville thinks, to that on Red River. About the middle of the day we struck the St. Peter's again, where it is not more than 20 yards wide & at a rapid one quarter of a mile below the mouth of the aux Liards [*Cottonwood R.*]. The valley of the St. Peter's is here less than a mile wide & 80 or 100 feet below the prairie. Forded the river & one mile beyond forded the Riviere aux Liards or W$\overset{3}{\text{a}}$rh$\overset{1}{\text{o}}$z$\overset{1}{\text{u}}$ i.e. abounding in Cottonwood. It is 15 yards wide & has sandy bottom. Directly after passed two inhabited lodges. Light rain throughout the day. Distance 21 miles.[51]

THURSDAY, JULY 17, 1823. Last night we occupied the site of a considerable settlement not long abandoned; we frequently see frames of lodges but no Indians; the great hunting season is commenced. Continued our march at 5:48 A.M. The prairie slightly undulated, ponds occassionally on either hand. The timber rapidly decreasing in quantity: the soil gravelly & many travelled masses of granite. Fair day; in forenoon wind N Easterly: in afternoon. N Westerly. At 8h. 2m. P.M. Mer[idian] Alt[itude] of the Moon's

[50] On the distribution of rattlesnakes and garter snakes in this area, see W. J. Breckenridge, *Reptiles and Amphibians of Minnesota*, 146–159 (Minneapolis, 1944). Colhoun's "Wotepah Makatooze" corresponds to "Makato Osa Watapa," Keating's more correct rendering of the Dakota name; see Keating, *Narrative*, 1:341. On the Swan Lake mounds, which numbered 11 in all, see Winchell, *Aborigines*, 199.

[51] The two lodges were inhabited by the Mdewakanton Chief Black Dog and his family; see Keating, *Narrative*, 1:345. The considerable settlement mentioned below was probably the village of Chief Sleepy Eyes; see Bray and Bray, eds., *Nicollet on the Plains*, 18n, 57.

Upper Limb 41° 2′ 30″; in[dex] error −3′ 30″. Distance travelled 22 miles.

FRIDAY, JULY 18, 1823. Fortunately the nights are sufficiently cool to permit our sleeping with our boots on & our heads covered with the blanket. It is hardly an exaggeration of the traders that in the summer season on the St. Peter's the one whose office it is to strike fire will find it impossible to perform his duties, unless protected from the mus-quitoes by some of his company. Although I have a veil for the purpose, I find it necessary to keep a soldier constantly employed to brush away these troublesome insects while I am making Observations, & even with that aid I am seldom able to make them in a satisfactory manner. So soon as supper is ended we hurry to our coverts. The horses crowd into the smoke of our fire, & several times have been so much distracted by stings of musquitoes as to rush over our baggage & into the midst of the party. They have no respite in the day time, for then they have to bear the torment of horseflies.

After a ride of 12 miles we forded the R. Bois Rouge [*Redwood R.*] one mile above its mouth, where it is 8 yards wide. The Sioux call it Chasiape (the first syllable nasal) that is, "the wood that is reddened." Its sources are in the Coteau des Prairies. Red pipestone is found on it three days' journey above. Saw, at its junction with the St. Peter's, granite in place. Rainville says it is also found extending on the latter several miles lower down. Schoolcraft (67th day) met with rugged peaks of granite only 20 or 30 miles above the Falls of St. Anthony. Which is in a direction from here, according to the best maps, about NNE. We have no accounts of this mass being traced southwest of us, but it strikes the Southeastern part of Lake Superior. I will not encroach on Mr. Keating's province.[52]

Patterson's Rapids on the St. Peter's are 4 or 5 miles above the Bois Rouge. We encamped on the bank of the St. Peter's, which is here 25 yds. wide & has gentle current. Its valley today has been generally a mile wide; the river continually divides it equally & has lost, for the most part, its tendency to deep curved & abrupt bends. No trees are to be seen except in a line frequently broken that marks

[52] The Redwood rises in the coteau northeast of Pipestone, near the site where the Indians mined pipestone. See Holmquist and Brookins, *Minnesota's Major Historic Sites*, 108–112. For a technical analysis and dating of the granite formations in the Redwood area, see Sims and Morey, eds., *Geology of Minnesota*, 184–190. See also Schoolcraft, *Narrative Journal*, 288 (1821). Keating was, of course, the expedition's geologist.

the course of the river, & in another attendant on the R. Bois Rouge. Fair weather; wind NE — Evening Amplitude W 18° N. At 8h. 53m. P.M. Mer[idian] Alt[itude] of the Moon's Upper Limb 37° 35′ 30″, index error −3′ 30″. Distance travelled 25 miles.

SATURDAY, JULY 19, 1823. Morning Amplitude E 38° 30′ N. Travelling 8 miles brought us to P$\overset{2}{\mathrm{a}}$z$\overset{1}{\mathrm{e}}\overset{1}{\mathrm{o}}t\overset{2}{\mathrm{a}}z\overset{1}{\mathrm{e}}z\overset{1}{\mathrm{e}}$ or Yellow Medicine River, which is 8 [*20?*] yards wide. A smaller stream [*Hawk Creek*] enters the St. Peter's nearly opposite. It is named by the natives Ch$\overset{2}{\mathrm{a}}$t$\overset{2}{\mathrm{a}}$b$\overset{4}{\mathrm{a}}$ (two first syllables nasal) which signifies "that hatches sparrow hawks." The traders call it R. de l'Eau de Vie. About sunset we encamped again on the river bank. After crossing the Pazeotazeze we travelled obliquely through the valley of the St. Peter's about 5 miles & found it rather more than a mile wide. In it were many piles of granite or sienite; the highest of them forming peaks that rose to 35 feet above the river, an elevation about 15 feet less than the summit of the prairie on which we see it only in rolled masses besides a good deal of sand. About our camp cottonwood & grapevines. Five miles below us there is a portage [*at Granite Falls*] about a mile long around 13 rapids; these 13 with 26 more complete the whole number of rapids below Lac Travers[e], but in a good stage of water there are only two portages & this is one.[53]

No wild quadrupeds; the few birds we see are sparrows, cow buntings, curlews, sand-hill cranes, a species of tern & the Bartram sand piper. The two last are the most numerous. No grouse for sometime past.[54]

In the evening a family of [*Gens du Lac*] Indians pitched their lodge near us & gave us an invitation to eat Buffalo meat, which was gladly accepted. The usual preliminaries of shaking hands & smoking gone through, pieces of dried meat, 1/8 of an inch thick some of them 8 inches wide & 18 inches long, were served up in a large wooden dish & surmounted with slices of fat without salt or any kind of bread. Boiling had been the preparation. I thought it better than any jerked beef I have ever tasted in South America; it was without the strong cod-fish smell so disagreeable in that. This, however, I believe had been smoked & was the spoils of buffalo killed near here

[53] On the names of Yellow Medicine River and Hawk or Chetambe Creek, see Keating, *Narrative*, 1:355, 356; Upham, *Minnesota Geographic Names*, 106, 593.

[54] The birds Colhoun refers to are the sparrow, cowbird (cow-bunting), long-billed curlew, sandhill crane, common tern, upland plover (Bartram sandpiper), and prairie sharp-tailed grouse; see Roberts, *Birds of Minnesota*, 1:395–402, 433–438, 482–484, 486–490, 559–564, 2:322–328, 333.

only three days ago. What remained of the repast, according to Indian custom, we took with us. Our entertainer informed us that the Buffalo has made his appearance above in unusual numbers. Clear day; wind SE. Distance today 23 miles.

SUNDAY, JULY 20, 1823. Our horses feasted last night on wild pea-vine. 18 miles to a stream [*Lac qui Parle R.*] 6 yards wide with sandy bottom. The traders call it Beaver River; the Sioux, $\overset{1}{\text{E}}\text{nt}\overset{4}{\text{a}}\text{p}\overset{4}{\text{a}}$, which signifies At the End, perhaps because [it is] the last of the tributaries of the St. Peters below the first lake. Half a mile before we reached it saw six artificial mounds in a line; on the two largest, which were 5 feet high & 30 feet diameter of base, I observed recent graves of the kind much used by the Sioux: stakes placed roof-wise over the interred like those described on page 50 [*288*]. This instance accounts for the presence of modern articles in ancient tumuli.[55]

Walking fourteen miles in the forenoon, the grass cut through my moccassins, which were good new ones. Saw frequently circular places of different growth from the general prairie. Rainville says they are caused by the Buffalo licking where there is saline exudation. Though this has the appearance of a secondary region, we see no limestone or sandstone in place. The monotony of scenery on the prairie is equalled by the absence of incident in our journey. On both accounts therefore, taking two young wolves [*coyotes*] caused no small commotion in the party. We encamped at the lower end of Lac qui parle, a name bestowed on the lower Lake of St. Peter's R. by the traders to interpret that given by the Sioux, $\text{M}\overset{2}{\text{u}}\text{nd}\overset{1}{\text{a}}\ \overset{1}{\text{E}}\overset{1}{\text{a}}\text{d}\overset{4}{\text{a}}\text{h}$. It is probable the high bluffs around this lake create an echo that may have caused its name. There is a tributary of the Assinniboin [*Assiniboine R.*], the Indian name of which the traders translate by Riviere qui Appelle [*Qu'Appelle R.*]: I do not know what suggested that appellation. Clear: wind S Easterly. Distance 20 miles.[56]

MONDAY, JULY 21, 1823. Morning Amplitude E 38° N. After riding about 16 miles we stopped to dine on the river bank. The river was there not more than 12 yards wide & so choaked with wild rice as to have no perceptible current. Lac qui parle appears to be about 7 [*13*] miles long & where broadest about 3/4 of a mile wide. The bluffs at its lower extremity were about 70 ft. high, but as we

[55] On the mounds, see Winchell, *Aborigines*, 121.

[56] For a discussion of the names of both Lac qui Parle and the Qu'Appelle River of Canada, which flows into the Assiniboine at Lazare, Man., see Upham, *Minnesota Geographic Names*, 288.

advanced they gradually lessened in elevation & in a manner disappeared, till in our mid-day journey they became gentle slopes blending the prairie with the valley of the river. 5 leagues above Lac qui parle, our guides say, the H$\overset{1}{\text{a}}$ W$\overset{3}{\text{a}}$k$\overset{2}{\text{u}}$h or Mountain Spirit Cr. [*Yellow Bank R.*] enters from the left [*southwest*]. It is the R. pome de Terre of the traders. In the afternoon buffalo bones were almost constantly in sight. Passed by a stone of sacrifice, a large conical rock, on which were drawn with red paint, crescents, horns down for the Moon, & circles & crosses for the Stars; Rainville say[s] it is dedicated to them. 5 miles from where we dined we struck the [Minnesota] River again with intention to cross to the other side, but found the bottom too boggy for fording. Observe three species of horse fly make appearance about 7 A. M. & continue throughout the day. Fair: wind SE. Distance 25 1/2 miles.[57]

TUESDAY, JULY 22, 1823. Last night's camp was on [a] high steep bluff over the river. Some rain in the night. Half a mile from camp to a stream [*Yellow Bank R.*] 6 yds. wide. 6 miles more to another [*Whetstone R.*] 5 yds. wide, which enters just below the Lake $\overset{1}{\text{E}}\overset{2}{\text{a}}t\overset{2}{\text{a}}kek\overset{2}{\text{a}}$ (third & last syllables nasal) which name the traders translate by L. des Grosses Roches [*Big Stone Lake*]. While approaching this last creek, my hopes were not a little excited when the more experienced ones of the party pronounced two animals curvetting on a high hill before us to be either Elks or buffalos. But my disappointment was not soured into chagrin when they were ascertained to be mounted Indians, the harbingers of a considerable band of friendly [Wahpeton] Sioux. On ascending the high bank from the creek we first came in view of the Coteau des Prairies on our left & like a range of mountains from their comparative height.[58]

We were soon met by more than 50 Indians, some on horseback, the greater part running afoot. The horsemen coursed around us, firing off their guns & drumming constantly with their heels on the horses' sides, for they carried neither whip nor spur. One of them

[57] Colhoun apparently mistook the Yellow Bank River for the Pomme de Terre; the latter flows into the Minnesota from the north just above Lac qui Parle. Although Say listed no horseflies in his catalog of insects published in Keating, *Narrative*, 2:268–378, he listed three species (*tabanus annulatus*, *tabanus molestus*, and *tabanus stygius*) in "Descriptions of Dipterous Insects of the United States," in Academy of Natural Sciences of Philadelphia, *Journal*, 1st series 3:31, 32, 33 (Philadelphia, 1823). These may have been the species referred to by Colhoun.

[58] On the name of Big Stone Lake, see Upham, *Minnesota Geographic Names*, 53. Colhoun's description of the Indians was used by Keating in *Narrative*, 1:368.

had a live Sparrow Hawk on his head by way of ornament; & over his shoulders a buffalo robe on which eight bear tracks were painted. Several young men had looking-glasses suspended to their belts. I observe none of these Indians having the fine bay color I remarked in the young men of the village near Rock R. & which I am half inclined to prefer to white. In general, however, they are good looking and straight, though none are large nor are any symmetrically formed. They have, like all the Indians I have seen, hollow hands & feet; those extremities are also small. The Malay, though he often has elegant legs, is disfigured by the spreading of his feet unrestrained by any kind of shoe, but the Indian moccassin, preventing expansion of the toes, enables its wearer to appear naked with advantage.

A troop of squaws met us half a mile from the village. They have no ornaments nor do they seem to value themselves on personal appearance, all vain display belonging exclusively to the young men. Their dress consists of a long wrapper of dark calico with short sleeves; a piece of blue broadcloth passed two or three times round the waist so as to show the list & the end tucked in; the first garment covering from the shoulders to the waist; the other thence to the knees; they have also leggings of blue or scarlet cloth. Without the exquisite waists of the women of the Philip[p]ines, they have equal breadth of hips, showing a capacious pelvis, which in some measure accounts for their comparative exemption from pain & danger in parturition. If judged according to Lord Bacon's idea of beauty, which he makes to consist in "decent motion," they certainly will not be admired. Their gait merits the praise in the song of the modern Greek, "My Love walks about like a goose."*[59]

We followed them to [the] village on the shore of Lac des Grosses Roches, consisting of about 25 skin lodges & containing between 100 & 200 inhabitants. An island in the Lake a quarter of a mile distant is their permanent residence because more secure, but they have encamped here for the hunting season. We delayed a short time, accepting [an] invitation to feast in one of the lodges. They presented to us buffalo meat & a hominy of tepsin, which the Canadians call *navet des prairies* [*prairie turnip*]. It is very abundant in the moist soil about the village. The Indians do not appear to culti-

*Dodwell's Tour through Greece. Lon. 1819. vol. 2.19. [*Colhoun's note.*]

[59] Francis Bacon, "Of Beauty," in Peter Shaw, ed., *The Philosophical Works of Francis Bacon*, 2:123 (London, 1733); Edward Dodwell, *A Classical and Topographical Tour through Greece*, 2:19 (London, 1819).

vate it. My companions speak well of its taste; it was not agreeable to me.[60]

Squaws & children crowded the door to look in at us & some raised the skins of the lodge to get a peep; the men confronting us inside were equally observant, but none of them partook of the meal. That they as well as all other human beings have some knowledge of physiognomy, we had a proof. Our interpreter [*Renville*] overheard them remark that one of our company [*Beltrami*] must be a foreigner, because he wanted the mild expression of countenance which they said is universal with Americans. Their judgment was correct.

Many of them had scars on their arms, pierced for grief at the death of relatives. I observed one of them sit for sometime with his legs crossed like an East-Indian. Hitherto that posture seems not to be the habitual one; I believe it never has been with any of the North American tribes. In cabins that have a raised seat, the legs are sometimes pendent; but they usually sit on the right buttock with the right leg bent & lying horizontally, the left leg doubled vertically & resting on the sole of the foot. The women d[ou]ble their legs & lay them horizontally both towards the same side. I saw no countenances that I though indicative of cunning, nor one full of dreadful looks like that of Metea; their faces are faithful indices to the equanimity of their souls. Yet the action of the muscles, the bones of the face are not concealed as often in the Whiteman by a load of flesh: this together with the deep-sunk eye, renders the Indian capable on great provocation of exhibiting the most terrific passion.

Left the village & proceeded about 10 miles over a finely waved prairie to the house of Mr. Moore [*Hazen Mooers*], a fur trader. A short time after our arrival we were summoned to the lodge of the Buffalo Man about a quarter of a mile distant to a feast given in honor of us. The buffalo meat, very finely cooked, was serve[d] out by a great Medicine or Magic man. We found no other individual in the lodge except an Assiniboin, a captive, & very old; his locks were hoary: we have seen some Indians bald. The Buffalo-Man made a pertinent speech. He sat while delivering it, his countenance inflexible, his gestures vehement & unmeaning. Around Mr.

[60] The island where the Indians lived is shown on Colhoun's sketch map of Big Stone Lake; Keating, *Narrative*, 1:369, calls it "Big Island." It may be present Kite Island.

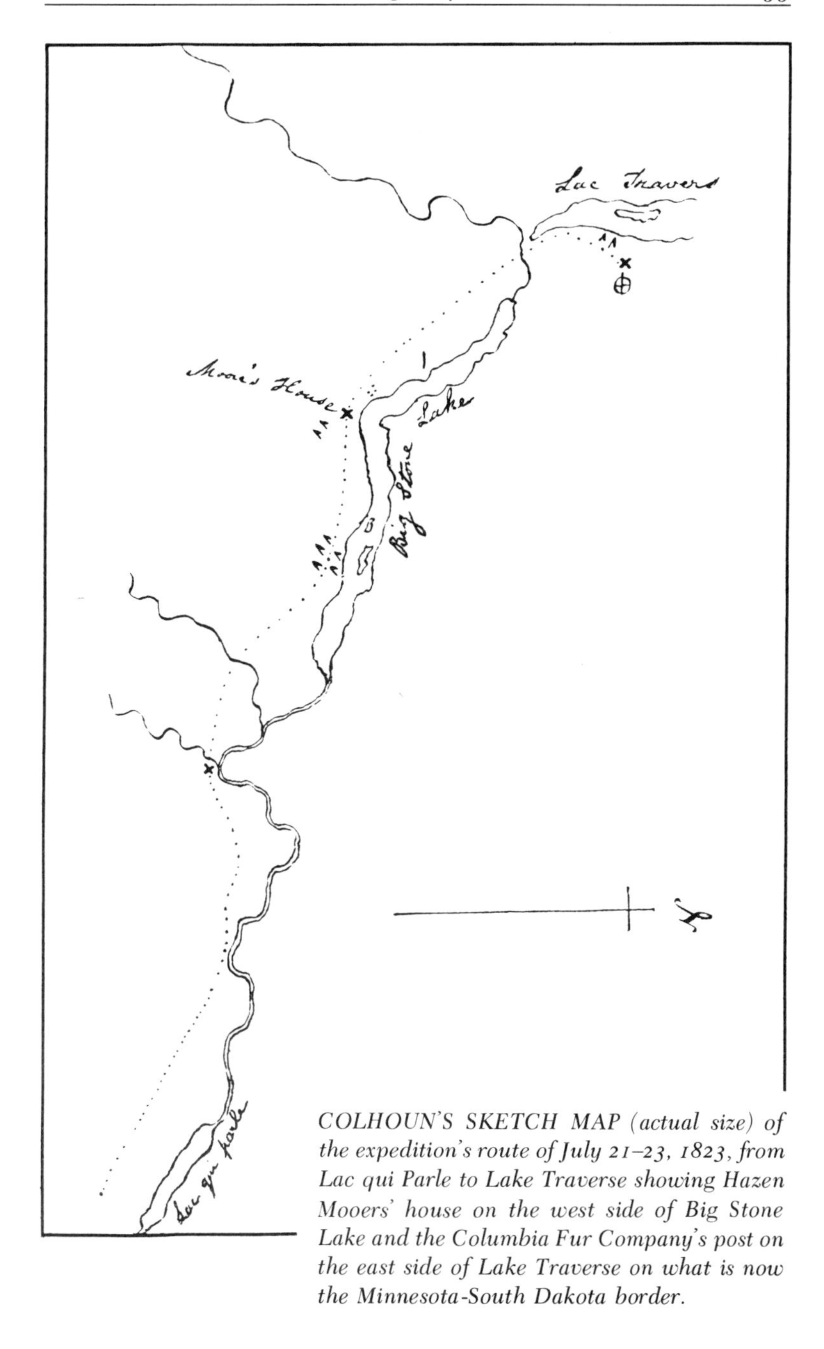

COLHOUN'S SKETCH MAP (actual size) of the expedition's route of July 21–23, 1823, from Lac qui Parle to Lake Traverse showing Hazen Mooers' house on the west side of Big Stone Lake and the Columbia Fur Company's post on the east side of Lake Traverse on what is now the Minnesota-South Dakota border.

Moore's house was Lamb's-quarter more than 7 feet high.[61] It is now almost too old to use, but heretofore in our meals it has been a valuable auxiliary to the fraction of biscuit. If to them be added a slice of fried ham, the whole bill of fare will be recited. Rain in the morning: throughout the day cloudy. Wind NNW. Distance travelled 22 miles.

[61] Lamb's quarter (*Chenopodium album* Linnaeus) is an edible plant sometimes called pigweed.

8. Down the Red River with Long

JULY 23 THROUGH 29, 1823

WEDNESDAY, JULY 23, 1823. Soon after we ascended the high prairie a short distance from Moore's [*Mooers'*] house we passed several small mounds. We then travelled over a prairie gently undulated about 14 miles to the upper part of Big Stone Lake, which as near as I can judge is 24 miles long, scarcely one mile wide, being a mere expansion of the river; however, it appears to be deep in some places. 3 miles further we crossed the St. Peter's where it is less than 7 yards wide; we crossed the Portage between Lac Travers[e] & Lac des Grosses Roches [*Big Stone Lake*], which is about 4 miles long. Early in the afternoon we reached an establishment [*of the Columbia Fur Company*] for Fur trade on the shore of Lac Travers, where we were welcomed by the discharge of fusils. Clear day: wind N Easterly. Distance 24 miles.[1]

The whole distance from the mouth of St. Peter's river to Lac Travers, as I travelled, is 302 miles in 15 days, giving a daily average of 20 miles: 70 miles were by water. But I am confident that one could travel from the mouth of that river to its source in less than 230 miles & I am equally confident that the St. Peter's, including its bends, does not exceed 500 miles in length. About three miles from Big Stone Lake & one mile from Lake Travers the St. Peter's turns roundly off. From that point the source of one Fork [*Jorgenson R.*] is at the foot of the Coteau des Prairies in a direction W by S & distant, say, 12 miles. The source of the northern or larger Fork [*Little Minnesota R.*] is at about twice that distance in Polecat [*Tewaukon?*] Lake bearing from the same point about W by N. This last Fork is 40 or 50 miles long counting its windings. Both Branches meet above,

[1] On the mounds, see Winchell, *Aborigines*, 119–121. By crossing the portage between Lakes Big Stone and Traverse, the party entered the Red River watershed.

where we last crossed. Polecat L. is at the base of the Coteau des Prairies, & does not exceed one mile & a half in length & half a mile in breadth.[2]

The River St. Peter's never can be made a commodious stream, for though it flows over gradations & not upon a slant, consequently has gentle current for the most part, yet those gradations are accumulated into the upper third of the distance between Big Stone Lake & its mouth, & although that portion of the river may be improved by locking & damming, no expense can supply a sufficiency of water throughout the summer, nor would it be worth while to attempt great amendment for the sake of short periods of the year just before & after the ice. If we were allowed to consider the Limestone stratum, which unde[r]lays the country through which the St. Peter's flows, horizontal, we could arrive near the true quantity of fall the river has below the Portage of Lac Travers. There appears to be little difference of elevation between Lac qui parle & that Portage. About the lower extremity of Lac qui parle, or rather about that portion of the river just below it, the average & general elevation of the prairie above the water is from 50 to 60 feet, while at the mouth of the St. Peter's it is about 110 feet. The stratum is disclosed only at the latter, therefore we have no means by which to judge accurately whether or not it is governed by the same ratio of difference; supposing that it is, the average fall does not exceed 2 or 3 [*9.3*] inches per mile. I am well satisfied with the result; however, the premises may be objected to.[3]

I am not qualified to judge of Prairie soil, having never seen it under cultivation. I remarked that pieces of woodland we occasionally met with were extremely fertile, & hence I infer favorably of the

[2] Keating gave the length of the Minnesota River as 325 miles in *Narrative*, 1:363; the figures in Long's journal total 298 1/4 miles traveled to Big Stone Lake. The length of the Minnesota is now calculated at 329 miles to Big Stone Lake. Mileages are shown on the maps in Greg Breining and Linda Watson, *A Gathering of Waters: A Guide to Minnesota's Rivers*, 54 (St. Paul, 1977).

The Little Minnesota River rises from several sources in Roberts and Marshall counties, S. Dak. Colhoun's "Polecat Lake" may be shown on Nicollet, "Hydrographical Basin," as "Makah Lake," which translates from the Dakota as "polecat" or "skunk." It was later called Skunk Lake. It is probably present Lake Tewaukon in southeastern Sargent County, N. Dak., which is not one of the sources of the Little Minnesota. See H. S. Morris, *Historical Stories Legends and Traditions: Roberts County and Northeastern South Dakota*, 25 (Sisseton, S. Dak., 1939).

[3] Later surveys of the navigational possibilities of the Minnesota echoed Colhoun's conclusions; see Warren, *Minnesota River*, 23. In 1978 the river is navigable only from its mouth to Shakopee. Its total fall is 274 feet, or 9.3 inches per mile; see Waters, *Streams and Rivers of Minnesota*, 313.

region bordering on the St. Peter's. Perhaps some of the species of grass indicate poverty of soil, & it is certain that the average height of all kinds is less than 12 inches, therefore, I would be understood to allude to its susceptibility of improvement & not to its present capacity. That stinted growth, however, may perhaps depend mainly on a degree of aridity, a chief defect in this country. Thirty or 40 miles above the river we found neither springs nor brooks. The roots of the grass are so closely matted that water cannot penetrate into the earth, & from the openness of the country evaporation is rapid & immense. To these remarks may be given more extensive application. The western tributaries of the Mississippi, therefore, contrast strikingly with the rivers east of the Alleghanies [*Allegheny Mountains*]: the latter are as superior to the former in body of water as they are inferior in length of course.[4]

Annual fires remove all vegetable deposit. The Indian sets fire to the prairie behind him to distract pursuit by the smoke & by destroying all trace of his passage; to keep the country open & thus invite the buffalo, and enable him to see & chace his game; to give notice to his friends of his approach or to warn them of the presence of the enemy; the traders by the same mean[s] bring to them the Indians; the prairies are often burnt by the spreading of the fires of encampments. By the operation of these numerous causes, we may safely say that all the prairies of the continent, with little exception, are burnt every year. Places that have had respite of only a few months are covered with dense thickets. Observation & reflexion, so far has [*as*] I have capacity in viewing a subject interesting to me, have convinced me that fire is the cause of the existence of prairies. The Indian summer has been generally attributed to the annual conflag[r]ations on them. If that kind of season be peculiar to this continent & the direction of the wind at the time ascertained to be favorable, I admit the sufficiency of the explanation: but I am not aware that the subject has been properly examined.

The St. Peter's is owned throughout its length by two or three bands of the Sioux nation. Charlevoix says the name by which we know them is an ab[b]reviation retaining only the two last syllables

[4] The soil of this region, as Colhoun suggested, was indeed very fertile. The theory expressed below that prairies were the result of repeated fires was common among 19th-century pioneers and explorers. Keating, *Narrative*, 2: 41, correctly deduced aridity as a cause. On these points and prairie grasses, see J. E. Weaver, *North American Prairie*, 3–17, 271–273 (Lincoln, Neb., 1954); David F. Costello, *The Prairie World*, 53, 195–199 (New York, 1969).

of Naudowessioux, a name given them I [think] by Otaways [*Ottawa*]. Hennepin gives that termination only once; all other instances he spells sies & says they were called Tint[h]onha, i.e. of the Prairies. [Louis-Armand de Lom d'Arce, Baron de] Lahontan always terminates with sie. They call themselves D$\overset{2}{a}$c$\overset{1}{o}$t$\overset{4}{a}$. I have not been able to learn whether they are confederate of other nations, as the Iroquois, or subdivided from one great original people. Should discrepancies of language be discovered in the several tribes, the conglomeration will appear more probable than a division & their name, which signifies United or Allied, would in my mind increase the probability. But all such inquiries belong to the duties of Mr. Keating. I shall content myself with reciting a few facts in their history.[5]

Du Pratz in the former part of the last century placed the Sioux on both sides of the Mississippi about 100 leagues above the Falls of St. Anthony.[α] Lewis & Clark consider that position to have been the original seat of the nation. They were first known to Europeans in 1660, & it was then said of them that they were not cruel to their prisoners,[β] nor do they appear to have ever been charged with eating them. It was also reported of them that they had better conception than any other Indians of the First Cause.[γ] Lahontan tells us that they destroyed a party of Iroquois on an island of the Mississippi prior to 1688. In 1697 they defeated a party of Miamis between St. Joseph's & Kikalemazo [*Kalamazoo*] Rivers on the Southeastern coast of Lake Michigan.[δ] In 1701 "the Sakis [*Sauk*], the Otchagras or Puants [*Winnebago*], the Malhomines or Folles Avoines [*Menominee*], the Outagamis [*Fox*], the Pouteouatamis [*Potawatomi*], & the Kichapous [*Kickapoo*]" assembled at Green

[5] For a discussion of Dakota subdivisions and the meanings of their names, see Hodge, *Handbook*, 1:376–378, 2:577–579; Bray and Bray, eds., *Nicollet on the Plains*, 252–263. All the Dakota tribes shared the same basic language. The authorities Colhoun cited are Charlevoix, *Histoire*, 5:270; Hennepin, *Description*, 204; Lahontan, *New Voyages to North-America*, 1:110, 129, 231 (London, 1703). Hennepin spelled the name in a variety of ways, including Nadouessiou, -siouz, -sans, and -sious. Lahontan used -sious or -sis.

[α]Hist. de la Louisiane. Tom. 2. Chap. 17.[α6]

[α6] Du Pratz, *Histoire*, 2:228. Footnotes α through η were supplied by Colhoun.

[β]Hist. de la N. France par Charlevoix Tom. 2. p. 98.[β7]

[β7] Allen, ed., *History of the Expedition under . . . Lewis and Clark*, 1:61; Charlevoix, *Histoire*, 2:100.

[γ]Journal Historique par Charlevoix Tom 2 L 26.[γ8]

[γ8] Charlevoix, *Histoire*, 6:64.

[δ]Histoire de la Nouvelle France par Charlevoix Tom. 3, p. 310.[δ9]

[δ9] Lahontan, *New Voyages*, 1:128; Charlevoix, *Histoire*, 3:310. Charlevoix calls the Kalamazoo River the Maramek.

Bay to go to war with them, but were prevailed on by a French emissary to remain at peace.[ε] The Chipéways informed Carver in 1767 that war had continued without interruption for "more than 40 winters" between themselves & the Sioux.[ζ] Pike says the Band at the mouth of St. Peter's river is the only one that "cultivates vegetables." I do not believe that to be strictly true, but most of the Bands are still erratic.

I have not the leisure to examine all the accounts of their numbers, but there can be little doubt that Rainville's [*Renville's*] estimate (30,000) is too great. He says also that they are divided into 21 Bands. Vast confusion exists as to the names & numbers of the Bands respectively,[η] which must be owing in some degree to the subdivisions of each; chiefly to the ignorance & carelessness of travellers. They have seldom discriminated between the names given by Indian tribes to themselves & those bestowed upon them by their neighbors. The practice also obtains among Indians generally of naming a few families from the chief of their village or the stream on which they are located. No less confusion prevails in their geography & in their claims of territory from one nation lending land to another & from the changes constantly produced by secession, emigration & conquest. Mr. [Lawrence] Taliaferro, the agent for this nation, thinks that Wabeshaw [*Wabasha*] is at present the most influential chief; he is so considered because his father was confessedly preeminent. Petit Corbeau [*Little Crow*] is thought to rank next.[13]

[ε]idem idem p. 405.[ε10]

[ε10] Charlevoix, *Histoire*, 3:405. Colhoun translated Charlevoix's text and added the common names of the Indian tribes.

[ζ]Travels p. 32.[ζ11]

[ζ11] Carver, *Three Years Travels*, 32.

[η]Compare together the Synopsis in Jefferson's Notes on Virginia, Carver's Travels pp. 30–40, Lewis' & Clark's Expedition Vol. 1. p. 61, Pike's Expeditions p. 59, Breckenridge's Views of Louisiana in loco.[η12]

[η12] Thomas Jefferson, *Notes on the State of Virginia*, 109, 112 (Philadelphia, 1788); Carver, *Three Years Travels*, 30, 40; Allen, ed., *History of the Expedition under . . . Lewis and Clark*, 1:61; Pike, *Expeditions*, part 1 appendix, 59, 61 (quotation); Brackenridge, *Views of Louisiana*, 87.

[13] Keating, *Narrative*, 1:380, gave Renville's figure for the Dakota population as 28,100; Keating listed only 14 "villages or parties" of the Dakota. There are seven generally recognized subdivisions of the Dakota: Mdewakanton, Wahpeton, Sisseton, Wahpekute, Yankton, Yanktonai, and Teton. On this and Dakota population, see Hodge, *Handbook*, 1:378; John R. Swanton, *Indian Tribes of North America*, 283 (Bureau of American Ethnology, *Bulletins*, no. 145—Washington, D.C., 1952). For Taliaferro's assessment of Wabasha and Little Crow, see Taliaferro Journal, undated entry (7:17), March 7, 1828 (8:176), Taliaferro Papers.

It is said that the Assiniboins wish to rejoin the confederacy & that negociations have commenced with that end. Rainville makes them equally numerous with the Sioux; whether or not his estimate be correct, the coalition will form a powerful nation & as it is on our frontier, it should occupy the constant attention of our government. I have been led to think that among the causes of the wars with the Indians, their ignorance of our power has been principal. Encouraging, therefore, frequent visits of the Chiefs to Washington will effectually belie the representations of British traders & preserve peace on our borders.[14]

The Coteau des Prairies has been continually in sight since we approached the lower end of Big Stone Lake. It is a remarkable feature of this region. The Indians, I am told, consider it a spur of the Rocky Mountains; that such is their opinion appears also from their telling Carver that the St. Peter's has its source in the "Shining Mountains," which is but another name for the same range. That opinion seems to me to be erroneous, or [at] least if an offset, that it is not continuous. The tributaries of the Missouri, of the Saskatchawan & of the Assiniboin[e] interlock. It is well known that a branch of the latter, la Riviere Sourie [*Souris*] has its source within less than a day's journey of the Missouri itself & that the country between them is practicable for wheels. Such is my impression of the facility of that communication, but I must confess I cannot say how I came by it, whether from hearing, reading or misapprehension.[15]

The western Branch of the Terre Bleue [*Blue Earth R.*] heads in the Coteau: the southern does not, & about there the range terminates. Here they represented it [to] be very broken & about 500 feet high; whether in ridges or in insulated hills was not satisfactorily explained. From its appearance at this distance I would [suppose] the former to be the formation. From this [Columbia Fur Company] trading establishment, the most northern part in sight, bears a little South of West. The base is about 15 miles distant; the central &

[14] According to tradition, the Assiniboin separated from the Yanktonai. They did not rejoin this group. Most estimates of their numbers are far less than the Dakota. See Swanton, *Indian Tribes*, 388; Hodge, *Handbook*, 1:102.

[15] The Coteau des Prairies is not a spur of the Rockies. For Carver's statement, see *Three Years Travels*, 38. Shining Mountains was a common early name for the Rockies. See James, *Account*, 2:361, 362 (1823). The tributaries of the Missouri, Assiniboine, and Saskatchewan come near each other in various places in southeastern Alberta, southern Saskatchewan, and northern North Dakota. The source of the Souris is far north of the Missouri in Saskatchewan, but at its most southern point (at Velva, N. Dak.) the Souris comes within 40 miles of the Missouri. See also Appendix 1, note 29, below.

highest part is 15 miles more in addition. It is probably primitive, & is thought to cause the swerving course of the Missouri. On many accounts, we have to regret that Mr. Keating was unable to examine it. Mr. Jeffries [*Joseph Jeffryes*], going to the Mandan villages on the Missouri not long since, found no difficulty in crossing it with his cart.[16]

The country gradually swelled as we advanced towards Big Stone L. Both about it & about Lac Travers the prairie is 100 feet above the water. Yet there is no just ground for the "Height of Land" laid down in most maps, a range of hills or mountains between the waters of the Mississippi & of Hudson's Bay. I speak in reference to this particular section of country. Both those Lakes are in the same valley, & it is still in the recollection of some persons that a boat once floated from Lac Travers to the St. Peter's R.[17]

Rainville established this trading post six years ago: a year since he joined the Columbia Fur Company of which a Mr. McKensie [*Kenneth McKenzie*] is principal. We found at it Messrs. Wm. Laidlaw & Jeffries, both of them in the employment of the Company. There were also several Canadian Engagés. We were treated with politeness. The houses, which are built of logs & covered with bark & earth, are enclosed by a sorry stockade. The parchment windows admit a mild light, very similar to that of windows formed out of the inner lamina of oyster shells I have seen at Macao & Manila, & which are the best kind for tropical climates. Fortunately for us, they have a good supply of buffalo meat, the produce of a hunt concluded a few days before our arrival. They were obliged to travel 5 days in a Northwestern direction to find the game, but then soon succeeded in killing 60 buffalo. They brought home a male buffalo calf, two or three months old. It is of a uniform dun color. The hump is not yet begun to form. It makes almost continually a grunting

[16] By the western branch of the Blue Earth Colhoun probably meant the Watonwan River, with sources in Watonwan and Cottonwood counties, Minn. At its most northern point the head of the coteau near present Rutland, N. Dak., rises close to 1,000 feet above the plain near Big Stone Lake. For the extent of the Coteau des Prairies, see Nicollet, "Hydrographical Basin"; Bray and Bray, eds., *Nicollet on the Plains*, 204.

[17] Many map makers of Colhoun's time represented heights of land as ranges of hills. See, for example, Wheat, *Mapping the Transmississippi West*, 2:facing pp. 10, 57. The inconspicuous divide between the Hudson Bay and Mississippi watersheds at Big Stone-Lake Traverse is now known as Browns Valley. Navigation across the four miles of swamp separating the lakes was possible during times of high water. See Chief of Engineers, *Report*, 443 (44 Congress, 1 session, *House Executive Documents*, no. 1, part 2—serial 1675); Upham, *Minnesota Geographic Names*, 7.

A SCAFFOLD BURIAL *at Lake Traverse, a drawing by Samuel Seymour engraved by J. Hill for publication in the* Narrative *of the 1823 expedition published in 1824.*

noise not unlike that of a hog. A domestic cow nourishes it without discovering anything more than uneasiness at its hard sucking, though at first she submitted only through force.[18]

We found here W$\overset{3}{a}$n$\overset{1}{o}$t$\overset{3}{o}$n (last syllable as in French) [*Waneta*]. He is Chief of the six bands of the "Y$\overset{4}{a}$nkt$\overset{4}{o}$ns [*Yanktonai*] of the plains," collectively seven or 8 thousand in number, according to Rainville. More than 6 feet high, he is altogether the finest looking Indian I have seen. His age does not exceed 28 years & yet he has performed more feats, is more distinguished in war than any of the Sioux except perhaps Petit Corbeau. His name, which signifies Charger, is expressive of his character.[19]

In the afternoon of our arrival, he invited us to a feast. They spread for us their buffalo robes. A good number of warriors were present but as usual no women. No speeches, nor much ceremony. Buffalo & dog meat very nicely boiled were presented us in wooden bowls without salt or any kind of bread. I overcame my repugnance to the novel dish so far as to eat a piece of dog's flesh. It was enticing in appearance & after having tasted it, I no longer wonder at the fattened Pups I saw in the market of Canton. It approached nearest to pork.

Giving a feast of dog's flesh is the most distinguished manner of receiving a stranger among many tribes this side of the Rocky Mountains, as in most of the Islands of the Pacific; not so West of those Mountains: the natives of Columbia River in derision called Lewis & Clark Dog-eaters. The Portuguese narrator of de Soto's Invasion of Florida tells us that at Guaxule, which was perhaps within the present limits of Alabama, the army was presented by the Indians with 300 dogs, because they saw that the Spaniards eat them, which they did not. It [is] probable, however, that the Spaniards were taught to eat them by the Indians of the Antilles, for Bernal Diaz [del Castillo] enumerates several times among the sea-

[18] On Renville's post see Nute, in *Minnesota History*, 22:282. Kenneth McKenzie, a Scotsman who emigrated in 1816, served the North West Company before participating in the organization of the Columbia Fur Company. See Ray H. Mattison, "Kenneth McKenzie," in Hafen, ed., *Mountain Men*, 2:217–224; Simpson to Colvile, May 20, 1822 (24:98–100), Selkirk Papers.

[19] Renville's population figure was too high for the Yanktonai alone, perhaps because of a confusion on Colhoun's part between the closely related Yankton and Yanktonai. Keating, *Narrative*, 1:380, gave Renville's estimate of Yanktonai population as 5,200 and the Yankton as 2,000. In Taliaferro, Sioux Census, September 1, 1834, OIA, St. Peter's Agency, Letters Received, NARG 75, the population of Waneta's people (the Pabaksa or Cut Head band) was given as 1,820. On subdivisions of the Yanktonai, see Hodge, *Handbook*, 2:990; Bray and Bray, eds., *Nicollet on the Plains*, 258.

stores, salted dogs. [Joannes] de Laet says from [Samuel] Champlain, speaking of a people on the River St. Lawrence, *Canes in deliciis habent & in festivitatibus mensis inferunt. . . . Ursos denique saginant aliquot annis, & in summis festivitatibus usurpant.*[20]

We were admonished by one of the traders, when we had finished eating, to gather all the bones into our dishes out of respect to a prejudice of the Indians: he was unable to assign upon what the prejudice is founded. Lawson relates that the Indians in the upper part of North Carolina carefully burnt the bones left from a repast, believing that if they did not the game would desert the country.[21] None of our entertainers partook with us: I do not believe it is customary for the Indian to eat with his guest, but he considers the food he presents as belonging exclusively to the one who enjoys his hospitality.

THURSDAY, JULY 24, 1823. Some rain in the morning; clear in the afternoon. About 5 P.M. ten warriors came within the pickets sent by Wanoton to perform for us the dance of the Brave. The Chief's son, a lad of about 12 years, came with them. He had on a bulky head dress of war-Eagle feathers precisely like that worn by Poulaho, king of the Friendly Islands, of which a drawing is given in [James] Cook's Voyages. The others had very little ornament. Wanoton made apology for the want of style in the exhibition; that the best dancers were employed in the chace & that this being the roving season, their finest dresses were not with them. Still, as the first I had seen, it was to me not devoid of interest.[22]

The performers stood in a ring, each with a fan in his hand, the wing of a bird, with which he beat time on his gun, arrow or some-

[20] Allen, ed., *History of the Expedition under . . . Lewis and Clark*, 2:269; Hakluyt, trans., *Virginia richly valued*, 58; Diaz del Castillo, *Historia Verdadera de la Conquista de la Nueva España*, 3:59, 4:65 (Madrid, 1795–96); De Laet, *Novvs Orbis seu Descriptionis Indiae Occidentalis*, 49 (Antwerp, 1633). There is considerable debate about where De Soto was, but most historians place Guaxule somewhere near the junction of present Georgia, Tennessee, and North Carolina. See Theodore H. Lewis, ed., "The Narrative of the Expedition of Hernando de Soto by the Gentleman of Elvas," in *Spanish Explorers in the Southern United States 1528–1543*, 177 (*Original Narratives of Early American History*—New York, 1907). The Latin passage means: "They are fond of dogs and in festivals they sacrifice them. In the same way . . . they fatten bears for several years and use them in the greatest festivities."

[21] Lawson, *New Voyage to Carolina*, 52. Carver attributed a similar custom to the Dakota in Parker, ed., *Carver Journals*, 103.

[22] The Dakota headdress was depicted in Keating, *Narrative*, 1:frontispiece. For Poulaho's headdress see James Cook and James King, *A Voyage to the Pacific Ocean . . . in the Years 1776, 1777, 1778, 1779, and 1780*, 1:plate 18 (3rd ed., London, 1785).

thing else that would emit sound. One supported a sort of standard; a piece of red cloth 6 inches wide & 8 or 10 ft. long having small black & also white feathers attached by their quills closely together to one edge as a fringe; the other edge was confined to a light pole 12 feet long. They commenced in a low tone, gradually raised it for a few minutes & concluded the singing with a shrill yell, when one would step into the area & recount his martial deeds. In the repetition of this the performance consisted, but there did not seem to be strict regard to rotation; it was varied only by dancing with little animation in the midst of some of the songs; they however kept time throughout by a sinking motion of the body, by genuflexion or by patting with the feet. In dancing they took no steps, nothing like *Chassez* [*chassé*] or *Rigodon*; the body was slightly bent & the feet were either raised together or *alterno terram quatiunt pede*. May the Graces & Nymphs forgive me! the transferring to these Savages what Horace said of them. The singing appeared to be painful effort; the mouth was kept constantly open, & the sound issued from the larynx. There were no words in their singing. They finished in about half an hour's time & after receiving a present of tobacco, they went away.[23]

Wanoton was present as a spectator, dressed & painted quite in chieftain style, but I recollect only the manly necklace of bear's claws & his enormous buffalo robe superbly buffed. Tufts of small feathers of different colors were quilted on the robe, probably the remnant of a fabric once general with the Aborigines of our territory & still common on the northeastern & Northwestern parts of this continent as well as in the South Sea Islands. I allude to what were called "feather mantles" & "feather blankets" by the first European visitors of North America & much admired by them. Among other writers, Captain [Bernard] Romans says the Chactaws [*Choctaw*] make them "by a process similar to that of our wig makers."

During our stay at Lac Travers I made the following Observations. . . . [*omitted*].

SATURDAY, JULY 26, 1823. At 8 A.M. We left the trading establishment to continue our journey: fired a salute when about to lose

[23] The Latin quotation means "they stamp on the earth one foot after another"; see Horace, *Odes*, book 1, ode 4, line 7. For a specimen of the music, see p. 171, above. On featherwork, below, see Bernard Romans, *A Concise Natural History of East and West Florida*, 85 (New York, 1775); Anne D. Harding and Patricia Bolling, *Bibliography of Articles and Papers on North American Indian Art*, 196 (Washington, D.C., [1938]). The editors are indebted to Alan R. Woolworth for the latter citation.

sight of it. Mr. Jeffries accompanies us as far as Pembina. We have also with us 4 Frenchmen or Canadians with their 6 carts returning to that place; they had brought thus far some Swiss emigrants from the British settlements [*Selkirk Colony*] to our territory. On the bluff above the Lake we saw several small tumuli: they are the last we shall see. I have made inquiry, but no one could tell me of the existence of any artificial mounds Northwest of this Lake: it is believed that there are none. As we are about to take leave of ancient remains & having omitted in the proper place, I will here mention that Mr. Schoolcraft heard report of "several antique mounds & circumvallations upon the bank of the St. Peter's" & the most remarkable were stated to be near the mouth of Carver's river. In page 45 [*287*], the most important antiquities we saw on the St. Peter's are noticed but there was no appearance of rampart so far as we observed.[24]

14 miles of travelling brought us to the M$\overset{2}{\text{u}}$sht$\overset{1}{\text{e}}$nch$\overset{4}{\text{a}}$ or aux Lièvres [*Mustinka*] River. Its waters are almost stagnant & much lower than usual; its bed is 15 yards wide; 20 leagues above the place we crossed, it issues from a small lake in a Northeastern direction, & runs into Swan [*Bois de Sioux*] River just after it commences out of Lake Travers. We stopped to dine on the banks of the Mushtencha. Our repast consisted of Pemican alone, which is jerked buffalo meat pounded until it resembles oakum. Generally, melted fat of the animal is poured over it, sometimes the marrow extracted by boiling the bones, often berries are mixed with it, but salt never, because the dried meat has naturally a saline taste. Chokecherries pounded stone & all were incorporated in this. I found it agreeable, though uncooked & without bread. In this country it is never cooked.[25]

We frequently see buffalo bones but not so thickly strewd as between the two Lakes [*Lac qui Parle and Big Stone*] of the St. Peter's. Occassionally buffalo roads lead over the prairie, well beaten & about a foot wide. Early in the afternoon we saw two buffalo bulls; Rainville & Mr. Jeffries immediately gave chace & turned them

[24] Winchell, *Aborigines*, 302–307, described several groups of mounds on the east side of Lake Traverse; see also Lloyd A. Wilford, *Burial Mounds of the Red River Headwaters*, 1, 24 (St. Paul, 1970). Colhoun was wrong in saying there were no mounds northwest of Lake Traverse; see, for example, Elden Johnson, *The Arvilla Complex*, 3, 6 (St. Paul, 1973). On the Minnesota River mounds, see Schoolcraft, *Narrative Journal*, 312 (1821).

[25] Swan Creek was a name applied to the Bois de Sioux on many early maps; see, for example, Lewis and Clark's map in Wheat, *Mapping the Transmississippi West*, 2: facing p. 57; and Arrowsmith's map in Warkentin and Ruggles, eds., *Manitoba Historical Atlas*, 141.

towards the party. The "hope deferred" ever since we left Great Swan Lake of seeing the game which was to furnish that enumerated rural pleasure, *dapes inemtas*;[26] of beholding the strange animal described as "resembling in some respect a Lion, in other the Camels, Horses, Oxen, Sheepe or Goats"* made the cry "buffalo!" supplant in me every previous thought and sensation.

I viewed the chace with intense interest; my imagination exaggerating all the chances of escape really in favor of the animals & creating many others. At last, I fancied that one of them with unwasted strength was leaving far behind the jaded horse of his pursuer. Sensible to nothing but the fear of his passing us & wishing to intercept him, I urged my horse to full speed. I soon arrived within a few paces of him & discharged my piece; but the poor animal was too far exhausted with fatigue to discover either pain or rage at the wound inflicted. I then galloped a good distance to view the other, which had been shot down at the same time.

Hardly had I satisfied curiosity before some one remarked that my saddle-bags were lost. When I could realize the fact, I cursed my thoughtlessness & the whole species of the animal that had caused it. Those Saddle-bags contained all the Astronomical Instruments of the Expedition & they were essential to the attainment of its main object. Could I succeed by searching in the long grass over a space of several miles, it was not to be hoped that in falling they had escaped injury from the horse's heels: within many hundred miles of that spot it was not possible to procure other instruments or to have these repaired. Some idea of the depression I experienced may be conceived, when I state that the joy I felt at finding them has not been surpassed on any former occassion. In this instance, Burke himself could not have denied that pleasure is relief from pain.[27]

Proceeding to rejoin my companions, I passed an enormous buffalo that had been killed by one of the party merely for its tongue. I over took some Squaws carrying slices of buffalo meat to jerk. Their fellow laborers were dogs. Each dog had the ends of two poles crossed & faste[ne]d over the shoulders, with a piece of hide underneath to prevent chafing; the other extremities dragged on the ground. This sort of vehicle was confined to the animal by a string passed round the breast & another under the belly. Sticks fastened

[26] *Dapes inemptas* means "unpurchased banquet"; see Horace, *Epodes*, epode 2, line 48.

* Purchas' Pilgrimage. London 1617. p. 967. [*Colhoun's note.*]

[27] Edmund Burke, "A Philosophical Inquiry into the Origin of our Ideas of the Sublime and Beautiful," in *Works*, 1:82 (Boston, 1806).

by their ends to the poles kept them at a proper distance & supported the burthen. This seems to be the only mode of harnessing dogs practised by the Sioux, never using them in teams as the traders do. In this defective manner, in which the dogs act singly, 60 lbs. is thought to be a good load, & they perhaps travel with more ease on the dry grass than on the snow.[28]

I found the party encamped near Lac des Boeufs [*Buffalo Lake*], which is merely a continuation of L. Travers. This last is called P$\overset{2}{e}$t$\overset{2}{a}$s$\overset{1}{e}$nt$\overset{1}{a}$ or Otter-tail from its shape by the Sioux: the Canadians have named it Lac Travers from the circumstance of its being stretched Northeast & Southwest, a direction opposite to that of Big Stone Lake. I do not think it can exceed 18 [*26*] miles in length & 2 in width. Two or three wooded islands were observed in it; there may be more. The outlet is Swan [*Bois de Sioux*] River, which is like a mere trench in the prairie, having no valley whatever, for the high prairie terminates at the northern extremity of the Lake. It is termed here Riviere des Sioux, but Swan is the name well established on maps & ought to be preferred, because the other has already been applied to several rivers. Not being able to procure wood, we were obliged to cook supper with buffalo dung. Our company consists of 28 persons & we have 24 horses & mules. The carts with the tent fly give shelter in the night to the whole party. They are precisely the Charettes of the north bank of the St. Lawrence very rudely constructed & have wrapped round the wheels raw hide for tire. Today calm & clear. Distance 19 miles.[29]

SUNDAY, JULY 27, 1823. At 3:56 A.M. Mer[idian] Alt[itude] of Moon's U[pper] L[imb] 88° 2′ 00″, index error −4′ 7″. The Observation was not satisfactory; the artificial horizon was too much agitated by a high southerly wind. The body of Lac Travers bore from the camp S 19° W. Morning Amplitude E 45° N. Soon after we started, we were overtaken by Lieut. Martin Scott, who after returning his men to Fort Crawford had received permission to rejoin us: he takes command of our guard. He brought a Thermometer which had been

[28] On the Dakota use of dogs and the travois, see Royal B. Hassrick, *The Sioux: Life and Customs of a Warrior Society*, 156–159, plate 10 (Norman, Okla., 1964).

[29] Colhoun's confusion of Lake Traverse with Otter Tail Lake in present Otter Tail County, Minn., may have been due to the fact that the latter was then considered the source of the Red River; see also p. 319, below. On Red River carts, see Giraud, *Le Métis Canadien*, 754; W. G. Fonseca, "On the St. Paul Trail in the Sixties," in Historical and Scientific Society of Manitoba, *Transactions*, no. 56, p. 2 (January, 1900). There is some controversy as to whether the origin of the carts was Scottish or French-Canadian.

left by us at Fort St. Anthony. Mr. Seymour has charge of it: he politely promises to communicate to me the daily temperature of the air in the shade, at Sunrise, Meridian & Sunset.

For a good part of the forenoon we travelled parellel to & not far from Swan River for some distance, having on our right a ridge 30 or 40 feet high, which as we advanced inclined to the Northeast & finally turned abruptly off. The Sioux call Swan River K$\overset{2}{\breve{a}}$nt$\overset{2}{\breve{o}}$k$\overset{2}{\breve{o}}$ from a thicket of Plum bushes at its commencement. Its bed, about the size of that of the Mushtencha, has now no running water & in some places is perfectly dry. We passed in sight of the Nid du Tonnere on the other [*west*] side of the river. It is an elevation of the prairie & has at its base a number of salt ponds. The French is the interpretation of its Indian name. Throughout the forenoon the "Islands" or patches of woods [*known as Bois des Sioux*] that marked the course of Psé or Wild Rice River could be seen in the West. It rises near Polecat Lake & runs into Red River, say 30 miles from our camp.[30]

Stopped for a short time at a lodge pitched by several Indian families [*of Waneta's Yanktonai*] in company for the purpose of hunting the buffalo & preparing store of the meat & skins. We regaled us with some delicious boiled flesh of a buffalo cow. Their manner of jerking the meat was to cut it into broad thin slices, which they laid over poles so as to hang down exposed to the sun. 2 days' sunning dry it sufficiently.

Some squaws were occupied scraping hides. They first stretched the skin while green by driving stakes through its margin into the ground; then with pieces of bone an inch wide & sharpened to an edge, they removed the softer portion of the flesh side &, with an instrument of iron like the bit of a plane, the hair from the outside. If the operation proceed no further it is parchment, but for clothing or moccassins the skin is afterwards worked with the hands in the brains of the animal. Smoking the dressed skin will qualify it better for exposure to moisture but destroys its beautiful soft white. A shirt & leggings of unsmoked skins, especially of deer, with broad pieces of the edge left without the seam & cut into fringe really compose a very handsome dress.

[30] Nid du Tonnere or Thunder Nest was located southwest of Hankinson, N. Dak.; see Morris, *Historical Stories*, 58. Nicollet, "Hydrographical Basin," called it Lightnings Nest. Salt springs and lakes were abundant along the Wild Rice River; see N[ewton] H. Winchell, *Report Concerning the Salt Spring Lands*, 10–13 (St. Paul, 1874). The source of the Wild Rice River is not in Polecat or Makah (Tewaukon) Lake, but the river does run through it. The mouth of the Wild Rice River is at Wild Rice, N. Dak.

Skins may be dressed equally well with soap suds. Lawson says that "young Indian corn, beaten to a pulp, will effect the same as the brains."* He also informs us that the Indians tanned with bark sometimes.† In the account of [William E.] Parry's Second voyage, we are told that the Esquimaux [*Eskimo*] "held up skins & small narrow strips of well tanned leather to exchange." And in same account p. 441 [*538*] it is said, that the Esquimaux dressed hides by steeping them in urine. What Bernal Diaz says with regard to this matter in Cap[itulo] 92, when describing the City of Mexico I give in his own language. *Tambien ve[n]dian canoas llenas de hienda de hombres que tenian en los esteros cerca de la plaça, y esto era para hazer ò para curtír cueros que sin ella dezian, que no se hazian buenos.*[32]

At this lodge we again saw Wanoton. In compliance with our request, he accompanied Messrs. Beltrami, Jeffries, Rainville & myself to show the manner of hunting buffalo with the arrow. He rode a very good horse &, according to the custom of the country, the long halter trailed on the ground for the greater facility of taking the animal when suffered to run at large. We passed solitary bulls scattered over the prairie, but as they are now lean, this being the rutting season, we did not regard them. Many of them seemed to be aware of the immunity they enjoy at this season & were undisturbed at our approach; others struck up a long gallop frequently shifting the leading leg. Seeing them banished far from their loves reminded me of that line in the Georgics, *Victus abit, longeque ignotis exsulat oris.*[33]

It was not long before we came in sight of a "band" which was known to be one of cows, because it was subdivided into close squads. They permitted us to get very near. We then went at full speed into the midst of them to single out the fattest. In running, they left behind a strong smell of musk & their feet made the grass crackle as if on fire. Wanoton killed them by shooting an arrow into

* New Voyage to N. Carolina. p. 209 [*Colhoun's note.*]*[31]

*[31] Lawson, *New Voyage to Carolina*, 209.

† idem idem [*Colhoun's note.*]

[32] William E. Parry, *Journal of a Second Voyage for the Discovery of a North-West Passage*, 14, 538 (London, 1824); Diaz del Castillo, *Historia Verdadera*, 2:107. The Spanish translates: "also they sold boats filled with human ordure in the inlet near the marketplace, and this was for use in tanning leather—without which, they said, good leather could not be made."

[33] See Virgil, *Georgics*, book 3, line 225. The passage, which refers to domestic bulls, translates: "The conquered one departs and lives in exile far away in unknown regions."

the flank, which, though it might not penetrate half its length, would be buried by the motion of the animal in running, notches being made in the arrow-head for that purpose. Mr. Beltrami gave this account when we met at supper, but it was in the presence of Mr. Jeffries & all the party & was admitted as a circumstance well known.

I did not stop to witness the Indian's feats but turned off to attempt something of myself, & with my rifle soon succeeded in obtaining some excellent veal. By the time that I alighted, not a single buffalo was to be seen nor a human being. Mr. Jeffries however came up before long & soon after an Indian. The latter proposed to butcher for me on condition that the hide should be given him. I gladly accepted the offer. My companion & I took pieces of the flesh, tied them behind our saddles & sat out to rejoin the party. We rode through a hard rain [a] good part of the distance & found the camp already formed in an "Island of Wood" called Bois des Sioux, on the bank of Swan River.

Wanoton used the common Sioux bow, which does not exceed 4 feet in length; the arrows were proportional. However, during our interview with Wabeshaw, the old chief was busily rasping to form a bow that must have been 5 or 6 feet long; whether it was to continue of that length or to be shortened, I know not. We have heard so often of these bows driving arrows through a buffalo that perhaps we must believe it, tho' I confess they appear to me too short to possess that power. I would be less incredulous if this were stated of the bows used by the Florida Indians, which Garcilaso de la Vega says were always of the length of the person who carried them. He makes frequent mention of the prodigious force of their bows & records instances which show that the Southern Indians had wonderful skill & vigor in the use of the weapon. In the authentic paintings of John With [*White*], who was sent in 1585 to Virginia by Queen Elizabeth to execute drawings, the Indians of that country were represented as having bows rather longer than themselves. Engravings from them were first made in 1590 for the Latin work of Theodore de Bry.[34]

Rainville did not rejoin us after the hunt, but went back. Mr. K.,

[34] On Sioux bows, see Hassrick, *The Sioux*, 198. Colhoun's references are to: Vega, *La Florida del Inca*, 7; Theodor de Bry, *Admiranda Narratio Fida Tamen, de Commodis et Incolarvm Ritibvs Virginiae*, plate 3 (Frankfurt, Germany, 1590). On White, see Randolph G. Adams, "An Effort to Identify John White," in *American Historical Review*, 41:87–91 (October, 1935).

who conversed with him most, speaks highly of his good sense. My good opinion of him is somewhat abated by a strange story he told me & which he recounted to several others of the party. I give it as a specimen of the tales of the country. He said that 16 or 18 years ago, when he was about 15, he shot a flying serpent at some small lakes near the St. Peter's two miles above the mouth of the Terre Bleue. It flew at some elevation above the ground to attack him making a hissing noise. Its length was between 7 & 8 feet; the head very round; the colors were blk. white & yellow, besides a deep green on the belly, & red on the throat & on the lower jaw. There was a membrane on each side about the width of the hand at its broadest part, & tapering: this could be folded at pleasure. He believes it to have been a land serpent. A brother of [Augustin] Ro[c]que was with him at the time; Mr. [Murdoch] Cameron, a trader, & several other persons saw it after it was killed. He said moreover that 20 years ago such a one was seen on Cannon R. by two Indians & a Squaw. Mr. Snelling has heard a trader say that he had killed three such at the Portage between Wisconsan & Fox rivers. So much for *les Serpens Volants.*[35]

This is not the only fable of the ancients to be met with in the New World. The region on the confines of Geography is always peopled with strange monsters, often heard of, never seen. In North America that portion contained, besides others, Pigmies, Monoceles [*Cyclops*] & Welch Indians. The two first have been chaced by successive discoverers till they are no longer to be found, but the latter, it seems, have "a local habitation and a name." In the Evangelical Magazine for January of this year [*1824*] there is a letter from the Rev. Epaphras Chapman, one of the U[nited] F[oreign] Missionary Society among the Osages, giving a description of the Navehoes [*Navaho*], a people unlike all other Indians & inhabiting the western aspect of the Rocky Mountains, 6 days' journey Northwest of Santa Fe. From the reciprocity of letters in the Spanish language, I take them to be the Nabijos of the Spaniards, a nation considerably advanced in the arts. Some are anxious to make them

[35] Renville may have been repeating the folk tale of the "hoop snake" or that of the flying serpent. See Breckenridge, *Reptiles and Amphibians*, 4; John S. Fox, ed., "Narrative of the Travels and Adventures of a Merchant Voyageur in the Savage Territories of Northern America," in *Michigan Pioneer and Historical Collections*, 37:547 (Lansing, Mich., 1909–10). Murdoch Cameron was a Scotsman associated with Robert Dickson in the fur trade. His post was near Lac qui Parle on the Minnesota River before his death in 1811. See Coues, ed., *Pike*, 1:66; Lavender, *Fist in the Wilderness*, 435.

the descendants of Madoc ap Owen Gwynedd & his followers. There has been a long-standing report that the Mandans speak the Welch language. But it is absurd; the thing has been pushed by the Welch, proverbially pertinacious geneologists. Forenoon fair; wind SE; afternoon rain; wind SW. Distance 21 miles.[36]

MONDAY, JULY 28, 1823. Proceeded 8 miles and forded Red River, where it is 25 yards wide about 5 miles by land below the mouth of Swan River. In crossing the cart containing all our dried buffalo meat upset & its contents fell into the water. The accident detained us for some time, for it was necessary to expose to the sun the meat that had been wet. From where we crossed, Otter-tail Lake, the source of Red River, bears northeasterly distant 70 or 80 miles. One of our Canadians who has seen it says that it is about 24 [*9*] miles long from North to South & 4 1/2 [*3*] wide. Mr. Jeffries describes the country lying in that direction as being full of small lakes & "Islands of Woods."

A Bald Eagle flew over our heads & alighted on her nest in our sight.[37] Travelled over level prairie: no trees to be seen except a strip of woods along Red River & the forest on the Montagnes des Feuilles [*Leaf Mountains*] a great distance to the Northeastward; the base of which range, that is, their southern [*western*] extreme, is washed by the [*Otter Tail*] River. We frequently see wolves [*coyotes*], & [the] horizon is occupied sometimes for several miles by a single "band" of buffalo. Bulls are sprinkled over the plain; they often advance within musket shot to look at us. Some of the party attribute this apparent boldness to the long hair hanging over their eyes & obstructing their vision, so as to hinder them from discovering, unless very near, that the moving crowd is not a band of cows. Others suppose them to have a degree of fearlessness in the rutting season.

[36] For reports of pygmies and monsters in the West, see, for example, Charlevoix, *Histoire*, 1:24–31. Monoceles (from *monos*, Greek for "one," and *oculus*, Latin for "eye") is an apparent reference to the Cyclops or mythical one-eyed giant, according to Professor George Rochefort, University of Minnesota Department of Classics, in a statement to the editors. For a survey of the extensive literature on the Welsh Indian myth, see Silverberg, *Mound Builders*, 84; David Williams, "John Evans' Strange Journey," in *American Historical Review*, 54:277–295, 508–529 (January, April, 1949). The quotation is from William Shakespeare, *A Midsummer Night's Dream*, act 5, scene 1, line 17. Chapman's letter appeared in *Evangelical Magazine and Missionary Chronicle*, new series 2:28 (January, 1824). Madoc ap Owen Gwynnedd was a 12th-century Welsh prince whose mythical colonizing expedition to America was first related in 1583 and taken seriously into the 20th century.

[37] The bald eagle (*Haliaeetus leucocephalus* Linnaeus) was formerly a common summer resident of this area; see Roberts, *Birds of Minnesota*, 1:335–340.

Early in the afternoon two of the party besides myself went in pursuit of a large herd of Elk. By creeping on our hands & knees a quarter of a mile leading our horses, we were enabled to approach within 80 yards. We then fired & one of the herd, a female, fell. As had been previously agreed, having the best horse & a pair of pistols, I mounted & chaced for more than a mile. I got up with them in half that distance, but my horse was so much afraid of them that the severest spurring did not urge him near enough: I flashed one pistol & discharged the other without effect. In the pursuit those in the rear repeatedly stopped to look at me. When in herds, it is not difficult to overtake them; it is otherwise when they are alone; however, they are said to be short-winded. The Elk is called in this country the Red Deer; the Virginia [*white-tailed*] Deer, the species common to the Southern States, is here termed the Jumping Deer. This last kind is said never to be found North of Lake Travers.[38] It is on account of creeping through the grass, so often to be done, that every body in this country has a leather cover for his piece, which must be dragged along: the cover protects the gun from the dew & secures the hunter from the danger of its being accidentally cocked.

We were occupied until sunset cutting up the carcase, & it was late in the night before we reached the camp on the bank of Red River, or rather somewhat removed without the skirt of woods lining the river bank. During our absence from the main body a strong war party of the Gens des Feuilles had conducted [themselves] in a very insolent manner towards our fellow travellers, demanding tobacco & whiskey, ordering them to go another way that the buffalo might not be driven off &c. After amusing them more than an hour, hoping myself & companions would come up, the Major left them. The Indians, awed by his firmness, committed no violence, though at first they discovered disposition to oppose & one of them cocked his gun.[39]

We made our supper of the spoils of the hunt, which we had brought fastened to our saddles. We found the elk-meat, though inferior to that of the buffalo, a lighter colored & better kind of

[38] The species hunted was the American elk (*Cervus canadensis* Erxleben), often compared to the European red deer. The Virginia or white-tailed deer is *Cervus virginianus* Boddart, whose range has extended farther north since Colhoun's time. See C. L. Herrick, *Mammals of Minnesota*, 278–282 (Geological and Natural History Survey of Minnesota, *Bulletins*, no. 7—Minneapolis, 1892); Harvey L. Gunderson and James R. Beer, *The Mammals of Minnesota*, 171–176 (Minnesota Museum of Natural History, *Occasional Papers*, no. 6—Minneapolis, 1953).

[39] On the confusing *Gens des Feuilles* and this incident, see Chapter 4, note 43.

venison; the chief objection to it was the too great taste of tallow. The udder was delicious, perhaps the more because our meal had been postponed & the appetite consequently increased. It was cooked in our usual way by inclining to the fire the sharpened stick thrust through it & stuck into the ground. Meals that I have ate with most zest have been those prepared in this rude manner, no doubt borrowing much from attendant circumstances. Cookery as an art is built up of the inventions of Civilization aiding languid appetite or ministering to the depraved palates of epicures. Among Savage nations all culinary improvements doubtless proceed from necessity in the first instance: to render less noxious or less unpleasant some kinds of food scarcity has reduced them to, or as a mean[s] to increase the quantity. Clear day: forenoon wind NW, afternoon SWd. Air at sunrise 62°, at Meridian 75°. Distance 22 miles.

TUESDAY, JULY 29, 1823. Apprehensive from the behaviour of the war party that they would steal our horses if not attack us before day, we left the camp at midnight & proceeded on our tour. After travelling 12 miles we stopped to breakfast on river bank. At 8 miles beyond, the Pse [*Wild Rice*] River comes in from the other [*west*] side. Where we encamped the [Red] River is 20 yards wide & has a current of about 1/2 knot an hour: the banks very boggy & the water thickened with particles of the rich light-blue clay through which it flows. No valley whatever to the river: on its banks, a flourishing growth of oak, elm, cottonwood, aspen &c. but no sugar-maple, walnut, hickory or beech. Travelled through flat rich prairie from one bend of the [Red] River to another. No granitic masses since the first day we left Lake Travers.

I repeatedly observed buffalo wallowing, throwing up the dust so as at a great distance to resemble the spouting of a whale. I killed a bull today that on counting the rugae on the horns proved to be 26 yrs. old; 4 rugae were allowed for the first year: it is probable that the domestic cattle never attain so great age. It is our practice to drive the bulls ahead of the party & kill them where we are to pass, so that there is little detention, especially as we take only the tongue & liver, rarely the marrow bones. We have not been able to procure a single cow, though in the forenoon I chased one in a band till my horse was tired & all my balls expended without wounding her sufficiently to disable her.

In this country a horse is valued in reference to his capacity for "running buffalo." If pushed, a buffalo soon tires down, otherwise he will run a long time. The hunter keeps within a few paces on the starboard quarter of the animal & aims to pass his ball from about the middle of the side to the heart or lungs. Should the discharge be ineffectual he loads while running: the powder is poured between the thumb & forefinger into the hand, clenched to form a cavity; the hand is emptied, resting the little finger & the lower part of the hand upon the muzzle of the gun: the ball is dropped from the mouth: no wadding, in general, & that is the reason the buffalo appears to be so hard to kill. In this kind of hunt, it is evident that the rifle cannot be used to advantage & therefore it is a species of firearm not to be seen in this country. The danger in running buffalo in herd is that by advancing too much on flank, a part may turn short & run over the pursuer, & if one were to fall from his horse after having wounded a buffalo, the enraged animal would be apt to gore. But I must think that the difficulty of killing the buffalo & the danger to be apprehended from him are greatly exaggerated. It is true that in one place, at least, he appears to be invulnerable: Lt. Scott fired a musket at the head of one within ten paces, but the ball did not penetrate. Buffalo have [a] larger frame than domestic cattle & though uncouth in the fore parts, they are handsomely formed in the hinder.

At Lac Travers it was estimated that the cows generally furnish from 250 to 300 wt. of meat, not counting the head & some other parts. Of the flesh, that upon the bones forming the hump is most esteemed. I thought the buffalo meat superior to any beef I have ever eaten, excelling even that of the wild cattle of the Pampas of Buenos Ayres; it has not the least taste of tallow. Salted tongues are sent in considerable quantities to New Orleans & are excellent.[40] Eight bones are enumerated as marrow bones. The flesh is chopped off them & they are thrown on the fire: the marrow, roasted in that manner, resembles in color & in consistence a custard & is even richer. It is eaten out of the bone with a stick splintered at the end & requires no accompaniament. I am unable to conjecture how much the bones yield singly or collectively, but the marrow of onc thigh-bone affords a sufficient meal to a hearty man.

Du Pratz is of [the] opinion that the flesh of the bulls is more delicate than that of the cows: of course he speaks in reference to the

[40] The weight of buffalo varied considerably; up to 800 pounds of meat could be taken from one animal. The marketing of salted tongue in New Orleans and St. Louis is well documented. See Frank G. Roe, *The North American Buffalo: A Critical Study of the Species in Its Wild State*, 58, 886 (Toronto, 1951).

animal being in good condition. It has already been said that they are now lean, & consequently it is needless to resort to his remedy against rankness of flavour; *aussi-tôt que la bête est morte, lui couper les suites, comme on fait aux Cerfs & aux Sangliers*, for that cannot make the flesh more tender. The Indians always prefer the flesh of the cows & they have probably done so from time immemorial & kill them alone, therefore the diminution of the species ought to have assigned for it a cause of as recent date as the alleged decay of numbers.[41]

All the buffalo we have seen were of a uniform dun color, lighter now because the animal is sunburnt & not fat. Mackensie [*Alexander Mackenzie*] makes frequent mention of small "white buffaloe," which the Indians told him occupied the Rocky Mountains while he was in Latitude say from 60° to 62° N. He probably labored under misapprehension for Lewis & Clark inform us that the Indians designate by that name the Mountain Sheep. In this country, we have been told the buffalo is sometimes spotted & has variegated horns; which if the fact we must perhaps attribute it to the reported practice of the Indians of castrating the male calves & letting them go, believing that it will improve the animal. De Laet says from [Francisco López de] Gomara that *fere nigri sunt, & raro albis quibusdam maculis distincti*, speaking of the animal west of the Rocky Mountains. A gentleman of the Hudson's Bay Company confirmed to us this account. Rainville informed me that one of the color of a beaver was killed last spring on the Missouri: the beaver of that river is, I believe, of a sort of sorrel color. The Missouri Fur Co. gave $200 for its hide. Of course according to valuation of their goods. Mr. [Kenneth?] McKensie told Mr. Snelling of the same animal.[42]

With regard to the primitive region of the Buffalo, Anthonie Park-

[41] Du Pratz, *Histoire*, 2:68, did not recommend the flesh of bulls, as Colhoun says. The passage translates, "As soon as the beast is dead, cut off the testicles as one does with stags and wild boars."

[42] Mackenzie, *Voyages from Montreal*, 40; Allen, ed., *History of the Expedition under . . . Lewis and Clark*, 2:325. As Colhoun surmised, Mackenzie's white buffalo were probably mountain sheep. White and pied buffalo were albinos or crosses with domestic cattle. Spots were not correlated with castration, though frequent claims were made that the Indians castrated buffalo to increase their size. The rare "beaver robe" bison skins were another variation from the norm. See Roe, *North American Buffalo*, 62–65, 715–728, 856. For the quotation see Laet, *Novus Orbis*, 303; the Latin translates, "They are nearly black, and rarely have white in certain separate spots." Gomara's book was originally published as *Primera y segunda parte dela historia general de las Indias* (Saragossa, 1553). On the Missouri Fur Company, see Hiram M. Chittenden, *The American Fur Trade of the Far West*, 1:138–154 (New York, 1902).

hurst, writing in 1578 to Hakluyt concerning Newfoundland, informs him that "there are mightie beastes like to Camels in greatnesse, & their feet cloven, I did see them farre off not able to discerne them perfectly, but their steps shewed that their feete were cloven, & bigger than the feete of Camels. I suppose them to be a kind of Buffes which I read to bee in the countreys adiacent, & very many in the firme land." Again in the account of Sir Humfrey Gilbert's voyage, which commenced in 1583, mention is made of "buttolfes or a beast it seemeth by the tract & foote very large in maner of an oxe." But I would be slow to believe that the Buffalo ever existed on that Island [*Newfoundland*]. Nor, so far as I have been able to discover, has the animal been seen east of Hudson's River & Lake Champlain, though with the exception of that region & of narrow strips of coast on the Atlantic & on the Gulf of Mexico that were swampy or had low thick woods, he was found perhaps throughout the present limits of our territory.[43]

With respect to those excepted parts the negative testimony I possess is voluminous; I believe that I have read nearly all the accounts written of the first visits to our coast. [William] Hubbard in his History, written to be sure subsequent to 1684, does not enumerate the Buffalo among the animals of New England. Thomas Morton, one of the early settlers of that country, says the Indians "have also made description of great heards of well growne beasts, that live about the parts of this Lake" Erocoise, as he terms Lake Ontario, "such as the Christian world (untill this discovery) hath not bin made acquainted with. These beasts are of the bigness of a Cowe, their flesh being very good foode, their hides good lether, their fleeces very usefull, being a kinde of wolle, as fine almost as the wolle of the Beaver, & the Salvages doe make garments thereof. It is tenne yeares since first the relation of these things came to the eares of the English." His "New English Canaan" was published in 1637: the quotation is introduced mainly to show that the fineness of the Buffalo wool was known to Europeans at least as far back as 6 or 7 years after the landing of the Pilgrims.[44]

[43] Parkhurst, "A letter . . . conteining a report of the true state and commodities of New found land," and Gilbert, "A report of the voyage and successe thereof, attempted in the yeere of our Lord, 1583," in Hakluyt, *Principall Navigations*, 676, 689. Although Colhoun's limited selection of travel accounts here and below sometimes led him to make incorrect inferences, his general delineation of the buffalo range was accurate. See Roe, *North American Buffalo*, 204–333.

[44] William Hubbard, *A General History of New England, from the Discovery to MDCLXXX*, 25 (Cambridge, Mass., 1815); Thomas Morton, *New English Canaan*, 98 (Amsterdam, 1637).

We are told that Captains Amadas & Barlowe in 1584 traded on the coast of Virginia for "Chammoys, *Buffe*, & Deere skinnes," but it appears to have been not till 1613 that the Colonists of that country discovered "a slow kind of cattle, as bigge as Kine." Lawson tells us under date of 1709 that the Toteros [*Tutelos*], living in the "Westward Mountains" of North Carolina, had "great plenty of Buffeloes, Elks, &c., but that the Buffelo seldom appears amongst the English Inhabitants:" some had been killed "on the Hilly Part of Cape-Fair [*Cape Fear*]-River [N. Car.]," & that two were killed one year at "Appamaticks [*Appomattox R.*] in Virginia." My Grandfather & his three brothers, who settled Abbeville District, South Carolina, in 1756, found the Buffalo in that country.[45]

I have not been able to discover that this animal has been seen on any part of the Atlantic coast; I do not believe that he ever frequented it, or even approached nearer to it than 60 or 80 miles. De Soto's party traversed East Florida, Georgia, Alabama, Mississippi, Arkansas Territory & Louisiana in 1539–43, but saw no Buffalo; they were told the animal was North of them; however, they often met with buffalo hides, particularly when west of the Mississippi. Yet Bernard Romans, who wrote in 1774, speaks of the Buffalo as a benefit of nature bestowed on Florida. Du Pratz, who published in 1758, says that he is unable to penetrate to Lower Louisiana on account of the thick woods & besides that the long grass he is fond of grows only in the meadows of the high lands. Yet on the other hand, Alvar Nuñez [Cabeza de Vaca] about 1535 found Buffalo not far from the coast of the Gulf of Mexico, probably near the Bay of St. Bernard [La.], where Joutel saw vast herds 150 years afterwards.[46]

It is only at that Bay or near to it that I can trace the Buffalo perhaps to the seacoast, & that is also the lowest Latitude he seems to me to have arrived at on this side [of] the Rocky Mountains. I think it highly probable that he ranged on the western side to quite as low a Latitude. De Laet says on the authority of [Antonio de] Herrera [y Tordesillas], *juxta Yaquimi fluminis* [Yaqui R., Sonora, Mex.] *ripas tauri vaccaeque & praegrandes cervi pascuntur.* He soon after states that the Yaquimi is said to be in Cinaloa, which province Martin Perez, he says in the same Chap[t]er, estimated to be 300 leagues

[45] "The first voyage made to the coastes of America," in Hakluyt, *Principall Navigations*, 730; Sir Samuell Argoll, "A Letter . . . touching his Voyage to Virginia," in Samuel Purchas, *Pvrchas his Pilgrimes*, 4:1765 (London, 1625); Lawson, *New Voyage to Carolina*, 47, 48, 115. Colhoun paraphrased Lawson's text.

[46] Hakluyt, trans., *Virginia richly valued*, 107, 112, 113; Romans, *Concise Natural History*, 174; Du Pratz, *Histoire*, 2:67; Cabeza de Vaca, *Navfragios*, 22; Joutel, *Journal Historique*, 52.

from the City of Mexico. He proceeds to say that [Nuño de] Guzman in 1532 (the year in which Buffalo was first known to Europeans) having marched 30 leagues from the river Tamochala [*Sinaloa R., Sinaloa, Mex.*] entered Cinaloa, then 30 leagues northwardly to a River, thence he travelled in 7 days to the Yaquimi. In one of the maps appended to his work, the River Tamochala is laid down in about 26° 35′ N. The Yaquimi may be that named in Tanner's map Hiaqui & which enters the Gulf of California between 27° & 28° N. Lat. Perhaps, however, it is the Rio Gila.[47]

Though we may not be able to fix the southern limit of the Buffalo region on the Pacific so clearly as on the Atlantic side of North America, it can be easily shown that the animal existed in abundance on the western side of the Rocky Mountains: vide de Laet Lib. 6, Cap. 17, which from Gomara, also Purchas' Pilgrimage p. 853 [778]. But in the middle of last century, Father [Miguèl] Venegas does not enumerate the Buffalo among the animals of California. At the time of Lewis & Clark's Expedition he did not exist on the west side of the Rocky Mountains, nor according to the reports of the Indians does he seem then to have roamed above the Falls of the Missouri [*at Great Falls, Mont.*]. [Daniel W.] Harmon does not name him among the animals of New Caledonia, a country of indefinite extent lying between the Pacific Ocean, the Rocky Mountains, our Possessions & those of Russia. Mackensie [*Alexander Mackenzie*] says expressly that neither the Buffalo nor Wolf are found in that country. Yet it is said they are now abundant about Columbia R., & if I am not misinformed, there is tradition in that country that shortly before the visit of our enterprising countrymen named above destructive fires drove the Buffalo this side of the Rocky Mountains.[48]

The animal did not exist in that immense region East of Lake Winipic [*Winnipeg*] & North of the Great Lakes. But West of Lake

[47] Laet, *Novvs Orbis*, 285–287; the Latin translates, "Near the banks of the river Yaquimi bulls and cows and huge stags graze." Herrera y Tordesillas' book was *Historia General de los Hechos de los Castellanos en las Islas i Tierra Firme del Mar Oceano* (Madrid, 1601–15). Martín Perez was a Jesuit missionary in Sinaloa, Mexico, and Guzmán was the governor of Pánuco and New Galicia. The boundaries of Sinaloa province were at that time more northerly than those of the present state and took in much of present Sonora. See also Tanner, "Map of North America," southwest sheet, in *New American Atlas*. The Rio Gila is in present Arizona.

[48] Laet, *Novvs Orbis*, 303; Purchas, *Pilgrimage*, 778 (1614); Venegas, *Noticia de la California*, 1:36–46 (Madrid, 1757); Allen, ed., *History of the Expedition under . . . Lewis and Clark*, 1:395; Harmon, *A Journal of Voyages and Travels in the Interiour of North America*, 190 (Andover, Mass., 1820); Mackenzie, *Voyages from Montreal*, cxxvii.

Winipic they ranged all over the Prairies, the northern Limit of which I take to be about 62° N. Lat., nor do they reach that high except at the eastern base of the Rocky Mountains, whence they run obliquely to the southern extreme of Lake Winipic, which is in little more than 50°. At present the Buffalo is not found east of the Mississippi & south of the St. Lawrence. But that subtraction from his roamings, great as it is, cannot be supposed to have made him feel confinement or to have sensibly diminished his means of subsistence; perhaps great diminution of his species may be doubted. When it shall be excessive & utter, it will be by the operation of a greater cause than exclusive slaughter of the females by Indian hunters. Civilization in its steady, deploying march destroys the larger gregarious animals, even exterminates venatic man unless he change his mode of life. If the Deer were more social in his habits, that interesting tenant of our forest would have been long since driven to the asylum of the buffalo, the elk & the beaver. Calm & hazy. Air 56, 88, 71. Distance 33 miles.

Appendix 1
Documents Relating to the 1817 Expedition

1. *Long to Brigadier General Thomas A. Smith, commander, Ninth Military Dept., St. Louis, Mo., May (n.d.), 1817.*[1]

DR. GENL.

I think I shall be able to procure a Skiff that will answer my purpose, and should be glad if you would allow two or three of the soldiers to come from the Garrison, and take the boat to Bellefontaine [Mo.], as I should like to meander the course of the [Mississippi] river between this place & that. I shall not be able to leave this place till monday.

Have seen your brother, & shown him the mineral.[2] But have said nothing more upon the subject.

Yours sincerely & respectfully
S. H. LONG

2. *Smith to Long, Belle Fontaine, Mo., May 31, 1817.*[3]

SIR,

You will proceed forthwith on your Tour up the Mississippi. You

[1] Smith Papers, joint Western Historical Manuscripts Collection-State Historical Society Manuscripts, University of Missouri Library, Columbia. Used with permission. Copy in MHS.

[2] Smith's brother was the famous duelist and mining speculator, John Smith T. See "Missouriana," in *Missouri Historical Review*, 25:634n, 32:228n (July, 1931, January, 1938). The "mineral" may have related to a "supposed Silver-mine" which Long was searching for; see Long to Brig. Gen. Joseph G. Swift, October 15, 1817, OCE, Miscellaneous Papers, Fortifications (Series A), NARG 77. See also p. 330, below.

[3] Copy in Long's hand in GAO, Second Auditor, Account No. 1433, NARG 217. Another copy in the Smith Papers varies in minor matters of spelling and punctuation and contains two significantly different readings: Under the sixth point, the first

will be governed by the inclosed Instructions.

I am, Sir, with high respect Yr. obt. Sert.
(Signed) T. A. SMITH
Brigr. General Commanding

INSTRUCTIONS FOR MAJ. LONG TOPL. ENGINEER

1st. A correct Chart of the Mississippi, shewing all situations that would be advantagious as Mily. Positions, as far as Fort Crawford.

2nd. A Chart of the Ouisconsin as far as the Portage between that & Fox River of the Lake [*Michigan*], with a particular description of the Portage, and the adjacent Country. Obtain the best information in your power, how far the Wisconsin can be navigated with Mackinaw boats above the Portage. Ascertain the general course of the river. A description of Fox River to Green Bay, depth of water, navigation, with such other information generally as can be advantagious in a military point of view.

3rd. Correct Plans of the Posts on the Mississippi noticing particularly the manner in which the works have been constructed, the number of Troops they are calculated to contain, the defects in the plans (if any) and the probable advantage or necessity of keeping them garrisoned, the country for some miles around each Post must be examined and particularly described.

4th. Ascertain the distance from Fort Armstrong to Fort Clark and obtain the best information generally in your power of the country East of the Mississippi, and South of the Ouisconsin, to the Illinois that it may be connected with your former researches.[4]

5th. You will take the Latitude of each Military Post.

6th. Ascertain the situation of the different Indian Towns & the numbers of the different Tribes, the best season of the year for a Military Force to march through the country, and generally a Sketch of the character and dispositions of the Indian Tribes. Obtain the best information in your power, how far the Ioway [*Iowa*], Demoine [*Des Moines*] and Rock Rivers are navigable.

sentence ends "Indian Traders" rather than "Indian tribes"; the seventh point reads "Give a general description of the country on the Mississippi and Ouisconsin," omitting any mention of Fort Crawford.

[4] The reference is to Long's 1816 trip to Fort Clark; see p. 7, above. On Fort Armstrong, see pp. 98–102, above.

7th. Give a general description of the country directly on the Mississippi as far as Fort Crawford.

3. *Long to Smith, Prairie du Chien, Wis., June 24, 1817.*[5]

DR. GENL.

I arrived at this place yesterday; myself and the Boat's Crew all in good health. In regard to *Minerals* I find every thing in a quiet condition at Forts Edwards & Armstrong. I had no time or other opportunities to make an investigation in relation to the subject. But left every thing in a favourable train to commence opperations in conjunction with Lt. [*Capt. Joseph*] Calhoun on my return.

Intend to set out on my trip up the Ouisconsin tomorrow or the day after. Cannot learn that there is any danger to be apprehend from the Indians in that quarter. Rumours at present, relative to the Indians above this on the Mississippi, are rather unsatisfactory, but I am in hopes they will be more flattering before my return, as I am very anxious to ascend to the Falls of St. Anthony.

There is some misunderstanding between the Foxes on the one point & the Sioux & Puants [*Winnebago*] on the other, on account of an [out]rage committed by the latter, upon a hunting party of the former, in which four foxes are said to have been killed & two others badly wounded. The Sioux & Soteurs [*Ojibway*] who are threating war with each other, and it is reported that they wish not to see any American soldiers in their country.

This letter, as I am under the necessity of writing it in haste, I beg leave to subscribe unoffic[i]ally.

Believe me Dr. Genl.

Your sincere friend & Humble Sert.
S. H. LONG

4. *VOUCHER A*[6]

Portage Des Sioux [Mo.] July

The United States To Joseph Goe Dr.

To my services on a Tour to Prairie Du Chien on the Mississippi, and to the Ouisconsin Portage in the employ of Maj. Long of the

[5] Smith Papers, joint Western Historical Manuscripts Collection-State Historical Society Manuscripts, University of Missouri Library, Columbia. Used with permission. Copy in MHS. On Fort Edwards and Joseph Calhoun, see pp. 104, 105, above. The outrage referred to below or a similar incident between the Dakota and Fox was reported by Charles Jouett, Indian agent at Chicago, on July 21. See Jouett to [Lewis Cass?], July 21, 1817, OIA, Michigan Superintendency, Letters Received and Sent, NARG 75.

[6] Vouchers A-J, here and below, are in GAO, Second Auditor, Account No. 1433,

Engineers, as Interpreter & Guide, forty five days at $1. pr. Day from the 1st June to 15 July, 1817. $45.00.

Portage des Sioux July 14, 1817. Received of Maj. S. H. Long forty five Dollars in full of the above account.

Attest. Scott Campbell

his
JOSEPH X GOE
mark

VOUCHER B

The United States To [Alexander] McNair & [Wilfred] Owens, Dr.[7]

For Twenty three pounds of Tobacco furnished Major Lon[g] of Engineers for the purpose of distributing to Indians, in voyaging up the Mississippi & Wisconsan Rivers, at Fifty Cents per lb. $11.50

Received Prairie Du Chien 22d July 1817, of S. H. Long, Major of Engineers, Eleven Dollars and Fifty Cents, in full of the above account. Signed Duplicates hereof.

Attest: $11.50 MCNAIR & OWENS

VOUCHER C

The United States To John Rollins a private of the Rifle Regt. Dr.

To Extra duty under the command of Maj. Long of the Engineers, in surveying the Mississippi & Wisconsan Rivers from June 18 to July 22, 1817. 34 Days at $\$\frac{15}{100}$ pr. D. $5.10.

Recd. July 23, 1817 of Maj. S. H. Long five Dollars and ten cents in full of the above account.

JOHN ROLLINS

Authorised — See page 85 of Rules & Regulations[8]

VOUCHER D

The United States To Augustus Rock [*Augustin Rocque*] Dr.[9]

To my Services on a Voyage from Prairie Du Chien to the Falls of St. Anthony, in the capacity of Indian Interpreter to Major Long of the Engineers from the 9th to the 24th July 1817. 15 Days at $1 pr. D. $15.00.

Prairie Du Chien July 24, 1817. Received of Major S. H. Long, fifteen Dollars in full of the above account.

Attest. Scott Campbell

his
AUGUSTUS X ROCK
mark

NARG 217. On Goe and the soldiers, see Chapter 1, notes 1, 2, above. On Scott Campbell, trader and interpreter, see Upham and Dunlap, *Minnesota Biographies*, 103. On Portage des Sioux, see Chapter 2, note 41.

[7] On McNair, the sutler at Fort Crawford, and his clerk Owens, see Chapter 2, note 22.

[8] AGO, *Articles of War, Military Laws, and Rules and Regulations*, 85.

[9] On Rock or Rocque, see Chapter 1, note 2.

VOUCHER E

United States Bot of Simpson & Quarles[10] 1 Quire Super Royal Paper 2.00.

Received of Majr. Long two dollars in full of the above.

St. Louis Aug. 26, 1817 SIMPSON & QUARLES

VOUCHER F

The United States, To Thomas Porter a private of the Rifle Regiment Dr.

To Extra duty under the Command of Major Long of the engineers in Surv[e]ying the Mississippi and Ouisconsin Rivers from June 1st to 15th Augst. 1817 76 days at 15 Cnts pr. day. $11.40 Cts.

Received of Major S. H. Long eleven Dollars, & forty Cents in full of the above accounts. Signed Duplicates.

$11.40 Attest W[illiam] L. Dufphey[11] Capt. R. R.

his
THOMAS X PORTER
mark

VOUCHER G

The United States To Zacheriah Stephens a private of the Rifle Regiment Dr.

To Extra duty under the Command of Major Long of the engineers in Surveying the Mississippi & Wisconsan Rivers, from June 1st to August 15th 1817. 76 Days at 15 Cents pr. day $11.40 Cts.

Recd. Septr. 14th 1817, of Major S. H. Long, eleven dollars & forty Cents, in full of the above account. Signed Duplicates.

$11.40 Attest. W. L. Dufphey Capt. R. R.

his
ZACHIRIAH X STEVENS
mark

VOUCHER H

The United States To Samuel Porter 1st a private of the Rifle Regt. Dr.

To Extra duty under the Command of Major Long of the engineers in Surveying the Mississippi & Wisconsan Rivers from June 1st to August 15th 1817. 76 Days at 15 Cents pr. day. $11.40

Received Septr. 14th 1817, of Majr. S. H. Long, eleven dollars & forty Cents in full of the above account. Signed Duplicates.

$11.40 Attest W. L. Dufphey Capt. R. R. SAMUEL PORTER

[10] Drs. Robert Simpson and Pryor Quarles opened the first drugstore on Main Street in St. Louis, according to *Missouri Gazette*, January 13, 1816; Irwin H. Pizer and Harriet Steuernagel, "Medical Journals in St. Louis Before 1900," in Missouri Historical Society, *Bulletins*, 20:221 (April, 1964).

[11] On Dufphey, see Chapter 2, note 8.

VOUCHER I
The United States To Samuel Love a private of the Rifle Regiment Dr.

To Extra duty under the Command of Major Long of the engineers in Surveying the Mississippi & Wisconsan Rivers, from June 1st to August 15th 1817. 76 Days at 15 Cents pr. day $11.40 Cts.

Recd. Septr. 14th 1817, of Majr. S. H. Long, eleven Dollars & forty Cents, in full of the above account. Signed Duplicates.
$11.40 Attest W. L. Dufphey Capt. R. R. Samuel Love

VOUCHER J
The United States To Andrew Love a private of the Rifle Regt. Dr.

To Extra duty under the Command of Major Long of the engineers in Surveying the Mississippi & Ouisconsin Rivers, from June 1st to August 15th 1817. 76 Days at 15 Cents pr. day. $11.40

Recd. Septr. 14th 1817, of Majr. S. H. Long, eleven dollars & forty Cents in full of the above account. Signed Duplicates.
$11.40 Attest W. L. Dufphey Capt. R. R. The United States

his
Andrew X Love
mark

5. *Long to Smith, Belle Fontaine, Mo., May 12, 1818.*[12]

Sir;

I have the honor to acknowledge the receipt of your letter of the 7th *inst.*, in which you intimate some doubts as to the eligibility of the positions on the Mississippi selected for Military purposes, and request my opinion to the following questions viz.

"What posts are necessary on the Mississippi to afford protection to the frontier, check unauthorized intercourse, and preserve friendly relations with the Indians?

["]Secondly. What posts are necessary on the Missouri between Fort Osage [Mo.] and the mouth of the yellow stone river to afford facilities in the transportation of supplies to the latter point and protect authorized traders?

["]Thirdly. What posts are necessary on the South Western frontier of this Territory to prevent illicit intercourse with the Indians, prevent intrusions on their lands as well as to afford protection to our settlers on that frontier?

[12] OCE, Buell Collection of Historical Documents Relating to the Corps of Engineers, 1801–19, NARG 77.

["]Fourthly. Is a Military establishment necessary on the Illinois so long as Fort Dearborn (Chicago) is Garrisoned?"

I am also instructed to give my opinion as to the number of troops necessary at each post, the establishment of which I may recommend. And in relation to supplying them with provisions I am directed to state what number of labourers will be necessary to raise by cultivation supplies sufficient for a Company, and how many months in a year it will be necessary to abstract such labourers from their professional duties, also to make such suggestions as may be of general benefit.

Before I reply to the several queries you have done me the honor to propose, I beg leave to offer a few general remarks relative to the section of Country comprised in the ninth Military Department & to the intercourse kept up between the whites and the Indian tribes situated therein. After which I will consider the several queries you have suggested and communicate all the intelligence bearing upon them which the nature of my services under your command has placed within my reach.[13]

The intelligence I shall communicate is founded principally upon personal observations that I have made in the following Tours to wit: From Belle Fontaine by water to the head of Lake Peoria in the Illinois and thence by land to Belle Fontaine again. From St. Louis by land to Lake Michigan and thence to Fort Wayne. From Nashville, Tenn., by land to St. Louis. From Belle Fontaine by water to the Falls of St. Anthony in the Mississippi and up the Wisconsan to the Portage between that river and Fox river of Green bay and return. From Belle Fontaine by water to the Arkansaw, thence up the Arkansaw to its forks and return to Belle Point on that river, thence by land to Red river [of the South], and thence on the west of the Mississippi to St. Louis. I shall also avail myself of such intelligence in relation to the queries as I have been able to collect transiently from other Sourses.[14]

The section of Country under consideration embraces an extent of not less than fifteen hundred miles in length from East to West and

[13] For a map showing the area for which the Ninth Military Department was responsible at this time, see Edgar B. Wesley, *Guarding the Frontier: A Study of Frontier Defense from 1815 to 1825*, 103 (Minneapolis, 1935).

[14] These tours, on which Long visited Forts Dearborn, Clark, and Wayne, were made in 1816–17. On them and for a discussion of this report, see p. 7, above; Wood, *Long*, 40–57. On his trip to Nashville in 1817, Long visited Andrew Jackson at the Hermitage. The junction of the Salt Fork of the Arkansas with the main stream is in north-central Oklahoma near present Ponca City.

of more than one thousand miles in breadth from north to South, and is situated between 33° and 48° of North Latt. The Southern part of this region bordering upon the Allegheny Mountains as also that West of the Mississippi, extending northwardly to the Missouri and westwardly four or five hundred miles from the Mississippi, is hilly and broken and in many places mountainous. Under this general character must be excepted many large tracts of rolling Country scattered in various directions, and the vallies of the large rivers, particularly that of the Mississippi which Spreads in some instances to the width of 40 or 50 miles, comprising large bodies of flat and marshy land more or less subject to inundation.

West of the Country above specified is situated a large tract of Country of a more level aspect, extending along the east side of the Rockey or Shining mountains from Red river northwardly to the Missouri, watered by many navigable tributaries of these and the Arkansaw rivers. In this tract are numerous Prairies and extensive sandy deserts.[15] Those parts of the Country situated north of the Ohio and East of the Mississippi, and between the latter and the Missouri, extending northward to the northern limits of the United States, present some few mountains, but in general are rolling or moderately hilly and abound in extensive tracts of Champaign or Prairie land. To the west of the Missouri the Country assumes a more uneaven appearance, and by degrees the habitable regions are intercepted by the rugged cliffs and snowcapped peaks of the rockey mountains.

The Rivers of this region proper to be noticed in this communication are the Mississippi, the Missouri, the Red [of the South], the Arkansaw, Illinois, Wisconsen, St. Croix, St. Peters [*Minnesota*], Fox of Green bay, the Red of Hudson bay, and several of their Tributaries, these being the channels thro' which an intercourse is kept up both by citizens of the United States and foreigners with the savages of this Country.

The Mississippi is navigable for boats of any burden from its mouth to its confluence with the Missouri, a distance of 1200 miles, in all stages of the water. Thro' out this distance, the average daily

[15] Long as yet had no firsthand knowledge of the Rocky Mountains or the western Great Plains. For a discussion of the reports of Lewis and Clark, Pike, and others from which he may have obtained the impression that the Great Plains offered "extensive sandy deserts," see G. Malcolm Lewis, "Early American Exploration and the Cis-Rocky Mountain Desert, 1803–1823," in *Great Plains Journal*, 5: 1–11 (Fall, 1965).

progress made by keel boats in asending the river may be rated at 12 miles. A voyage from New Orleans to St. Louis 1180 miles requires from 90 to 100 days in the performance. Favourable winds render it somewhat more expeditious. That part of the Mississippi situated above the mouth of the Missouri, and commonly denominated the upper Mississippi, requires boats of moderate draught in navigating it, otherwise their passage would be obstructed by Sand bars and shoals with which it abounds in the lower stages of the water. In assending the upper Mississippi from the Missouri to the falls of St. Anthony, its current gradually becomes more moderate, decreasing in rapidity from 3 to 1 1/2 miles per hour. Its navigation throughout this part has no very serious obstruction except in a very low stage of the water, when the De Moyen [*Des Moines*] & Rock Island rapids are impassable for boats of any considerable burden. The distance from the mouth of the Missouri to that of the St. Peters nine miles below the Falls of St. Anthony has usually been rated at something more than 1000 miles. But agreeably to my estimate founded on corrections for the latitude, it does not exceed 750 miles. A boat of suitable construction and properly loaded for the upper Mississippi may without dificulty ascend this distance in 45 or 50 days.[16]

The Red river or river of Nachitoches is navigable about 500 miles to the great raft, at which the navigation for boats of any considerable burden is obstructed during the lower stages of the water. At other times keel boats may ascend without much difficulty several hundred miles farther. Their progress in ascending may be rated at 16 miles per day; a voyage from its mouth to the Pawney nation 1000 miles requireing about 60 Days. To Natchitoches—15 Days.[17]

The Arkansaw is navigable at all stages of the water for keel boats and barges of 15 or 20 tons burden from its mouth to the Forks, a distance of 600 miles agreeable to my own estimate as above. The average daily progress of boats in assending this river is 15 miles,

[16] Long's figures, probably based upon his own measurements of the Mississippi, were quite accurate. Modern comparisons may be found in U.S. Army Corps of Engineers, *The Middle and Upper Mississippi Rivers* (Washington, D.C., 1940).

[17] The Natchitoches, a Caddoan tribe, lived near the northwestern Louisiana city of that name; Hodge, *Handbook*, 2:36. On the Great Raft, a driftwood obstruction in the Red River near present Campti, La., and Long's later work to clear it, see Wood, *Long*, 199, 244, 247–250. For a map showing the locations of the Pawnee villages on the Platte River in what is now Nebraska, see George E. Hyde, *Pawnee Indians*, facing p. 130 (Denver, 1951). Long had visited the Red River of the South and the Arkansas in the fall of 1817, at which time he named Belle Point, mentioned in the paragraph below. See Wood, *Long*, 50–52.

requiring 42 days to ascend the whole of the above distance, or 34 Days to Belle Point, 130 miles below the forks. During very high water or when Contrary winds prevail, more time is required. For a description of the Illinois, I beg leave to refer to my report of the 4th March 1817.[18]

The Wisconsan is navigable for Mackinaw boats about 350 miles. Its navigation dureing the lower stages of the water is much obstructed by sand bars. At the distance of 160 miles from its mouth is the portage between this and Fox river of Green bay, 1 1/2 miles in extent. The latter is a very crooked river and its navigation is also much obstructed by shoals and rapids. Boats can ascend these rivers at the rate of 14 miles per day in the former, & 12 miles per day in the latter, from their mouths to the portage, the distance in both being nearly the same. A voyage from the mouth of the Wisconsan to the Portage requires 12 days, from that of the Fox to the same place 15 or 16.

The St. Croix, entering the Mississippi about 45 miles below the mouth of the St. Peters, is navigable for Perogues and Mackinaw boats about 50 miles, when the navigation is obstructed by rapids [*St. Croix Falls*]. Above this it is again navigable for Perogues to a considerable distance, and affords a communication with the navigable waters of Lake Superior by means of a short Portage.[19]

The St. Peters is navigable for perogues in all stages of the water between two and three hundred miles, and in time of floods nearly to its sourse, as also to the sourses of many of its tributaries. Its head branches interlock with the waters of the Missouri and with those also of Red river of Hudson bay, affording easy communication with both by means of portages.

In regard to the Missouri, my information is extracted principally from "Lewis & Clarks Expedition."[20] This river is navigable to the Great Falls [Mont.], 2575 miles. Its current for many hundred miles above its mouth is considerably more rapid and difficult of

[18] This report, dated March 4, 1817, was enclosed with Long to James Monroe, March 15, 1817, Secretary of War, Letters Received, NARG 107.

[19] On the St. Croix-Brule Portage, see Chapter 1, note 34. The St. Peter's or Minnesota River mentioned here and below had not yet been officially explored; it proved to be shorter and less navigable than Long stated. Its headwaters and those of the Big Sioux River in the Missouri watershed are indeed close together on the Coteau des Prairies in southeastern South Dakota.

[20] The distances given in this paragraph appear in Allen, ed., *History of the Expedition under . . . Lewis and Clark*, 2:462–465. Fort Mandan, mentioned below, was erected by the explorers as a temporary wintering post on the Missouri River south of present Stanton, N. Dak.

ascent than that of the Lower Mississippi. Sails can seldom be used to advantage, owing to the frequent changes in course of the river. As an order has recently been issued for the establishment of Military posts along this river between its mouth and its confluence with the Yellow stone, it may be proper to notice that part of the Missouri only situated between these two points.[21]

The Point of confluence between these two rivers is at the distance of 1880 miles above the mouth of the Missouri, pursuing its meanders. In ascending this distance with loaded boats, it will require at least 150 days. An outward and return voyage may be performed possibly in one season of boating. In the neighbourhood of the Mandans at the wintering Post [*Fort Mandan*] of Captains Lewis & Clark is a point where the road and main pass between Red River [of the North] and the Missouri strikes the latter.

From the mouth of the Missouri to this point the distance is 1600 miles, through which a boat may ascend in 132 days. An intermediate post between this and the mouth of the river Platte may be estimated at the distance of 1100 miles, through which a boat may decend in 100 days. The Confluence of the Platte & the Missouri is 600 miles from the mouth of the latter, requiring 54 days in ascending to this point. The distance as above to the Kansaw [*Kansas R.*] is 340 miles and may be ascended in 32 days.

The rivers above mentioned are the principal channels of intercourse between the whites & the Indians within the limits of the ninth Military Department. Those frequented by foreigners imployed in the Indian trade are the Mississippi above Prairie Du Chien, the St. Croix, and St. Peters of the Mississippi, The Missouri and its tributaries above the Kansaw, to all of which they have easy access from the establishments of the North West & Hudson bay Companies situated upon the Head waters of the Mississippi, upon those of Red River of Hudson bay interlocking with the tributaries

[21] An order to establish "a permanent military post" at the mouth of the Yellowstone was sent by Secretary of War Calhoun to Gen. Smith on March 16, 1818. It is printed in Hemphill, ed., *Calhoun Papers*, 2:194 (Columbia, S.C., 1963). The project, in which Long played a role in 1819–20, was beset with difficulties and was not completed. In 1829 the American Fur Company built Fort Union near the Yellowstone's mouth. An important fur post and rendezvous point on the northern plains, it was briefly garrisoned by troops during the Civil War, but not until 1867—49 years after Calhoun's order—did the army erect Fort Buford at the mouth of the Yellowstone. For summary information, see Robert G. Ferris, ed., *Soldier and Brave: Historic Places Associated with Indian Affairs*, 240, 244–247 (National Park Service, *National Survey of Historic Sites and Buildings*, vol. 12—Washington, D.C., 1971), and note 26, below.

both of the Mississippi and Missouri, and upon the Shores of Lake Superior. An illicit trade is also carried on thro' the same channels by individuals, both foreigners and citizens of the United States, who embark in the Indian trade as principals or engagees, and illude the restrictive Laws of the Union by prosecuting their business beyond the reach both of civil and Military authority.

Upon many other rivers of this Country, where no Military posts have been established for the suppression of illicit trade and intercourse with the Indians, similar violations are committed, but not to so great an extent as upon those above mentioned. I beg leave on some future occasion to communicate my ideas concerning the policy proper to be pursued by our government, for the purpose of regulating our trade and intercourse with the Indians, upon which the efficacy of all measures for conciliating and civilizing the savages exclusively depends.[22]

In regard to the section of Country in which the Military operations of this Department are to take effect, no part of the U. States is more exposed both in peace and war to the insults and depredations of the savages. At the same time its vast extent, the numberless avenues it affords thro' which an influence pernicious to the welfare of the Country is circulated amongst the Indians, and the various points at which savage annoyance is to be apprehended, render it impracticable for the Military force assigned to this department to enforce an observance of the laws in every place where a violation is to be apprehended, or resist the aggressions of our treacherous neighbours at every vulnerable point.

It is highly probable from the importance attached to this part of the Country in the late negociations at Ghent [*for the 1814 treaty*], as also from the exertions made by the N. West trading Companies

[22] For general background on the relationship of the fur trade to frontier defense during this period and the largely unenforceable 1816 law restricting foreigners from participating in the Indian trade, see Wesley, *Guarding the Frontier*, 56–64. British traders, particularly Robert Dickson, were of special concern to the Ninth Military Department and to the Indian affairs office at St. Louis. William Clark, superintendent of Indian affairs there and governor of Missouri, dispatched Indian agent Benjamin O'Fallon to the upper Mississippi to look into the situation and give him a firsthand report. O'Fallon described the "exertions" of British traders, the word Long used below; the agent also arrested Dickson and took him to St. Louis. Long was to become well acquainted with O'Fallon on his 1819–20 trip up the Missouri. See Clark to Secretary of War, September 28, 1816, and O'Fallon to Clark, May 10, 1817, May 20, 1818, in Carter, ed., *Territorial Papers of the United States (Missouri)*, 15:175, 262–266, 407–413; James, *Account*, 126 (Thwaites, ed., *Early Western Travels*, vol. 14—Cleveland, 1905). The editors have been unable to locate any further report incorporating Long's views on the Indian trade.

to engross the whole of the Indian trade, that in the event of another War with Great Briton, strenuous attempts will be made to wrest a portion of it from our possession. These considerations shew the importance of selecting such positions for Military posts as will effectually guard the most important passes, and also the importance of constructing works of a formidable as well as permanent character in those situations when the attack of a Regular Army is to be apprehended.[23]

As it does not comport with the principles of our Government to Support large armies in time of peace, and as the distribution of an army into numerous Small detachments to be kept constantly Seperate from each other if Subversive of Military order and dicipline, and more over, as a small and inefficient military force is invariably viewed with contempt by the Indians and liable to be crushed in a moment whenever they see cause to exert their Strength, it becomes essential to a well organized system of Military operations to reduce the number of Posts as much as the nature of the service will admit, and concentrate the forces as much as possible at those points where annoyance is most to be apprehended.

Having taken the preceeding view of several subjects intimately connected with the Queries you have proposed, I am in some measure prepared to offer an opinion in answer to the queries themselves, which I beg leave to do with the utmost deference in the same order in which they are presented.

In reply to the first question I feel myself justified in stating that the Posts already established at Green bay [*Fort Howard*] and Chicago [*Fort Dearborn*], which ought to be of a permanent and formidable character and calculated not only for Indian defence but also for defence against a regular force both by land and water, are better situated to effect the objects specified in the question, so far as it respects operations carried on thro' the medium of the Great Water communications between the [Great] Lakes and the Mississippi passing in their neighbourhood, than any other posts that are or can be established for the same objects; and that fort Clarke on the Illinois, Fort Edwards near the confluence of the De Moyen & Mississippi, and Fort Crawford at Prairie Du Chien on the latter river, if they can be considered as having any weight in furtherence

[23] On the Treaty of Ghent and the problem of the boundary between British Canada and the U.S., which was not resolved until 1842, see a useful summary in Folwell, *History of Minnesota*, 1:500–502. The negotiations concerning the Ghent treaty are printed in *American State Papers: Foreign Relations*, 3:709–726.

of the objects proposed, must be considered as merely auxiliary to the posts above specified. Fort Clark is so situated as to afford a tolerable command of the Illinois, and may be of some service in regulating an inconsiderable portion of domestic trade with the Indians; but the number of Indians in its neighbourhood is too small to render this an object worthy of attention. And since there are objects of far greater moment to the attainment of which the services of the troops may be advantagiously applied, it would be expedient to abandon this post. The same remarks are equally as applicable to Fort Edwards, with the exception perhaps that this post is situated near the De Moyen rapids and may be of service during low water in aiding boats laden with Military Supplies in their passage up the rapids. This however should be considered of little importance, since such aid is seldom required. It should also be remarked of this post that it has no command of the enterance into the De Moyen.[24]

Fort Crawford possesses even fewer advantages in a Military point of view than either of the last mentioned posts. It has no command either of the Mississippi or the Wisconsan, thus being destitute of one of the most essential requisites of a Military post, Vizt. that of commanding the passage of the river upon which it is situated. The protection of the village of Prairie Du Chien may be urged as an argument in favour of keeping up a Garrison at this place: but since the establishment of the Garrison, the village has been deserted by nearly half its former inhabitants. This place it is true was once a rendezvous for unauthorized traders, but the outlets of trade in this quarter are sufficiently barricaded by the posts at Green bay and Rock Island in the Mississippi, so that the same evil is no more to be apprehended in case this post should be abandoned. The Indians frequently resort to this place, but without any other inducement than that of trading with the whites, and receiveing presents, annuities &c.

I would therefore recommend the adoption of measures leading directly or eventually to the abandonment of the three posts above mentioned, and to the arrangement of the troops now required to man them at other points where they would be able to render more essential service to the Country.

[24] For Long's more detailed remarks on Forts Edwards and Crawford, see pp. 88–90, 164–107, above. As the frontier shifted westward, Forts Clark, Wayne, and Edwards were abandoned by 1824; Crawford was temporarily abandoned in 1826–27 and rebuilt on higher ground in 1830; and Long himself recommended closing Howard and Dearborn in 1823. See Prucha, *Guide to the Military Posts*, 66, 69, 73, 115; Keating, *Narrative*, 2:243.

With this view I would propose that the number of Posts to be kept up on the upper Mississippi and its waters should be reduced to two, one of which should be Fort Armstrong situated on Rock Island in Latt. 41° 27′ and the other should be located at the confluence of the Mississippi & St. Peters in Latt. 45° 6′ North. These two are the only positions I have been able to discover on that part of the Mississippi that appear to combine healthfulness, Security, and a Complete command of the river. At the same time the facilities of communication from one to the other afforded by the river, also their relation to other parts of the Country, give them a decided preference over any other positions that might be selected for Military purposes.[25]

Rock Island is not only situated in the immediate neighbourhood of the largest body of [*Sauk and Fox*] Indians to be found on the Mississippi, but is also central to a large extent of Country inhabited by savages thro' which there are easy communications either by land or water in almost every direction. The Position at the confluence of the Mississippi and St. Peters is not only well adapted to the command of both these rivers, but is also admirably calculated to intercept the most important line of communication within our Territory thro' which an intercourse is kept up between foreign traders and the Indians.

Between this point and rock Island the rivers falling into the Mississippi from the west are small and navigable only a short distance, so that there is no channel thro' which trade can be diverted from its present course and carried on with any degree of advantage or security between foreigners & the Indians living on the Missouri and its waters. The establishment of respectable and commanding posts at these positions, especially at the mouth of the St. Peters, I consider absolutely essential to the attainment of the objects Specified in the question and am convinced that the success of our Military operations upon the Mississippi in the prosecution of the objects of Government depends in a great degree on the adoption of this measure.

The second question embraces an enterprize in regard to which the administration have recently taken a step worthy of the aspireing and honorable spirit of our Government. Altho' the establishment of Military Posts on the Missouri, embracing an extent of nearly 2000 miles along that river, is to be viewed as one of the most

[25] For Long's description of Fort Armstrong and the future site of Fort Snelling, see pp. 76, 98–102, above.

arduous undertakings that ever was encountered in the Military operations of the Country and will require a proportionate expence of treasure and labour, possibly of blood, in the achievement, yet we may flatter our selves with the pleasing prospect of being amply renumerated [*remunerated*] in the advantages that will result to the nation in the enjoyment of a valuable trade, and in the Security from savage spoliations which it promises.[26]

The points proper to be occupied on the Missouri as Military positions, so far as I am able to judge from the best information I can obtain, both on account of their Geographical situation and their local advantages are at least four Vizt. at the mouth of the river Platte, at the Grand Detour or big bend, at or near Fort Mandan, and at the confluence of the Yellow Stone & Missouri.[27]

The first of these points is 600 miles distant from the mouth of the Missouri, and should be so selected if possable as to afford a command of the Missouri and of the mouth of the Platte, by means of which the outlet of an important part of the Indian trade, extending along the western frontier from the head waters of the Arkansaw to the Missouri, would be effectually guarded. The number of Indians residing upon the Platte and its waters agreeably to Lewis and Clarke, amounts to more than 10,000 Souls.[28] The Second point is about 570 miles above the first and is noted only on account of its being situated in the neighbourhood of a large number of Indians and of its convenient situation for an intermediate post.

The third Vizt. The Position at or near Fort Mandan about 430 miles above the last mentioned is deserving of more particular consideration than any other on the Missouri. Its proximity to the boundary line and its exposed situation, together with the necessity

[26] Long himself was to be associated with the "arduous undertaking" when he led the scientific complement of the so-called Yellowstone Expedition, which was under the command of Col. Henry Atkinson. The latter had orders to take up to 1,100 men by steamboat to the Yellowstone and establish a post there in 1819. The literature on the ill-fated venture is extensive. For a recent review, see Lamar, "Introduction," in James, *Account*, xv–xxxvi (1972).

[27] Long expanded upon his suggestions here in a document he prepared describing "the extent of the line of our frontier," which was submitted by Calhoun to the House of Representatives on December 11, 1818; see *American State Papers: Military Affairs*, 1:779, 791. Fort Atkinson was built at the mouth of the Platte in Nebraska by troops of the Yellowstone Expedition in 1819. The big bend area of the Missouri became the site of a major fur trade post, Fort Pierre (S. Dak.), which was taken over by the army in 1855. The site of Fort Mandan was never occupied by troops, although Fort Stevenson was built not far away in 1867. On the Yellowstone posts, see note 21, above. For background on the defense of the northwestern frontier in this period, see Beers, *Western Military Frontier*, 27–53.

[28] Allen, ed., *History of the Expedition under . . . Lewis and Clark*, 1:33.

of commanding effectually this part of the river in order to controul the trade above and prevent an enemy from cutting off necessary supplies destined for the establishment at the confluence of the Yellow Stone & the Missouri, contribute to render it more important than any other position on the Northern frontier between the Lakes and the Rockey Mountains.

If the U. States boundary on this frontier pass along the dividing ridge situated between the waters of Red river of Hudson bay and those of the Missouri and Mississippi, it will pass within a few miles of this position. The distance from this point to several establishments of the N.W. & Hudson bay company's upon the Assiniboin[e] of Red River is about 150 miles thro' which there is a good road leading direct to some of their establishments. Between this point and the head of navigation in Mouse [*Souris*] river, a tributary of the Assinboin, is a portage of an extent probably not exceeding 60 miles, which is the principal line of communication between the British traders and the Indians of the upper Missouri. The N.W. & H.B. Companies have on several occasions signified a determination to fortify at this place, in order to carry on their operations in this quarter with greater security and monopolize more effectually the Indian trade. Other considerations might be urged in favour of occupying this position with a formidable Military force but these may be deemed sufficient.[29]

The fourth point, which is at the junction of the Yellow stone and Missouri, is 280 miles above Fort Mandan. A post at this place is necessary in order to guard the outlets of two of the most prolific sources of the fur trade, as also to intercept the line of communication between foreign traders and the western Indians extending along our western frontier from the northern boundary to the waters of the Platte. Altho' the trade & intercourse which has heretofore been kept up between the Indians & the foreign trading Companies direct from Fort Mandan to the establishments of the latter on the assiniboin, may be effectually obstructed by a Military force at the

[29] On the boundary uncertainty; see note 23, above. On the portage, see p. 306, above. A portage of approximately 60 miles would have taken a traveler from Fort Mandan to the Souris River near present Minot, N. Dak. The route from Fort Mandan to the Assiniboine River posts is described, the posts are located, and much the same anti-British point of view is reflected in Ernest S. Osgood, ed., *The Field Notes of Captain William Clark, 1803–1805*, 166, 169, 172 (New Haven and London, 1964). It seems probable that Long was indebted to Lewis and Clark for this information. If so, the posts referred to were Brandon House of the Hudson's Bay Company and Forts Assiniboine and Souris of the North West Company, located just above the junction of the Souris and Assiniboine rivers in present Manitoba.

third point specified, yet the trade of these companies may be diverted into other channels more remote, and be carried on to great advantage with the upper Indians of the Missouri, provided it be not checked at the point last under consideration.

In regard to the site of Fort Osage, I am inclined to think, should it be deemed expedient to maintain a garrison on this point of the river, that this post is not so advantagiously situated as it would be at the mouth of the Kansaw river. Could an eligible and commanding site be selected at the latter place, which is about 30 miles above the former, I would recommend the removal of the Garrison to that place in order to barricade another important outlet of the Missouri trade, and more effectually controul the intercourse with the Indians residing between the Missouri and Arkansaw rivers.[30]

By occupying the positions above pointed out, particularly the four first mentioned, in a suitable manner, we should be able almost effectually to controul the trade and intercourse, not only with the Indians residing immediately on the Missouri, but also with those inhabiting a vast extent of Country to the South and West of it, as we should command the most important avanues thro' which such intercourse is kept up. These positions have been recommended, not from any personal knowledge I have of them, but from a general idea of the Topography of the Country & of the representations made of it by travellers.

The intermediate distances between the posts above proposed may be deemed too great to afford all the aid that may be thought needful in the transportation of provisions & Military stores up the turbulent current of the Missouri, but when we consider the size of our army, and the inefficiency that must necessarily result from its being divided into a multiplicity of seperate detachments, we are constrained to view the number of posts here proposed even greater than it ought to be, should a reduction be found practicable without a manifest injury to the service.

In answer to the third question, it may be remarked that the object of Military establishments in the South Western parts of the Missouri Territory is not to prevent foreign intercourse with the indians, but to check illicit trade on the part of our own citizens, also to restrain them from hunting & committing other trespasses on

[30] After Fort Osage near present Sibley, Mo., was largely abandoned in 1819 and Atkinson in 1827, Fort Leavenworth not far from the mouth of the Kansas River became important in the development of the West. Beers, *Western Military Frontier*, 53, 94–96; Wesley, *Guarding the Frontier*, 140.

Indian lands. These being the objects, it is obvious that all Military Posts intended to operate as a check upon this kind of intercourse should be located between the whites and the Indians. And I conceive it would be highly expedient to prohibit citizens of the United States in future from settling beyond the range of our exterior posts. As a general principle, this remark is applicable to every part of our inland frontier, but more particularly so to those parts exposed to Savage depredations, not only because we should then be able more effectually to prevent illicit proceedings between our Citizens & the Indians, but because the latter in advancing upon our frontier settlements must thus "leave a post in their rear," a circumstances that uniformly imposes a powerful restraint upon their operations. I would therefore recommend two posts only in this quarter, one of which should be situated upon Red River above the american settlements, and the other on the Arkansaw either at Belle Point, or higher up, should we extend the limits of our Territory in that direction by extinguishing the Osage claims.[31]

Having anticipated a reply to the 4th question, I shall only observe in this place that the works of Fort Clarke are so injudiciously constructed & are so nearly decayed that if the post be not abandoned, the immediate construction of new works will be necessary.

As to the number and description of the troops proper to man the posts above proposed, I would recommend the following arrangement Viz.

At the confluence of the Mississippi and St. Peters four companies of Infantry.

At Fort Armstrong two companies of Infantry.

At the confluence of the yellow stone & the Missouri two companys of Riflemen.

At Fort Mandan five companies of Riflemen.

At the Great bend of the Missouri one company of Riflemen.

At the mouth of the Platte two companies of Riflemen.

At Fort Osage or the mouth of the Kansaw a Sergeants guard of Riflemen.

At the Depot of the ninth Military department one Company of Infantry. (As Belle Fontaine is by no means an eligible situation for a

[31] Largely because of the powerful Osage tribe, Fort Smith (Ark.) was built in the fall of 1817 at Belle Point on the Arkansas River; Long selected the site and helped establish the post. A second post, Fort Gibson, was built on the Red River in Oklahoma in 1824. On these posts and the southwestern frontier in this period, see Beers, *Western Military Frontier*, 57–72; Wesley, *Guarding the Frontier*, 178–182.

depot I would advise the establishment of one at some other point.)[32]

On the Arkansaw two companys of Infantry. And on Red River one Company of Infantry, amounting to a force of two Regiments for the Department. When we consider that this department comprises more than one third part of the Territory of the United States and contains at least four fifths of the Indians residing within the limits of the Same, we cannot but view the force here proposed not only as necessary to the performance of the arduous duties required, but also as a reasonable proportion to be allowed to the Department under the Military Peace establishment.

I beg leave on this occasion to offer a few remarks relative to the construction of works at the positions above pointed out, the means of transportation with which they should be furnished, and the plan of Military operations proper to be adopted.

At the positions most exposed Viz. At the junction of the Mississippi & St. Peters and at Fort Mandan, I would advise the erection of Regular fortifications on a respectable scale, both in regard to their Size and manner of construction. They should each be furnished with quarters and other appendages necessary for the accommodation of at least two companies in addition to the permenant force respectively stationed at them, and as the term of service for which they are required will be coextensive with that of reclaiming and settling the vast wilderness in which they are situated, they ought to be constructed of dureable materials and in other respects possess a permanent as well as formidable character. At the other positions stockade works calculated for Indian defence and carefully constructed with a view to render them inaccessable to an enemy designing to attack with fire would be sufficient.

The Garrisons on the Mississippi should be furnished with fortified boats sufficient for the transportation of all the troops stationed at them. Their form and construction being such as are best adapted to the navigation of the upper Mississippi in all stages of the water. Their width should be greater in proportion to their length than those heretofore constructed for the same purpose. Their draught when loaded with the necessary Stores, provision &c. should not exceed twenty inches, the bulwarks upon their sides should be no thicker than is necessary to render them impervious to musket balls,

[32] Belle Fontaine was replaced in 1826 by Jefferson Barracks on the west bank of the Mississippi below St. Louis. See Beers, *Western Military Frontier*, 53; Prucha, *Guide to the Military Posts*, 81.

& should be so constructed by means of hinges or slides, as that they may be drawn aside when there is no danger to be apprehended from an enemy in ambush. Their size also should be much less than that of the fortified boats now in use upon the Mississippi. Boats of a similar construction should also be furnished to the posts on the Missouri, except that these should be fitted up with running boards attached to their sides, as the use of polls will be necessary in stemming the rapid current of this river.[33]

The Garrisons on each river should be furnished with horses enough to mount at least one Company of troops. The expence of furnishing these would be merely the prime Cost of the horses, as they may be subsisted upon the grass and fodder suitable for that purpose with which the Country every where abounds, and the necessary corn may be raised by the troops.

In regard to the system of Military operations proper to be adopted, in addition to regular drills, police, and a limited fatiegue duty, the troops should be required to Serve regular campaigns in traversing the Country either by land or water, visiting the various Indian settlements, and aiding in the execution of such regulations as Government may think proper to prescribe in relation to trade and intercourse with the Indians, by bringing offenders of every description to condign punishment. In order the more effectually to strike a dread upon the Savages and command their respect, it would be essential that the force on Such occasions should be as large as possible and move in a body, also that expeditions of this kind should be conducted with the utmost secrecy that the Indians may not be apprised of the intended visit, and thus have an opportunity to avoid the interview or make preparations to annoy the party. The advantages resulting from such a plan of operations are obvious, not only as it respects the ascendency it is calculated to yield us over our Indian neighbours, but also as it respects a knowledge of the Country, the acquirement of which is essential to a well concerted plan of operations in time of war, when, in order to act with decision & Judgment, our officers must be acquainted with the ground that constitutes their field of action.

In answer to the subjoined Querry regarding the expedients proper to be adopted for the procurement of the necessary supplies of provision, I fully concur with you in the opinion that "the difficulty of procureing them at the most remote Posts renders a

[33] On Long's keen interest in boat design and his successful development of the "Western Engineer" and other steamboats, see Wood, *Long*, 59–84, 212–214, 266.

different mode of Supply necessary and that the troops stationed at these Posts should depend for subsistence upon resources within their own controul.["] The quantity of corn requisite for the subsistence of a man for one year, including what may be required to fatten his meat, would not exceed 35 bushels or the avarage produce of 1 1/4 acres. Agreeably to this estimate the quantity required annually for each company will be 3100 bushels or the produce of 112 acres, which would require the labour of 12 men dureing eight months of the year and ten yoke of oxen in cultivating, fencing and tending, besides the occasional assistance of as many more. The cultivation of Wheat, Rye, Pulse &c. may be subsisted in part for that of Indian corn, in which case the number of acres should be some what greater. The quantity of corn necessarily appropriated to the fattening of meat will depend in a great measure upon the quantity of game afforded by the Country in the vicinity of each Garrison, which in all probability will be abundant at first but will soon become scarce.[34]

The climate of the Country must be regarded in the selection of seeds adapted to agriculture at the several posts. Seeds never succeed well in a climate situated in a Latitude much higher than that in which they were matured. It will therefore be necessary to procure seeds of all kinds from climates corresponding with those in which the posts are to be established in order to ensure success in cultivation. Such as may be imported from Canada, or the Northern parts of New England & New York, would no doubt succeed better at the upper posts on the Mississippi & Missouri than those from any other part of the Country.

Any arrangements that may be made for Supplying provisions in this way should by no means supercede the necessity of transmitting regular Supplies up the rivers, for the uncertainty of raising a crop in these northern regions where an appropriate mode of cultivation is yet to be learnt, added to the treacherous disposition of the Savages who on the slightest pretence might be induced to cut off a whole years Supply of provisions by laying waste the fields, killing the cattle, &c. either by day or night, renders a dependence upon resources of this kind very precarious. In order to save the expence of furnishing Supplies not needed, returns should be forwarded immediately after the crops are secured, stating the quantity of

[34] Secretary of War Calhoun issued a general order on September 11, 1818, requiring all permanent posts to cultivate gardens. For comment on the results, see Prucha, *Broadax and Bayonet*, 120–128; Chapter 7, note 33, above.

provisions on hand at the several posts, in order that the contractor might be regulated by this Intelligence in furnishing the Supplies next due.

In connection with my reply to this subject I beg leave to suggest the propriety of encourageing settlements in the neighbourhood of each garrison by allowing to citizens the priviledge of cultivating certain parcels of Land, and to Soldiers who may have served out either the whole or part of their time at any of the Garrisons and obtained an honorable discharge, the right of improveing at least one hundred acres in the vicinity of either post. This measure would not only be calculated to aid in Supplying the posts with provisions, but would add greatly to their strength as the settlers may be called upon in case of emergency to cooperate with the troops.

In view of the hardships, exposures, and privations that must necessarily be encountered by every soldier embarking in the expedition, as also the great benefit that must result to the United States in consequence of their Services in this cause, I think it would accord with the views and policy of a liberal Government to allow them a generous recompence for such meritorious service. It is therefore to be hoped that the attention of the Legislature will be directed to this subject, and that every soldier who shall have served faithfully on this frontier dureing the period of his enlistment will be rewarded by a bounty of at least 100 acres of Land situated as above mentioned, whenever the Indian claims to the same shall have been extinguished.[35]

In offering the foregoing remarks and opinions I have been prompted by a conviction that they are well founded, and a desire of communicating such intelligence as would prove beneficial in the adoption of measures calculated "to afford protection to the frontiers, check unlawful intercourse, and preserve friendly relations with the Indians." Should they meet your approbation and have any weight in bringing about events so desireable, it will afford me the highest Satisfaction.

A Topographical sketch of the Country through which I have

[35] Beginning with the Revolutionary War, noncomissioned officers and privates were granted 100 acres of free land as a reward for service under a system of military bounty warrants. The system was extended with some modifications to veterans of the War of 1812, with the exception of commissioned officers, who were excluded. The United States at the time Long wrote had an all-volunteer army, and soldiers who served during times of peace were not entitled to free land. See Paul W. Gates, *History of Public Land Law Development*, 249–263 (Washington, D.C., 1968).

travelled shall be submitted as soon as a reasonable time shall have elapsed for its completion.[36]

I have the honor to be, Sir, very respectfully

Your most obedient and very humble Servant,
S. H. Long Major T. Engineers

[36] The sketch has not been located. Secretary Calhoun, writing to Brown, October 17, 1818, Letter Book, p. 123, Brown Papers, stated that he transmitted to Brown "a sketch of the country," but he does not identify it as Long's.

Appendix 2
Documents Relating to the 1823 Expedition

1. *Alexander Macomb to Long, Washington, D.C., March 8, 1823.*[1]

SIR

From your knowledge & experience in the mode of exploring the Western regions it has been proposed to order you on an expedition up the St. Peters [*Minnesota R.*] this season but as you have so lately been employed on those arduous undertakings, it is conceived reasonable to give you an option in this matter, & therefore I wou'd desire you'll inform this Department as early as possible, whether such duty would at this time be agreeable to you.

ALEX MACOMB M[ajor] G[eneral]
Chf. Engr.

2. *Long to Macomb, Philadelphia, Pa., March 11, 1823.*[2]

DR. GENL/

I this day received your official communication of the 8th inst. and beg leave to trouble you with a few remarks connected with the subject of it, while I am forming a decision in relation to the service you have so kindly submitted to my choice. I also beg you will excuse an unofficial reply, for a few days, that I may have the better opportunity of deliberately weighing the matter submitted to my option.

The service contemplated in your letter will probably admit of the

[1] OCE, Letters to Officers of Engineers, NARG 77. On this letter and the one below, see p. 13, above.

[2] OCE, Letters Received, NARG 77.

following details as it relates to the general outfit and objects of the Expedition, viz. — The *party* to consist of myself as comdg. officer, Lt. [Andrew] Talcott as Assistant, Dr. [Edwin] James as Botanist & Geologist, Prof. [Thomas] Say *perhaps* as Naturalist and Antiquary, Capt. [Matthew J.] Magee or some other enterprising & active officer, as commandant of an escort consisting of not more than 20 or 30 men to be selected from the troops either at Fort Armstrong, Prairie du Chien or St. Peters [*Fort St. Anthony*], together with suitable guides & interpreters. The Instruments for observation, to consist of on[e] small sea and a snuff-box sextant, one mercurial Horizon, two or three small thermometers, and as many travelling compasses, one or two good patent lever watches, a small apparatus for determining the weight of the atmosphere by means of boiling water, instead of a barometer (which cannot be transported with safety) — together with such instruments as the naturalists may deem indispensable, also a limited quantity of necessary baggage and apparatus, which need not be specified.[3]

The route of the Expedition to commence at this place, proceed to Wheeling on the Ohio, thence to Fort Wayne on the Maumee, thence to Chicago, thence to Fort Armstrong or Prairie du Chien, and thence to Fort St. Anthony. Thence up the St. Peters to its source, thence northwardly to the 49th deg. N. Lat., thence eastwardly on that parallel and the northern boundary of the U[nited] States to Lake Superior, and thence by way of the Lakes homeward.

The objects of research to be similar to those of the late Expedition I had the honour to command.

The comdg. officer to be allowed to call on the officers of the military posts for such assistance as may be deemed necessary.

A digest of the proceedings and discoveries of the expedition to be published under the auspices of the Department.

Such is the plan that I should be happy to be instrumental in executing should it meet your approbation, in case no opportunity should offer for establishing myself permanently in a regular routine of business. You are already aware of my having applied for the appointment of Civl. Engr. for Virginia, and that the office is again vacant. Many of my friends are still urgent that I should renew my

[3] Talcott and Magee were both experienced in exploration, having accompanied the 1819–20 "Yellowstone Expedition" under Col. Henry Atkinson, where Long probably met both of them. Magee had commanded a party (including Talcott) that explored the route between Council Bluffs and Fort St. Anthony. See Porter, ed., in *Missouri Historical Collections*, 3:12. On these men and the instruments mentioned here, see pp. 19–26, above, p. 362, below.

application for that appointment, but as yet no opportunity has been presented, and I have of course done nothing more in relation to it. In order to satisfy the exigencies and claims of a rising family, I am extremely anxious for such a course of life & pursuits as will enable me to afford them every reasonable provision and protection.[4] Yet I am not disposed to swerve from any line of duty in which I can render myself useful, or for which I may be deemed qualified. Nevertheless, I would not have any claims that I may be thought to possess exclude the pretentions of any other officer who may wish to be indulged in the contemplated service.

I beg you will excuse the haste of this communication, and do me the favour to acquaint me with your sentiments in relation to it, while I remain Dr. Genl. very truly and respectfully

Your much obliged and very humble Sert.
S. H. Long

3. *Macomb to Long, Washington, D.C., March 17, 1823.*[5]

Sir

I have received your letter of the 11th inst in reply to mine of the 8th upon the subject of an expedition up the St. Peters river. The outline of your project being approved, the expedition will be commenced as soon as the necessary arrangements can be made, in order to effect which you will, should you not be appointed Civil Engineer to the State of Virginia, come on to Washington & report to me immediately upon determination of the latter point.

Alex Macomb M[ajo]r G[eneral]
Chf. Engr.

4. *Long to Macomb, Philadelphia, Pa., March 19, 1823.*[6]

Sir

I have just received your letter of the 17th Inst. in which you have done me the honour to signify your approbation of the plan of an Expedition suggested in my letter of the 11th. The indulgence you have extended in regard to my taking charge of the Expedition, as

[4] Long and his wife had two children at this time—William D., born in 1820, and Henry C., born in 1822. See Reid, *Biographical Sketch of Enoch Long*, 33. Long did not get the position of civil engineer for Virginia; see p. 13, above.

[5] OCE, Letters to Officers of Engineers, NARG 77.

[6] OCE, Letters Received, NARG 77.

also to my being allowed to wait the event of the election of a Civil Engineer for the State of Virginia, an office for which I have been an applicant, is highly gratifying, while it claims my warmest acknowledgements.

In reply, I beg leave to suggest that it would be desirable that the Expedition should be commenced as early as practicable in the month of April next, and that no time should be lost in making the necessary preparations for the enterprise. Accordingly I take the liberty to request that I may be allowed to make arrangements for purchasing and constructing such apparatus as may be deemed indispensable in the contemplated service. Some of the articles suitable for the purpose cannot be obtained except by order on the manufacturer, for example, Thermometers proper for measuring the boiling temperature at different altitudes, Travelling compasses, Portfolios & Packing cases for plants, Packing cases for insects, & Small blank books & cases for journals, and various other instruments and articles of less note. Some time will be requisite to select a good Patent Lever Watch and adjust it accurately. A snuff-box sextant accurately constructed may be difficult to find. Travelling apparatus of various kinds is to be procured, all of which will require considerable time and attention. In case the charge of the Expedition should devolve upon some other officer, he might avail himself of the preparations already made, and the sooner complete his outfit.

I should have troubled you again on this subject previously to this time, but have been waiting Dr. Jame's [*Edwin James's*] return from N. York, in order to ascertain his views and wishes in relation to it. He has not yet returned but is daily expected.

With sentiments of the highest respect, I have the honor to be Sir,

Your obedient and Humble Sert.
S. H. Long
M[ajor] T[opographical] Engr.

5. *Long to Macomb, Washington, D.C., April 15, 1823.*[7]

Sir:

I beg leave to submit the following Project of an Expedition for exploring the river St. Peter's and the country situated on the Northern Boundary of the United States between Red River of Hudsons Bay and Lake Superior.

[7] OCE, Letters Received, NARG 77.

Route of the Expedition.

Commencing at Philadelphia, thence proceed to Wheeling, thence to Chicago via Fort Wayne, thence to Fort Armstrong or Dubuques Lead Mines, thence up the Mississippi to Fort St. Anthony, thence to the source of St. Peter's River, thence to the point of intersection between Red River [of the North] and the 49th deg. of N. Lat., thence along the northern boundary of the United States to Lake Superior, and thence homeward by the [Great] Lakes.

Objects of the Expedition.

To make a general Survey of the Country on the proposed route, together with a topographical description of the same. To ascertain the Lat. and Longitude of remarkable points. To examine and describe its productions, animal, vegetable and mineral, and to enquire into the character, customs, &c. of the Indian tribes inhabiting the same. The time required to perform the route will not probably exceed eight months.[8]

Means of accomplishing those objects.

The commanding Officer of the Expedition should be authorised to call on the commanding officer of any post in the contemplated route for such supplies and assistance, whether of men, horses, camp equipage, provisions, boats, clothing, medicine, or other aids as he may deem needful to the success of the Expedition, and upon the Indian Agents for such goods (not exceeding in the aggregate $300) as he may deem expedient as presents to the Indians. He should also be authorised to call on the comdg. officers of Fort Crawford or St. Anthony, for a guard not exceeding thirty men, armed and equiped for the service of the Expedition in such manner as may be deemed appropriate, to be commanded by some active and enterprising officer eager to embark in the Expedition. In addition to the above, the sum of $1500 at least, will be necessary to defray the contingent expenses of the Expedition incurred in the purchase of horses, saddles and other equipments, in procuring subsistence for the party, in the hiring of guides and interperters, and in various other contingencies.

Individuals of the Expedition.

Comdg. Officer	Major S. H. Long
Assistant	Lieut. A. Talcott
Botanist & Geologist	Dr. E. James
Zoologist & Antiquary	Professor T. Say, at 2 dolls. per day

[8] Long modified the route outlined; see p. 15, above. The expedition took only six months, not the eight Long allowed.

Landscape Painter [Samuel] Seymour or Reader [*Alexander Rider?*] at $1.50 pr. day.

In case Dr. James should not accompany the Expedition, a substitute might be made in the selection of another person or persons at the rate of $2 per day each.[9]

Recapitulation embracing the several items of Expenditure.

		D C
Q.M. Dept.	The cost of 4 horses, including saddles, bridles, saddlebags, holsters &c. will probably amount to $80 each	320.00
	Four additional horses on leaving the Settlement $50 each	200.00
	Contingencies chargable to Q. M. Dept. on account of transportation of Guides, interpreters, baggage &c.	180.00
		700.00
Engr. Dept.	One Patent Lever Watch	75.00
	One Surveyors Compass small	17.00
	One Plotting Instrument [*protractor*]	12.00
	One Small Box Sextant	25.00
	Blank books, Mercury for horizon, Port Folios &c.	31.00
		160.00
Subsistence	Travelling Expenses of Zoologist & Landscape painter one month onward & one month returning at $1 per day each	120.00
	Steam Boat & Stage fare from Detroit to Philadelphia for Zoologist & Painter	110.00
		230.00
Ind. Dept.	Guides & Interpreters 3-4 months at $30 per mo. each	360.00
	Goods for presents to the Indians	300.00
		660.00
Amount of Expenditure as above		1750.00
Individual Charges		250.00
		2000.00

Blankets & other articles of clothing for the use of the Party, also

[9] See note 12, below; see also "Abstract," below, for the final expedition accounts, including the expenses of William H. Keating, who took James's place. On Seymour and Rider, see p. 29, 30, above.

provisions when required in kind to be drawn from the Public Stores.

In case Dr. James should not accompany the Expedition, a Botanist and Zoologist being substituted in his place, the expense will be enhanced about $1000.

The foregoing estimate is intended to embrace only the expenditures incident to the performance of the contemplated route.

I have the honor to be, Sir, very respectfully
Your most obdt. & humble Servt.
S. H. LONG Maj. T. Engrs.

P. S. It would be expedient that orders issue from the Adjt. Genls. Office to the comdg. officers of Forts Wayne, Dearborn, Armstrong, Crawford, St. Anthony, Sault St. Mary [*Fort Brady*], Mackinaw, and Gratoit [*Gratiot*], authorizing them to furnish to the Expedition such assistance & supplies as may be deemed necessary.

6. *Long to Macomb, Philadelphia, Pa., April 24, 1823.*[10]

DR. GENL.

I have nearly completed the arrangements for the contemplated Expedition, and shall be ready to start on Monday morning. The commission you proposed together with your instructions will no doubt be received by to-morrow's mail. I am very anxious to commence the journey immediately lest we should be overtaken by cold weather before we shall have accomplished it. I hope you will not forget the letter of credence and pass-port, for which we must be indebted to the politeness of Mr. [Stratford] Canning.

I have procured three horses with suitable equipments, together with such apparatus as may be easily transported, but am under the necessity of waiting for funds to defray their expense. I purpose to transmit an account of our outfit at the time of our departure.

I remain Dr. Sir, very respectfully Your obt. and humble Sert.
S. H. LONG Maj. T. Engrs.

7. *John C. Calhoun to Long, Washington, D.C., April 25, 1823.*[11]

SIR

It is determined by the Executive that an Expedition be im-

[10] OCE, Letters Received, NARG 77. The Canning letter is printed below, p. 363.

[11] OCE, Letters to Officers of Engineers, NARG 77.

mediately fitted out for exploring the River St. Peters and the country situated on the Northern Boundary of the United States between the Red River of Hudsons Bay and Lake Superior. For the important service you have been selected, and you are hereby specially charged and entrusted with the conduct, command, and direction of the party which shall compose the Expedition.

The Route of the Expedition will be as follows. Commencing at Philadelphia, thence proceeding to Wheeling in Virginia; thence to Chicago via Fort Wayne; thence to Fort Armstrong or Dubouque's Lead Mines; thence up the Mississippi to Fort St. Anthony; thence to the source of the St. Peters river; thence to the point of intersection between Red River and the 49th degree of North Latitude; thence along the Northern Boundary of the United States to Lake Superior, and thence homeward by the Lakes.

The object of the Expedition is to make a general Survey of the Country on the Route pointed out, together with a Topographical description of the same. To ascertain the Latitude and Longitude of all the remarkable points. To examine and describe its productions, animal, vegetable and Mineral, and to enquire into the character, customs, &c. of the Indian Tribes inhabiting the same. In order to accomplish these objects you are authorised to call on the Commanding Officer of any post in the contemplated route for such supplies and assistance, whether of Men, horses, Camp Equipage, provisions, Boats, clothing, medicines or other aids, as you may deem essential to the success of the Expedition; and on the Indian Agents for such goods (not exceeding in the aggregate the value of $300) as you may deem expedient as presents for the Indians. You are likewise authorised to call on the commanding officer of Fort Crawford or St. Anthony for a Guard not exceeding Thirty Men, to be armed and equipped for the service of the Expedition, in such manner as may be judged appropriate, to be commanded by such officer as you may select for his activity & enterprizing disposition and possessing a willingness to embark on the expedition; which officer & men you will leave at the Sau[l]t of St. Mary, Mackinaw or some other post from which they can most conveniently rejoin their respective companies.[12]

[12] Post commandants were notified of Long's instructions to call on them for supplies and assistance in Special Order No. 27, April 28, 1823, AGO, Special Orders, 1:49, NARG 94. An extract from the letter published here was sent to Lawrence Taliaferro at Fort St. Anthony and probably to other Indian agents. The undated extract can be found under April 25, 1823, in the Taliaferro Papers. There is no covering letter in the papers.

Lieutenant A. Talcot[t] of the Corps of Engineers is ordered to join you as an Assistant, and will be considered as second in Command in conducting the Expedition. Docter E. James will accompany the Expedition as Botanist, Geologist and Phisician. In addition, you may engage Professor T. Say at two dollars p. day, Mr. Seymour or Mr. Reader at one dollar and an half p. day, and in case that Dr. James should not be able to accompany the party a Substitute may be selected by you at the rate of Two dollars p. day.

For the purchase of Horses, Saddles, Bridles, bags, Holsters, & Contingencies on Account of Transportation of Guides, Interpreters Baggage &c. For the purchase of Instruments, Viz. One Patent Lever Watch, One Surveyors compass, one plotting Instrument, one small box Sextant, Blank Books, Port folio, Artificial Horizon &c. The Travelling expenses of Zoologist & Landscape Painter, The Guides and Interpreters (3) & for Individual charges not enumerated making in all *Seventeen hundred Dollars*, the sum estimated by you, you are authorized to draw on the Department. It is desirable that as far as possible, you will keep within the Estimate which you left with the Engineer Department.

The experience which you possess in undertakings of this sort renders it now unnecessary to be more particular in these instructions, as you can always have recourse to those which you received on the former expedition, for such suggestions as will naturally claim your attention in the present enterprize; & every hope is indulged that the additional skill and practical knowledge of the manner of conducting an expedition which you must necessarily have acquired, and the great confidence reposed in the acquirements, talents, and zeal of the scientific Gentlemen who will accompany you, that the expedition will be conducted in such a manner as to give additional character and reputation to all concerned.

I have the honor to be &c.
J. C. CALHOUN [*Secretary of War*]

8. *Long to Macomb, Philadelphia, Pa., April 28, 1823.*[13]

DR. GENL.

Your kind favour of the 26th inst. came to hand this day, and with it, the Secy's Instructions relative to the contemplated Expedition. The receipt of them gave me much pleasure; as I had completed my

[13] OCE, Letters Received, NARG 77.

arrangements and was only waiting for funds and orders to enable me to commence the tour. I shall no doubt be able to settle my bills in the course of to morrow, and purpose to take my departure on the day following.

Lt. Talcott has not yet arrived but no doubt will be here to morrow. In case he should not come in season to start with us, I purpose to leave instructions for him to join us at Wheeling, which he can easily effect by taking passage in the Stage. Prof. Say and Mr. Seymour are ready to start with me, also Prof. [William H.] Keating who accompanies us in the capacity of Mineralogist & Geologist. I have been induced to offer him the place from a conviction that Dr. James will not be able to join the party, the latter having taken his departure from Albany on the 18th inst. with the view of travelling to Belle Fontaine via Niagara and the Lakes. I very much regret that we have no better prospect of his being able to join our party, as he would prove an invaluable acquisition. We are not without some hopes that he will be of the party, as we have written several letters to intercept his march. Prof. Keating stands deservedly high as a Geologist and I have no doubt but that he will fill the station assigned him to great advantage. I have no doubt that the step I have taken in this matter will meet your approbation, considering the circumstances under which I am placed.[14]

I hope the names of our friends in the Administration will remain as long as the "perpetual hills["] and never be forgotten till "the rivers shall cease to flow." Should I find any rivers, mountains, cataracts, caverns or fountains worthy to bear their names, I shall cheerfuly assume the functions of the priest, so far as to christen them.[15]

In case Mr. Canning should favour us with the letter formerly suggested, I beg you will do me the favour to forward it, with any additional intelligence, or instructions, to Columbus Ohio.

With sentiments of the highest esteem

I remain Dr. Genl. in haste
Your Obedt. Sert.
S. H. LONG

[14] In 1824 a stagecoach to Pittsburgh left daily (except Sunday) from Philadelphia. From Pittsburgh connections could be made to Wheeling via mail coach. See Robert De Silver, *The Philadelphia Directory, for 1824,* n.p. (Philadelphia, 1824).

[15] The two quotations are probably intended to refer to the Bible; "perpetual hills" can be found in Habakkuk, 3:6; "the rivers shall cease to flow" may be a paraphrase of such passages as Nahum, 1:4, or Isaiah, 19:5.

9. *Macomb to Long, Washington, D.C., April 30, 1823.*[16]

SIR

It is with much regret that I have to acquaint you that the services of Lieut. Talcott of the Corps of Engineers are deemed of such indispensable importance at Old Point Comfort that it is found inconsistent with the publick interest to remove him from that place — in consequence of this circumstance, he will not be able to join the expedition.[17]

Your Draft on the Secy. of War for One thousand dollars has just come to hand & it will be duly honored. From the manner in which you was authorised to draw & from the plan of your estimate founded on the mode in which the funds were to have been supplied to you, it was expected that you would have accompanied your draft with the several bills, or at least with statements under what heads the several expenditures were to be charged, as for instance the Qr. Masters department, the Subsistence Dept. &c. as arranged in your projects. As far as practicable it is desirable that the remainder of your funds may be obtained in that way.

ALEX MACOMB
Mr. G. Chf. Eng.

10. *Long to Macomb, Lancaster, Pa., May 1, 1823.*[18]

DR. GENL.

I take the liberty to apprise you that the Expedition have proceeded thus far on their way to the St. Peters. We left Philadelphia yesterday morning, and purpose to prosecute our journey at the rate of about 30 miles per day.

The party with me consists of Professors Say and Keating and Mr. Seymour. Fearing that it would not be practicable for Dr. James to join us in season, and believing it of the utmost importance to the Expedition that it should have a Geologist & Mineralogist attached to it, I took occasion to accept of the services of Prof. Keating, who volunteered to officiate in those capacities. The arrangement I made with him is of the following import, viz. that his travelling expenses should be defrayed and that he should serve as Geologist for the

[16] OCE, Letters to Officers of Engineers, NARG 77.

[17] Old Point Comfort, at the mouth of the James River near Hampton, Va., was the site of Fort Monroe, which was under construction in 1823.

[18] OCE, Letters Received, NARG 77.

Expedition. That he should receive a compensation at the rate of $2 per day for any term of actual service not exceeding eight months, provided Dr. James should not be able to join us; otherwise that he should be entitled to no compensation, unless it should be hereafter authorized by the War Department. Messrs. Say and Keating are also to act conjointly as Literary journalists for the Expedition.

Dr. James has taken his departure from Albany with the expectation no doubt that he will be able to join us at St. Louis, but as our route will not lead us within 500 miles of that place, and as we shall probably be at Chicago as soon as he can expect to reach St. Louis, there is little hope that he will be able to join the party. I have written letters with the view of interrupting his march, but as I could not learn the route he intended to take, have little expectation of their reaching him. Thus have I been induced to accept the offer of Prof. Keating.

Lt. Talcott had not arrived at Philadelphia at the time of our departure. I left orders for him in the Post Office at that place, requiring him to repair to Wheeling or Columbus, where he will be able to overtake us by travelling in the stage. I purpose to trouble you from time to time as we advance on our journey, and will therefore detain you no longer on this occasion

I remain Dr. Genl.

Very respectfully Your obt. humble Sert.
S. H. LONG

11. *Stratford Canning to "Any officer of His Majesty or other person having authority in the Posts or Settlements situated within His Majesty's North Western American Territories," Washington, D.C., May 1, 1823.*[19]

SIR,

This letter will be exhibited to you by Major Stephen H. Long of the United States Topographical Engineers, who for objects purely scientific, has been ordered to conduct an exploring expedition up the St. Peters' River, thence to proceed to the 49th degree of North Latitude, and thence to the Lakes on his return home. The American Government, conceiving it possible that Major Long may have occasion to pass on his way through some of the British Posts or Settlements along the frontiers, have requested me to state the

[19] OCE, Letters Received, NARG 77. See also p. 16, above; p. 364, below.

nature of the Expedition, and to recommend that officer and his party to the civilities of His Majesty's Officers and subjects in the Northwest territory. It is on this account that I furnish Major Long with the present Letter, not doubting that it will afford you pleasure to treat both him and the Party which he conducts, in case of their approaching your Station, with attention and good offices suitable to the friendly relations subsisting between the two Countries.

I am, Sir, with truth and regard
Your most obedient Humble Servant
STRATFORD CANNING

12. *Macomb to Long, Washington, D.C., May 3, 1823.*[20]

SIR

Mr. James Calhoun of the Navy having volunteered his services to join the expedition under your command, he is appointed to take the place therein assigned to Lt. Talcott of the Corps of Engineers. Mr. Calhoun will proceed forthwith to join you, & will be the bearer of the British Ministers letter to the Officers of his Britanick Majesty's on the Canadian frontier, recommending the party to their kind offices.

By Order of the Secy. of War
ALEX MACOMB, Mr. G. Chf. Engr.

13. *Stratford Canning to George Canning, Washington, D.C., May 5, 1823.*[21]

SIR,

I have received within the last few days a written communication from the American Secretary of State [*John Quincy Adams*] informing me that his Government was on the point of sending out an Exploring Party through a section of the North Western Country, by the River St. Peters, as far as the 49th degree of Latitude, and requesting, as the party might possibly fall in with some of the British Stations or Settlements near the frontier, that I would fur-

[20] OCE, Letters to Officers of Engineers, NARG 77. On Colhoun, see pp. 24–26, above.

[21] Foreign Office, 5:176; this transcript of Crown-copyright records in the Public Record Office appears by permission of the Controller of H. M. Stationary Office. The *Account* of the 1819–20 expedition referred to below was that authored by Edwin James and published in 1823.

nish it's Commander, Major Long, with a letter recommending him to the friendly attention of His Majesty's Subjects in that quarter. Major Long is an officer of the topographical engineers, the same individual who in the years 1819 and 1820 conducted a similar expedition through the Country of the Arkansas, an account of which is before the public. On the present occasion he is to be accompanied by several Gentlemen of Science, together with a military party of thirty men and an officer. The American Government have stated the object of his journey to be purely scientific.

Under these circumstances I have thought it most consistent with the friendly relations of the two Countries to comply with the request conveyed to me by Mr. Adams. The expedition was wholly independent of my assent, and in the present indeterminate state of the frontiers adjacent to Red River, the American party may easily approach Lord Selkirk's settlement, a part of which is supposed to be South of 49, or some of the trading posts established by His Majesty's subjects, without having any particular purpose in view, though I think it not unlikely that a visit to the British settlement on Red River, may form one of the express objects of Major Long's Instructions. At the same time, therefore, that I have furnished that officer with an open letter addressed in general terms to such British Subjects, invested with any kind of authority, as may be stationed along the northwestern frontier, I have written to apprize Lord Dalhousie [*George Ramsay, Earl of Dalhousie*] of the expedition, and to submit to His Lordship's judgment how far it may be worth while to give directions for observing it's movements, and Endeavouring to ascertain more particularly the extent of its views.[22]

I have the honour to be with the highest Respect, Sir,
Your most obedient humble servant,
Stratford Canning

14. *Long to Macomb, Wheeling*, [now W. Va.], *May 12, 1823.*[23]

Sir:

I have the honour to inform you that the Expedition under my command arrived at this place on the evening of the 10th inst. Having written letters in various directions with the view of in-

[22] On the border situation between Canada and the United States, see above, pp. 15–17. No letter from Canning to Dalhousie has been located. The latter was governor-in-chief of Canada.

[23] OCE, Letters Received, NARG 77.

terupting Dr. James in his progress westward, I expected to find him here waiting the arrival of the Expedition, but have been disappointed. He has no doubt proceeded directly to Belle Fountaine. I also anticipated the pleasure of meeting Lt. Talcott here, but he has not yet arrived. We purpose to resume our march towards Columbus to morrow morning, when we shall probably be overtaken by Lt. T. I purpose to write Dr. J. at Belle Fontaine, requiring him to repair with as little delay as possible to Prairie du Chien or Fort St. Anthony, with the hope that he will be able to join us at one of these places.

I have the honour to be Sir very respectfully
Your obedt. & humble Servant
S. H. LONG Maj. T. Engs.

15. *Long to Macomb, Piqua, Ohio, May 23, 1823.*[24]

SIR:

At Columbus I had the honour to receive by the hand of Mr. James Calhoun your letters of the 30th Apr. and 3rd May, together with the highly gratifying and distinguished favor of the Rt. Hon. Mr. Canning. Altho' I much regret that we cannot avail ourselves of the assistance of Lt. Talcott, yet we are hig[h]ly gratified at the attainment of so valuable an acquisition to our part[y] as that afforded by the substitution of Mr. Calhoun.

The circumstances under which my draft on the War Department for $1000 was made were such as precluded the practicability of transmitting either the vouchers or statement that appear to have been expected. I had immediate occasion for funds to complete the outfit for the Expedition, and necessarily must have recourse to the draft in order to obtain an immediate supply; otherwise I should have been delayed many days in order to accomplish this part of the business. The several articles of our outfit having been procured at a variety of places occasioned a multiplicity of accounts which could not be receipted till the sums they called for were paid, and I had no funds in hand for this purpose. Moreover, funds must be procured for the purchase of horses and for defraying the traveling expenses of the gentlemen of the party, the accounts for which could not be rendered, nor the amount stated, till the expenses should have actually been incurred. These are among the considerations which I

[24] OCE, Letters Received, NARG 77.

trust will be admitted as a reasonably apology for the step I have taken in relation to the draft.

I have the satisfaction to inform you, that the Expedition has proceeded thus far without accident, and that the gentlemen of the party are all in good health; and that, altho' the roads are exceedingly bad, owing to the wetness of the season, yet our progress is equally as rapid as I had anticipated.

I should have replied to your letters immediately on the receipt of them, but for a temporary indisposition I experienced at Columbus.

I have the honour to be Sir, very respectfully
Your most obedient and humble Sert.
S. H. LONG Maj. T. Engs.

16. *Long to Macomb, Fort Wayne, Ind., May 29, 1823.*[25]

SIR:

I beg leave to represent that our expenses thus far on the journey have considerably exceeded my estimate, the reasons whereof are, first, that I omitted to include the expense of horse-keeping on the route, and second, I have the travelling expenses of four persons instead of two, as exhibited in the estimate, to defray.[26]

I accordingly beg leave to request that funds to the amount of at least five hundred dollars may be transmitted to Detroit, that they may be in readiness for us on our return.

We are about taking our departure for Chicago, where we shall probably arrive in the course of eight days.

I have the honour to be Sir very respectfully
Your obedt. & humble Sert.
S. H. LONG Maj. T. Engs.

17. *Long to Macomb, "Fort Dearborn Chicago," Ill., June 10, 1823.*[27]

SIR

I have the honor to inform you that the Expedition arrived at this place on the 5th Inst. and purpose to resume their march tomorrow

[25] OCE, Letters Received, NARG 77.

[26] Long's estimate of April 15, printed above, included traveling expenses for Say and Seymour. His final accounts also included Keating and Colhoun. The extra funds he requested below did not arrive; see Long to Macomb, October 18, 1823, below.

[27] OCE, Letters Received, NARG 77.

in a direction for Pra[i]rie Du Chien. The roads having been very muddy and the streams high, our progress has been necessarily slow. Our Horses have suffered considerably. Four of them have been so much injured by the journey that we are compelled to leave them here and obtain others which we have effected thro the aid of the Commanding Officer Col. [John] McNeil. I wrote you from Fort Wayne, requesting that funds might be transmitted to Detroit for the use of the Expedition.[28]

I have the honor to be Sir
Yr. mo. Obt. humble Servt:
[UNSIGNED]

18. *Long to Macomb, Prairie du Chien, Wis., June 24, 1823.*[29]

SIR:

I have the honour to inform you that the Explg. Party reached this place on the 19th inst. after a march of nine days from Chicago. We purpose to take our departure hence to-morrow morning, accompanied by a detachment from this Post consisting of 1 Subaltern, 1 non-commissioned officer & 9 privates. Mr. Calhoun and myself purpose to travel hence to Fort St. Anthony by land, while the other gentlemen of the party will proceed thither by water.[30]

I have the honour to be Sir respectfully
Your obt. and humble Sert.
S. H. Long, Maj. T. Eng.

P. S. I beg you will do me the favour of forwarding the accompanying letter to Mrs. L. per Mail. S.H.L.[31]

19. *Long to Macomb, Fort St. Anthony, July 9, 1823.*[32]

SIR:

I have the honour to inform you that the Expedition arrived at this Post in safety on the 2nd Inst.

[28] On McNeil, see Heitman, *Historical Register*, 1:679; Quaife, *Chicago and the Old Northwest*, 282.

[29] OCE, Letters Received, NARG 77.

[30] On the men Long took with him from Fort Crawford and the water party, see Chapter 3, notes 61, 62, above. The subaltern was probably Lt. Martin Scott, and the noncommissioned officer was Corp. Joshua Sanders.

[31] Mrs. Long was probably living in Philadelphia at this time. See Long to Macomb, August 8, 1823, below; De Silver, *Philadelphia Directory, 1824*, n.p.; Reid, *Biographical Sketch of Enoch Long*, 33.

[32] OCE, Letters Received, NARG 77.

Soon after our arrival, Lt. [Martin] Scott and the guard detailed at Fort Crawford for the service of the Expedition were ordered back to Fort Crawford by the comdg. Officer of this Post, Lt. Scott being ordered to return to this post with the least possible delay for the purpose of rejoining the Expedition. In the mean time, a guard consisting of two non commissioned officers and nineteen privates, has been detailed for the service of the Expedition, and placed under the immediate command of 2nd Lt. [St. Clair] Denny who has reported for duty. With this detachment we purpose to take our departure hence this day with the expectation that Lt. Scott will overtake us on the march. The men appear to be well selected, and their number accords with my requisition. Twelve horses & mules have also been added to the Expedition, together with such stores &c. as were deemed requisite.[33]

Mr. [Giacomo C.] Beltrami, an Italian gentleman, and Mr. [William] J. Snelling son of Col. S. have volunteered to accompany us, and join our party at this place.

Mr. [Lawrence] Taliaferro Ind. Agt. also accompanies us up the St. Peters, about 8 days, with the view of councilling with the Sussaton [*Sisseton*] Indians.

A Guide and two interpreters are also added to our party.[34]

I have the honour to be Sir, very respectfully
Your obt. and humble Sert.
S. H. LONG, Maj. T. Engrs.

Private

I transmit the enclosed for the sake of a more safe conveyance. I beg you will do me the favour to forward them. S.H.L.

20. *Long to Macomb, "Camp on the St. Peters 130 miles from its mouth"* [Traverse des Sioux], *July 15, 1823.*[35]

SIR:

The Exploring Party reached this point last evening having sustained no other misfortune but the loss of a part of our ammunition

[33] The guard included three noncommissioned officers (one sergeant and two corporals) in addition to 19 privates and Lt. Denny. See p. 155, above.

[34] On Beltrami and William J. Snelling, see pp. 31, 35, 154, 184, above. Taliaferro did not accompany the expedition beyond the first day; see p. 157, above. Joseph Renville served as guide and Dakota interpreter and Louis Demarest or Desmarais as Ojibway interpreter, a total of two persons rather than three. See p. 155, above.

[35] OCE, Letters Received, NARG 77. Long mentions writing this letter on p. 162, above.

and all the tobacco we took with us for presents to the Indians, occasioned by the oversetting of the canoe on board of which it was transported. Some damage was also done to our provisions by a violent storm that immediately succeeded the accident just mentioned.

Thus far we have proceeded up the St. Peter's in two parties, one by land and the other by water. Finding the ascent by water very tedious and slow, on account of the crookedness of the river and the obstructions occasioned by shoals, I am induced to prosecute our journey by land exclusively. We have been informed that the Indians generally have withdrawn from the river to perform their summer hunt, also that little danger is to be apprehended from any with whom we are likely to meet; I have accordingly thought it best to send back nine men out of the number furnished at Fort St. Anthony as our guard. I am the more inclined to this measure, in consequence of the rumour spread by the Indians, that game is exceedingly scarse on the upper part of the river. Our party will now consist of 24 persons including Interpreters, and the 12 soldiers that we retain.[36]

I have the pleasure to add that we are all in good health.

I have the honour to be sir very respectfully
Your most obedt. and humble Sert.
S. H. LONG Maj. T. Engs.

21. *Long to Macomb, "Camp Monroe near Pembina on Red river," August 8, 1823.*[37]

SIR:

I have the honour to report that the Exploring Expedition under my command reached this place in safety on the morning of the 5th inst. On our march up the St. Peter's, several of our horses failed, and some of them since our departure from the source of that river. From the gens de la fieulle [*Gens des Feuilles*], a wandering band of the Sioux notorious for their insolence and depredations, we rec[e]ived some slight annoyanc[e], not injurious, however, either to

[36] The guard which accompanied Long from Fort St. Anthony consisted of 23 men, including Lt. St. Clair Denny. When nine were sent back to the fort, the guard numbered 14. With the five gentlemen of the party, two interpreters, Snelling, and Beltrami, the expedition numbered 23. See p. 155, above.

[37] OCE, Letters Received, NARG 77.

our persons or property, but merely calculated to excite in us some apprehension for our safety.[38]

Our Camp (Monroe) is situated just below the village of Pembina, and immediately on the bank of Red river of Hudson's Bay. By a series of observations for Latitude as complete as the weather (which has been very changeable since our arrival) would permit, the site of our Camp has been ascertained to be within 10″ seconds of the 49th deg. of N. Lat. A line of 207 1/2 feet, running N 18° 25′ E carries us from the site of our Flag Staff to a point on the bank of the river, where we have erected a Post of demarkation inscribed with the letters G.B. on the north and U.S. on the South side.

We find it necessary at this place to change our means of conveyance and to prosecute our journey by water. I have accordingly disposed of most of our horses for the purchase of provisions, employing of boatmen &c. The residue (4 horses & 2 mules) I have delivered to Mr. [William] Joseph Snelling, with instructions to proceed with three of the soldiers of my command on their return to Fort St. Anthony, and to report there to the Comdg. officer of that Post.

We purpose to resume our march to-morrow, and to proceed via Ft. Douglass, Lake Winnipeg, Lake of the Woods &c. with all convenient dispach on our way homeward.

I have the honour to be Sir very respectfully
Your most obt. and humble Sert.
S. H. LONG Maj. T. Engs.

P. S. I beg you will do me the favour to forward the enclosed by mail to Philadelphia.

22. *Major General Edmund P. Gaines, "Hd. Qtrs. Western Department" to John C. Calhoun, Secretary of War, Louisville, Ky., October 18, 1823.*[39]

SIR —

A report has this day reached this city from St. Louis, that the exploring party under Major Long of the Topographical Engineers,

[38] On the *Gens des Feuilles*, the marking of the boundary, and the rearrangements at Pembina mentioned below, see pp. 20, 176, 183, 184, above.

[39] Secretary of War, Letters Received, NARG 107. Gaines commanded the U.S. Army's Western Department at this time. Louisville was one of several points from which he administered the unit. See James W. Silver, *Edmund Pendleton Gaines: Frontier General*, 90, 91 ([Baton Rouge], 1949).

had been attacked and cut off by the Indians of the Red River of Lake Winnipeg.

Although the report comes to this place unsupported by any account of the source or channel by which it found its way to St. Louis, or any other particulars calculated to give it authenticity, yet it is stated by Mr. [George K.] McGunnegle of St. Louis, in a letter that I have just now seen, that Governor [William] Clark deems the report to be entitled to credit. And when it is recollected that the distance from the Ricaras [*Arikara*] to the Indian villages on the Red River is less than 300 miles; that the Indians of these villages are understood to have been in habits of friendly and frequent intercourse with the Ricaras; and that an account of the successful outrage on General [William H.] Ashleys trading company may have reached the Red River previous to the arrival of Major Long, and may have prepared the minds of the Indians there for a similar outrage upon his party; there is too much reason to apprehend the report to be true.[40]

Immediately on the receipt of this painful report, I wrote to Colonel Snelling, commanding at St. Anthony, by express, directing him that should any such outrage have been or in future be committed to adopt the most effectual measures the force and other means under his controul would permit to afford relief to the survivors of the party, and to inflict exemplary punishment on the offenders. For this purpose I directed him to employ the Indian country men near him, with from one to two hundred friendly Indian warriors, to co-operate with the disposable regular force under him, and I authorised him moreover to call to his aid Lieut. Colonel [Willoughby] Morgan with one company from Prairie du Chien.[41]

With great respect I have the honor to be
E. P. GAINES Maj. Genl. by Brevet
Commanding

[40] Gaines was probably referring to an exaggerated report on the threatening attitude of the *Gens des Feuilles* which the expedition experienced on July 28; see p. 176, above. McGunnegle went to St. Louis in 1821 as a clerk; see his obituary in *Missouri Republican*, December 13, 1878. The Arikara, whose villages were located near the Grand River in present Corson County, S. Dak., on June 2, 1823, attacked a fur trading party led by Ashley, a general in the Missouri militia and a partner of Andrew Henry. See Richard A. Krause, *The Leavenworth Site: Archaeology of an Historic Arikara Community*, 15 (University of Kansas, *Publications in Anthropology*, no. 3—Lawrence, Kan., 1972); Chittenden, *American Fur Trade*, 1:247–249, 264–269.

[41] See Gaines to Snelling, October 18, 1823, in AGO, Letters Received, NARG 94.

23. *Long to Macomb, Buffalo, N.Y., October 18, 1823.*[42]

SIR/.

I have the satisfaction to inform you that the Expedition I have the honour to command reached this place in good health this morning, having in their tour traversed the valley of St. Peter's river from its mouth to its source about 300 miles, that of Red river thro' its whole length 400 miles, Lake Wenepeek [*Winnipeg*] across its southerly extremity 65 miles, Wenepeek river from its mouth to the Lake of the Woods 175 miles, thence thro' the Lake of the Woods, Rainy river and Lake, Kamana [*Kaministikwia*] river &c. to Lake Superior 600 miles, and thence the Sault de St. Marie, Mackinaw and Detroit, to this place more than 1000 miles. At Mackinaw Lts. Scott and Denny and the guard detailed for the service of the Expedition at Fort St. Anthony separated from the party with orders to rejoin their regiment on the Mississippi.

I take the liberty herewith to enclose an Abstract of expenditures necessarily incurred by the Expedition in the performance of their duties, with an ardent desire that you will with the least possible delay forward to Philadelphia the means necessary to avert the shower of demands that is ready to break over me on my arrival at that place. Of the sum of one thousand dollars for which I drew on the War Department in favour of J. M. Wright Esq. in April last, upwards of $500 were expended in making our outfit from Philadelphia. The residue, something less than $500, is all the pecuniary aid hitherto received from Government to defray the whole of the charges specified in the enclosed Abstract, for the payment of which I have had occasion to make myself individually responsible. The sum of $500, which I requested might be transmitted to Detroit to enable me to defray the expenses of the Expedition thence homeward, I am sorry to state, has never come to hand.[43]

It will readily be perceived that the expenses of the Expedition will far exceed the amount contemplated in the Estimate made by myself at Washington in April last. That amount, so far as I can

[42] OCE, Letters Received, NARG 77.

[43] The $1,000 was received on May 10 from Wright, who was probably the Jonathan M. Wright, a Philadelphia merchant, mentioned in Voucher No. 59, in "Abstract," below. See "The United States in Account Current with the Exploring Expedition Commanded by S. H. Long Maj. Topographical Engineers, in 1823," December 5, 1823, in GAO, Third Auditor, Account No. 2303, NARG 217; De Silver, *Philadelphia Directory, 1824*, n.p. The Philadelphia expenditures, recorded in Vouchers No. 1–15, 59, in "Abstract," below, totaled $584.60. For the April estimate of expenses mentioned below, see Long to Macomb, April 15, 1823, above.

Abstract of Expenditures incurred by the Explg. Expedition subsequently to their departure from Philadelphia in April 1823.

No. of vouch.	*Date 1823*	*To whom paid*	*On what account*	*Dol.*	*Cts.*	*Dol.*	*Cts.**
1	May	F. Fogle	Two Horses	130	00		
2	"	F. Hughes	One Horse	75	—		
3	"	Do.	Horse-shoeing &c.	8	87		
4	"	S. Dugan	Saddle & Bridle	10	—		
5	"	James Robinson	One Horse, Sad. & Brid.	87	50		
6	"	Thomas Say	Travelling Expenses	45	26		
7	"	Samuel Seymour	Do. do.	45	26		
8	"	Wm. H. Keating	Do. do.	45	26		
9	June 22	J. St. P. Le Sellier	Services as Guide &c.	30	—		
10	July 9	Augustus Roque	Services as Interpreter	15	—		
11	" 26	Cola. Fur Company	Provisions &c.	234	75	234	75
12	Aug. 5	Anthony Le Gros	Transportation of Baggage &c.	108	—	108	—
13	" 7	—— Beltrami	One Horse, Sad. & Bridle	90	—		
14	" 14	Charles Ferdinand	Provisions &c.	114	32	114	32
15	" "	Benjamin Jervais	One North Canoe &c.	59	—		
16	" 16	Hudson B. Company	Provisions &c.	196	89	196	89
17	" "	Paul Bauche	One North Canoe	30	—		
18	" "	Andrew M[c]Dermont	Tobacco &c. for presents	42	—	42	—
19	Sept. 2	Hudson B. Company	Provisions &c.	77	90	77	90
20	" 13	Baptiste Demarest	Services as Pilot	141	33	141	33

21	"	"	Francis Frenier	Services as Bowsman	66	66	66	66
22	"	"	Louis Morain	Do. do.	66	66	66	66
23	"	"	Antoine La Frenier	Do. do.	66	66	66	66
24	"	"	John B. Robillard	Services as Steersman	66	66	66	66
25	"	"	Peter George	Do. do.	66	66	66	66
26	"	"	Joachim Ranger	Do. do.	66	66	66	66
27	"	"	Charles G. Bruce	Services as Interpreter	56	—		
28	"	15	Hudson B. Company	Provisions &c.	119	11	119	11
29	Oct.	1	Baptiste Fontaine	Services as Voyageur	54	—	54	—
30	"	"	Joachim Ranger	Do. do.	24	—	24	—
31	"	"	Moses Le Febre	Do. do.	46	—	46	—
32	"	"	Joseph Plante	Do. do.	46	—	46	—
33	"	"	Hudson B. Company	Provisions &c.	29	91	29	91
34	"	17	Thomas Say	Travelling Expenses	82	63		
35	"	"	W. H. Keating	Do. do.	82	63		
36	"	"	Saml. Seymour	Do. do.	82	63		
37	"	"	J. E. Calhoun	Do. do.	90	37		
				Amount	$2699	58	$1634	17

I certify that the above is an accurate statement of Expenditures that have actually been incurred by the Expedition I have the honour to command, since its departure from Philadelphia up to the 18th October 1823.

S. H. LONG Maj. Topl. Engineers

*Note. The Expenses carried out in this column were not anticipated at the time of making the estimate of the Expenses of the Expedition, which I had the honour to submit to the War Dept. S.H.L.

recollect, was something more than $1700, or if we include our Geologist and Astronomer agreeably to the purport of the Estimate a little more than $2700, nearly the Amount specified in the accompanying Abstract. But there are many items of expenditure in this document that could not be anticipated at the time the estimate was made. These constitute a seperate column in the Abstract and much increase the amount as may be seen by recurring to that instrument. Besides it was expected in the out-set that we should be supplied at the several Posts in our route with many articles of clothing, camp-equippage, Indian goods, and other out-fits, very few of which could be obtained except by special purchase.

I beg leave to subjoin a brief recapitulation, in order to show more plainly the amount of Funds necessary to relieve me from impending embarrassments.[44]

	D.C.
Amount of Expenditures as per Abstract herewith submitted	2699.58
Do. of Pecuniary aid received from War Department for the disbursement of the above expenditures	500.00
Balance required to meet the payment of expenses actually incurred by the expedition as pr. Abstract	2199.58

Permit me to request that the sum of $2000, or $1500 at least, may be transmitted to me at Philadelphia with as little delay as practicable that I may be enabled to settle the demands now against me on account of the Expedition. I shall embrace the earliest opportunity to render my accounts in a more complete form embracing all the expenses I have already incurred, or may hereafter be subjected to on account of the Expedition.

I have the honour to be Sir:
Very respectfully Your most obedt. Servant
S. H. LONG Maj. T. Engrs.

[44] Some of the figures here, as well as the voucher numbers in the abstract on pp. 374–375, are incorrect. For a complete and correct listing with identification of persons, see "Abstract," pp. 378–385. In saying that he had received only $500 of "Pecuniary aid" from the War Department, Long was subtracting the Philadelphia expenses (which he miscalculated) from the $1,000 he received on May 10. He received an additional $2,000 from the U.S. treasurer on November 5, 1823; see "The United States in Account Current with the Exploring Expedition," December 5, 1823, in GAO, Third Auditor, Account No. 2303, NARG 217.

24. *Macomb to Long, Washington, D.C., October 31, 1823.*[45]

SIR

Your letter of the 18th instant has been received together with its enclosure. The whole has been laid before the Secretary of War, who is much gratified to learn that you and your party have returned in safety, and trusts that the information and materials collected will enable you to make a very interesting report of your expedition. The Amount of your requisition for funds to defray the expences of the expedition viz. $2000 Dollars will be sent to you immediately. In the settlement of your Accounts, you will take care to arrange the several items under their proper heads, as Subsistance, Quarter Master's Dept. &c. &c. No transportation is to be allowed when the Public have furnished the transport, and to the Gentlemen who accompanied you you will allow the Amount of the sum actually paid for Stage fare, and the Actual expences where there were no stages, provided the said expences do not exceed the rate of ten cents p. mile. I avail myself of this occasion to congratulate you on the happy issue of your enterprize, and the fortunate return of all who accompanied you, assuring you at the same time of the respect and esteem with which I remain Sir

Yr. obt. Sert.
ALEX MACOMB
Maj. Genl. Chf. Engr.

NB. A copy of this letter will be sent to the 3rd Auditor to govern in the settlement of your accounts.

25. *Long to Macomb, Philadelphia, Pa., October 31, 1823.*[46]

SIR:

I have the honour to report that the Exploratory Tour authorized by the War Department in April last has been performed, and that the gentlemen of the Expedition, with the exception of Mr. J. E. Calhoun who had occasion to delay a short time at N. York, have arrived in good health at this place.

In connexion with the service in which we have been engaged, copious notes have been taken, together with such records as were deemed essential to a geographical delineation and description of the country traversed by the party. I therefore take the liberty to

(*continued on page 388*)

[45] OCE, Letters to Officers of Engineers, NARG 77.
[46] OCE, Letters Received, NARG 77.

26. *Abstract of Expenditures incurred by the Exploring Expedition commanded by Major S. H. Long in 1823, exhibiting a List of the several articles &c. purchased and the disposition made of them, together with the Departments &c. to which they are respectively chargeable* [47]

Dates 1823	No. of Vouchr.	To whom paid	For what Articles and Services	To what Department &c. chargeable												How disposed of and appropriated	Amount	
				Q. Masters Department		Contingencies				Ordnance Department		Indian Departmt.		S.H. Long's Personl. Acct.				
						Engr. Dept.		War Dept.										
				Dol	Cts	Dol	Cts	Dol	Cts	Dol	Cts	Dol	Cts	Dol	Cts		Dol	Cts
Apr. 10	1	Thomas Whitney[48]	One Small Surveyor's Compass	—	—	17	00	—	—	—	—	—	—	—	—	On hand: Damaged in the Service	17	00
" 25	2	Anthony Finley	Blank Books, Lead Pencils, Camels-Hair Do.	—	—	13	26	—	—	—	—	—	—	—	—	Expended in the Service	13	26
" "	3	John H. Schrader	One Mercurial Case, Box-wood	—	—	2	—	—	—	—	—	—	—	—	—	Delivered to Mr. J. E. Calhoun	2	00
" 26	4	James C. Wood	Four Oil-Cloth Capes	22	93	—	—	—	—	—	—	—	—	—	—	Worn out in the Service	22	93
" 28	5	Asher Atkinson	Three Saddles and three Bridles	—	—	—	—	—	—	—	—	—	—	24	00	Accounted for in Account Current		
" "	"	Do.	Breast-Plates, Valices, Sadl. Bags, Coat-Pads, Holsters, Bearskins, Cyrcingles [*sursingles*] &c.[49]	47	68	—	—	—	—	—	—	—	—	—	—	2 Valices & 2 Sad.-Bags on hand. Residue expended in Service	71	68
" 29	6	George W. Tryon	One Rifle, one Pr. Bayonet Pistols	—	—	—	—	—	—	24	25	—	—	—	—	Damaged in the Service. Delivered to Lt. Scott		

																	pr. Receipt (A)[50]		
〃	〃	〃	Do.	One Double Gun, one Percussion Pistol	—	—	—	—	—	—	29	75	—	—	—	—	On hand. Damaged in the Service	63	25
〃	〃	〃	Do.	Primg. Caps, Drink. Cups, Screw driver, Primg. Wires & Brushes, Repairs &c.[51]	—	—	—	—	—	—	9	25	—	—	—	—	Expended in the Service, or unavoidably lost		
〃	〃	7	Isaiah Lukens	One Small Gun	—	—	—	—	—	—	—	—	—	—	16	—	Accounted for in Acct. Current	16	00
〃	〃	8	John Harned	Tin Canisters, Boxes, Memorandum Case	3	62½	—	—	—	—	—	—	—	—	—	—	Ex[p]ended in the service or unavoidably lost	3	62½
〃	〃	9	Wickham & Co.	Two Canisters of Powder	—	—	—	—	—	—	1	50	—	—	—	—	Do. do.	1	50
〃	〃	10	William Davenport	Pocket Sextant, Protractor, Nautical Almanac	—	—	31	50	—	—	—	—	—	—	—	—	Almanac deld. to J. E. Calhoun. Residue on hand	31	50
〃	〃	11	Charles A. Droz	One Patent Leaver Watch	—	—	66	—	—	—	—	—	—	—	—	—	On hand, in good condition	66	00
〃	〃	12	Joseph Tyson	One Horse	—	—	—	—	—	—	—	—	—	—	68	—	Accounted for in Account Current	68	00
〃	〃	13	M. Fisher & Son	Thermometers, Lenses, Pocket Compass[52]	—	—	11	—	—	—	—	—	—	—	—	—	1 Thermr. unavoidably lost. Residue on hand	11	00
〃	〃	14	John Dupuy	Portable Soupe (for the subsistence of the Party)	15	—	—	—	—	—	—	—	—	—	—	—	Expended in the Service	15	00
〃	〃	15	William Snowdon	Two Horses	170	—	—	—	—	—	—	—	—	—	—	—	Damaged in the Service, & turned over to Pubc. pr. Rect. (B)	170	00
May	13	16	Francis Fogle[53]	Do. do.	—	—	—	—	—	—	—	—	—	—	130	—	Accounted for in Account Current	130	00

Dates 1823	No. of Vouchr.	To whom paid	For what Articles and Services	To what Department &c. chargeable: Q. Masters Department Dol	Cts	Contingencies: Engr. Dept. Dol	Cts	Contingencies: War Dept. Dol	Cts	Ordnance Department Dol	Cts	Indian Departmt. Dol	Cts	S.H. Long's Personl. Acct. Dol	Cts	How disposed of and appropriated	Amount Dol	Cts
″ 17	17	Thomas Hughes	Horse-shoeing, Bag, Pack-Saddle, Saddle Blankets	8	87½	—	—	—	—	—	—	—	—	—	—	2 Blankts. deld. to Capt. Perkins, pr. Receipt (C) Residue expended	8	87½
″ ″	18	J. S. Dugan	One Saddle and one Bridle	10	—	—	—	—	—	—	—	—	—	—	—	Worn out and expended in the Service	10	00
″ ″	19	Thomas Hughes	One Horse	—	—	—	—	—	—	—	—	—	—	75	—	Accounted for in Account Current	75	00
″ 20	20	James Robinson	One Horse, Saddle and Bridle	—	—	—	—	—	—	—	—	—	—	87	50	Do. do.	87	50
″ 27	21	William Suttonfield[54]	One Horse	—	—	—	—	—	—	—	—	—	—	30	—	Do. do.	30	00
″ ″	22	Thomas Say	Travelling Expenses (exclusive of Transportation)	—	—	—	—	45	26	—	—	—	—	—	—	Expended between Philadelphia & Fort Wayne	45	26
″ ″	23	Saml. Seymour	Do. Do. do.	—	—	—	—	45	26	—	—	—	—	—	—	Do. Do. do.	45	26
″ ″	24	Wm. H. Keating	Do. Do. do.	—	—	—	—	45	26	—	—	—	—	—	—	Do. Do. do.	45	26
″ 28	25	James Hackley	Cotton (Cloth), Thread, Buttons, Tomahks. Bridle, Girths, Cord, Br. Skins, Pk. Saddle	20	41	—	—	—	—	—	—	—	—	—	—	Expended in the Service or unavoidably lost }	50	41
″ ″	″	Do.	5 Large Blankets, and two small Do.	30	—	—	—	—	—	—	—	—	—	—	—	Delivered to Capt. Perkins Mily. Str. Keepr. pr Rect. (C) }		

June 22	26	J. St. P. Le Sellier[55]	Services as Indn. Interpreter & Guide	—	—	—	—	—	—	—	—	30	—	—	—	Expended between Chicago & Prairie du Chien	30	00
July 9	27	Augustus Roque	Do. do. do.	—	—	—	—	—	—	—	—	15	—	—	—	Do. Prairie du Chien & Ft. St. Anthony	15	00
" 26	28	Columbia Fur Compy.	Tobacco, Powder, Balls, Indn. Interr. & Guide, Silk Hkf. (Indn. Presents)	—	—	—	—	—	—	—	—	115	25	—	—	Expended in the Service		
" "	"	Do. Do.	Dry Buffalo Meat, Pemakin, Horse-hire, Grease, 2 Blankets	87	50	—	—	—	—	—	—	—	—	—	—	Expended between Lake Traverse & Pembina	234	75
" "	"	Do. Do.	Four Blankets (appropriated by Major Long)	—	—	—	—	—	—	—	—	—	—	32	—	Accounted for in Account Current		
Aug. 7	29	Beltrami	One Horse, Saddle & Bridle	—	—	—	—	—	—	—	—	—	—	90	—	Do. do.	90	00
" 14	30	Charles Ferdinand[56]	Sugar, Pemican, Meat, Fat, Salt	114	32	—	—	—	—	—	—	—	—	—	—	Expended in the Service	114	32
" "	31	Benjamin Jervais	One North Canoe, and Voyageurs Kettle	59	—	—	—	—	—	—	—	—	—	—	—	Canoe left at Ft. William. Kettle expended in Service	59	00
" 16	32	H. Bay Company	Pemican, Line, N. Canoe, Buffo. Shoes, Buffo. Cloth, Wheat	196	89	—	—	—	—	—	—	—	—	—	—	Buffo. Cloth on hand. Residue expended in the Service	196	89
" "	33	Paul Bauché	One North Canoe	30	—	—	—	—	—	—	—	—	—	—	—	Worn out in the Service	30	00
" "	34	Andw. McDermont	Pitch, Nails, Moose-skin	14	—	—	—	—	—	—	—	—	—	—	—	Expended in the Service	42	—
" "	"	Do.	Tobacco (Indn. Presents)	—	—	—	—	—	—	—	—	28	—	—	—	Expanded in Do.		
" 5	35	Antoine Le Gros[57]	Transportation of Baggage, one Canoe &c.	108	—	—	—	—	—	—	—	—	—	—	—	Do. between Lake Traverse & Pembina	108	00
Sept. 2	36	H. Bay Company	Gum, Bark, Whatapp, Grease, Salt, Flour, Corn	77	90	—	—	—	—	—	—	—	—	—	—	Do. in the Service	77	90

Dates 1823	No. of Vouchr.	To whom paid	For what Articles and Services	To what Department &c. chargeable												How disposed of and appropriated	Amount	
				Q. Masters Department		Contingencies				Ordnance Department		Indian Departmt.		S.H. Long's Personl. Acct.				
						Engr. Dept.		War Dept.										
				Dol	Cts	Dol	Cts	Dol	Cts	Dol	Cts	Dol	Cts	Dol	Cts		Dol	Cts
" 13	37	Francois Fournier[58]	Services as Bowsman (Voyageur)	—	—	66	66	—	—	—	—	—	—	—	—	Expended between Ft. Douglass & Lake Superior	66	66
" "	38	Louis Morain	Do. do. do.	—	—	66	66	—	—	—	—	—	—	—	—	Do. Do. do.	66	66
" "	39	John B. Robillard	Do. as Steerman do.	—	—	66	66	—	—	—	—	—	—	—	—	Do. Do. do.	66	66
" "	40	Peter George	Do. do. do.	—	—	66	66	—	—	—	—	—	—	—	—	Do. Do. do.	66	66
" "	41	Antoine Le Frenier	Do. as Bowsman do.	—	—	66	66	—	—	—	—	—	—	—	—	Do. Do. do.	66	66
" "	42	Baptiste Demarest	Do. as Pilot do.	—	—	141	33	—	—	—	—	—	—	—	—	Do. Do. do.	141	33
" "	43	Charles G. Brouss	Do. as Indian Interpreter	—	—	—	—	—	—	—	—	56	—	—	—	Do. Do. do.	56	00
" "	44	Joachim Ranger	Do. as Steersman (Voyageur)	—	—	66	66	—	—	—	—	—	—	—	—	Do. Do. do.	66	66
" 15	45	H. Bay Company	Corn, Pitch, Oakum, Block, Nails, Soap, Flour, Pork, Grease, Sugar, Salt, Candles &c.	100	71	—	—	—	—	—	—	—	—	—	—	Expended between Fort William & Mackinaw		
" "	"	Do. Do.	Note to Baptiste Demarest, charged in this Account	—	—	—	—	—	—	—	—	—	—	14	—	Accounted for in Account Current	119	11
" "	"	Do. Do.	Tobacco (Indian Presents)	—	—	—	—	—	—	—	—	4	40	—	—	Expended between Fort William & Mackinaw		
Octor. 1	46	Baptiste Fontaine[59]	Services as Voyageur and Pilot	—	—	54	—	—	—	—	—	—	—	—	—	Expended between Ft. Douglass & Mackinaw	54	00
" "	47	Joachim Ranger	Do. do. and Guide	—	—	24	—	—	—	—	—	—	—	—	—	Do. Fort William & Do.	24	00

"	"	48	Moses Le Fevre	Do. do.	—	—	46	—	—	—	—	—	—	—	—	—	Do. Fort Douglass & Do.	46	00
"	"	49	Joseph Plante	Do. do.	—	—	46	—	—	—	—	—	—	—	—	—	Do. Do. Do.	46	00
"	"	50	H. Bay Company	Corn, Flour, Grease, Sugar, Butter, Tea, Gum, Salt, Fish, Potatoes	23	91	—	—	—	—	—	—	—	—	—	—	Do. Fort William & Do.	29	91
"	"	"	Do. Do.	Two Blankets charged in this account, £ 1.10s Halifax Cury.	—	—	—	—	—	—	—	—	—	—	6	—	Accounted for in Account Current		
"	17	51	Wm. H. Keating[60]	Travelling Expenses (not included in any of the foregoing charges)	—	—	—	—	82	63	—	—	—	—	—	—	Expended on the Route from Ft. Wayne to Buffalo	82	63
"	"	52	Thomas Say	Do. do.	—	—	—	—	82	63	—	—	—	—	—	—	Do. do. Do.	82	63
"	"	53	Samuel Seymour	Do. do.	—	—	—	—	82	63	—	—	—	—	—	—	Do. do. Do.	82	63
"	"	54	James E. Calhoun	Do. do.	—	—	—	—	90	37	—	—	—	—	—	—	Do. do. from Columbus to Buffalo	90	37
"	26	55	Do.	Do. (inclusive of Transportation)	—	—	—	—	38	88	—	—	—	—	—	—	Expended between Buffalo & New York	38	88
"	29	56	Samuel Seymour	Do. do.	—	—	—	—	45	52	—	—	—	—	—	—	Do. Do. & Philadelphia	45	52
"	"	57	Thomas Say	Do. do.	—	—	—	—	45	52	—	—	—	—	—	—	Do. Do. Do.	45	52
"	"	58	William H. Keating	Do. do.	—	—	—	—	45	52	—	—	—	—	—	—	Do. Do. Do.	45	52
Apr.	24	59	Jonathan M. Wright	Knives, Dirk, Fish-hooks, Powder Flasks, Fishing Lines &c.[61]	11	86	—	—	—	—	—	—	—	—	—	—	Expended in the Service, or unavoidably lost	11	86
Received at Chicago				One Public Horse. Disabled in the Service and Sold at Pembina	—	—	—	—	—	—	—	—	—	—	35	—	Accounted for in Account Current.	35	00
Received at Fort St. Anthony				One Pub. Mule & 2 Horses. Do. do. do.	—	—	—	—	—	—	—	—	—	—	100	—	Do. Do.	100	00
				Amounts. $	1152	61	852	05	649	48	64	75	248	65	707	50	Total Amount $	3675	04

Dates 1823 / No. of Vouchr. / To whom paid	For what Articles and Services	To what Department &c. chargeable												How disposed of and appropriated	Amount	
		Q. Masters Department		Contingencies				Ordnance Department		Indian Departmt.		S. H. Long's Personl. Acct.				
				Engr. Dept.		War Dept.										
		Dol	Cts	Dol	Cts	Dol	Cts	Dol	Cts	Dol	Cts	Dol	Cts		Dol	Cts
The Amount charged to S. H. Long, deducible from that chargd. to Q. M. Department. Deduct		707	50											Expended in defraying a part of the foregoing charges	707	50
Balance due from Q. M. Department		$ 445	11											Amount expended by Major S. H. Long, and chargeable on Account of the Expedition $	2967	54
Abstract supplementary of Accounts outstanding on the first day of November 1823, and chargeable to the Explg. Expedition commanded by Major S. H. Long in 1823	Thomas Say's Account for Services as Zoologist &c. for the Expedn.	—	—	—	—	374	—	—	—	—	—	—	—	To be transmitted to Washington for payment	374	00
	Wm. H. Keating's Do. do. as Geologist &c. for Do.	—	—	—	—	374	—	—	—	—	—	—	—	Do. do. do.	374	00
	J. E. Calhoun's Do. do. as Astronomer for Do.	—	—	374	—	—	—	—	—	—	—	—	—	Do. do. do.	374	00
	Saml. Seymour's Do. do. as Landp. Painter for Do.	—	—	280	50	—	—	—	—	—	—	—	—	Do. do. do.	280	50
Amounts expended by the Expedition prior to the 1st Nov. 1823		$ 445	11	1506	55	1397	48	64	75	248	65	707	50	Total amt. of Expenditures $	4370	04

I certify that the foregoing Abstract exhibits a true Statement of the Accounts of the late Expedition under my command, and that the Expenditures therein charged were actually made by me in behalf of the said Expedition, for the several considerations therein specified, that the vouchers therein referred to are severally, original and genuine, and that the several articles &c. purchased were disposed of, and appropriated, in the manner therein stated. I further certify that the above Abstract Supplementary contains a correct statement of the Accounts outstanding on the first day of Nov. 1823, and chargeable on Account of the said Expedition, and that the several sums therein specified are estimated agreeably to Instructions from the War Department, authorizing a compensation to the scientific gentlemen of the said Expedition.

Philadelphia November 1st 1823

S. H. LONG Major of the
Topl. Engineers

Invoice of Public Horses & Mules furnished for the use of the Expedition, 1823

At what Post or Place.	By whom furnished	No. of Horses	No. of Mules
Fort Dearborn, Chicago	Col. John McNeal[62]	4	—
Ft. Crawford Pr. du Chien	Col. W. Morgan	1	1
Ft. St. Anthony St. Pr. Riv.	Col. J. Snelling	10	2
	Total	15	3

Philadelphia Nov. 1, 1823

Certificate and Statement relative to the Horses, Mules, and other Public property furnished for the use of the Expedition.

I hereby certify that fifteen Horses and three Mules as specified in the Invoice herein annexed, include the whole number of Horses and Mules furnished by the Public for the use of the late Expedition under my command; and [*ms. illegible*] four horses were received at Chicago in place of four other horses that had been damaged in the service of the said Expedition and receipted for by Lt. Hobson, Actg. Q. Master, as pr. Receipt marked (B), that one horse & one mule were received at Prairie du Chien in place of two other horses that had also been damaged in the said service, and receipted for by Col. Morgan, as pr. Receipt marked (D), that two horses failed in the said service and were necessarily left in the wilderness, that three horses and one mule were disabled in the said service and sold for $135, viz. one [*ms. illegible*] for $35.00, & 2 horses & 1 mule for $100.00, and are accounted for in the Account Current herewith transmitted. And that the residue, viz. four horses and two mules were delivered to Joseph Snelling as Public Property, pr. Receipt &c. marked (E). Also I further certify that all articles of Public property, both Military & Indian Stores, have been furnished for the use of, and may stand charged against the said expedition, were either expended or unavoidably lost in the Public Service, or else have been restored again to the Public.

S. H. LONG, Maj. Topographical
Engineers

[47] GAO, Third Auditor, Account No. 2303, NARG 217. The vouchers cited in footnotes below are in the same account, with the exception of No. 27 and 36, which are in Account No. 2332. They are itemized lists of purchases and give quantity as well as price for each category.

[48] The place of payment of Vouchers No. 1–15 and 56–59 was Philadelphia. The people mentioned in Vouchers No. 1–15 and 59 can be found in [William] M'Carty and [Thomas] Davis, *The Philadelphia Directory and Register, for 1821* (Philadelphia, 1821); De Silver, *Philadelphia Directory, 1824*; and Thomas Wilson, ed., *The Philadelphia Directory and Stranger's Guide, for 1825* (Philadelphia, 1825). They are identified as follows: Thomas Whitney, mathematical instrument maker; Anthony Finley, bookseller; John H. Schrader, turner; James Wood, merchant; Asher Atkinson, saddler; George W. Tryon, gun manufacturer; Isaiah Lukens, town clockmaker and mechanist; John Harned, tinplate worker; Wickham & Co., sellers of military and fancy hardware; William Davenport, mathematical instrument maker; Charles A. Droz, clock and watch maker; Joseph Tyson, accountant; Martin Fisher, thermometer and spectacle maker; John Dupuy, cook and confectioner; William Snowden (as he signed the voucher), laborer; Jonathan M. Wright, merchant.

[49] The bearskins were covers for saddles. Listed also in Voucher No. 5 were neck straps, coat straps, compass cases, and saddle repairs.

[50] Receipts A, B, C, D, and E, mentioned here and below, have not been located.

[51] Also listed in Voucher No. 6 were flints, balls, a hunter's canteen, a rifle cover, and a bullet mold for the percussion pistol.

[52] Voucher No. 13 stated that one lens was "common," the other French cylinder.

[53] The place of payment of Voucher No. 16 was Wheeling, Va.; of Vouchers No. 17–19, Zanesville, Ohio; of Voucher No. 20, Columbus, Ohio. No further information on Fogle and Robinson has been found. For Hughes, see U.S. Manuscript Census Schedules, 1830, Muskingum County, Ohio, p. 276A, National Archives Microfilm Roll No. 137. On tavernkeeper Dugan, see Chapter 3, note 12, above. Capt. Samuel Perkins, mentioned opposite, was a military storekeeper for the Ordnance Department. See Heitman, *Historical Register*, 1:784.

[54] Vouchers No. 21–25 were paid at Fort Wayne. William Suttenfield (as he signed the voucher) went to Fort Wayne with Maj. John Whistler's troops and stayed to become one of the first settlers of the town. See Griswold, *Pictorial History of Fort Wayne*, 1:226. On Hackley, see Chapter 3, note 23, above. In the separate Vouchers No. 22–24, Long clarified that "Transportation" meant "the purchase of horses."

[55] Voucher No. 26, paid at Fort Crawford, gave the payee's name as Joseph St. Peter Le Sellier (see above, Chapter 3, note 45), and indicated he received $24.00 for services as interpreter and guide and $6.00 for the use of his horse. Voucher No. 27 was paid to Augustin Rocque (see Chapter 1, note 2, above) at Fort St. Anthony; Voucher No. 28 was paid at Lake Traverse with Joseph Jeffryes, clerk (see Chapter 4, note 36), signing the voucher for the Columbia Fur Co.; and Giacomo C. Beltrami (see p. 31, above) was paid at Pembina by Voucher No. 29.

[56] Vouchers No. 30–34 were paid at "Fort Douglas," by which Long probably meant Fort Garry. No further information on Charles Ferdinand has been found. Benjamin Gervais is identified in Joseph Tassé, *Les Canadiens de L'Ouest*, 2:9–11 (2nd ed., Montreal, 1878); Morice, *Dictionnaire Historique*, 121, 339. Donald McKenzie (see Chapter 4, note 62) signed Voucher No. 32 for the Hudson's Bay Company. By Bauché Long may have meant Paul Bouché or Boucher, also called Lamallice; see "Mackinac Register," in *WHC*, 19:91; Red River Census, 1838, p. 7, 1840, p. 7; Rich, ed., *Journal of . . . Athabasca Department*, 430, 445. Andrew McDermot, as he signed Voucher No. 34, is identified in Ross, *Red River Settlement*, 400–403. Voucher No. 34 also listed Long's purchase of bark for canoe repair.

[57] Voucher No. 35, on which Le Gros's first name was written "Anthony," was paid at Pembina. On Le Gros, see Red River Census, 1840, p. 29; Morice, *Dictionnaire*

Historique, 178; Lake Traverse Account Book, 1820–21, p. 33, in Hudson's Bay Company Archives, Winnipeg. Voucher No. 36 was signed for the Hudson's Bay Company by Simon McGillivray, Jr. (see Chapter 5, note 32, above). It covered purchases made on August 20 at Bas de la Rivière and on September 2 at Rainy Lake. The place of payment was not specified.

[58] Vouchers No. 37–45 were paid at Fort William, which was specified in the vouchers as the terminal point. Except in No. 43, the return trips were included as part of the expenditure. On Jean Baptiste Robillard, Jean Baptiste Desmarais, and Charles G. Brousse, see Chapter 5, note 1, above. Fournier's name was spelled Frenier on p. 375, above; he signed Voucher No. 37 with an X. Louis Morain may be the man (otherwise known as Louis Perrault) who was involved in disturbances at Red River in 1816. See *Report of the . . . Disputes between the Earl of Selkirk and the North-West Company*, 111, appendix p. 3. For Peter or Pierre George, see Red River Census, 1838, p. 21; Canada, Dominion Lands Office, "Claimants to Land Scrip, Red River Settlement, 1790–1860," p. 49, in Provincial Library of Manitoba, Winnipeg, copy in MHS. For Antoine La Frenier, see Red River Census, 1840, p. 59. His name is spelled La and Le Freniere on Voucher No. 41; he signed with an X. A Joachim Rangé of Longueuil signed a contract with the Michilimackinac Company in 1812; this may be Joachim Ranger. See *Rapport de L'Archiviste de la Province de Quebec pour 1945–1946*, 327 (Quebec, 1946).

Roderick McKenzie (see Chapter 5, note 52, above), signed Voucher No. 45 for the Hudson's Bay Company. Also included in Long's purchases were coffee, juniper spirits, a caulking iron, a mallet, and blacksmith work.

[59] Vouchers No. 46–50 were paid at Cantonment Brady, Sault Ste. Marie. On Baptiste Fontaine or La Fontaine, see Chapter 5, note 1, above. No information on Le Fevre has been located. A Joseph La Plante was a voyageur for the North West Company in the early 1800s; see Louis R. Masson, *Les Bourgeois de la Compagnie du Nord-Ouest*, 1:400 (New York, 1960); Coues, ed., *New Light*, 1:268n.

Although Voucher No. 50 was paid at Sault Ste. Marie, the purchases were made at the Michipicoten post (see p. 242, above). The voucher was signed by John McBean (see Chapter 6, note 20) for the Hudson's Bay Company. Halifax currency was the standard Canadian medium of exchange, worth four American dollars to the pound in 1823. See Adam Shortt and Arthur G. Doughty, eds., *Canada and Its Provinces*, 4:600–603 (Toronto, 1914).

[60] Vouchers No. 51–54 were paid at Buffalo, N.Y., Voucher No. 55 at New York City, and Vouchers No. 56–59 in Philadelphia.

[61] The knives were butcher knives and a sportsman's knife.

[62] On McNeil, see note 28, above. On Morgan and Snelling, see Chapter 3, note 60, and Chapter 4, note 3. On Lt. John D. Hopson, mentioned opposite, see Keating, *Narrative*, 1:166; Heitman, *Historical Register*, 1:542.

solicit your instructions relative to the disposition proper to be made of the documents alluded to.

Thinking it probable that some account of our researches, in a popular form, will be required, I have already made some arrangements with a view to that object, but can do nothing decisive till authorized by the Department. In addition to the authority solicited, I beg leave to ask the indulgence of an Office and fuel during the time necessary for compiling and publishing the work in contemplation. It is moreover desirable that some compensation may be allowed to the gentlemen whose services will be indispensable in executing the work, and should it be consistent to authorize any compensation of the kind, I beg you will specify the rate and restrictions agreeably to which it may be made.

As no funds have yet been received for the disbursment of certain expenses of the Expedition (a list of which I forwarded from Buffalo) I entreat your immediate attention to the subject. Agreeably to that list and the statement accompanying it, my circumstances in relation to funds are of the most pressing nature, which is the only apology I can offer for again repeating my application for relief.

I have the honour to be Sir: respectfully
Your obt. and humble Sert.
S. H. LONG Maj. T. Engineers

27. *Long to Macomb, Philadelphia, Pa., November 20, 1823.*[63]

SIR/

In relation to a part of your Instructions of the 31st Ult. viz. "no transportation is to be allowed where the Public have furnished the transport, and to the gentlemen who accompanied you, you will allow the amount of the sums actually paid for Stage-fare, and the actual expenses where there were no stages, provided the said expenses do not exceed the rate of 10 cts. pr. mile," I conceive it my duty to submit the following Statement, in order to show that the expenses actually incurred on account of the Transportation of the gentlemen of the party do not exceed the rate of 10 cts. per mile.

[63] OCE, Letters Received, NARG 77.

Statement	Dols. Cts.
The actual distance travelled by the Expedition is at least 4550 miles, which at the rate of ten cents pr. mile each for Messrs. Say, Keating, Calhoun and Seymour will cost	1820.00
The actual distance travelled by Lieut. Scott and Denny while connected with the Expedition is 2000 miles, which at the rate of 10 cts. pr. mile each will cost	400.00
Amount of Transportation at the rate of 10 cts. pr. mile on the supposition that no Public Transportation has been furnished to the above named gentlemen of the Party	2220.00
By recurring to the charges contained in the Abstract herewith transmitted, it will appear that the several sums charged on account of Travelling Expenses amount to	649.48
To which may be added the charges for Transportation of Baggage viz. $108 and the several charges for the services of Voyageurs, amounting in all, to the sum of	819.29[64]
Also the amount paid for 3 north canoes of Bark & 1 Wooden Canoe, employed in the transportation of the Party	173.00[65]
And we have for the aggregate expense actually incurred in the transportation of the Gentlemen of the Party a considerable proportion of which, bye the bye, is chargeable on account of the Transportation of Public Baggage for which no other provision was made, the sum of	1641.77
Balance resulting in favour of the Public by charging the actual expense of Transportation, rather than that of mileage, at the rate above mentioned — is	570.83

This Balance will more than compensate for the wear and failure of the Public horses employed on the Expedition.

[64] Although this figure agrees with the separate charges on the vouchers, it includes $18.00 for a canoe purchased from Antoine Le Gros which should not be in this account. See Voucher No. 35, in "Abstract," above.

[65] In this sum Long included canoes purchased from Benjamin Gervais, Paul Bouché, Antoine Le Gros, and the Hudson's Bay Company, the latter costing £17 10s., which Long translated as $73.00. If, however, the canoe's price is figured at the same exchange rate used for the rest of the Hudson's Bay Company bill, it appears that it really cost him $77.78, and the total would thus be $177.78, not $173.00.

It should moreover be considered that the Travelling Expenses as charged in the Abstract include the expense for Subsistence as well as Transportation to both of which the gentlemen of the Party were entitled. From this view of the matter it is manifest that the real Balance in favour of the Public is much greater than that above stated.

By a recurrence to a copy of the Estimate I had the honour to submit in April last, relative to the expenses of the Expedition — agreeably to which I was directed to regulate as nearly as practicable the disbursements on account of this Service, I find that the sum estimated as necessary to cover the expenses of the out fit and contingences of the Expedition, not including compensation to the Scientific gentlemen of the Party, was 2000.00

To this sum should be added the Travelling expenses of Messrs. Keating and Calhoun, which were not included in the Estimate, but should have been estimated at the same rate as those of the Zoologist and Painter, viz. 230.00[66]

To these sums may also be added the amount allowable, by way of compensation to the Zoologist, Geologist, Astronomer and Landscape Painter of the Expedition for a term not exceeding eight months, agreeably to the Estimate 1830.00[67]

And the Amount agreeably to the intent and spirit of the Estimate, exclusive of Provisions Clothing and other Military Stores, will be 4060.00

Amount of expenses actually incurred as pr. Abstract 4370.04

Hence it appears that the excess of the Expenditures over and above the amount provided for and implied by the Estimate, is only $310.04

This Excess may be satisfactorily accounted for and the occasion of it very readily explained in the variety of emergencies encountered by the Expedition that could not be foreseen or provided for at the time of making the Estimate; for Example: we had the misfortune to loose by the upsetting of one of our canoes in St. Peters river a considerable quantity of Tobacco and Ammunition which could not

[66] The total of Colhoun's and Keating's vouchers (No. 24, 51, 55, and 58, in "Abstract," above) is $302.66 rather than $230.00.

[67] The compensation paid to Say, Colhoun, Keating, and Seymour for a six-month period ending November 1, 1823, was $1,402.50 in "Abstract," above.

be replaced but by purchase at remote Trading Establishments, when we had to procure them at extravagant prices. Also instead of finding game sufficient to supply our demands for provisions, as was anticipated, we were compelled to purchase the necessaries for the Subsistence of the Party at a very exorbitant rate: as may be seen by recurring to the vouchers referred to in the Abstract.

Thus have I endeavoured to show that the allowance for Travelling Expenses and Transportation, as stated in the Abstract, fall far short of the charges that would result from an allowance of ten cents per mile to the several gentlemen of the Party: And that the actual expenditures incurred by the Expedition exceed but very little, if any, those that were implied in the Estimate; altho they may have been in some respects of a different nature from those contemplated in that Instrument.

I have the honour to be Sir:
Very respectfully Your obedient Servant
S. H. Long Maj. T. Engs.

28. *Long to Macomb, Philadelphia, Pa., April 23, 1825.* [68]

Sir/

By the instructions authorizing the publication of The Narrative of the 2nd. Expedition I had the honour to command, I entered into an arrangement with Mr. Seymour, relative to a number of Drawings to be completed from the sketches taken by himself on the Expedition. They were to have been made ready for delivery at the time of the publication of the work just mentioned. But were never received till yesterday. Having closed the accounts of the Expedition, I have deemed it not proper to take any steps in relation to the drawings but such as would meet your approbation: and it is with a view of ascertaining your pleasure in regard to this matter, that I now trouble you. The arrangement with Mr. S. provided that a compensation of $3.50 should be allowed him for each drawing.

The Pictures furnished by Mr. S. are enumerated in the following List, viz.[69]

[68] OCE, Letters Received, NARG 77. No response to this letter has been located.

[69] On the Seymour works known to exist, see Introduction, note 69. Several of the works listed here were referred to by Long in his journal; see pp. 153, 196, 214, 236, 247, 266, above. On Cape Garlic (No. 3), see Chapter 1, note 6, above; Keating, *Narrative*, 1:267. On Nolin (No. 8), see Chapter 4, note 53, above. The spot mentioned in No. 13 is near Tanner Lake, Ont. See p. 219, above.

No. 1. Carey Mission Station
″ 2. Prairie du Chien
″ 3. Cape Garlic, Mis. riv.
″ 4. Falls of St. Anthony
″ 5. Funeral Scaffold of Sioux
″ 6. View of Big Stone Lake
No. 7. Sioux Infant, and other scenery
″ 8. Mr. Knolan [*Augustin Nolin*], Scot, at Pembina
″ 9. View on St. Peter's [*Minnesota*] riv.
″ 10. Lower [*Silver*] Falls of Winnepeek [*Winnipeg*] R.
″ 11. Rainy Lake [*Koochiching*] Falls.
″ 12. View on Rainy Lake.
No. 13. View of the place [*Twin Falls*] where [John] Tanner received his wound.
″ 14. View on Hyodon [*Pickerel*] Lake
″ 15. View on Dog Lake.
″ 16. View from Dog Portage
″ 17. View on Lake Superior
No. 18. View on Lake Superior
″ 19. Sault de St. Marie
″ 20. Distant view of Mackinac I.
″ 21. View of Sugar Loaf Rock, Mack. I.
″ 22. Cohoez [*Cohoes Falls*] of Mohawk river.

The drawings are very well executed, and make very handsome pictures. Their cost will be $77 agreeably to contract with Mr. S. I will endeavour to retain them, subject to your instructions, but consider myself under no obligation to Mr. S. There is little doubt, however, that the drawings will command the price above mentioned.

I have the honour to be Sir
Very respectfully Your most obt. Sevt.
S. H. Long Maj. T. Engrs.

Index

The type for this book was set on a Mergenthaler VIP phototypesetter with text in Caledonia and headings in Bembo. It is printed by offset lithography on Warren's Old Style stock. The paper is manufactured with controlled pH for maximum shelf life. The book was designed by Alan Ominsky and manufactured by North Central Publishing Company, St. Paul, Minnesota.

STEPHEN H. LONG'S ROUTES, 1817, 1823

(continued on front endsheet)